THE COMPLETE RESULTS

& LINE-UPS OF THE

EUROPEAN FAIRS CUP

1955-1971

Romeo Ionescu

About the author

Romeo Ionescu was born in Ploiesti, Romania, on 19th December 1962. He fell in love with football statistics the first time he held a sports newspaper in 1970 and since then has collected a great number of sports newspapers, magazines and books, now possessing around 20,000 items. He began to collate statistics when he was a schoolboy and continued as a student in Bucuresti, where he completed his Romanian football statistics, spending hundreds of hours in two national libraries. Romeo began to exchange magazines and footballing material with other enthusiasts overseas in 1985 including his Dutch friend Kees Doeleman. Kees sparked Romeo's interest with European Cup line-ups and provided a lot of match details, which eventually led to production of a book about this competition. After collaborating on several books including *The European Football Yearbook*, *Annuario del Calcio Mondiale*, and a Romanian yearbook, Romeo published his first book, *An Encyclopedia of Romanian Football*, in 2000, followed by books on The European Cup and The European Championship amongst others. By profession a mechanical engineer, he now works as a full-time football statistician and is seeking an appointment with an international agency.

Also available from Soccer Books Limited in the same series:

The Complete Results & Line-ups of the European Cup-Winners' Cup 1960-1999
(ISBN 1-86223-087-0)   *Softback Price £29.50*

The Complete Results & Line-ups of the European Champion Clubs' Cup 1955-1991
(ISBN 1-86223-089-7)   *Softback Price £28.00*

The Complete Results & Line-ups of the European Champions League 1991-2004
(ISBN 1-86223-114-1)   *Softback Price £27.50*

The Complete Results & Line-ups of the UEFA Cup 1971-1991
(ISBN 1-86223-109-5)   *Softback Price £29.50*

The Complete Results & Line-ups of the UEFA Cup 1991-2004
(ISBN 1-86223-115-X)   *Softback Price £29.50*

The Complete Results & Line-ups of the Olympic Football Tournaments 1900-2004
(ISBN 1-86223-088-9)   *Softback Price £18.95*

The Complete Results & Line-ups of the European Football Championships 1958-2004
(ISBN 1-86223-108-7)   *Softback Price £24.50*

British Library Cataloguing in Publication Data
A catalogue record for this book is available from the British Library

ISBN 1-86223-085-4

Copyright © 2003, SOCCER BOOKS LIMITED. (01472 696226)
72 St. Peter's Avenue, Cleethorpes, N.E. Lincolnshire, DN35 8HU, England

Printed by 4edge Ltd. www.4edge.co.uk

AN INTRODUCTION TO THE FAIRS CUP

The Idea

The underlying idea behind the creation of the "Fairs Cup" was the provision of inter-cities' matches to entertain and to promote international sports' relations, thus contributing to the bringing together of peoples by means of football. Furthermore, it was intended to give businessmen an opportunity to make contacts where international fairs were held.

During the period immediately after World War II, far fewer football matches between towns were played than during pre-war years. Director Ernst Thommen of Basel, Switzerland, had been studying this problem for a long time and thought that the interest of the public could be stimulated again by arranging matches to be played either by clubs or selected teams who represented towns on an international basis.

At that time UEFA did not exist so Dir. Thommen discussed the project of an "Inter-Cities Fairs Cup Competition" with various representatives of national associations on the occasion of the 50th Anniversary of the Swedish FA in Stockholm.

The proposal was well received as it was thought that such a tournament would give an opportunity to talented young players to get experience in international football.

Foundation

Dir. Thommen contacted Sir Stanley Rous in London and Dr.ing. O. Barassi in Roma, who were then acting as joint honorary Secretaries of FIFA. These three formed an "Initiative Committee" and contacted the national associations and also the committees of towns and clubs which might be interested in the idea of this new competition. Great interest was shown and the Initiative Committee decided (with the consent of the national associations) to arrange a meeting with all the interested organisations.

A meeting took place in Basel, Switzerland on 18th April 1955 and the Inter-Cities Fairs Cup Competition was founded. The following twelve towns were represented by a delegate or by a representative of their national association: Barcelona, Basel, Birmingham, København, Frankfurt, Lausanne, Leipzig, London, Milano, Stockholm, Wien, Zagreb.

The first decisions taken by the foundation assembly were the forming of groups for the first competition and the nomination of a committee under the presidency of Director Ernst Thommen composed of four representative members of the participating teams and the two members of the "Initiative Committee".

This was the beginning of the administrative side of the INTER-CITIES FAIRS CUP.

The years passed

Almost 50 years have now passed since the first match between the selected teams representing Basel and London was played at the St. Jakob Stadium in Basel. This match took place during the visit of the Lord Mayor of London to the Rhine City on 4th June, 1955 and marked the beginning of the FAIRS CUP proper.

During the life of the Cup, 13 competitions took place during which a total of 1,036 matches were played by 207 clubs or selected teams from towns. After the first competition, the representative teams of towns were replaced by club teams, one by one.

The number of participating teams increased from 10 in the first competition to 64 in the final year. CF Barcelona appeared in the competition 11 times and won the trophy 3 times. It is followed by Valencia CF and Lausanne Sports with 9 appearances, Wiener SK, AS Roma, Hannover 96 and Hibernian Edinburgh with 7.

The trophy

The Competition was presented with a trophy of solid silver with gold wings (value Swiss Fr. 10,000) by the sportsman and friend of football, Mr. Noel Béard, a Swiss industrialist of Montreux. After the 1970-71 season, the autonomous committee sponsored by FIFA which had organized the Fairs Cup was replaced by UEFA. The European football organisation preserved the competition format for the tournament, but renamed it UEFA Cup and created a new trophy for the winner. In order to decide which team would keep the old Fairs Cup trophy permanently, a game was played between the first ever winner of this competition (CF Barcelona, 1958) and the last one (Leeds United AFC, 1971). Barcelona duly won the match to become permanent holders of the Fairs Cup.

This book

The story of football, of both domestic and international competitions is followed by many statisticians. But there are a lot of gaps in the story of all competitions played. A match paper contains the full names of every player as well as the full names of the three referees, attendance, goalscorers, stadium and town. To collect all this information about a competition like the Fairs Cup is, unfortunately, quite impossible so there are some minor parts of the data missing for a few games. The statistics have been cross-checked in different newspapers and other books and also with information provided by some of my penpals to make this book the most comprehensive record of this competition.

Thoughout this book, rather than use English spellings, I have used the correct spelling of Club names and places as used in the country of origin. For example, Rome is Roma, Copenhagen is København etc. If a club's name does not include the name of the town or city from which they originate, this name has been appended. For example, Chelsea and Hibernian become Chelsea London and Hibernian Edinburgh accordingly.

Romeo Ionescu

FAIRS CUP 1955-1958

FIRST ROUND

GROUP I

BASEL v LONDON 0-5 (0-3)

St.Jakob, Basel   4.6.55

Referee: Alois Penning (WG)   Attendance: 12,500

BASEL: Werner Schley; Werner Bopp, Hansruedi Fitze; Peter Redolfi, Hans Weber, Richard Zingg; Walter Bannwart, Josef Hügi II (Cap), Juan Monros, Hansueli Oberer, Kurt Thalmann. Trainers: René Bader, Ernst Hufschmid

LONDON: Ronald Reynolds; Richard Peter Sillett, James Fotheringham; Stanley Willemse, Kenneth Armstrong, Derek Saunders (65 Brian Nicholls); Harry Hooper, John Norman Haynes (Cap), Clifford Holton, Edwing Ronald Firmani, William Kiernan. Manager: Joseph Mears

Goals: Firmani (35, 81), Holton (37, 43, 74)

LONDON v FRANKFURT 3-2 (0-2)

Wembley, London   26.10.55

Referee: Fritz Buchmüller (Swi)   Attendance: 42,000

LONDON: Edward Ditchburn; Richard Peter Sillett, Stanley Willemse; Robert Daniel Blanchflower, Charles Hurley, Cyril Hammond; Victor Groves, Robert Robson, Bedford Jezzard, Royston Thomas Frank Bentley (Cap), Charles Mitten. Manager: Joseph Mears

FRANKFURT: Willi Rado; Helmut Sattler, Willi Magel; Willi Keim, Günter Lurz, Willi Weber; Engelbert Kraus, Gerhard Kaufhold, Richard Kress, Alfred Pfaff (Cap), Richard Herrmann. Trainer: Paul Osswald

Goals: Pfaff (25 pen), Kaufhold (30), Jezzard (46, 76), Robson (60)

LONDON v BASEL 1-0 (0-0)

White Hart Lane, London   4.05.56

Referee: Vincenzo Orlandini (Ita)   Attendance: 16,730

LONDON: John Alfred Kelsey; Richard Peter Sillett, John Hewie; Robert Daniel Blanchflower (Cap), Stanley Wicks, Kenneth Coote; James Lewis, Derek Tapscott, Clifford Holton, Robert Cameron, George Robb. Manager: Joseph Mears

BASEL: Karl Oeschger; Hansruedi Fitze, René Brodmann; Peter Redolfi, Hansueli Oberer (46 Richard Zingg), Silvan Thüler; Jürgen Sanmann, Josef Hügi II (Cap), Rolf Gronau, Werner Kirchhofer, Gottlieb Stäuble. Trainer: Béla Sárosi

Goal: Robb (87)

FRANKFURT v BASEL 5-1 (2-1)

Bornheimer Hang, Frankfurt   20.06.56

Referee: Arthur Edward Ellis (Eng)   Attendance: 7,000

FRANKFURT: Willi Rado; Hermann Höfer, Horst Krone; Werner Mayer, Hans Wloka, Eberhard Schymick; Richard Kress, Erich Bäumler (31 Ernst Wade), Berthold Buchenau, Alfred Pfaff (Cap), Richard Herrmann. Trainer: Rudolf Gellesch

BASEL: Karl Oeschger; René Brodmann, Hansruedi Fitze; Peter Redolfi, Richard Zingg, Silvan Thüler; Walter Bannwart, Rolf Gronau, Josef Hügi II (Cap), Jürgen Sanmann, Gottlieb Stäuble. Trainer: Ernst Hufschmid

Goals: Buchenau (19, 80), Pfaff (31, 73), J. Hügi II (35 pen), Herrmann (52)

FRANKFURT v LONDON 1-0 (0-0)

Waldstadion am Riederwald, Frankfurt am Main   27.03.57

Referee: Gottfried Dienst (Swi)   Attendance: 13,900

FRANKFURT: Walter Zimmermann; Helmut Sattler, Hermann Höfer (40 Horst Krone); Hans Weilbächer, Hans Wloka, Werner Mayer; Richard Kress, Berthold Buchenau, Helmut Preisendörfer, Alfred Pfaff (Cap), Engelbert Kraus. Trainer: Paul Osswald

LONDON: Ronald Reynolds; John Bond, Richard Peter Sillett; Kenneth Armstrong, Malcolm Allison, Anthony Marchi; Terence Medwin, Stuart Leary, David George Herd, John Norman Haynes (Cap), William Kiernan. Manager: Joseph Mears

Goal: Preisendörfer (72)

BASEL v FRANKFURT 6-2 (2-1)

Landhof, Basel   12.06.57

Referee: Pierre Mourat (Fra)   Attendance: 4,500

BASEL: Karl Oeschger (66 Hansruedi Blatter); René Brodmann, Hans Hügi I; Hansueli Oberer, Rudolf Burger, Richard Zingg; Jürgen Sanmann, Josef Hügi II (Cap), Anton Allemann, Hermann Suter, Gottlieb Stäuble. Trainer: Béla Sárosi

FRANKFURT: Karlheinz Leichum; Peter Wagner (35 Karl-Heinz Lidynski), Horst Krone; Erwin Tilke, Günter Lurz (Cap), Phillip Nold; Werner Hofmann, Friedel Kabatzki, Berthold Buchenau, Werner Mayer, Engelbert Kraus. Trainer: Rudolf Gellesch

Goals: Allemann (10, 47, 66), Kraus (32), Sanmann (33), J. Hügi II (64), Mayer (65), Burger (88)

GROUP II

LEIPZIG v LAUSANNE SPORTS 6-3 (4-3)

Bruno-Plache-Stadion, Leipzig 6.03.56

Referee: Bengt Lundell (Swe)   Attendance: 28,000

LEIPZIG: Günter Busch; Manfred Bauer, Werner Knaust, Karl-Heinz Brandt; Horst Scherbaum (Cap), Siegfried Fettke; Horst Lemke, Rudolf Krause, Günther Konzack, Rainer Baumann, Werner Walter. Trainer: Heinz Krügel

LAUSANNE: Georges Stuber; Roger Mathis, Marc Perruchoud; Jean-Jacques Maurer, Hans Weber, Gaston Magnin; Gilbert Rey (46 Ricardo Poma), Norbert Eschmann (Cap), Joseph Zürcher, René Maillard II, Willy Monti (76 Rey). Trainer: Fernand Jaccard

Goals: Walther (5), Konzack (9, 82), Maillard (11), Krause (23, 36), Rey (31), Eschmann (43), Fettke (69 pen)

LAUSANNE SPORTS v LEIPZIG 7-3 (4-1)

Stade Olympique de la Pontaise, Lausanne 21.10.56

Referee: Francesco Liverani (Ita)   Attendance: 4,500

LAUSANNE: Georges Stuber; Roger Mathis, Hans Weber; Roger Reymond, Marcel Vonlanden, Peter Roesch; Aldo Tedeschi (46 Pierre Stefano), Norbert Eschmann (Cap), Todor Zivanovic (80 Maillard), Hans Moser, Gilbert Fesselet. Trainer: Fernand Jaccard

LEIPZIG: Günter Busch; Manfred Bauer, Dieter Busch, Karl-Heinz Brandt; Siegfried Fettke, Horst Scherbaum (Cap); Günter Behne, Werner Walter (46 Arnolf Pahlitzsch), Rainer Baumann, Günther Konzack, Heinz Fröhlich. Trainer: Fritz Wittenbecher

Goals: Walter (13), Tedeschi (28), Eschmann (37, 43, 55), Moser (38), Behne (58), Stefano (60, 62), Fröhlich (70)

GROUP III

CF BARCELONA v KØBENHAVN 6-2 (4-0)

Campo de Las Corts, Barcelona 25.12.55

Referee: Armando Marchetti (Ita)   Attendance: 27,750

CF BARCELONA: Antonio RAMALLETS Simón; José SEGUER Sanz, Gustavo BIOSCA Pagés (46 Joaquín BRUGUÉ Heras), Sigfrido GRACIA Royo; Andrés BOSCH Pujol, Juan SEGARRA Iraceta (Cap); Justo TEJADA Martínez, Ramón Alberto VILLAVERDE Vázquez, László KUBALA Stecz, Esteban ARETA Vélez, Eduardo MANCHÓN Molina. Trainer: Domingo Balmanya

KØBENHAVN: Per Henriksen (Frem); Erik Køppen (KB), Verner Nielsen (AB); Flemming Nielsen (B93), John Jørgensen (Skovshoved IF), Børge Christensen (B93); Einer Jensen (VIF), Jørgen Jacobsen (B93), Ove Andersen (Brønshøj BK), Knud Lundberg (Cap-AB)), Holger Seebach (AB). Trainers: Oscar Olsen, Aage Strebøl, Aksel Bjerregaard

Goals: Areta (9, 12), Tejada (32, 81), Villaverde (40), Kubala (59), Lundberg (65 pen), Jacobsen (75)

KØBENHAVN v CF BARCELONA 1-1 (0-0)

Idraetspark, København 26.04.56

Referee: John Erik Andersson (Swe)   Attendance: 15,500

KØBENHAVN: Per Henriksen (Frem); Erik Køppen (KB), Verner Nielsen (AB); Erik Pondal Jensen (AB), Bent Jørgensen (Frem), Leif Tønnesen (Frem); Ejner Jensen (VIF), Bent Ib Jørgensen (Frem), Ove Andersen (Brønshøj) (75 Henning Jensen), Knud Lundberg (Cap-AB), Kaj Lerby (1903). Trainers: Oscar Olsen, Aage Strebøl, Aksel Bjerregaard

CF BARCELONA: Antonio RAMALLETS Simón; José SEGUER Sanz, Gustavo BIOSCA Pagés, Sigfrido GRACIA Royo; Andrés BOSCH Pujol, Juan SEGARRA Iraceta (Cap); Estanislao BASORA Brunet, Ramón Alberto VILLAVERDE Vázquez, Esteban ARETA Vélez, Mariano GONZALVO Falcón, Eduardo MANCHÓN Molina. Trainer: Domingo Balmanya

Goals: Lundberg (60 pen), Villaverde (85)

GROUP IV

INTERNAZIONALE MILANO v BIRMINGHAM CITY 0-0

Arena Civica, Milano 15.05.56

Referee: Paul Wyssling (Swi)   Attendance: 8,000

INTERNAZIONALE: Giorgio Ghezzi; Livio Fongaro, Giovanni Giacomazzi (Cap); Enea Masiero, Rino Ferrario, Giovanni Invernizzi; Benito Lorenzi, Roger Vonlanthen, Achille Fraschini, Celestino Celio, Lennart Skoglund. Trainer: Giuseppe Meazza

BIRMINGHAM CITY: Gilbert Harold Merrick; Jack Badham, Kenneth Green (Cap); John Watts, John Newman, Peter Warmington; Geoffrey Cox, Noel Kinsey, Edward Brown, Peter Murphy, Alexander Govan. Manager: Arthur Turner

ZAGREB v BIRMINGHAM CITY 0-1 (0-1)

Maksimir, Zagreb 22.05.56

Referee: Friedrich Seipelt (Aus)   Attendance: 12,000

ZAGREB: Branko Kralj; Franjo Beseredi, Tomislav Crnković (Cap); Branko Rezek, Ivan Horvat, Ivan Šantek; Vladimir Čonč, Kadro Abadžić, Vladimir Firm (46 Savo Joksimović), Vilim Medved, Luka Lipošinović (46 Franjo Spirk). Trainer: Rudolf Sabljak

BIRMINGHAM CITY: Gilbert Harold Merrick; Jack Badham, George Allen; Leonard Boyd (Cap), John Newman, Roy Warhurst; John Lane, William Finney, Edward Brown, Noel Kinsey, Peter Murphy. Manager: Arthur Turner

Goal: Brown (8)

ZAGREB v INTERNAZIONALE MILANO 0-1 (0-0)

Maksimir, Zagreb   6.06.56

Referee: Ezio Damiani (Ita)   Attendance: 40,000

ZAGREB: Vladimir Macek; Mladen Koscak, Svemir Delić; Ivan Šantek (Cap), Ante Vidosević, Branko Rezek; Vilim Medved, Vladimir Čonč, Drazan Jerković, Zdravko Prelcek (46 Ljubomir Bencić), Franjo Spirk.   Trainer: Rudolf Sabljak

INTERNAZIONALE: Giorgio Ghezzi; Livio Fongaro, Giovanni Giacomazzi (10 Celestino Celio); Enea Masiero, Guido Vincenzi, Fulvio Nesti; Roger Vonlanthen, Giovanni Invernizzi, Oscar Massei, Cesare Campagnoli, Lennart Skoglund.   Trainer: Giuseppe Meazza

Goal: Campagnoli (74)

BIRMINGHAM CITY v ZAGREB 3-0 (1-0)

St.Andrew's, Birmingham   3.12.56
Referee: Paul Wyssling (Swi)   Attendance: 40,144

BIRMINGHAM CITY: Gilbert Harold Merrick; Brian Farmer, George Allen; John Watts, Kenneth Green (Cap), Roy Warhurst; George Cox, Brian Orritt (.. Noel Kinsey), Edward Brown, Peter Murphy, Alexander Govan.
Manager: Arthur Turner

ZAGREB: Gordan Irović; Ivica Banozić, Tomislav Crnković (Cap); Branko Rezek, Ivan Horvat (46 Vladimir Klaić), Lav Mantula; Vilim Medved, Aleksandar Benko, Drazan Jerković, Branko Rezar, Marijan Kolonić.   Trainer: Rudolf Sabljak

Goals: Orritt (3), Brown (60), Murphy (67)

INTERNAZIONALE MILANO v ZAGREB 4-0 (2-0)

Arena Civica, Milano   19.03.57

Referee: Josef Gulde (Swi)   Attendance: 5,000

INTERNAZIONALE: Enzo Matteucci; Guido Vincenzi (46 Livio Fongaro), Giovanni Giacomazzi (Cap); Giovanni Invernizzi, Vasco Tagliavini, Aldo Dorigo; Roger Vonlanthen, Egisto Pandolfini, Benito Lorenzi, Cesare Campagnoli, Lennart Skoglund.   Trainer: Ferrero

ZAGREB: Branko Kralj; Josip Šikić, Tomislav Crnković (Cap); Ivan Šantek, Ivan Horvat, Branko Rezek; Vilim Medved (46 Dionizije Dvornic), Vladimir Čonč (46 Željko Matuš), Luka Lipošinović, Lav Mantula, Aleksandar Benko.
Trainer: Rudolf Sabljak

Goals: Skoglund (8, 89), Lorenzi (43, 50)

BIRMINGHAM CITY v INTERNAZIONALE MILANO 2-1 (1-0)

St.Andrew's, Birmingham   17.04.57

Referee: Juan Gardeazabal (Spa)   Attendance: 30,858

BIRMINGHAM CITY: Gilbert Harold Merrick; Jeffrey Hall, Kenneth Green; John Watts, Trevor Smith (Cap), Roy Warhurst; Gordon Astall, Noel Kinsey, Edward Brown, Peter Murphy, Alexander Govan.   Manager: Arthur Turner

INTERNAZIONALE: Giorgio Ghezzi (60 Enzo Matteucci); Livio Fongaro, Giovanni Invernizzi (Cap); Enzo Bearzot, Giorgio Bernardin, Fulvio Nesti; Aldo Dorigo, Roger Vonlanthen, Benito Lorenzi, Cesare Campagnoli, Marco Savioni.   Trainer: Ferrero

Goals: Govan (44, 53), Lorenzi (88)

SEMI-FINALS

LAUSANNE SPORTS v LONDON 2-1 (1-0)

Stade Olympique de la Pontaise, Lausanne   16.09.57

Referee: Jacques Devillers (Fra)   Attendance: 9,200

LAUSANNE: René Schneider; Jean-Pierre Magada II, Gilbert Fesselet, Gaston Magnin; Roland Stalder, Peter Roesch; Aldo Tedeschi, Heinz Roth, Mario Bernasconi, Marcel Vonlanden (Cap), Bernard Coutaz.   Trainer: Walter Presch

LONDON: Edward Ditchburn; Stanley Charlton, James Fotheringham; Dennis Evans, Brian Nicholls (Cap), Philip McKnight; Peter Berry, Geoffrey Truett, Leslie Stubbs, Phillip Abraham Woosnam, Joseph Haverty.   Trainer: Joseph Mears

Goals: Vonlanden (6, 73), Haverty (70)

LONDON v LAUSANNE SPORTS 2-0 (1-0)

Highbury, London   23.10.57

Referee: Albert Dusch (WG)   Attendance: 16,723

LONDON: John Alfred Kelsey, Stanley Charlton, John Sillett; Kenneth Coote, William Dodgin, Derek Saunders; Royston Dwight, James Peter Greaves, Clifford Holton, John Norman Haynes (Cap), William Kiernan.   Trainer: Joseph Mears

LAUSANNE: René Schneider; Jean-Pierre Magada II, Gilbert Fesselet, Gaston Magnin; Rémy Uldry, Peter Roesch; Oscar Klein, Roland Stalder, Mario Bernasconi, Marcel Vonlanden (Cap), Marc Perruchoud.   Trainer: Walter Presch

Goals: Greaves (10), Holton (76)

BIRMINGHAM CITY v CF BARCELONA 4-3 (3-3)

St.Andrew's, Birmingham   23.10.57

Referee: Josef Gulde (Swi)   Attendance: 28,791

BIRMINGHAM CITY: Gilbert Harold Merrick; Brian
Farmer, George Allen; Bernard Larkin, Trevor Smith (Cap),
John Watts; Gordon Astall, Brian Orritt, Edward Brown,
Richard Neal, Peter Murphy.   Manager: Arthur Turner

CF BARCELONA: Antonio RAMALLETS Simón; Juan
SEGARRA Iraceta (Cap), Fernando OLIVELLA Pons,
Sigfrido GRACIA Royo; Isidro FLOTATS Villanova, Andrés
BOSCH Pujol; Estanislao BASORA Brunet, Ramón Alberto
VILLAVERDE Vázquez, EULOGIO Ramiro MARTÍNEZ,
EVARISTO Juan de Macedo Filho, Justo TEJADA Martínez.
Trainer: Domingo Balmanya

Goals: Brown (2), Tejada (12), Evaristo (27), Orritt (35),
E. Martínez (40), Murphy (43, 60)

CF BARCELONA v BIRMINGHAM CITY 1-0 (0-0)

Camp Nou, Barcelona   13.11.57

Referee: Manuel ASENSI Martin (Spa)   Attendance: 45,000

CF BARCELONA: Pedro ESTREMS Navarro; Juan SEGARRA
Iraceta (Cap), Fernando OLIVELLA Pons, Sigfrido GRACIA
Royo; Isidro FLOTATS Villanova, Martín VERGÉS Massa;
Estanislao BASORA Brunet, EVARISTO Juan de Macedo Filho,
EULOGIO Ramiro MARTÍNEZ, László KUBALA Stecz, Justo
TEJADA Martínez.   Trainer: Domingo Balmanya

BIRMINGHAM CITY: Gilbert Harold Merrick; Jeffrey Hall,
George Allen; Bernard Larkin, Trevor Smith (Cap), Richard
Neal; Gordon Astall, Noel Kinsey, Edward Brown, Peter
Murphy, Alexander Govan.   Manager: Arthur Turner

Goal: Kubala (86)

CF BARCELONA v BIRMINGHAM CITY 2-1 (1-0)

St.Jakob, Basel   26.11.57

Referee: Gottfried Dienst (Swi)   Attendance: 20,000

CF BARCELONA: Antonio RAMALLETS Simón; Juan
SEGARRA Iraceta (Cap), Joaquín BRUGUÉ Heras, Sigfrido
GRACIA Royo; Martín VERGÉS Massa, Andrés BOSCH
Pujol; Estanislao BASORA Brunet, László KUBALA Stecz,
EVARISTO Juan de Macedo Filho, Luis SUÁREZ Miramontes,
Justo TEJADA Martínez.   Trainer: Domingo Balmanya

BIRMINGHAM CITY: Gilbert Harold Merrick; Jeffrey Hall,
Brian Farmer; John Watts, Trevor Smith (Cap), Richard Neal;
Gordon Astall, Brian Orritt, Edward Brown, Peter Murphy,
Alexander Govan.   Manager: Arthur Turner

Goals: Evaristo (33), Murphy (48), Kubala (83)

FINAL

LONDON v CF BARCELONA 2-2 (1-2)

Stamford Bridge, London   5.03.58

Referee: Albert Dusch (WG)   Attendance: 45,466

LONDON: John Alfred Kelsey (Arsenal); Richard Peter
Sillett (Chelsea), Ernest James Langley (Fulham); Robert
Daniel Blanchflower (Cap-Tottenham), Maurice Norman
(Tottenham), Kenneth Coote (Bentford); Victor Groves
(Arsenal), James Peter Greaves (Chelsea), Robert Alfred Smith
(Tottenham), John Norman Haynes (Fulham), George Robb
(Tottenham).   Manager: Joseph Mears

CF BARCELONA: Pedro ESTREMS Navarro; Fernando
OLIVELLA Pons, Enrique GENSANA Meroles, Juan
SEGARRA Iraceta (Cap); Martín VERGÉS Massa, Enrique
RIBELLES Sero; Justo TEJADA Martínez, Ramón Alberto
VILLAVERDE Vázquez, EULOGIO Ramiro MARTÍNEZ,
Everisto de Macedo, Estanislao BASORA Brunet.
Trainer: Domingo Balmanya

Goals: Tejada (4), Greaves (5), E. Martínez (35),
Langley (85 pen)

CF BARCELONA v LONDON 6-0 (3-0)

Camp Nou, Barcelona   1.05.58

Referee: Albert Dusch (WG)   Attendance: 62,000

CF BARCELONA: Antonio RAMALLETS Simón (Cap);
Fernando OLIVELLA Pons, Joaquín BRUGUÉ Heras,
Juan SEGARRA Iraceta; Martín VERGÉS Massa, Enrique
GENSANA Meroles; Justo TEJADA Martínez, EVARISTO
Juan de Macedo Filho, EULOGIO Ramiro MARTÍNEZ, Luis
SUÁREZ Miramontes, Estanislao BASORA Brunet.
Trainer: Domingo Balmanya

LONDON: John Alfred Kelsey; George Wright (West Ham
United), Noel Cantwell (West Ham United); Robert Daniel
Blanchflower (Cap-Tottenham), Kenneth Brown (West Ham
United), David Lloyd Bowen (Arsenal); Terence Cameron
Medwin (Tottenham), Victor Groves (Arsenal), Robert Alfred
Smith (Tottenham), James Robert Bloomfield (Arsenal), James
Leonard Lewis (Chelsea).   Manager: Joseph Mears

Goals: Suárez (6, 8), E. Martínez (43), Evaristo (52, 80),
Vergés (67)

Goalscorers Fairs Cup 1955-58:

4 goals: Norbert Eschmann (Lausanne Sports), Clifford
Holton (London), EVARISTO Juan de Macedo Filho,
Justo TEJADA Martínez (CF Barcelona), Peter Murphy
(Birmingham City)

3 goals: Anton Allemann (Basel), László KUBALA Stecz,
EULOGIO Ramiro MARTÍNEZ (CF Barcelona), Benito
Lorenzi (Internazionale Milano), Alfred Pfaff (Frankfurt),
Edward Brown (Birmingham City)

2 goals: Firmani, Jezzard, Greaves (London), Buchenau (Frankfurt), J.Hügi (Basel), Walter, Konzack, Krause (Leipzig), Stefano, Vonlanden (Lausanne), Areta, Villaverde, Suárez (CF Barcelona), Lundberg (Kobenhavn), Orritt, Govan (Birmingham City), Skoglund (Internazionale Milano)

1 goal: Robson, Robb, Haverty, Langley (London), Kaufhold, Herrmann, Preisendörfer, Kraus, Mayer (Frankfurt), Sanmann, Burger (Basel), Fettke, Fröhlich, Behne (Leipzig), Maillard, Rey, Tedeschi, Moser (Lausanne), Vergés (CF Barcelona), Jacobsen (København), Campagnoli (Inter)

KØBENHAVN v CHELSEA LONDON 1-3 (1-1)

Idraetspark, København 30.09.58

Referee: Pierre Schwinte (Fra)   Attendance: 19,200

KØBENHAVN: Bent Koch; Arne Kjeldsen, Verner Nielsen; Harald Gronemann (Cap); George Lees, Egon Henriksen; Knud Petersen, Mogens Machon, Søren Andersen, John Hansen, Jens Peder Hansen.   Trainer: Svend Frederiksen

CHELSEA: Reginald Matthews; Richard Peter Sillett (Cap), John Sillett; Clifford Huxford, Melvyn Scott, Derek Saunders; Colin Court, James Peter Greaves, Ronald Tindall, Anthony Nicholas, Michael Harrison.   Manager: Edward Drake

Goals: Harrison (13), Gronemann (25), Greaves (54), Nicholas (90)

FAIRS CUP 1958-60

FIRST ROUND

BEOGRAD v LAUSANNE SPORTS 6-1 (1-1)

JNA, Beograd 24.09.58

Referee: Kurt Tschenscher (WG)   Attendance: 22,000

BEOGRAD: Slavko Stojanović; Bruno Belin, Vasilije Šijaković; Tomislav Kaloperović, Milorad Milutinović, Lazar Tasić, Aleksandar Petaković, Rajko Mitić (Cap); Miloš Milutinović, Dragoslav Šekularac (46 Ljubomir Ognjanović), Bora Kostić.   Trainer: Predrag Djajić

LAUSANNE: René Schneider; André Grobéty, Gilbert Fesselet (Cap), Jean-Pierre Magada II; Walter Fischli, Gino Monti; Mario Bernasconi, Charles Hertig, Egon Jonsson, Rolf Willimann, René Regamey.   Trainer: Walter Presch

Goals: Jonsson (2), Miloš Milutinović (40, 88), Kostić (58, 63), Mitić (65), Ognjanović (67 pen)

LAUSANNE SPORTS v BEOGRAD 3-5 (1-2)

Stade Olympique de la Pontaise, Lausanne 22.10.58

Referee: José González Etcheverria (Spa)   Attendance: 3,000

LAUSANNE: Joseph Fischli; André Grobéty, Gilbert Fesselet, Jean-Pierre Magada II; Bruno Michaud, Gino Monti; Oscar Klein, Charles Hertig, Roland Stalder, Marcel Vonlanden (Cap), René Regamey.   Trainer: Walter Presch

BEOGRAD: Petar Radenković (46 Slavko Stojanović); Bruno Belin, Miljan Zeković; Rajko Mitić (Cap), Milorad Milutinović, Vladimir Popović (46 Ljubisa Spajić); Živko Josić, Dragoslav Šekularac, Anton Rudinski, Bora Kostić, Ljubomir Ognjanović.   Trainer: Prvoslav Mihajlović

Goals: Rudinski (13, 75), Regamey (29), Kostić (32, 88), Stalder (53, 62), Šekularac (87)

CHELSEA LONDON v KØBENHAVN 4-1 (2-1)

Stamford Bridge, London 4.11.58

Referee: Alois Smidts (Bel)   Attendance: 13,104

CHELSEA: Reginald Matthews; Richard Peter Sillett (Cap), John Sillett; John Mortimore, Melvyn Scott, Derek Saunders; Peter Brabrook, James Peter Greaves, Leslie Allen, Ronald Tindall, Michael Block.   Manager: Edward Drake

KØBENHAVN: Per Henriksen; Arne Kjeldsen, Christian Brøgger; Harald Gronemann (Cap), Georges Lees, Egon Henriksen; Jens Peder Hansen, Villy Schóne Hansen, Søren Andersen, John Hansen, Poul Mejer.   Trainer: Svend Frederiksen

Goals: Lees (6 og), Schøne (7), Greaves (44, 69), P.Sillett (72)

KÖLN v BIRMINGHAM CITY 2-2 (2-1)

Müngersdorferstadion, Köln 14.10.58

Referee: Gottfried Dienst (Swi)   Attendance: 12,500

KÖLN: Fritz Ewert; Georg Stollenwerk, Günter Wagner; Bernhard Schwier, Fritz Breuer, Herbert Dörner; Franz Brungs, Hans Sturm, Ernst-Günter Habig, Hans Schäfer (Cap), Hans Pfeiffer.   Trainer: Johannes Weisweiler

BIRMINGHAM CITY: Gilbert Harold Merrick; Jeffrey Hall, Kenneth Green (Cap); John Watts, Graham Sissons, Richard Neal; Harry Hooper, John Gordon, Edward Brown, Brian Orritt, Peter Murphy.   Manager: Arthur Turner

Goals: Brungs (7), Pfeiffer (12), Neal (40), Hooper (60)

BIRMINGHAM CITY v KÖLN 2-0 (0-0)

St.Andrew's, Birmingham   11.11.58

Referee: Concetto Lo Bello (Ita)   Attendance: 20,266

BIRMINGHAM CITY: Gilbert Harold Merrick; Jeffrey Hall, George Allen; John Watts, Trevor Smith (Cap), Richard Neal; Harry Hooper, John Gordon, Edward Brown, Bernard Larkin, Brian Taylor.   Manager: Arthur Turner

KÖLN: Fritz Ewert; Hans Kessler, Karl-Heinz Schnellinger; Bernhard Schwier, Heinz Schumacher, Günter Mühlenbock; Ernst-Günter Habig, Hans Sturm (Cap), Heinz Lorenz, Herbert Dörner, Helmut Fendel.   Trainer: Johannes Weisweiler

Goals: Larkin (59), Taylor (67)

UNION SAINT GILLOISE BRUSSEL v LEIPZIG 6-1 (3-0)

Stade Joseph Mariën, Brussel   29.10.58

Referee: Kenneth Aston (Eng)   Attendance: 3,000

UNION ST.GILLOISE: Willy Bruggeman; Henri Dirickx (Cap), Theo Van Rooy; Jozef Torfs, Jozef Oversteyns, Léon Close; Antoine Diegenant, Remy Van de Weyer, Hubert Vandormael, Paul Vandenberg, Roger Van Cauwelaert. Trainer: André Van de Wijer

LEIPZIG: Wolfgang Pröhl (64 Günter Busch); Manfred Bauer, Horst Scherbaum (Cap), Claus Pfeufer; Siegfried Fettke, Dieter Fischer; Werner Gase, Rudolf Krause, Dieter Scherbarth, Rolf Nitzsche, Rainer Trölitzsch.
Trainers: Alfred Kunze, Johannes Studener.

Goals: Vandenberg (12, 51), Van Cauwelaert (16, 62), Vandormael (40, 59), Scherbarth (86)

LEIPZIG v UNION ST.GILLOISE BRUSSEL 1-0 (0-0)

Zentralstadion, Leipzig   4.03.59

Referee: Helge Andersen (Dan)   Attendance: 35,000

LEIPZIG: Wolfgang Klank; Heinz Herrmann, Karl-Heinz Brandt, Manfred Bauer; Dieter Fischer, Siegfried Fettke (Cap); Werner Gase, Rudolf Krause, Dieter Scherbarth, Günter Stiller, Günter Behne.   Trainer: Alfred Kunze

UNION ST.GILLOISE: Fernand Decorte; Georges René Seeraert, Theo Van Rooy; André Masset, Jozef Oversteyns, Willy Depauw; Jean-Pierre Janssens, Hubert Vandormael, Frans Laureys, Henri Dirickx (Cap), Claude Geeraert. Trainer: André Van de Wijer

Goal: Scherbarth (64)

BASEL v CF BARCELONA 1-2 (0-0)

St.Jakob, Basel   12.11.58

Referee: Gastone Grandain (Bel)   Attendance: 9,600

BASEL: Kurt Stettler; Werner Bopp, Hans Weber; Fredy Kehrli, Hanspeter Füri, Silvan Thüler; Robert Hosp, Hansueli Oberer, Josef Hügi II (Cap), Rudolf Burger, Gottlieb Stäuble. Trainer: Rudolf Strittich

CF BARCELONA: Antonio RAMALLETS Simón; Fernando OLIVELLA Pons, Francisco Rodríguez García "RODRI", Sigfrido GRACIA Royo; Juan SEGARRA Iraceta (Cap), Enrique GENSANA Meroles; Justo TEJADA Martínez, László KUBALA Stecz, EVARISTO Juan de Macedo Filho, Luis SUÁREZ Miramontes, Ramón Alberto VILLAVERDE Vázquez. Trainer: Helenio Herrera

Goals: Evaristo (51), Hosp (71), Gensana (80)

CF BARCELONA v BASEL 5-2 (3-0)

Camp Nou, Barcelona   6.01.59

Referee: Leo Lemešić (Jug)   Attendance: 45,000

CF BARCELONA: Antonio Larraz; Juan SEGARRA Iraceta (Cap), Joaquín RIFÉ Climent, Sigfrido GRACIA Royo; Enrique RIBELLES Sero, Isidro Flotas; HERMES GONZÁLEZ Flores, Ramón Alberto VILLAVERDE Vázquez, EVARISTO Juan de Macedo Filho, László KUBALA Stecz, Zoltán Czibor. Trainer: Helenio Herrera

BASEL: Kurt Stettler; Werner Bopp, Hans Weber; Hanspeter Füri, Hansueli Oberer, Fredy Kehrli; Robert Hosp, Rudolf Burger, Josef Hügi II (Cap), Antoine Kohn, Gottlieb Stäuble. Trainer: Rudolf Strittich

Goals: Villaverde (15), Czibor (23, 86), Evaristo (36), Hermes González (55), J. Hügi II (69 pen), Burger (77)

HANNOVER SPORT-VEREIN 1896 v AS ROMA 1-3 (0-1)

Niedersachsenstadion, Hannover   9.11.58

Referee: Carl Frederik Jørgensen (Dan)   Attendance: 15,000

HANNOVER SV: Ewald Stiller; Helmuth Geruschke, Rudolf Fassnacht; Friedel Schicks, Heinz Elzner, Ulrich Kühn; Heinz Wewetzer (Cap), Walter Gawletta, Hans Tkotz, Horst Wenker, Georg Kellermann.   Trainer: Fritz Silken

ROMA: Fabio Cudicini; Giovanni Griffith, Giacomo Losi (Cap); Mario David, Giosué Stucchi, Franco Zaglio; Alcide Ghiggia, Paolo Pestrin, Dino Da Costa, Filippo Tasso, Arne Selmosson.   Trainer: Gunnar Nordahl

Goals: Tasso (25), Kellermann (69), Da Costa (74, 78)

AS ROMA v HANNOVER 96   1-1 (1-1)

Stadio Olimpico, Roma   7.01.59

Referee: John Clough (Eng)   Attendance: 8,000

ROMA: Fabio Cudicini; Giovanni Griffith, Giacomo Losi (Cap) (20 Silvio Franchi); Mario David, Giosué Stucchi, Enzo Menegotti; Lamberto Leonardi, Paolo Pestrin, Alcide Ghiggia, Filippo Tasso, Severino Lojodice.   Trainer: Gunnar Nordahl

HANNOVER 96: Hans Krämer; Helmuth Geruschke, Ulrich Kühn; Horst Wenker, Hubert Wiezorek, Heinz Elzner; Heinz Wewetzer (Cap), Friedel Schicks, Gerd Gollnow, Wilfried Schott, Georg Kellermann.   Trainer: Fritz Silken

Goals: Gollnow (4), Tasso (23)

ZAGREB v ÚJPESTI DÓZSA BUDAPEST   4-2 (2-2)

Maksimir, Zagreb   26.11.58

Referee: Giulio Campanatti (Ita)   Attendance: 25,000

ZAGREB: Gordan Irović; Josip Šikić, Mladen Koscak; Ivan Šantek, Tomislav Crnković (Cap), Franjo Gašpert; Vilim Medved, Vladimir Čonč (46 Ivica Zuban), Drazan Jerković, Željko Matuš, Vladimir Lacković.   Trainer: Momčilo Pazur

ÚJPESTI DÓZSA: Gábor Török; Pál Várhidi, Kálmán Sóvári, József Györvári; József Szini, György Borsányi; Károly Nagy, János Göröcs, Béla Kuharszki, Ferenc Szusza (Cap), József Bencsics.   Trainer: István Balogh

Goals: Gyorvári (19 og), Szusza (31), Jerković (33, 55), Bencsics (40), Lacković (70)

ÚJPESTI DÓZSA BUDAPEST v ZAGREB   1-0 (0-0)

Megyeri út, Budapest   3.12.58

Referee: Victor Schicker (Swi)   Attendance: 8,000

ÚJPESTI DÓZSA: Gábor Török; Pál Várhidi (Cap), Kálmán Sóvári, József Györvári; József Szini, György Borsányi; Károly Nagy, János Göröcs, Béla Kuharszki, István Halápi (25 Ferenc Szusza), József Bencsics.   Trainer: István Balogh

ZAGREB: Gordan Irović; Josip Šikić, Mladen Koscak; Ivan Šantek, Tomislav Crnković (Cap), Franjo Gašpert; Vilim Medved, Vladimir Čonč, Drazan Jerković, Željko Matuš, Vladimir Lacković.   Trainer: Momčilo Pazur

Goal: Szini (73)

INTERNAZIONALE MILANO v OLYMPIQUE LYON   7-0 (3-0)

Arena Civica, Milano   10.12.58

Referee: Vilmos Hernadi (Hun)   Attendance: 4,000

INTER: Natale Nobili; Livio Fongaro, Aristide Guarneri; Enea Masiero, Vasco Tagliavini, Bruno Bolchi (Cap); Renzo Rovatti, Edwing Ronald Firmani, Antonio Valentin Angelillo, Bengt Lindskog, Mario Corso.   Trainer: Giuseppe Bigogno

OLYMPIQUE: Robert Sabathier; Robert Mouynet, Aimé Mignot; Emile Antonio, Camille Ninel, André Lerond; Marcel Le Borgne (Cap), Emile Daniel, Pires Constantinho, Henri Levandowitz, Lucien Cossou.   Trainer: Lucien Troupel

Goals: Angelillo (17, 28), Firmani (37, 72, 75, 79), Lindskog (56)

OLYMPIQUE LYON v INTERNAZIONALE MILANO   1-1 (1-0)

Stade Gerland, Lyon   14.01.59

Referee: Daniel Mellet (Swi)   Attendance: 2,000

OLYMPIQUE: Eleftherios Manolios; Robert Mouynet, Aimé Mignot; Emile Antonio, Antoine Dalla Cieka, André Lerond; Marcel Le Borgne (Cap), Emile Daniel, Pires Constantinho, Henri Levandowitz, Lucien Cossou.   Trainer: Lucien Troupel

INTER: Natale Nobili; Luigi Robbiati, Aristide Guarneri; Enea Masiero, Vasco Tagliavini, Italo Galbiati; Osvaldo Verdi, Renzo Rovatti, Edwing Ronald Firmani (Cap), Arcadio Venturi, Mario Mereghetti.   Trainer: Giuseppe Bigogno

Goals: Cossou (19), Rovatti (70)

QUARTER FINALS

CHELSEA LONDON v BEOGRAD   1-0 (1-0)

Stamford Bridge, London   29.04.59

Referee: Gunther Ternieder (WG)   Attendance: 25,771

CHELSEA: Reginald Matthews; Richard Peter Sillett (Cap), Richard Whittaker; Sylvan Anderton, John Mortimore, Stanley Crowther; Peter Brabrook, James Peter Greaves, Leslie Allen, Frank Blunstone, Michael Harrison.   Manager: Edward Drake

BEOGRAD: Blagoje Vidinić; Bruno Belin, Fahrudin Jusufi; Jovan Miladinović, Vasilije Šijaković, Bozidar Pajević; Aleksandar Petaković, Milan Galić, Tomislav Kaloperović, Branko Zebec (Cap), Branislav Mihajlović.   Trainer: Rajko Mitić

Goal: Brabrook (30)

BEOGRAD v CHELSEA LONDON 4-1 (2-0)

JNA, Beograd 13.05.59

Referee: Antonio Moriconi (Ita)   Attendance: 10,000

BEOGRAD: Vladimir Beara; Bruno Belin, Vladimir Durković; Lazar Tasić, Vasilije Šijaković, Bozidar Pajević; Dragoslav Šekularac, Aleksandar Petaković, Branko Zebec (Cap), Bora Kostić, Branislav Mihajlović.   Trainer: Rajko Mitić

CHELSEA: William George Robertson; Richard Peter Sillett (Cap), Richard Whittaker; Sylvan Anderton, John Mortimore, Stanley Crowther; Peter Brabrook, Anthony Nicholas, Leslie Allen, Frank Blunstone, Michael Harrison.
Manager: Edward Drake

Goals: Petakovic (3), Mihajlovic (42, 86), Brabrook (51), Kostic (65)

BIRMINGHAM CITY v ZAGREB 1-0 (1-0)

St.Andrew's, Birmingham 6.05.59

Referee: Gérard Versyp (Bel)   Attendance: 21,411

BIRMINGHAM CITY: John Schofield; Brian Farmer, George Allen; John Watts (Cap), Graham Sissons, Richard Neal; Harry Hooper, John Gordon, Robin Stubbs, Bernard Larkin, Brian Taylor.   Manager: Albert Beasley

ZAGREB: Gordon Irovic; Josip Šikić, Mladen Koscak; Ivan Šantek (Cap), Franjo Gašpert, Željko Perušić; Luka Lipošinovic, Vladimir Čonč, Dionizije Dvornic, Željko Matuš, Vladimir Lackovic.   Trainer: Momčilo Pazur

Goal: Larkin (41)

UNION ST.GILLOISE BRUSSEL
v AS ROMA 2-0 (1-0)

Stade Joseph Mariën, Brussel 22.04.59

Referee: Helmut Köhler (DDR)   Attendance: 6,000

UNION: Fernand Decorte; Henri Dirickx (Cap), Theo Van Rooy; André Masset, Jozef Oversteyns, Léon Close; Jean-Pierre Janssens, Remy Van de Weyer, Hubert Vandormael, Paul Vandenberg, Roger Van Cauwelaert.
Trainer: André Van de Wijer

AS ROMA: Fabio Cudicini; Giovanni Griffith, Giulio Corsini; Egidio Guarnacci, Giacomo Losi (Cap), Luigi Giuliano; Lamberto Leonardi, Enzo Menegotti, Dino Da Costa, Arne Selmosson, Alcide Ghiggia.   Trainer: Sarosi

Goals: Vandormael (35), Janssens (61)

ZAGREB v BIRMINGHAM CITY 3-3 (0-1)

Maksimir, Zagreb 24.05.59

Referee: János Pósa-Polareczki (Hun)   Attendance: 18,000

ZAGREB: Gordon Irović; Josip Šikić, Vladimir Marković; Ivan Šantek (Cap), Franjo Gašpert, Hrvoje Jukić; Zdravko Rauš, Vladimir Čonč, Dionizije Dvornić, Željko Matuš, Željko Perušić.   Trainer: Momčilo Pazur

BIRMINGHAM CITY: John Schofield; Brian Farmer, George Allen; John Watts, Trevor Smith (Cap), Richard Neal; Gordon Astall, John Gordon, Robin Stubbs, Bernard Larkin, Harry Hooper. Smith sent off (65)   Trainer: Albert Beasley

Goals: Larkin (32, 62), Hooper (47), Dvornic (52, 72), Gašpert (87)

AS ROMA
v UNION ST.GILLOISE BRUSSEL 1-1 (1-0)

Stadio Olimpico, Roma 13.05.59

Referee: Manuel Asensi (Spa)   Attendance: 6,000

AS ROMA: Fabio Cudicini; Giovanni Griffith, Giulio Corsini; Egidio Guarnacci, Giacomo Losi (Cap), Franco Zaglio; Alcide Ghiggia, Paolo Pestrin, Dino Da Costa, Mario David, Severino Lojodice.   Trainer: Sarosi

UNION: Fernand Decorte (29 Willy Bruggeman); Henri Dirickx (Cap), Theo Van Rooy; André Masset, Jozef Oversteyns, Léon Close; Jean-Pierre Janssens, Remy Van de Weyer, Hubert Vandormael, Paul Vandenberg, Roger Van Cauwelaert. Trainer: André Van de Wijer

Goals: Da Costa (23), Vandenberg (49)

CF BARCELONA
v INTERNAZIONALE MILANO 4-0 (2-0)

Cump Nou, Barcelona 7.05.59

Referee: Louis Fauquembergue (Fra)   Attendance: 50,000

CF BARCELONA: Antonio RAMALLETS Simón; Fernando OLIVELLA Pons, Francisco Rodríguez García «RODRI», Sigfrido GRACIA Royo; Juan SEGARRA Iraceta (Cap), Martín VERGÉS Massa; Justo TEJADA Martínez, Enrique RIBELLES Sero, EULOGIO Ramiro MARTÍNEZ, Luis SUÁREZ Miramontes, Ramón Alberto VILLAVERDE Vázquez.
Trainer: Helenio Herrera

INTERNAZIONALE: Enzo Matteucci; Livio Fongaro, Ambrogio Valadé; Giovanni Invernizzi, Amos Cardarelli, Arcadio Venturi; Mauro Bicicli, Edwing Ronald Firmani, Antonio Valentin Angelillo (Cap), Bengt Lindskog, Lennart Skoglund.   Trainer: Aldo Campatelli

Goals: Ribelles (10, 34), Villaverde (77), Segarra (81)

INTERNAZIONALE MILANO v CF BARCELONA 2-4 (0-1)

San Siro, Milano 30.09.59

Referee: Kenneth George Aston (Eng)   Attendance: 30,000

INTERNAZIONALE: Enzo Matteucci; Aristide Guarneri, Livio Fongaro; Enea Masiero, Amos Cardarelli, Giovanni Invernizzi; Eugenio Rizzolini, Edwing Ronald Firmani, Antonio Valentin Angelillo (Cap), Arcadio Venturi, Mario Mereghetti.   Trainer: Aldo Campatelli

CF BARCELONA: Antonio RAMALLETS Simón; Fernando OLIVELLA Pons, Francisco Rodríguez García "RODRI", Sigfrido GRACIA Royo; Juan SEGARRA Iraceta (Cap), Enrique GENSANA Meroles; Justo TEJADA Martínez, László KUBALA Stecz, EULOGIO Ramiro MARTÍNEZ, Luis SUÁREZ Miramontes, Zoltán Czibor.   Trainer: Helenio Herrera

Goals: Martínez (7, 74), Firmani (50), Kubala (51, 88), Mereghetti (58)

BEOGRAD v CF BARCELONA 1-1 (0-1)

JNA, Beograd 28.10.59

Referee: Joseph Barbéran (Fra)   Attendance: 40,000

BEOGRAD: Vladimir Beara (FK Crvena Zvezda); Vladimir Durković (CZ), Fahrudin Jusufi (FK Partizan Beograd); Lazar Tasić (CZ), Ljubomir Spajić (CZ), Vasilije Šijaković (OFK Beograd); Dragoslav Šekularac (CZ), Aleksandar Petaković (Cap-FK Radnički), Tomislav Kaloperović (Partizan), Bora Kostić (CZ), Ljubomir Ognjanović (FK Radnički). Trainer: Rajko Mitić

CF BARCELONA: Antonio RAMALLETS Simón (Cap); Fernando OLIVELLA Pons, Francisco Rodríguez García "RODRI", Sigfrido GRACIA Royo; Martín VERGÉS Massa, Enrique GENSANA Meroles; Enrique RIBELLES Sero, EVARISTO Juan de Macedo Filho, EULOGIO Ramiro MARTÍNEZ, Luis SUÁREZ Miramontes, Ramón Alberto VILLAVERDE Vázquez.   Trainer: Helenio Herrera

Goals: Evaristo (44), Kostić (69)

SEMI-FINALS

UNION ST.GILLOISE BRUSSEL v BIRMINGHAM CITY 2-4 (1-2)

Stade Joseph Mariën, Brussel 7.10.59

Referee: Albert Guinnard (Swi)   Attendance: 20,000

UNION ST.GILLOISE: Fernand Decorte; Henri Dirickx (Cap), Theo Van Rooy; André Masset, Jean Claes, Léon Close; Jean-Pierre Janssens, Remy Van de Weyer, Luc Mertens, Paul Vandenberg, Roger Van Cauwelaert.   Trainer: Henri Dekens

BIRMINGHAM CITY: Gilbert Harold Merrick; Graham Sissons, Brian Farmer; John Watts, Trevor Smith (Cap), Richard Neal; Harry Hooper, John Gordon, Brian Orritt, James Barrett, Brian Taylor.   Manager: Albert Beasley

Goals: Janssens (9), Hooper (25), Gordon (39), Van Cauwelaert (46), Taylor (73), Barrett (79)

BIRMINGHAM CITY v UNION ST.GILLOISE BRUSSEL 4-2 (2-0)

St.Andrew's, Birmingham 11.11.59

Referee: Johannes Malka (WG)   Attendance: 14,152

BIRMINGHAM CITY: John Schofield; Brian Farmer, George Allen; John Watts, Trevor Smith (Cap), Bernard Larkin; Michael Hellawell, James Barrett, John Gordon, Harry Hooper, Brian Taylor.   Manager: Albert Beasley

UNION ST.GILLOISE: Fernand Decorte; Henri Dirickx (Cap), Theo Van Rooy; André Masset, Jean Claes, Willy Depauw; Camille Van Vaerenberg, Remy Van de Weyer, Claude Lenglet, Luc Martens, Jean-Pierre Janssens. Trainer: Henri Dekens

Goals: Gordon (15, 63), Larkin (32), Janssens (60), Dirickx (78 pen), Hooper (89 pen)

CF BARCELONA v BEOGRAD 3-1 (1-1)

Camp Nou, Barcelona 9.12.59

Referee: Concetto lo Bello (Italia)   Attendance: 60,000

CF BARCELONA: Antonio RAMALLETS Simón (Cap); Fernando OLIVELLA Pons, Francisco Rodríguez García "RODRI", Sigfrido GRACIA Royo; Martín VERGÉS Massa, Enrique GENSANA Meroles; EULOGIO Ramiro MARTÍNEZ, László KUBALA Stecz, EVARISTO Juan de Macedo Filho, Luis SUÁREZ Miramontes, Zoltán Czibor.   Trainer: Helenio Herrera

BEOGRAD: Milutin Šoškić (Partizan); Vladimir Durković, Fahrudin Jusufi; Lazar Tasić, Ljubisa Spajić, Jovan Miladinović (Partizan); Aleksandar Petaković, Dragoslav Šekularac, Branko Zebec (Cap), Dušan Maravić (CZ), Branislav Mihajlović (Partizan).   Trainer: Milorad Pavić.   Tasić sent off (82).

Goals: Kubala (5), Mihajlović (43), Evaristo (57), Martínez (85)

FINAL

BIRMINGHAM CITY v CF BARCELONA 0-0

St.Andrew's Ground, Birmingham   *29.03.60*   *Hour: 19,15*

Referee: Lucien Van Nuffel (Bel)   Attendance: 40,524

BIRMINGHAM CITY: John Schofield; Brian Farmer, George Allen; John Watts, Trevor Smith (Cap), Richard Neal; Gordon Astall, John Gordon, Donald Weston, Brian Orritt, Harry Hooper.   Manager: Albert Beasley

CF BARCELONA: Antonio RAMALLETS Simón; Fernando OLIVELLA Pons, Francisco Rodríguez García "RODRI", Sigfrido GRACIA Royo; Juan SEGARRA Iraceta (Cap), Enrique GENSANA Meroles, Luis COLL Hortal, Sándor Kocsis, EULOGIO Ramiro MARTÍNEZ, Enrique RIBELLES Sero, Ramón Alberto VILLAVERDE Vázquez.
Trainer: Helenio Herrera

CF BARCELONA v BIRMINGHAM CITY 4-1 (2-0)

Camp Nou, Barcelona   *4.05.60*

Referee: Lucien van Nuffel (Bel)   Attendance: 70,000

CF BARCELONA: Antonio RAMALLETS Simón; Fernando OLIVELLA Pons, Francisco Rodríguez García "RODRI", Sigfrido GRACIA Royo; Martín VERGÉS Massa, Juan SEGARRA Iraceta (Cap); Luis COLL Hortal, Enrique RIBELLES Sero, EULOGIO Ramiro MARTÍNEZ, László KUBALA Stecz, Zoltán Czibor.   Trainer: Helenio Herrera

BIRMINGHAM CITY: John Schofield; Brian Farmer, George Allen; John Watts, Trevor Smith (Cap), Richard Neal; Gordon Astall, John Gordon, Donald Weston, Peter Murphy, Harry Hooper.   Manager: Albert Beasley

Goals: Martínez (3, 78), Czibor (7, 51), Hooper (83)

Goalscorers Fairs Cup 1958-60

6 goals: Bora Kostić (Beograd)

5 goals: Edwing Ronald Firmani (Internazionale Milano), Bernard Larkin, Harry Hooper (Birmingham City), EULOGIO Ramiro MARTÍNEZ (CF Barcelona)

4 goals: Zoltán Czibor, EVARISTO Juan de Macedo Filho (CF Barcelona)

3 goals: Dino Da Costa (Roma), Peter Brabrook, James Peter Greaves (Chelsea) Branislav Mihajlovic (Beograd), Roger Van Cauwelaert, Hubert Vandormael, Paul Vandenberg, Jean-Pierre Janssens (Union St.Gilloise), László KUBALA Stecz (CF Barcelona), John Gordon (Birmingham City)

2 goals: Miloš Milutinović, Rudinski (Beograd), Stalder (Lausanne), Brabrook (Chelsea), Taylor (Birmingham City), Scherbarth (Leipzig), Villaverde, Ribelles (CF Barcelona), Tasso (Roma), Jerković, Dvornic (Zagreb), Angelillo (Inter Milano)

1 goal: Mitic, Ognjanovic, Šekularac, Petakovic (Beograd), Jonsson, Regamey (Lausanne), Gronemann, Schøne (Frem), Harrison, Nicholas, P.Sillett (Chelsea), Pfeiffer, Brungs (Köln), Neal, Barrett (Birmingham City), Hosp, J.Hügi II, Burger (Basel), Kellermann, Gollnow (Hannover 96), Szusza, Bencsics, Szini (Újpesti Dózsa Budapest), Cossou (Olympique Lyon), Dirickx (Union St.Gilloise), Gensana, González, Segarra (CF Barcelona), Lackovic, Gašpert (Zagreb), Lindskog, Rovatti, Mereghetti (Inter Milano)

Own Goals: Lees (Fram) for Chelsea, Györvari (Újpesti Dózsa) for Zagreb

FAIRS CUP 1960-61

FIRST ROUND

LEIPZIG XI v BEOGRAD XI 5-2 (3-1)

Zentralstadion, Leipzig   *11.09.60*

Referee: Karl Keller (Swi)   Attendance: 35,000

LEIPZIG XI: Dieter Sommer; Heinz Herrmann, Dieter Scherbarth, Claus Pfeufer, Dieter Fischer, Michael Faber, Werner Gase, Rudolf Krause, Rainer Trölitzsch, Henning Frenzel, Klaus Heydenreich.

BEOGRAD XI: Srboljub Krivokuća; Vasilije Šijaković, Milan Zeković (40 Ljubisa Spajić), Rajko Mitić, Golubović, Velibor Vasović, Aleksandar Petaković, Vladimir Kovačević, Milan Vukelić, Ljubomir Ognjanović, Branislav Mihajlović.

Goals: Heydenreich (29, 38), Kovacevic (33), Frenzel (34), Mihajlovic (73), Krause (76), Trölitzsch (87 pen)

BEOGRAD XI v LEIPZIG XI 4-1 (1-1)

JNA, Beograd   *19.10.60*

Referee: Marian Koczner (Pol)   Attendance: 16,000

BEOGRAD XI: Blagoje Vidinić (46 Milutin Šoškić); Vasilije Šijaković, Fahrudin Jusufi; Jovan Miladinović, Branko Zebec, Lazar Tasić; Vladimir Kovačević, Milan Galić, Zoran Prljinčević, Bora Kostić, Branislav Mihajlović.

LEIPZIG XI: Dieter Sommer; Manfred Bauer, Horst Scherbaum, Claus Pfeufer, Dieter Fischer, Michael Faber, Günter Stiller, Rudolf Krause, Rainer Trölitzsch, Karl Drössler, Klaus Heydenreich.

Goals: Tasić (12), Stiller (24), Mihajlović (60, 90), Prljinčević (73 pen)

BEOGRAD XI v LEIPZIG XI 2-0 (1-0)

Budapest 9.11.60

Referee: Ferdinand Marschall (Aus)   Attendance: 3,500

BEOGRAD XI: Milutin Šoškić (84 Srboljub Krivokuća); Vladimir Durković, Fahrudin Jusufi; Lazar Tasić, Vasilije Šijaković, Velibor Vasović; Josip Skoblar, Vladimir Kovačević, Zoran Prljinčević, Branko Zebec, Bora Kostić.

LEIPZIG XI: Dieter Sommer; Manfred Bauer, Horst Scherbaum, Claus Pfeufer, Michael Faber, Heinz Herrmann, Henning Frenzel, Rudolf Krause, Rainer Trölitzsch, Karl Drössler, Klaus Heydenreich.

Goals: Skoblar (10), Kostić (49)

INTERNAZIONALE MILANO
v HANNOVER 96 8-2 (1-0)

San Siro, Milano 13.09.60

Referee: Arthur Edward Ellis (Eng)   Attendance: 17,000

INTER: Lorenzo Buffon; Picchi, Livio Fongaro; Franco Zaglio, Aristide Guarneri, Bruno Bolchi; Mauro Bicicli, Edwing Ronald Firmani, Valentin Angelillo, Bengt Lindskog, Mario Corso.   Trainer: Helenio Herrera

HANNOVER 96: Dieter Meyer; Siegfried Korff, Hubert Wiezorek, Manfred Kowol, Heinz Steinwedel, Klaus Bohnsack, Viktor Schmidtke, Heinz Fischer, Friedrich Heiser, Gerd Gollnow, Georg Kellermann.

Goals: Bicicli (21), Heiser (49), Zaglio (55), Fischer (61), Lindskog (63 pen, 73), Corso (70, 76), Firmani (79), Angelillo (90)

HANNOVER 96
v INTERNAZIONALE MILANO 1-6 (1-2)

Niedersachsenstadion, Hannover 5.10.60

Referee: Gérard Versyp (Bel)   Attendance: 12,000

HANNOVER 96: Dieter Meyer; Peter Flegel, Hubert Wiezorek; Manfred Kowol, Heinz Steinwedel, Klaus Bohnsack; Herbert Weinberg, Viktor Schmidtke, Friedrich Heiser, Heinz Fischer, Georg Kellermann.

INTER: Lorenzo Buffon; Mauro Gatti, Remo Bicchierai, Enea Masiero, Aristide Guarneri, Giovanni Invernizzi, Mauro Bicicli, Edwing Ronald Firmani, Valentin Angelillo, Bengt Lindskog, Mario Corso.   Trainer: Helenio Herrera

Goals: Heiser (4), Angelillo (25), Corso (40), Lindskog (55), Bicchierai (75), Wieczorek (77 og), Firmani (85)

UNION ST.GILLOISE BRUSSEL v AS ROMA 0-0

Parc Duden, Brussel 4.10.60

Referee: Werner Treichel (WG)   Attendance: 5,000

UNION: Willy Bruggeman; Henri Diricx, Marcel Dries, Camille Van Vaerenberg, Jean Claes, Léon Close, Roger Van Cauwelaert, Paul Vandenberg, Lucien Mertens, Hans Gerard, Roger Janssens.

AS ROMA: Luciano Panetti; Giosué Stucchi, Guido Corsini, Alfio Fontana, Giacomo Losi, Luigi Giuliano, Alcide Edgardo Ghiggia, Paolo Pestrin, Pedro Waldemar Manfredini, Juan Alberto Schiaffino, Arne Selmosson.
Trainer: Luis Antonio Carniglia

AS ROMA
v UNION ST.GILLOISE BRUSSEL 4-1 (3-0)

Stadio Olimpico, Roma 1.11.60

Referee: Daniel Mellet (Swi)   Attendance: 20,000

AS ROMA: Luciano Panetti, Giosué Stucchi, Guido Corsini, Luigi Giuliano, Giacomo Losi, Juan Alberto Schiaffino, Alberto Orlando, Francisco Ramon Lojacono, Pedro Waldemar Manfredini, Arne Selmosson, Giampaolo Menichelli.
Trainer: Luis Antonio Carniglia

UNION: Willy Bruggeman; Henri Diricx, Claude Langlet, Camille Van Vaerenberg, Jean Claes, Léon Close, Jean-Pierre Janssens, Paul Vandenberg, Lucien Mertens, Hans Gerard, Roger Janssens.

Goals: Giuliano (6), Menichelli (21), Manfredini (38), Lojacono (76), Dirickx (81 pen)

ZAGREB-CF BARCELONA 1-1 (0-1)

Maksimir, Zagreb 12.10.60

Referee: Gino Rigato (Ita)   Attendance: 15,000

ZAGREB: Mirko Stojanović; Josip Šikić, Tomislav Crnković, Vlatko Marković; Ivan Šantek, Željko Perušić; Ivica Cvitković, Drazan Jerković, Željko Matuš, Stjepan Lamza, Dragan Blažić.
Trainer: Milan Antolković

CF BARCELONA: Antonio RAMALLETS Simón; José PINTO, Jesús GARAY Vecino, Sigfrido GRACIA Royo; Martín VERGÉS Massa, Enrique GENSANA Meroles; Andres Paredes Alvite "SUCO", Enrique RIBELLES Sero, EVARISTO Juan de Macedo Filho, Juan SEGARRA Iraceta, Ramón Alberto VILLAVERDE Vázquez.   Trainer: Ljubiša Broćić

Goals: Villaverde (25), Gensana (61 og)

CF BARCELONA v ZAGREB 4-3 (1-2)

Camp Nou, Barcelona 19.10.60

Referee: Michel Devillers (Fra) Attendance: 50,000

CF BARCELONA: Antonio RAMALLETS Simón; José PINTO, Jesus GARAY Vecino, Sigfrido GRACIA Royo; Martín VERGÉS Massa, Enrique GENSANA Meroles; Justo TEJADA Martínez, EVARISTO Juan de Macedo Filho, EULOGIO Ramiro MARTÍNEZ, Luis SUÁREZ Miramontes, Zoltán Czibor. Trainer: Ljubiša Bročić

ZAGREB: Gordan Irović; Josip Šikić, Tomislav Crnković, Vlatko Marković; Ivan Šantek, Željko Perušić; Vladimir Čonč, Željko Matuš, Dragan Blažić, Stjepan Lamza, Ilijas Pasić. Trainer: Milan Antolković

Goals: Lamza (18), Markovic (27), Suárez (38), E. Martínez (53), Gensana (65), Czibor (70), Pasic (83)

BIRMINGHAM CITY v ÚJPESTI DÓZSA BUDAPEST 3-2 (1-1)

St.Andrew's, Birmingham 19.10.60

Referee: Arthur Blavier (Bel) Attendance: 23,381

BIRMINGHAM: John Schofield; Brian Farmer, Graham Sissons, George Allen; John Watts, Richard Neal; Michael Hellawell, William Rudd, John Gordon, James Singer, Gordon Astall. Manager: Gil Merrick

ÚJPESTI DÓZSA: Gábor Török; Károly Rajna, Pál Várhidi, József Györvári; József Szini, György Borsányi; László Jagodics, János Göröcs, Ferenc Szusza, Béla Kuharszki, József Bencsics. Trainer: László Fenyvesi

Goals: Göröcs (15, 49), Gordon (29, 83), Astall (62)

OLYMPIQUE LYON v KÖLN 1-3 (1-0)

Stade Gerland, Lyon 12.10.60

Referee: John Kelly (Eng) Attendance: 1,100

OLYMPIQUE: Claude Abbes (46 Claude Hugues); Milan Grobarcik, Aimé Mignot, Jean Camilla, Jacques Solas, Camille Ninel; Jean Louis Rivoire, Bernard Roubaud, Nestor Combin, Eugene N'jo-Lea, Emile Daniel. Trainer: Gaby Robert

KÖLN: Fritz Ewert; Fritz Pott, Heinz Schumacher, Fritz Breuer; Günter Mühlenbock, Hans Sturm; Karl-Heinz Rühl, Bernhard Schwier, Christian Müller, Willi Wrenger, Otto Neteler.

Goals: Roubaud (4 pen), Müller (55), Rühl (70), Schwier (76)

ÚJPESTI DÓZSA BUDAPEST v BIRMINGHAM CITY 1-2 (1-1)

Megyeri út, Budapest 26.10.60

Referee: Helmut Köhler (DDR) Attendance: 25,000

ÚJPESTI DÓZSA: Gábor Török; Károly Rajna, Pál Várhidi, Kálmán Sóvári; József Szini, György Borsányi; László Jagodics, Béla Kuharszki, Ferenc Szusza, László Pataki, Ferenc Horváth. Trainer: László Fenyvesi

BIRMINGHAM: John Schofield; Brian Farmer, Trevor Smith, George Allen; John Watts, Richard Neal; Michael Hellawell, Raymond Barlow, John Gordon, James Singer, William Rudd. Gordon sent off (83). Manager: Gil Merrick

Goals: Szusza (63), Rudd (88), Singer (90)

KÖLN v OLYMPIQUE LYON 1-2 (1-1)

Mungersdorferstadion, Köln 19.10.60

Referee: Frede Hansen (Dan) Attendance: 8,900

KÖLN: Siegfried Ernst; Fritz Pott, Heinz Schumacher, Günter Mühlenbock, Fritz Breuer, Georg Stollenwerk, Karl-Heinz Rühl, Bernhard Schwier, Christian Müller, Hans Sturm, Ernst-Günter Habig.

OLYMPIQUE: Claude Hugues; Milan Grobarcik, Aimé Mignot, Jean Camilla, Raymond Gardon, Camille Ninel, Jean Louis Rivoire, Bernard Roubaud, Lucien Gardon, Nestor Combin, Eugene N'jo-Lea. Trainer: Gaby Robert

Goals: Sturm (20), L. Gardon (67), Njo-Lea (80)

KB KØBENHAVN v BASEL XI 8-1 (2-1)

Idraetsparken, København 26.10.60

Referee: Gerhard Schulenburg (WG) Attendance: 2,600

KB KØBENHAVN: Niels Jensen; Henning Hellbrandt, Ib Kjøge, Bent Poulsen, Bent Krog, Vagn Petersen, Eyvind Clausen, Jørgen Ravn, Jørn Sørensen, Ole Sørensen, Leif Mortensen.

BASEL: Kurt Stettler; Bruno Michaud, Hans Weber, Horst Fischer, Hansueli Oberer, Paul Speidel, Hanspeter Stocker, Guido Kiefer, Josef Hügi II, Eduard Vogt, Antonio Danani. Trainer: Jenő Vincze (Hun)

Goals: V. Petersen (18, 44, 89), J. Hügi II (34), O. Sørensen (62), Clausen (66), J. Sørensen (72, 76, 86)

BASEL XI v KB KØBENHAVN 3-3 (2-2)

St.Jakob, Basel   3.11.60

Referee: Pierre Schwinte (Fra)   Attendance: 4,000

BASEL: Kurt Mayer (70 Kurt Stettler); Horst Fischer, Hans Weber, Ruedi Rickenbacher, Hansueli Oberer, Paul Speidel, Hanspeter Stocker, Silvan Thüler, Josef Hügi II, Gerhard Siedl, Werner Kirchhofer.   Trainer: Jenő Vincze

KB KØBENHAVN: Niels Jensen; Henning Hellbrandt, Ib Kjøge, Bent Poulsen, Bent Krog, Klaus Busk, Eyvind Clausen, Jørgen Ravn, Jørn Sørensen, Ole Sørensen, Leif Mortensen.

Goals: J.Hügi II (..), Siedl (..), Kirchhofer (..), Ravn (.., ..), O.Sørensen (..)

Hibernian Edinburgh walk over, Lausanne Sports forfeited

**CF BARCELONA
v HIBERNIAN EDINBURGH 4-4** (1-2)

Camp Nou, Barcelona   27.12.60

Referee: Cesare Jonni (Ita)   Attendance: 32,000

CF BARCELONA: Antonio RAMALLETS Simón; Juan SEGARRA Iraceta, Sigfrido GRACIA Royo, Martín VERGÉS Massa, Jesus GARAY Vecino, Enrique GENSANA Meroles, Ramón Alberto VILLAVERDE Vázquez, Sándor Kocsis, EVARISTO Juan de Macedo Filho, László KUBALA Stecz, Gonzalo Díaz BEITIA.   Trainer: Ljubiša Broćić

HIBERNIAN: Ronald Campbell Simpson; John Fraser, Joseph McClelland, John Grant, James Easton, Samuel Baird, James Scott, Thomas Preston, Joe Baker, John Baxter, John Murdoch MacLeod.

Goals: Baker (7, 74), MacLeod (19), Kocsis (36, 53, 83), Preston (72), Evaristo (89)

QUARTER-FINALS

KB KØBENHAVN v BIRMINGHAM CITY 4-4 (1-1)

Idraetsparken, København   23.11.60

Referee: Raymond Lespineux (Bel)   Attendance: 2,200

KB KØBENHAVN: Niels Jensen; Henning Hellbrandt, Bent Poulsen, Bent Krogh, Ib Kjøge, Klaus Busk, Eyvind Clausen, Jørgen Ravn, Jens Thorstensen, Ole Sørensen, Leif Mortensen. Trainer: Carlos Pinter

BIRMINGHAM: Colin Withers; Brian Farmer, George Allen, John Watts, Trevor Smith, Richard Neal, Michael Hellawell, John Gordon, James Singer, James Bloomfield, Brian Taylor. Manager: Gil Merrick

Goals: Ravn (34), Gordon (36, 71), Singer (49, 61), Clausen (65, 79), Thorstensen (73)

BIRMINGHAM CITY v KB KØBENHAVN 5-0 (1-0)

St.Andrew's, Birmingham   7.12.60

Referee: Frank Crossley (Sco)   Attendance: 22,486

BIRMINGHAM: Colin Withers; Brian Farmer, George Allen; John Watts, Trevor Smith, Richard Neal; Michael Hellawell, Robin Stubbs, James Harris, James Bloomfield, Brian Taylor. Manager: Gil Merrick

KB KØBENHAVN: Niels Jensen; Henning Hellbrandt, Bent Poulsen, Bent Krog, Ib Kjøge, Vagn Petersen, Eyvind Clausen, Jørgen Ravn, Jørn Sørensen, Ole Sørensen, Leif Mortensen. **Trainer**: Carlos Pinter

Goals: Stubbs (4, 67), Harris (48), Hellawell (51), Hellbrandt (53 og)

**HIBERNIAN EDINBURGH
v CF BARCELONA 3-2** (1-2)

Easter Road Park, Edinburgh   22.02.61

Referee: Johnnes Malka (WG)   Attendance: 45,000

HIBERNIAN: Ronald Campbell Simpson; John Fraser, Joseph McClelland, John Baxter, James Easton, Samuel Baird, John Murdoch MacLeod, Thomas Thomas Preston, Joe Baker, Robert Kinloch, William Ormond.

CF BARCELONA: Carlos Domingo MEDRANO; Alfonso María Rodríguez Salas "FONCHO", Enrique GENSANA Meroles, Martín VERGÉS Massa, Jesus GARAY Vecino, Juan SEGARRA Iraceta, EVARISTO Juan de Macedo Filho, Sándor Kocsis, EULOGIO Ramiro MARTÍNEZ, Luis SUÁREZ Miramontes, Ramón Alberto VILLAVERDE Vázquez. Trainers: Bradock & Enrique Orizaola

Goals: Baker (10), E. Martínez (29), Kocsis (44), Preston (72), Kinloch (85 pen)

KÖLN v AS ROMA 0-2 (0-0)

Mungersdorfenstadion, Köln   18.01.61

Referee: George McCabe (Eng)   Attendance: 13,000

AS ROMA: Luciano Panetti (46 Fabio Cudicini); Alfio Fontana, Guido Corsini, Paolo Pestrin, Giosué Stucchi, Luigi Giuliano, Alcide Edgardo Ghiggia, Francisco Ramon Lojacono, Pedro Waldemar Manfredini, Juan Alberto Schiaffino, Giampaolo Menichelli.   Trainer: Luis Antonio Carniglia

KÖLN: Günter Klemm; Georg Stollenwerk, Karl-Heinz Schnellinger, Christian Breuer, Günter Mühlenbock, Friedel Giegeling, Karl-Heinz Rühl, Hans Schäfer, Christian Müller, Hans Sturm, Willibert Kremer.

Goals: Manfredini (51), Stollenwerk (70 og)

AS ROMA v KÖLN 0-2 (0-0)

Stadio Olimpico, Roma   8.02.61

Referee: Trajan Ivanovski (Jug)   Attendance: 9,000

KÖLN: Günter Klemm; Georg Stollenwerk, Karl-Heinz Schnellinger, Christian Breuer, Leo Wilden, Günter Mühlenbock, Karl-Heinz Rühl, Hans Sturm, Christian Müller, Friedel Giegeling, Willibert Kremer.

AS ROMA: Luciano Panetti; Giosué Stucchi, Guido Corsini, Alfio Fontana, Giacomo Losi, Luigi Giuliano, Giancarlo De Sisti, Paolo Pestrin, Alberto Orlando, Francisco Ramon Lojacono, Arne Selmosson.   Trainer: Luis Antonio Carniglia

Goals: Kremer (58), Schnellinger (82)

AS ROMA v KÖLN 4-1 (1-0)

Stadio Olimpico, Roma   1.03.61

Referee: Victor Schicker (Swi)   Attendance: 20,000

AS ROMA: Fabio Cudicini; Giosué Stucchi, Guido Corsini; Alfio Fontana, Giacomo Losi, Luigi Giuliano; Giampaolo Menichelli, Francisco Ramon Lojacono, Pedro Waldemar Manfredini, Paolo Pestrin, Juan Alberto Schiaffino. Trainer: Luis Antonio Carniglia

KÖLN: Günter Klemm (36 Toni Schumacher); Georg Stollenwerk, Dieter Nasdella, Christian Breuer, Günter Mühlenbock, Friedel Giegeling, Karl-Heinz Rühl, Karl-Heinz Ripkens, Christian Müller, Hans Sturm, Willibert Kremer.

Goals: Manfredini (42, 70), Lojacono (60), Pestrin (71), Müller (83)

INTERNAZIONALE MILANO v BEOGRAD XI 5-0 (1-0)

San Siro, Milano   1.03.61

Ref: José María Ortiz de Mendibil (Spa)   Attendance: 21,000

INTER: Lorenzo Buffon; Armando Picchi, Livio Fongaro, Bruno Bolchi, Aristide Guarneri, Costanzo Balleri, Mauro Bicicli, Bengt Lindskog, Edwing Ronald Firmani, Mario Corso, Egidio Morbello. Trainer: Helenio Herrera

BEOGRAD: Milutin Šoškić; Vladimir Durković, Novak Tomić; Tomislav Kaloperović, Vasilije Šijaković, Velibor Vasović; Aleksandar Petaković, Vladimir Kovačević, Zoran Prljinčević, Bora Kostić, Branislav Mihajlović.

Goals: Morbello (8), Bicicli (51, 80), Firmani (74, 87)

BEOGRAD XI v INTERNAZIONALE MILANO 1-0 (0-0)

JNA, Beograd   8.03.61

Referee: Gottfried Dienst (Swi)   Attendance: 30,000

BEOGRAD: Milutin Šoškić; Fahrudin Jusufi, Vasilije Šijaković; Tomislav Kaloperović, Vladimir Durković, Lazar Tasić; Josip Skoblar, Sava Antić, Branislav Mihajlović, Milan Galić, Bora Kostić.

INTER: Lorenzo Buffon; Armando Picchi, Mauro Gatti; Bruno Bolchi, Aristide Guarneri, Costanzo Balleri; Mauro Bicicli, Valentin Angelillo, Edwing Ronald Firmani, Mario Corso, Enea Masiero.   Trainer: Helenio Herrera

Goals: Skoblar (54)

SEMI-FINALS

HIBERNIAN EDINBURGH v AS ROMA 2-2 (1-0)

Easter Road, Edinburgh   19.04.61

Referee: Daniel Mellet (Swi)   Attendance: 40,000

HIBERNIAN: Ronald Campbell Simpson; John Fraser, Davin, John Grant, James Easton, Samuel Baird, James Scott, Thomas Preston, Joe Baker, John Baxter, John MacLeod.

AS ROMA: Fabio Cudicini; Leopoldo Raimondi, Guido Corsini; Alfio Fontana, Giacomo Losi, Luigi Giuliano; Alberto Orlando, Paolo Pestrin, Juan Alberto Schiaffino, Francisco Ramon Lojacono, Giampaolo Menichelli. Trainer: Luis Antonio Carniglia

Goals: Lojacono (14, 63), Baker (47), MacLeod (82)

AS ROMA v HIBERNIAN EDINBURGH 3-3 (1-1)

Stadio Olimpico, Roma   26.04.61

Referee: Marcel Lequesne (Fra)   Attendance: 22,000

AS ROMA: Fabio Cudicini; Alfio Fontana, Leopoldo Raimondi; Paolo Pestrin, Giacomo Losi, Luigi Giuliano; Alberto Orlando, Francisco Ramon Lojacono, Pedro Waldemar Manfredini, Juan Alberto Schiaffino, Giampaolo Menichelli. Trainer: Luis Antonio Carniglia

HIBERNIAN: Ronald Campbell Simpson; John Fraser, Davin; Robert Kinloch, James Easton, Samuel Baird, John MacLeod, Joe Baker, John Baxter, David Gibson, William Ormond.

Goals: Manfredini (23, 67), Kinloch (31), Baker (59, 62), Lojacono (72)

AS ROMA v HIBERNIAN EDINBURGH 6-0 (3-0)

Stadio Olimpico, Roma   27.05.61

Referee: Dittmar Huber (Swi)   Attendance: 50,000

AS ROMA: Luciano Panetti; Alfio Fontana, Leopoldo Raimondi; Paolo Pestrin, Giacomo Losi, Luigi Giuliano; Giampaolo Menichelli, Francisco Ramon Lojacono, Pedro Waldemar Manfredini, Juan Alberto Schiaffino, Arne Selmosson.   Trainer: Luis Antonio Carniglia

HIBERNIAN: Ronald Campbell Simpson; John Fraser, Joseph McClelland; John Baxter, James Easton, Samuel Baird; John MacLeod, Robert Kinloch, Joe Baker, David Gibson, Eric Stevenson.

Goals: Manfredini (1, 9, 35, 57), Menichelli (69), Selmosson (72)

INTERNAZIONALE MILANO v BIRMINGHAM CITY 1-2 (0-2)

San Siro, Milano   19.04.61

Referee: Carl Frederik Jørgensen (Dan)   Attendance: 20,000

INTER: Mario Da Pozzo; Armando Picchi, Mauro Gatti; Bruno Bolchi, Aristide Guarneri, Costanzo Balleri; Mauro Bicicli, Mario Corso, Edwing Ronald Firmani, Enea Masiero, Egidio Morbello.   Trainer: Helenio Herrera

BIRMINGHAM: Colin Withers; Brian Farmer, George Allen; Terence Hennessey, Trevor Smith, Richard Neal; Michael Hellawell, Robin Stubbs, James Harris, James Bloomfield, Bryan Orritt.   Manager: Gil Merrick

Goals: Harris (12), Balleri (42 og), Firmani (75)

BIRMINGHAM CITY v INTERNAZIONALE MILANO 2-1 (1-0)

St.Andrew's, Birmingham   3.05.61

Referee: Raymond Lespineux (Bel)   Attendance: 29,530

BIRMINGHAM: John Schofield; Brian Farmer, George Allen; Terence Hennessey, Trevor Smith, Richard Neal; Michael Hellawell, Bryan Orritt, James Harris, James Bloomfield, Robert Auld.   Manager: Gil Merrick

INTER: Lorenzo Buffon; Mauro Gatti, Giacinto Facchetti; Bruno Bolchi, Aristide Guarneri, Costanzo Balleri; Orazio Rancati, Egidio Morbello, Edwing Ronald Firmani, Bengt Lindskog, Enea Masiero.   Trainer: Helenio Herrera

Goals: Harris (5, 64), Masiero (63)

FINAL

BIRMINGHAM CITY v AS ROMA 2-2 (0-1)

St.Andrew's, Birmingham   27.09.61

Referee: Robert Holley Davidson (Sco)   Attendance: 21,055

BIRMINGHAM: John Schofield; Brian Farmer, Graham Sissons; Terence Hennessey, Winston Foster, Malcolm Beard; Michael Hellawell, Bryan Orritt, James Harris, James Bloomfield, Robert Auld.   Manager: Gilbert Harold Merrick

AS ROMA: Fabio Cudicini; Alfio Fontana, Guido Corsini; Luigi Giuliano, Giacomo Losi (Cap), Sergio Carpanesi; Alberto Orlando, Dino Da Costa, Pedro Waldemar Manfredini, Antonio Angelillo, Giampaolo Menichelli. Trainer: Luis Antonio Carniglia

Goals: Manfredini (30, 56), Hellawell (78), Orritt (86)

AS ROMA v BIRMINGHAM CITY 2-0 (0-0)

Stadio Olimpico, Roma   11.10.61

Referee: Pierre Schwinte (Fra)   Attendance: 60,000

AS ROMA: Fabio Cudicini; Alfio Fontana, Guido Corsini; Sergio Carpanesi, Giacomo Losi (Cap), Paolo Pestrin; Alberto Orlando, Antonio Angelillo, Pedro Waldemar Manfredini, Francisco Ramon Lojacono, Giampaolo Menichelli. Trainer: Luis Antonio Carniglia

BIRMINGHAM: John Schofield; Brian Farmer, Graham Sissons, Terence Hennessey, Trevor Smith, Malcolm Beard, Michael Hellawell, James Bloomfield, James Harris, James Singer, Bryan Orritt.   Manager: Gil Merrick

Goals: Farmer (56 og), Pestrin (90)

Goalscorers Fairs Cup 1960-61:

12 goals: Pedro Waldemar Manfredini (AS Roma)

6 goals: Joe Baker (Hibernian Edinburgh)

5 goals: Edwing Roland Firmani (Internazionale Milano), Francisco Ramon Lojacono (AS Roma)

4 goals: Sándor Kocsis (C.F. Barcelona), John Gordon, James Harris (Birmingham City)

3 goals: Vagn Petersen, Eyvind Clausen, Jørn Sørensen, Jørgen Ravn (KB København), Branislav Mihajlovic (Beograd), Mauro Bicicli, Bengt Lindskog, Mario Corso (Inter Milano), Kinloch (Hibernian), James Singer (Birmingham City)

2 goals: Heydenreich (Leipzig), Heiser (Hannover 96), Göröcs (Újpesti Dózsa), J. Hügi II (Basel), O. Sørensen (KB København), E. Martínez (CF Barcelona), Müller (FC Köln), Skoblar (Beograd), Angelillo (Inter), Menichelli, Pestrin (Roma), MacLeod (Hibernian), Stubbs, Hellawell (Birmingham City)

1 goal: Frenzel, Krause, Trölitzsch, Stiller (Leipzig), Dirickx (Union St.Gilloise), Lamza, Markovic, Pasic (Zagreb), Roubaud, L.Gardon, N'jo-Lea (Olympique Lyon), Szusza (Újpesti Dózsa), Siedl, Kirchofer (Basel), Thorstensen (KB København), Villaverde, Suárez, Gensana, Czibor, Evaristo (CF Barcelona), Kremer, Schnellinger, Ruhl, Schwier, Sturm (Köln), Kovačević, Tasić, Prljinčević, Kostić (Beograd), Fischer (Hannover 96), Zaglio, Bicchierai, Morbello, Masiero (Inter Milano), Prestin (Hibernian), Astall, Rudd, Orritt (Birmingham City), Giuliani, Stollenwerk, Selmosson (Roma)

Own Goals: Wieczorek (Hannover 96) for Inter Milano, Gensana (Barceona) for Zagreb, Balleri (Inter) & Hellbrandt (BK København) for Birmingham City, Farmer (Birmingham City) & Stollenwerk (Köln) for Roma

FAIRS CUP 1961-62

FIRST ROUND

AC MILAN v NOVI SAD 0-0

San Siro, Milano   30.08.61

Referee: Henri Faucheux (FRA)   Attendance: 15,000

AC MILAN: Mario Liberalato; Cesare Maldini, Francesco Zagatti, Ambrogio Pelagalli, Sandro Salvadore, Luigi Radice, Gianni Rivera, Gino Pivatelli, José Altafini, James Peter Greaves, Oliviero Conti.   Trainer: Nereo Rocco

NOVI SAD: Andrija Vereš; Novak Roganovic, Stevan Bena, Zarko Nikolic, Slavko Svinjarevic, Branimir Vratnijan, Dobrosav Krstic, Silvester Takac, Djordje Pavlic, Borbelj, Klipa.

NOVI SAD v AC MILAN 2-0 (1-0)

Gradski, Novi Sad   20.09.61

Referee: Ernst Chebat (AUS)   Attendance: 15,000

NOVI SAD: Ilija Pantelić; Novak Roganovic, Stevan Bena, Zarko Nikolic, Slavko Svinjarevic, BranimirVratnijan, Dobrosav Krstic, Silvester Takac, Djordje Pavlic, Borbelj, Klipa.

AC MILAN: Mario Liberalato; Cesare Maldini, Francesco Zagatti, Ambrogio Pelagalli, Sandro Salvadore, Giovanni Trapattoni, Giancarlo Danova, James Peter Greaves, José Altafini, Mario David, Gianni Rivera.   Trainer: Nereo Rocco

Goals: Takac (20), Pavlic (50)

HIBERNIAN EDINBURGH
v BELENENSES LISBOA 3-3 (0-3)

Easter Road, Edinburgh   4.09.61

Referee: Kevin Howley (Eng)   Attendance: 20,000

HIBERNIAN: Ronald Campbell Simpson; Patrick Hughes, Joseph McClelland; John Baxter, John Grant, Samuel Baird; James Scott, Eric Stevenson, John Fraser, David Gibson, Ally McLeod.

BELENENSES: José Pereira; João Rosendo, Jose Manuel CASTRO Silva Soares; José CORDEIRO Duarte, Alfredo Abrantes, Vicente Lucas; António Fernandes Yauca; António Vitor CARVALHO Junior, Lucas Sebastiao da Fonseca "MATATEU", Salvador Martins, ESTEVÃO António Espírito Santo Mansidão.   Trainer: Enrico Vega (Arg)

Goals: Matateu (13, 26), Yauca (15), Fraser (47, 53), Baird (60 pen)

BELENENSES LISBOA
v HIBERNIAN EDINBURGH 1-3 (1-1)

Estádio do Restelo, Lisboa   27.09.61

Referee: José Caballero (Spa)   Attendance: 25,000

BELENENSES: José Pereira; Francisco Pires, João Rosendo; José CORDEIRO Duarte, Alfredo Abrantes, Vicente Lucas; António Fernandes Yauca; António Vitor CARVALHO Junior, Lucas Sebastiao da Fonseca "MATATEU", Salvador Martins, ESTEVÃO António Espírito Santo Mansidão.   Trainer: Enrico Vega

HIBERNIAN: Ronald Campbell Simpson; John Grant, Joseph McClelland; Davin, James Easton, Samuel Baird; James Scott, Eric Stevenson, John Fraser, John Baxter, Ally McLeod.

Goals: Baxter (20,61), Matateu (28), E. Stevenson (74)

BASEL XI v CRVENA ZVEZDA BEOGRAD 1-1 (1-1)

St.Jakob, Basel   6.09.61

Referee: Roger Machin (FRA)   Attendance: 3,500

BASEL: René Jecker; Bruno Michaud, Hans Weber, Markus Pfirter, Hansueli Oberer, Silvan Thüler, Fernando Kranichfeldt, Karl Odermatt, Josef Hügi II, Hanspeter Stocker, Wilfried Fritz.   Trainer: Georges Sobotka (Ces)

CRVENA ZVEZDA: Petar Cosić; Dimitrije Stojanović, Vladimir Durković, Novak Tomić, Lazar Tasić, Vladimir Popović, Vojislav Melić, Dušan Maravić, Anton Rudinski, Dragoslav Šekularac, Nikola Stipić.

Goals: Odermatt (8), Maravic (32)

CRVENA ZVEZDA BEOGRAD v BASEL XI 4-1 (2-1)

JNA, Beograd   18.10.61

Referee: Kurt Tschenscher (WG)   Attendance: 6000

CRVENA ZVEZDA: Dragomir Vukicević; Dimitrije Stojanović, Tomislav Milićević, Dušan Maravić, Lazar Tasić, Vladimir Popović, Svetozar Andrejić, Vojislav Melić, Anton Rudinski, Dragoslav Šekularac, Nikola Stipić.

BASEL: René Jecker; Hans Weber, Bruno Michaud, Markus Pfirter, Hanspeter Füri, Hanspeter Stocker, Wifried Fritz, Karl Odermatt, Maier, Wolfgang Walther, Heinz Blumer. Trainer: Georges Sobotka (Ces)

Goals: Stipic (6), H. Blumer (23), Melic (42, 69), Rudinski (60)

**OLYMPIQUE LYON
v SHEFFIELD WEDNESDAY 4-2** (3-0)

Stade de Gerland, Lyon   12.09.61

Referee: Albert Guinnard (SWI)   Attendance: 3,000

OLYMPIQUE: Jean Sabathier; Raymond Gardon, Aimé Mignot, Marcel Le Borgne, Alexandre Viala, Lucien Degeorges, Robert Salen, Jean Djorkaeff, Nestor Combin, Eugène Njo-Léa, Angel Rambert.   Trainer: Manuel Fernández

SHEFFIELD: Ronald Springett; Peter Johnson, Donald Megson, Thomas McAnearney, Peter Swan, Anthony Kay, Derek Wilkinson, Robert Craig, Keith Ellis, Gerry Young, Alan Finney.   Manager: Vic Buckingham

Goals: Rambert (19), Njo-Lea (22, 38), Young (47), Ellis (63), Combin (90)

STAEVNET KØBENHAVN v DINAMO ZAGREB 2-7

Idraetsparken, København   7.09.61

Referee: Gerhard Schulenburg (WG)   Attendance: 12,000

STAEVNET: Jørn Larsen; Henning Hellbrandt, Øyvind Fangel, Bent Hansen, Birger Larsen, Bent Krog, Finn Møller, Jørgen Ravn, Jørn Sørensen, Ole Sørensen, Eyvind Clausen.

DINAMO: Mirko Stojanović; Josip Šikić, Mirko Braun, Ivan Šantek, Vlatko Marković, Željko Perušić, Ivica Cvitković, Petar Remete, Drazan Jerković, Željko Matuš, Tomislav Knez. Trainer: Milan Antolković

Goals: Ole Sørensen (..), Ravn (..), Jerković (..,..), Cvitković (..,..), Šantek (..), Knez (..), Matuš (..)

**SHEFFIELD WEDNESDAY
v OLYMPIQUE LYON 5-2** (3-1)

Hillsborough, Sheffield   4.10.61

Referee: Arthur Crossman (SCO)   Attendance: 30,303

SHEFFIELD: Ronald Springett; Peter Johnson, Donald Megson, Thomas McAnearney, Peter Swan, Anthony Kay, Alan Finney, Robert Craig, John Fantham, William Griffin, Colin Dobson.   Manager: Vic Buckingham

OLYMPIQUE: Claude Hugues; Roger Duffez, Aimé Mignot, Marcel Le Borgne, Raymond Gardon, Lucien Degeorges, Robert Salen, Jean Djorkaeff, Nestor Combin, Bernard Roubaud, Angel Rambert.   Trainer: Manuel Fernández

Goals: Salen (6), Fantham (9, 85), Griffin (14), McAnearney (20 pen), Dobson (78), Djorkaeff (81)

**DINAMO ZAGREB
v STAEVNET KØBENHAVN 2-2** (1-2)

Maksimir, Zagreb   4.10.61

Referee: Gyula Gere (HUN)   Attendance: 5,000

DINAMO: Zlatko Škorić; Josip Šikić, Mirko Braun, Ivan Šantek, Vlatko Marković, Željko Perušić, Ivica Cvitković, Slaven Zambata, Drazan Jerković, Petar Remete, Luka Lipošinović.   Trainer: Milan Antolković

KØBENHAVN: Jørn Larsen; Poul Andersen, Øyvind Fangel, Mogens Johansen, Birger Larsen, Borge Rasmussen, Leif Holten, Willi Schøne, Egon Rasmussen, Hans Andersen, Kaj Lerby.

Goals: Remete (29), Egon Rasmussen (31), Hans Andersen (40), Marković (70)

**RACING CLUB STRASBOURG
v MTK BUDAPEST 1-3** (0-2)

Stade Meinau, Strasbourg   13.09.61

Referee: Victor Schicker (SWI)   Attendance: 20,000

RACING: Francis Matéo; Raymond Stieber, Gines Gonzales; Roland Merschel, Robert Jonquet, Michel Leblond; Casimir Novotarski, Pierre Nabat, Michel Lachot, Gerard Coinçon, Charles Isel.   Trainer: Emile Veinante

MTK: Ferenc Kovalik; György Keszei, Ferenc Sipos, Tibor Palicskó; István Nagy, Ferenc Kovács III; Károly Sándor, István Kuti, Gyula Sas, János Molnár, István Szimcsák. Trainer: Gyula Szűcs

Goals: Sándor (20), Gonzales (23 og), Lachot (73), Kuti (90)

MTK BUDAPEST
v RACING CLUB STRASBOURG 10-2 (3-1)

Népstadion, Budapest   17.09.61
Referee: Mach (CZE)   Attendance: 18,000

MTK: Ferenc Kovalik; László Szimcsák II, Ferenc Sipos, Tibor Palicskó; István Nagy, Gyula Sas; Károly Sándor, Gábor Arató, István Kuti, János Molnár, István Szimcsák I.
Trainer: Gyula Szűcs

RACING: François Remetter; Gines Gonzales, Robert Jonquet, René Hauss; Raymond Stieber, Roland Merschel; Michel Leblond, Pierre Nabat, Michel Lachot, Gerard Coinçon, Casimir Novotarski.   Trainer: Emile Veinante

Goals: Kuti (13, 60), Sándor (17, 83), Nabat (21), Molnár (37, 69), Szimcsak I (47, 53, 68), Hauss (75 pen), Sas (82)

HANNOVER 96 v ESPAÑOL BARCELONA 0-1 (0-0)

Niedersachsenstadion, Hannover   13.09.61

Referee: Jozef Casteleyn (Bel)   Attendance: 12,000

HANNOVER: Dieter Meyer; Peter Flegel, Harald Jörss, Hubert Wiezorek, Manfred Kowol, Manfred Fahrtmann, Friedrich Heiser, Otto Hartz, Viktor Schmidtke, Fred Hoff, Udo Nix.   Trainer: Grotkopp

ESPAÑOL: Rafael PIRIS Esteva; Antonio ARGILÉS Antón, Juan BARTOLÍ Figueras, Amaro DAUDER Guardiola, José SASTRE Sanz, Luis MUÑOZ Grau, Zoltán CZIBOR Suhai, Ernesto DOMÍNGUEZ Hernández, Aloísio Francisco da Luz "ÍNDIO", Ramón Sergio CARRANZA Semprini, Antonio CAMPS Bau.   Trainer: José Luis SASO

Goal: Camps (52)

ESPAÑOL BARCELONA v HANNOVER 96 2-0 (1-0)

Estadio de Sarriá, Barcelona   27.09.61

Referee: Gino Rigato (Ita)   Attendance: 12,000

ESPAÑOL: Benito JOANET Jiménez; Antonio ARGILÉS Antón, Juan BARTOLÍ Figueras, Amaro DAUDER Guardiola, José SASTRE Sanz, Luis MUÑOZ Grau, Zoltán CZIBOR Suhai, VIÑAS, Aloísio Francisco da Luz "ÍNDIO", Ramón Sergio CARRANZA Semprini, Antonio CAMPS Bau.
Trainer: José Luis SASO

HANNOVER: Dieter Meyer; Peter Flegel, Harald Jörss, Heinz Steinwedel, Manfred Kowol, Manfred Fahrtmann, Bernd Kettler, Otto Hartz, Friedrich Heiser, Kurt Handke, Viktor Schmidtke.   Trainer: Grotkopp

Goals: Camps (27), Índio (61)

VALENCIA CF v NOTTINGHAM FOREST 2-0 (2-0)

Campo de Mestalla, Valencia   13.09.61

Ref: Joaquim Fernandes de Campos (Por)   Att: 46,000

VALENCIA CF: José GINESTÁ Andreu; Vicente PIQUER Mora, Manuel MESTRE Torres, Francisco SENDRA Corbera, Juan Carlos Díaz QUINCOCES, Décio Quaresma RECAMAN, HÉCTOR NÚÑEZ Bello, Enrique RIBELLES Sero, WALDO Machado da Silva, José PAREDES Gimeno, Vicente GUILLOT Fabián.   Trainer: Domingo Balmanya Parera

FOREST: Peter Grummit; Calvin Palmer, William Gray, Jeffrey Whitefoot, Robert McKinlay, James Iley, Geoffrey Vowden, Colin Booth, Colin Addison, John Quigley, Richard Le Flem.   Manager: Andy Beattie

Goals: Waldo (14, 42)

NOTTINGHAM FOREST v VALENCIA CF 1-5 (0-3)

City Ground, Nottingham   4.10.61

Referee: Robert Smith (WAL)   Attendance: 36,158

FOREST: Peter Grummit; Douglas Baird, William Gray, Jeffrey Whitefoot, Robert McKinlay, James Iley, William Cobb, Colin Booth, Colin Addison, John Quigley, Richard Le Flem.   Manager: Andy Beattie

VALENCIA CF: José GINESTÁ Andreu; Bautista VERDÚ Panadero, SÓCRATES Belenguer Pérez, Manuel MESTRE Torres, Francisco SENDRA Corbera, Enrique RIBELLES Sero, HÉCTOR NÚÑEZ Bello, José PAREDES Gimeno, WALDO Machado da Silva, Décio Quaresma RECAMAN, José Santiago Baeza "FICHA".   Trainer: Domingo Balmanya Parera

Goals: Waldo (11, 13), Núñez (30, 49, 68), Cobb (56)

BERLIN WEST v CF BARCELONA 1-0 (0-0)

Olympiastadion, Berlin West   20.09.61

Referee: Leopold Silvayn Horn (HOL)   Attendance: 30,289

BERLIN: Hans-Joachim Posinski (Ta); Rudolf Deinert (TB), Hans-Günter Schimmöller (H); Rudolf Zeiser (H), Günter Schüler (H), Hans Eder (H); Wolfgang Neumann (Ta), Lutz Steinert (H), Wolfgang Rosenfeldt (Ta), Helmut Faeder (H), Foit (TB).   Trainer: Schneider.
H=Hertha, Ta=Tasmania, TB=Tennis Borussia

CF BARCELONA: José Manuel PESUDO Soler; Alfonso María Rodríguez Salas FONCHO, Sigfrido GRACIA Royo; Martín VERGÉS Massa, Francisco Rodríguez García "RODRI", Enrique GENSANA Meroles; José Antonio ZALDÚA Urdanavia, Sándor KOCSIS, EVARISTO do Macedo Filho, Antonio PAÍS Castroagudin, Ramón Alberto VILLAVERDE Vázquez.   Trainer: Luis Miró

Goal: Steinert (84)

CF BARCELONA v BERLIN WEST 3-0 (1-0)

Camp Nou, Barcelona 4.10.61

Referee: Giulio Campanati (ITA)   Attendance: 46,000

CF BARCELONA: José Manuel PESUDO Soler; Alfonso María Rodríguez Salas FONCHO, Sigfrido GRACIA Royo; Antonio PAÍS Castroagudin, Enrique GENSANA Meroles, Jesús GARAY Vicino; Pedro ZABALLA Barquín, José Antonio ZALDÚA Urdanavia, EVARISTO do Macedo Filho, Sándor KOCSIS, VICENTE González Sosa.   Trainer: Luis Miró

BERLIN: Wolfgang Tillich (H); Rudolf Deinert, Hans-Günter Schimmöller; Rudolf Zeiser, Günter Schüler, Hans Eder; Wolfgang Neumann, Peter Engler (Ta), Helmut Faeder, Lutz Steinert (H), Wolfgang Rosenfeldt (Ta).   Trainer: Mnrpschat

Goals: Evaristo (9, 75), Zaldúa (90)

SPARTAK BRNO v LEIPZIG XI 2-2 (1-2)

Luzankani, Brno 27.09.61

Referee: Gyula Balla (HUN)   Attendance: 1,500

SPARTAK: Přeček; Přibyl, Sobotka, Dobrodka, Skarba, Kocman I, Handl, Kocman II, Hermann, Rudolf Schejbal, Ryc. Trainer: Síma

LEIPZIG: Dieter Sommer; Dieter Scherbarth, Michael Faber, Heinz Herrmann, Peter Giessner, Karl Drössler, Dieter Engelhardt, Rainer Trölitzsch, Arno Zerbe, Dieter Fischer, Werner Gase.

Goals: Schejbal (9, 46 pen), Trölitzsch (13, 44 pen)

UNION ST.GILLOISE v HEART OF MIDLOTHIAN EDINBURGH 1-3 (1-2)

Parc Duden, Brussel 27.09.61

Referee: Pieter Paulus Roomer (HOL)   Attendance: 4000

UNION: André Vanderstappen; Charles De Vogelaere, Alfons Bruylandts, Paul Schraepen, Jean Claes, Lucien Haeck, Julien Kialunda, Camille Van Vaerenbergh, Lucien Mertens, Philippe Van Wilder, Roger Janssens.

HEARTS: Gordon Marshall; Robert Kirk, David Holt, John Cumming, William Polland, William Higgins, Ross, John Hamilton, Norman Davidson, John Docherty, Robert Blackwood.

Goals: Van Vaerenberg (18), Blackwood (23), Davidson (30, 76)

LEIPZIG XI v SPARTAK BRNO 4-1 (3-0)

Zentralstadion, Leipzig 4.10.61

Referee: Marcel Raeymaekers (BEL)   Attendance: 15,000

LEIPZIG: Wolfgang Klank; Dieter Scherbarth, Michael Faber, Claus Pfeufer, Peter Giessner, Karl Drössler, Werner Gase, Rainer Trölitzsch, Henning Frenzel, Dieter Fischer, Arno Zerbe.

SPARTAK: Sova (22 Přeček); Přibyl, Vonarchetz, Dobrodka, Sobotka, Kocman I, Handl, Kocman II, Hermann, Rudolf Schejbal, Ryc.   Trainer: Síma

Goals: Frenzel (17, 21), Zerbe (36, 55), Schejbal (64)

HEART OF MIDLOTHIAN EDINBURGH v UNION ST.GILLOISE 2-0 (0-0)

Tynecastle Park, Edinburgh 4.10.61

Referee: Aage Poulsen (Dan)   Attendance: 18,000

HEARTS: Gordon Marshall; Robert Kirk, David Holt, John Cumming, William Polland, William Higgins, John Hamilton, Robin Stenhouse, William Bauld, William Wallace, John Docherty.

UNION: André Vanderstappen; Paul Schraepen, Alfons Bruylandts, Lucien Haeck, Jean Claes, Léon Close, Roger Van Cauwelaert, Camille Van Vaerenbergh, Lucien Mertens, Julien Kialunda, Roger Janssens.

Goals: Wallace (71), Stenhouse (87)

FC KÖLN v INTERNAZIONALE MILANO 4-2 (3-1)

Mungersdorferstadion, Köln 27.09.61

Referee: James Finney (ENG)   Attendance: 31,000

KÖLN: Fritz Ewert; Ernst-Günter Habig, Fritz Pott, Hans Sturm, Georg Stollenwerk, Karl-Heinz Schnellinger, Karl-Heinz Thielen, Karl-Heinz Ripkens, Christian Müller, Matthias Hemmersbach, Fritz Breuer.

INTER: Ottavio Bugatti; Luigi Caloi, Giacinto Facchetti, Costanzo Balleri, Remo Bicchierai, Giorgio Della Giovanni, Mauro Bicicli, Guido Gratton, Bruno Petroni, Giorgio Brigo, Egidio Morbello.   Trainer: Helenio Herrera

Goals: Sturm (2), Morbello (19), Müller (23), Hemmersbach (36), Petroni (63), Thielen (71)

INTERNAZIONALE MILANO v FC KÖLN 2-0 (1-0)

San Siro, Milano 11.10.61

Referee: Alexandar Škorić (IUG) Attendance: 21,000

INTER: Ottavio Bugatti; Enea Masiero, Giacinto Facchetti, Franco Zaglio, Aristide Guarneri, Costanzo Balleri; Mauro Bicicli, Raggi Giorgio Humberto, Gerald Hitchens, Luis SUÁREZ Miramontes, Egidio Morbello.
Trainer: Helenio Herrera

KÖLN: Fritz Ewert; Ernst-Günter Habig, Fritz Pott, Hans Sturm, Georg Stollenwerk, Karl-Heinz Schnellinger, Karl-Heinz Thielen, Hans Schäfer, Christian Müller, Karl-Heinz Ripkens, Anton Regh.

Goals: Suárez (4, 59 pen)

NOVI SAD v IRAKLIS THESSALONIKI 9-1 (3-0)

Gradski, Novi Sad 15.11.61

Referee: Helmut Köhler (WG) Attendance: 3,000

NOVI SAD: Andrija Vereš; Stevan Sekereš, Milosević, Dobrosav Krstić, Sentin, Borbelj, Veljko Aleksić, Jergić, Djordje Pavlić, Petar Mijatović, Dimitrije Radović.

IRAKLIS: Kostas Karapatis; Ioannidis, Beredimas, Nikos Liaros, Lolos Hasekidis, Asvestas, Plastizas Xilas, Stathis Hasekidis, Mihalis Bellis, Tsigkos, Plutazhos Karavergos.

Goals: Radović (8, 46, 53), Aleksić (22), Pavlić (38, 57, 58), Mijatović (55, 77), S. Hasekidis (60)

INTERNAZIONALE MILANO v FC KÖLN 5-3 (4-1)

San Siro, Milano 25.10.61

Referee: John Kelly (ENG) Attendance: 23,000

INTER: Ottavio Bugatti; Giacinto Facchetti, Enea Masiero, Franco Zaglio, Remo Bicchierai, Costanzo Balleri, Mario Mereghetti, Egidio Morbello, Raggi Giorgio Humberto, Luis SUÁREZ Miramontes, Mario Corso. Trainer: Helenio Herrera

KÖLN: Fritz Ewert; Ernst-Günter Habig, Fritz Pott, Hans Sturm, Georg Stollenwerk, Karl-Heinz Schnellinger, Karl-Heinz Thiellen, Hans Schäfer, Christian Müller, Karl-Heinz Ripkens, Anton Regh.

Goals: Humberto (2, 32, 63), Suárez (16), Morbello (40), Regh (42, 54), Ripkens (73)

CRVENA ZVEZDA BEOGRAD v HIBERNIAN EDINBURGH 4-0 (3-0)

JNA, Beograd 1.11.61

Referee: Fritz Seipelt (Aus) Attendance: 25,000

CRVENA ZVEZDA: Dragomir Vukićević; Dimitrije Stojanović, Tomislav Milićević, Lazar Tasić, Vladimir Durković, Vladimir Popović, Svetozar Andrejić, Dušan Maravić, Vojislav Melić, Dragoslav Šekularac, Nikola Stipić.

HIBERNIAN: William Muirhead; John Fraser, Joseph McClelland, Davin, James Easton, Patrick Hughes, Eric Stevenson, David Gibson, John Baxter, Thomas Preston, Ally McLeod.

Goals: Maravic (17, 55), Melic (24), Tasic (42)

SECOND ROUND

IRAKLIS THESSALONIKI v NOVI SAD 2-1 (1-1)

Kautatzogleio, Thessaloniki 26.10.61

Referee: Giuseppe Adami (Ita) Attendance: 18,000

IRAKLIS: Kostas Karapatis; Ioannidis, Beredimas, Haralampidis, Nikos Liaros, Lolos Hasekidis, Asvestas, Plastizas Xilas, Stathis Hasekidis, Tsigkos, Plutazhos Karavergos.

NOVI SAD: Andrija Vereš; Milosević, Mladen Vucinić, Jergić, Zarko Nikolić, Sentin, Veljko Aleksić, Borbelj, Stefanović, Petar Mijatović, Silvester Takac.

Goals: Xilas (9 pen), Takac (43), Asvestas (48)

HIBERNIAN EDINBURGH v CRVENA ZVEZDA BEOGRAD 0-1 (0-0)

Easter Road, Edinburgh 15.11.61

Referee: Clive W. Kingston (Wal) Attendance: 9,000

HIBERNIAN: Ronald Campbell Simpson; John Fraser, Joseph McClelland, John Grant, James Easton, Davin, Eric Stevenson, Ian Cuthbert, Thomas Preston, David Gibson, Ally McLeod.

CRVENA ZVEZDA: Dragomir Vukićević, Tomislav Milićević, Novak Tomić, Vladimir Popović, Jovan Cokić, Lazar Tasić, Svetozar Andrejić, Dušan Maravić, Anton Rudinski, Vojislav Melić, Zoran Prljinčević.

Goal: Prljinčević (77)

HEART OF MIDLOTHIAN EDINBURGH v INTERNAZIONALE MILANO 0-1 (0-1)

Tynecastle Park, Edinburgh 6.11.61

Referee: Kevin Howley (Eng)   Attendance: 20,500

HEARTS: Gordon Marshall; Robert Kirk, David Holt, John Cumming, William Polland, William Higgins, Daniel Ferguson, Maurice Elliott, William Bauld, William Wallace, John Hamilton.

INTER: Ottavio Bugatti; Armando Picchi, Giacinto Facchetti, Enea Masiero, Aristide Guarneri, Costanzo Balleri, Mauro Bicicli, Lorenzo Bettini, Raggi Giorgio Humberto, Mario Mereghetti, Egidio Morbello. Trainer: Helenio Herrera

Goal: Humberto (33)

INTERNAZIONALE MILANO v HEART OF MIDLOTHIAN EDINBURGH 4-0 (2-0)

San Siro, Milano 22.11.61

Referee: Kevin Howley (Eng)   Attendance: 12,000

INTER: Ottavio Bugatti; Giacinto Facchetti, Giorgio Della Giovanni, Enea Masiero, Remo Bicchierai, Costanzo Balleri, Bruno Petroni, Raggi Giorgio Humberto, Gerald Hitchens, Franco Zaglio, Egidio Morbello. Trainer: Helenio Herrera

HEARTS: Gordon Marshall, Robert Kirk, David Holt, John Cumming, William Polland, William Higgins, John Docherty, Robert Blackwood, Maurice Elliott, William Wallace, John Hamilton.

Goals: Hitchens (11, 86), Morbello (31), Humberto (75)

MTK BUDAPEST v LEIPZIG XI 3-0 (1-0)

Népstadion, Budapest 8.11.61

Referee: Borce Nedelkovski (Jug)   Attendance: 3,000

MTK: Sándor Gellér; György Keszei, Tibor Palicskó, István Jenei; Ferenc Sipos, Ferenc Kovács III; Károly Sándor, Mihály Laczkó, János Molnár, László Povázsai, István Szimcsák I. Trainer: Gyula Szűcs

LEIPZIG: Wolfgang Klank; Karl Drössler, Michael Faber, Claus Pfeufer; Peter Giessner, Manfred Geisler; Werner Gase, Dieter Fischer, Rainer Trölitzsch, Arno Zerbe, Dieter Engelhardt.

Goals: Povázsai (37, 59), Sándor (81)

LEIPZIG XI v MTK BUDAPEST 3-0 (1-0)

Zentralstadion, Leipzig 15.11.61

Referee: Alois Obtulovič (Cze)   Attendance: 12,000

LEIPZIG: Dieter Sommer; Karl Drössler, Michael Faber, Claus Pfeufer; Peter Giessner, Manfred Geisler; Dieter Engelhardt, Dieter Fischer, Rainer Trölitzsch, Henning Frenzel, Arno Zerbe.

MTK: Sándor Gellér (84 László Takács); György Keszei, Tibor Palicskó, István Jenei; Ferenc Sipos, Ferenc Kovács III; Károly Sándor, Gábor Arató, Mihály Laczkó, László Povázsai, István Szimcsák I. Trainer: Gyula Szűcs

Goals: Frenzel (18, 81), Engelhardt (76)

MTK BUDAPEST v LEIPZIG 2-0 (1-0)

Tehelné pole, Bratislava 30.11.61

Referee: Karol Galba (Cze)   Attendance: 10,000

MTK: Sándor Gellér; Tibor Palicskó, Ferenc Sipos, István Jenei; István Nagy, Ferenc Kovács III; Károly Sándor, László Bödör, Mihály Laczkó, János Molnár, István Szimcsák I. Trainer: Gyula Szűcs

LEIPZIG: Dieter Sommer; Dieter Scherbarth, Michael Faber, Claus Pfeufer; Peter Giessner, Karl Drössler; Werner Gase, Dieter Fischer, Rainer Trölitzsch, Henning Frenzel, Arno Zerbe.

Goals: Sándor (40), Bödör (57)

ESPAÑOL BARCELONA v BIRMINGHAM CITY 5-2 (3-1)

Estadio de Sarriá, Barcelona 15.11.61

Referee: Jean Tricot (Fra)   Attendance: 30,000

ESPAÑOL: Benito JOANET Jiménez; Antonio ARGILÉS Antón, Juan BARTOLÍ Figueras, Julián RIERA Navarro, Fermín GORDEJUELA Roncal, José SASTRE Sanz, José Antonio CASTAÑOS Alarcón, SANTOS Bedoya López, Aloísio Francisco da Luz «ÍNDIO», Ramón Sergio CARRANZA Semprini, Antonio CAMPS Bau. Trainer: José Luis SASO

BIRMINGHAM: John Schofield; Stan Lynn, Graham Sissons, Terence Hennessey, Trevor Smith, Malcolm Beard, Michael Hellawell, James Bloomfield, James Harris, Bryan Orritt, Robert Auld. Manager: Gil Merrick

Goals: Bloomfield (20), Castaños (24), Carranza (26), Camps (32, 80, 85), Harris (75 pen)

BIRMINGHAM CITY
v ESPAÑOL BARCELONA 1-0 (0-0)

St.Andrew's, Birmingham   7.12.61

Referee: Thomas Wharton (SCO)   Attendance: 16,874

BIRMINGHAM: John Schofield; Stan Lynn, Graham Sissons, Terence Hennessey, Trevor Smith, Malcolm Beard, Michael Hellawell, Bryan Orritt, James Harris, Kenneth Leek, Robert Auld.   Manager: Gil Merrick

ESPAÑOL: Rafael PIRIS Esteva; José SASTRE Sanz, Julián RIERA Navarro, Fermín GORDEJUELA Roncal, ABEL Hérnandez Sanchís, SANTOS Bedoya López, Carlos TORRES Barallobre, Víctor Manuel RIVAS Sanmeterio, Aloísio Francisco da Luz "ÍNDIO", Zoltán CZIBOR Suhai, Antonio CAMPS Bau.   Trainer: Ricardo Zamora

Sent off: Harris (53), Abel (53), Auld (64), Ribas (64)

Goal: Auld (59)

SHEFFIELD WEDNESDAY v AS ROMA 4-0 (3-0)

Hillsborough, Sheffield   29.11.61

Referee: Arthur Blavier (BEL)   Attendance: 42,589

WEDNESDAY: Ronald Springett; Peter Johnson, Donald Megson, Thomas McAnearney, Peter Swan, Anthony Kay, Alan Finney, Robert Craig, Gerald Young, John Fantham, Derek Wilkinson.   Manager: Vic Buckingham

AS ROMA: Fabio Cudicini; Alfio Fontana, Leopoldo Raimondi, Paolo Pestrin, Giacomo Losi, Sergio Carpanesi, Alberto Orlando, Valentin Angelillo, Francisco Lojacono, Giancarlo De Sisti, Giampaolo Menichelli.
Lojacono sent off (65).   Trainer: Luis Antonio Carniglia

Goals: Fantham (6), Young (33, 35, 79)

AS ROMA v SHEFFIELD WEDNESDAY 1-0 (1-0)

Stadio Olimpico, Roma   13.12.61

Referee: Dittmar Huber (SWI)   Attendance: 45,000

AS ROMA: Fabio Cudicini; Alfio Fontana, Giulio Corsini, Torbjörn Jönsson, Giacomo Losi, Paolo Pestrin, Alberto Orlando, Valentin Angelillo, Pedro Manfredini, Giancarlo De Sisti, Giampaolo Menichelli.   Trainer: Luis Antonio Carniglia

WEDNESDAY: Ronald Springett; Peter Johnson, Donald Megson, Thomas McAnearney, Peter Swan, Anthony Kay, Alan Finney, Robert Craig, Gerald Young, John Fantham, Colin Dobson. Manager: Vic Buckingham

Goal: Swan (80 og)

CF BARCELONA v DINAMO ZAGREB 5-1 (4-0)

Camp Nou, Barcelona   13.12.61

Referee: Günther Ternieden (WG)   Attendance: 50,000

CF BARCELONA: José Manuel PESUDO Soler; Alfonso María Rodríguez Salas FONCHO, Sigfrido GRACIA Royo, Enrique GENSANA Meroles, Francisco Rodríguez García "RODRI", Juan SEGARRA Iraceta, Jesús María PEREDA Ruiz de Temiño, Sándor KOCSIS, EVARISTO do Macedo Filho, Jesús GARAY Vicino, Ramón Alberto VILLAVERDE Vázquez. Trainer: László KUBALA Stecz

DINAMO: Mirko Stojanović (31 Zlatko Škorić); Željko Matuš, Vlatko Marković, Mirko Braun, Ivan Šantek, Željko Perušić, Luka Lipošinović, Rudolf Belin, Drazan Jerković, Slaven Zambata, Stjepan Lamza.   Trainer: Milan Antolković

Goals: Pereda (15), Evaristo (19, 28, 33), Kocsis (68), Jerković (87)

DINAMO ZAGREB v CF BARCELONA 2-2 (1-1)

Maksimir, Zagreb   20.12.61

Referee: Demostene Stathos (GRE)   Attendance: 5,000

DINAMO: Mirko Stojanović; Josip Šikić, Vlatko Markovic, Željko Matuš, Ivan Šantek, Željko Perušić, Luka Lipošinovic, Slaven Zambata, Drazan Jerković, Rudolf Belin, Stjepan Lamza. Trainer: Milan Antolković

CF BARCELONA: José Manuel PESUDO Soler; Alfonso María Rodríguez Salas FONCHO, Sigfrido GRACIA Royo, Juan SEGARRA Iraceta, Enrique GENSANA Meroles, Martín VERGÉS Massa; Pedro ZABALLA Barquín, Jesús María PEREDA Ruiz de Temiño, EVARISTO do Macedo Filho, Ramón Alberto VILLAVERDE Vázquez, VICENTE González Sosa.   Trainer: Isidro FLOTATS

Goals: Lamza (24, 47), Evaristo (37), Zaballa (69)

VALENCIA CF v LAUSANNE SPORTS 4-3 (2-0)

Estadio de Mestalla, Valencia   23.12.61

Referee: Décio Bentes de Freitas (POR)   Attendance: 17,500

VALENCIA CF: Gregorio Vergel Serrano "GOYO"; Vicente PIQUER Mora, SÓCRATES Belenguer Pérez, Manuel MESTRE Torres, ROBERTO Gil Esteve, Décio Quaresma RECAMAN, José Santiago Baeza "FICHA", Enrique RIBELLES Sero, WALDO Machado da Silva, HÉCTOR NÚÑEZ Bello, Luis COLL Hortal.   Trainer: Domingo Balmanya Parera

LAUSANNE: René Künzi; André Grobéty, Ely Tacchella, Kurt Hunziker, Richard Dürr, Marcel Vonlanden, Robert Hosp, Gilbert Rey, Miodrag Glišović, Roger Vonlanthen, Charles Hertig.   Trainer: Marmier / Franckie Sechehaye

Dürr sent off (89)

Goals: Ribelles (20 pen, 37), Vonlanthen (47 pen), Coll (57), Dürr (60), Hosp (63), Waldo (82)

QUARTER-FINALS

ESPAÑOL BARCELONA
v CRVENA ZVEZDA BEOGRAD 2-1 (0-1)

Estadio Sarriá, Barcelona   1.02.62

Referee: Raoul Righi (ITA)   Attendance: 30,000

ESPAÑOL: Benito JOANET Jiménez; Victor Manuel RIVAS Sanmeterio, Juan BARTOLÍ Figueras, Amaro DAUDER Guardiola, ABEL Hérnandez Sanchís, José SASTRE Sanz, Zoltán CZIBOR Suhai, SANTOS Bedoya López, Ramón Sergio CARRANZA Semprini, José Héctor RIAL Laguia, Antonio CAMPS Bau.   Trainer: Ricardo Zamora

CRVENA ZVEZDA: Dragomir Vukićević; Vladimir Durković, Novak Tomić, Slobodan Škrbić, Vasilije Šijaković, Vladimir Popović, Nikola Stipić, Dušan Maravić, Anton Rudinski, Dragoslav Šekularac, Vojislav Melić.

Sent off: Carranza and Šijaković (85)

Goals: Stipic (11), Camps (55, 76)

CRVENA ZVEZDA BEOGRAD
v ESPAÑOL BARCELONA 5-0 (1-0)

JNA, Beograd   14.03.62

Referee: Albert Guinnard (SUI)   Attendance: 5,000

CRVENA ZVEZDA: Mirko Stojanović; Vladimir Durković, Novak Tomić, Luka Malesev, Vasilije Šijaković, Vladimir Popović, Nikola Stipić, Dušan Maravić, Milan Galić, Dragoslav Šekularac, Vojislav Melić.

ESPAÑOL: Benito JOANET Jiménez (46 Rafael PIRIS Esteva); Antonio ARGILÉS Antón, Juan BARTOLÍ Figueras, ABEL Hérnandez Sanchís, Luis MUÑOZ Grau, Victor Manuel RIVAS Sanmeterio, Ernesto DOMÍNGUEZ Hernández, José SASTRE Sanz, SANTOS Bedoya López, Ramón Sergio CARRANZA Semprini, Antonio CAMPS Bau.
Trainer: Ricardo Zamora

Goals: Šekularac (24, 56), Abel (46 og), Galic (49), Stipic (81)

NOVI SAD v MTK BUDAPEST 1-4 (1-1)

Gradski, Novi Sad   11.02.62

Referee: Ferdinand Marschall (AUS)   Attendance: 20,000

NOVI SAD: Andrija Vereš, Stevan Sekereš, Zarko Nikolić, Slavko Svinjarević; Stevan Bena, Sentin; Veljko Aleksić, Silvester Takac, Petar Mijatović, Jergić, Dimitrije Radović.

MTK: Ferenc Kovalik; Tibor Palicskó, Ferenc Sipos, István Jenei; István Nagy, Ferenc Kovács III; Károly Sándor, Mihály Vasas, László Bödör, István Kuti, István Szimcsák I.
Trainer: Gyula Szűcs

Goals: Aleksić (22), Bödör (35), Kuti (55), Vasas (75, 80)

MTK BUDAPEST - NOVI SAD 2-1(1-1)

Hungária körút, Budapest   18.02.62

Referee: Werner Bergmann (DDR)   Attendance: 3,000

MTK: Ferenc Kovalik; Tibor Palicskó, Ferenc Sipos, István Jenei; István Nagy, Ferenc Kovács III; László Bödör, Mihály Vasas, István Kuti, János Molnár, István Szimcsák I.

Trainer: Gyula Szűcs

NOVI SAD: Andrija Vereš, Dimitrije Radović, Stevan Sekereš, Slavko Svinjarević; Jergić, Sentin; Veljko Aleksić, Silvester Takac, Stefanović, Djordje Milić, Dugandzija.

Goals: Milić (10), Molnár (35), Bödör (67)

VALENCIA CF
v INTERNAZIONALE MILANO 2-0 (2-0)

Estadio de Mestalla, Valencia   14.02.62

Referee: James Finney (ENG)   Attendance: 56,000

VALENCIA CF: Gregorio Vergel Serrano "GOYO"; Vicente PIQUER Mora, Manuel MESTRE Torres, Décio Quaresma RECAMAN, Juan Carlos Díaz QUINCOCES, Francisco Amáncio dos Santos "CHICÃO"; HÉCTOR NÚÑEZ Bello, Enrique RIBELLES Sero, WALDO Machado da Silva, Vicente GUILLOT Fabián, José Santiago Baeza "FICHA".
Trainer: Domingo Balmanya Parera

INTER: Lorenzo Buffon; Armando Picchi, Giacinto Facchetti, Giorgio Della Giovanni, Aristide Guarneri, Costanzo Balleri, Bruno Petroni, Luis SUÁREZ Miramontes, Raggi Giorgio Humberto, Franco Zaglio, Mario Mereghetti.
Trainer: Helenio Herrera

Goals: Guillot (4), Waldo (7)

INTERNAZIONALE MILANO
v VALENCIA CF 3-3 (2-2)

San Siro, Milano   21.03.62

Referee: Gérard Versyp (BEL)   Attendance: 20,000

INTER: Lorenzo Buffon (46 Ottavio Bugatti); Armando Picchi, Enea Masiero, Bruno Bolchi, Aristide Guarneri, Costanzo Balleri, Mauro Bicicli, Lorenzo Bettini, Gerald Hitchens, Luis SUÁREZ Miramontes, Mario Corso.
Trainer: Helenio Herrera

VALENCIA CF: Gregorio Vergel Serrano "GOYO"; Bautista VERDÚ Panadero, Manuel MESTRE Torres, Vicente PIQUER Mora, Juan Carlos Díaz QUINCOCES, Francisco Amáncio dos Santos "CHICÃO", José Santiago Baeza "FICHA", Enrique RIBELLES Sero, WALDO Machado da Silva, Décio Quaresma RECAMAN, Vicente GUILLOT Fabián.
Trainer: Domingo Balmanya Parera

Goals: Chicão (4), Bettini (7, 51), Suárez (26 pen), Recaman (34), Ficha (90)

SHEFFIELD WEDNESDAY
v CF BARCELONA 3-2 (2-2)

Hillsborough, Sheffield 28.02.62

Referee: Albert Dusch (WG) Attendance: 28,956

WEDNESDAY: Ronald Springett; Peter Johnson, Donald Megson, Robin Hardy, Peter Swan, Anthony Kay, Derek Wilkinson, Colin Dobson, Gerald Young, John Fantham, Alan Finney. Manager: Vic Buckingham

CF BARCELONA: Juan Antonio CELDRÁN Montoya; Julio César BENÍTEZ Amoedo, Sigfrido GRACIA Royo, Juan SEGARRA Iraceta, Francisco Rodríguez García "RODRI", Jesús GARAY Vicino, Jesús María PEREDA Ruiz de Temiño, Martín VERGÉS Massa, EVARISTO do Macedo Filho, Sándor KOCSIS, Ramón Alberto VILLAVERDE Vázquez.
Trainer: László KUBALA Stecz

Goals: Villaverde (14), Fantham (28, 50), Evaristo (35), Finney (43)

CF BARCELONA
v SHEFFIELD WEDNESDAY 2-0 (2-0)

Camp Nou, Barcelona 28.03.62

Referee: Gottfried Dienst (SWI) Attendance: 75,000

CF BARCELONA: Salvador SADURNÍ Urpi; Julio César BENÍTEZ Amoedo, Jesús GARAY Vicino, Martín VERGÉS Massa, Enrique GENSANA Meroles, Juan SEGARRA Iraceta, Jesús María PEREDA Ruiz de Temiño, Sándor KOCSIS, EVARISTO do Macedo Filho, Ramón Alberto VILLAVERDE Vázquez, VICENTE González Sosa.
Trainer: László KUBALA Stecz

WEDNESDAY: Ronald Springett; Peter Johnson, Donald Megson, Robin Hardy, Peter Swan, Anthony Kay, Alan Finney, Colin Dobson, Keith Ellis, John Fantham, Edwin Holliday. Manager: Vic Buckingham

Goals: Evaristo (11), Kocsis (33)

SEMI-FINALS

CRVENA ZVEZDA BEOGRAD
v CF BARCELONA 0-2 (0-0)

JNA, Beograd 18.04.62

Referee: Gottfried Dienst (SUI) Attendance: 20,000

CRVENA ZVEZDA: Mirko Stojanović (46 Dragomir Vukićević); Novak Tomić, Tomislav Milićević, Luka Malesev, Vladimir Durković, Vladimir Popović, Nikola Stipić, Dušan Maravić, Anton Rudinski, Dragoslav Šekularac, Vojislav Melić.

CF BARCELONA: Salvador SADURNÍ Urpi; Fernando OLIVELLA Pons, Sigfrido GRACIA Royo, Ramón de Pablo MARAÑÓN, Francisco Rodríguez García "RODRI", Jesús GARAY Vicino, Pedro ZABALLA Barquín, José Antonio ZALDÚA Urdanavia, EVARISTO do Macedo Filho, Ramón Alberto VILLAVERDE Vázquez, Jesús María PEREDA Ruiz de Temiño. Trainer: László KUBALA Stecz

Goals: Zaldúa (81), Pereda (87)

CF BARCELONA
v CRVENA ZVEZDA BEOGRAD 4-1 (2-1)

Camp Nou, Barcelona 25.04.62

Referee: Kenneth George Aston (ENG) Attendance: 50,000

CF BARCELONA: José Manuel PESUDO Soler; Alfonso María Rodríguez Salas FONCHO, Fernando OLIVELLA Pons; Ramón de Pablo MARAÑÓN, Francisco Rodríguez García "RODRI", Jesús GARAY Vicino; Pedro ZABALLA Barquín, José Antonio ZALDÚA Urdanavia, EVARISTO do Macedo Filho, Sándor KOCSIS, VICENTE González Sosa.
Trainer: Isidro FLOTATS

CRVENA ZVEZDA: Dragomir Vukicević; Novak Tomić, Tomislav Milićević, Luka Malesev, Vladimir Durković, Vladimir Popović, Nikola Stipić, Svetozar Andrejić, Selimir Milošević, Dušan Maravić, Vojislav Melić.

Goals: Kocsis (8), Maravić (27 pen), Zaldúa (36, 70), Vicente (57 pen)

VALENCIA CF
v MTK BUDAPEST 3-0 (0-0)

Estadio de Mestalla, Valencia 25.04.62

Referee: Concetto lo Bello (ITA) Attendance: 50,000

VALENCIA CF: José GINESTÁ Andreu; Vicente PIQUER Mora, Juan Carlos Díaz QUINCOCES, Manuel MESTRE Torres; Vicente GUILLOT Fabián, Francisco Amáncio dos Santos «CHICÃO»; HÉCTOR NÚÑEZ Bello, Décio Quaresma RECAMAN, WALDO Machado da Silva, Enrique RIBELLES Sero, Luis COLL Hortal. Trainer: Domingo Balmanya Parera

MTK: László Takács; György Keszei, Ferenc Sipos, István Jenei; István Nagy, Ferenc Kovács III; Károly Sándor, László Bödör, István Kuti, Mihály Laczkó, István Szimcsák I.
Trainer: Gyula Szűcs

Goals: Guillot (55), Coll (69), Waldo (73)

MTK BUDAPEST v VALENCIA CF 3-7 (1-3)

Népstadion, Budapest 2.05.62

Referee: Günther Ternieden (WG) Attendance: 20,000

MTK: László Takács (46 Ferenc Kovalik); György Keszei, Ferenc Sipos, István Jenei; István Nagy, Ferenc Kovács III; Károly Sándor, László Bödör, Ferenc Machos, János Farkas, István Szimcsák I. Trainer: Gyula Szűcs

VALENCIA CF: José GINESTÁ Andreu; Vicente PIQUER Mora, Juan Carlos Díaz QUINCOCES, Manuel MESTRE Torres; ROBERTO Gil Esteve, Francisco Amáncio dos Santos "CHICÃO"; HÉCTOR NÚÑEZ Bello, Décio Quaresma RECAMAN, WALDO Machado da Silva, Vicente GUILLOT Fabián, Luis COLL Hortal.
Trainer: Domingo Balmanya Parera

Goals: Héctor Núñez (6, 60, 75), Guillot (25, 46), Machos (28, 52), Waldo (32, 49), Bödör (82)

FINAL

VALENCIA CF v CF BARCELONA 6-2 (3-2)

Estadio de Mestalla, Valencia   8.09.62

Referee: Joseph Barberan (FRA)   Attendance: 65,000

VALENCIA CF: Ricardo ZAMORA de Grassa; Vicente PIQUER Mora, Manuel MESTRE Torres, José SASTRE Sanz, Juan Carlos Díaz QUINCOCES (Cap); Francisco Amáncio dos Santos "CHICÃO", HÉCTOR NÚÑEZ Bello; Enrique RIBELLES Sero, WALDO Machado da Silva, Vicente GUILLOT Fabián, Fernando Trío "YOSU".   Trainer: Alejandro Scopelli

CF BARCELONA: José Manuel PESUDO Soler; Julio César BENÍTEZ Amoedo, Fernando OLIVELLA Pons, Martín VERGÉS Massa, Francisco Rodríguez García "RODRI", Sigfrido GRACIA Royo; Luis CUBILLA, Sándor Kocsis, Cayetano RE Rodríguez, Ramón Alberto VILLAVERDE Vázquez, Antonio CAMPS Bau.
Trainer: László KUBALA Stecz

Goals: Kocsis (4, 20), Yosu (14, 42), Guillot (35, 54, 67), Núñez (78)

CF BARCELONA
v VALENCIA CF 1-1 (0-0)

Camp Nou, Barcelona   12.09.62

Referee: Giulio Campanati (ITA)   Attendance: 60,000

CF BARCELONA: José Manuel PESUDO Soler; Julio César BENÍTEZ Amoedo, Sigfrido GRACIA Royo, Martín VERGÉS Massa, Jesús GARAY Vicino; José María FUSTÉ Blanch, Luis CUBILLA; Fernand GOYWAERTS, Sándor Péter Kocsis, Ramón Alberto VILLAVERDE Vázquez, Antonio CAMPS Bau.
Trainer: László KUBALA Stecz

VALENCIA CF: Ricardo ZAMORA de Grassa; Vicente PIQUER Mora, Manuel MESTRE Torres, José SASTRE Sanz, Juan Carlos Díaz QUINCOCES (Cap); Francisco Amáncio dos Santos "CHICÃO", HÉCTOR NÚÑEZ Bello; Enrique RIBELLES Sero, WALDO Machado da Silva, Vicente GUILLOT Fabián, Fernando Trío "YOSU".   Trainer: Alejandro Scopelli

Goals: Kocsis (47), Guillot (88)

Goalscorers Fairs Cup 1961/62

9 goals: WALDO Machado da Silva (Valencia CF)

8 goals: EVARISTO do Macedo Filho (CF Barcelona), Vicente GUILLOT Fabián (Valencia CF)

7 goals: Antonio CAMPS Bau (Español Barcelona), HÉCTOR NÚÑEZ Bello (Valencia CF)

6 goals: Sándor KOCSIS (CF Barcelona)

5 goals: John Fantham (Sheffield Wednesday), Raggi Giorgio Humberto (Inter Milano), Károly Sándor (MTK Budapest), José Antonio ZALDÚA Urdanavia (CF Barcelona)

4 goals: Henning Frenzel (Leipzig), Gerald Young (Sheffield Wednesday), Djordje Pavlic (Novi Sad), Luis SUÁREZ Miramontes (Inter Milano), Dušan Maravic (Crvena Zvezda), István Kuti, László Bödör (MTK Budapest)

3 goals: Lucas Sebastiao da Fonseca Matateu (Belenenses); Rudolf Schejbal (Spartak Brno); Dimitrije Radovic (Novi Sad); Egidio Morbello (Inter Milano); Nikola Stipic, Vojislav Melic (Crvena Zvezda); János Molnár, István Szimcsak (MTK Budapest); Drazan Jerković (Dinamo Zagreb)

2 goals: Njo-Lea (Olympique Lyon); Fraser, Baxter (Hibernian); Cvitkovic, Lamza (Dinamo Zagreb); Davidson (Hearts); Trölitzsch, Zerbe (Leipzig); Regh (Köln); Takac, Aleksic, Mijatovic (Novi Sad); Hitchens, Bettini (Inter); Šekularac (Crvena Zvezda); Povazsai, Vasas, Machos (MTK Budapest); Pereda (CF Barcelona); Coll, Ribelles, Yosu (Valencia)

1 goal: Yauca (Belenenses), Odermatt, Blumer (Basel); O. Sørensen, Ravn, E. Rasmussen, H. Andersson (Staevnet København); Rambert, Combin, Djorkaeff, Salen (Olympique Lyon); Lachot, Nabat, Hauss (Strasbourg); Cobb (Nottingham Forest); Baird, E. Stevenson (Hibernian); Šantek, Knez, Matuš, Remete, Markovic (Dinamo Zagreb); Lutz Steinert (Berlin); Van Vaerenberg (Union St.Gilloise); Blackwood, Wallace, Stenhouse (Hearts); Engelhardt (Leipzig); Sturm, Müller, Hemmersbach, Thielen, Ripkens (Köln); Xilas, Asvestas, S.Hasekidis (Iraklis); Bloomfield, Harris, Auld (Birmingham); M.Vonlanden, Dürr, Hosp (Lausanne Sports); Índio, Castaños, Carranza (Español); Ellis, Griffin, Finney, Dobson, McAnearney (Sheffield Wednesday), Milic (Novi Sad); Petroni (Inter); Rudinski, Tasić, Prljinčević, Galić (Crvena Zvezda); Sas (MTK Budapest); Villaverde, Vicente (CF Barcelona); Chicão, Recaman, Ficha (Valencia)

Own Goals: Gonzales (Strasbourg) for MTK; Swan (Sheffield Wednesday) for Roma; Abel (Español) for Crvena Zvezda Beograd

29

FAIRS CUP 1962-63

FIRST ROUND

UTRECHT XI
v TASMANIA 1900 BERLIN WEST 3-2 (1-1)

Galgenwaard, Utrecht   12.09.62

Referee: George McCabe (ENG)   Attendance: 7,300

UTRECHT: Nico van Zoghel; Charles Smits, Joop Gademans; Joop Jochems, Humphrey Mijnals, Willem van Arnhem; Frans Geurtsen, Jozef Siahaya, Tonny Van der Linden, Leen Morelissen, Gerard Weber.   Trainer: Daan Van Beek

TASMANIA: Klaus Basikow; Hans-Jürgen Bäsler, Horst Talaszus; Hans-Günter Becker, Eckhardt Peschke, Horst Greuel; Wolfgang Neumann, Erwin Bruske, Helmut Fiebach, Wolfgang Rosenfeldt, Bernd Brückner.

Goals: Geurtsen (6, 77), Greuel (43), Neumann (55), Siahaya (61)

TASMANIA 1900 BERLIN WEST
v UTRECHT XI 1-2 (1-2)

Olympiastadion, Berlin West   17.10.62

Referee: Frede Hansen (DAN)   Attendance: 6,000

TASMANIA: Hans-Joachim Posinski; Hans-Jürgen Bäsler, Horst Talaszus; Hans-Günter Becker, Klaus Konieczka, Horst Greuel; Wolfgang Neumann, Bernd Wüstenhagen, Bernd Brückner, Wolfgang Rosenfeldt, Erich Reimer.

UTRECHT: Nico van Zoghel; Martin Ockhuysen, Georgi Liptak; Joop Jochems, Humphrey Mijnals, Willem van Arnhem; Frans Geurtsen, Leen Morelissen, Tonny Van der Linden, Jozef Siahaya, Cor Luiten.   Trainer: Daan Van Beek

Goals: Rosenfeldt (17), Luiten (33), Van der Linden (35)

SAMPDORIA GENOVA
v ARIS BONNEVOIE 1-0 (1-0)

Luigi Ferraris, Genova   26.09.62

Referee: Félix Birigay Nieva (SPA)   Attendance: 2,500

SAMPDORIA: Francesco Sattolo; Guido Vincenzi, Paolo Marocchi, Giancarlo Prato, Gaudenzio Bernasconi, Azeglio Vicini, Luigi Toschi, Jorge Toro, José Ricardo Da Silva, Sergio Brighenti, Ernesto Tito Cucchiaroni. Trainer: Ocinirk

ARIS: Théo Stendebach; Ernest Brenner, Brech, Jean-Pierre Hoffstetter, Fernand Brosius, Friedrich, Francis Kohl, Joseph Kunnert, Nicolas Hoffmann, J. Müller, Josy Kirchens.

Goal: Brighenti (36)

ARIS BONNEVOIE
v SAMPDORIA GENOVA 0-2 (0-0)

Stade Camille Polfer, Luxembourg   3.10.62

Referee: Rudolf Kreitlein (WG)   Attendance: 5,000

ARIS: Théo Stendebach; Ernest Brenner, Brech, Jean-Pierre Hoffstetter, Fernand Brosius, Friedrich, Francis Kohl, Joseph Kunnert, Paul May, Müller, Josy Kirchens.

SAMPDORIA: Francesco Sattolo; Francesco Vincenzi, Paolo Marocchi, Manlio Vigna, Gaudenzio Bernasconi, Giancarlo Prato, Luigi Toschi, Jorge Toro, José Ricardo Da Silva, Sergio Brighenti, Ernesto Tito Cucchiaroni.   Trainer: Ocinirk

Goals: Da Silva (52), Brenner (80 og)

GLENTORAN BELFAST
v REAL ZARAGOZA 0-2 (0-1)

The Oval, Belfast   26.09.62

Referee: William Mullan (SCO)   Attendance: 7,000

GLENTORAN: Roy Rea; Roy Borne, Victor Wilson; William McCullough, James Murdough, Arthur Stewart; Richard Warburton, Walter Bruce, Trevor Thompson, William Hume, Matt Doherty.

REAL ZARAGOZA: Juan VISA; Joaquín CORTIZO, Juan ZUBIAURRE Jáuregui; Antonio de la Torre Muñoz "TUCHO", Francisco SANTAMARÍA Briones, Antonio GONZÁLEZ Sanromán; MIGUEL González Pérez, Adualdo Barbosa da Silva "DUCA", MARCELINO Martínez Cao, Juan Roberto SEMINARIO Rodríguez, Carlos LAPETRA Coarasa. Trainer: César Rodríguez

Goals: Borne (40 og), Duca (85)

REAL ZARAGOZA
v GLENTORAN BELFAST 6-2 (2-1)

Estadio La Romareda, Zaragoza 10.10.62

Ref: Hermínio Henrique Soares (POR)   Attendance: 16,000

REAL ZARAGOZA: Enrique YARZA Soraluce (46 Juan VISA); Severino REIJA Vázquez, Joaquín CORTIZO; Santiago ISASI Salazar, José Cuéllar González PEPÍN, Antonio de la Torre Muñoz "TUCHO"; MIGUEL González Pérez, Juan Manuel VILLA Gutiérrez, Joaquín MURILLO Pascual, José Sigfredo Martínez "SIGI", Juan Roberto SEMINARIO Rodríguez.   Trainer: César Rodríguez

GLENTORAN: Roy Rea; Roy Borne, Victor Wilson; William Neill, William McCullough, Arthur Stewart; Richard Warburton, Walter Bruce, Trevor Thompson, William Hume, Matt Doherty.

Goals: Doherty (7, 81), Murillo (20, 28, 66, 79), Villa (56, 71)

OLYMPIQUE MARSEILLE v UNION ST.GILLOISE 1-0 (0-0)

Stade Vélodrome, Marseille   26.09.62

Referee: Pietro Bonetto (ITA)   Attendance: 1,000

OLYMPIQUE: Joseph Moreira; Daniel Ugolini, Max Alauzun, Jean Pierre Knayer, André Moulon, Regis Bruneton, Daniel Viaene, Julien Stopyra, Serge Roy, Pierre Dogliani, Etienne Sansonetti.   Trainer: Armand Penverne

UNION: André Vanderstappen; Charles De Vogelaere, Marcel Dries, Alfons Bruylandts, Jean Claes, Philippe van Wilder, Camille Van Vaerenbergh, Paul Vandenberg, Paul Schraepen, Julien Kialunda, Lucien Mertens.
Trainer: François Edmond Delfour

Goal: Sansonetti (63)

CELTIC GLASGOW v VALENCIA CF 2-2 (0-0)

Celtic Park, Glasgow   24.10.62

Referee: Pieter Paulus Roomer (HOL)   Attendance: 45,000

CELTIC: Frank Haffey; Duncan MacKay, William O'Neill, Patrick Crerand, John McNamee, John Clark, Stephen Chalmers, Robert Craig, John Divers, Charles Gallacher, Alexander Byrne.   Trainer: Robert Rooney

VALENCIA: Ricardo ZAMORA de Grassa; Bautista VERDÚ Panadero, Manuel MESTRE Torres, Francisco Amáncio dos Santos "CHICÃO", Vicente PIQUER Mora, Décio Quaresma RECAMÁN, Enrique RIBELLES Sero, ROBERTO Gil Esteve, WALDO Machado da Silva, Vicente GUILLOT Fabián, José Santiago Baeza "FICHA".

Goals: Verdú (48 og), Guillot (63), Waldo (80), Crerand (85)

UNION ST.GILLOISE v OLYMPIQUE MARSEILLE 4-2 (2-1)

Parc Duden, Brussel   17.10.62

Referee: Karl Keller (SWI)   Attendance: 3,000

UNION: André Vanderstappen; Charles De Vogelaere, Marcel Dries, Alfons Bruylandts, Jean Claes, Philippe van Wilder, Camille Van Vaerenbergh, Julien Kialunda, Paul Vandenberg, Lucien Mertens, Roger Van Cauwelaert.
Trainer: François Edmond Delfour

OLYMPIQUE: Joseph Moreira; Daniel Ugolini, Max Alauzun, Jean Pierre Knayer, André Moulon, Regis Bruneton, Daniel Viaène, Julien Stopyra, Serge Roy, Lucien Temarii, Gérard Aygoui.   Trainer: Armand Penverne

Goals: Van Cauwelaert (25), Mertens (26, 48), Aygoui (44), Kialunda (50), Roy (72)

ALTAY IZMIR v AS ROMA 2-3 (1-3)

Alsançak, Izmir   26.09.62

Referee: Faruk Talu (TUR)   Attendance: 4,500

ALTAY: Varol Ürkmez; Yilmaz Canlisoy, Numan Okumus; Cahit Dikici, Kazim Yildiz, Ertan Adatepe; Gönen Ucer, Nazmi Bilge, Bekir Turkgeldi, Önder, Coskun Esenler.

AS ROMA: Enzo Matteucci; Alfio Fontana, Sergio Carpanesi; Egidio Guarnacci, Giacomo Losi, Paolo Pestrin; Alberto Orlando, Giancarlo De Sisti, Francisco Ramon Lojacono, Valentin Angelillo, Giampaolo Menichelli.
Trainer: Alfredo Foni

Goals: Nazmi (19, 55), Orlando (20), Lojacono (32), Menichelli (41)

VALENCIA CF v CELTIC GLASGOW 4-2 (3-1)

Estadio de Mestalla, Valencia   26.09.62

Referee: François Eurdekian (FRA)   Attendance: 25,000

VALENCIA: Ricardo ZAMORA; Vicente PIQUER Mora, Juan Carlos Díaz QUINCOCES, Manuel MESTRE Torres, José SASTRE Sanz, Francisco Amáncio dos Santos «CHICÃO», José Santiago Baeza «FICHA», Enrique RIBELLES Sero, José Antonio URTIAGA, Vicente GUILLOT Fabián, Luis COLL Hortal.

CELTIC: John Fallon; Duncan MacKay, James Kennedy, Patrick Crerand, William McNeill, William O'Neill, Stephen Chalmers, Mike Jackson, Robert Carroll, Charles Gallacher, Alexander Byrne.   Trainer: Robert Rooney

Goals: Coll (9, 26), Carroll (27, 74), Guillot (31, 46)

AS ROMA v ALTAY IZMIR 10-1 (5-0)

Stadio Olimpico, Roma   7.11.62

Referee: Živko Bajić (JUG)   Attendance: 7,000

AS ROMA: Fabio Cudicini; Alfio Fontana, Giulio Corsini; Torbjörn Jönsson, Giacomo Losi, Paolo Pestrin; Lamberto Leonardi, Francisco Ramon Lojacono, Pedro Waldemar Manfredini, Valentin Angelillo, Giancarlo De Sisti.
Trainer: Alfredo Foni

ALTAY: Varol Ürkmez (46 E.Duder); Yilmaz Canlisoy, Numan Okumus; Cahit Dikici, Kazim Yildiz, Ertan Adatepe; Ali Itiker, Nazmi Bilge, Bekir Turkgeldi, Uail, Coşkun Esenler.

Goals: Manfredini (2, 41, 56, 82), Jönsson (16, 22), Lojacono (30 pen, 74, 89), Angelillo (69), Uail (55)

PETROLUL PLOIEŞTI v SPARTAK BRNO 4-0 (2-0)

Petrolul Ploieşti   3.10.62

Referee: Gyula Balla (HUN) Attendance: 11000

PETROLUL: Vasile Sfetcu; Gheorghe Pahonţu (Cap), Alexandru Fronea, Gheorghe Florea; Dumitru Munteanu, Nicolae Ivan; Alexandru Badea, Constantin Tabarcea, Mircea Dridea, Anton Munteanu, Virgil Dridea.   Trainer: Ilie Oană

SPARTAK: František Schmucker; Miroslav Vítů, Karel Kohlík, Juraj Janoščin; Bohumil Pišek, Karel Komárek; Jozef Haspra, Kulan, Karel Lichtnégl, Jan Stloukal, Vognar. Trainer: R. Krčil

Goals: M. Dridea (6), Badea (38, 40), Tabarcea (58)

SPARTAK BRNO v PETROLUL PLOIEŞTI 0-1 (0-0)

Luzankani, Brno   10.10.62

Referee: Dimitris Wlachojanis (AUS)   Attendance: 2,500

SPARTAK: František Schmucker; Miroslav Vítů, Karel Kohlík, Bohumil Pišek; František Majer, Jan Stloukal; Kulan, Karel Kolácek, Karel Lichtnégl, Vognar, Barstak.   Trainer: R. Krčil

PETROLUL: Vasile Sfetcu; Gheorghe Pahonţu (Cap), Alexandru Fronea, Gheorghe Florea; Dumitru Munteanu, Marin Marcel; Alexandru Badea, Constantin Tabarcea, Mircea Dridea, Anton Munteanu, Virgil Dridea.   Trainer: Ilie Oană

Goal: Tabarcea (71)

BELENENSES LISBOA v CF BARCELONA 1-1 (1-1)

Estádio do Restelo, Lisboa   3.10.62

Referee: Raymond Lespineux (BEL)   Attendance: 35,000

BELENENSES: José Pereira; Francisco Torrão PIRES, Manuel de Sousa RODRIGUES; VICENTE Lucas, Mário Melo PAZ, Jose Manuel CASTRO Silva Soares; ADELINO Ferreira, Antonio Fernandes YAUCA, RAFAEL Fernandes, Fernando PERES, ESTEVÃO António Espírito Santo Mansidão. Trainer: Fernando Vaz

CF BARCELONA: Salvador SADURNÍ Urpi; Alfonso María Rodríguez Salas "FONCHO", Julio César BENÍTEZ Amoedo; Martín VERGÉS Massa, Francisco Rodríguez García "RODRI", Jesús GARAY Vicino; Luis CUBILLA, Jesús María PEREDA Ruiz de Temiño, José Antonio ZALDÚA Urdanavia, José María FUSTÉ Blanch, Antonio CAMPS Bau. Trainer: László KUBALA Stecz

Goals: Fusté (8), Estevão (11)

CF BARCELONA v BELENENSES LISBOA 1-1 (1-1)

Camp Nou, Barcelona   11.10.62

Referee: Anton Bucheli (SWI)   Attendance: 26,000

CF BARCELONA: Salvador SADURNÍ Urpi; Alfonso María Rodríguez Salas «FONCHO», Julio César BENÍTEZ Amoedo; Martín VERGÉS Massa, Francisco Rodríguez García «RODRI», Jesús GARAY Vicino; Pedro ZABALLA Barquín, Jesús María PEREDA Ruiz de Temiño, Cayetano RE Rodríguez, José María FUSTÉ Blanch, Antonio CAMPS Bau. Trainer: László KUBALA Stecz

BELENENSES: José Pereira; Francisco Torrão PIRES, Manuel de Sousa RODRIGUES; Jose Manuel CASTRO Silva Soares, Mário Melo PAZ, VICENTE Lucas; ADELINO Ferreira, António Vitor CARVALHO Junior, RAFAEL Fernandes, Antonio Fernandes YAUCA, Fernando PERES. Trainer: Fernando Vaz

Goals: Ré (11), Peres (36)

CF BARCELONA v BELENENSES LISBOA 3-2 (2-1)

Camp Nou, Barcelona   31.10.62

Referee: Albert Guinnard (SWI)   Attendance: 23,000

CF BARCELONA: José Manuel PESUDO Soler; Alfonso María Rodríguez Salas «FONCHO», Julio César BENÍTEZ Amoedo; Ramón Alberto VILLAVERDE Vázquez, Fernando OLIVELLA Pons, Jesús GARAY Vicino; Pedro ZABALLA Barquín, Sándor KOCSIS, Cayetano RE Rodríguez, José María FUSTÉ Blanch, Antonio CAMPS Bau. Trainer: László KUBALA Stecz

BELENENSES: José Pereira; Francisco Torrão PIRES, Jose Manuel CASTRO Silva Soares, Manuel de Sousa RODRIGUES; Osvaldo Dias "PELEZINHO", VICENTE Lucas; RAFAEL Fernandes, ADELINO Ferreira, Paulo Lourenço "PALICO", Antonio Fernandes YAUCA, Fernando PERES. Trainer: Fernando Vaz

Goals: Palico (8, 62), Pereda (15), Benítez (20), Kocsis (55)

VIKTORIA KÖLN
v FERENCVÁROS BUDAPEST 4-3 (4-2)

Viktoria-stadion, Köln   3.10.62

Referee: Joseph Barberan (FRA)   Attendance: 20000

VIKTORIA: Günter Klemm; Dieter Klever, Hans-Günter Diegel, Erich Ribbek; Jürgen Sundermann, Werner Maes; Karl-Heinz Rühl, Horst Hülss, Klaus Matischack, Willibert Kremer, Manfred Lefkes.

FERENCVÁROS: György Horváth; Dezső Novák, Ferenc Ormai, Sándor Havasi; Oszkár Vilezsál, György Kocsis; Sándor Mátrai, Pál Orosz, Flórián Albert, Gyula Rákosi, Máté Fenyvesi. Trainer: József Mészáros

Goals: Mátrai (6), Rühl (16), Kremer (19), Matischack (25, 33 pen), Albert (31, 53)

FERENCVÁROS BUDAPEST
v VIKTORIA 04 KÖLN 4-1 (1-0)

Népstadion, Budapest   17.10.62

Referee: Karl Kainer (AUS)   Attendance: 25,000

FERENCVÁROS: György Száger; Sándor Mátrai, Ferenc Ormai, Dezső Novák; Oszkár Vilezsál, György Kocsis; József Kökény, Pál Orosz, Flórián Albert, Gyula Rákosi, Máté Fenyvesi.   Trainer: József Mészáros

VIKTORIA: Bernd Koch; Dieter Klever, Erich Ribbek, Hans-Günter Diegel; Gero Bisanz, Werner Maes; Karl-Heinz Rühl, Horst Hülss, Klaus Matischack, Jürgen Sundermann, Willibert Kremer.

Goals: Novák (14), Kökény (67), Fenyvesi (73), Albert (80), Rühl (81)

DRUMCONDRA DUBLIN
v STAEVNET ODENSE 4-1 (3-0)

Tolka Park, Dublin   3.10.62

Referee: Alan Howells (WAL)   Attendance: 12,000

DRUMCONDRA: William Murphy; Christopher Fullam, Alfred Girvan; Paddy Byrne, Kevin Smith, Robert Prole; Raymond Keogh, William Dixon, Michael Rice, James Morrissey, James McCann.

ODENSE: Erik Lykke Sørensen; Kaj Johansen, Finn Helweg; Kurt Grønning Hansen, A. Hansen, Kaj Andersen; H. Hansen, John Danielsen, Kjeld Petersen, Helge Jørgensen, Palle Bruun.

Goals: Dixon (12, 38), Morrissey (26), McCann (79), Bruun (74)

FC PORTO v DINAMO ZAGREB 1-2 (1-1)

Estádio das Antas, Porto   3.10.62

Referee: Gennaro Marchese (ITA) Attendance: 33,000

FC PORTO: RUI Fernando Sousa Teixeira; VIRGÍLIO Mendes, António Duarte MESQUITA; Jorge GOMES, Alberto Augusto FESTA, JOAQUIM Antonio JORGE; CARLOS Domingos DUARTE, João Custódio PINTO, Fernando Júlio PERDIGÃO, HERNÂNI Ferreira Silva, Manuel SERAFIM Monteiro Pereira.   Trainer: Jenő Kalmar

DINAMO: Zlatko Škorić; Rudolf Belin, Mirko Braun; Željko Matuš, Vlatko Marković, Ivan Šantek; Zdenko Kobešćak, Slaven Zambata, Željko Perušić, Berislav Ribić, Ilijas Pasić.

Goals: Serafim (26), Ribić (44), Pasić (55)

STAEVNET ODENSE
v DRUMCONDRA DUBLIN 4-2 (2-2)

Odense Stadion   17.10.62

Referee: Gösta Ackerborn (SWE)   Attendance: 5,200

ODENSE: Erik Lykke Sørensen; Kaj Johansen, Finn Helweg; Kurt Grønning Hansen, H.Hansen, Kaj Andersen; Jørgen Rasmussen, E. Andersen, Kjeld Petersen, Helge Jørgensen, Palle Bruun.

DRUMCONDRA: William Murphy; Christopher Fullam, Alfred Girvan; Paddy Byrne, Kevin Smith, Robert Prole; Raymond Keogh, William Dixon, Michael Rice, James Morrissey, James McCann.

Goals: Prole (3 og), Petersen (6), Bruun (76), Jørgensen (85), Rice (20), Morrissey (33)

DINAMO ZAGREB v FC PORTO 0-0

Dinamo Zagreb   17.10.62

Referee: Walter Meissner (DDR)   Attendance: 10,000

DINAMO: Zlatko Škorić; Rudolf Belin, Mirko Braun; Željko Matuš, Vlatko Marković, Ivan Šantek; Berislav Ribić, Slaven Zambata, Drazan Jerković, Željko Perušić, Ilijas Pasić.

FC PORTO: AMÉRICO Ferreira Lopes; Alberto Augusto FESTA, António Duarte MESQUITA; Jorge GOMES, Miguel ARCANJO, JOAQUIM Antonio JORGE; JAIME Ferreira Silva, João Custódio PINTO, Manuel SERAFIM Monteiro Pereira, HERNÂNI Ferreira Silva, Francisco Lage Pereira da NOBREGA.   Trainer: Jenő Kalmar

HIBERNIAN EDINBURGH
v STAEVNET KØBENHAVN 4-0 (4-0)

Easter Road, Edinburgh 3.10.62

Referee: Joseph Hannet (BEL)   Attendance: 10,000

HIBERNIAN: Ronald Campbell Simpson; John Fraser, Joseph McClelland; John Grant, Patrick Hughes, Ally McLeod; James Scott, John Byrne, Gerry Baker, Morris Stevenson, Eric Stevenson.   Trainer: Calabraith

KØBENHAVN: Jørn Larsen; Ronnow, Kaj Hansen; Bent Hansen, Erik Sparring, Rasmussen; Ole Jørgensen, Hans Andersen, Arvid Christensen, Jacobsen, Ussing.

Goals: Byrne (17), Baker (20), M.Stevenson (24), Ronnow (30 og)

STAEVNET KØBENHAVN
v HIBERNIAN EDINBURGH 2-3 (1-2)

Idraetsparken, København 23.10.62

Referee: Laurens van Ravens (BEL)   Attendance: 4,500

KØBENHAVN: Johansen; Bent Hansen, Øyvind Fangel, Jacobsen, Erik Sparring, Hans Andersen; B. Jørgensen, Arne Dyremose, Arvid Christensen, Hans Andersen, Ussing.

HIBERNIAN: Ronald Simpson; John Fraser, Joseph McClelland; John Grant, Patrick Hughes, Ally McLeod; James Scott, Duncan Falconer, Gerry Baker, Morris Stevenson, John Byrne. Trainer: Calabraith

Goals: Dyremose (17), Byrne (33), M. Stevenson (47, 63), A. Christensen (67)

RAPID WIEN
v CRVENA ZVEZDA BEOGRAD 1-1 (0-0)

Prater, Wien   10.10.62

Referee: Jean Tricot (Fra)   Attendance: 20,000

RAPID: Hans-Peter Gürtler; Paul Halla, Walter Glechner, Josef Höltl; Franz Hasil, Karl Gieβer; Karl Bader, Rudolf Flögel, Max Schmid, Gerhard Hanappi, Peter Rehnelt.
Trainer: Robert Körner

CRVENA ZVEZDA: Dragomir Vukicević; Novak Tomić, Milan Čop, Tomislav Milićević, Luka Malesev, Dragoslav Šekularac, Svetozar Andrejić, Slobodan Škrbić, Zoran Prljinčević, Bora Kostić, Vojislav Melic.

Goals: Flögel (48), Kostić (75)

VOJVODINA NOVI SAD v LEIPZIG XI 1-0 (1-0)

Gradski, Novi Sad   3.10.62

Referee: Atanas Kiriakov (BUL)   Attendance: 6,000

VOJVODINA: Andrija Vereš; Stevan Sekereš, Slavko Svinjarevic, Stevan Bena, Zarko Nikolic, Dimitrije Radovic, Silvester Takac, Djordje Milic, Djordje Pavlic, Radivoj Radosav, Dugandzija.

LEIPZIG: Horst Weigang; Peter Giessner, Michael Faber, Claus Pfeufer, Karl Drössler, Manfred Geisler, Werner Gase, Dieter Fischer, Rainer Trölitzsch, Henning Frenzel, Dieter Engelhardt.

Goal: Pavlic (23)

CRVENA ZVEZDA BEOGRAD
v RAPID WIEN 1-0 (0-0)

JNA, Beograd   13.11.62

Referee: Carlo Gambarotta (Ita)   Attendance: 6,200

CRVENA ZVEZDA: Mirko Stojanović; Novak Tomić, Tomislav Milićević, Luka Malesev, Milan Čop, Vladimir Popovic, Josip Skoblar, Ljubomir Ognjanović, Vojislav Melić, Svetozar Andrejić, Bora Kostić.

RAPID: Hans-Peter Gürtler; Paul Halla, Walter Glechner, Josef Höltl; Franz Hasil, Karl Gieβer; Rudolf Flögel, Franz Wolny, Max Schmid, Gerhard Hanappi, Walter Seitl.
Trainer: Robert Körner

Goal: Melic (55)

LEIPZIG XI v VOJVODINA NOVI SAD 2-0 (1-0)

Zentralstadion, Leipzig   17.10.62

Referee: Milan Kusak (CZE)   Attendance: 25,000

LEIPZIG: Horst Weigang; Peter Giessner, Michael Faber, Claus Pfeufer, Karl Drössler, Manfred Geisler, Werner Gase, Dieter Fischer, Rainer Trölitzsch, Henning Frenzel, Dieter Engelhardt.

VOJVODINA: Andrija Vereš; Stevan Sekereš, Slavko Svinjarevic, Mladen Vucinic, Stevan Bena, Zarko Nikolic, Novak Roganovic, Silvester Takac, Djordje Milic, Radivoj Radosav, Veljko Aleksic.

Goals: Fischer (3), Trölitzsch (76 pen)

FC BASEL v BAYERN MÜNCHEN 0-3 (0-1)

St. Jakob, Basel   16.10.62

Referee: Norman Mootz (LUX)   Attendance: 5,800

FC BASEL: Kurt Stettler; Hanspeter Füri, Bruno Michaud; Hanspeter Stocker, Wolfgang Walther, Carlo Porlezza; Otto Ludwig, Roland Denicola, Markus Pfirter, Heinz Blumer, Wilfried Fritz.   Trainer: Georges Sobotka (Ces)

BAYERN: Fritz Kosar; Heinz Ostner, Peter Kupferschmidt; Peter Fröhlich, Adolf Kunstwadl, Willi Giesemann; Rainer Ohlhauser, Harry Sieber, Dieter Brenninger, Jakob Drescher, Peter Grosser.

Goals: Brenninger (41, 70), Drescher (86)

FC Basel forfeited the second match

EVERTON LIVERPOOL
v DUNFERMLINE ATHLETIC 1-0 (1-0)

Goodison Park, Liverpool   24.10.62

Referee: John Meighan (Eire)   Attendance: 40,240

EVERTON: Gordon West; Alexander Parkerker, George Thomson, James Gabriel, Brian Labone, Brian Harris, William Bingham, Dennis Stevens, Alexander Young, Roy Vernon, John Morrissey.   Manager: Harry Catterick

DUNFERMLINE: James Herriot; William Callaghan, William Cunningham, James Thomson, James McLean, George Miller, Dan McLindon, Alexander Smith, Charles Dickson, Harry Melrose, George Peebles.   Manager: Jock Stein

Goal: Stevens (25)

DUNFERMLINE ATHLETIC
v EVERTON LIVERPOOL 2-0 (1-0)

East End Park, Dunfermline   31.10.62

Referee: Samuel Carswell (NIR)   Attendance: 21,813

DUNFERMLINE: James Herriot; William Callaghan, William Cunningham, James Thomson, James McLean, George Miller, Dan McLindon, Alexander Smith, Charles Dickson, Harry Melrose, George Peebles.   Manager: Jock Stein

EVERTON: Gordon West; Alexander Parkerker, Michael Meagan, James Gabriel, Brian Labone, Brian Harris, William Bingham, Dennis Stevens, Alexander Young, Roy Vernon, John Morrissey.   Manager: Harry Catterick

Goals: Miller (5), Melrose (87)

SECOND ROUND

DINAMO ZAGREB
v UNION ST.GILLOISE BRUSSEL 2-1 (1-0)

Maksimir, Zagreb   7.11.62

Referee: Dimitris Wlachojanis (Aus)   Attendance: 8,500

DINAMO: Zlatko Škorić; Rudolf Belin, Vlatko Marković, Mirko Braun, Željko Matuš, Ivica Cvitković, Ivan Šantek, Slaven Zambata, Željko Perušić, Berislav Ribić, Ilijas Pasić.

UNION: André Vanderstappen; Alfons Bruylandts, Charles De Vogelaere, Jean Claes, Marcel Dries, Julien Kialunda, Paul Schraepen, Camille Van Vaerenbergh, Lucien Mertens, Paul Vandenberg, Roger Van Cauwelaert.
Trainer: François Edmond Delfour

Goals: Zambata (3), Pasic (64), Schraepen (75)

UNION ST.GILLOISE BRUSSEL
v DINAMO ZAGREB 1-0 (1-0)

Parc Duden, Brussel   21.11.62

Referee: Werner Treichel (DDR)   Attendance: 2,000

UNION: André Vanderstappen; Paolo Zalamena, Jean Claes, Charles De Vogelaere, Alfons Bruylandts, Camille Van Vaerenbergh, Firmin Thiels, Julien Kialunda, Lucien Mertens, Paul Vandenberg, Roger Van Cauwelaert.
Trainer: François Edmond Delfour

DINAMO: Zlatko Škorić; Rudolf Belin, Mestrović, Željko Matuš, Vlatko Marković, Ivan Šantek, Zdenko Kobešćak, Slaven Zambata, Željko Perušić, Zlatko Haramincić, Ilijas Pasić.

Goal: Van Cauwelaert (43)

DINAMO ZAGREB
v UNION ST.GILLOISE BRUSSEL 3-2 (1-2)

Stadion Auf der Gugl, Linz   13.02.63

Referee: Karl Kainer (Aus)   Attendance: 1,500

DINAMO: Zlatko Škorić; Rudolf Belin, Mirko Braun, Željko Matuš, Vlatko Marković, Željko Perušić, Ivica Cvitković, Zdenko Kobešćak, Drazan Jerković, Zlatko Haramincić, Ilijas Pasić.

UNION: André Vanderstappen; Charles De Vogelaere, Jean Claes, Claude Langlet, Alfons Bruylandts, Philippe van Wilder, Camille Van Vaerenbergh, Julien Kialunda, Paul Vandenberg, Lucien Mertens, Roger Van Cauwelaert.
Trainer: François Edmond Delfour

Goals: Mertens (15), Braun (25 og), Kobešćak (28, 50), Pasic (62)

PETROLUL PLOIEŞTI v LEIPZIG XI 1-0 (1-0)

Petrolul Ploieşti   7.11.62

Referee: Lajos Aranyosi (HUN)   Attendance: 15,000

PETROLUL: Vasile Sfetcu; Gheorghe Pahonţu (Cap), Alexandru Fronea, Gheorghe Florea; Dumitru Munteanu, Nicolae Ivan; Alexandru Badea, Constantin Tabarcea, Mircea Dridea, Anton Munteanu, Constantin Moldoveanu.
Trainer: Ilie Oană

LEIPZIG XI: Horst Weigang (R); Peter Giessner (L), Michael Faber (R), Claus Pfeufer (R); Karl Drössler (L), Manfred Geisler (R); Klaus Lisiewicz (R), Dieter Fischer (L), Rainer Trölitzsch (R), Arno Zerbe (R), Dieter Engelhardt (R).
R = Rotation Leipzig, L = Lokomotive Leipzig

Goal: A. Munteanu (36)

LEIPZIG XI v PETROLUL PLOIEŞTI 1-0 (1-0)

Zentralstadion, Leipzig   28.11.1962

Referee: Alois Obtulovič (CZE)   Attendance: 30,000

LEIPZIG XI: Horst Weigang; Peter Giessner, Michael Faber, Claus Pfeufer; Karl Drössler, Manfred Geisler; Henning Frenzel (Lok), Dieter Fischer, Rainer Trölitzsch, Arno Zerbe, Dieter Engelhardt.

PETROLUL: Vasile Sfetcu; Gheorghe Pahonţu (Cap), Alexandru Fronea, Gheorghe Florea; Dumitru Munteanu, Nicolae Ivan; Alexandru Badea, Anton Munteanu, Mircea Dridea, Marin Marcel, Constantin Moldoveanu. Trainer: Ilie Oană

Goal: Fischer (25)

PETROLUL PLOIEŞTI v LEIPZIG XI 1-0 (0-0)

MTK Budapest   9.12.62

Referee: Lajos Aranyosi (HUN)   Attendance: 3,000

PETROLUL: Vasile Sfetcu; Gheorghe Pahonţu (Cap), Alexandru Fronea, Gheorghe Florea; Dumitru Munteanu, Nicolae Ivan; Alexandru Badea, Marin Marcel, Mircea Dridea, Anton Munteanu, Virgil Dridea.   Trainer: Ilie Oană

LEIPZIG XI: Peter Nauert; Peter Giessner, Michael Faber, Claus Pfeufer; Karl Drössler, Manfred Geisler; Werner Gase, Dieter Fischer, Wolfgang Behla, Arno Zerbe, Kurt Seidlitz.

Goal: V. Dridea (48)

UTRECHT XI v HIBERNIAN EDINBURGH 0-1 (0-1)

Galgenwaard, Utrecht   27.11.62

Referee: Jozef Casteleyn (BEL)   Attendance: 10,000

UTRECHT: Nico van Zoghel; Georgi Liptak, Martin Ockhuysen, Joop Jochems, Humphrey Mijnals, Willem van Arnhem, Leen Morelissen, Frans Geurtsen, Chris Geutjes, Jozef Siahaya, Cor Luiten.   Trainer: Daan Van Beek

HIBERNIAN: Ronald Simpson; John Fraser, Joseph McClelland; John Grant, Patrick Hughes, Ally McLeod; James Scott, Duncan Falconer, Thomas Preston, John Byrne, Morris Stevenson.   Trainer: Calabraith

Goal: Falconer (11)

HIBERNIAN EDINBURGH v UTRECHT XI 2-1 (1-1)

Easter Road, Edinburgh   12.12.62

Referee: Geoffrey Powell (WAL)   Attendance: 10,000

HIBERNIAN: Ronald Simpson; John Fraser, Joseph McClelland; John Grant, George Muir, Ally McLeod; James Scott, Duncan Falconer, Gerry Baker, James O'Rourke, Morris Stevenson.   Trainer: Calabraith

UTRECHT: Nico van Zoghel; Georgi Liptak, Martin Ockhuysen, Joop Jochems, Niclos Dacsev, Sjaak Westphaal, Frans Geurtsen, Benjamin Aarts, Tonny Van der Linden, Chris Geutjes, Jozef Siahaya.   Trainer: Daan Van Beek

Goals: Geurtsen (21), Baker (23), M. Stevenson (48)

SAMPDORIA GENOVA v FERENCVÁROS BUDAPEST 1-0 (1-0)

Stadio Luigi Ferraris, Genova   1.12.62

Referee: François Eurdekian (FRA)   Attendance: 10,000

SAMPDORIA: Francesco Sattolo; Francesco Vincenzi, Glauco Tomasin, Mario Bergamaschi, Gaudenzio Bernasconi, Giancarlo Prato; Luigi Toschi, Jorge Toro, José Ricardo Da Silva, Giuseppe Tamborini, Ernesto Tito Cucchiaroni. Trainer: Ocinirk

FERENCVÁROS: György Száger; Sándor Havasi, László Kiss III, Jenő Dálnoki; Oszkár Vilezsál, György Kocsis; József Kökény, Pál Orosz, Sándor Mátrai, Zoltán Friedmanszky, Máté Fenyvesi.   Trainer: József Mészáros

Goal: Da Silva (18)

FERENCVÁROS BUDAPEST v SAMPDORIA GENOVA 6-0 (2-0)

Üllói út, Budapest   12.12.62

Referee: Karl Kainer (AUS)   Attendance: 20,000

FERENCVÁROS: István Géczi; Dezső Novák, Sándor Mátrai, Jenő Dálnoki; Oszkár Vilezsál, György Kocsis; József Kökény, Pál Orosz, Flórián Albert, Zoltán Friedmanszky, Máté Fenyvesi.   Trainer: József Mészáros

SAMPDORIA: Francesco Sattolo; Francesco Vincenzi, Paolo Marocchi, Azeglio Vicini, Gaudenzio Bernasconi, Giancarlo Prato, Luigi Toschi, Jorge Toro, Sergio Brighenti, Santino Maestri, Ernesto Tito Cucchiaroni.   Trainer: Ocinirk

Goals: Kökény (15, 61), Friedmanszky (16, 60), Vilezsál (70), Fenyvessi (71)

REAL ZARAGOZA v AS ROMA 2-4 (1-1)

Estadio La Romareda, Zaragoza 2.12.62

Referee: Henri Faucheux (FRA)   Attendance: 21,000

REAL ZARAGOZA: Juan VISA; Joaquín CORTIZO, Juan ZUBIAURRE Jáuregui, Santiago ISASI Salazar, José Cuéllar González PEPÍN, Antonio GONZÁLEZ Sanromán, MIGUEL González Pérez, MARCELINO Martínez Cao, Joaquín MURILLO Pascual, Juan Manuel VILLA Gutiérrez, Carlos LAPETRA Coarasa.   Trainer: César Rodríguez

AS ROMA: Fabio Cudicini; Alfio Fontana, Giulio Corsini, Paolo Pestrin, Giacomo Losi, Torbjörn Jönsson, John William Charles, Antonio Valentin Angelillo, Pedro Waldemar Manfredini, Francisco Ramón Lojacono, Giancarlo de Sisti. Trainer: Alfredo Foni

Goals: Lojacono (1), Villa (30), Manfredini (57), De Sisti (60), Charles (78), Marcelino (81)

AS ROMA v REAL ZARAGOZA 1-2 (1-1)

Stadio Olimpico, Roma 19.12.62

Referee: Alexandar Škorić (JUG)   Attendance: 16,000

AS ROMA: Fabio Cudicini; Alfio Fontana, Giulio Corsini, Paolo Pestrin, Giacomo Losi, Torbjörn Jönsson, Alberto Orlando, Antonio Valentin Angelillo, Pedro Waldemar Manfredini, Giancarlo de Sisti, Giampaolo Menichelli. Trainer: Alfredo Foni

REAL ZARAGOZA: Vicente CARDOSO Sánchez; Severino REIJA Vázquez, Juan ZUBIAURRE Jáuregui, Santiago ISASI Salazar, Francisco SANTAMARÍA Briones, Antonio de la Torre Muñoz "TUCHO", MIGUEL González Pérez, Juan Manuel VILLA Gutiérrez, MARCELINO Martínez Cao, José Sigfredo Martínez "SIGI", Carlos LAPETRA Coarasa. Trainer: César Rodríguez

Goals: Angelillo (5), Corsini (40 og), Sigi (83)

CRVENA ZVEZDA BEOGRAD v CF BARCELONA 3-2 (0-1)

JNA, Beograd 2.12.62

Referee: Joseph Heymann (SWI)   Attendance: 10,000

CRVENA ZVEZDA: Mirko Stojanović; Novak Tomić, Milan Čop, Tomislav Milićević, Svetozar Andrejić, Vladimir Popović, Spasoje Samardžić, Ljubomir Ognjanović, Bora Kostić, Vojislav Melić, Josip Skoblar.

CF BARCELONA: Juan Antonio CELDRÁN Montoya; Alfonso María Rodríguez Salas "FONCHO", Francisco Rodríguez García "RODRI", Fernando OLIVELLA Pons, Martín VERGÉS Massa, Sigfrido GRACIA Royo, Ramón Alberto VILLAVERDE Vázquez, Alcides SILVEIRA, Luis CUBILLA, José María FUSTÉ Blanch, Antonio CAMPS Bau. Trainer: Isidro FLOTATS

Goals: Cubilla (17), Villaverde (54), Samardžić (57), Skoblar (65), Ognjanović (66)

CF BARCELONA CRVENA ZVEZDA BEOGRAD 1-0 (0-0)

Camp Nou, Barcelona 19.12.62

Referee: Gino Rigato (Ita)   Attendance: 28,000

CF BARCELONA: Salvador SADURNÍ Urpi; Alfonso María Rodríguez Salas "FONCHO", Jesús GARAY Vicino, Sigfrido GRACIA Royo, Alcides SILVEIRA, Martín VERGÉS Massa, Luis CUBILLA, Jesús María PEREDA Ruiz de Temiño, Julio César BENÍTEZ Amoedo, José María FUSTÉ Blanch, VICENTE González Sosa.   Trainer: László KUBALA Stecz

CRVENA ZVEZDA: Mirko Stojanović; Novak Tomić, Tomislav Milićević, Slobodan Škrbić, Milan Čop, Vladimir Popović, Vojislav Melić, Vladimir Kovačevic, Milan Galić, Ljubomir Ognjanović, Bora Kostić. Pereda sent off (82)

Goal: Cubilla (86)

CF BARCELONA v CRVENA ZVEZDA BEOGRAD 0-1 (0-0)

Stade Municipal du Ray, Nice 2.01.63

Referee: Joseph Barberan (Fra)   Attendance: 6,000

CF BARCELONA: Salvador SADURNÍ Urpi; Alfonso María Rodríguez Salas "FONCHO", Enrique GENSANA Meroles, Sigfrido GRACIA Royo, Martín VERGÉS Massa, Juan SEGARRA Iraceta, Pedro ZABALLA Barquín, Julio César BENÍTEZ Amoedo, Cayetano RE Rodríguez, José María FUSTÉ Blanch, Luis CUBILLA. Trainer: László KUBALA Stecz

CRVENA ZVEZDA: Mirko Stojanović; Novak Tomić, Tomislav Milićević, Luka Malesev, Milan Čop, Vladimir Popović, Jovan Andjelković, Sreten Djurica, Vojislav Melić, Zoran Prljinčević, Bora Kostić.   Sent off: Benítez (53)

Goal: Kostić (72)

BAYERN MÜNCHEN v DRUMCONDRA DUBLIN 6-0 (1-0)

Grünwalderstadion, München 4.12.62

Referee: Anton Bucheli (SWI)   Attendance: 2,500

BAYERN: Fritz Kosar; Adolf Kunstwadl, Werner Olk, Karl Borutta, Heinz Ostner, Willi Giesemann, Peter Grosser, Harry Sieber, Rainer Ohlhauser, Jakob Drescher, Dieter Brenninger.

DRUMCONDRA: William Murphy; Christopher Fullam, Alfred Girvan, Francis Brennan, Sean Smith, Robert Prole, James McCann, Edward Halpin, Michael Rice, William Dixon, Hendrick.

Goals: Ohlhauser (12), Kosar (47 pen), Borutta (57), Brenninger (77), Grosser (80), Giesemann (83)

Ohlhauser became goalkeeper in the second half instead of Kosar who was injured. Kosar took Ohlhauser's place in the field instead.

DRUMCONDRA DUBLIN
v BAYERN MÜNCHEN 1-0 (0-0)

Tolka Park, Dublin 12.12.62

Referee: Robert Holley Davidson (SCO) Attendance: 3,500

DRUMCONDRA: Eamonn Darcy; Christopher Fullam, Francis Brennan, Paddy Byrne, Sean Smith, Robert Prole, Raymond Keogh, William Dixon, Michael Rice, James Morrissey, James McCann.

BAYERN: Fritz Kosar; Adolf Kunstwadl, Werner Olk, Karl Borutta, Heinz Ostner, Willi Giesemann, Jakob Drescher, Harry Sieber, Dieter Brenninger, Peter Grosser, Peter Kupferschmidt.

Goal: Dixon (58)

VALENCIA CF
v DUNFERMLINE ATHLETIC 4-0 (3-0)

Estadio de Mestalla, Valencia 12.12.62

Referee: Joseph Barberan (Fra) Attendance: 25,000

VALENCIA CF: Ricardo ZAMORA de Grassa; Bautista VERDÚ Panadero, Manuel MESTRE Torres, Vicente PIQUER Mora, Juan Carlos Díaz QUINCOCES, Francisco Amáncio dos Santos «CHICÃO», HÉCTOR NÚÑEZ Bello, Enrique RIBELLES Sero, WALDO Machado da Silva, Vicente GUILLOT Fabián, José Santiago Baeza «FICHA».

DUNFERMLINE: James Herriot; William Callaghan, William Cunningham, James Thomson, James McLean, George Miller, Dan McLindon, Alexander Smith, Charles Dickson, Harry Melrose, George Peebles. Manager: Jock Stein

Goals: Núñez (2), Waldo (36, 50), Ficha (44)

DUNFERMLINE ATHLETIC
v VALENCIA CF 6-2 (5-1)

East End Park, Dunfermline 19.12.62

Referee: James Finney (Eng) Attendance: 14,826

DUNFERMLINE: James Herriot; William Callaghan, William Cunningham, James Thomson, James McLean, George Miller, Alexander Edwards, George Peebles, Alexander Smith, John Sinclair, Harry Melrose. Manager: Jock Stein

VALENCIA CF: José GINESTÁ; Bautista VERDÚ Panadero, Manuel MESTRE Torres, Vicente PIQUER Mora, Juan Carlos Díaz QUINCOCES, José SASTRE Sanz; HÉCTOR NÚÑEZ Bello, José Antonio URTIAGA, WALDO Machado da Silva, Vicente GUILLOT Fabián, José Santiago Baeza "FICHA".

Goals: Melrose (10), Sinclair (15, 17), Guillot (20), J. McLean (34), Peebles (37), Mestre (50), Smith (56)

VALENCIA CF
v DUNFERMLINE ATHLETIC 1-0 (0-0)

Estádio do Restelo, Lisboa 6.02.63

Referee: Raul Martins (POR) Attendance: 3,000

VALENCIA CF: Ricardo ZAMORA de Grassa; Manuel MESTRE Torres, Vicente PIQUER Mora, Juan Carlos Díaz QUINCOCES, José SASTRE Sanz, Francisco Amáncio dos Santos "CHICÃO", José Santiago Baeza "FICHA", HÉCTOR NÚÑEZ Bello, WALDO Machado da Silva, Vicente GUILLOT Fabián, Luis COLL Hortal.

DUNFERMLINE: James Herriot; William Callaghan, William Cunningham, Ronald Mailer, James McLean, George Miller, Alexander Edwards, George Peebles, Alexander Smith, John Sinclair, Harry Melrose. Manager: Jock Stein

Goal: Mestre (62)

QUARTER-FINALS

AS ROMA v CRVENA ZVEZDA BEOGRAD 3-0 (2-0)

Stadio Olimpico, Roma 6.03.63

Referee: Gyula Gere (UNG) Attendance: 28,000

AS ROMA: Fabio Cudicini; Alfio Fontana, Sergio Carpanesi, Torbjörn Jönsson, Giacomo Losi, Paolo Pestrin, Alberto Orlando, Francisco Ramon Lojacono, Pedro Waldemar Manfredini, Antonio Valentin Angelillo, Giampaolo Menichelli Trainer: Alfredo Foni

CRVENA ZVEZDA: Mirko Stojanović; Novak Tomić, Tomislav Milićević, Luka Malesev, Milan Čop, Vladimir Popović, Blagoje Mitić, Ljubomir Ognjanović, Vojislav Melić, Sreten Djurica, Bora Kostić.

Goals: Manfredini (21), Lojacono (24), Menichelli (47)

CRVENA ZVEZDA BEOGRAD v AS ROMA 2-0 (1-0)

JNA, Beograd 20.03.63

Referee: Kurt Tschenscher (WG) Attendance: 18,000

CRVENA ZVEZDA: Mirko Stojanović; Novak Tomić, Tomislav Milićević, Blagoje Mitić, Milan Čop, Vladimir Popović, Jovan Andjelković, Sreten Djurica, Luka Malesev, Bora Kostić, Vojislav Melić.

AS ROMA: Fabio Cudicini; Alfio Fontana, Sergio Carpanesi, Torbjörn Jönsson, Giacomo Losi, Paolo Pestrin, Alberto Orlando, Francisco Ramon Lojacono, Pedro Waldemar Manfredini, Antonio Valentin Angelillo, Giampaolo Menichelli Trainer: Alfredo Foni

Goals: Malesev (12, 74)

VALENCIA CF
v HIBERNIAN EDINBURGH 5-0 (4-0)

Estadio de Mestalla, Valencia   13.03.63

Referee: Giuseppe Adami (ITA)   Attendance: 13,000

VALENCIA CF: Ricardo ZAMORA de Grassa; Vicente PIQUER Mora, Manuel MESTRE Torres, José SASTRE Sanz, Antonio SALVADOR Ruiz, Francisco Amáncio dos Santos «CHICÃO», Daniel MAÑÓ Villagrasa, ROBERTO Gil Esteve, WALDO Machado da Silva, Vicente GUILLOT Fabián, Fernando Trío "YOSU".

HIBERNIAN: Ronald Simpson; John Grant, Joseph McClelland, Thomas Leishman, Patrick Hughes, John Baxter, James Scott, Gerry Baker, Thomas Preston, James O'Rourke, Ally McLeod.   Trainer: Calabraith

Goals: Roberto (15, 21), Chicão (39), Waldo (44, 65)

HIBERNIAN EDINBURGH
v VALENCIA CF 2-1 (2-1)

Easter Road, Edinburgh   3.04.63

Referee: Kenneth Dagnall (ENG)   Attendance: 4,000

HIBERNIAN: Ronald Simpson; Alex Cameron, Davin; John Grant, William Toner, Thomas Leishman; James O'Rourke, Morris Stevenson, Gerry Baker, Thomas Preston, Eric Stevenson.   Trainer: Calabraith

VALENCIA CF: Ricardo ZAMORA de Grassa; Manuel MESTRE Torres, Bautista VERDÚ Panadero, José SASTRE Sanz, Juan Carlos Díaz QUINCOCES, Francisco Amáncio dos Santos "CHICÃO", José Antonio URTIAGA, ROBERTO Gil Esteve, WALDO Machado da Silva, Vicente GUILLOT Fabián, HÉCTOR NÚÑEZ Bello.

Goals: Preston (11), Baker (25), Núñez (30)

BAYERN MÜNCHEN v DINAMO ZAGREB 1-4 (0-2)

Grünwalderstadion, München   13.03.63

Referee: Joseph Heymann (SWI)   Attendance: 10,000

BAYERN: Josef Maier (46 Fritz Kosar); Adolf Kunstwadl, Werner Olk, Karl Borutta, Herbert Erhardt, Willi Giesemann, Rudolf Grosser, Jakob Drescher, Alfred Brecht, Rainer Ohlhauser, Peter Grosser.

DINAMO: Zlatko Škorić; Rudolf Belin, Mirko Braun, Željko Matuš, Vlatko Markovic, Željko Perušić, Ivica Cvitkovic, Slaven Zambata, Drazan Jerković, Tomislav Knez, Zdenko Kobešćak.

Goals: Zambata (19, 45), Jerković (52), Kobešćak (66), Brecht (86)

DINAMO ZAGREB v BAYERN MÜNCHEN 0-0

Maksimir, Zagreb   3.04.63

Referee: Mustafa Gerçeker (TUR)   Attendance: 12,000

DINAMO: Zlatko Škorić; Rudolf Belin, Mirko Braun, Željko Matuš, Mestrovic, Željko Perušić, Ivica Cvitković, Slaven Zambata, Stjepan Lamza, Zdenko Kobešćak, Ilijas Pasic.

BAYERN: Fritz Kosar; Adolf Kunstwadl, Peter Kupferschmidt, Karl Borutta, Herbert Erhardt, Willi Giesemann, Norbert Wodarczik, Jakob Drescher, Dieter Brenninger, Rainer Ohlhauser, Peter Grosser.

FERENCVÁROS BUDAPEST
v PETROLUL PLOIEŞTI 2-0 (2-0)

Üllői út, Budapest   27.03.63

Referee: Borce Nedelkovski (Jug)   Attendance: 30,000

FERENCVÁROS: László Aczél; Dezső Novák, Sándor Mátrai, Jenő Dálnoki; Oszkár Vilezsál, György Kocsis; József Kökény, Fenyvesi II, Zoltán Friedmanszki, János Farkás, dr. Máté Fenyvesi. Trainer: József Mészáros

PETROLUL: Vasile Sfetcu; Gheorghe Pahonţu (Cap), Alexandru Fronea, Gheorghe Florea; Dumitru Munteanu, Marin Marcel; Vasile Anghel, Constantin Tabarcea, Alexandru Badea, Nicolae Ivan, Virgil Dridea.   Trainer: Ilie Oană

Goals: dr. Fenyvesi (2), Novák (19)

PETROLUL PLOIEŞTI
v FERENCVÁROS BUDAPEST 1-0 (0-0)

Petrolul Ploieşti   3.04.63

Referee: Anastasios Faturos (Gre)   Attendance: 20,000

PETROLUL: Vasile Sfetcu; Gheorghe Pahonţu (Cap), Marin Marcel, Gheorghe Florea; Dumitru Munteanu, Nicolae Ivan; Alexandru Badea, Constantin Tabarcea, Mircea Dridea, Anton Munteanu, Virgil Dridea. Trainer: Ilie Oană

FERENCVÁROS: László Aczél; Dezső Novák, Sándor Mátrai, Jenő Dálnoki; Sándor Havasi, György Kocsis; József Kökény, Gyula Rákosi, Oszkár Vilezsál, Fenyvesi II, dr. Máté Fenyvesi. Rákosi sent off (42).   Trainer: József Mészáros

Goal: Ivan (61)

SEMI-FINALS

FERENCVÁROS BUDAPEST
v DINAMO ZAGREB 0-1 (0-0)

Népstadion, Budapest   24.04.63

Referee: Adolf Mach (Cze)   Attendance: 25,000

FERENCVÁROS: László Aczél; Dezső Novák, Sándor Mátrai, Sándor Havasi; Oszkár Vilezsál, György Kocsis; József Kökény, Gyula Rákosi, Flórián Albert, Pál Orosz, Máté Fenyvesi.
Trainer: József Mészáros

DINAMO: Zlatko Škorić; Rudolf Belin, Mestrović, Mirko Braun; Željko Matuš, Željko Perušić; Ivica Cvitković, Slaven Zambata, Zdenko Kobešćak, Berislav Ribić, Stjepan Lamza.

Goal: Lamza (85)

DINAMO ZAGREB
v FERENCVÁROS BUDAPEST 2-1 (0-1)

Maksimir, Zagreb   5.06.63

Referee: Alois Kessler (AUS)   Attendance: 18,000

DINAMO: Zlatko Škorić; Rudolf Belin, Vlatko Marković, Mirko Braun; Marijan Biščan, Željko Perušić; Zdenko Kobešćak, Slaven Zambata; Tomislav Knež, Željko Matuš, Stjepan Lamza.

FERENCVÁROS: László Aczél; Dezső Novák, Sándor Mátrai, Sándor Havasi; Oszkár Vilezsál, Pál Orosz; Fenyvesi II, Zoltán Varga, Flórián Albert, Gyula Rákosi, Máté Fenyvesi.
Trainer: József Mészáros

Goals: Fenyvesi (27), Zambata (55), Kobešćak (75)

VALENCIA CF v AS ROMA 3-0 (0-0)

Estadio de Mestalla, Valencia   25.04.63

Referee: Thomas Wharton (SCO)   Attendance: 40,000

VALENCIA CF: Ricardo ZAMORA de Grassa; Bautista VERDÚ Panadero, Manuel MESTRE Torres, José SASTRE Sanz, Juan Carlos Díaz QUINCOCES, Francisco Amáncio dos Santos "CHICÃO", Daniel MAÑÓ Villagrasa, Enrique RIBELLES Sero, WALDO Machado da Silva, Vicente GUILLOT Fabián, HÉCTOR NÚÑEZ Bello.

AS ROMA: Fabio Cudicini; Alfio Fontana, Sergio Carpanesi, Egidio Guarnacci, Giacomo Losi, Torbjörn Jönsson, Alberto Orlando, Giancarlo De Sisti, Pedro Waldemar Manfredini, Antonio Valentin Angelillo, John William Charles.
Trainer: Alfredo Foni

Goals: Losi (78 og), Núñez (84), Guillot (88)

AS ROMA v VALENCIA CF 1-0 (1-0)

Stadio Olimpico, Roma   16.05.63

Referee: Rudolf Kreitlein (WG)   Attendance: 35,000

AS ROMA: Enzo Matteucci; Alfio Fontana, Sergio Carpanesi, Paolo Pestrin, Giacomo Losi, Egidio Guarnacci, Alberto Orlando, Torbjörn Jönsson, Pedro Waldemar Manfredini, Antonio Valentin Angelillo, Giampaolo Menichelli.
Trainer: Alfredo Foni

VALENCIA CF: Ricardo ZAMORA de Grassa; Vicente PIQUER Mora, Bautista VERDÚ Panadero, José SASTRE Sanz, Juan Carlos Díaz QUINCOCES, Francisco Amáncio dos Santos "CHICÃO", HÉCTOR NÚÑEZ Bello, Enrique RIBELLES Sero, WALDO Machado da Silva, Vicente GUILLOT Fabián, José Santiago Baeza "FICHA".

Goal: Angelillo (25)

FINAL

DINAMO ZAGREB v VALENCIA CF 1-2 (1-0)

Maksimir, Zagreb   12.06.63

Referee: Giuseppe Adami (ITA)   Attendance: 40,000

DINAMO: Zlatko Škorić; Rudolf Belin, Mirko Braun, Marijan Biščan, Vlatko Marković; Željko Perušić, Zdenko Kobešćak; Slaven Zambata, Tomislav Knez, Željko Matuš, Stjepan Lamza.

VALENCIA CF: Ricardo ZAMORA de Grassa; Vicente PIQUER Mora, Francisco Amáncio dos Santos "CHICÃO", Francisco García Gómez "PAQUITO", Juan Carlos Díaz QUINCOCES (Cap); José SASTRE Sanz, Daniel MAÑÓ Villagrasa; José María SÁNCHEZ LAGE, WALDO Machado da Silva, Enrique RIBELLES Sero, José Antonio URTIAGA.
Trainer: Alejandro Scopelli

Goals: Zambata (14), Waldo (62), Urtiaga (75)

VALENCIA CF v DINAMO ZAGREB 2-0 (0-0)

Estadio de Mestalla, Valencia   26.06.63

Referee: Kevin Howley (ENG)   Attendance: 55,000

VALENCIA CF: Ricardo ZAMORA de Grassa; Vicente PIQUER Mora, Francisco Amáncio dos Santos "CHICÃO", Francisco García Gómez "PAQUITO", Juan Carlos Díaz QUINCOCES (Cap); José SASTRE Sanz, Daniel MAÑÓ Villagrasa; José María SÁNCHEZ LAGE, WALDO Machado da Silva, Enrique RIBELLES Sero, HÉCTOR NÚÑEZ Bello.
Trainer: Alejandro Scopelli

DINAMO: Zlatko Škorić; Rudolf Belin, Mirko Braun, Željko Matuš, Vlatko Marković; Željko Perušić, Zdenko Kobešćak; Drazan Jerković, Stjepan Lamza, Zdravko Rauš, Tomislav Knez.

Goals: Mañó (69), Núñez (78)

Goalscorers Fairs Cup 1962/63

6 goals: Francisco Ramon Lojacono, Pedro Waldemar Manfredini (Roma), Waldo Machado da Silva (Valencia)

5 goals: Slaven Zambata (Dinamo Zagreb), Vicente Guillot (Valencia)

4 goals: Joaquín Murillo Pascual (Real Zaragoza), John Byrne (Hibernian), Máté Fenyvesi (Ferencváros), Zdenko Kobešćak (Dinamo Zagreb), Héctor Núñez Bello (Valencia)

3 goals: Frans Geurtsen (Utrecht), Palle Bruun (Odense), William Dixon (Drumcondra), Lucien Mertens (Union), Gerry Baker (Hibernian), Dieter Brenninger (Bayern), Flórián Albert, József Kökény (Ferencváros), Antonio Valentin Angelillo (Roma), Ilijas Pasic (Dinamo Zagreb)

2 goals: Da Silva (Sampdoria), Doherty (Glentoran), Nazmi (Altay Izmir), Palico (Belenenses), Rühl, Matischack (Viktoria Köln), Jørgensen (Odense), Morrissey (Drumcondra), Van Cauwelaert (Union), Fischer (Leipzig), Villa, Sigi (Real Zaragoza), Cubilla (Barcelona), Melrose, Sinclair (Dunfermline), Kostic, Malesev (Crvena Zvezda), M. Stevenson (Hibernian), Badea, Tabarcea (Petrolul), Novák, Friedmanszky (Ferencváros), Menichelli, Jönsson (Roma), Coll, Mestre, Roberto (Valencia)

1 goals: Greuel, Neumann, Rosenfeldt (Tasmania), Siahaya, Luiten, Van der Linden (Utrecht), Brighenti (Sampdoria), Sansonetti, Viaene, Roy (Marseille), Carroll, Crerand (Celtic), Uail (Altay Izmir), Estevão, Peres (Belenenses), Kremer (Viktoria Köln), Serafim (FC Porto), Dyremose, Christensen (København), Pavlic (Vojvodina Novi Sad), Flögel (Rapid Wien), McCann, Rice (Drumcondra), Stevens (Everton), Kialunda, Schraepen (Union), Trölitzsch (Leipzig), Duca, Marcelino (Real Zaragoza), Fusté, Re, Pereda, Benítez, Kocsis, Villaverde (Barcelona), Miller, J. McLean, Peebles, Smith (Dunfermline), Melić, Samardžić, Skoblar, Ognjanović (Crvena Zvezda), Falconer, Preston (Hibernian), Drescher, Ohlhauser, Kosar, Borutta, Grosser, Giesemann, Brecht (Bayern), M. Dridea, A. Munteanu, V. Dridea, Ivan (Petrolul), Mátrai, Vilezsál (Ferencváros), Orlando, De Sisti, Charles (Roma), Ribić, Jerković, Lamza (Dinamo Zagreb), Ficha, Chicão, Urtiaga, Mañó (Valencia)

Own Goals: Brenner (Aris Bonnevoie) for Sampdoria, Borne (Glentoran) for Zaragoza, Mestre & Verdú (Valencia) for Celtic, Hansen (København) for Hibernian, Braun (Dinamo Zagreb) for Union, Corsini (Roma) for Zaragoza, Losi (Roma) for Valencia

FAIRS CUP 1963-64

FIRST ROUND

SC LEIPZIG v ÚJPESTI DOZSA BUDAPEST 0-0

Georg Schwarz Sportpark, Leipzig   4.09.63

Referee: Alois Obtulovič (CZE)   Attendance: 20,000

SC LEIPZIG: Peter Nauert; Michael Faber, Peter Giessner, Volker Trojan; Arno Zerbe, Karl Drössler; Jürgen Albrecht, Rainer Trölitzsch, Dieter Fischer, Dieter Engelhardt, Werner Gase.   Trainer: Rudolf Krause

ÚJPESTI DÓZSA: Ferenc Lung; Mátyás Csordás, Károly Rajna, Pál Várhidi; Benő Káposzta, József Szini; Ferenc Horváth, János Göröcs, Béla Kuharszki, Ferenc Bene, Sándor Zámbó.   Trainer: Ferenc Szusza

ÚJPESTI DÓZSA BUDAPEST v SC LEIPZIG 3-2 (1-0)

Megyeri út, Budapest   11.09.63

Referee: Atanas Dinev (BUL)   Attendance: 15,000

ÚJPESTI DÓZSA: Ferenc Lung; Pál Várhidi, Károly Rajna, Kálmán Sóvári; Benő Káposzta, József Szini; Ferenc Horváth, János Göröcs, Sándor Lenkei, Ferenc Bene, Mihály Tóth. Trainer: Ferenc Szusza

SC LEIPZIG: Peter Nauert; Michael Faber, Peter Giessner, Volker Trojan; Arno Zerbe, Karl Drössler; Werner Gase, Henning Frenzel, Rainer Trölitzsch, Dieter Fischer, Dieter Engelhardt.

Goals: Várhidi (1 pen), Bene (46), Trölitzsch (63), Káposzta (68), Frenzel (89)

ARIS BONNEVOIE v RFC LIÈGE 0-2 (0-0)

Stade Camille Polfer, Luxembourg   4.09.63

Referee: Rudolf Kreitlein (WG)   Attendance: 1,800

ARIS: Théo Stendebach; Fernand Brosius, Ernest Brenner, Francis Kohl, Jean-Pierre Hoffstetter; Emile Wagner, Johny Hilbert, Joseph Kunnert, Nicolas Hoffmann, Josy Kirchens, Maller.

RFC LIÈGE: Guy Delhasse; Yves Baré, Albert Sulon, Emile Lejeune, Lambert Defraigne; Julien Onclin, Gérard Sulon, Muana Dominique Mutschi, Victor Wegria, Jean-Marie Letawe, Henri Depireux.   Trainer: Jean Cornilli

Goals: Wegria (50), G. Sulon (68)

RFC LIÈGE v ARIS BONNEVOIE 0-0

Stade Jules George, Liège   2.10.63

Referee: Albert Guinnard (SWI)   Attendance: 3,000

RFC LIÈGE: Guy Delhasse; Yves Baré, Lambert Defraigne, Albert Sulon, Emile Lejeune, Jean Neys; Claude Croté, Muana Dominique Mutschi, Hector Cribioli, Jean-Marie Letawe, Henri Depireux.   Trainer: Jean Cornilli

ARIS: Théo Stendebach; Ernest Brenner, Jean-Pierre Hoffstetter, Fernand Jeitz, Fernand Brosius, Emile Wagner, Klein, Joseph Kunnert, Nicolas Hoffmann, Johny Schreiner, Paul Hoscheit.

Brenner from Stade Dudelange, Brossius from Spora Luxembourg, Klein from US Dudelange

1.FC KÖLN v ARA LA GANTOISE 3-1 (1-0)

Müngersdorferstadion, Köln   4.09.63

Referee: Pierre Schwinte (Fra)   Attendance: 7,500

FC KÖLN: Toni Schumacher; Toni Regh, Helmut Benthaus, Leo Wilden, Wolfgang Weber, Georg Stollenwerk, Hans Schäfer, Hans Sturm, Karl-Heinz Ripkens, Fritz Pott, Heinz Hornig.   Trainer: Georg Knöpfle

ARA LA GANTOISE: Armand Seghers; Noël van de Velde, Eric Delmulle, Lucien Ghellynck, Richard De Nayer, Albert Mayama, Robert Mahieu, Urbain Seghers, Eric Lambert, Norbert Delmulle, James Storme.

Goals: Sturm (21 pen, 63 pen), Delmulle (53), Weber (55)

ARA LA GANTOISE v 1.FC KÖLN 1-1 (0-0)

Jules Ottenstadion, Gent   16.10.63

Referee: Samuel Carswell (NIr)   Attendance: 3,500

ARA LA GANTOISE: Armand Seghers; Raymond Debaets, Roger Debaets, Norbert van Nuffel, Noël van de Velde, Lucien Ghellynck, Robert Mahieu, André De Vos, Carlos Lua, Roger Van Gansbeke, James Storme.

Lua from Racing White, De Vos from White Star Ieper, van Gansbeke from KSC Eendracht Aalst

FC KÖLN: Toni Schumacher; Georg Stollenwerk, Toni Regh, Matthias Hemmersbach, Leo Wilden, Helmut Benthaus, Karl-Heinz Thielen, Hans Sturm, Christian Müller, Wolfgang Overath, Heinz Hornig.   Trainer: Georg Knöpfle

Goals: Overath (55), De Vos (57)

IRAKLIS THESSALONIKI v REAL ZARAGOZA 0-3 (0-1)

Kautatzogleio, Thessaloniki   8.09.63

Referee: Živko Bajić (JUG)   Attendance: 15,800

IRAKLIS: Gavrigiorgos; Tsatalis, Nikos Liaros, Spiridakis, Mihalis Bellis, Ioannidis, Lolos Hasekidis, Kasapis, Giorgos Lianis, Rougklos, Plastizas Xilas.   Trainer: Takac

REAL ZARAGOZA: Vicente CARDOSO Sánchez; Joaquín Cortizo, Juan ZUBIAURRE Jáuregui, Santiago ISASI Salazar, Francisco SANTAMARÍA Briones, José Luis VIOLETA Lajusticia, Darcy Silveira dos Santos "CANARIO", Adualdo Barbosa da Silva "DUCA", MARCELINO Martínez Cao, Juan Manuel VILLA Gutiérrez, Carlos LAPETRA Coarasa. Trainer: Antonio RAMALLETS Simón

Goals: Villa (44, 87), Marcelino (60)

REAL ZARAGOZA v IRAKLIS THESSALONIKI 6-1 (2-0)

Estadio La Romareda, Zaragoza   9.10.63

Referee: Gennaro Marchese (ITA) Attendance: 16,000

REAL ZARAGOZA: Enrique YARZA Soraluce; Juan ZUBIAURRE Jáuregui, Francisco SANTAMARÍA Briones, Severino REIJA Vázquez; Antonio PAÍS Castroagudin, Eduardo Bibiano ENDÉRIZ Cortajarena; Darcy Silveira dos Santos "CANARIO", Eleuterio SANTOS Brito, Joaquín MURILLO Pascual, José Sigifredo Martínez "SIGI", Carlos LAPETRA Coarasa.   Trainer: Antonio RAMALLETS Simón

IRAKLIS: Gavrigiorgos; Tsatalis, Mihalis Bellis, Kasapis, Giorgos Lianis, Rougklos, Ioannidis, Beredimas, Plastizas Xilas, Nikos Liaros, Tsigkos.   Trainer: Takac

Goals: Canario (17), Murillo (36, 47), Sigi (58), Liaros (62), Endériz (83, 90)

RAPID WIEN v RACING CLUB PARIS 1-0 (0-0)

Prater, Wien   11.09.63

Referee: Vaclav Korelus (CZE)   Attendance: 25,000

RAPID: Andrija Vereš; Paul Halla, Walter Glechner, Josef Höltl; Gerhard Hanappi, Karl Gießer; Max Schmid, Walter Seitl, Franz Hasil, Rudolf Flögel, Peter Rehnelt. Trainer: Robert Körner

RACING: Jean Taillandier; Bernard Lelong, Umberto Melloni, Pierre Bodin, Jean Louis Lagadec, Edouard Kula, François Heutte, Jean Jacques Marcel, Abderrhaman Mahjoub, Guy Van Sam, Francis Magny.   Trainer: André Jeampierre

Goal: Flögel (87)

RACING CLUB PARIS v RAPID WIEN 2-3 (1-2)

Parc des Princes, Paris   2.10.63

Referee: Andries van Leeuwen (HOL)   Attendance: 5,000

RACING: Jean Taillandier; Bernard Lelong, Umberto Melloni, Pierre Bodin, Jean Louis Lagadec, Bruno Bollini, Jean Topka, Abderrhaman Mahjoub, Guy Van Sam, Jean Jacques Marcel, Francis Magny.   Trainer: André Jeampierre

RAPID: Andrija Vereš; Paul Halla, Walter Glechner, Josef Höltl, Gerhard Hanappi, Karl Gießer; Max Schmid, Walter Seitl, Franz Hasil, Rudolf Flögel, Branko Milanovic. Trainer: Robert Körner

Goals: Van Sam (17), Schmid (17), Hasil (20), Flögel (55), Mahjoub (85)

GLENTORAN BELFAST
v PARTICK THISTLE GLASGOW 1-4 (1-1)

The Oval, Belfast   16.09.63

Referee: Jack Lowry (WAL)   Attendance: 5,000

GLENTORAN: Albert Finlay; Harold Creighton, Victor Wilson, William McCullough, Eamon Byrne, Walter Bruce, Richard Warburton, Anthony Curley, Trevor Thompson, Roy McDowell, Gerry Green.

PARTICK THISTLE: George Niven; Douglas Wright, George Muir, John Harvey, Donald McKinnon, William Cunningham, David McParland, William Hainey, Ernie Yard, Neil Duffy, Ronald Hume.

Goals: Thompson (39), Hainey (7), Yard (58, 74), Wright (78)

PARTICK THISTLE GLASGOW
v GLENTORAN BELFAST 3-0 (0-0)

Firhill Park, Glasgow   30.09.63

Referee: Kevin Howley (ENG)   Attendance: 10,500

PARTICK THISTLE: George Niven; Thomas Gibb, George Muir, John Harvey, William Cunningham, David McParland, Ian Cowan, William Hainey, Ernie Yard, James Fleming, George Smith.

GLENTORAN: Albert Finlay; Harold Creighton, Victor Wilson, Thomas Brannigan, Eamon Byrne, Walter Bruce, Richard Warburton, William Hume, Roy McDowell, Eric Ross, Albert Mitchell.

Goals: Smith (52, 67), Harvey (74 pen)

SHAMROCK ROVERS DUBLIN
v VALENCIA CF 0-1 (0-0)

Dalymount Park, Dublin   18.09.63

Referee: Franz Geluck (BEL)   Attendance: 26,000

SHAMROCK ROVERS: Patrick Dunne; John Keogh, Patrick Courtney, Ronald Nolan, Thomas Farrell, John Fullam, Francis O'Neill, John Mooney, Edward Bailham, William Tuohy, Anthony O'Connell.

VALENCIA CF: Cipriano González Rivero "ÑITO"; Vicente PIQUER Mora, Alberto ARNAL Andrés; Francisco García Gómez "PAQUITO", Juan Carlos Díaz QUINCOCES II, José SASTRE Sanz; HÉCTOR NÚÑEZ Bello, José María SÁNCHEZ LAGE, WALDO Machado da Silva, Vicente GUILLOT Fabián, Andres Paredes Alvite "SUCO".
Trainer: Bernardino Pérez "Pasieguito"

Goal: Suco (51)

VALENCIA CF
v SHAMROCK ROVERS DUBLIN 2-2 (0-1)

Estadio de Mestalla, Valencia   10.10.63

Referee: Clemente Henriques (POR)   Attendance: 45,000

VALENCIA CF: José MARTÍNEZ Palomar; Javier GARCÍA VERDUGO Garrido, Alberto ARNAL Andrés, ROBERTO Gil Esteve, Juan Carlos Díaz QUINCOCES II, José SASTRE Sanz, Daniel MAÑO Villagrasa, José María SÁNCHEZ LAGE, WALDO Machado da Silva, Vicente GUILLOT Fabián, Andres Paredes Alvite «SUCO».
Trainer: Bernardino Pérez «Pasieguito»

SHAMROCK ROVERS: Patrick Dunne; John Keogh, Patrick Courtney, Ronald Nolan, Thomas Farrell, John Fullam, Francis O'Neill, John Mooney, Edward Bailham, William Tuohy, Anthony O'Connell.

Goals: Tuohy (39), Mooney (56), Guillot (63), Arnal (81)

STEAGUL ROŞU BRAŞOV
v LOKOMOTIV PLOVDIV 1-3 (1-3)

Braşov   19.09.63

Referee: György Vadas (HUN)   Attendance: 12,000

STEAGUL ROŞU: Stere Adamache; Octavian Zaharia, Iuliu Jenei, Nicolae Pescaru; Vasile Seredai, Ion Szigeti; Emanoil Haşoti, Iuliu Năftănăilă, Dorin Necula, Alexandru Meszaros, Nicolae Selimesi.   Trainer: Nicolae Proca

LOKOMOTIV: Stancho Bonchev; Ilia Bekiarov, Georgi Mizin, Ivan Manolov; Ivan Boiadjiev, Dimitar Mladenov; Ivan Kanchev, Ivan Bachkov, Hristo Andonov, Hristo Iliev, Petar Kolev.

Goals: Meszaros (4), P. Kolev (14, 37), Kanchev (30)

LOKOMOTIV PLOVDIV
v STEAGUL ROŞU BRAŞOV 2-1 (2-0)

Deveti Septemvri, Plovdiv 9.10.63

Referee: Milan Fencl (CZE)   Attendance: 8,200

LOKOMOTIV: Stancho Bonchev; Ilia Bekiarov, Georgi Mizin, Ivan Manolov; Boitsev, Ivan Boiadjiev; Dimitar Mladenov, Ivan Kanchev, Hristo Andonov, Hristo Iliev, Petar Kolev.

STEAGUL ROŞU: Carol Haidu; Nicolae Campo, Iuliu Jenei, Ion Nagy; Nicolae Pescaru, Ion Szigeti; Emanoil Haşoti, Iuliu Năftănăilă, Vasile Seredai, Gheorghe Ciripoi, Nicolae Selimesi. Trainer: Nicolae Proca

Goals: Mizin (38), Kolev (39), Seredai (89)

LAUSANNE SPORTS
v HEART OF MIDLOTHIAN EDINBURGH 2-2 (0-1)

Stade Olympique La Pontaise, Lausanne 25.09.63

Referee: Giuseppe Adami (ITA)   Attendance: 5,000

LAUSANNE SPORTS: René Künzi; André Grobéty, Ely Tacchella, Kurt Hunziker, Kurt Armbruster, Heinz Schneiter, Vittore Gottardi, Richard Dürr, Robert Hosp, Peter Engler, Charles Hertig.   Trainer: Jean Luciano (Fra)

HEARTS: James Fergus Cruickshank; William Polland, Christopher Shevlane, Roy Barry, John Cumming, William Higgins, John Hamilton, Daniel Ferguson, Norman Davidson, William Wallace, Thomas Traynor.

Goals: Traynor (25), Ferguson (47), Hertig (56), Gottardi (74)

NK TREŠNJEVKA ZAGREB
v BELENENSES LISBOA 0-2 (0-1)

Dinamo, Zagreb 25.09.63

Referee: Carlo Gambarotta (ITA)   Attendance: 2,100

TREŠNJEVKA: Mrdjias; Cranić, Branko Gracanin; Kovac, Popović, Balent; Stampfelj, Bradac, Jovićić, Judik, Ivica Pintarić.

BELENENSES: Alfredo José Henriques NASCIMENTO; João ROSENDO, Manuel Sousa RODRIGUES; ABDUL ZUBAIDA, Mário Melo PAZ, ALBERTO LUÍS Pinto Ferro; Adelino Ferreira, Paulo Lourenço "PALICO", ESTEVÃO António Espírito Santo Mansidão, Fernando PERES, Vítor Manuel Cruz GODINHO.   Trainer: Fernando Vaz

Goals: Peres (17), Estevão (40)

HEART OF MIDLOTHIAN EDINBURGH
v LAUSANNE SPORTS 2-2 (1-0)

Tynecastle Park, Edinburgh 9.10.63

Referee: Kenneth Dagnall (ENG)   Attendance: 10,500

HEARTS: James Fergus Cruickshank; William Polland, Christopher Shevlane, Roy Barry, John Cumming, William Higgins, John Hamilton, Daniel Ferguson, Norman Davidson, William Wallace, Thomas Traynor.

LAUSANNE SPORTS: René Künzi; André Grobéty, Ely Tacchella, Kurt Hunziker, Eric Polencent, Heinz Schneiter, Vittore Gottardi, Richard Dürr, Roberto Frigerio, Robert Hosp, Charles Hertig.   Trainer: Jean Luciano

Goals: Cumming (19), Gottardi (62), Hosp (88), Hamilton (90)

BELENENSES LISBOA
v NK TREŠNJEVKA ZAGREB 2-1 (1-1)

Estádio do Restelo, Lisboa 9.10.63

Ref: José González Echeverría (SPA)   Attendance: 10,000

BELENENSES: Alfredo José Henriques NASCIMENTO; João ROSENDO, Manuel Sousa RODRIGUES; ABDUL ZUBAIDA, Mário Melo PAZ, ALBERTO LUÍS Pinto Ferro; Carlos António Silva ANGEJA, Osvaldo Dias PELEZINHO, Paulo Lourenço "PALICO", Fernando PERES, ESTEVÃO António Espírito Santo Mansidão.   Trainer: Fernando Vaz

TREŠNJEVKA: Bilić; Cranić, Kovac; Muskovic, Popović, Jurić; Jovićić, Vicević, Juckov, Ivica Pintarić, Repar.

Goals: Palico (4), Pintarić (28), Estevão (70)

LAUSANNE SPORTS v HEART OF MIDLOTHIAN
EDINBURGH 3-2 (2-1, 2-2 aet)

Stade Olympique La Pontaise, Lausanne 15.10.63

Referee: Rudolf Kreitlein (WG)   Attendance: 6,200

LAUSANNE SPORTS: René Künzi; André Grobéty, Ely Tacchella, Kurt Hunziker, Kurt Armbruster, Heinz Schneiter, Vittore Gottardi, Richard Dürr, Roberto Frigerio, Robert Hosp, Charles Hertig.   Trainer: Jean Luciano

HEARTS: James Fergus Cruickshank; Christopher Shevlane, David Holt, Daniel Ferguson, Roy Barry, John Cumming, Thomas Traynor, William Murdoch Hamilton, William Wallace, Alan Gordon, John Hamilton.

Goals: Frigerio (13), Dürr (20 pen), Wallace (30), Ferguson (70), Schneiter (103)

DOS UTRECHT
v SHEFFIELD WEDNESDAY 1-4 (0-2)

Municipal, Utrecht   25.09.63

Referee: André Hauben (BEL)   Attendance: 13,000

UTRECHT: Nico Van Zoghel; Martin Ockhuysen, Georgi Liptak, Sjaak Westphaal, Humphrey Mijnals, Wim Visser, Michel Kruin, Hans Sleven, Tonny Van der Linden, Cor De Meulemeester, Cor Luiten.   Trainer: Wilhelm Kment

WEDNESDAY: Ronald Springett; Brian Hill, Donald Megson, Thomas McAnearney, Peter Swan, Gerald Young, Alan Finney, John Quinn, David Layne, John Fantham, Edwin Holliday. Trainer: Vic Buckingham

Goals: Holliday (5), Layne (20), Quinn (49), Mijnals (64 og), Westphaal (65)

SHEFFIELD WEDNESDAY
v DOS UTRECHT 4-1 (2-0)

Hillsborough, Sheffield   15.10.63

Referee: Thomas Wharton (SCO)   Attendance: 20,643

WEDNESDAY: Ronald Springett; Brian Hill, Donald Megson, Thomas McAnearney, Peter Swan, Gerald Young, Alan Finney, John Quinn, David Layne, Colin Dobson, Edwin Holliday. Trainer: Vic Buckingham

UTRECHT: Nico Van Zoghel; Sjaak Westphaal, Joop Rooders, Georgi Liptak, Humphrey Mijnals, Wim Visser, Hans Sleven, Michel Kruin, Tonny Van der Linden, Ries van de Bogert, Gerard Weber.   Trainer: Wilhelm Kment

Goals: Layne (9, 52, 56 pen), Dobson (16), van de Boogert (84)

STAEVNET KØBENHAVN
v ARSENAL LONDON 1-7 (0-5)

Idraetsparken, København   25.09.63

Referee: John Meighan (EIRE)   Attendance: 11,300

KØBENHAVN: Niels Jensen (KB); Øyvind Fangel (B1903), Kaj Hansen (Frem), Bent Hansen (B1903), Finn Willy Sørensen (Frem), Finn Nielsen (AB), Leif Holten (Fremad Amager), Ole Jørgensen (Køge BK), Keld Petersen (Køge BK), Ole Sørensen (KB), Flemming Jensen (AB).

ARSENAL: Ian McKechnie; Edward Magill, William McCullough, Laurence Brown, Ian Ure, Victor Groves, John MacLeod, Geoffrey Strong, Joseph Baker, George Eastham, George Armstrong.   Manager: William Wright

Goals: MacLeod (9), Baker (24, 46, 71), Strong (27, 35, 40), O. Jørgensen (81)

ARSENAL LONDON
v STAEVNET KØBENHAVN 2-3 (1-1)

Highbury, London   22.10.63

Referee: Pieter Paulus Roomer (HOL)   Attendance: 13,569

ARSENAL: Ian McKechnie; Edward Magill, William McCullough, Laurence Brown, Ian Ure, Victor Groves, Alan Skirton, Geoffrey Strong, David Court, John Barnwell, George Eastham.   Manager: William Wright

KØBENHAVN: Leif Nielsen (Frem); Karl Hansen (Køge BK), Birger Larsen (Frem), Bent Hansen, Finn Willy Sørensen, Kaj Hansen, Leif Holten, Arne Dyrmose (AB), Ole Jørgensen, Keld Petersen, Henning Stilling (AB).

Goals: Skirton (1), A. Dyrmose (30, 88), Barnwell (53), O. Jørgensen (78)

ATLÉTICO MADRID v FC PORTO 2-1 (2-1)

Estadio Metropolitano, Madrid   2.10.63

Referee: François Eurdekian (FRA)   Attendance: 21,000

ATLÉTICO: Edgardo Mario MADINABEYTIA Bassi; Feliciano RIVILLA Muñoz, José Antonio RODRÍGUEZ Lopez; RAMIRO Rodríguez Valente, Jorge Bernardo GRIFFA Monferoni, Jesús GLARÍA Roldán; Aramburu, ADELARDO Rodríguez Sánchez, Jorge Alberto MENDOZA Paulino, José RIBES Flores, Enrique COLLAR Monterrubio. Trainer: Rafael Tinté

FC PORTO: AMÉRICO Ferreira Lopes; Alberto Augusto FESTA, António Duarte MESQUITA; João Custódio PINTO, Miguel ARCANJO, António Manuel PAULA; CARLOS Domingos DUARTE, JAIME Ferreira Silva, VALDIR Araújo Sousa, ROMEU Gibim, HERNÂNI Ferreira Silva. Trainer: Jenő Kalmar

Goals: Ribes (7, 29), Romeu (23)

FC PORTO v ATLÉTICO MADRID 0-0

Estádio das Antas, Porto   9.10.63

Referee: Cesare Jonni (ITA)   Attendance: 35,000

FC PORTO: RUI Fernando Sousa Teixeira; Alberto Augusto FESTA, JOAQUIM Antonio JORGE; João Custódio PINTO, Miguel ARCANJO, António Manuel PAULA; CARLOS Domingos DUARTE, HERNÂNI Ferreira Silva, VALDIR Araújo Sousa, ROMEU Gibim, Francisco Lage Pereira da NOBREGA.   Trainer: Jenő Kalmar

ATLÉTICO: Edgardo Mario MADINABEYTIA Bassi; Feliciano RIVILLA Muñoz, Jesús MARTÍNEZ JAYO; RAMIRO Rodríguez Valente, Jorge Bernardo GRIFFA Monferoni, Jesús GLARÍA Roldán; Aramburu, ADELARDO Rodríguez Sánchez, Jorge Alberto MENDOZA Paulino, José RIBES Flores, Enrique COLLAR Monterrubio.   Trainer: Rafael Tinté

SPARTAK BRNO v SERVETTE GENÈVE 5-0 (3-0)

Spartak, Brno   2.10.63

Referee: Gerhard Kunze (DDR)   Attendance: 5,400

SPARTAK: František Schmucker; Miroslav Vítů, Karel Kohlík, Hájek; Bohumil Pišek, Karel Komárek; Karel Koláček, Karel Lichtnégl, Pando Jankulovský, Jan Brada, Bohumil Hlaváč.
Trainer: Sezemský

SERVETTE: René Schneider; Raymond Maffiolo, Robert Kaiserauer, Maurice Meylan; Jean-Marie Schaller, Bernard Mocellin; Michel Desbiolles, Walter Heuri, André Bosson, Bernard Rahis, Jean-Claude Schindelholz.
Trainer: Lucien Leduc (Fra)

Goals: Brada (5), Jankulovský (18), Komarek (43), Pišek (50), Hlaváč (54)

SERVETTE GENEVE v SPARTAK BRNO 1-2 (1-1)

Stade des Charmilles, Genève   16.10.63

Referee: Michel Kitabdjian (FRA)   Attendance: 5,200

SERVETTE: René Schneider; Raymond Maffiolo, Robert Kaiserauer, Jacques Desbaillet, Maurice Meylan, Peter Pazmandy, Valer Nemeth, André Bosson, Michel Desbiolles, Walter Heuri, Jean-Claude Schindelholz.
Trainer: Lucien Leduc

SPARTAK: František Schmuker; Miroslav Vítů, Karel Komárek, Hájek, Bohumil Pišek, Jan Stloukal, Karel Koláček, Karel Lichtnégl, Pando Jankulovský, Jan Brada, Bohumil Hlaváč.   Trainer: Sezemský

Goals: Desbiolles (14), Komárek (39), Hlaváč (70)

JUVENTUS TORINO v OFK BEOGRAD 2-1 (1-1)

Stadio Comunale, Torino   2.10.63

Referee: Josef Kandlbinder (WG)   Attendance: 2,062

JUVENTUS: L. Ferrero; Renato Caocci, Giancarlo Bercellino, Adolfo Gori, Giovanni Sacco, Gianfranco Leoncini, Carlo Dell'Omodarme, Luis Cascajares Del Sol, Cláudio Olinto de Carvalho NENÉ, Gianfranco Zigoni, Giampaolo Menichelli.
Trainer: Eraldo Monzeglio

OFK: Blagoje Vidinić; Čolić, Momčilo Gavrić, Dragoljub Marić, Blagomir Krivokuća, Miroslav Milovanović, Spasoje Samardžić, Dragan Gugleta, Stojan Milosev, Sreten Banović, Josip Skoblar.

Goals: Nené (34), Gugleta (39), Zigoni (53)

OFK BEOGRAD v JUVENTUS TORINO 2-1 (1-1)

OFK, Beograd   16.10.63

Referee: Gyula Emsberger (HUN)   Attendance: 40,000

OFK: Blagoje Vidinić; Čolić, Momčilo Gavrić, Dragoljub Marić, Blagomir Krivokuća, Miroslav Milovanović, Spasoje Samardžić, Dragan Gugleta, Stojan Milosev, Sreten Banović, Josip Skoblar.

JUVENTUS: Roberto Anzolin; Adolfo Gori, Benito Sarti, Ernesto Castano, Giancarlo Bercellino, Gianfranco Leoncini, Gino Stacchini, Luis Cascajares Del Sol, Dino Da Costa, Omar Enrique Sívori, Giampaolo Menichelli.
Trainer: Eraldo Monzeglio

Goals: Stacchini (17), Gugleta (31), Milosev (83)

JUVENTUS TORINO v OFK BEOGRAD 1-0 (0-0)

Stadio Pinzo Grezar, Trieste   13.11.63

Referee: Gottfried Dienst (SWI)   Attendance: 16,000

JUVENTUS: Roberto Anzolin; Adolfo Gori, Benito Sarti, Ernesto Castano, Sandro Salvadore, Gianfranco Leoncini, Gino Stacchini, Luis Cascajares Del Sol, Cláudio Olinto de Carvalho NENÉ, Omar Enrique Sívori, Giampaolo Menichelli.
Trainer: Eraldo Monzeglio

OFK: Blagoje Vidinić; Čolić, Momčilo Gavrić, Dragoljub Marić, Blagomir Krivokuća, Miroslav Milovanović, Spasoje Samardžić, Dragan Gugleta, Stojan Milosev, Sreten Banović, Josip Skoblar.

Goal: Menichelli (82)

HERTHA BERLIN WEST v AS ROMA 1-3 (1-1)

Olimpiastadion, Berlin West   16.10.63

Referee: Frede Hansen (DAN)   Attendance: 7,300

HERTHA: Wolfgang Tillich; Otto Rehhagel, Hans-Günter Schimmöller, Uwe Klimaschefski, Hans Eder, Peter Schlesinger, Karl-Heinz Rühl, Helmut Faeder, Hans-Joachim Altendorf, Lutz Steinert, Harald Beyer.
Trainer: Josef Schneider

ROMA: Enzo Matteucci; Saul Malatrasi, Mario Ardizzon, Alfio Fontana, Giacomo Losi, Sergio Frascoli, Alberto Orlando, Antonio Valentin Angelillo, Jürgen Schütz, Giancarlo De Sisti, Lamberto Leonardi.   Trainer: Luis Miró

Goals: Schütz (21), Rühl (32), De Sisti (60), Leonardi (72)

AS ROMA v HERTHA BERLIN WEST 2-0 (1-0)

Stadio Olimpico, Roma 30.10.63

Referee: Gottfried Dienst (SWI)   Attendance: 3,200

ROMA: Enzo Matteucci; Saul Malatrasi, Mario Ardizzon; Sergio Carpanesi, Giacomo Losi, Sergio Frascoli; Alberto Orlando, Antonio Valentin Angelillo, Pedro Waldemar Manfredini, Jürgen Schütz, Giancarlo De Sisti. Trainer: Luis Miró

HERTHA: Wolfgang Tillich; Klaus Heuer, Hans-Günter Schimmöller, Hans-Joachim Altendorf, Otto Rehhagel, Peter Schlesinger, Karl-Heinz Rühl, Uwe Klimaschefski, Harald Beyer, Helmut Faeder, Lutz Steinert. Trainer: Josef Schneider

Goals: Schütz (4), Orlando (70)

1.FC KÖLN v SHEFFIELD WEDNESDAY 3-2 (3-0)

Müngersdorferstadion, Köln 6.11.63

Referee: Leopold Silvayn Horn (HOL)   Attendance: 8,500

FC KÖLN: Toni Schumacher; Matthias Hemmersbach, Toni Regh, Helmut Benthaus, Leo Wilden, Hans Sturm, Karl-Heinz Thielen, Hans Schäfer, Christian Müller, Wolfgang Overath, Heinz Hornig. Trainer: Georg Knöpfle

WEDNESDAY: Ronald Springett; Brian Hill, Donald Megson, Thomas McAnearney, Peter Swan, Gerald Young, Alan Finney, Colin Dobson, Derek Wilkinson, Mark Pearson, Edwin Holliday. Manager: Vic Buckingham

Goals: Müller (28), Hornig (35), Sturm (44 pen), Pearson (81, 86)

SECOND ROUND

LAUSANNE SPORTS v REAL ZARAGOZA 1-2 (1-2)

Stade Olympique de la Pontaise, Lausanne 6.11.63

Referee: Giuseppe Adami (ITA)   Attendance: 7,500

LAUSANNE SPORTS: René Künzi; André Grobéty; Heinz Schneiter, Kurt Hunziker, Eric Polencent, Richard Dürr, Albert Bonny, Peter Engler, Roberto Frigerio, Robert Hosp, Charles Hertig. Trainer: Jean Luciano

REAL ZARAGOZA: Vicente CARDOSO Sánchez; Joaquín Cortizo, Francisco SANTAMARÍA Briones, Severino REIJA Vázquez; Santiago ISASI Salazar, José Luis VIOLETA Lajusticia; Darcy Silveira dos Santos "CANARIO", Adualdo Barbosa da Silva "DUCA", MARCELINO Martínez Cao, Juan Manuel VILLA Gutiérrez, Carlos LAPETRA Coarasa. Trainer: Antonio RAMALLETS Simón

Goals: Canario (12), Cortizo (32 og), Marcelino (33)

SHEFFIELD WEDNESDAY v 1.FC KÖLN 1-2 (1-0)

Hillsborough, Sheffield 27.11.63

Referee: William Syme (SCO)   Attendance: 36,929

WEDNESDAY: Ronald Springett; Peter Johnson, Donald Megson, Robin Hardy, Peter Swan, Gerald Young, Alan Finney, Colin Dobson, David Layne, Mark Pearson, Edwin Holliday. Manager: Vic Buckingham

FC KÖLN: Toni Schumacher; Matthias Hemmersbach, Wolfgang Weber, Helmut Benthaus, Leo Wilden, Hans Sturm, Karl-Heinz Thielen, Hans Schäfer, Christian Müller, Wolfgang Overath, Toni Regh. Trainer: Georg Knöpfle

Goals: Layne (16), Thielen (59), Overath (66)

REAL ZARAGOZA v LAUSANNE SPORTS 3-0 (2-0)

Estadio La Romareda, Zaragoza 20.11.63

Referee: Décio Bentes de Freitas (POR)   Attendance: 17,500

REAL ZARAGOZA: Enrique YARZA Soraluce; Severino REIJA Vázquez, Francisco SANTAMARÍA Briones, Juan ZUBIAURRE Jáuregui; Santiago ISASI Salazar, José Luis VIOLETA Lajusticia; Darcy Silveira dos Santos «CANARIO», Eduardo Bibiano ENDÉRIZ Cortajarena, Joaquín MURILLO Pascual, MARCELINO Martínez Cao, Carlos LAPETRA Coarasa. Trainer: Antonio RAMALLETS Simón

LAUSANNE SPORTS: René Künzi; André Grobéty; Heinz Schneiter, Kurt Hunziker, Ely Tacchella, Eric Polencent, Vittore Gottardi, Kurt Armbruster, Roberto Frigerio, Robert Hosp, Charles Hertig. Trainer: Jean Luciano

Goals: Endériz (30), Murillo (33), Marcelino (52)

RAPID WIEN v VALENCIA CF 0-0

Prater, Wien 6.11.63

Referee: Alois Obtulovič (CZE)   Attendance: 40,000

RAPID: Andrija Vereš; Paul Halla, Walter Glechner, Josef Höltl, Gerhard Hanappi, Karl Gießer; Max Schmid, Walter Seitl, Franz Hasil, Rudolf Flögel, Branko Milanovic. Trainer: Robert Körner

VALENCIA CF: Ricardo ZAMORA de Grassa; Vicente PIQUER Mora, Juan Carlos Díaz QUINCOCES II, Manuel MESTRE Torres; ROBERTO Gil Esteve, José SASTRE Sanz; José Santiago Baeza "FICHA", Enrique RIBELLES Sero, WALDO Machado da Silva, José María SÁNCHEZ LAGE, Andres Paredes Alvite "SUCO". Trainer: Bernardino Pérez "Pasieguito"

VALENCIA CF v RAPID WIEN 3-2 (1-1)

Estadio de Mestalla, Valencia   27.11.63

Referee: Arthur Blavier (BEL)   Attendance: 18,000

VALENCIA CF: Ricardo ZAMORA de Grassa; Vicente PIQUER Mora, Juan Carlos Díaz QUINCOCES II, Bautista VERDÚ Panadero; ROBERTO Gil Esteve, José SASTRE Sanz, Daniel MAÑO Villagrasa, Vicente GUILLOT Fabián, WALDO Machado da Silva, José María SÁNCHEZ LAGE, José Santiago Baeza «FICHA». Trainer: Bernardino Pérez «Pasieguito»

RAPID: Andrija Vereš; Paul Halla, Walter Glechner, Josef Höltl; Gerhard Hanappi, Wilhelm Zaglitsch; Walter Seitl, Franz Wolny, Walter Skocik, Rudolf Flögel, Peter Rehnelt. Trainer: Robert Körner

Goals: Wolny (6, 61), Sánchez Lage (25 pen), Waldo (48), Roberto (71)

PARTICK THISTLE GLASGOW v SPARTAK BRNO 3-2 (2-0)

Firhill Park, Glasgow   18.11.63

Referee: John K. Taylor (ENG)   Attendance: 8,000

PARTICK THISTLE: George Niven; George Muir, Hugh Tinney, Martin Ferguson, John Harvey; William Cunningham, Ian Cowan, Ernie Yard; William Hainey, Neil Duffy, David McParland.

SPARTAK: František Schmucker; Bohumil Pišek, Karel Kohlík, Miroslav Vítů, Karel Komárek; František Majer, Karel Koláček, Karel Lichtnégl; Farmačka, Jan Brada, Bohumil Hlaváč.   Trainer: Sezemský

Goals: Yard (29), Harvey (37 pen), Ferguson (51), Koláček (65), Lichtnégl (74)

ARSENAL LONDON v RFC LIÈGE 1-1 (0-1)

Highbury, London   13.11.63

Referee: Jack Lowry (WAL)   Attendance: 22,003

ARSENAL: Robert Wilson; Edward Magill, William McCullough, Laurence Brown, Ian Ure, John Barnwell, John MacLeod, Geoffrey Strong, Joseph Baker, George Eastham, Terence Anderson.   Manager: William Wright

RFC LIÈGE: Guy Delhasse; Yves Baré, Gérard Sulon, Emile Lejeune, Lambert Defraigne, Julien Onclin, Henri Depireux, Albert Sulon, Victor Wegria, Jean-Marie Letawe, Sebastien Kilola.   Trainer: Jean Cornilli

Goals: Kilola (11), Anderson (67)

SPARTAK BRNO v PARTICK THISTLE GLASGOW 4-0 (3-0)

Spartak Brno   27.11.63

Referee: János Fehérvári (HUN)   Attendance: 4,100

SPARTAK: František Schmucker; Bohumil Pišek, Karel Kohlík, Miroslav Vítů; Karel Komárek, Jan Stloukal; Karel Koláček, Karel Lichtnégl, Pando Jankulovský, Jan Brada, Bohumil Hlaváč.   Trainer: Sezemský

PARTICK THISTLE: George Niven; George Muir, Hugh Tinney; David Closs, John Harvey, William Cunningham; Ian Cowan, Ernie Yard, William Hainey, Neil Duffy, David McParland.

Goals: Brada (1927), Jankulovský (40), Lichtnégl (49)

RFC LIÈGE v ARSENAL LONDON 3-1 (2-1)

Stade Jules Georges, Liège   18.12.63

Referee: Jean Tricot (Fra)   Attendance: 7,600

RFC LIÈGE: Guy Delhasse; Yves Baré, Gérard Sulon, Emile Lejeune, Lambert Defraigne, Julien Onclin, Henri Depireux, Albert Sulon, Victor Wegria, Jean-Marie Letawe, Claude Croté. Trainer: Jean Cornilli

ARSENAL: James Furnell; Edward Magill, William McCullough, John Barnwell, Ian Ure, John Snedden, John MacLeod, Geoffrey Strong, David Court, George Eastham, George Armstrong.   Manager: William Wright

Goals: McCullough (32), Croté (42), G. Sulon (43), Wegria (67)

ÚJPESTI DÓZSA BUDAPEST v LOKOMOTIV PLOVDIV 0-0

Megyeri út, Budapest   20.11.63

Referee: Paul Schiller (AUS)   Attendance: 10,000

ÚJPESTI DÓZSA: György Cselényi; Mátyás Csordás, Károly Rajna, Kálmán Sóvári; Ernő Solymosi, József Lutz; Ferenc Bene, János Göröcs, Béla Kuharszki, József Szini, Sándor Zámbó.   Trainer: Ferenc Szusza

LOKOMOTIV: Stancho Bonchev; Ilia Bekiarov, Georgi Mizin, Ivan Manolov; Ivan Boiadjiev, Dimitar Mladenov; Ivan Kanchev, Ianko Dzoglev, Ivan Grancharov, Hristo Iliev, Dimitar Chobanov.

LOKOMOTIV PLOVDIV
v ÚJPESTI DÓZSA BUDAPEST 1-3 (0-1)

Deveti Septemvri, Plovdiv   27.11.63

Referee: Mihai Popa (ROM)   Attendance: 35,000

LOKOMOTIV: Stancho Bonchev; Ilia Bekiarov, Georgi Mizin, Ivan Manolov; Ivan Boiadjiev, Dimitar Mladenov; Ivan Kanchev, Ivan Grancharov, Hristo Iliev, Dimitar Chobanov, Petar Kolev.

ÚJPESTI DÓZSA: Ferenc Lung; Pál Várhidi, Károly Rajna, Kálmán Sóvári; Ernő Solymosi, József Szini; Sándor Lenkei, János Göröcs, Ferenc Bene, Béla Kuharszki, Sándor Zámbó.
Trainer: Ferenc Szusza

Goals: Bene (41, 71), Zámbó (65), Chobanov (89)

AS ROMA v BELENENSES LISBOA 2-1 (1-0)

Stadio Olimico, Roma   4.12.63

Referee: Joseph Heymann (SWI)   Attendance: 4,600

AS ROMA: Enzo Matteucci; Alfio Fontana, Mario Ardizzon; Saul Malatrasi, Giacomo Losi, Antonio Valentin Angelillo; Alberto Orlando, Jürgen Schütz, Pedro Waldemar Manfredini, Giancarlo De Sisti, Angelo Benedicto Sormani.
Trainer: Luis Miró

BELENENSES: Alfredo José Henriques NASCIMENTO; João ROSENDO, ALBERTO LUÍS Pinto Ferro; VICENTE Lucas, Mário Melo PAZ, Orlando Dias PELEZINHO; ADELINO Ferreira, Paulo Lourenço PALICO, ESTEVÃO António Espírito Santo Mansidão, Fernando PERES, Vítor Manuel Cruz GODINHO.

Goals: Schütz (20), Peres (58, 86 og)

BELENENSES LISBOA v AS ROMA 0-1 (0-1)

Estádio do Restelo, Lisboa   11.12.63

Ref: José González Echevarría (SPA)   Attendance: 13,000

BELENENSES: Alfredo José Henriques NASCIMENTO; João ROSENDO, Manuel Sousa RODRIGUES; VICENTE Lucas, Mário Melo PAZ, ALBERTO LUÍS Pinto Ferro; ADELINO Ferreira, Abdul Renan Nhassengo, ESTEVÃO António Espírito Santo Mansidão, Osvaldo Dias PELEZINHO, Vítor Manuel Cruz GODINHO.

AS ROMA: Fabio Cudicini; Alfio Fontana, Mario Ardizzon; Saul Malatrasi, Giacomo Losi, Antonio Valentin Angelillo; Lamberto Leonardi, Jürgen Schütz, Angelo Benedicto Sormani, Giancarlo De Sisti, Sergio Carpanesi.
Trainer: Luis Miró

Goal: De Sisti (19)

JUVENTUS TORINO
v ATLÉTICO MADRID 1-0 (1-0)

Stadio Comunale, Torino   4.12.63

Referee: Alexandros Monastiriotis (Gre)   Attendance: 7,000

JUVENTUS: Carlo Mattrel; Adolfo Gori, Gianfranco Leoncini, Ernesto Castano, Sandro Salvadore, Giovanni Sacco, Gino Stacchini, Dino Da Costa, Cláudio Olinto de Carvalho NENÉ, Omar Enrique Sívori, Giampaolo Menichelli.
Trainer: Eraldo Monzeglio

ATLÉTICO: Edgardo Mario MADINABEYTIA Bassi; Feliciano RIVILLA Muñoz, Isacio CALLEJA García; RAMIRO Rodríguez Valente, Jorge Bernardo GRIFFA Monferoni, Jesús GLARÍA Roldán; José RIBES Flores, ADELARDO Rodríguez Sánchez, Jorge Alberto MENDOZA Paulino, Jesús MARTÍNEZ JAYO, Enrique COLLAR Monterrubio.   Trainer: Rafael Tinté

Goal: Stacchini (30)

ATLÉTICO MADRID
v JUVENTUS TORINO 1-2 (0-2)

Estadio Santiago Bernabéu, Madrid   1.01.64

Referee: Kurt Tschenscher (WG)   Attendance: 50,000

ATLÉTICO: Edgardo Mario MADINABEYTIA Bassi; Feliciano RIVILLA Muñoz, Isacio CALLEJA García; RAMIRO Rodríguez Valente, Jorge Bernardo GRIFFA Monferoni, Jesús GLARÍA Roldán; Benito BEITIA Goenaga, Manuel Bermúdez Arias "POLO", Jorge Alberto MENDOZA Paulino, Jesús MARTÍNEZ JAYO, Enrique COLLAR Monterrubio.
Trainer: Rafael Tinté

JUVENTUS: Roberto Anzolin; Adolfo Gori, Benito Sarti, Ernesto Castano, Giancarlo Bercellino, Gianfranco Leoncini, Carlo dell'Omodarme, Luis DEL SOL Cascajares, Dino da Costa, Cláudio Olinto de Carvalho NENÉ, Giampaolo Menichelli.   Trainer: Eraldo Monzeglio

Goals: Dell'Omodarme (5), Menichelli (9), Beitia (64)

QUARTER-FINALS
REAL ZARAGOZA v JUVENTUS TORINO 3-2 (1-0)

Estadio La Romareda, Zaragoza   29.01.64

Referee: Thomas Wharton (SCO)   Attendance: 28,000

REAL ZARAGOZA: Enrique YARZA Soraluce; Joaquín Cortizo, Severino REIJA Vázquez; Santiago ISASI Salazar, Francisco SANTAMARÍA Briones, José Luis VIOLETA Lajusticia, Darcy Silveira dos Santos "CANARIO", Adualdo Barbosa da Silva "DUCA", MARCELINO Martínez Cao, Juan Manuel VILLA Gutiérrez, Carlos LAPETRA Coarasa.
Trainer: Antonio RAMALLETS Simón

JUVENTUS: Roberto Anzolin; Adolfo Gori, Benito Sarti, Ernesto Castano, Sandro Salvadore, Gianfranco Leoncini, Carlo dell'Omodarme, Luis Del Sol Cascajares, Cláudio Olinto de Carvalho NENÉ, Giovanni Sacco, Giampaolo Menichelli.
Trainer: Eraldo Monzeglio

Goals: Isasi (10), Marcelino (57), Villa (60), Menichelli (75 pen), Dell'Omodarme (82)

JUVENTUS TORINO v REAL ZARAGOZA 0-0

Stadio Comunale, Torino   12.02.64

Referee: Karl Kainer (AUS)   Attendance: 14,000

JUVENTUS: Roberto Anzolin; Adolfo Gori, Benito Sarti, Ernesto Castano, Sandro Salvadore, Gianfranco Leoncini, Carlo dell'Omodarme, Luis Del Sol Cascajares, Cláudio Olinto de Carvalho NENÉ, Omar Enrique Sívori, Giampaolo Menichelli.   Trainer: Eraldo Monzeglio

REAL ZARAGOZA: Enrique YARZA Soraluce; Joaquín Cortizo, Severino REIJA Vázquez; Santiago ISASI Salazar, Francisco SANTAMARÍA Briones, José Cuéllar González "PEPÍN"; Darcy Silveira dos Santos "CANARIO", Adualdo Barbosa da Silva "DUCA", MARCELINO Martínez Cao, Juan Manuel VILLA Gutiérrez, Carlos LAPETRA Coarasa.
Trainer: Antonio RAMALLETS Simón

AS ROMA v FC KÖLN 3-1 (2-0)

Stadio Olimpico, Roma   29.01.64

Referee: Cezmi Basar (TUR)   Attendance: 4,800

AS ROMA: Fabio Cudicini; Alfio Fontana, Mario Ardizzon, Sergio Carpanesi, Giacomo Losi, Antonio Valentin Angelillo, Alberto Orlando, Jürgen Schütz, Angelo Benedicto Sormani, Giancarlo De Sisti, Lamberto Leonardi.   Trainer: Luis Miró

FC KÖLN: Toni Schumacher; Matthias Hemmersbach, Toni Regh, Helmut Benthaus, Leo Wilden, Hans Sturm, Karl-Heinz Thielen, Hans Schäfer, Karl-Heinz Ripkens, Wolfgang Overath, Heinz Hornig.   Trainer: Georg Knöpfle

Goals: Schütz (8, 48 pen), Sormani (19), Thielen (75)

FC KÖLN v AS ROMA 4-0 (1-0)

Müngersdorferstadion, Köln   5.03.64

Referee: Andries van Leeuwen (HOL)   Attendance: 20,000

FC KÖLN: Fritz Ewert; Fritz Pott, Toni Regh, Helmut Benthaus, Leo Wilden, Wolfgang Weber, Karl-Heinz Thielen, Hans Schäfer, Hans Sturm, Wolfgang Overath, Christian Müller. Trainer: Georg Knöpfle

AS ROMA: Fabio Cudicini; Saul Malatrasi, Giulio Corsini, Alfio Fontana, Mario Ardizzon, Sergio Frascoli, Alberto Orlando, Antonio Valentin Angelillo, Pedro Waldemar Manfredini, Sergio Carpanesi, Lamberto Leonardi.
Trainer: Luis Miró

Goals: Benthaus (45), Pott (67), Müller (85, 90)

FC LIÈGE v SPARTAK BRNO 2-0 (1-0)

Stade Jules Georges, Liège   19.02.64

Referee: Pieter Paulus Roomer (Hol)   Attendance: 8,800

RFC LIÈGE: Guy Delhasse; Yves Baré, Albert Sulon, Emile Lejeune, Jean Neys; Julien Onclin, Hector Cribioli, Auguste Goessens, Victor Wegria, Gérard Sulon, Jean-Marie Letawe.
Trainer: Jean Cornilli

SPARTAK: František Schmucker; Sněhota, Bohumil Pišek, Karel Kohlík, Miroslav Vítů; Karel Komárek, Jan Stloukal, Karel Koláček, Karel Lichtnégl, Pando Jankulovský, Bohumil Hlaváč.   Trainer: Sezemský

Goals: Letawe (10), Cribioli (57)

SPARTAK BRNO v RFC LIÈGE 2-0 (1-0)

Spartak Brno   11.03.64

Referee: Bozidar Botić (JUG)   Attendance: 7,500

SPARTAK: František Schmucker, Bohumil Pišek, Karel Kohlík, Miroslav Vítů, Karel Komárek, Jan Stloukal, Karel Koláček, Karel Lichtnégl, Pando Jankulovský, Jan Brada, Bohumil Hlaváč.   Trainer: Sezemský

RFC LIÈGE: Guy Delhasse; Yves Baré, Albert Sulon, Emile Lejeune, Jean Neys, Julien Onclin, Hector Cribioli, Auguste Goessens, Victor Wegria, Gérard Sulon, Jean-Marie Letawe.
Trainer: Jean Cornilli

Goals: Lichtnégl (23), Jankulovský (37)

RFC LIÈGE v SPARTAK BRNO 1-0 (0-0)

Stade Jules Georges Rocourt, Liège   25.03.64

Referee: Günther Baumgärtel (WG)   Attendance: 13,000

RFC LIÈGE: Guy Delhasse; Yves Baré, Albert Sulon, Emile Lejeune, Jean Neys, Julien Onclin, Hector Cribioli, Victor Wegria, Gérard Sulon, Henri Depireux, Claude Croté.
Trainer: Jean Cornilli

SPARTAK: František Schmucker, Miroslav Vítů, Hájek, Juraj Janoščin, Bohumil Pišek, Jan Stloukal, Jaroslav Vojta, Karel Lichtnégl, Farmačka, Jan Brada, Bohumil Hlaváč.
Trainer: Sezemský

Goal: G. Sulon (70)

VALENCIA CF
v ÚJPESTI DOZSA BUDAPEST 5-2 (3-1)

Estadio de Mestalla, Valencia   8.03.64

Referee: Kevin Howley (ENG)   Attendance: 22,500

VALENCIA CF: Ricardo ZAMORA de Grassa; Vicente PIQUER Mora, Juan Carlos Díaz QUINCOCES II, Francisco VIDAGAŇY Hernández; Francisco García Gómez «PAQUITO», ROBERTO Gil Esteve; Manuel CABELLO Carbonell, Vicente GUILLOT Fabián, WALDO Machado da Silva, José María SÁNCHEZ LAGE, HÉCTOR NÚÑEZ Bello. Trainer: Edmundo Suárez «Mundo»

ÚJPESTI DÓZSA: Ferenc Lung; Benő Káposzta, Károly Rajna, Pál Várhidi; Ernő Solymosi, József Szini; Sándor Faliszek, János Göröcs, Ferenc Bene, Béla Kuharszki, Sándor Zámbó.   Trainer: Ferenc Szusza

Goals: Núñez (4, 74 pen), Waldo (20, 27, 80), Göröcs (35), Bene (55)

ÚJPESTI DÓZSA BUDAPEST
v VALENCIA CF 3-1 (2-0)

Megyeri út, Budapest   8.04.64

Referee: Rudolf Glöckner (WG)   Attendance: 17,000

ÚJPESTI DÓZSA: Ferenc Lung; Benő Káposzta, Károly Rajna, Pál Várhidi; Attila Borsányi II, József Szini; Sándor Lenkei, János Göröcs, Ferenc Bene, Béla Kuharszki, Sándor Zámbó.   Trainer: Ferenc Szusza

VALENCIA CF: Ricardo ZAMORA de Grassa; Vicente PIQUER Mora, Juan Carlos Díaz QUINCOCES II, Francisco VIDAGAŇY Hernández; Francisco García Gómez "PAQUITO", ROBERTO Gil Esteve; HÉCTOR NÚÑEZ Bello, Enrique RIBELLES Sero, WALDO Machado da Silva, José María SÁNCHEZ LAGE, José Santiago Baeza "FICHA".
Trainer: Edmundo Suárez "Mundo"

Goals: Bene (12), Kuharszki (35), Núñez (48 pen), Göröcs (80)

SEMI-FINALS

RFC LIÈGE v REAL ZARAGOZA 1-0 (1-0)

Stade Rocourt, Liège   22.04.64

Referee: Rudolf Kreitlein (WG)   Attendance: 20,000

RFC LIÈGE: Guy Delhasse; Yves Baré, Albert Sulon, Emile Lejeune, Jean Neys, Julien Onclin, Hector Cribioli, Victor Wegria, Gérard Sulon, Henri Depireux, Jean-Marie Letawe. Trainer: Jean Cornilli

REAL ZARAGOZA: Vicente CARDOSO Sánchez; Joaquín Cortizo, José Cuéllar González «PEPÍN», Severino REIJA Vázquez, Santiago ISASI Salazar; Antonio PAÍS Castroagudin, Darcy Silveira dos Santos "CANARIO", Eleuterio SANTOS Brito, MARCELINO Martínez Cao, Juan Manuel VILLA Gutiérrez, Carlos LAPETRA Coarasa.
Trainer: Antonio RAMALLETS Simón

Goal: Wegria (44)

REAL ZARAGOZA v RFC LIÈGE 2-1 (0-1)

Estadio La Romareda, Zaragoza   7.05.64

Referee: William Syme (SCO)   Attendance: 25,800

REAL ZARAGOZA: Enrique YARZA Soraluce, José Cuéllar González "PEPÍN", Severino REIJA Vázquez; Santiago ISASI Salazar, Francisco SANTAMARÍA Briones, Antonio PAÍS Castroagudin; Darcy Silveira dos Santos "CANARIO", Eleuterio SANTOS Brito, MARCELINO Martínez Cao, Adualdo Barbosa da Silva "DUCA", Carlos LAPETRA Coarasa.
Trainer: Antonio RAMALLETS Simón

RFC LIÈGE: Guy Delhasse; Yves Baré, Jean Neys, Albert Sulon, Emile Lejeune, Hector Cribioli, Julien Onclin, Victor Wegria, Henri Depireux, Jean-Marie Letawe, Gérard Sulon.
Trainer: Jean Cornilli

Goals: G. Sulon (6), Santos (62), Lapetra (77)

REAL ZARAGOZA v RFC LIÈGE 2-0 (1-0)

Estadio La Romareda, Zaragoza   28.05.64

Referee: Joseph Barbéran (Fra)   Attendance: 25,000

REAL ZARAGOZA: Enrique YARZA Soraluce; Joaquín Cortizo, Severino REIJA Vázquez; José Cuéllar González «PEPÍN», Francisco SANTAMARÍA Briones, Antonio PAÍS Castroagudin; MARCELINO Martínez Cao, Adualdo Barbosa da Silva "DUCA", Eleuterio SANTOS Brito, Juan Manuel VILLA Gutiérrez, Carlos LAPETRA Coarasa.
Trainer: Luis BELLÓ Martínez

RFC LIÈGE: Guy Delhasse; Jean Neys, Albert Sulon, Emile Lejeune; Lambert Defraigne, Gérard Sulon, Hector Cribioli, Gilbert Zenthner, Sebastien Kilola, Victor Wegria, Claude Croté.   Trainer: Jean Cornilli

Goals: Duca (42), Santos (52)

VALENCIA CF v 1.FC KÖLN 4-1 (1-0)

Estadio de Mestalla, Valencia   6.05.64

Referee: Pieter Paulus Roomer (HOL)   Attendance: 40,000

VALENCIA CF: Ricardo ZAMORA de Grassa; Vicente PIQUER Mora, Juan Carlos Díaz QUINCOCES II, Francisco VIDAGAŇY Hernández; Francisco García Gómez «PAQUITO», ROBERTO Gil Esteve; HÉCTOR NÚÑEZ Bello, Vicente GUILLOT Fabián, WALDO Machado da Silva, José María SÁNCHEZ LAGE, José Santiago Baeza «FICHA».
Trainer: Edmundo Suárez «Mundo»

FC KÖLN: Fritz Ewert; Fritz Pott, Toni Regh, Matthias Hemmersbach, Wolfgang Weber, Hans Sturm, Karl-Heinz Thielen, Hans Schäfer, Helmut Benthaus, Wolfgang Overath, Christian Müller.   Trainer: Georg Knöpfle

Goals: Waldo (15, 68), Ficha (59), Roberto (65), Schäfer (82)

1.FC KÖLN v VALENCIA CF 2-0 (2-0)

Müngersdorferstadion, Köln   14.05.64

Referee: John K. Taylor (ENG)   Attendance: 30,000

FC KÖLN: Toni Scumacher; Hans Sturm, Matthias Hemmersbach, Toni Regh, Fritz Pott, Helmut Benthaus, Jürgen Rumor, Hans Schäfer, Christian Müller, Wolfgang Weber, Heinz Hornig.   Trainer: Georg Knöpfle

VALENCIA CF: Ricardo ZAMORA de Grassa; Vicente PIQUER Mora, Juan Carlos Díaz QUINCOCES II, Francisco VIDAGAÑY Hernández, Francisco García Gómez "PAQUITO", ROBERTO Gil Esteve, Daniel MAÑO Villagrasa, HÉCTOR NÚÑEZ Bello, WALDO Machado da Silva, José María SÁNCHEZ LAGE, José Santiago Baeza "FICHA".
Trainer: Edmundo Suárez "Mundo"

Goals: Benthaus (27), Müller (37)

FINAL

REAL ZARAGOZA v VALENCIA CF 2-1 (1-1)

Camp Nou, Barcelona   24.06.64

Ref: Joaquim Fernandes de CAMPOS (POR)   Att: 50,000

REAL ZARAGOZA: Enrique YARZA Soraluce; Joaquín CORTIZO, Severino REIJA Vázquez; Santiago ISASI Salazar, Francisco SANTAMARÍA Briones, José Cuéllar González «PEPÍN»; Darcy Silveira dos Santos «CANARIO», Adualdo Barbosa da Silva «DUCA», MARCELINO Martínez Cao, Juan Manuel VILLA Gutiérrez, Carlos LAPETRA Coarasa.
Trainer: Luis BELLÓ Martínez

VALENCIA CF: Ricardo ZAMORA de Grassa; Alberto ARNAL Andrés, Francisco García Gómez «PAQUITO», Juan Carlos Díaz QUINCOCES (Cap); ROBERTO Gil Esteve, Francisco VIDAGAÑY Hernández; Andrés Paredes Alvite «SUCO», Vicente GUILLOT Fabián, WALDO Machado da Silva, José Antonio URTIAGA, José Santiago Baeza «FICHA».
Trainer: Alejandro Scopelli

Suco sent off (89)

Goals: Villa (41), Urtiaga (44), Marcelino (63)

Goalscorers Fairs Cup 1963-64

6: goals ALDO Machado da Silva (Valencia)

5 goals: David Layne (Sheffield), Jürgen Schütz (Roma), Ferenc Bene (Újpesti Dózsa), MARCELINO Martínez Cao (Real Zaragoza)

4 goals: Gérard Sulon (RFC Liège), Christian Müller (FC Köln), Juan Manuel Villa Gutiérrez (Real Zaragoza)

3 goals: Baker, Strong (Arsenal), Ernie Yard (Partick Thistle), Petar Kolev (Lokomotiv), Menichelli (Juventus), Jan Brada, Pando Jankulovský, Lichtnégl (Spartak Brno), Wegria (RFC Liège), Sturm (FC Köln), Murillo, Endériz (Real Zaragoza), Núñez (Valencia)

2 goals: Mooney (Shamrock Rovers), Ferguson (Hearts), O. Jørgensen, A. Dyrmose (Staevnet København), Gugleta (OFK Beograd), Gottardi (Lausanne), Pearson (Sheffield), Wolny, Flögel (Rapid Wien), Harvey, Smith (Partick Thistle), Estevão, Peres (Beleneneses), Ribes (Atlético Madrid), Stacchini, Dell'Omodarme (Juventus), De Sisti (Roma), Koláček, Hlaváč (Spartak), Göröcs (Ujpesti), Benthaus, Overath, Thielen (FC Köln), Canario, Santos (Real Zaragoza), Roberto (CF Valencia)

1 goals: Trölitzsch, Frenzel (SC Leipzig), Delmulle, Devos (ARA La Gantoise), Lianis (Iraklis), Van Sam, Mahjoub (RC Paris), Thompson (Glentoran), Meszaros, Seredai (Steagul Roşu), Pintaric (NK Tresnjevka Zagreb), Traynor, Cumming, John Hamilton, Wallace (Hearts), Ries van de Boogert, Westphal (DOS), Romeu (FC Porto), Desbiolles (Servette), Milosev (OFK Beograd), Rühl (Hertha), Hertig, Hosp, Frigerio, Dürr, Schneiter (Lausanne), Holliday, Quinn, Dobson (Sheffield), Schmid, Hasil (Rapid Wien), MacLeod, Skirton, Barnwell, McCullough, Anderson (Arsenal), Hainey, Wright, Ferguson (Partick Thistle), Kanchev, Mizin, Chobanov (Lokomotiv), Palico (Belenenses), Beitia (Atlético Madrid), Nené, Zigoni (Juventus), Leonardi, Orlando, Sormani (Roma), Pišek, Komárek (Spartak), Várhidi, Káposzta, Zámbó, Kuharszki (Ujpesti), Kilola, Croté, Letawe, Cribioli (RFC Liège), Duca, Lapetra, Isasi, Sigi (Real Zaragoza), Ficha, Guillot, Arnal, Suco, Sánchez-Lage, Urtiaga (Valencia), Weber, Hornig, Pott, Schäfer (FC Köln)

Own Goals: Mijnals (DOS) for Sheffield, Cortizo (Real Zaragoza) for Lausanne, Peres (Belenenses) for Roma

FAIRS CUP 1964-65

FIRST ROUND

WIENER SK v SC LEIPZIG 2-1 (0-0)

Prater, Wien 2.09.64

Referee: Rudolf Kreitlein (WG)   Attendance: 11,500

WIENER SK: Rudolf Szanwald; Wilhelm Kainrath, Webora, Cizl; Helmut Weiss, Johann Windisch; Friedrich Rafreider, Adolf Knoll, Peter Schmidt, Wolfgang Gayer, Johann Hörmayer.

SC LEIPZIG: Horst Weigang; Michael Faber, Peter Giessner, Manfred Geisler, Karl Drössler, Volker Trojan, Dieter Engelhardt, Jürgen Naumann, Henning Frenzel, Rainer Trölitzsch, Arno Zerbe.   Trainer: Rudolf Krause

Goals: Hörmayer (47), Naumann (60), Knoll (86)

SC LEIPZIG v WIENER SK 0-1 (0-0)

Bruno Plache, Leipzig 9.09.64

Referee: Gyula Gere (Hun)   Attendance: 15,000

SC LEIPZIG: Horst Weigang; Michael Faber, Peter Giessner, Manfred Geisler, Karl Drössler, Volker Franke, Dieter Engelhardt, Jürgen Naumann, Henning Frenzel, Rainer Trölitzsch, Arno Zerbe.   Trainer: Rudolf Krause

WIENER SK: Rudolf Szanwald; Wilhelm Kainrath, Webora, Anton Linhart; Rudolf Oslansky, Johann Windisch; Friedrich Rafreider, Adolf Knoll, Wolfgang Gayer, Josef Hamerl, Johann Hörmayer.

Goal: Gayer (57)

EINTRACHT FRANKFURT v FC KILMARNOCK 3-0 (0-0)

Waldstadion, Frankfurt 2.09.64

Referee: André Hauben (Bel)   Attendance: 11,800

EINTRACHT: Egon Loy; Richard Weber, Hermann Höfer, Dieter Lindner, Ludwig Landerer, Dieter Stinka, Erwin Stein, Horst Trimhold, Wilhelm Huberts, Wolfgang Solz, Lothar Schämer.   Trainer: Ivica Horvath

KILMARNOCK: Campbell Forsyth; Andrew King, Matthew Watson, James McFadzean, John McGrory, Frank Beattie, Eric Murray, John McInnaly, Robert Black, David Sneddon, Brian McIlroy.   Manager: William Waddell

Goals: Stein (53), Trimhold (55), Stinka (77)

FC KILMARNOCK v EINTRACHT FRANKFURT 5-1 (2-1)

Rugby Park, Kilmarnock 22.09.64

Referee: John Adair (NIrl)   Attendance: 15,000

KILMARNOCK: Campbell Forsyth; Andrew King, James McFadzean, Eric Murray, John McGrory, Frank Beattie, Thomas McLean, John McInnaly, Ronald Hamilton, David Sneddon, Brian McIlroy.   Manager: William Waddell

EINTRACHT: Egon Loy; Peter Blusch, Willi Herbert, Dieter Lindner, Richard Weber, Dieter Stinka, Helmut Kraus, Horst Trimhold, Erwin Stein, Wilhelm Huberts, Lothar Schämer.   Trainer: Ivica Horvath

Goals: Huberts (2), Hamilton (13, 87), McIlroy (16), McFazdean (51), McInally (81)

B 1913 ODENSE v VfB STUTTGART 1-3 (1-2)

Odense 8.09.64

Referee: Adrianus Aalbrecht (Hol)   Attendance: 5,500

B 1913: Knud Engedahl; Kurt Grønning Hansen, Finn Helweg, John Ejlertsen, Knud Naeshave, István Kaibinger, N.C. Nielsen, Jørgen Rasmussen, Kjeld Petersen, Kent Hansen, Erik Dyrholm.

VfB: Günter Sawitzki; Hans Eisele, Günter Seibold, Eberhard Pfisterer, Klaus-Dieter Sieloff, Hans Arnold, Helmut Siebert, Siegfried Böhringer, Helmut Huttary, Rolf Geiger, Dieter Höller.   Trainer: Kurt Baluses

Goals: Geiger (16), Dyrholm (20), Höller (30, 88)

VfB STUTTGART v B 1913 ODENSE 1-0 (0-0)

Neckarstadion, Stuttgart 22.09.64

Referee: Albert Guinnard (Swi)   Attendance: 7,200

VfB: Werner Pfeifer; Hans Eisele, Gerd Menne, Werner Walter, Klaus-Dieter Sieloff, Eberhard Pfisterer, Erwin Waldner, Theodor Hoffmann, Rolf Geiger, Helmut Huttary, Manfred Reiner.   Trainer: Kurt Baluses

B 1913: Knud Engedahl; Kurt Grønning Hansen, John Ejlertsen, Finn Helweg, Knud Naeshave, István Kaibinger, N.C. Nielsen, Jørgen Rasmussen, Kjeld Petersen, Kent Hansen, Erik Dyrholm.

Goal: Hoffmann (56)

FERENCVÁROS BUDAPEST
v SPARTAK BRNO 2-0 (2-0)

Népstadion, Budapest   9.09.64

Referee: Andonis Kitsoukalis (Gre)   Attendance: 45,000

FERENCVÁROS: István Géczi; Sándor Havasi, Sándor Mátrai, Jenő Dálnoki; Tibor Perecsi, Pál Orosz; József Fenyvesi II, Zoltán Varga, Flórián Albert, Oszkár Vilezsál, dr. Máté Fenyvesi.   Trainer: József Mészáros

SPARTAK: Pavel Spisiak; Miroslav Vítů, Karel Kohlík, Tomas Hradský; Bohumil Pišek, Karel Komárek; Sněhota, Pando Jankulovský, Bohumil Hlaváč, Jan Brada, Jaroslav Vojta. Trainer: Karel Kolský

Goals: Varga (10), Albert (20)

SPARTAK BRNO
v FERENCVÁROS BUDAPEST 1-0 (1-0)

Spartak Brno   16.09.64

Referee: Octavian Comşa (Rom)   Attendance: 15,000

SPARTAK: František Schmucker; Miroslav Vítů, Karel Kohlík, Tomas Hradský; Bohumil Pišek, Karel Komárek; Sněhota, Karel Lichtnégl, Bohumil Hlaváč, Jan Brada, Jaroslav Vojta. Trainer: Karel Kolský

FERENCVÁROS: István Géczi; Dezső Novák, Sándor Mátrai, Jenő Dálnoki; Tibor Perecsi, Pál Orosz; József Kökény, Zoltán Varga, Flórián Albert, Gyula Rákosi, dr. Máté Fenyvesi. Trainer: József Mészáros

Goal: Vojta (24)

GÖZTEPE IZMIR v PETROLUL PLOIEŞTI 0-1 (0-1)

Alsançak, Izmir   9.09.64

Referee: Faruk Talu (Tur)   Attendance: 8,500

GÖZTEPE: Nevzat Okuyucu; Sönmezler Kâmil, Koldaş Ekrem, Sedat Çaglayan, Sabahattin Kuruoglu, Nevzat Güselirmak, Ceyhan Yazar, Nihat Yayöz, Fevzi Zemzem, Gürsel Aksel, Cengiz Kayalar.

PETROLUL: Mihai Ionescu; Gheorghe Pahonţu (Cap), Alexandru Fronea, Bujor Hălmăgeanu, Gheorghe Florea; Eduard Juhasz, Nicolae Ivan; Camil Oprişan, Mircea Dridea, Alexandru Badea, Mihai Mocanu.   Trainer: Ilie Oană

Goal: M. Dridea (22)

PETROLUL PLOIEŞTI v GÖZTEPE IZMIR 2-1 (2-0)

Petrolul Ploieşti   23.09.64

Referee: Mihai Popa (Rom)   Attendance: 3,300

PETROLUL: Mihai Ionescu; Gheorghe Pahonţu (Cap), Alexandru Fronea, Gheorghe Florea, Alexandru Pall; Eduard Juhasz, Petre Dragomir; Camil Oprişan, Mircea Dridea, Alexandru Badea, Mihai Mocanu.   Trainer: Ilie Oană

GÖZTEPE: Seyfettin Talay; Kamil Sönmezler, Ekrem Koldaş, Çaglayan Sedat; Sabahattin Kuruoglu, Nevzat II Güselirmak; Ceyhan Yazar, Nihat Yayöz, Fevzi Zemzem, Gürsel Aksel, Cengiz Kayalar.

Goals: Mocanu (5), M. Dridea (40), Nihat (62)

REAL BETIS BALOMPIE SEVILLA
v STADE FRANÇAIS PARIS 1-1 (0-0)

Estadio Heliópolis, Sevilla   9.09.64

Ref: Francisco Guerra Gonçalves (POR)   Attendance: 30,000

BETIS: José Casas Gris «PEPÍN»; Francisco Aparicio, Eusebio RÍOS Fernández, Francisco Faleato Ochoantesana Paquito, José Lopez Hidalgo, Suárez, Breval, Francisco Ortiz Vázquez FRASCO, Fernando ANSOLA Sanmartín, Manuel Azcárate Izeta, ROGELIO Sosa Ramírez.   Trainer: Louis Hon

STADE FRANÇAIS: George Carnus; François Stasiak, Bronas Trusas, Jean Bacconnier, Prudent Bacquet, Edouard Stachowitz «Stako», René Bérangé, Robert Peri, André Fefeu, Phillipe Pottier, Jean Pierre Alba.   Trainer: Henri Priami

Goals: Lopez-Hidalgo (46), Pottier (78)

STADE FRANÇAIS PARIS
v REAL BETIS SEVILLA 2-0 (1-0)

Parc des Princes, Paris   30.09.64

Referee: Günther Baumgärtel (WG)   Attendance: 6,000

STADE FRANÇAIS: George Carnus; François Stasiak, Bronas Trusas, Jean Bacconnier, Maryan Synakowski, Edouard Stachowitz «Stako», André Fefeu, René Bérangé, Georges Peyroche, Phillipe Pottier, Jean Pierre Alba. Trainer: Henri Priami

BETIS: José Casas Gris «PEPÍN»; Francisco GRAU Plá, Eusebio RÍOS Fernández, Francisco Faleato Ochoantesana «PAQUITO», José Lopez Hidalgo, Andrés BOSCH Pujol, BREVAL, Antonio Pallarés Huerta, Fernando ANSOLA Sanmartín, Francisco Ortiz Vázquez FRASCO, Léon LASA Mújica.   Trainer: Louis Hon

Goals: Pottier (18), Stasiak (76)

RACING CLUB STRASBOURG
v AC MILAN 2-0 (1-0)

Stade Meinau, Strasbourg   9.09.64

Referee: Gottfried Dienst (Swi)   Attendance: 14,800

RACING: Johnny Schuth; René Hauss, Gines Gonzales, Raymond Stieber, Denis Devaux, Raymond Kaelbel, Jozef Zsamboki, Gilbert Gress, José Farias, Roland Merschel, Gérard Hausser.   Trainer: Paul Frantz

AC MILAN: Mario Barluzzi; Gilberto Noletti, Ambrogio Pelagalli, Bruno Bacchetta, Cesare Maldini, Giovanni Trapattoni, Giancarlo Salvi, Morales Victor Benítez, Amarildo Tavares de Silveira, Mario David, Germano de Sales José.   Trainer: Nils Liedholm

Goals: Merschel (30), Hausser (82)

AC MILAN
v RACING CLUB STRASBOURG 1-0 (1-0)

San Siro, Milano   30.09.64

Referee: Stjepan Varaždinec (Jug)   Attendance: 27,800

AC MILAN: Mario Barluzzi; Mario David, Mario Trebbi, Gilberto Noletti, Cesare Maldini, Ambrogio Pelagalli, Bruno Mora, Giovanni Lodetti, Amarildo Tavares de Silveira, Moreno Ferrario, Giuliano Fortunato.   Trainer: Nils Liedholm

RACING: Johnny Schuth; René Hauss, Gines Gonzales, Raymond Stieber, Denis Devaux, Raymond Kaelbel, Gilbert Gress, Roland Merschel, José Farias, Robert Szczepaniak, Gérard Hausser.   Trainer: Paul Frantz

Goal: Ferrario (9)

ATHLETIC BILBAO v OFK BEOGRAD 2-2 (0-0)

Estadio San Mamés, Bilbao   9.09.64

Ref: Hermínio Henrique Soares (Por)   Attendance: 24,500

ATHLETIC: José Ángel IRÍBAR Cortajarena; José María ORUE Aranguren, Manuel González ETURA, Meltzer, Luis María AGUIRRE Vidaurrazaga, Luis María ECHEBERRÍA Igartua; José Luis ARTECHE Muguirre, Fidel URIARTE Macho, Ignacio ARIETA I Araunabeña Piedra, José María ARGOITIA Acha, Fernando Trío "YOSU".
Trainer: Antonio Barrios

OFK: Vucicović; Miroslav Milovanović, Blagomir Krivokuća, Momčilo Gavrić, Zoran Dakić, Stojan Vukašinović, Spasoje Samardžić, Petrović, Stojan Milošev, Čolić, Josip Skoblar.   Trainer: Ciril Milovan

Goals: Aguirre (53 pen), Skoblar (56 pen), Argoitia (58), Vukašinović (76)

OFK BEOGRAD v ATHLETIC BILBAO 0-2 (0-1)

JNA, Beograd   30.09.64

Referee: Karl Kainer (Aus)   Attendance: 40,000

OFK: Vucicović; Miroslav Milovanović, Momčilo Gavrić, Dragoljub Marić, Zoran Dakić, Stojan Vukašinović, Dragan Gugleta, Petrović, Stojan Milošev, Sreten Banović, Josip Skoblar.   Trainer: Ciril Milovan

ATHLETIC: José Ángel IRÍBAR Cortajarena; José María ORUE Aranguren, Manuel González ETURA, Jesús ARANGUREN Merino, Juan María ZORRIQUETA Azpiazu, Luis María ECHEBERRÍA Igartua, Luis María AGUIRRE Vidaurrazaga, Fidel URIARTE Macho, Antonio María ARIETA II Araunabeña Piedra, José María ARGOITIA Acha, Fernando Trío "YOSU".   Trainer: Juan Antonio Ipiña

Goals: Uriarte (12, 54)

FC BASEL v SPORA LUXEMBOURG 2-0 (1-0)

St.Jakob, Basel   9.09.64

Referee: Pierre Schwinte (Fra)   Attendance: 1,700

FC BASEL: Jean-Paul Laufenburger; Walter Baumann, Carlo Porlezza, Hanspeter Stocker, Werner Decker, Helmut Hauser, Markus Pfirter, Roberto Frigerio, Crava, Bruno Gabrieli, Aldo Moscatelli.   Trainer: Georges Sobotka (Cze)

SPORA: Romain Schoder; Norbert Neumann, Bernard Ruhe, Fernand Wambach, Fernand Brosius, Victor Nürenberg, Jean Leer, Norbert Wampach, Kirsch, Johny Hilbert, Emile Meyer.

Goals: Crava (14, 66)

SPORA LUXEMBOURG v FC BASEL 1-0 (1-0)

Stade Municipal, Luxembourg   8.10.64

Referee: Robert Schaut (Bel)   Attendance: 700

SPORA: Romain Schoder; Bernard Ruhe, Fernand Wambach, Mario Morocutti, Paul Ludwig, Johny Hilbert, Emile Meyer, Josy Krier, Portz, Norbert Wampach, Norbert Neumann.

FC BASEL: Jean-Paul Laufenburger; Walter Baumann, Bruno Michaud, Heinz Blumer, Josef Kiefer, Werner Decker, Helmut Hauser, Markus Pfirter, Roberto Frigerio, Crava, Aldo Moscatelli.   Trainer: Georges Sobotka

Goal: Krier (20)

VOJVODINA NOVI SAD
v LOKOMOTIV PLOVDIV 1-1 (0-0)

Gradski, Novi Sad   16.09.64

Referee: Aleksandar Škorić (Jug)   Attendance: 4,500

VOJVODINA: Ilija Pantelić; Nacević, Mladen Vucinić, Stevan Nešticki, Stevan Sekereš, Sentin, Silvester Takac, Ljubomir Milić, Djordje Pavlić, Radivoj Radosav, Veljko Aleksić.

LOKOMOTIV: Stancho Bonchev; Ilia Bekiarov, Georgi Mizin, Ivan Manolov, Ivan Boiadjiev, Ianko Dzoglev, Kolchev, Ivan Enchev, Ivan Grancharov, Hristo Iliev, Petar Kolev.

Goals: Kolev (51), D. Pavlic (71)

LOKOMOTIV PLOVDIV
v VOJVODINA NOVI SAD 1-1 (0-0)

9 Septemvri, Plovdiv   23.09.64

Referee: Gábor Soos (Hun)   Attendance: 10,000

LOKOMOTIV: Stancho Bonchev; Ilia Bekiarov, Georgi Mizin, Ivan Manolov, Ivan Boiadjiev, Ijerev, Kolchev, Ivan Enchev, Ivan Grancharov, Hristo Iliev, Petar Kolev.

VOJVODINA: Stanković; Tomce Stamenski, Dimitrije Radović, Stevan Sekereš, Zarko Nikolić, Stevan Nešticki, Veljko Aleksić, Radivoj Radosav, Ljubomir Milić, Adolf Lambi, Vasa Pušibrk.

Goals: L. Milic (76), Kolchev (88)

LOKOMOTIV PLOVDIV
v VOJVODINA NOVI SAD 2-0 (1-0)

Vasil Levski, Sofia   7.10.64

Referee: Vasile Dumitrescu (Rom)   Attendance: 10,200

LOKOMOTIV: Stancho Bonchev; Ilia Bekiarov, Ivan Manolov, Ivan Tsanev, Georgi Mizin, Ivan Boiadjiev, Kolchev, Ivan Enchev, Ivan Grancharov, Hristo Iliev, Petar Kolev.

VOJVODINA: Ilija Pantelić; Tomce Stamenski, Dimitrije Radović, Stevan Sekereš, Jergić, Stevan Nešticki, Veljko Aleksić, Radivoj Radosav, Ljubomir Milić, Adolf Lambi, Vasa Pušibrk.

Goals: Georgi Mizin (30), Enchev (80)

ARIS THESSALONIKI v AS ROMA 0-0

Harilaou, Thessaloniki   16.09.64

Referee: Konstantin Zecević (Jug) Attendance: 15,000

ARIS: Giorgos Pantelakos; Hristos Kambourlazos, Vasilis Psifidis, Kostas Hatzikostas, Kemalidis, Dimitris Grimbelakos, Giorgos Konstantinidis, Alekos Alexiadis, Stefanos Demiris, Vaggelis Tsistoumis, Katama.

AS ROMA: Enzo Matteucci; Francesco Carpenneti, Mario Ardizzon, Sergio Carpanesi, Giacomo Losi, Karl Heinz Schnellinger, Lamberto Leonardi, Giuseppe Tamborini, Bruno Nicolé, Antonio Valentin Angelillo, Fulvio Francesconi. Trainer: Juan Carlos Lorenzo

AS ROMA v ARIS THESSALONIKI 3-0 (0-0)

Stadio Olimpico, Roma   30.09.64

Referee: Daniel Mellet (Swi)   Attendance: 10,800

AS ROMA: Fabio Cudicini; Glauco Tomasin, Mario Ardizzon, Sergio Carpanesi, Giacomo Losi, Karl Heinz Schnellinger, Elvio Salvori, Giancarlo De Sisti, Giuseppe Tamborini, Antonio Valentin Angelillo, Lamberto Leonardi. Trainer: Juan Carlos Lorenzo

ARIS: Giorgos Pantelakos; Hristos Kambourlazos, Vasilis Psifidis, Kostas Hatzikostas, Kemalidis, Dimitris Grimbelakos, Alekos Alexiadis, Theodoros Spanopoulos, Stefanos Demiris, Vaggelis Tsistoumis, Katama.

Goals: Tamborini (58), Schnellinger (69), Leonardi (71)

BELENENSES LISBOA
v SHELBOURNE DUBLIN 1-1 (0-0)

Estadio do Restelo, Lisboa   16.09.64

Referee: Ruiz Casasola (Spa)   Attendance: 6,500

BELENENSES: José Pereira; Manuel Sousa Rodrigues, Agostinho Pereira Ribeiro, ALBERTO LUÍS Pinto Ferro, ALFREDO Nunes VITORINO, Osvaldo Dias Pelezinho, Alfredo Abrantes, Paulo Lourenço PALICO, José TEODORO Ribeiro, Fernando Peres, Vítor Manuel Cruz Godinho. Trainer: Franz Fuchs

SHELBOURNE: Leo Byrne; Patrick Bonham, Brendan O'Brien, Patrick Roberts, Frederick Strahan, John Hennessey, Theo Dunne, Bernard Hannigan, Eric Barber, Michael Conroy, Mick McGrath.   Trainer: Gerard Doyle

Goals: Palico (62), Barber (80)

SHELBOURNE DUBLIN
v BELENENSES LISBOA 0-0

Dalymount Park, Dublin   14.10.64

Referee: Jack Lowry (Wal)   Attendance: 12,900

SHELBOURNE: John Heavey; Patrick Bonham, Brendan O'Brien, Patrick Roberts, Frederick Strahan, John Hennessey, Paddy Dowling, Bernard Hannigan, Eric Barber, Michael Conroy, Mick McGrath.   Trainer: Gerard Doyle

BELENENSES: José Pereira; Alfredo Abrantes, Manuel Sousa Rodrigues, ALBERTO LUÍS Pinto Ferro, Abdul Zubaida, Agostinho Pereira Ribeiro, ESTEVÃO António Espírito Santo MANSIDÃO, José TEODORO Ribeiro, José Rodrigues LIRAS, Fernando Peres, Vítor Manuel Cruz Godinho. Trainer: Franz Fuchs

SHELBOURNE DUBLIN
v BELENENSES LISBOA 2-1 (2-1)

Dalymount Park, Dublin   28.10.64

Referee: Jack Lowry (Wal)   Attendance: 14,400

SHELBOURNE: John Heavey; Paddy Dowling, Brendan O'Brien, Patrick Roberts, Patrick Bonham, John Hennessey, Oliver Conroy, Bernard Hannigan, Eric Barber, Michael Conroy, Mick McGrath.   Trainer: Gerard Doyle

BELENENSES: José Pereira; Alfredo Abrantes, Manuel Sousa Rodrigues, ALBERTO LUÍS Pinto Ferro, Abdul Zubaida, Agostinho Pereira Ribeiro, José TEODORO Ribeiro, José Rodrigues LIRAS, Fernando Peres, Osvaldo Dias Pelenzinho, Vítor Manuel Cruz Godinho.   Trainer: Franz Fuchs

Goals: Hannigan (5), M. Conroy (25), Teodoro (35)

BORUSSIA DORTMUND
v GIRONDINS DE BORDEAUX 4-1 (1-0)

Rote Erde, Dortmund   23.09.64

Referee: Adrianus Boogaerts (Hol)   Attendance: 5,500

BORUSSIA: Heinrich Kwiatkowski; Wolfgang Paul, Manfred Pfeiffer, Wilhelm Sturm, Rudolf Assauer, Hermann Straschitz, Reinhold Wosab, Alfred Schmidt, Franz Brungs, Friedhelm Konietzka, Lothar Emmerich.   Trainer: Hermann Eppenhoff

GIRONDINS: Jean-Claude Ranouilh; Gilbert Moevi, André Chorda, Guy Calleja, Claude Rey, Francisco Navarro, Didier Couécou, Gabriel Abossolo, Aimé Gori, Roland Guillas, Laurent Robuschi.   Trainer: Salvador Artigas (SPA)

Goals: Straschitz (29 pen), Couécou (49), Konietzka (82), Brungs (85, 89)

GIRONDINS DE BORDEAUX
v BORUSSIA DORTMUND 2-0 (1-0)

Stade Municipal, Bordeaux   30.09.64

Referee: Adolfo Bueno Perales (Spa)   Attendance: 11,900

GIRONDINS: Jean-Claude Ranouilh; Gilbert Moevi, Jean Bidegarray, Guy Calleja, Jean-Claude Dubouil, Gabriel Abossolo, Karounga Keita, Hector De Bourgoing, Didier Couécou, Roland Guillas, Laurent Robuschi. Trainer: Salvador Artigas (SPA)

BORUSSIA: Hans Tilkowski; Lothar Geisler, Manfred Pfeiffer, Dieter Kurrat, Wolfgang Paul, Hermann Straschitz, Wilhelm Sturm, Franz Brungs, Harald Beyer, Friedhelm Konietzka, Lothar Emmerich.   Trainer: Hermann Eppenhoff

Goals: Keita (40), Guillas (62)

CF BARCELONA
v AC FIORENTINA FIRENZE 0-1 (0-1)

Camp Nou, Barcelona   23.09.64

Referee: Marcel du Bois (Fra)   Attendance: 27,000

CF BARCELONA: Salvador SADURNÍ Urpi; ELADIO Silvestre Graels, Sigfrido GRACIA Royo, Martín VERGÉS Massa, Fernando OLIVELLA Pons, José María FUSTÉ Blanch; Joaquín RIFÉ Climent, Jesús María PEREDA Ruiz de Temiño, Juan Roberto SEMINARIO Rodríguez, Julio César BENÍTEZ Amoedo, Cayetano RE Rodríguez.   Trainer: César Rodríguez

FIORENTINA: Enrico Albertosi; Enzo Robotti, Sergio Castelletti, Giovan Battista Pirovano, Egidio Guarnacci, Rino Marchesi, Kurt Hamrin, Humberto Dionisio Maschio, Alberto Orlando, Renato Benaglia, Juan Carlos Morrone. Trainer: Giuseppe Chiapella

Goal: Hamrin (26)

AC FIORENTINA FIRENZE
v CF BARCELONA 0-2 (0-1)

Stadio Comunale, Firenze   7.10.64

Referee: Branko Tešanić (Jug)   Attendance: 13,100

FIORENTINA: Enrico Albertosi; Enzo Robotti, Sergio Castelletti, Giovan Battista Pirovano, Egidio Guarnacci, Rino Marchesi, Kurt Hamrin, Mario Bertini, Paolo Nuti, Renato Benaglia, Juan Carlos Morrone.   Trainer: Giuseppe Chiapella

CF BARCELONA: Salvador SADURNÍ Urpi, Alfonso María Rodríguez Salas «FONCHO», ELADIO Silvestre Graels; Martín VERGÉS Massa, Fernando OLIVELLA Pons, Juan TORRENT Solé; Pedro ZABALLA Barquín, Jesús María PEREDA Ruiz de Temiño, Juan Roberto SEMINARIO Rodríguez, José María FUSTÉ Blanch, Cayetano RE Rodríguez. Trainer: César Rodríguez

Goals: Seminario (8, 60)

LEIXÕES PORTO v CELTIC GLASGOW 1-1 (1-1)

Estadio do Mar Matosinhos, Porto 23.09.64

Referee: Joseph Barberan (Fra)   Attendance: 10,000

LEIXÕES: José Nunes Rosas; GERALDO Melo Medeiros, RAÚL Martins MACHADO, Agostino PEREIRA Ribeiro, MANUEL Fernando Martins MOREIRA, José Carlos MARÇAL, João ESTEVES Galego, VAGNER Canotilho, MANUEL OLIVEIRA Santos, MÁRIO Soares VENTURA, Mateus.   Trainer: José Maria Pedroto

CELTIC: John Fallon; Ian Young, Thomas Gemmell, John Clark, John Cushley, James Kennedy, James Johnstone, Robert Murdoch, Stephen Chalmers, Charles Gallacher, Robert Lennox.   Trainer: Robert Rooney

Goals: Esteves (6), Murdoch (31)

CELTIC GLASGOW v LEIXÕES PORTO 3-0 (1-0)

Celtic Park, Glasgow 7.10.64

Referee: Ernest Crawford (Eng)   Attendance: 30,000

CELTIC: John Fallon; Ian Young, Thomas Gemmell, John Clark, John Cushley, James Kennedy, James Johnstone, Robert Murdoch, Stephen Chalmers, Charles Gallacher, Robert Lennox.   Trainer: Robert Rooney

LEIXÕES: José Nunes Rosas; GERALDO Melo Medeiros, RAÚL Martins MACHADO, Agostino PEREIRA Ribeiro, Manuel Moreira, José Carlos MARÇAL, João ESTEVES Galego, VAGNER Canotilho, Juan CAMBRES, MÁRIO Soares VENTURA, CARLOS Domingos DUARTE.
Trainer: José Maria Pedroto

Goals: Chalmers (14, 83), Murdoch (88 pen)

UNION SAINT GILLOISE BRUSSEL v JUVENTUS TORINO 0-1 (0-1)

Parc Duden, Brussel 23.09.64

Referee: James Finney (Eng)   Attendance: 8600

UNION: André Vanderstappen; Firmin Thiels, Alfons Bruylandts, Fernand Verleysen, René Delbrouck, Tomislav Kaloperovic, Julien Kialunda, Philippe Van Wilder, Todor Veselinovic, Paul Vandenberg, Roger Van Cauwelaert.

JUVENTUS: Roberto Anzolin; Adolfo Gori, Benito Sarti, Ernesto Castano, Sandro Salvadore, Gianfranco Leoncini, Carlo Dell'Omodarme, Dino Da Costa, Nestor Combin, Giovanni Sacco, Giampaolo Menichelli.
Trainer: Heriberto Herrera

Goal: Combin (35)

JUVENTUS TORINO UNION SAINT GILLOISE BRUSSEL 1-0 (1-0)

Stadio Comunale, Torino 7.10.64

Referee: Kurt Tschenscher (WG)   Attendance: 4,100

JUVENTUS: Roberto Anzolin; Adolfo Gori, Benito Sarti, Giancarlo Bercellino, Ernesto Castano, Gianfranco Leoncini, Dino Da Costa, Giovanni Sacco, Nestor Combin, Cascajares Luis Del Sol, Giampaolo Menichelli.
Trainer: Heriberto Herrera

UNION: André Vanderstappen; Firmin Thiels, Fernand Verleysen, René Delbrouck, Alfons Bruylandts, Tomislav Kaloperovic, Raymond Best, Julien Kialunda, Jozef Daniels, Todor Veselinovic, Roger Janssens.

Goal: Menichelli (18)

VALENCIA CF v RFC LIEGE 1-1 (1-0)

Estadio de Mestalla, Valencia 23.09.64

Referee: Henri Faucheux (Fra)   Attendance: 14,800

VALENCIA CF: Cipriano González Rivero «ÑITO»; Vicente PIQUER Mora, Luis VILAR Botet, Francisco VIDAGAÑY Hernández; Alberto ARNAL Andrés, ROBERTO Gil Esteve, HÉCTOR NÚÑEZ Bello, Vicente GUILLOT Fabián, WALDO Machado da Silva, José María SÁNCHEZ LAGE, Andres Paredes Alvite «SUCO».   Trainer: Edmundo Suárez «Mundo»

RFC LIÈGE: Guy Delhasse; Yves Baré, Albert Sulon, Emile Lejeune, Lambert Defraigne, Hector Cribioli, Julien Onclin, Gérard Sulon, Jean-Marie Letawe, Georget Bertoncello, Henri Depireux.   Trainer: Jean Cornilli

Goals: Waldo (23), Depireux (87)

RFC LIÈGE v VALENCIA CF 3-1 (1-0)

Stade Rocourt, Liège 8.10.64

Referee: Thomas Wharton (Sco)   Attendance: 14,800

RFC LIÈGE: Guy Delhasse; Yves Baré, Albert Sulon, Emile Lejeune, Lambert Defraigne, Julien Onclin, Hector Cribioli, Henri Depireux, Gérard Sulon, Denis Houf, Georget Bertoncello.   Trainer: Jean Cornilli

VALENCIA CF: Cipriano González Rivero "ÑITO"; Alberto ARNAL Andrés, Francisco VIDAGAÑY Hernández; ROBERTO Gil Esteve, Manuel MESTRE Torres, Francisco García Gómez "PAQUITO"; Manuel Polinario Muñoz "POLI", José Antonio URTIAGA, Valentín García Pascual "TOTÓ", José María SÁNCHEZ LAGE, HÉCTOR NÚÑEZ Bello.
Trainer: Edmundo Suárez "Mundo"

Goals: Bertoncello (4), Depireux (73, 75), Vidagañy (74)

VÅLERENGENS IF OSLO
v EVERTON LIVERPOOL 2-5 (1-1)

Bislett, Oslo   23.09.64

Referee: Einar Boström (Swe)   Attendance: 17,952

VÅLERENGENS: Helge Sørlie; Nils Arne Eggen, Jack Kramer, Thorvald Larsen, Bjarne Hansen, Arne Jakobsen, Per Knudsen, Einar Bruno Larsen, Leif Eriksen, Svein Lauvsnes, Age Sørensen.   Trainer: Anton Ploderer

EVERTON: Andrew Rankin; Brian Harris, Alexander Brown, James Gabriel, Brian Labone, Dennis Stevens, Alex Scott, Colin Harvey, Frederick Pickering, Derek Temple, John Morrissey. Manager: Harry Catterick

Goals: E.B. Larsen (26), Pickering (36, 71), Eriksen (46), Harvey (77), Temple (84), Scott (89)

MANCHESTER UNITED
v DJURGARDENS STOCKHOLM 6-1 (1-0)

Old Trafford, Manchester   27.10.64

Referee: Franz Geluck (Bel)   Attendance: 38,437

UNITED: Patrick Dunne; Seamus Brennan, Tony Dunne, Patrick Crerand, William Foulkes, Norbert Stiles, John Connelly, Robert Charlton, David Herd, Denis Law, George Best.   Manager: Matt Busby

DJURGARDENS: Arne Arvidsson; Jan Karlsson, Lars Arnesson, Torsten Furukrantz, Hans Mild, Gösta Sandberg, Bernt Andersson, Hans Karlsson, Leif Eriksson, Peder Persson, Boris Johansson.   Manager: Torsten Lindberg

Goals: Law (21, 68, 69 pen), R. Charlton (63, 73), Best (86), H. Karlsson (89)

EVERTON LIVERPOOL
v VÅLERENGENS IF OSLO 4-2 (1-2)

Goodison Park, Liverpool   14.10.64

Referee: Willem Schalks (Hol)   Attendance: 20,717

EVERTON: Andrew Rankin; Thomas Wright, Alexander Brown, Dennis Stevens, Brian Labone, Brian Harris, Alex Scott, Alexander Young, Frederick Pickering, Roy Vernon, Derek Temple.   Manager: Harry Catterick

VÅLERENGENS: Helge Sørlie; Nils Arne Eggen, Age Sørensen, Thorvald Larsen, Bjarne Hansen, Arne Jakobsen, Per Knudsen, Einar Bruno Larsen, Terje Hellerud, Leif Eriksen, Egil Olsen.   Trainer: Anton Ploderer

Goals: Young (15, 61), Eriksen (32), Olsen (35), Jacobsen (66 og), Vernon (86)

NK ZAGREB v GRAZER AK 3-2 (1-0)

Zagreb   24.09.64

Referee: Günter Männig (DDR)   Attendance: 4,400

NK ZAGREB: Zoran Misić; Galeković, Aumiler, Susa, Stanisić, Klobucar, Kralj, Stanislav Bubanj, Mladen Wacha, Zlatko Dracić, Mladen Azinović.

GRAZER AK: Juric; Weiss, Erich Frisch, Ernst Wenzlmaier, Gerald Erkinger; Erwin Ninaus, Günther Klug; Günther Iberer, Walter Koleznik, Kauzil, Wilhelm Sgerm.
Trainer: Milan Zeković

Goals: Dracić (35), Bubanj (51, 62), Sgerm (53), Iberer (84)

DJURGARDENS IF STOCKHOLM
v MANCHESTER UNITED 1-1 (1-0)

Råsunda, Stockholm   23.09.64

Referee: Åge Poulsen (Dan)   Attendance: 6,537

DJURGARDENS: Arne Arvidsson; Jan Karlsson, Lars Arnesson, Torsten Furukrantz, Hans Mild, Gösta Sandberg, Bernt Andersson, Hans Karlsson, Leif Eriksson, Hans Nilsson, Boris Johansson.   Manager: Torsten Lindberg

UNITED: Patrick Dunne; Seamus Brennan, Tony Dunne, Patrick Crerand, William Foulkes, Norbert Stiles, John Connelly, Robert Charlton, David Herd, Maurice Setters, George Best.   Manager: Matt Busby

Goals: Johansson (8), Herd (87)

GRAZER AK v NK ZAGREB 0-6 (0-2)

Bundesstadion Liebenau, Graz   7.10.64

Referee: Lajos Aranyosi (Hun)   Attendance: 2,400

GRAZER AK: Reinprecht; Weiss, Erich Frisch, Stefan Kölly, Gerald Erkinger; Erwin Ninaus, Walter Koleznik; Ernst Wenzlmaier, Bernard Vukas, Günther Iberer, Wilhelm Sgerm.
Trainer: Milan Zeković

NK ZAGREB: Zoran Misić; Galeković, Čepelja, Susa, Stanisić, Klobucar, Kralj, Stanislav Bubanj, Mladen Wacha, Zlatko Dracić, Mladen Azinović.

Goals: Bubanj (30, 32), Dracić (54, 57, 65), Azinović (77)

SERVETTE GENÈVE
v ATLÉTICO MADRID 2-2 (0-2)

Stade des Charmilles, Genève   30.09.64

Referee: Robert Lacoste (FRA)   Attendance: 15,742

SERVETTE: Jacques Barlie; Raymond Maffiolo, Robert Kaiserauer, Peter Pazmandy, Bernard Mocellin, Anton Schnyder, Roger Vonlanthen, Michel Desbiolles, André Bosson, André Daina, Jean-Claude Schindelholz.
Trainer: Lucien Leduc (Fra)

ATLÉTICO: Edgardo Mario MADINABEYTIA Bassi; Feliciano RIVILLA Muñoz, Jorge Bernardo GRIFFA Monferoni, Isacio CALLEJA García, Jesús MARTÍNEZ JAYO, ADELARDO Rodríguez Sánchez, Luis Armando UFARTE Ventoso, José Enrique CARDONA Gutiérrez, Jorge Alberto MENDOZA Paulino, Enrique COLLAR Monterrubio, RAMIRO Rodríguez Valente.   Trainer: Otto Bumbel

Goals: Adelardo (5, 37), Schindelholz (64), Daina (74)

ATLÉTICO MADRID
v SERVETTE GENÈVE 6-1 (2-1)

Estadio Metropolitano, Madrid   7.10.64

Referee: Bruno de Marchi (ITA)   Attendance: 21,000

ATLÉTICO: Edgardo Mario MADINABEYTIA Bassi; Feliciano RIVILLA Muñoz, RAMIRO Rodríguez Valente, Jorge Bernardo GRIFFA Monferoni, Isacio CALLEJA García, Jesús GLARÍA Roldán, Luis Armando UFARTE Ventoso, LUIS Aragonés Suárez, Jorge Alberto MENDOZA Paulino, ADELARDO Rodríguez Sánchez, Enrique COLLAR Monterrubio.   Trainer: Otto Bumbel

SERVETTE: Jacques Barlie; Raymond Maffiolo, Robert Kaiserauer, Jacques Desbaillet, Anton Schnyder, Peter Pazmandy, Michel Desbiolles, André Bosson, André Daina, Roger Vonlanthen, Jean-Claude Schindelholz.
Trainer: Lucien Leduc

Goals: Schindelholz (13), Luis (17), Mendoza (28, 81), Ramiro (48), Adelardo (54, 66)

KB KØBENHAVN v DOS UTRECHT 3-4 (2-4)

Idraetsparken, København   30.09.64

Referee: Hans Grandlund (Nor)   Attendance: 9,200

KB KØBENHAVN: Niels Jensen; Tommy Jørgensen, Bent Poulsen, Johansen, Henning Hellbrandt, Niels Møller, Eyvind Clausen, Finn Møller, Jørgen Ravn, Ole Sørensen, Leif Mortensen.

DOS: Wim Ruitenbeek; Leo Kuhnen, Martin Ockhuysen, Sjaak Westphaal, Joop Rooders, Ries van de Bogert, Ger Fahrenhorst, Hans Sleven, Tonny Van der Linden, Wim Visser, Henk Wery.   Trainer: de Vroet

Goals: Mortensen (13), Visser (19), Van der Linden (20), Wery (21), Poulsen (35 pen), Sleven (43), F. Møller (63)

DOS UTRECHT v KB KØBENHAVN 2-1 (1-1)

Galgenwaard, Utrecht   14.10.64

Referee: Antoine Quedeville (Lux)   Attendance: 11,000

DOS: Wim Ruitenbeek; Leo Kuhnen, Martin Ockhuysen, Sjaak Westphaal, Joop Rooders, Henk Vonk, Ger Fahrenhorst, Wim Visser, Tonny Van der Linden, Ries van de Bogert, Henk Wery.   Trainer: de Vroet

KB KØBENHAVN: Niels Jensen; Tommy Jørgensen, Bent Poulsen, Johansen, Henning Hellbrandt, Niels Møller, Eyvind Clausen, Finn Møller, Jørgen Ravn, Ole Sørensen, Leif Mortensen.

Goals: Sørensen (34), Wery (34, 87)

HERTHA BERLIN WEST
v ROYAL ANTWERP FC 2-1 (2-0)

Olympischstadion, Berlin West   3.10.64

Referee: Hansen (Dan)   Attendance: 9,200

HERTHA: Wolfgang Fahrian; Otto Rehhagel, Hans-Günter Schimmöller, Lothar Gross, Hans Eder, Uwe Klimaschefski, Kurt Schulz, Jürgen Sundermann, Hans-Joachim Altendorf, Lutz Steinert, Eberhard Borchert.   Trainer: Josef Schneider

ANTWERP: Willy Coremans; Maurice Renier, Jozef Janssens, Werner Deprez, Walter Noels, Ludo Stuyck, Jean-François Tonnelet, Wally Listhaegen, Eddy Van De Putte, Florent Bohez, Theofiel van de Velde.   Trainer: Fraipons

Goals: Steinert (5, 27), Bohez (57)

ROYAL ANTWERP FC
HERTHA BERLIN WEST 2-0 (1-0)

Bosuil, Antwerp   14.10.64

Referee: Hugh Philips (Sco)   Attendance: 2,200

ANTWERP: Willy Coremans; Maurice Renier, Jozef Janssens, Ludo Stuyck, Walter Noels, Jozef Deckers, Eddy Van De Putte, Ivo Stockbroeckx, Florent Bohez, Theofiel van de velde, Werner Deprez.   Trainer: Fraipons

HERTHA: Wolfgang Fahrian; Otto Rehhagel, Hans-Günter Schimmöller, Lothar Gross, Hans Eder, Jürgen Sundermann, Karl-Heinz Rühl, Helmut Faeder, Michael Krampitz, Lutz Steinert, Eberhard Borchert.   Trainer: Josef Schneider

Goals: Bohez (24), Van de Velde (75)

DUNFERMLINE ATHLETIC
v ÖRGRYTE GÖTEBORG 4-2 (2-2)

East End Park, Dunfermline   13.10.64

Referee: Owen McCarthy (Eire)   Attendance: 8,500

DUNFERMLINE: James Herriot; James Thomson, William Callaghan, Alexander Smith, James McLean, George Miller, George Peebles, John Kilgannon, John McLaughlin, Harry Melrose, John Sinclair.   Manager: Victor Cunningham

ÖRGRYTE: Kurt Johansson; Bertil Jansson, Helge Börjesson, Anders Svensson, Vilgot Schwartz, Lennart Wing, Lars Olofsson, Jen Söderberg, Agne Simonsson, Stig Jonsson, Örjan Persson.   Trainer: Walter Probst

Goals: Persson (19), McLaughlin (21, 46), Simonsson (25), Sinclair (29, 81)

FERENCVÁROS BUDAPEST
v WIENER SK 2-1 (1-1)

Népstadion, Budapest   4.11.64

Referee: Fritz Köpcke (DDR)   Attendance: 20,000

FERENCVÁROS: István Géczi; Dezső Novák, Sándor Mátrai, Jenő Dálnoki; Oszkár Vilezsál, Tibor Perecsi; József Kökeny, Zoltán Varga, Flórián Albert, Gyula Rákosi, dr. Máté Fenyvesi.   Trainer: József Mészáros

WIENER SK: Rudolf Szanwald; Wilhelm Kainrath, Webora, Erich Hasenkopf; Johann Windisch, Rudolf Oslansky; Adolf Knoll, Wolfgang Gayer, Peter Schmidt, Helmut Weiss, Johann Hörmayer.

Goals: Hörmayer (32), Novak (33 pen), Varga (65)

ÖRGRYTE GÖTEBORG
v DUNFERMLINE ATHLETIC 0-0

Ullevi, Göteborg   20.10.64

Referee: Gunnar Michaelsen (Dan)   Attendance: 1,341

ÖRGRYTE: Lars-Olof Gunnskog; Rolf Wetterlind, Bo Åkervall, Anders Svensson, Vilgot Schwartz, Bertelsen, Jen Söderberg, Rolf Hansson, Agne Simonsson, Roger Karlsson, Örjan Persson.   Trainer: Walter Probst

DUNFERMLINE: James Herriot; James Thomson, William Callaghan, John Lunn, James McLean, George Miller, Harry Melrose, Alexander Smith, John McLaughlin, Alexander Ferguson, John Sinclair.   Manager: Victor Cunningham

FERENCVÁROS BUDAPEST
v WIENER SK 2-0 (0-0)

Népstadion, Budapest   18.11.64

Referee: Josef Krnavec (Cze)   Attendance: 40,000

FERENCVÁROS: István Géczi; Dezső Novák, Sándor Mátrai, Jenő Dálnoki; Oszkár Vilezsál, Tibor Perecsi; József Kökény, István Juhász, Flórián Albert, Zoltán Friedmanszky, Máté Fenyvesi.   Trainer: József Mészáros

WIENER SK: Rudolf Szanwald; Wilhelm Kainrath, Webora, Erich Hasenkopf; Rudolf Oslansky, Johann Windisch; Adolf Knoll, Peter Schmidt, Wolfgang Gayer, Josef Hamerl, Johann Hörmayer.

Goals: Albert (59, 75)

SECOND ROUND

WIENER SK
v FERENCVÁROS BUDAPEST 1-0(1-0)

Prater, Wien   28.10.64

Referee: Karl Keller (Swi)   Attendance: 12,000

WIENER SK: Rudolf Szanwald; Wilhelm Kainrath, Webora, Erich Hasenkopf; Rudolf Oslansky, Johann Windisch; Anton Linhart, Adolf Knoll, Peter Schmidt, Wolfgang Gayer, Johann Hörmayer.

FERENCVÁROS: István Géczi; Sándor Havasi, Sándor Mátrai, Jenő Dálnoki; Oszkár Vilezsál, Tibor Perecsi; József Fenyvesi II, István Juhász, Flórián Albert, Gyula Rákosi, dr. Máté Fenyvesi.   Trainer: József Mészáros

Goal: Hörmayer (35)

NK ZAGREB v AS ROMA 1-1 (1-0)

Zagreb   28.10.64

Referee: Joseph Heymann (Swi)   Attendance: 4,000

ZAGREB: Zoran Misić; Galeković, Mestrović, Klobucar, Stanisić, Susa, Kralj, Stanislav Bubanj, Dušan Beslac, Zlatko Dracić, Mladen Azinović.

AS ROMA: Enzo Matteucci; Glauco Tomasin, Mario Ardizzon, Sergio Carpanesi, Giacomo Losi, Karl Heinz Schnellinger, Giuseppe Tamborini, Giancarlo De Sisti, Bruno Nicolé, Antonio Valentin Angelillo, Fulvio Francesconi.   Trainer: Juan Carlos Lorenzo

Goals: Beslac (6), Nicolé (52)

AS ROMA v NK ZAGREB 1-0 (0-0)

Stadio Olimpico, Roma   25.11.64

Referee: Gerhard Schulenburg (WG)   Attendance: 9,200

AS ROMA: Fabio Cudicini; Glauco Tomasin, Mario Ardizzon, Sergio Carpanesi, Giacomo Losi, Karl Heinz Schnellinger, Lamberto Leonardi, Giancarlo De Sisti, Bruno Nicolé, Antonio Valentin Angelillo, Fulvio Francesconi.
Trainer: Juan Carlos Lorenzo

ZAGREB: Zoran Misić; Mestrović, Galeković, Klobucar, Stanisić, Susa, Kralj, Nedov, Mladen Wacha, Zlatko Dracić, Dušan Beslac.

Goal: Angelillo (82)

STADE FRANÇAIS PARIS
v JUVENTUS TORINO 0-0

Parc des Princes, Paris   28.10.64

Referee: Laurens Van Ravens (Hol)   Attendance: 17,000

STADE FRANÇAIS: George Carnus; Prudent Bacquet, Serge Dumas, Robert Peri, François Stasiak, Edouard Stachowitz «Stako», André Fefeu, René Berangé, Miloš Milutinović, Philippe Pottier, Jean Pierre Alba.   Trainer: Henri Priami

JUVENTUS: Roberto Anzolin; Adolfo Gori, Benito Sarti, Giancarlo Bercellino, Ernesto Castano, Gianfranco Leoncini, Dino Da Costa, Giovanni Sacco, Nestor Combin, Cascajares Luis Del Sol, Gino Stacchini.   Trainer: Heriberto Herrera

JUVENTUS TORINO
v STADE FRANÇAIS PARIS 1-0 (0-0)

Stadio Comunale, Torino   2.12.64

Referee: Živko Bajić (Jug)   Attendance: 2,300

JUVENTUS: Roberto Anzolin; Adolfo Gori, Benito Sarti, Giancarlo Bercellino, Ernesto Castano, Gianfranco Leoncini, Giovanni Sacco, Dino Da Costa, Nestor Combin, Cascajares Luis Del Sol, Giampaolo Menichelli.   Trainer: Heriberto Herrera

STADE FRANÇAIS: René Gallina; Prudent Bacquet, François Stasiak, Synakowski Maryan, Bronas Trusas, Edouard Stachowitz «Stako», Georges Peyroche, René Berangé, Miloš Milutinović, Philippe Pottier, Jean Bacconnier.
Trainer: Henri Priami

Goal: Da Costa (49)

FC BASEL
v RACING CLUB STRASBOURG 0-1 (0-0)

St.Jakob, Basel   3.11.64

Referee: Helmut Fritz (WG)   Attendance: 2,700

FC BASEL: Jean-Paul Laufenburger; Walter Baumann, Carlo Porlezza, Josef Kiefer, Helmut Hauser, Werner Decker, Markus Pfirter, Bruno Gabrieli, Roberto Frigerio, Heinz Blumer, Aldo Moscatelli.   Trainer: Georges Sobotka

RACING: Johnny Schuth; Gines Gonzales, Pierre Sbaïz, Raymond Kaelbel, Denis Devaux, Michel Leblond, Gilbert Gress, Roland Merschel, Jozef Zsamboki, Robert Szczepaniak, Gérard Hausser.   Trainer: Paul Frantz

Goal: Hausser (48)

RACING CLUB STRASBOURG
v FC BASEL 5-2 (3-2)

Stade Meinau, Strasbourg   11.11.64

Referee: Joseph Hannet (Bel)   Attendance: 5,300

RACING: Johnny Schuth; Gines Gonzales, Pierre Sbaïz, Raymond Kaelbel, Denis Devaux, Michel Leblond, Gilbert Gress, Roland Merschel, José Farias, Robert Szczepaniak, Gérard Hausser.   Trainer: Paul Frantz

FC BASEL: Jean-Paul Laufenburger; Carlo Porlezza, Hanspeter Stocker, Bruno Michaud, Helmut Hauser, Werner Decker, Markus Pfirter, Bruno Gabrieli, Roberto Frigerio, Heinz Blumer, Aldo Moscatelli.   Trainer: Georges Sobotka

Goals: Farias (13), Sbaïz (21), Frigerio (22 pen), Hausser (30, 53), Blumer (35), Szczepaniak (83)

KILMARNOCK FC
v EVERTON LIVERPOOL 0-2 (0-0)

Rugby Park, Kilmarnock   11.11.64

Referee: Adrianus Aalbrecht (Hol)   Attendance: 20,000

KILMARNOCK: Campbell Forsyth; Andrew King, Matthew Watson, Eric Murray, John McGrory, Frank Beattie, Brian McIlroy, Robert Black, Ronald Hamilton, James McFadzean, David Sneddon.   Manager: William Waddell

EVERTON: Andrew Rankin; Dennis Stevens, Alexander Brown, James Gabriel, Brian Labone, Brian Harris, Derek Temple, Alexander Young, Frederick Pickering, Roy Vernon, John Morrissey.   Manager: Harry Catterick

Goals: Temple (55), Morrissey (59)

EVERTON LIVERPOOL
v KILMARNOCK FC 4-1 (2-1)

Goodison Park, Liverpool   23.11.64

Referee: Kurt Tschenscher (WG)   Attendance: 30,727

EVERTON: Andrew Rankin; Brian Harris, Alexander Brown, James Gabriel, Brian Labone, Dennis Stevens, Derek Temple, Alexander Young, Frederick Pickering, Colin Harvey, John Morrissey.   Manager: Harry Catterick

KILMARNOCK: Campbell Forsyth; Andrew King, Matthew Watson, Eric Murray, John McGrory, Pat O'Connor, Brian McIlroy, John McInnaly, Ronald Hamilton, James McFadzean, David Sneddon.   Manager: William Waddell

Goals: McIlroy (6), Harvey (24), Pickering (34, 70), Young (64)

BORUSSIA DORTMUND
v MANCHESTER UNITED 1-6 (0-2)

Rote Erde, Dortmund   11.11.64

Referee: Gino Rigato (Ita)   Attendance: 18,000

BORUSSIA: Bernhard Wessel; Gerhard Cyliax, Theodor Redder, Dieter Kurrat, Wolfgang Paul, Wilhelm Sturm, Reinhold Wosab, Franz Brungs, Harald Beyer, Friedhelm Konietzka, Lothar Emmerich.   Trainer: Hermann Eppenhoff

UNITED: Patrick Dunne; Seamus Brennan, Tony Dunne, Patrick Crerand, William Foulkes, Norbert Stiles, John Connelly, Robert Charlton, David Herd, Denis Law, George Best.   Manager: Matt Busby

Goals: Herd (12), R. Charlton (30, 79, 85), Best (49), Kurrat (52 pen), Law (77)

PETROLUL PLOIEŞTI
v LOKOMOTIV PLOVDIV 1-0 (0-0)

Petrolul Ploieşti   11.11.64

Referee: György Müncz (Hun)   Attendance: 3,000

PETROLUL: Mihai Ionescu; Gheorghe Pahonţu (Cap), Alexandru Fronea, Bujor Hălmăgeanu, Gheorghe Florea; Petre Dragomir, Nicolae Ivan; Alexandru Badea, Eduard Juhasz, Mircea Dridea, Mihai Mocanu.   Trainer: Ilie Oană

LOKOMOTIV: Stancho Bonchev; Ilia Bekiarov, Georgi Mizin, Ivan Manolov; Ivan Boiadjiev, Dimitar Mladenov; Denev, Ivan Grancharov, Ivan Kanchev, Hristo Iliev, Petar Kolev.

Goal: M. Dridea (66 pen)

MANCHESTER UNITED
v BORUSSIA DORTMUND 4-0 (2-0)

Old Trafford, Manchester   2.12.64

Referee: Vital Loraux (Bel)   Attendance: 31,896

UNITED: Patrick Dunne; Seamus Brennan, Tony Dunne, Patrick Crerand, William Foulkes, Norbert Stiles, John Connelly, Robert Charlton, David Herd, Denis Law, George Best.   Manager: Matt Busby

BORUSSIA: Hans Tilkowski; Wilhelm Burgsmüller, Manfred Pfeiffer, Gerhard Cyliax, Wolfgang Paul, Hermann Straschitz, Wilhelm Sturm, Alfred Schmidt, Franz Brungs, Harald Beyer, Reinhold Wosab.   Trainer: Hermann Eppenhoff

Goals: R. Charlton (1, 19), Law (68), Connelly (80)

LOKOMOTIV PLOVDIV
v PETROLUL PLOIEŞTI 2-0 (1-0)

9 Septemvri, Plovdiv   2.12.64

Referee: Nejat Sener (Tur)   Attendance: 6,200

LOKOMOTIV: Stancho Bonchev; Ilia Bekiarov, Georgi Mizin, Ivan Boiadjiev, Ivan Manolov; Ivan Tsanev, Hristo Iliev; Ivan Kanchev, Ivan Enchev, Ivan Grancharov, Petar Kolev.

PETROLUL: Mihai Ionescu; Gheorghe Pahonţu (Cap), Alexandru Fronea, Bujor Hălmăgeanu, Gheorghe Florea; Petre Dragomir, Nicolae Ivan; Alexandru Badea, Eduard Juhasz, Mircea Dridea, Constantin Moldoveanu.   Trainer: Ilie Oană

Goals: Manolov (33 pen), Kolev (85)

DUNFERMLINE ATHLETIC
v VfB STUTTGART 1-0 (0-0)

East End Park, Dunfermline   17.11.64

Referee: John Adair (NIrl)   Attendance: 15,000

DUNFERMLINE: James Herriot; William Callaghan, John Lunn, Alexander Smith, James McLean, Thomas Callaghan, Alexander Edwards, Alexander Ferguson, Robert Paton, Harry Melrose, George Peebles.   Manager: Victor Cunningham

VfB: Günter Sawitzki; Gerd Menne, Günter Seibold, Willi Entenmann, Theodor Hoffmann, Eberhard Pfisterer, Erwin Waldner, Hans Eisele, Rolf Geiger, Hans Krauss, Manfred Reiner.   Trainer: Kurt Baluses

Goal: T. Callaghan (70)

VfB STUTTGART
v DUNFERMLINE ATHLETIC 0-0

Neckarstadion, Stuttgart 1.12.64

Referee: Anton Bucheli (Swi)   Attendance: 10,000

VfB: Günter Sawitzki; Gerd Menne, Günter Seibold, Willi Entenmann, Klaus-Dieter Sieloff, Eberhard Pfisterer, Helmut Siebert, Siegfried Böhringer, Erwin Waldner, Hans Eisele, Dieter Höller.   Trainer: Kurt Baluses

DUNFERMLINE: James Herriot; William Callaghan, John Lunn, James Thomson, James McLean, Thomas Callaghan, Alexander Edwards, Alexander Smith, John McLaughlin, John Kilgannon, John Sinclair.   Manager: Victor Cunningham

CF BARCELONA v CELTIC GLASGOW 3-1 (2-0)

Camp Nou, Barcelona 18.11.64

Referee: Antonio Sbardella (Ita)   Attendance: 21,000

CF BARCELONA: Salvador SADURNÍ Urpi; Alfonso María Rodríguez Salas «FONCHO», Julio César BENÍTEZ Amoedo, Juan TORRENT Solé, ELADIO Silvestre Graels, Martín VERGÉS Massa, Joaquín RIFÉ Climent, Jesús María PEREDA Ruiz de Temiño, José Antonio ZALDÚA Urdanavia, Juan Roberto SEMINARIO Rodríguez, Cayetano RE Rodríguez. Trainer: Vicente Sasot

CELTIC: Ronald Simpson; Ian Young, Thomas Gemmell, John Clark, William McNeill, James Kennedy, James Johnstone, John Cushley, Stephen Chalmers, Robert Murdoch, John Hughes.   Trainer: Robert Rooney

Goals: Zaldúa (12), Seminario (23), Hughes (55), Rifé (83)

CELTIC GLASGOW v CF BARCELONA 0-0

Celtic Park, Glasgow 2.12.64

Referee: Tage Sørensen (Dan)   Attendance: 42,500

CELTIC: Ronald Simpson; Ian Young, Thomas Gemmell, Robert Murdoch, William McNeill, William O'Neill, James Johnstone, Stephen Chalmers, John Hughes, Charles Gallacher, Robert Lennox.   Trainer: Robert Rooney

CF BARCELONA: Salvador SADURNÍ Urpi; Julio César BENÍTEZ Amoedo, ELADIO Silvestre Graels, Martín VERGÉS Massa, Fernando OLIVELLA Pons, Jesús GARAY Vicino, Fernand Goywaerts, Sándor Kocsis, Cayetano RE Rodríguez, José María FUSTÉ Blanch, Juan Roberto SEMINARIO Rodríguez.   Trainer: Vicente Sasot

ATHLETIC BILBAO
v ROYAL ANTWERP FC 2-0 (1-0)

Estadio San Mamés, Bilbao 18.11.64

Ref: Joaquim Fernandes de Campos (Por)   Att: 22,500

ATHLETIC: José Ángel IRÍBAR Cortajarena; José María ORUE Aranguren, Manuel González ETURA, Jesús ARANGUREN Merino, Luis María ECHEBERRÍA Igartua, Juan María ZORRIQUETA Azpiazu, Jesús María ECHEVARRÍA, Luis María AGUIRRE Vidaurrazaga, Antonio María ARIETA II Araunabeña Piedra, Fidel URIARTE Macho, Fernando Trío "YOSU".   Trainer: Antonio Barrios

ANTWERP: Willy Coremans; Maurice Renier, Edward Wauters, Jozef Deckers, Werner Deprez, Jozef Janssens, Ludo Stuyck, Karel Beyers, Florent Bohez, Marcel Janssen, Theofiel van de Velde.   Trainer: Fraipons

Goals: Aguirre (6, 48)

ROYAL ANTWERP FC
v ATHLETIC BILBAO 0-1 (0-1)

Bosuil, Antwerp 9.12.64

Referee: William O'Neill (Eire)   Attendance: 4,100

ANTWERP: Willy Coremans; Edward Wauters, Jozef Janssens, Jozef Deckers, Werner Deprez, Jean-François Tonnelet, Raymond Goris; Karel Beyers, Florent Bohez, Jozef Van Gool, Ivo Stockbroeckx.   Trainer: Fraipons

ATHLETIC: José Ángel IRÍBAR Cortajarena; José María ORUE Aranguren, Jesús María ECHEVARRÍA, Jesús ARANGUREN Merino, Luis María ECHEBERRÍA Igartua, Juan María ZORRIQUETA Azpiazu, Fernando Trío "YOSU", Luis María AGUIRRE Vidaurrazaga, Ignacio ARIETA I Araunabeña Piedra, Antonio María ARIETA II Araunabeña Piedra, Fidel URIARTE Macho.   Trainer: Antonio Barrios

Goal: Echevarría (33)

DOS UTRECHT v RFC LIÈGE 0-2 (0-1)

Galgenwaard, Utrecht 19.11.64

Referee: George McCabe (Eng)   Attendance: 7,500

DOS: Wim Ruitenbeek; Leo Kuhnen, Joop Rooders, Niclos Dacsev, Martin Ockhuysen, Sjaak Westphaal, Henk Vonk, Ger Fahrenhorst, Tonny Van der Linden, Wim Visser, Henk Wery. Trainer: de Vroet

RFC LIÈGE: Claude Coulonval; Yves Baré, Albert Sulon, Emile Lejeune, Lambert Defraigne, Julien Onclin, Hector Cribioli, Gérard Sulon, Denis Houf, Victor Wegria, Georget Bertoncello.   Trainer: Jean Cornilli

Goals: Bertoncello (31), Wegria (73)

RFC LIÈGE v DOS UTRECHT 2-0 (1-0)

Stade Rocourt, Liège   9.12.64

Referee: Leo Callaghan (Wal)   Attendance: 5,700

RFC LIÈGE: Guy Delhasse; Yves Baré, Albert Sulon, Emile Lejeune, Jean Neys, Julien Onclin, Hector Cribioli, Claude Croté, Gérard Sulon, Jean-Marie Letawe, Georget Bertoncello. Trainer: Jean Cornilli

DOS: Wim Ruitenbeek; Leo Kuhnen, Joop Rooders, Niclos Dacsev, Martin Ockhuysen, Henk Vonk, Wim Visser, Ger Fahrenhorst, Sjaak Westphaal, Tonny Van der Linden, Henk Wery. Trainer: de Vroet

Goals: G. Sulon (38, 67)

SHELBOURNE DUBLIN v ATLÉTICO MADRID 0-1 (0-0)

Dalymount Park, Dublin   25.11.64

Referee: William Syme (Sco)   Attendance: 19,800

SHELBOURNE: John Heavey; Patrick Bonham, Brendan O'Brien, Patrick Roberts, Frederick Strahan, John Hennessey, Oliver Conroy, Bernard Hannigan, Eric Barber, Michael Conroy, Mick McGrath. Trainer: Gerard Doyle

ATLÉTICO: Miguel SAN ROMÁN Núñez; Julio Santaella Benítez "COLO", Jesús MARTÍNEZ JAYO, Manuel RUIZ-SOSA, Jorge Bernardo GRIFFA Monferoni, Jesús GLARÍA Roldán, Luis Armando UFARTE Ventoso, José Enrique CARDONA Gutiérrez, EULOGIO Ramiro MARTÍNEZ, ADELARDO Rodríguez Sánchez, Enrique COLLAR Monterrubio. Trainer: Otto Bumbel

Goal: Cardona (71)

ATLÉTICO MADRID v SHELBOURNE DUBLIN 1-0 (0-0)

Estadio Metropolitano, Madrid   2.12.64

Referee: Pierre Schwinte (Fra)   Attendance: 10,800

ATLÉTICO: Miguel SAN ROMÁN Núñez, Feliciano RIVILLA Muñoz, Isacio CALLEJA García; Manuel RUIZ-SOSA, Julio Santaella Benítez «COLO», Jesús GLARÍA Roldán; Luis Armando UFARTE Ventoso, LUIS Aragonés Suárez, Jorge Alberto MENDOZA Paulino, ADELARDO Rodríguez Sánchez, Enrique COLLAR Monterrubio. Trainer: Otto Bumbel

SHELBOURNE: John Heavey; Patrick Bonham, Brendan O'Brien; Patrick Roberts, Frederick Strahan, John Hennessey; Paddy Dowling, Oliver Conroy, Bernard Hannigan, Eric Barber, Michael Conroy. Trainer: Gerard Doyle

Goal: Adelardo (85)

THIRD ROUND

RFC LIÈGE v ATLETICO MADRID 1-0 (0-0)

Rocourt, Liège   13.01.65

Referee: James Finney (Eng)   Attendance: 18,300

RFC LIÈGE: Guy Delhasse; Yves Baré, Albert Sulon, Emile Lejeune, Lambert Defraigne, Hector Cribioli, Denis Houf, Claude Croté, Gérard Sulon, Jean-Marie Letawe, Georget Bertoncello. Trainer: Jean Cornilli

ATLÉTICO: Miguel SAN ROMÁN Núñez; Julio Santaella Benítez «COLO», Isacio CALLEJA García; Feliciano RIVILLA Muñoz, Jorge Bernardo GRIFFA Monferoni, Jesús GLARÍA Roldán; Luis Armando UFARTE Ventoso, Manuel RUIZ-SOSA, LUIS Aragonés Suárez, ADELARDO Rodríguez Sánchez, José Enrique CARDONA Gutiérrez. Trainer: Adrián ESCUDERO Garcia

Goal: Bertoncello (87)

ATLETICO MADRID v RFC LIÈGE 2-0 (1-0)

Estadio Metropolitano, Madrid   3.03.65

Referee: Giulio Campanati (Ita)   Attendance: 15,000

ATLÉTICO: Edgardo Mario MADINABEYTIA Bassi; Julio Santaella Benítez «COLO», RAMIRO Rodríguez Valente; Manuel Bermúdez Arias «POLO», Isacio CALLEJA García, Manuel RUIZ-SOSA, LUIS Aragonés Suárez, Luis Armando UFARTE Ventoso, Jorge Alberto MENDOZA Paulino, ADELARDO Rodríguez Sánchez, José Enrique CARDONA Gutiérrez. Trainer: Adrián ESCUDERO Garcia

RFC LIÈGE: Guy Delhasse; Yves Baré, Albert Sulon, Emile Lejeune, Lambert Defraigne, Julien Onclin, Hector Cribioli, Claude Croté, Gérard Sulon, Denis Houf, Georget Bertoncello. Trainer: Jean Cornilli

Croté sent off (88)

Goal: Luis (45 pen), Ufarte (47)

RACING CLUB STRASBOURG v CF BARCELONA 0-0

Meinau, Strasbourg   20.01.65

Referee: Pieter Paulus Roomer (Hol)   Attendance: 18,800

RACING: Johnny Schuth, René Hauss, Pierre Sbaïz, Ginés González, Raymond Kaelbel, Denis Devaux, Gilbert Gress, Roland Merschel, José Farias, Robert Szczepaniak, Gérard Hausser. Trainer: Paul Frantz

CF BARCELONA: Salvador SADURNÍ Urpi; Julio César BENÍTEZ Amoedo, ELADIO Silvestre Graels; Martín VERGÉS Massa, Fernando OLIVELLA Pons, Jesús GARAY Vicino; Joaquín RIFÉ Climent, Sándor Kocsis, Fernand Goywaerts, José María FUSTÉ Blanch, Juan Roberto SEMINARIO Rodríguez. Trainer: Vicente Sasot

CF BARCELONA
v RACING CLUB STRASBOURG 2-2 (0-2)

Camp Nou, Barcelona   10.02.65

Referee: Vital Loraux (Bel)   Attendance: 26,300

CF BARCELONA: Salvador SADURNÍ Urpi; Julio César BENÍTEZ Amoedo, ELADIO Silvestre Graels; Martín VERGÉS Massa, Fernando OLIVELLA Pons, Jesús GARAY Vicino; Joaquín RIFÉ Climent, Sándor Kocsis, Cayetano RE Rodríguez, Fernand Goywaerts, Juan Roberto SEMINARIO Rodríguez.   Trainer: Vicente Sasot

RACING: Johnny Schuth, René Hauss, Pierre Sbaïz, Ginés González, Raymond Kaelbel, Denis Devaux, Gilbert Gress, Roland Merschel, José Farias, Robert Szczepaniak, Gérard Hausser.   Trainer: Paul Frantz

Goals: Hausser (17), Farias (21), Benítez (53), Seminario (89)

CF BARCELONA
v RACING CLUB STRASBOURG 0-0

Camp Nou, Barcelona   18.03.65

Referee: Concetto Lo Bello (Ita) Attendance: 38,000

CF BARCELONA: Salvador SADURNÍ Urpi; Julio César BENÍTEZ Amoedo, Fernando OLIVELLA Pons, Jesús GARAY Vicino, ELADIO Silvestre Graels, Martín VERGÉS Massa, José María FUSTÉ Blanch, Joaquín RIFÉ Climent, Luis VIDAL Planella, Cayetano RE Rodríguez, Juan Roberto SEMINARIO Rodríguez.   Trainer: Vicente Sasot

RACING: Johnny Schuth; Denis Devaux, René Hauss, Raymond Stieber, Gines Gonzales, Pierre Sbaïz, Gilbert Gress, Roland Merschel, Robert Szczepaniak, José Farias, Gérard Hausser.   Trainer: Paul Frantz

Racing Strasbourg qualified on the toss of a coin

MANCHESTER UNITED
v EVERTON LIVERPOOL 1-1 (1-1)

Old Trafford, Manchester   20.01.65

Referee: Gerhard Schulenburg (WG)   Attendance: 49,075

UNITED: Patrick Dunne; Seamus Brennan, Tony Dunne, Patrick Crerand, William Foulkes, Norbert Stiles, John Connely, Robert Charlton, David Herd, Denis Law, George Best.   Manager: Matt Busby

EVERTON: Gordon West; Thomas Wright, Ramon Wilson, James Gabriel, Brian Labone, Dennis Stevens, Alex Scott, Colin Harvey, Frederick Pickering, Derek Temple, John Morrissey.   Manager: Harry Catterick

Goals: Pickering (14), Connely (33)

EVERTON LIVERPOOL
v MANCHESTER UNITED 1-2 (0-1)

Goodison Park, Liverpool   9.02.65

Referee: Thomas Wharton (Sco)   Attendance: 54,397

EVERTON: Gordon West; Thomas Wright, Ramon Wilson, James Gabriel, Brian Labone, Dennis Stevens, Alex Scott, Colin Harvey, Frederick Pickering, Roy Vernon, Derek Temple.   Manager: Harry Catterick

UNITED: Patrick Dunne; Seamus Brennan, Tony Dunne, Patrick Crerand, William Foulkes, Norbert Stiles, John Connely, Robert Charlton, David Herd, Denis Law, George Best.   Manager: Matt Busby

Goals: Connely (6), Pickering (54), Herd (69)

ATHLETIC BILBAO
v DUNFERMLINE ATHLETIC 1-0 (0-0)

Estadio San Mamés, Bilbao   27.01.65

Referee: Karl Keller (Swi)   Attendance: 23,700

ATHLETIC: José Ángel IRÍBAR Cortajarena; José María ORUE Aranguren, Jesús ARANGUREN Merino; Luis María ECHEBERRÍA Igartua, Manuel González ETURA, Juan María ZORRIQUETA Azpiazu; Jesús María ECHEVARRÍA, Luis María AGUIRRE Vidaurrazaga, Antonio María ARIETA II Araunabeña Piedra, Fidel URIARTE Macho, Fernando Trío "YOSU".   Trainer: Antonio Barrios

DUNFERMLINE: James Herriot; William Callaghan, John Lunn, James Thomson, James McLean, Thomas Callaghan, Alexander Edwards, Robert Paton, John McLaughlin, Alexander Ferguson, John Sinclair.   Manager: Victor Cunningham

Goal: Yosu (87)

DUNFERMLINE ATHLETIC
v ATHLETIC BILBAO 1-0 (1-0)

East End Park, Dunfermline   3.03.65

Referee: Leo Callaghan (Wal)   Attendance: 17,000

DUNFERMLINE: James Herriot; William Callaghan, John Lunn, James Thomson, James McLean, Thomas Callaghan, Alexander Edwards, Alexander Smith, John McLaughlin, Alexander Ferguson, John Sinclair.   Manager: Victor Cunningham

ATHLETIC: José Ángel IRÍBAR Cortajarena; Meltzer, Jesús ARANGUREN Merino, Luis María ECHEBERRÍA Igartua, Luis María ZUGAZAGA Martínez, Luis María AGUIRRE Vidaurrazaga, Jesús María ECHEVARRÍA, José María ARGOITIA Acha, Antonio María ARIETA II Araunabeña Piedra, Fidel URIARTE Macho, Fernando Trío "YOSU".   Trainer: Antonio Barrios

Goal: Smith (19)

ATHLETIC BILBAO
v DUNFERMLINE ATHLETIC 2-1 (1-0)

Estadio San Mamés, Bilbao   16.03.65

Referee: Anton Bucheli (Swi)   Attendance: 28,000

ATHLETIC: José Ángel IRÍBAR Cortajarena; José María ORUE Aranguren, Jesús ARANGUREN Merino; Luis María ECHEBERRÍA Igartua, Manuel González ETURA, Luis María AGUIRRE Vidaurrazaga; José Ignacio SÁEZ Ruiz, Antonio María ARIETA Piedra, Ignacio ARIETA Piedra, Fidel URIARTE Macho, Fernando "YOSU".
Trainer: Antonio Barrios

DUNFERMLINE: James Herriot; William Callaghan, John Lunn, James Thomson, James McLean, Thomas Callaghan, Alexander Edwards, George Peebles, John Kilgannon, Harry Melrose, Alexander Smith.   Manager: Victor Cunningham

Goals: Aguirre (32 pen), Smith (50), Uriarte (85)

JUVENTUS TORINO
v LOKOMOTIV PLOVDIV 2-1 aet (1-1, 1-1)

Stadio Comunale, Torino   14.04.65

Referee: Anton Bucheli (Swi)   Attendance: 10,300

JUVENTUS: Roberto Anzolin; Adolfo Gori, Bruno Mazzia, Sandro Salvadore, Ernesto Castano, Gianfranco Leoncini, Nestor Combin, Cascajares Luis Del Sol, Dino Da Costa, Enrique Omar Sívori, Carlo Dell'Omodarme.
Trainer: Heriberto Herrera

LOKOMOTIV: Stancho Bonchev; Ilia Bekiarov, Ivan Manolov, Ivan Tsanev, Dimitar Mladenov, Ivan Boiadjiev, Ivan Enchev, Ivan Grancharov, Ivan Kanchev, Hristo Iliev, Petar Kolev.

Goals: Kanchev (17), Sívori (23, 101)

JUVENTUS TORINO
v LOKOMOTIV PLOVDIV 1-1 (1-0)

Stadio Comunale, Torino   17.02.65

Referee: José Barberan (Fra)   Attendance: 4,500

JUVENTUS: Roberto Anzolin; Adolfo Gori, Benito Sarti, Sandro Salvadore, Ernesto Castano, Gianfranco Leoncini, Gino Stacchini, Cascajares Luis Del Sol, Dino Da Costa, Enrique Omar Sívori, Giampaolo Menichelli.
Trainer: Heriberto Herrera

LOKOMOTIV: Stancho Boncev; Ilia Bekiarov, Ivan Manolov, Ianko Dzoglev, Georgi Mizin, Ivan Boiadjiev, Ivan Kanchev, Ivan Enchev, Dimitar Muletarov, Hristo Iliev, Petar Kolev.

Goals: Menichelli (36), Muletanov (71)

AS ROMA v FERENCVÁROS BUDAPEST 1-2 (0-1)

Stadio Olimpico, Roma   10.03.65

Referee: Daniel Zariquieguizco (Spa)   Attendance: 20,000

AS ROMA: Fabio Cudicini; Glauco Tomasin, Mario Ardizzon, Giuseppe Tamborini, Giacomo Losi, Sergio Carpanesi, Bruno Nicolé, Giancarlo De Sisti, Pedro Waldemar Manfredini, Antonio Valentin Angelillo, Lamberto Leonardi.
Trainer: Juan Carlos Lorenzo

FERENCVÁROS: István Géczi; Dezső Novák, Sándor Mátrai, Jenő Dálnoki, Tibor Perecsi, Pál Orosz; János Karába, Zoltán Varga, István Juhász, László Rátkai, Máté Fenyvesi.
Trainer: József Mészáros

Goals: Rátkai (37), dr. Fenyvesi (79), De Sisti (81)

LOKOMOTIV PLOVDIV
v JUVENTUS TORINO 1-1 (1-1)

9 September, Plovdiv   10.03.65

Referee: Vasile Dumitrescu (Rom)   Attendance: 22,000

LOKOMOTIV: Stancho Bonchev; Ilia Bekiarov, Ivan Boiadjiev, Ivan Manolov, Ivan Tsanev, Dimitar Mladenov, Dimitar Muletarov, Ivan Enchev, Ivan Kanchev, Hristo Iliev, Petar Kolev.

JUVENTUS: Roberto Anzolin; Adolfo Gori, Benito Sarti, Sandro Salvadore, Ernesto Castano, Gianfranco Leoncini, Gino Stacchini, Cascajares Luis Del Sol, Dino Da Costa, Bruno Mazzia, Giampaolo Menichelli.   Trainer: Heriberto Herrera

Goals: Manolov (4), Mazzia (44)

FERENCVÁROS BUDAPEST v AS ROMA 1-0 (1-0)

Népstadion, Budapest   16.03.65

Referee: Božidar Botić (Jug)   Attendance: 30,000

FERENCVÁROS: István Géczi; Dezső Novák, Sándor Mátrai, Jenő Dálnoki, Tibor Perecsi, Pál Orosz; János Karába, Zoltán Varga, Flórián Albert, Oszkár Vilezsál, Máté Fenyvesi.
Trainer: József Mészáros

AS ROMA: Fabio Cudicini; Glauco Tomasin, Francesco Carpenneti, Giuseppe Tamborini, Giacomo Losi, Karl Heinz Schnellinger, Fulvio Francesconi, Giancarlo De Sisti, Bruno Nicolé, Antonio Valentin Angelillo, Mauro Nardoni.
Trainer: Juan Carlos Lorenzo

Goal: Albert (42)

QUARTER-FINALS

FERENCVÁROS BUDAPEST
v ATHLETIC BILBAO 1-0 (1-0)

Népstadion, Budapest   7.04.65

Referee: Konstantin Zecević (Jug)   Attendance: 35,000

FERENCVÁROS: István Géczi; Dezső Novák, Sándor Mátrai, László Horváth; Oszkár Vilezsál, Tibor Perecsi; János Karába, Zoltán Varga, Flórián Albert, István Juhász, Gyula Rákosi. Trainer: József Mészáros

ATHLETIC: José Ángel IRÍBAR Cortajarena; José María ORUE Aranguren, Luis María ECHEBERRÍA Igartua, Jesús ARANGUREN Merino; Luis María AGUIRRE Vidaurrazaga, Luis María ZUGAZAGA Martínez; José María ARGOITIA Acha, Antonio María ARIETA II Araunabeña Piedra, Ignacio ARIETA I Araunabeña Piedra, Fidel URIARTE Macho, Fernando Trío "YOSU". Trainer: Antonio Barrios

Goal: Juhász (25)

ATHLETIC BILBAO
v FERENCVÁROS BUDAPEST 2-1 (1-1)

Estadio San Mamés, Bilbao   21.04.65

Referee: Gottfried Dienst (Swi)   Attendance: 30,000

ATHLETIC: José Ángel IRÍBAR Cortajarena; José María ORUE Aranguren, Luis María ECHEBERRÍA Igartua, Jesús ARANGUREN Merino; Luis María AGUIRRE Vidaurrazaga, Luis María ZUGAZAGA Martínez; José María ARGOITIA Acha, Antonio María ARIETA II Araunabeña Piedra, Ignacio ARIETA I Araunabeña Piedra, Fidel URIARTE Macho, Fernando Trío "YOSU". Trainer: Antonio Barrios

FERENCVÁROS: István Géczi; Dezső Novák, Sándor Mátrai, Jenő Dálnoki; István Juhász, László Horváth; László Rátkai, Zoltán Varga, Flórián Albert, Gyula Rákosi, Máté Fenyvesi. Trainer: József Mészáros

Goals: Varga (14), Arieta I (44, 76)

FERENCVÁROS BUDAPEST
v ATHLETIC BILBAO 3-0 (2-0)

Népstadion, Budapest   13.05.65

Referee: Gerhard Schulenburg (WG)   Attendance: 38,000

FERENCVÁROS: István Géczi; Dezső Novák, Sándor Mátrai, László Horváth; István Juhász, Pál Orosz; János Karába, Zoltán Varga, Flórián Albert, Gyula Rákosi, Máté Fenyvesi. Trainer: József Mészáros

ATHLETIC: José Ángel IRÍBAR Cortajarena; José María ORUE Aranguren, Luis María ECHEBERRÍA Igartua, Jesús ARANGUREN Merino; Luis María AGUIRRE Vidaurrazaga, Luis María ZUGAZAGA Martínez; José María ARGOITIA Acha, Antonio María ARIETA II Araunabeña Piedra, Ignacio ARIETA I Araunabeña Piedra, Fidel URIARTE Macho, Fernando Trío "YOSU". Trainer: Antonio Barrios

Goals: Echeberría (19 og), dr. Fenyvesi (44, 62)

RACING CLUB STRASBOURG
v MANCHESTER UNITED 0-5 (0-2)

Meinau, Strasbourg   12.05.65

Referee: Günther Baumgärtel (WG)   Attendance: 29,000

RACING: Johnny Schuth; René Hauss, Gines Gonzales, Raymond Kaelbel, Denis Devaux, Raymond Stieber, Gilbert Heiné, Roland Merschel, Gilbert Gress, Robert Szczepaniak, Gérard Hausser. Trainer: Paul Frantz

UNITED: Patrick Dunne; Seamus Brennan, Tony Dunne, Patrick Crerand, William Foulkes, Norbert Stiles, John Connelly, Robert Charlton, David Herd, Denis Law, George Best. Manager: Matt Busby

Goals: Connelly (20), Herd (40), Law (61, 89), R. Charlton (73)

MANCHESTER UNITED
v RACING CLUB STRASBOURG 0-0

Old Trafford, Manchester   19.05.65

Referee: Franz Geluck (Bel)   Attendance: 34,188

UNITED: Patrick Dunne; Seamus Brennan, Tony Dunne, Patrick Crerand, William Foulkes, Norbert Stiles, John Connelly, Robert Charlton, David Herd, Denis Law, George Best. Manager: Matt Busby

RACING: Johnny Schuth; Gines Gonzales, Pierre Sbaïz, Raymond Stieber, Denis Devaux, Raymond Kaelbel, Gilbert Gress, Roland Merschel, Edmond Biernat, Robert Szczepaniak, Gérard Hausser. Trainer: Paul Frantz

Atlético Madrid and Juventus Torino both received byes

SEMI-FINALS

ATLÉTICO MADRID
v JUVENTUS TORINO 3-1 (0-1)

Estadio Metropolitano, Madrid   19.05.65

Referee: Albert Guinnard (Swi)   Attendance: 50,000

ATLÉTICO: Edgardo Mario MADINABEYTIA Bassi; Feliciano RIVILLA Muñoz, Isacio CALLEJA García; Manuel RUIZ-SOSA, Jorge Bernardo GRIFFA Monferoni, Jesús GLARÍA Jordén; Luis Armando UFARTE Ventoso, LUIS Aragonés Suárez, YANKO DAUCIK Ciboch, Jorge Alberto MENDOZA Paulino, José Enrique CARDONA Gutiérrez. Trainer: Otto BUMBEL

JUVENTUS: Roberto Anzolin; Adolfo Gori, Benito Sarti, Giancarlo Bercellino, Ernesto Castano, Gianfranco Leoncini, Nestor Combin, Cascajares Luis Del Sol, Dino Da Costa, Enrique Omar Sívori, Giampaolo Menichelli. Trainer: Heriberto Herrera

Goals: Combin (43), Luis (47 pen, 52, 62)

JUVENTUS TORINO
v ATLÉTICO MADRID 3-1 (0-0)

Stadio Comunale, Torino   26.05.65

Referee: James Finney (Eng)   Attendance: 12,000

JUVENTUS: Roberto Anzolin; Adolfo Gori, Sandro Salvadore, Giancarlo Bercellino, Ernesto Castano, Gianfranco Leoncini, Carlo Dell'Omodarme, Cascajares Luis Del Sol, Nestor Combin, Bruno Mazzia, Giampaolo Menichelli.
Trainer: Heriberto Herrera

ATLÉTICO: Edgardo Mario MADINABEYTIA Bassi; Feliciano RIVILLA Muñoz, Isacio CALLEJA García; Manuel RUIZ-SOSA, Jorge Bernardo GRIFFA Monferoni, Jesús GLARÍA Roldán; Luis Armando UFARTE Ventoso, LUIS Aragonés Suárez, ADELARDO Rodríguez Sánchez, Jorge Alberto MENDOZA Paulino, José Enrique CARDONA Gutiérrez.   Trainer: Otto BUMBEL

Goals: Menichelli (50), Combin (54), Bercellino (58), Luis (83)

JUVENTUS TORINO
v ATLÉTICO MADRID 3-1 (1-1)

Stadio Comunale, Torino   3.06.65

Referee: Joseph Heymann (Swi)   Attendance: 11,000

JUVENTUS: Carlo Mattrel; Adolfo Gori, Sandro Salvadore, Giancarlo Bercellino, Ernesto Castano, Gianfranco Leoncini, Carlo Dell'Omodarme, Cascajares Luis Del Sol, Nestor Combin, Bruno Mazzia, Gino Stacchini.
Trainer: Heriberto Herrera

ATLÉTICO: Edgardo Mario MADINABEYTIA Bassi; Feliciano RIVILLA Muñoz, Isacio CALLEJA García; Manuel RUIZ-SOSA, Jorge Bernardo GRIFFA Monferoni, Jesús GLARÍA Roldán; Luis Armando UFARTE Ventoso, LUIS Aragonés Suárez, ADELARDO Rodríguez Sánchez, Jorge Alberto MENDOZA, José Enrique CARDONA Gutiérrez.
Trainer: Otto BUMBEL

Goals: Mendoza (13), Salvadore (81), Stacchini (34), Calleja (75 og)

MANCHESTER UNITED
FERENCVÁROS BUDAPEST 3-2 (1-1)

Old Trafford, Manchester   31.05.65

Referee: Hubert Burguet (Bel)   Attendance: 39,902

UNITED: Patrick Dunne; Seamus Brennan, William Foulkes, Tony Dunne; Patrick Crerand, Norbert Stiles, John Connelly, Robert Charlton, David Herd, Denis Law, George Best.
Manager: Matt Busby

FERENCVÁROS: István Géczi; Dezső Novák, Sándor Mátrai, László Horváth; István Juhász, Pál Orosz; László Rátkai, Zoltán Varga, Flórián Albert, Gyula Rákosi, Máté Fenyvesi.
Trainer: József Mészáros

Goals: Novák (23), Law (34 pen), Herd (61, 69), Rákosi (76)

FERENCVÁROS BUDAPEST
v MANCHESTER UNITED 1-0 (1-0)

Népstadion, Budapest   6.06.65

Referee: Michel Kitabdjian (Fra)   Attendance: 55,000

FERENCVÁROS: István Géczi; Dezső Novák, Sándor Mátrai, László Horváth; István Juhász, Pál Orosz; József Fenyvesi II, Zoltán Varga, Flórián Albert, Gyula Rákosi, Máté Fenyvesi.
Trainer: József Mészáros

UNITED: Patrick Dunne; Seamus Brennan, William Foulkes, Tony Dunne; Patrick Crerand, Norbert Stiles; John Connelly, Robert Charlton, David Herd, Denis Law, George Best.
Manager: Matt Busby

Orosz and Crerand sent off (73)

Goal: Novák (44 pen)

FERENCVÁROS BUDAPEST
v MANCHESTER UNITED 2-1 (1-0)

Népstadion, Budapest   16.06.65

Referee: Gerhard Schulenburg (WG) Attendance: 72,318

FERENCVÁROS: István Géczi; Dezső Novák, Sándor Mátrai, László Horváth; István Juhász, Pál Orosz; János Karába, Zoltán Varga, Flórián Albert, Gyula Rákosi, Máté Fenyvesi.
Trainer: József Mészáros

UNITED: Patrick Dunne; Seamus Brennan, William Foulkes, Tony Dunne; Patrick Crerand, Norbert Stiles; John Connelly, Robert Charlton, David Herd, Denis Law, George Best.
Manager: Matt Busby

Goals: Karába (44), dr. Fenyvesi (54), Connelly (86)

FINAL

JUVENTUS TORINO
FERENCVÁROS BUDAPEST 0-1 (0-0)

Stadio Comunale, Torino   23.06.65

Referee: Gottfried Dienst (Swi)   Attendance: 25.000

JUVENTUS: Roberto Anzolin; Adolfo Gori, Benito Sarti; Giancarlo Bercellino, Ernesto Castano (Cap), Gianfranco Leoncini; Gino Stacchini, Cascajares Luis Del Sol, Nestor Combin, Bruno Mazzia, Giampaolo Menichelli.
Trainer: Heriberto Herrera

FERENCVÁROS: István Géczi; Dezső Novák (Cap), Sándor Mátrai, László Horváth; István Juhász, Pál Orosz; János Karába, Zoltán Varga, Flórián Albert, Gyula Rákosi, Máté Fenyvesi.   Trainer: József Mészáros

Goal: M. Fenyvesi (74)

Goalscorers Fairs' Cup 1964-65

8 goals: Denis Law, Robert Charlton (Manchester United)

6 goals: LUIS Aragonés Suárez (Atlético Madrid), David Herd (Manchester United), Frederick Pickering (Everton Liverpool)

5 goals: ADELARDO Rodríguez Sánchez (Atlético Madrid), John Connelly (Manchester United), Gérard Hausser (Strasbourg), Máté Fenyvesi (Ferencváros)

4 goals: Stanislav Bubanj, Zlatko Dracic (NK Zagreb), Juan Roberto SEMINARIO Rodríguez (Barcelona), Luis María AGUIRRE Vidaurrazaga (Athletic Bilbao), Flórián Albert (Ferencváros)

3 goals: Henk Wery (DOS Utrecht), Alexander Young (Everton), Georget Bertoncello, Henri Depireux (RFC Liège), Nestor Combin, Giampaolo Menichelli (Juventus), Fidel URIARTE Macho (Athletic Bilbao), Mircea Dridea (Petrolul Ploieşti), Johann Hörmayer (Wiener SK), Dezső Novák, Zoltán Varga (Ferencváros)

2 goals: McLaughlin, Sinclair, Smith (Dunfermline), Steinert (Hertha), Bohez (Antwerp), Schindelholz (Servette Genève), Mendoza (Atlético Madrid), Best (Manchester United), Eriksen (Vålerengen), Harvey, Temple (Everton), Sívori (Juventus), Chalmers, Murdoch (Celtic), Brungs (Borussia), Kolev, Manolov (Lokomotiv Plovdiv), Crava (FC Basel), Arieta I (Athletic Bilbao), Farias (Strasbourg), G.Sulon (RFC Liége), Pottier (Stade Français Paris), Höller (VfB Stuttgart), McIlroy (Kilmarnock)

1 goals: Persson, Simonsson (Örgryte Göteborg), T. Callaghan (Dunfermline), Van de Velde (Antwerp), Mortensen, Poulsen, F. Møller, Sørensen (KB København), Visser, Van der Linden, Sleven (DOS Utrecht), Daina (Servette Genève), Ramiro, Cardona, Ufarte (Atlético Madrid), Sgerm, Iberer (AK Graz), Azinovic, Beslac (NK Zagreb), Johansson, H.Karlsson (Djurgardens), Olsen, E.B.Larsen (Vålerengen), Scott, Vernon, Morrissey (Everton), Vidagañy, Waldo (Valencia), Wegria (RFC Liége), Da Costa, Mazzia, Bercellino, Salvadore, Stacchini (Juventus), Esteves (Leixões), Hughes (Celtic), Hamrin (Fiorentina), Zaldúa, Rifé, Benítez (CF Barcelona), Couécou, Keita, Guillas (Bordeaux), Straschitz, Konietzka, Kurrat (Borussia), Teodoro, Palico (Belenenses), Barber, Hannigan, M.Conroy (Shelbourne), Tamborini, Schnellinger, Leonardi, Nicolé, Angelillo, De Sisti (Roma), L. Milic, D. Pavlic (Vojvodina), Kolchev, Mizin, Enchev, Muletanov, Kanchev (Lokomotiv Plovdiv), Krier (Spora), Frigerio, Blumer (FC Basel), Skoblar, Vukašinović (OFK Beograd), Argoitia, Echevarría, Yosu (Athletic Bilbao), Ferrario (Milan), Merschel, Sbaïz, Szczepaniak (Strasbourg), Lopez-Hidalgo (Betis Sevilla), Stasiak (Stade Français Paris), Nihat (Göztepe), Mocanu (Petrolul), Knoll, Gayer (Wiener SK), Naumann (SC Leipzig), Vojta (Spartak Brno), Dyrholm (B 1913 Odense), Hoffmann, Geiger (VfB Stuttgart), Stein, Trimhold, Stinka, Huberts (Eintracht), Hamilton, McFazdean, McInally, Sneddon (Kilmarnock), Rátkai, Juhász, Rákosi, Karába (Ferencváros)

Own Goals: Salvadore (Juventus) for Atlético Madrid, Calleja (Atlético Madrid) for Juventus, Echeberría (Athletic Bilbao) for Ferencváros, Jacobsen (Vålerengen) for Everton Liverpool

FAIRS CUP 1965-66

FIRST ROUND

RFC LIÈGE v NK ZAGREB 1-0 (1-0)

Stade Rocourt, Liège   8.09.65

Referee: Kevin Howley (Eng)   Attendance: 7,500

RFC LIÈGE: Guy Delhasse; Auguste Goessens, Albert Sulon, Emile Lejeune, Yves Baré, Gérard Sulon, Denis Houf, Horatio Schéna, Raoul Lolinga, François Demarteau, Henri Klein.

NK ZAGREB: Zoran Misić; Galeković, Mestrović, Klobucar, Stanisić, Suša, Kralj, Stanislav Bubanj, Mladen Vaha, Zlatko Dracić, Mladen Azinović.   Trainer: Gustav Lechner

Goal: Demarteau (15)

NK ZAGREB v RFC LIEGE 2-0 (0-0)

Zagreb   29.09.65

Referee: Gerhard Kunze (DDR)

NK ZAGREB: Harar; Galeković, Mestrović, Klobucar, Stanisić, Suša, Kralj, Stanislav Bubanj, Mladen Vaha, Zlatko Dracić, Mladen Azinović.   Trainer: Gustav Lechner

RFC LIÉGE: Guy Delhasse; Auguste Goessens, Gérard Sulon, Emile Lejeune, Yves Baré, Hector Cribioli, Denis Houf, Horatio Schéna, François Demarteau, Henri Depireux, Georget Bertoncello.

Goals: Vaha (61), Azinovic (88)

UNION SPORTIVE LUXEMBOURG v FC KÖLN 0-4 (0-3)

Stade Municipal, Luxembourg   8.09.65

Referee: Gottfried Dienst (SWI)   Attendance: 4,463

US: Armand Olinger; Ady Colas, Mathias Ewen, Becker, René Schneider, Paul Ries, Jean-Pierre Hemmerling, Johny Leonard, Jean-Pierre Mertl, Marco Funck, Paul Goedert.

FC KÖLN: Toni Schumacher; Fritz Pott, Matthias Hemmersbach, Leo Wilden, Hans Sturm, Wolfgang Weber, Karl-Heinz Thielen, Johannes Löhr, Franz Krauthausen, Wolfgang Overath, Heinz Hornig.   Trainer: Georg Knopfle

Goals: Krauthausen (14, 80), Thielen (28), Löhr (35)

1.FC KÖLN
v UNION SPORTIVE LUXEMBOURG 13-0 (8-0)

Mungersdorferstadion, Köln 5.10.65

Referee: Bengt Lundell (Swe) Attendance: 4,448

FC KÖLN: Fritz Ewert; Fritz Pott, Anton Regh, Wolfgang Weber, Leo Wilden, Hans Sturm, Karl-Heinz Thielen, Franz-Peter Neumann, Christian Müller, Wolfgang Overath, Johannes Löhr. Trainer: Georg Knopfle

US: Armand Olinger; Ady Colas, Paul Ries, René Schneider, Mathias Ewen, Becker, Jean-Pierre Hemmerling, Johny Leonard, Kohl, Jean-Pierre Mertl, Marco Funck.

Goals: Thielen (2, 6, 23, 31), Löhr (12, 15, 57), Overath (16, 87), Neumann (44, 78), Müller (72), Weber (88)

HIBERNIAN EDINBURGH
v VALENCIA CF 2-0 (1-0)

Easter Road, Edinburgh 8.09.65

Referee: Hubert Burguet (Bel) Attendance: 19,000

HIBERNIAN: William Wilson; William Simpson, Joseph Davis, Patrick Gordon Stanton, John McNamee, John Baxter, Peter Cormack, Patrick Quinn, James Scott, Neil Martin, Eric Stevenson. Manager: William Shankly

VALENCIA CF: Ricardo ZAMORA de Grassa; Javier GARCÍA VERDUGO Garrido, Francisco VIDAGAÑY Hernández; ROBERTO Gil Esteve, Manuel MESTRE Torres, Francisco García Gómez "PAQUITO"; José Antonio URTIAGA Albizei, José María SÁNCHEZ LAGE, WALDO Machado da Silva, Juan Cruz SOL Oria, Manuel Polinario Muñoz "POLI". Trainer: Sabino Barinaga

Goals: Scott (4), McNamee (88)

VALENCIA CF
v HIBERNIAN EDINBURGH 2-0 (1-0)

Estadio de Mestalla, Valencia 12.10.65

Referee: Gottfried Dienst (Swi) Attendance: 44,000

VALENCIA CF: Ricardo ZAMORA de Grassa; Javier GARCÍA VERDUGO Garrido, Manuel MESTRE Torres, Francisco VIDAGAÑY Hernández, ROBERTO Gil Esteve, Francisco García Gómez "PAQUITO", Manuel Polinario Muñoz "POLI", José María SÁNCHEZ LAGE, WALDO Machado da Silva, Vicente GUILLOT Fabián, Juan MUÑOZ Cerdá. Trainer: Sabino Barinaga

HIBERNIAN: William Wilson; William Simpson, Joseph Davis, Patrick Gordon Stanton, John McNamee, John Baxter, Peter Cormack, Patrick Quinn, James Scott, Neil Martin, Eric Stevenson. Manager: William Shankly

Goals: Waldo (15), Sánchez Lage (74 pen)

VALENCIA CF
v HIBERNIAN EDINBURGH 3-0 (1-0)

Estadio de Mestalla, Valencia 3.11.65

Referee: Jean Tricot (Fra) Attendance: 43,100

VALENCIA CF: Ricardo ZAMORA de Grassa; Javier GARCÍA VERDUGO Garrido, Manuel MESTRE Torres, Francisco VIDAGAÑY Hernández, ROBERTO Gil Esteve, Francisco García Gómez «PAQUITO», Manuel Polinario Muñoz «POLI», José María SÁNCHEZ LAGE, WALDO Machado da Silva, Vicente GUILLOT Fabián, Juan MUÑOZ Cerdá. Trainer: Sabino Barinaga

HIBERNIAN: William Wilson; William Simpson, Joseph Davis, Patrick Gordon Stanton, John McNamee, John Baxter, Peter Cormack, Patrick Quinn, James Scott, James O'Rourke, Eric Stevenson. Manager: William Shankly

Goals: Muñoz (11, 72), Guillot (66)

STADE FRANÇAIS PARIS v FC PORTO 0-0

Parc des Princes, Paris 14.09.65

Referee: Jack D. Russell (NIr) Attendance: 6,993

STADE FRANÇAIS: Georges Carnus; Prudent Bacquet, François Stasiak; Serge Dumas, Robert Peri, André Boragno; Dominique Rustichelli, Jacky Lemée, Phillipe Pottier, Jean Pierre Alba, André Fefeu. Trainer: André Gérard

FC PORTO: AMÉRICO Ferreira Lopes; Alberto Augusto FESTA, António Manuel PAULA, ALÍPIO Vasconcelos Santos Monteiro, João Eleutério Luis ATRACA; José ROLANDO Andrade Gonçalves, CUSTÓDIO João PINTO; JAIME Ferreira Silva, CARLOS MANUEL Gomes Dias, MANUEL ANTÓNIO Leitão da Silva, Francisco Lage Pereira da NÓBREGA. Trainer:Flavio Costa (Bra)

FC PORTO v STADE FRANÇAIS PARIS 1-0 (1-0)

Estadio das Antas, Porto 6.10.65

Referee: Antonio Sbardella (Ita) Attendance: 25,000

FC PORTO: AMÉRICO Ferreira Lopes; Alberto Augusto FESTA, João Luís Pinto ALMEIDA, ALÍPIO Vasconcelos Santos Monteiro, João Eleutério Luis ATRACA; Fernando Neves PAVÃO, CUSTÓDIO João PINTO; JAIME Ferreira Silva, AMAURI Silva, MANUEL ANTÓNIO Leitão da Silva, Francisco Lage Pereira da NÓBREGA. Trainer: Flavio Costa

STADE FRANÇAIS: Georges Carnus; Prudent Bacquet, Jacques Ratajczak, François Stasiak; Girard, Serge Dumas; André Boragno, Dominique Rustichelli, Philippe Pottier, Jean Pierre Alba, André Fefeu. Trainer: André Gérard

Goal: Manuel António (12)

CRVENA ZVEZDA BEOGRAD
v AC FIORENTINA FIRENZE 0-4 (0-0)

Crvena Zvezda, Beograd 15.09.65

Referee: Alfred Haberfellner (Aus) Attendance: 25,000

CRVENA ZVEZDA: Mirko Stojanović; Aleksandar
Stojanović, Živorad Jevtić, Dragan Stojanović, Milan Čop,
Dejan Bekić, Dragoljub Živković, Branko Klenkovski, Selimir
Milosević, Jovan Aćimović, Trifun Mihajlović.

FIORENTINA: Enrico Albertosi; Bernardo Rogora, Sergio
Castelletti, Giovan Battista Pirovano, Piero Gonfiantini,
Giuseppe Brizi, Kurt Hamrin, Mario Bertini, Paolo Nuti,
Giancarlo De Sisti, Juan Carlos Morrone.
Trainer: Giuseppe Chiapella

Goals: Bertini (67, 86), Hamrin (70), Nuti (83)

TSV MÜNCHEN 1860 v MALMÖ FF 4-0 (2-0)

Grünwalderstadion, München 28.09.65

Referee: Lajos Aranyosi (HUN) Attendance: 8,500

TSV 1860: Petar Radenković; Manfred Wagner, Bernd
Patzke, Hans Reich, Otto Luttrop, Željko Perušić, Alfred Heiss,
Friedhelm Konietzka, Rudolf Brunnenmeier, Peter Grosser,
Hans Rebele. Trainer: Max Merkel

MALMÖ FF: Nils Hult; Jörgen Ohlin, Rolf Björklund, Rolf
Eriksson, Gert-Åke Nilsson, Prawitz Öberg, Bertil Elmstedt,
Bertil Nilsson, Lars Granström, Jan Ekström, Ingvar Svahn.
Trainer: Antonio Durán

Goals: Brunnenmeier (7), Heiss (24), Grosser (58),
Rebele (88)

AC FIORENTINA FIRENZE
v CRVENA ZVEZDA BEOGRAD 3-1 (2-1)

Stadio Comunale, Firenze 22.09.65

Referee: Daniel Zariquiegui (Spa) Attendance: 35,000

FIORENTINA: Enrico Albertosi; Marcello Diomedi, Sergio
Castelletti, Giovan Battista Pirovano, Piero Gonfiantini,
Giuseppe Brizi, Kurt Hamrin, Humberto Maschio, Mario
Brugnera, Mario Bertini, Juan Carlos Morrone.
Trainer: Giuseppe Chiapella

CRVENA ZVEZDA: Mirko Stojanović; Aleksandar
Stojanović, Živorad Jevtić, Slobodan Škrbić, Milan Čop,
Branko Klenkovski, Dragan Dzajić, Jovan Aćimović, Selimir
Milosević, Dragoslav Šekularac, Bora Kostić.

Goals: Hamrin (6), Pirovano (26), Milosević (42),
Brugnera (48)

PAOK THESSALONIKI v WIENER SK 2-1 (0-0)

Toumpas, Thessaloniki 15.09.65

Referee: Božidar Botić (Jug) Attendance: 21,051

PAOK: Mouselemidis; Nikos Mitrakas, Apostolos Vasileiadis,
G. Mouratidis, Giannis Giakoumis, Giannis Nikolaidis,
Emilios Theofanidis, Anastasios Afentoulidis, Giorgos Koudas,
Leandros Symeonidis, Kiriakos Apostolidis.

WIENER: Rudolf Szanwald; Wilhelm Kainrath, Webora,
Anton Linhart; Adolf Blutsch, Johann Windisch, Helmuth
Mätzler, Friedrich Rafreider, Erich Hof, Norbert Hof, Johann
Hörmayer. Trainer: Karl Schlechta

Goals: Rafreider (51), Koudas (62), Mouratidis (75)

MALMÖ FF v TSV MÜNCHEN 1860 0-3 (0-2)

Malmö Stadion 15.09.65

Referee: Marcel Zeimes (Lux) Attendance: 8,500

MALMÖ FF: Nils Hult; Jörgen Ohlin, Rolf Björklund;
Lennart Svensson, Gert-Åke Nilsson, Prawitz Öberg, Bertil
Elmstedt, Bertil Nilsson, Lars Granström, Bo Larsson, Ingvar
Svahn. Trainer: Antonio Durán

TSV 1860: Petar Radenković; Bernd Patzke, Hans Reich,
Hans Küppers, Željko Perušić, Alfred Heiss, Wilfried Kohlars,
Friedhelm Konietzka, Rudolf Brunnenmeier, Peter Grosser,
Hans Rebele. Trainer: Max Merkel

Goals: Heiss (23), Rebele (27), Grosser (64)

WIENER SK v PAOK THESSALONIKI 6-0 (3-0)

Prater, Wien 29.09.65

Referee: Bruno de Marchi (Ita) Attendance: 5,750

WIENER: Rudolf Szanwald; Wilhelm Kainrath, Johann
Windisch, Anton Linhart; Adolf Blutsch, Norbert Hof;
Friedrich Rafreider, Adolf Knoll, Erich Hof, Wolfgang Gayer,
Johann Hörmayer. Trainer: Karl Schlechta

PAOK: Mouselemidis; Nikos Mitrakas, Apostolos Vasileiadis,
G. Mouratidis, Giannis Giakoumis, Giannis Nikolaidis,
Emilios Theofanidis, Anastasios Afentoulidis, Giorgos Koudas,
Onufrios Haralampidis, Kiriakos Apostolidis.

Goals: E. Hof (3, 27, 74, 89), Gayer (13, 73)

DOS UTRECHT v CF BARCELONA 0-0

Galgenwaard, Utrecht 16.09.65

Referee: Leo Callaghan (Wal)   Attendance: 20,000

DOS: Wim Ruitenbeek; Boelie van Vulpen, Joop Rooders, Louis van Plateringen, Eddy Achterberg, Bennie Aarts, Eddie van Stijn, Dick Weijman, Tonny van der Linden, Cees Loffeld, Henk Wery.   Trainer: Jovanović

CF BARCELONA: Salvador SADURNÍ Urpi; Julio César BENÍTEZ Amoedo, ELADIO Silvestre Graells, Lucien MULLER Schmidt, Fernando OLIVELLA Pons, Francisco Fernández Rodríguez "GALLEGO", Joaquín RIFÉ Climent, Jesús María PEREDA Ruíz de Temiño, José Antonio ZALDÚA Urdanavia, Juan Roberto SEMINARIO Rodríguez, VICENTE González Sosa.   Trainer: Roque Olsen

CF BARCELONA v DOS UTRECHT 7-1 (3-1)

Camp Nou, Barcelona 6.10.65

Referee: Anton Bucheli (Swi)   Attendance: 45,000

CF BARCELONA: Salvador SADURNÍ Urpi; Julio César BENÍTEZ Amoedo, ELADIO Silvestre Graells, Martín VERGÉS Massa, Fernando OLIVELLA Pons, Francisco Fernández Rodríguez «GALLEGO», SERAFÍN García Muñoz, Jesús María PEREDA Ruíz de Temiño, José Antonio ZALDÚA Urdanavia, Juan Roberto SEMINARIO Rodríguez, VICENTE González Sosa.   Trainer: Roque Olsen

DOS: Wim Ruitenbeek; Louis Van Plateringen, Eddie van Stijn, Joop Rooders, Leo Kuhnen, Joop van de Bogert, Bennie Aarts, Cees Loffeld, Eddy Achterberg, Tonny van der Linden, Henk Wery.   Trainer: Jovanović

Goals: Vergés (10), Zaldúa (14, 17, 55, 59, 82), Van der Linden (39), Pereda (85)

GIRONDINS DE BORDEAUX v SPORTING LISBOA 0-4 (0-1)

Stade Municipal, Bordeaux 22.09.65

Referee: Juan Gardeazábal Garay (Spa)   Attendance: 12,069

GIRONDINS: Jean-Claude Ranouilh; Bernard Baudet, André Chorda; Jean-Louis Leonetti, Claude Rey, Guy Calleja; Karounga Keita, Gabriel Abossolo, Henry Duhayot, Roland Guillas, Laurent Robuschi.   Trainer: Salvador Artigas (SPA)

SPORTING: Joaquim da Silva CARVALHO; Mário Goulart LINO, HILÁRIO Rosário da Conceição, Daniel Afonso da Silva DANI, José ALEXANDRE da Silva BAPTISTA, Osvaldo Silva, Fernando FERREIRA PINTO, JOSÉ CARLOS da Silva José, Ernesto FIGUEIREDO, Fernando PERES, Joaquim António OLIVEIRA DUARTE.   Manager: Otto Gloria, Trainer: Júlio Cernades Pereira "JUCA"

Goals: Figueiredo (7, 87), Oliveira Duarte (47), Peres (80)

SPORTING LISBOA v GIRONDINS BORDEAUX 6-1 (3-0)

Estadio José Alvalade, Lisboa 6.10.65

Referee: Adolfo Bueno Perales (Spa)   Attendance: 15,000

SPORTING: Joaquim da Silva CARVALHO; JOÃO Pedro MORAIS, José ALEXANDRE da Silva BAPTISTA, HILÁRIO Rosário da Conceição; JOSÉ CARLOS da Silva José, Fernando FERREIRA PINTO, Ernesto Figueiredo, João de Matos Moura LOURENÇO, Fernando PERES, Osvaldo Silva, Joaquim António OLIVEIRA DUARTE.   Manager: Otto Gloria, Trainer: Júlio Cernades Pereira "JUCA"

GIRONDINS: Jean-Claude Ranouilh; Gilbert Moevi, Jean-Claude Dubouil; Guy Calleja, Claude Rey, Francisco Navarro; Claude Noleau, Gabriel Abossolo, Bernard Baudet, Roland Guillas, Laurent Robuschi.   Trainer: Salvador Artigas (SPA)

Goals: Lourenço (15, 78), Peres (24 pen), Oliveira Duarte (26), Abossolo (47), Figueiredo (53), Ferreira Pinto (60)

CHELSEA LONDON v AS ROMA 4-1 (2-1)

Stamford Bridge, London 22.09.65

Referee: Willem Schalks (Hol)   Attendance: 32,753

CHELSEA: Peter Bonetti; Kenneth Shellito, Edward McCreadie, John Hollins, Allan Young, Ronald Harris, Barry Bridges, George Graham, Peter Osgood, Terence Venables, Joseph Fascione. McCreadie sent off (28). Manager: Thomas Docherty

AS ROMA: Enzo Matteucci; Francesco Carpenneti, Mario Ardizzon, Sergio Carpanesi, Giacomo Losi, Renato Benaglia, Lamberto Leonardi, Glauco Tomasin, Fulvio Francesconi, Morales Victor Benítez, Paolo Barison. Trainer: Oronzo Pugliese

Goals: Venables (31, 39, 46), Barison (33), Graham (66)

AS ROMA v CHELSEA LONDON 0-0

Stadio Olimpico, Roma 6.10.65

Referee: Günther Baumgärtel (WG)   Attendance: 40,000

AS ROMA: Fabio Cudicini; Francesco Carpennetti, Glauco Tomasin, Sergio Carpanesi, Giacomo Losi, Renato Benaglia, Giuseppe Tamborini, Lamberto Leonardi, Fulvio Francesconi, Morales Victor Benítez, Mauro Nardoni. Trainer: Oronzo Pugliese

CHELSEA: Peter Bonetti; Kenneth Shellito, Edward McCreadie, John Hollins, Marvin Hinton, Ronald Harris, Bert Murray, George Graham, Barry Bridges, Terence Venables, John Boyle.   Manager: Thomas Docherty

AC MILAN v RACING STRASBOURG 1-0 (1-0)

San Siro, Milano   22.09.65

Referee: Thomas Wharton (Sco)   Attendance: 17,500

AC MILAN: Luigi Balzarini; Alberto Grossetti, Mario Trebbi, Ambrogio Pelagalli, Cesare Maldini, Nello Santin, Bruno Mora, Giovanni Lodetti, Antonio Valentin Angelillo, Gianni Rivera, Giuliano Fortunato.   Trainer: Nils Liedholm

RC STRASBOURG: Johnny Schuth; René Hauss, Gines Gonzales, Raymond Stieber, Denis Devaux, Raymond Kaelbel, Gilbert Gress, Philippe Piat, José Farias, Robert Szczepaniak, Gerard Hausser.   Trainer: Paul Frantz

Goal: Fortunato (41)

RACING STRASBOURG v AC MILAN 2-1 (0-0)

Stade Meinau, Strasbourg   27.10.65

Referee: Anibal da Silva Oliveira (Por)   Attendance: 21,000

RC STRASBOURG: Johnny Schuth; René Hauss, Gines Gonzales, Raymond Stieber, Denis Devaux, Raymond Kaelbel, Gilbert Gress, Roland Merschel, José Farias, Robert Szczepaniak, Gerard Hausser.   Trainer: Paul Frantz

AC MILAN: Luigi Balzarini; Alberto Grossetti, Nevio Scala, Ambrogio Pelagalli, Cesare Maldini, Giovanni Trapattoni, Urano Benigni, Antonio Valentin Angelillo, Angelo Benedicto Sormani, Fausto Daolio, Giuliano Fortunato.
Trainer: Nils Liedholm

Goals: Benigni (59), Hauss (70 pen), Farias (89)

AC MILAN v RACING STRASBOURG 1-1 (0-0)

San Siro, Milano   7.11.65

Referee: Othmar Huber (Swi)   Attendance: 12,500

AC MILAN: Claudio Mantovani; Alberto Grossetti, Karl Heinz Schnellinger, Ambrogio Pelagalli, Cesare Maldini, Nello Santin, Angelo Benedicto Sormani, Luigi Maldera, AMARILDO Tavares de Silveire, Antonio Valentin Angelillo, Giuliano Fortunato.   Trainer: Nils Liedholm

RC STRASBOURG: Johnny Schuth; René Hauss, Gines Gonzales, Raymond Stieber, Denis Devaux, Raymond Kaelbel, Gilbert Gress, Roland Merschel, José Farias, Robert Szczepaniak, Gerard Hausser.   Trainer: Paul Frantz

Goals: Angelillo (59), Szczepaniak (80)

Milan won on the toss of a coin

**DARING CLUB DE BRUSSEL
v AIK SOLNA 1-3** (1-2)

Oscar Bossaert, Brussel   23.09.65

Referee: Patrick Graham (Eire)   Attendance: 3,000

DARING: Jean-Pierre Goossens; Jean Van Achter, Gustave Bauweraerts, Julien Wauters, Donald De Vlegelaere, Etienne Coppens, Pierre Michelin, Armand Randoux, Roger Foulon, Mohamed Ben Salen, Roland Coclet.

AIK: Arne Lundqvist; Tommy Stenborg, Allan Wikström, Björn Anlert, Bengt Westerberg, Kjell Pettersson, Bo Holmberg, Owe Ohlsson, Björn Carlsson, Jim Nildén, Lennart Backman.   Trainer: Henry Carlsson

Goals: Randoux (10), Carlsson (17), Nilden (27), Backman (75)

AIK SOLNA v DARING CLUB DE BRUSSEL 0-0

Råsunda, Stockholm   19.10.65

Referee: Erling Rolf Olsen (Nor)   Attendance: 992

AIK: Arne Lundqvist; Lennart Söderberg, Bengt Westerberg, Lennart Hemming, Kjell Pettersson, Bo Holmberg, Lars Sjöström, Owe Ohlsson, Björn Carlsson, Jim Nildén, Lennart Backman.   Trainer: Henry Carlsson

DARING: Jean-Pierre Goossens; Jean Van Achter, Gustave Bauweraerts, Julien Wauters, Donald De Vlegelaere, Etienne Coppens, Pierre Michelin, Gilbert De Brandt, Roger Foulon, Mohamed Ben Salen, Florent van de Velde.

**ROYAL ANTWERP FC
v GLENTORAN BELFAST 1-0** (0-0)

Bosuil, Antwerp   28.09.65

Referee: Tage Sørensen (Dan)   Attendance: 5,000

ANTWERP: Willy Coremans; Maurice Renier, Werner Deprez, Jozef Janssens, Jozef Deckers, Willy Van der Wee, Florent Bohez, Theofiel van de Velde, Jozef Van Gool, Urbain Segers, Marcel Janssen.   Trainer: Harry Game

GLENTORAN: Albert Finlay; Harold Creighton, William McKeag, Arthur Stewart, Harry Millar, Walter Bruce, Eric Ross, Patrick Turner, Trevor Thompson, Thomas Dickson, Ken Hamilton.

Goal: Van de Velde (85)

GLENTORAN BELFAST
v ROYAL ANTWERP FC 3-3 (1-1)

The Oval, Belfast   6.10.65

Referee: William E.M. Syme (Sco)   Attendance: 12,000

GLENTORAN: Albert Finlay; Harold Creighton, William McKeag; Arthur Stewart, Harry Millar, Walter Bruce, Richard Warburton, Eric Ross, Trevor Thompson, Samuel Lunn, Ken Hamilton.

ANTWERP: Willy Coremans; Maurice Renier, Werner Deprez, Jozef Janssens, Jozef Deckers, Wilfried Van Moer, Willy Van der Wee, Florent Bohez, Theofiel van de Velde, Urbain Segers, Marcel Janssen.   Trainer: Harry Game

Goals: Segers (12), Hamilton (44), Thompson (55, 60), Van Moer (68), Van de Velde (87)

FC NÜRNBERG v EVERTON LIVERPOOL 1-1 (1-0)

Stadtisches, Nürnberg   28.09.65

Referee: Karol Galba (Cze)   Attendance: 10,000

FC NÜRNBERG: Roland Wabra; Horst Leupold, Helmut Hilpert, Tasso Wild, Ferdinand Wenauer, Stefan Reisch, Anton Allemann, Franz Brungs, Heinz Strehl, Gustav Flachenecker, Manfred Greif.   Trainer: Jenő Csaknady

EVERTON: Gordon West; Thomas Wright, Ramon „Ray" Wilson, James Gabriel, Alexander Brown, Brian Harris, Derek Temple, Dennis Stevens, Frederick Pickering, Colin Harvey, John Morrissey.   Manager: Harry Catterick

Goals: Greif (24), Harris (50)

SPARTAK BRNO
v LOKOMOTIV PLOVDIV 2-0 (1-0)

Spartak Brno   28.09.65

Referee: Marin Niţă (Rom)   Attendance: 1,000

SPARTAK: František Schmucker; Miroslav Vítů, Tomas Hradský, Juraj Janoščin; Bohumil Pišek, Karel Komárek; Lunda, Cestmir Chaloupka, Farmačka, Viliam Hrnčár, Jaroslav Vojta.   Trainer: Karel Kolský

LOKOMOTIV: Stancho Bonchev; Dimitar Mladenov, Georgi Mizin, Ivan Manolov; Vasil Ankov, Ivan Boiadjiev; Ivan Kanchev, Tsonio Stoinov, Hristo Andonov, Ivan Enchev, Petar Kolev.

Goals: Chaloupka (25), Vojta (72)

EVERTON LIVERPOOL v FC NÜRNBERG 1-0 (0-0)

Goodison Park, Liverpool   12.10.65

Referee: Marcel du Bois (Fra)   Attendance: 39,033

EVERTON: Gordon West (33 Andrew Rankin); Thomas Wright, Ramon „Ray" Wilson, James Gabriel, Brian Labone, Brian Harris, Alexander Scott, Colin Harvey, Frederick Pickering, Alexander Young, Derek Temple.   Manager: Harry Catterick

FC NÜRNBERG: Roland Wabra; Helmut Hilpert, Karl-Heinz Ferschl, Horst Leupold, Ferdinand Wenauer, Tasso Wild, Franz Brungs, Gustav Flachenecker, Rudolf Bast, Heinz Strehl, Manfred Greif.   Trainer: Jenő Csaknady

Goal: Gabriel (62)

LOKOMOTIV PLOVDIV
v SPARTAK BRNO 1-0 (1-0)

Lokomotiv Plovdiv   6.10.65

Referee: Demostene Stathatos (Gre)   Attendance: 10,300

LOKOMOTIV: Stancho Bonchev; Ilia Bekiarov, Georgi Mizin, Ivan Manolov; Vasil Ankov, Ivan Boiadjiev; Tsonio Stoinov, Ivan Enchev, Ivan Kanchev, Spas Iliev, Dimitar Muletarov.

SPARTAK: František Schmucker; Miroslav Vítů, Tomas Hradský, Juraj Janoščin; Bohumil Pišek, Karel Komárek; Lunda, Karel Lichtnégl, Cestmir Chaloupka, Jan Brada, Viliam Hrnčár.   Trainer: Karel Kolský

Goal: Kanchev (40)

LEEDS UNITED v AC TORINO 2-1 (1-0)

Elland Road, Leeds   29.09.65

Referee: Michel Kitabdjian (Fra)   Attendance: 33,852

UNITED: Gary Sprake; Paul Reaney, Paul Madeley, William Bremner, Jack Charlton, Norman Hunter, Alan Peacock, Robert Collins, Terence Cooper, Peter Lorimer, John Giles.   Manager: Don Revie

TORINO: Lido Vieri; Fabrizio Poletti, Natalino Fossati, Roberto Rosato, Giorgio Puia, Bruno Bolchi, Luigi Simoni, Paolo Pestrin, Alberto Orlando, Amilcare Ferretti, Jürgen Schütz.   Trainer: Nereo Rocco

Goals: Bremner (25), Peacock (48), Orlando (78)

AC TORINO v LEEDS UNITED 0-0

Stadio Comunale, Torino   6.10.65

Referee: Pieter Paulus Roomer (Hol)   Attendance: 26,000

AC TORINO: Lido Vieri; Fabrizio Poletti, Natalino Fossati, Giorgio Puia, Luciano Teneggi, Amilcare Ferretti, Luigi Meroni, Giorgio Ferrini, Alberto Orlando, Paolo Pestrin, Luigi Simoni.   Trainer: Nereo Rocco

UNITED: Gary Sprake; Paul Reaney, Paul Madeley, William Bremner, Jack Charlton, Norman Hunter, Alan Peacock, Robert Collins, Terence Cooper, Peter Lorimer, John Giles. Manager: Don Revie

ARIS THESSALONIKI v FC KÖLN 2-1 (1-0)

Harilaou, Thessaloniki   26.10.65

Referee: Alessandro d'Agostini (Ita)   Attendance: 20,000

ARIS: Giorgos Pantelakos; Hristos Kambourlazos, Dimitris Grimbelakos, Kostas Hatzikostas, Sofoklis Semertzis, Giorgos Konstantinidis, Theodoros Spanopoulos, Stefanos Demiris, Vasilis Psifidis, Nikos Filippou, Theofanis Athanasiadis.

FC KÖLN: Toni Schumacher; Fritz Pott, Jürgen Rumor, Herbert Bönnen, Wolfgang Weber, Matthias Hemmersbach, Karl-Heinz Thielen, Hans Sturm, Ole Sørensen, Wolfgang Overath, Johannes Löhr.   Trainer: Georg Knopfle

Goals: Konstantinidis (29), Filippou (71), Sturm (82)

SECOND ROUND

HEART OF MIDLOTHIAN EDINBURGH v VÅLERENGENS IF OSLO 1-0 (1-0)

Tynecastle Park, Edinburgh   18.10.65

Referee: William A. O'Neill (Eire)   Attendance: 10,000

HEARTS: James Fergus Cruickshank; Daniel Ferguson, David Duff Holt, William Polland, Alan Anderson, John Cumming, Donald Ford, Thomas Traynor, William Wallace, Donald Kerrigan, John Hamilton.   Manager: Thomas Walker

VÅLERENGENS: Helge Sørlie; Nils Arne Eggen, Arild Mathisen, Thorvald Larsen, Knut Presterud, Arne Jakobsen, Per Knudsen, Einar Bruno Larsen, Kjell Marcussen, Trond Børresen, Aage Sørensen.

Goal: Wallace (43)

FC KÖLN v ARIS THESSALONIKI 2-0 (0-0)

Mungersdorferstadion, Köln   16.11.65

Referee: Samuel H. Carswell (NIrl)   Attendance: 11,000

FC KÖLN: Toni Schumacher; Fritz Pott, Jürgen Rumor, Hans Sturm, Leo Wilden, Matthias Hemmersbach, Karl-Heinz Thielen, Franz-Peter Neumann, Christian Müller, Wolfgang Overath, Johannes Löhr.   Trainer: Georg Knopfle

ARIS: Giorgos Pantelakos; Hristos Kambourlazos, Dimitris Grimbelakos, Kostas Hatzikostas, Sofoklis Semertzis, Giorgos Konstantinidis, Theodoros Spanopoulos, Stefanos Demiris, Vasilis Psifidis, Nikos Filippou, Theofanis Athanasiadis.

Goals: Thielen (57, 83)

VÅLERENGENS IF OSLO v HEART OF MIDLOTHIAN EDINBURGH 1-3 (0-2)

Ulleval, Oslo   27.10.65

Referee: Willem Schalks (Hol)   Attendance: 15,000

VÅLERENGENS: Helge Sørlie; Nils Arne Eggen, Arild Mathisen, Thorvald Larsen, Knut Presterud, Arne Jakobsen, Per Knudsen, Einar Bruno Larsen, Egil Roger Olsen, Aage Sørensen, Trond Børresen.

HEARTS: James Fergus Cruickshank, Daniel Ferguson, David Duff Holt, William Polland, Alan Anderson, John Cumming, Donald Ford, Thomas Traynor, William Wallace, Donald Kerrigan, John Hamilton.   Manager: Thomas Walker

Goals: Kerrigan (9, 89), Traynor (19), P. Knudsen (72)

ÚJPESTI DÓZSA BUDAPEST v EVERTON LIVERPOOL 3-0 (2-0)

Népstadion, Budapest   3.11.65

Referee: Konstantin Zecević (Jug)   Attendance: 5,000

ÚJPESTI DÓZSA: Antal Szentmihályi; Benő Káposzta, Matyas Csordás, Gyula Solymosi; Ernő Solymosi, Ernő Noskó; Béla Kuharszki, János Göröcs, Ferenc Bene, Sándor Lenkei, Sándor Zámbó.   Trainer: Sándor Balogh

EVERTON: Andrew Rankin; Thomas Wright, Brian Labone, Ramon „Ray" Wilson; Dennis Stevens, Brian Harris; Alexander Scott, Colin Harvey, Frederick Pickering, Derek Temple, John Morrissey.   Manager: Harry Catterick

Goals: Solymosi (9), Bene (23), Kuharszki (62)

EVERTON LIVERPOOL
v ÚJPESTI DÓZSA BUDAPEST 2-1 (1-1)

Goodison Park, Liverpool   16.11.65

Referee: Laurens van Ravens (Hol)   Attendance: 24,201

EVERTON: Andrew Rankin; Thomas Wright, Brian Labone, Ramon „Ray" Wilson; Colin Harvey, Brian Harris; Derek Temple, James Gabriel, Alexander Young, James Husband, John Morrissey.   Manager: Harry Catterick

ÚJPESTI DÓZSA: Antal Szentmihályi; Benő Káposzta, Matyas Csordás, Kálmán Sóvári; Ernő Solymosi, Sándor Lenkei, Ernő Noskó; Béla Kuharszki, János Göröcs, Ferenc Bene, Sándor Zámbó.   Trainer: Sándor Balogh

Goals: Harris (4), Kuharszki (31), Noskó (83 og)

DUNFERMLINE ATHLETIC
v B 1903 KØBENHAVN 5-0 (1-0)

East End Park, Dunfermline   3.11.65

Referee: Leopold Horn (Hol)   Attendance: 14,000

DUNFERMLINE: Eric Martin; James Thomson, John Lunn, Alexander Smith, James McLean, Thomas Callaghan, Pat Wilson, Robert Paton, James Fleming, Alexander Ferguson, Hugh Robertson.   Manager: William Cunningham

B 1903: Torben Jensen; Oyvind Fangel, Palle Frederiksen, Bent Hansen, Henrik Vestergaard, Erik Larsen, John Jensen, Ivan Hattens, Per Petersen, Kristian Andersen, Einer Holt.

Goals: Fleming (23), Robertson (57), Paton (70, 89), T. Callaghan (73)

B 1903 KØBENHAVN
v DUNFERMLINE ATHLETIC 2-4 (1-2)

Idraetsparken, København   17.11.65

Referee: Robert Schaut (Bel)   Attendance: 2,000

B 1903: Torben Jensen; Oyvind Fangel, Torben Nielsen, Bent Hansen, Henrik Vestergaard, Erik Larsen, John Jensen, Ole Forsing, Per Petersen, Kristian Andersen, Einer Holt.

DUNFERMLINE: Eric Martin; William Callaghan, James Thomson, John Lunn, Alexander Smith, James McLean, Alexander Edwards, Robert Paton, James Fleming, Alexander Ferguson, Hugh Robertson.   Trainer: William Cunningham

Goals: P. Petersen (10), Edwards (29), Paton (32), K. Andersen (50), Fleming (55), A. Ferguson (61)

AIK SOLNA v SERVETTE GENÈVE 2-1 (2-0)

Nya Råsunda, Stockholm   4.11.65

Referee: William Syme (Sco)   Attendance: 1,000

AIK: Arne Lundqvist; Lennart Söderberg, Bengt Westerberg, Jim Nildén, Lennart Hemming, Kjell Pettersson, Bo Holmberg, Owe Ohlsson, Björn Eriksson, Björn Carlsson, Lennart Backman.   Trainer: Henry Carlsson

SERVETTE: Jacques Barlie; Raymond Maffiolo, Georges Martignano, Robert Kaiserauer, Bernard Mocellin, Anton Schnyder, Roger Vonlanthen, Valer Nemeth, Deszö Makay, André Daina, Jean-Claude Schindelholz.

Goals: Backman (40), Ohlsson (41), Schindelholz (57)

SERVETTE GENÈVE v AIK SOLNA 4-1 (2-0)

Stade des Charmilles, Genève   13.11.65

Referee: Concetto lo Bello (Ita)   Attendance: 3,000

SERVETTE: Jacques Barlie; Raymond Maffiolo, Georges Martignano, Robert Kaiserauer, Bernard Mocellin, Anton Schnyder, Pierre-Maurice Georgy, Valer Nemeth, Deszö Makay, André Daina, Charles Kvicinsky.

AIK: Arne Lundqvist; Lennart Söderberg, Bengt Westerberg, Tommy Stenborg, Lennart Hemming, Kjell Pettersson, Bo Holmberg, Owe Ohlsson, Björn Eriksson, Björn Carlsson, Jim Nildén.   Trainer: Henry Carlsson

Goals: Georgy (1), Makay (21), Eriksson (50), Nemeth (64), Daina (67)

SPORTING LISBOA
v ESPAÑOL BARCELONA 2-1 (0-0)

Estadio José Alvalade, Lisboa   10.11.65

Referee: William J. Mullan (Sco)   Attendance: 40,000

SPORTING: Joaquim da Silva CARVALHO; JOÃO Pedro MORAIS, HILÁRIO Rosário da Conceição, Daniel Afonso da Silva DANI, José ALEXANDRE da Silva BAPTISTA, Fernando FERREIRA PINTO; JOSÉ CARLOS da Silva José, João de Matos Moura LOURENÇO, Ernesto FIGUEIREDO, Fernando PERES, Joaquim António OLIVEIRA DUARTE.
Manager: Otto Gloria, Trainer: Júlio Cernades Pereira "JUCA"

ESPAÑOL: CARMELO Cedrún Ochandategui; Ignacio María BERGARA de Medina, José MINGORANCE Chimeno, ÁLVAREZ; Carlos RAMÍREZ Zancas, Julián RIERA Navarro; Carmelo AMAS Méndez, José María Sánchez RODILLA, Alfredo DI STÉFANO Lahule, Ramón MIRALLES, JOSÉ MARÍA García Lavilla.   Trainer: Fernando Argila

Goals: Oliveira Duarte (63), Lourenço (67), Miralles (74)

ESPAÑOL BARCELONA
v SPORTING LISBOA 4-3 (0-2)

Estadio Sarriá, Barcelona   24.11.65

Referee: Ernest Crawford (Eng)   Attendance: 30,000

ESPAÑOL: CARMELO Cedrún Ochandategui; Ignacio María BERGARA de Medina, José MINGORANCE Chimeno, ÁLVAREZ; Julián RIERA Navarro, Carlos RAMÍREZ Zancas; Carmelo AMAS Méndez, José María Sánchez RODILLA, Alfredo DI STÉFANO Lahule, Ramón MIRALLES, JOSÉ MARÍA García Lavilla.   Trainer: Fernando Argila

SPORTING: Joaquim da Silva CARVALHO; JOÃO Pedro MORAIS, José ALEXANDRE da Silva BAPTISTA, HILÁRIO Rosário da Conceição; Daniel Afonso da Silva DANI, JOSÉ CARLOS da Silva José; Fernando FERREIRA PINTO, João de Matos Moura LOURENÇO, Ernesto FIGUEIREDO, Fernando PERES, Joaquim António OLIVEIRA DUARTE.
Manager: Otto Gloria, Trainer: Júlio Cernades Pereira "JUCA"

Goals: Lourenço (27), Figueiredo (35), Oliveira Duarte (48), José María (55 pen), Miralles (63), Rodilla (70, 73)

ESPAÑOL BARCELONA
v SPORTING LISBOA 2-1 (2-1)

Estadio Sarría, Barcelona   15.12.65

Referee: Pierre Schwinte (Fra)   Attendance: 20,200

ESPAÑOL: CARMELO Cedrún Ochandategui; Ignacio María BERGARA de Medina, José MINGORANCE Chimeno, ÁLVAREZ; Julián RIERA Navarro, Carlos RAMÍREZ Zancas; Carmelo AMAS Méndez, José María Sánchez RODILLA, Alfredo DI STÉFANO Lahule, Ramón MIRALLES, JOSÉ MARÍA García Lavilla.   Trainer: Fernando Argila

SPORTING: Joaquim da Silva CARVALHO; JOÃO Pedro MORAIS, HILÁRIO Rosário da Conceição; Lourenço Salvador SITOE, José ALEXANDRE da Silva BAPTISTA, Fernando Ferreira Pinto; João de Matos Moura LOURENÇO, JOSÉ CARLOS da Silva José, Ernesto FIGUEIREDO, Fernando PERES, Joaquim António OLIVEIRA DUARTE.
Manager: Otto Gloria, Trainer: Júlio Cernades Pereira "JUCA"

Goals: Rodilla (36, 45), Lourenço (37)

HANNOVER 96 v FC PORTO 5-0 (2-0)

Niedersachsenstadion, Hannover   10.11.65

Referee: Einar Poulsen (Dan)   Attendance: 5,000

HANNOVER 96: Horst Grunenberg; Bodo Fuchs, Stefan Bena, Peter Kronsbein, Winfried Mittrowski, Karl-Heinz Mülhausen, Heiner Klose, Hans Siemensmeyer, Walter Rodekamp, Udo Nix, Jürgen Bandura.
Trainer: Helmut Kronsbein

FC PORTO: RUI Fernando Sousa Teixeira; Luís Pinto, João Eleutério Luis ATRACA; João CUSTÓDIO PINTO, João Luís Pinto ALMEIDA, VALDEMAR Pacheco; JAIME Ferreira Silva, AMAURI Silva, MANUEL ANTÓNIO Leitão da Silva, ERNESTO Fernando Pereira, Francisco Lage Pereira da NÓBREGA.   Trainer: Flavio Costa

Goals: Rodekamp (5), Siemensmayer (7, 79), Bandura (65), Nix (74)

FC PORTO v HANNOVER 96 2-1 (1-1)

Estadio das Antas, Porto   8.12.65

Referee: Manuel Gomez Arribas (Spa)   Attendance: 25,000

FC PORTO: AMÉRICO Ferreira Lopes; Alberto Augusto FESTA, João Luís Pinto ALMEIDA, VALDEMAR Pacheco, João Eleutério Luis ATRACA; José ROLANDO Andrade Gonçalves, João CUSTÓDIO PINTO; JAIME Ferreira Silva, AMAURI Silva, MANUEL ANTÓNIO Leitão da Silva, Francisco Lage Pereira da NÓBREGA.   Trainer: Flavio Costa

HANNOVER 96: Horst Podlasly; Bodo Fuchs, Peter Kronsbein, Stefan Bena, Otto Laszig, Karl-Heinz Mülhausen, Werner Gräber, Hans Siemensmayer, Walter Rodekamp, Udo Nix, Jürgen Bandura.   Trainer: Helmut Kronsbein

Goals: Manuel Antonio (21), Nix (42), Pinto (66 pen)

GÖZTEPE IZMIR v TSV 1860 MÜNCHEN 2-1 (0-0)

Alsançak, Izmir   3.11.65

Referee: Josef Tittl (Aus)   Attendance: 7,500

GÖZTEPE: Ali Artuner; Mehmet Aydin, Caglayan Derebaşi, Izzet Kayli, Sabahattin Kuruoglu, Nevzat Güzelirmak, Ertan Öznur, Nihat Yayöz, Cengiz Kayalar, Gürsel Aksel, Halil Kiraz.

TSV 1860: Petar Radenković; Manfred Wagner, Bernd Patzke, Rudolf Zeiser, Wilfried Kohlars, Željko Perušić, Rudolf Brunnenmeier, Hans Küppers, Friedhelm Konietzka, Peter Grosser, Hans Rebele.   Trainer: Max Merkel

Goals: Cengiz (63), Ertan (70), Brunnenmeier (72)

78

TSV 1860 MÜNCHEN v GÖZTEPE IZMIR 9-1 (5-1)

Grünwalderstadion, München   23.11.65

Referee: Joseph Heymann (Swi)   Attendance: 7,800

TSV 1860: Petar Radenković; Manfred Wagner, Bernd Patzke, Otto Luttrop, Wilfried Kohlars, Željko Perušić, Alfred Heiss, Hans Küppers, Friedhelm Konietzka, Hans Rebele, Peter Grosser.   Trainer: Max Merkel

GÖZTEPE: Ali Artuner; Mehmet Aydin, Caglayan Derebaşi, Izzet Kayli, Sabahattin Kuruoglu, Nevzat Güzelirmak, Ertan Öznur, Nihat Yayöz, Fevzi Zemzem, Gürsel Aksel, Halil Kiraz.

Goals: Rebele (1, 29, 58), Konietzka (5, 36, 44, 65), Ertan (6), Radenkovic (73 pen), Heiss (87)

NK ZAGREB v STEAGUL ROŞU BRAŞOV 2-2 (0-0)

Zagreb   17.11.65

Referee: Sándor Petri (Hun)   Attendance: 1,000

NK ZAGREB: Zoran Misić, Galeković, Čepelja, Suša, Ilić; Dušan Beslac, Klobucar; Mladen Vaha, Stanislav Bubanj, Zlatko Dracić, Mladen Azinović.   Trainer: Gustav Lechner

STEAGUL ROŞU: Stere Adamache; Octavian Zaharia, Mihai Ivăncescu, Nicolae Campo, Ion Nagy; Iuliu Năftănăilă, Ion Szigeti; Emanoil Haşoti, Dorin Necula, Marcel Goran, Nicolae Pescaru.   Trainer: Silviu Ploeşteanu

Goals: Goran (65), Vaha (65, 84), Năftănăilă (83)

SHAMROCK ROVERS DUBLIN REAL ZARAGOZA 1-1 (1-0)

Dalymount Park, Dublin   17.11.65

Referee: Marcel Deckx (Bel)   Attendance: 10,000

SHAMROCK ROVERS: Michael Smyth; John Keogh, Patrick Courtney, Patrick Mulligan, Ronald Nolan, John Fullam, Francis O'Neill, Brian Tyrell, Robert Gilbert, William Tuohy, Anthony O'Connell.

REAL ZARAGOZA: Enrique YARZA Sorlauce; José Ramón IRUSQUIETA García, Severino REIJA Vázquez, Santiago ISASI Salazar, Francisco SANTAMARÍA Briones, José Luis VIOLETA Lajusticia, Antonio GOZALO, Eleuterio SANTOS Brito, MARCELINO Martínez Cao, Eduardo Bibiano ENDÉRIZ Cortajarena, Carlos LAPETRA Coarasa.   Trainer: Louis Hon

Goals: Tuohy (44), Reija (88)

STEAGUL ROŞU BRAŞOV v NK ZAGREB 1-0 (1-0)

Braşov   24.11.65

Referee: Pavol Spotak (Cze)   Attendance: 3,200

STEAGUL ROŞU: Stere Adamache; Mihai Ivăncescu, Iuliu Jenei, Nicolae Campo, Octavian Zaharia; Iuliu Năftănăilă, Ion Szigeti; Emanoil Haşoti, Dorin Necula, Marcel Goran, Nicolae Pescaru.   Trainer: Silviu Ploeşteanu

NK ZAGREB: Zoran Misić; Galeković, Mestrović, Suša, Ilić, Klobucar, Dušan Beslac, Nedov, Stanislav Bubanj, Mladen Vaha, Zlatko Dracić.   Trainer: Gustav Lechner

Goal: Haşoti (14)

REAL ZARAGOZA v SHAMROCK ROVERS DUBLIN 2-1 (1-1)

Estadio La Romareda, Zaragoza   24.11.65

Referee: Günther Baumgärtel (WG)   Attendance: 18,700

REAL ZARAGOZA: Enrique YARZA Sorlauce; José Ramón IRUSQUIETA García, Severino REIJA Vázquez, Santiago ISASI Salazar, Francisco SANTAMARÍA Briones, José Luis VIOLETA Lajusticia, Darcy Silveira dos Santos "CANARIO", MARCELINO Martínez Cao, Antonio GOZALO, Eleuterio SANTOS Brito, Carlos LAPETRA Coarasa.   Trainer: Louis Hon

SHAMROCK ROVERS: Michael Smyth; John Keogh, Patrick Courtney, Patrick Mulligan, Ronald Nolan, John Fullam, Francis O'Neill, Brian Tyrell, Robert Gilbert, William Tuohy, Anthony O'Connell.

Goals: Santos (11), Fullam (22), Canario (77)

ANTWERP FC v CF BARCELONA 2-1 (2-1)

Bosuilstadion, Antwerp   17.11.65

Referee: Kevin Howley (Eng)   Attendance: 10,000

ANTWERP: Willy Coremans; Maurice Renier, Jozef Janssens, Jozef van Gool, Werner Deprez, Willy Van der Wee, Theofiel van de Velde, Florent Bohez, Wilfried van Moer, Urbain Segers, Karel Beyers.   Trainer: Harry Game

CF BARCELONA: José Manuel PESUDO Soler; Julio César BENÍTEZ Amoedo, ELADIO Silvestre Graells, Antonio TORRES García, Fernando OLIVELLA Pons, Martín VERGÉS Massa, Joaquín RIFÉ Climent, Jesús María PEREDA Ruíz de Temiño, José Antonio ZALDÚA Urdanavia, Ramón MONTESINOS Calaf, SERAFÍN García Muñoz.   Trainer: Roque Olsen

Goals: Van der Wee (8), Segers (15), Rifé (43)

CF BARCELONA v ANTWERP FC 2-0 (1-0)

Camp Nou, Barcelona   1.12.65

Referee: Alfred Haberfellner (Aus)   Attendance: 19,100

CF BARCELONA: José Manuel PESUDO Soler; Julio César BENÍTEZ Amoedo, ELADIO Silvestre Graells, Martín VERGÉS Massa, Fernando OLIVELLA Pons, Antonio TORRES García, Joaquín RIFÉ Climent, Jesús María PEREDA Ruíz de Temiño, José Antonio ZALDÚA, Luis PUJOL Codina, Pedro ZABALLA Barquín Marín.   Trainer: Roque Olsen

ANTWERP: Willy Coremans; Maurice Renier, Jozef Janssens, Jozef van Gool, Werner Deprez, Willy van der Wee, Theofiel van de Velde, Florent Bohez, Wilfried van Moer, Urbain Segers, Karel Beyers.   Trainer: Harry Game

Goals: Rifé (7), Zaballa (50)

WIENER SK v CHELSEA LONDON 1-0 (0-0)

Prater, Wien   17.11.65

Referee: Gyula Gere (Hun)   Attendance: 4,000

WIENER: Rudolf Szanwald; Wilhelm Kainrath, Johann Windisch, Anton Linhart; Adolf Knoll, Norbert Hof; Helmuth Mätzler, Erich Hof, Wolfgang Gayer, Friedrich Rafreider, Johann Hörmayer.   Trainer: Karl Schlechta

CHELSEA: Peter Bonetti; Kenneth Shellito, Edward McCreadie, John Hollins, Allan Young, Marvin Hinton, Joseph Fascione, George Graham, Peter Osgood, John Boyle, Robert Tambling. Hinton sent off (81).   Manager: Thomas Docherty

Goal: Gayer (82 pen)

CHELSEA LONDON v WIENER SK 2-0 (2-0)

Stamford Bridge, London   1.12.65

Referee: Joseph Barberan (Fra)   Attendance: 28,254

CHELSEA: Peter Bonetti; Kenneth Shellito, Edward McCreadie, Marvin Hinton, John Hollins, John Boyle, Bert Murray, George Graham, Peter Osgood, Terence Venables, Robert Tambling.   Manager: Thomas Docherty

WIENER: Rudolf Szanwald; Wilhelm Kainrath, Johann Windisch, Anton Linhart; Adolf Knoll, Norbert Hof; Helmuth Mätzler, Erich Hof, Wolfgang Gayer, Friedrich Rafreider, Johann Hörmayer. Knoll sent off (76). Trainer: Karl Schlechta

Goals: Murray (5), Osgood (30)

SC LEIPZIG v LEEDS UNITED 1-2 (0-0)

Georg Schwarz Sportpark, Leipzig   24.11.65

Referee: Anton Bucheli (Swi)   Attendance: 8,000

SC LEIPZIG: Horst Weigang; Michael Faber, Claus Pfeufer, Hans-Jürgen Naumann, Peter Giessner, Manfred Geisler, Dieter Engelhardt, Rainer Trölitzsch, Henning Frenzel, Arno Zerbe, Wolfram Löwe.   Trainer: Günter Konzack

UNITED: Gary Sprake; Paul Reaney, Paul Madeley, William Bremner, Jack Charlton, Norman Hunter, James Storrie, Peter Lorimer, William Bell, John Giles, Michael O'Grady.   Manager: Don Revie

Goals: Lorimer (80), Bremner (81), Frenzel (83)

LEEDS UNITED v SC LEIPZIG 0-0

Elland Road, Leeds   1.12.65

Referee: Adrianus Boogaerts (Hol)   Attendance: 32,111

UNITED: Gary Sprake; Paul Reaney, William Bell, William Bremner, Jack Charlton, Norman Hunter, James Storrie, Alan Peacock, John Giles, Michael O'Grady, Peter Lorimer.   Manager: Don Revie

SC LEIPZIG: Horst Weigang; Michael Faber, Peter Giessner, Claus Pfeufer, Hans-Jürgen Naumann, Manfred Geisler, Dieter Engelhardt, Rainer Trölitzsch, Henning Frenzel, Arno Zerbe, Wolfram Löwe.   Trainer: Günter Konzack

---

**AC FIORENTINA FIRENZE
v SPARTAK BRNO 2-0** (1-0)

Stadio Comunale, Firenze   24.11.65

Referee: Božidar Botić (Jug)   Attendance: 3,500

FIORENTINA: Enrico Albertosi; Bernardo Rogora, Egidio Guarnacci, Giovan Battista Pirovano, Ugo Ferrante, Giuseppe Brizi, Kurt Hamrin, Giancarlo De Sisti, Mario Brugnera, Mario Bertini, Juan Carlos Morrone.   Trainer: Giuseppe Chiapella

SPARTAK: František Schmucker; Miroslav Vítů, Tomas Hradský, Juraj Janoščin, Bohumil Pišek, Karel Komárek, Jaroslav Vojta, Karel Lichtnégl, Cestmir Chaloupka, Jan Brada, Viliam Hrnčár.   Trainer: Karel Kolský

Goals: De Sisti (15), Hamrin (89)

SPARTAK BRNO
v AC FIORENTINA FIRENZE 4-0 (1-0)

Spartak Brno 5.12.65

Referee: Bertil Lööw (Swe) Attendance: 2,700

SPARTAK: František Schmucker; Miroslav Vítů, Karel Kohlík, Juraj Janoščin, Bohumil Pišek, Karel Komárek, Jaroslav Vojta, Karel Lichtnégl, Cestmir Chaloupka, Tomas Hradský, Viliam Hrnčár. Trainer: Karel Kolský

FIORENTINA: Francesco Superchi; Bernardo Rogora, Sergio Castelletti, Giovan Battista Pirovano, Ugo Ferrante, Giuseppe Brizi, Kurt Hamrin, Giancarlo De Sisti, Mario Brugnera, Mario Bertini, Juan Carlos Morrone. Trainer: Giuseppe Chiapella

Goals: Hradský (29, 70), Lichtnégl (79, 83)

FC BASEL v VALENCIA CF 1-3 (1-2)

St.Jakob Stadium, Basel 24.11.65

Referee: Kurt Handwerker (WG) Attendance: 4,500

FC BASEL: Jean-Paul Laufenburger; Josef Kiefer, Hanspeter Stocker, Bruno Michaud, Markus Pfirter, Helmut Hauser, Helmut Benthaus, Hanspeter Vetter, Karl Odermatt, Bruno Gabrieli, Roberto Frigerio. Trainer: Helmut Benthaus

VALENCIA CF: Ricardo ZAMORA de Grassa; Javier GARCÍA VERDUGO Garrido, Manuel MESTRE Torres, Francisco VIDAGAŇY Hernández, ROBERTO Gil Esteve, Francisco García Gómez "PAQUITO", Manuel Polinario Muñoz "POLI", José María SÁNCHEZ LAGE, WALDO Machado da Silva, Vicente GUILLOT Fabián, Juan MUÑOZ Cerdá. Trainer: Sabino Barinaga

Goals: Benthaus (6), Waldo (17, 80), Muñoz (23)

VALENCIA CF v FC BASEL 5-1 (4-0)

Estadio de Mestalla, Valencia 8.12.65

Referee: Robert Lacoste (Fra) Attendance: 19,700

VALENCIA CF: Ricardo ZAMORA de Grassa; Javier GARCÍA VERDUGO Garrido, Manuel MESTRE Torres, Alberto ARNAL Andrés, José María SÁNCHEZ LAGE, Francisco García Gómez «PAQUITO», Manuel Polinario Muñoz «POLI», José Antonio URTIAGA Albizei, WALDO Machado da Silva, Vicente GUILLOT Fabián, Juan MUÑOZ Cerdá. Trainer: Sabino Barinaga

FC BASEL: Marcel Kunz; Josef Kiefer, Bruno Michaud, Schwager, Helmut Benthaus, Helmut Hauser, Karl Odermatt, Bruno Gabrieli, Markus Pfirter, Hanspeter Stocker, Roberto Frigerio. Trainer: Helmut Benthaus

Goals: Waldo (1, 79), Urtiaga (18), Muñoz (31), Guillot (33), Hauser (53)

CUF BARREIRO v AC MILAN 2-0 (0-0)

Estadio Alfredo da Liloa, Barreiro 1.12.65

Referee: Dittmar Huber (Swi) Attendance: 12,500

CUF: VÍTOR MANUEL Lopes Marques; António BAMBO Cassama, Francisco ABALROADO, MÁRIO JOÃO Sousa Alves, António Esteves DURAND, António José Santos MEDEIROS, José Diogo MADEIRA, António Sá VASCONCELOS, FERNANDO Oliveira, Alfredo Agostinho ESPÍRITO SANTO, Emidio Simoes URIA. Trainer: Manuel Oliveira

AC MILAN: Luigi Balzarini; Karl Heinz Schnellinger, Mario Trebbi, Nello Santin, Cesare Maldini, Luigi Maldera, Urano Benigni, Sergio Maddé, Angelo Benedicto Sormani, Antonio Valentin Angelillo, AMARILDO Tavares de Silveire. Trainer: Nils Liedholm

Goals: Fernando (61), Abalroado (89p)

AC MILAN v CUF BARREIRO 2-0 (1-0)

Stadio San Siro, Milano 8.12.65

Referee: Norman Mootz (Lux) Attendance: 9,500

AC MILAN: Luigi Balzarini; Mario Trebbi, Ambrogio Pelagalli, Nello Santin, Cesare Maldini, Karl Heinz Schnellinger, Urano Benigni, Sergio Maddé, Angelo Benedicto Sormani, Antonio Valentin Angelillo, AMARILDO Tavares de Silveire. Trainer: Nils Liedholm

CUF: VÍTOR MANUEL Lopes Marques; António BAMBO Cassama, António Esteves DURAND, Francisco ABALROADO, MÁRIO JOÃO Sousa Alves, António José Santos MEDEIROS, José Diogo MADEIRA, António VIEIRA DIAS, FERNANDO Oliveira, Alfredo Agostinho ESPÍRITO SANTO, Emidio Simoes URIA. Trainer: Manuel Oliveira

Goals: Sormani (18 pen), Angelillo (87)

AC MILAN v CUF BARREIRO 1-0 (0-0)

Stadio San Siro, Milano 29.12.65

Referee: Gerhard Schulenburg (WG) Attendance: 6,400

AC MILAN: Luigi Balzarini; Mario Trebbi, Karl Heinz Schnellinger, Nello Santin, Cesare Maldini, Giovanni Trapattoni, Sergio Maddé, Antonio Valentin Angelillo, Giovanni Lodetti, Gianni Rivera, AMARILDO Tavares de Silveire. Trainer: Nils Liedholm

CUF: VÍTOR MANUEL Lopes Marques; António BAMBO Cassama, António Esteves DURAND, Francisco ABALROADO, MÁRIO JOÃO Sousa Alves, António José Santos MEDEIROS, José Diogo MADEIRA, António VIEIRA DIAS, FERNANDO Oliveira, Alfredo Agostinho ESPÍRITO SANTO, Emidio Simoes URIA. Trainer: Manuel Oliveira

Goal: Lodetti (76)

THIRD ROUND

HEART OF MIDLOTHIAN EDINBURGH
v REAL ZARAGOZA 3-3 (0-2)

Tynecastle Park, Edinburgh   12.01.66

Referee: Aranth Jensen (Dan)   Attendance: 17,000

HEARTS: James Fergus Cruickshank; Daniel Ferguson, David Duff Holt, John Cumming, Alan Anderson, George Miller, John Hamilton, William Higgins, William Wallace, Donald Kerrigan, Thomas Traynor. Manager: Thomas Walker

REAL ZARAGOZA: Víctor ALDEA (59 Vicente CARDOSO Sánchez); José Ramón IRUSQUIETA García, Severino REIJA Vázquez, Santiago ISASI Salazar, Francisco SANTAMARÍA Briones, José Luis VIOLETA Lajusticia, Darcy Silveira dos Santos "CANARIO", Eleuterio SANTOS Brito, MARCELINO Martínez Cao, Eduardo Bibiano ENDÉRIZ Cortajarena, Carlos LAPETRA Coarasa.   Trainer: Louis Hon

Goals: Lapetra (10, 86), Endériz (30), Anderson (50), Wallace (59), Kerrigan (80)

REAL ZARAGOZA
v HEART OF MIDLOTHIAN EDINBURGH 2-2 (2-1)

Estadio La Romareda, Zaragoza   26.01.66

Referee: Michel Kitabdjian (Fra)   Attendance: 25,200

REAL ZARAGOZA: Andrés Rodríguez «RODRI»; José Ramón IRUSQUIETA García, Severino REIJA Vázquez, Santiago ISASI Salazar, Francisco SANTAMARÍA Briones, José Luis VIOLETA Lajusticia, Darcy Silveira dos Santos «CANARIO», Eleuterio SANTOS Brito, MARCELINO Martínez Cao, Eduardo Bibiano ENDÉRIZ Cortajarena, Carlos LAPETRA Coarasa.   Trainer: Louis Hon

HEARTS: James Fergus Cruickshank; Daniel Ferguson, Christopher Shevlane, John Cumming, Alan Anderson, George Miller, John Hamilton, William Higgins, William Wallace, Donald Kerrigan, Thomas Traynor. Manager: Thomas Walker

Goals: Santos (4), Marcelino (22), Anderson (26), Wallace (77)

REAL ZARAGOZA
v HEART OF MIDLOTHIAN EDINBURGH 1-0 (0-0)

Estadio La Romareda, Zaragoza   2.03.66

Referee: Bruno de Marchi (Ita)   Attendance: 25,000

REAL ZARAGOZA: Andrés Rodríguez «RODRI»; José Ramón IRUSQUIETA García, Juan ZUBIAURRE Jáuregui, José Cuéllar González «PEPÍN», Francisco SANTAMARÍA Briones, José Luis VIOLETA Lajusticia, Darcy Silveira dos Santos «CANARIO», Eleuterio SANTOS Brito, MARCELINO Martínez Cao, Juan Manuel VILLA Gutiérrez, Carlos LAPETRA Coarasa.   Trainer: Fernando Daučik

HEARTS: James Fergus Cruickshank; William Polland, David Holt, John Cumming, Alan Anderson, George Miller, John Hamilton, William Higgins, William Wallace, Donald Kerrigan, Thomas Traynor. Trainer: Thomas Walker

Goal: Marcelino (83)

ESPAÑOL BARCELONA
v STEAGUL ROȘU BRAȘOV 3-1 (0-0)

Estadio Sarriá, Barcelona   26.01.66

Referee: Francesco Francescon (Ita)   Attendance: 14,800

ESPAÑOL: Rafael PIRIS Esteva; JUAN MANUEL Tartillán Requejo, José MINGORANCE Chimeno, Rafael GRANERO Bellver; Jaime SABATÉ Mercadé, Julián RIERA Navarro (Cap); Carmelo AMAS Méndez, Carlos RAMÍREZ Zancas, Alfredo DI STÉFANO Lahule, José María Sánchez RODILLA, JOSÉ MARÍA García Lavilla.   Trainer: Fernando Argila

STEAGUL ROȘU: Stere Adamache; Octavian Zaharia, Iuliu Jenei, Nicolae Campo, Ion Nagy; Nicolae Pescaru, Ion Szigeti; Emanoil Hașoti, Iuliu Năftănăilă, Marcel Goran, Csaba Györffi.   Trainer: Silviu Ploeșteanu

Goals: Amas (59, 82, 87), Zaharia (62)

STEAGUL ROȘU BRAȘOV
v ESPAÑOL BARCELONA 4-2 (1-1)

Tractorul, Brașov   16.02.66

Referee: Stjepan Varaždinec (Jug)   Attendance: 13,800

STEAGUL ROȘU: Stere Adamache; Mihai Ivăncescu, Iuliu Jenei, Ion Nagy, Octavian Zaharia; Nicolae Pescaru, Nicolae Campo; Emanoil Hașoti, Dorin Necula, Marcel Goran, Csaba Györffi.   Trainer: Silviu Ploeșteanu

ESPAÑOL: CARMELO Cedrún Ochandategui; JUAN MANUEL Tartillán Requejo, José MINGORANCE Chimeno, ÁLVAREZ, Jaime SABATÉ Mercadé, Julián RIERA Navarro (Cap); Rodri, Boy, Alfredo DI STÉFANO Lahule, JOSÉ MARÍA García Lavilla, EULOGIO Ramiro MARTÍNEZ.   Trainer: Fernando Argila

Goals: Eulogio Martínez (21), Pescaru (23), José María (49), Ivăncescu (52, 60 pen), Goran (80)

STEAGUL ROȘU BRAȘOV
v ESPAÑOL BARCELONA 0-1 (0-0)

Tractorul, Brașov   2.03.66

Referees: Othmar Huber; Luigi Grassi, Otto Segginger (Swi)   Attendance: 13,000

STEAGUL ROȘU: Stere Adamache; Mihai Ivăncescu, Iuliu Jenei, Ion Alecu, Ion Nagy; Nicolae Pescaru, Nicolae Campo; Emanoil Hașoti, Dorin Necula, Marcel Goran, Csaba Györffi.   Trainer: Silviu Ploeșteanu

ESPAÑOL: CARMELO Cedrún Ochandategui; JUAN MANUEL Tartillán Requejo, José MINGORANCE Chimeno, Rafael GRANERO Bellver, Jaime SABATÉ Mercadé, Julián RIERA Navarro (Cap); RODRI, IDÍGORAS, Cayetano RE Rodríguez, EULOGIO Ramiro MARTÍNEZ, JOSÉ MARÍA García Lavilla.   Trainer: Alfredo di STÉFANO

Goal: Ré (54)

DUNFERMLINE ATHLETIC
v SPARTAK BRNO 2-0 (0-0)

East End Park, Dunfermline   26.01.66

Referee: H.D. Davies (Wal)   Attendance: 15,000

DUNFERMLINE: Eric Martin; William Callaghan, John Lunn, Alexander Smith, James McLean; Thomas Callaghan, Alexander Edwards, Robert Paton; James Fleming, Alexander Ferguson, Hugh Robertson. Manager: William Cunningham

SPARTAK: František Schmucker; Miroslav Vítů, Juraj Janoščin, Bohumil Pišek, Karel Kohlík; Karel Komárek, Jaroslav Vojta, Karel Lichtnégl; Cestmir Chaloupka, Tomas Hradský, Viliam Hrnčár. Trainer: Karel Kolský

Goals: Paton (61), A. Ferguson (88 pen)

SPARTAK BRNO
v DUNFERMLINE ATHLETIC 0-0

Spartak, Brno   16.02.66

Referee: Fritz Köpcke (DDR)   Attendance: 7,000

SPARTAK: František Schmucker; Miroslav Vítů, Juraj Janoščin, Bohumil Pišek, Karel Kohlík, Karel Komárek; Farmacka, Karel Lichtnégl, Cestmir Chaloupka, Tomas Hradský, Jan Brada. Trainer: Karel Kolský

DUNFERMLINE: Eric Martin; William Callaghan, John Lunn, Alexander Smith; James McLean, James Thomson; Alexander Edwards, Robert Paton, James Fleming, Alexander Ferguson, George Peebles. Manager: William Cunningham

FC KÖLN v ÚJPESTI DÓZSA BUDAPEST 3-2 (3-1)

Müngersdorferstadion, Köln   2.02.66

Referee: George McCabe (Eng)   Attendance: 25,000

FC KÖLN: Toni Schumacher; Fritz Pott, Wolfgang Weber, Leo Wilden; Hans Sturm, Matthias Hemmersbach; Karl-Heinz Thielen, Christian Müller, Johannes Löhr, Wolfgang Overath, Heinz Hornig. Trainer: Georg Knopfle

ÚJPESTI DÓZSA: Antal Szentmihályi; Benő Káposzta, Matyas Csordás, Ernő Noskó, Kálmán Sóvári; Ernő Solymosi, József Szini; Béla Kuharszki, Ferenc Bene, János Göröcs, Sándor Zámbó. Trainer: Sándor Balogh

Goals: Löhr (18, 31), Göröcs (30), Sturm (43), Solymosi (81 pen)

ÚJPESTI DÓZSA BUDAPEST v FC KÖLN 4-0 (1-0)

Megyeri út, Budapest   16.02.66

Referee: Ferdinand Marschall (Aus)   Attendance: 35,000

ÚJPESTI DÓZSA: Antal Szentmihályi; Benő Káposzta, Matyas Csordás, Kálmán Sóvári; Ernő Noskó, Ernő Solymosi; Béla Kuharszki, Ferenc Bene, János Göröcs, Antal Dunai, Sándor Zámbó. Trainer: Sándor Balogh

FC KÖLN: Fritz Ewert; Fritz Pott, Wolfgang Weber, Leo Wilden; Hans Sturm, Matthias Hemmersbach; Franz Krauthausen, Ole Sørensen, Christian Müller, Johannes Löhr, Heinz Hornig. Trainer: Georg Knopfle

Goals: A. Dunai (13), Bene (46, 70), Kuharszki (62)

LEEDS UNITED v VALENCIA CF 1-1 (1-1)

Elland Road, Leeds   2.02.66

Referee: Leopold Silvayn Horn (Hol)   Attendance: 34,414

UNITED: Gary Sprake; Paul Reaney, William Bell, William Bremner, Jack Charlton, Norman Hunter, James Storrie, Peter Lorimer, Rodney Belfitt, John Giles, Michael O'Grady. Manager: Don Revie

VALENCIA CF: Cipriano González Rivero "ÑITO"; Alberto ARNAL Andrés, Francisco VIDAGAÑY Hernández, ROBERTO Gil Esteve, Manuel MESTRE Torres, Francisco García Gómez "PAQUITO", Vicente GUILLOT Fabián, José PALAU Busquet, Valentín García Pascual "TOTÓ", José María SÁNCHEZ LAGE, Juan MUÑOZ Cerdá. Trainer: Sabino Barinaga

Charlton (75), Vidagañy (75) and Sánchez Lage (83) sent off

Goals: Muñoz (17), Lorimer (65)

VALENCIA CF v LEEDS UNITED 0-1 (0-0)

Estadio de Mestalla, Valencia   16.02.66

Referee: Othmar Huber (Swi)   Attendance: 45,000

VALENCIA CF: Cipriano González Rivero «ÑITO»; Javier GARCÍA VERDUGO Garrido, Valentín García Pascual «TOTÓ», ROBERTO Gil Esteve, Manuel MESTRE Torres, Francisco García Gómez «PAQUITO», Manuel Polinario Muñoz «POLI», José María SÁNCHEZ LAGE, WALDO Machado da Silva, Vicente GUILLOT Fabián, Juan MUÑOZ Cerdá. Trainer: Sabino Barinaga

UNITED: Gary Sprake; Paul Reaney, William Bell, William Bremner, Jack Charlton, Norman Hunter, James Storrie, Peter Lorimer, Paul Madeley, John Giles, Michael O'Grady. Manager: Don Revie

Goal: O'Grady (75)

HANNOVER 96 v CF BARCELONA 2-1 (1-1)

Niedersachsenstadion, Hannover   2.02.66

Referee: Franz Geluck (Bel)   Attendance: 40,000

HANNOVER 96: Horst Podlasly; Heinz Steinwedel, Stefan Bena; Winfried Mittrowski, Otto Laszig, Bodo Fuchs; Fred Hoff, Werner Gräber, Walter Rodekamp, Hans Siemensmeyer, Jürgen Bandura.   Trainer: Helmut Kronsbein

CF BARCELONA: José Manuel PESUDO Soler; Julio César BENÍTEZ Amoedo, ELADIO Silvestre Graells; Francisco Fernández Rodríguez "GALLEGO", Fernando OLIVELLA Pons, Antonio TORRES García; Joaquín RIFÉ Climent, Martín VERGÉS Massa, José Antonio ZALDÚA Urdanavia, José María FUSTÉ Blanch, Pedro ZABALLA Barquín Marín.   Trainer: Roque Olsen

Goals: Siemensmeyer (15, 55), Zaldúa (44)

CF BARCELONA v HANNOVER 96   1-0 (0-0)

Camp Nou, Barcelona   16.02.66

Referee: Hugh Phillips (Sco)   Attendance: 38,600

CF BARCELONA: José Manuel PESUDO Soler; Julio César BENÍTEZ Amoedo, ELADIO Silvestre Graells; Martín VERGÉS Massa, Fernando OLIVELLA Pons, Antonio TORRES García; Joaquín RIFÉ Climent, Lucien MULLER Schmidt, José Antonio ZALDÚA Urdanavia, José María FUSTÉ Blanch, Pedro ZABALLA Barquín Marín.   Trainer: Roque Olsen

HANNOVER 96: Horst Podlasly; Stefan Bena, Winfried Mittrowski, Otto Laszig, Klaus Bohnsack; Bodo Fuchs, Karl-Heinz Mülhausen, Werner Gräber, Walter Rodekamp, Hans Siemensmayer, Jürgen Bandura.   Trainer: Helmut Kronsbein

Goal: Fusté (61)

HANNOVER 96 v CF BARCELONA 1-1 (1-0, 1-1) a.e.t.

Niedersachsenstadion, Hannover   2.03.66

Referee: John Taylor (Eng)   Attendance: 38,100

HANNOVER 96: Horst Podlasly; Stefan Bena, Otto Laszig, Klaus Bohnsack, Winfried Mittrowski, Bodo Fuchs, Friedrich Heiser, Werner Gräber, Walter Rodekamp, Hans Siemensmayer, Jürgen Bandura.   Trainer: Helmut Kronsbein

CF BARCELONA: Miguel REINA Santos; Julio César BENÍTEZ Amoedo, Alfonso María Rodríguez Salas "FONCHO"; Ramón MONTESINOS Calaf, Fernando OLIVELLA Pons, Antonio TORRES García; Joaquín RIFÉ Climent, Jesús María PEREDA Ruíz de Temiño, Luis PUJOL Codina, Lucien MULLER Schmidt, Pedro ZABALLA Barquín Marín.   Trainer: Roque Olsen

Goals: Bandura (11), Pujol (88)

Barcelona won on the toss of a coin

SERVETTE GENEVE v TSV MÜNCHEN 1860   1-1 (0-1)

Stade des Charmilles, Genève   8.02.66

Referee: Marcel du Bois (Fra)   Attendance: 4,500

SERVETTE: Jacques Barlie; Raymond Maffiolo, Anton Schnyder, Bernard Mocellin, Deszö Makay, Robert Kaiserauer, Valer Nemeth, Pierre-Maurice Georgy, André Daina, Roger Vonlanthen, Jean-Claude Schindelholz.

TSV: Petar Radenković; Manfred Wagner, Bernd Patzke, Željko Perušić, Otto Luttrop, Wilfried Kohlars, Rudolf Steiner, Hans Reich, Rudolf Brunnenmeier, Friedhelm Konietzka, Peter Grosser.   Trainer: Max Merkel

Goals: Konietzka (39), Daina (89)

TSV MÜNCHEN 1860 v SERVETTE GENÈVE 4-1 (2-1)

Grünwalderstadion, München   15.02.66

Referee: Mayer (Aus)   Attendance: 15,000

TSV: Petar Radenković; Rudolf Zeiser, Bernd Patzke, Željko Perušić, Hans Küppers, Wilfried Kohlars, Alfred Heiss, Hans Reich, Rudolf Brunnenmeier, Friedhelm Konietzka, Peter Grosser.   Trainer: Max Merkel

SERVETTE: Jacques Barlie; Raymond Maffiolo, Anton Schnyder, Bernard Mocellin, Deszö Makay, Robert Kaiserauer, Valer Nemeth, Pierre-Maurice Georgy, André Daina, Roger Vonlanthen, Jean-Claude Schindelholz.

Goals: Konietzka (16), Grosser (35), Georgy (40), Brunnenmeier (58, 87)

AC MILAN v CHELSEA LONDON 2-1 (0-0)

Stadio San Siro, Milano   9.02.66

Referee: Rudolf Kreitlein (WG)   Attendance: 11,411

AC MILAN: Luigi Balzarini; Ambrogio Pelagalli, Mario Trebbi, Nello Santin, Cesare Maldini, Sergio Maddé, Urano Benigni, Giovanni Lodetti, Antonio Valentin Angelillo, Gianni Rivera, AMARILDO Tavares de Silveire.   Trainer: Nils Liedholm

CHELSEA: Peter Bonetti; Ronald Harris, Edward McCreadie, John Hollins, Marvin Hinton, John Boyle, Barry Bridges, George Graham, Peter Osgood, Terence Venables, Robert Tambling.   Manager: Thomas Docherty

Goals: Amarildo (58), Rivera (75), Graham (89)

CHELSEA LONDON v AC MILAN 2-1 (2-1)

Stamford Bridge, London 16.02.66

Referee: Einar Boström (Swe)   Attendance: 59,541

CHELSEA: Peter Bonetti; Ronald Harris, Edward McCreadie, John Hollins, Marvin Hinton, John Boyle, Barry Bridges, George Graham, Peter Osgood, Terence Venables, Robert Tambling.   Manager: Thomas Docherty

AC MILAN: Luigi Balzarini; Karl Heinz Schnellinger, Mario Trebbi, Nello Santin, Cesare Maldini, Sergio Maddé, Angelo Benedicto Sormani, Giovanni Lodetti, Antonio Valentin Angelillo, Gianni Rivera, AMARILDO Tavares de Silveire. Trainer: Nils Liedholm

Goals: Graham (9), Osgood (18), Sormani (43)

AC MILAN v CHELSEA LONDON 1-1 (0-1, 1-1)

Stadio San Siro, Milano 2.03.66

Referee: Günther Baumgärtel (WG)   Attendance: 35,000

AC MILAN: Luigi Balzarini; Ambrogio Pelagalli, Mario Trebbi, Nello Santin, Cesare Maldini, Alberto Grossetti, Sergio Maddé, Giovanni Lodetti, Angelo Benedicto Sormani, Antonio Valentin Angelillo, Giuliano Fortunato. Trainer: Nils Liedholm

CHELSEA: Peter Bonetti; Ronald Harris, Edward McCreadie, John Hollins, Marvin Hinton, John Boyle, Barry Bridges, George Graham, Peter Osgood, Bert Murray, Robert Tambling. Manager: Thomas Docherty

Goals: Bridges (10), Fortunato (90)

Chelsea London won on the toss of a coin

QUARTER-FINALS

LEEDS UNITED v ÚJPESTI DÓZSA BUDAPEST 4-1 (4-0)

Elland Road, Leeds 2.03.66

Referee: Gerhard Schulenburg (WG)   Attendance: 40,462

UNITED: Gary Sprake; Paul Reaney, Jack Charlton, William Bell; William Bremner, Norman Hunter; Michael O'Grady, Peter Lorimer, James Storrie, John Giles, Terence Cooper. Manager: Don Revie

ÚJPESTI DÓZSA: Antal Szentmihályi; Benő Káposzta, Matyas Csordás, Kálmán Sóvári; Ernő Solymosi, Ernő Noskó; Béla Kuharszki, János Göröcs, Ferenc Bene, Antal Dunai, Sándor Zámbó.   Trainer: Sándor Balogh

Goals: Cooper (7), Bell (35), Storrie (42), Bremner (43), A. Dunai (74)

ÚJPESTI DÓZSA BUDAPEST v LEEDS UNITED 1-1 (1-0)

Megyeri út, Budapest 9.03.66

Referee: Gottfried Dienst (Swi)   Attendance: 30,000

ÚJPESTI DÓZSA: Antal Szentmihályi; Benő Káposzta, Matyas Csordás, Kálmán Sóvári; Ernő Solymosi, Sándor Lenkei; Béla Kuharszki, János Göröcs, Ferenc Bene, László Fazekas, Sándor Zámbó.   Trainer: Sándor Balogh

UNITED: Gary Sprake; Paul Reaney, Jack Charlton, William Bell; William Bremner, Norman Hunter; Michael O'Grady, Peter Lorimer, James Storrie, John Giles, Terence Cooper. Manager: Don Revie

Goals: Fazekas (38), Lorimer (72)

TSV MÜNCHEN 1860 v CHELSEA LONDON 2-2 (1-1)

Grünwalderstrassestadion, München 15.03.66

Referee: Robert Schaut (Bel)   Attendance: 11,000

TSV: Petar Radenković; Manfred Wagner, Rudolf Steiner, Wilfried Kohlars, Hans Reich, Željko Perušić, Alfred Heiss, Hans Küppers, Friedhelm Konietzka, Peter Grosser, Hans Rebele.   Trainer: Max Merkel

CHELSEA: Peter Bonetti; Joseph Kirkup, Edward McCreadie, John Hollins, Marvin Hinton, Ronald Harris, Barry Bridges, George Graham, Peter Osgood, Terence Venables, Robert Tambling.   Manager: Thomas Docherty

Goals: Kohlars (17), Tambling (36, 55), Konietzka (75)

CHELSEA LONDON v TSV MÜNCHEN 1860 1-0 (0-0)

Stamford Bridge, London 29.03.66

Referee: István Zsolt (Hun)   Attendance: 42,224

CHELSEA: Peter Bonetti; Joseph Kirkup, Edward McCreadie, John Hollins, Marvin Hinton, Ronald Harris, Barry Bridges, George Graham, Peter Osgood, Terence Venables, Robert Tambling.   Manager: Thomas Docherty

TSV: Petar Radenković; Wilfried Kohlars, Bernd Patzke, Otto Luttrop, Hans Reich, Željko Perušić, Alfred Heiss, Hans Küppers, Friedhelm Konietzka, Peter Grosser, Hans Rebele. Trainer: Max Merkel

Goal: Osgood (78)

CF BARCELONA
v ESPAÑOL BARCELONA 1-0 (1-0)

Camp Nou, Barcelona   16.03.66

Referee: Adrianus Aalbrecht (Hol)   Attendance: 62,600

CF BARCELONA: Miguel REINA Santos; Julio César
BENÍTEZ Amoedo, Francisco Fernández Rodríguez
«GALLEGO», ELADIO Silvestre Graells, Martín VERGÉS
Massa, Antonio TORRES García, Joaquín RIFÉ Climent,
Lucien MULLER Schmidt, Luis PUJOL Codina, José María
FUSTÉ Blanch, Pedro ZABALLA Barquín Marín.
Trainer: Roque Olsen

ESPAÑOL: CARMELO Cedrún Ochandategui; JUAN
MANUEL Tartillán Requejo, José MINGORANCE Chimeno,
Rafael GRANERO Bellver, Jaime SABATÉ Mercadé, Julián
RIERA Navarro, Rodri, Carlos RAMÍREZ Zancas, IDIGORAS,
JOSÉ MARÍA García Lavilla, Cayetano RE Rodríguez.
Trainer: Pepe Espada

Goal: Benítez (43)

ESPAÑOL BARCELONA
v CF BARCELONA 0-1 (0-0)

Estadio de Sarría, Barcelona   23.03.66

Referee: James Finney (Eng)   Attendance: 26,000

ESPAÑOL: CARMELO Cedrún Ochandategui; JUAN
MANUEL Tartillán Requejo, José MINGORANCE Chimeno,
Rafael GRANERO Bellver, Jaime SABATÉ Mercadé,
IDIGORAS, Cayetano RE Rodríguez, Carlos RAMÍREZ
Zancas, Alfredo DI STÉFANO Lahule, José María Sánchez
RODILLA, JOSÉ MARÍA García Lavilla.   Trainer: Pepe Espada

CF BARCELONA: Miguel REINA Santos; Julio César
BENÍTEZ Amoedo, Francisco Fernández Rodríguez
«GALLEGO», ELADIO Silvestre Graells; Ramón
MONTESINOS Calaf, Antonio TORRES García; Joaquín RIFÉ
Climent, Lucien MULLER Schmidt, Luis VIDAL Planella, Juan
Roberto SEMINARIO Rodríguez, Pedro ZABALLA Barquín
Marín.   Trainer: Roque Olsen

Goal: Vidal (49)

DUNFERMLINE ATHLETIC
v REAL ZARAGOZA 1-0 (1-0)

East End Park, Dunfermline   16.03.66

Referee: Robert Lacoste (Fra)   Attendance: 18,000

DUNFERMLINE: Eric Martin; William Callaghan, John
Lunn, Alexander Smith, James McLean, James Thomson,
Alexander Edwards, Robert Paton, James Fleming, Alexander
Ferguson, Hugh Robertson.   Manager: William Cunningham

REAL ZARAGOZA: José María GOICOECHEA Ibarguren;
José Ramón IRUSQUIETA García, Juan ZUBIAURRE Jáuregui,
José Luis VIOLETA Lajusticia, Francisco SANTAMARÍA
Briones, Antonio PAÍS Castroagudin, Darcy Silveira dos
Santos "CANARIO", Eleuterio SANTOS Brito, MARCELINO
Martínez Cao, Juan Manuel VILLA Gutiérrez, Carlos
LAPETRA Coarasa.   Trainer: Fernando Daučik

Goal: Paton (86)

REAL ZARAGOZA
v DUNFERMLINE ATHLETIC 4-2 (0-0, 2-1) a.e.t.

Estadio La Romareda, Zaragoza   30.03.66

Referee: Alessandro d'Agostini (Ita)   Attendance: 27,100

REAL ZARAGOZA: José María GOICOECHEA Ibarguren;
José Ramón IRUSQUIETA García, Santiago ISASI Salazar,
José Luis VIOLETA Lajusticia, Francisco SANTAMARÍA
Briones, Antonio PAÍS Castroagudin, Darcy Silveira dos
Santos «CANARIO», Eleuterio SANTOS Brito, MARCELINO
Martínez Cao, Juan Manuel VILLA Gutiérrez, Carlos
LAPETRA Coarasa.   Trainer: Fernando Daučik

DUNFERMLINE: Eric Martin; William Callaghan, John
Lunn, Alexander Smith, James McLean, James Thomson,
Alexander Edwards, Robert Paton, Thomas Callaghan,
Alexander Ferguson, George Peebles.
Manager: William Cunningham

Goals: Santos (57), Marcelino (82), A. Ferguson (89, 103),
Villa (92, 118)

SEMI-FINALS

REAL ZARAGOZA v LEEDS UNITED 1-0 (0-0)

Estadio La Romareda, Zaragoza   20.04.66

Referee: Marcel du Bois (Fra)   Attendance: 35,000

REAL ZARAGOZA: Enrique YARZA Sorlauce; José Ramón
IRUSQUIETA García, Severino REIJA Vázquez, Antonio PAÍS
Castroagudin, Francisco SANTAMARÍA Briones, José Luis
VIOLETA Lajusticia, Darcy Silveira dos Santos «CANARIO»,
Eleuterio SANTOS Brito, MARCELINO Martínez Cao, Juan
Manuel VILLA Gutiérrez, Carlos LAPETRA Coarasa.
Trainer: Fernando Daučik

UNITED: Gary Sprake; Paul Reaney, William Bell, William
Bremner, Jack Charlton, Norman Hunter, James Greenhoff,
Edward Gray, James Storrie, John Giles, Albert Johanneson.
Manager: Don Revie

Violeta and Giles sent off (85)

Goal: Lapetra (59 pen)

LEEDS UNITED v REAL ZARAGOZA 2-1 (1-0)

Elland Road, Leeds   27.04.66

Referee: Günther Baumgärtel (WG)   Attendance: 45,008

UNITED: Gary Sprake; Paul Reaney, William Bell, William
Bremner, Jack Charlton, Norman Hunter, James Greenhoff,
Edward Gray, James Storrie, John Giles, Albert Johanneson.
Manager: Don Revie

REAL ZARAGOZA: José María GOICOECHEA Ibarguren;
José Ramón IRUSQUIETA García, Severino REIJA Vázquez,
Antonio PAÍS Castroagudin, Francisco SANTAMARÍA
Briones, José Luis VIOLETA Lajusticia, Darcy Silveira dos
Santos "CANARIO", Eleuterio SANTOS Brito, MARCELINO
Martínez Cao, Juan Manuel VILLA Gutiérrez, Carlos
LAPETRA Coarasa.   Trainer: Fernando Daučik

Goals: Johanneson (23), Canario (60), Charlton (63)

LEEDS UNITED v REAL ZARAGOZA 1-3 (0-1)

Elland Road, Leeds   11.05.66

Referee: Hans Carlsson (Swe)   Attendance: 43,046

UNITED: Gary Sprake; Paul Reaney, William Bell, William Bremner, Jack Charlton, Norman Hunter, James Greenhoff, Peter Lorimer, James Storrie, John Giles, Michael O'Grady. Manager: Don Revie

REAL ZARAGOZA: Enrique YARZA Sorlauce; José Ramón IRUSQUIETA García, Severino REIJA Vázquez, Antonio PAÍS Castroagudin, Francisco SANTAMARÍA Briones, José Luis VIOLETA Lajusticia, Darcy Silveira dos Santos "CANARIO", Eleuterio SANTOS Brito, MARCELINO Martínez Cao, Juan Manuel VILLA Gutiérrez, Carlos LAPETRA Coarasa. Trainer: Fernando Daučik

Goals: Marcelino (1), Villa (5), Santos (14), Charlton (79)

CF BARCELONA v CHELSEA LONDON 2-0 (1-0)

Camp Nou, Barcelona   27.04.66

Referee: Karl Keller (Swi)   Attendance: 70,000

CF BARCELONA: Miguel REINA Santos; Julio César BENÍTEZ Amoedo, ELADIO Silvestre Graells, Ramón MONTESINOS Calaf, Francisco Fernández Rodríguez "GALLEGO", Antonio TORRES García, Joaquín RIFÉ Climent, Lucien MULLER Schmidt, José Antonio ZALDÚA Urdanavia, José María FUSTÉ Blanch, Pedro ZABALLA Barquín Marín. Trainer: Roque Olsen

CHELSEA: Peter Bonetti; Joseph Kirkup, Marvin Hinton, Allan Young, Ronald Harris, John Hollins, Terence Venables, John Boyle, Peter Houseman, Peter Osgood, Robert Tambling. Manager: Thomas Docherty

Goals: Fusté (34), Zaldúa (89)

CHELSEA LONDON v CF BARCELONA 2-0 (0-0)

Stamford Bridge, London   11.05.66

Referee: Dittmar Huber (Swi)   Attendance: 40,073

CHELSEA: Peter Bonetti; Joseph Kirkup, Alan Harris, John Hollins, Marvin Hinton, Ronald Harris, Peter Houseman, George Graham, Peter Osgood, Charles Cooke, Robert Tambling.   Manager: Thomas Docherty

CF BARCELONA: Miguel REINA Santos; Julio César BENÍTEZ Amoedo, ELADIO Silvestre Graells, Ramón MONTESINOS Calaf, Francisco Fernández Rodríguez "GALLEGO", Antonio TORRES García, Joaquín RIFÉ Climent, Lucien MULLER Schmidt, José Antonio ZALDÚA Urdanavia, José María FUSTÉ Blanch, Pedro ZABALLA Barquín Marín. Eladio sent off (40).   Trainer: Roque Olsen

Goals: Torres (70 og), Reina (76 og)

CF BARCELONA v CHELSEA LONDON 5-0 (3-0)

Camp Nou, Barcelona   25.05.66

Referee: Kurt Tschentscher (WG)   Attendance: 40,000

CF BARCELONA: Salvador SADURNÍ Urpi; Alfonso María Rodríguez Salas "FONCHO", ELADIO Silvestre Graells, Ramón MONTESINOS Calaf, Francisco Fernández Rodríguez "GALLEGO", Antonio TORRES García, Joaquín RIFÉ Climent, Lucien MULLER Schmidt, José Antonio ZALDÚA Urdanavia, José María FUSTÉ Blanch, Pedro ZABALLA Barquín Marín. Trainer: Roque Olsen

CHELSEA: Peter Bonetti; Joseph Kirkup, Alan Harris, John Hollins, Marvin Hinton, Ronald Harris, John Boyle, George Graham, Peter Osgood, Charles Cooke, Robert Tambling. Manager: Thomas Docherty

Goals: Fusté (5, 74), Zaballa (18), Rifé (43, 50)

FINAL

CF BARCELONA v REAL ZARAGOZA 0-1 (0-1)

Camp Nou, Barcelona   14.09.66

Referee: István Zsolt (Hun)   Attendance: 50,000

CF BARCELONA: Salvador SADURNÍ Urpi; Julio César BENÍTEZ Amoedo, ELADIO Silvestre Graells, Ramón MONTESINOS Calaf, Francisco Fernández Rodríguez "GALLEGO", Antonio TORRES García, Pedro ZABALLA Barquín Marín, Lucien MULLER Schmidt, José Antonio ZALDÚA Urdanavia, José María FUSTÉ Blanch, Luis VIDAL Planella.   Trainer: Roque Olsen (Arg)

REAL ZARAGOZA: Enrique YARZA Sorlauce; José Ramón IRUSQUIETA García, Severino REIJA Vázquez, Antonio PAÍS Castroagudín, Francisco SANTAMARÍA Briones; José Luis VIOLETA Lajusticia, Darcy Silveira dos Santos "CANARIO"; Eleuterio SANTOS Brito, MARCELINO Martínez Cao, Juan Manuel VILLA Gutiérrez, Carlos LAPETRA Coarasa. Trainer: Ferdinand Daučik (Cze)

Goal: Canario (40)

REAL ZARAGOZA
v CF BARCELONA 2-4 (1-1, 2-3)

La Romareda, Zaragoza   21.09.66

Referee: Concetto lo Bello (Ita)   Attendance: 33,000

REAL ZARAGOZA: Enrique YARZA Sorlauce; José Ramón IRUSQUIETA García, Severino REIJA Vázquez, Antonio PAÍS Castroagudin, Francisco SANTAMARÍA Briones; José Luis VIOLETA Lajusticia, Darcy Silveira dos Santos "CANARIO"; Eleuterio SANTOS Brito, MARCELINO Martínez Cao, Juan Manuel VILLA Gutiérrez, Carlos LAPETRA Coarasa.
Trainer: Fernando Daučik

CF BARCELONA: Salvador SADURNÍ Urpi; Alfonso María Rodríguez Salas "FONCHO", ELADIO Silvestre Graells, Ramón MONTESINOS Calaf, Francisco Fernández Rodríguez "GALLEGO"; Antonio TORRES García, Pedro ZABALLA Barquín Marín; Pedro MAS Pujol, José Antonio ZALDÚA Urdanavia, José María FUSTÉ Blanch, Luis PUJOL Codina.
Trainer: Roque Olsen

Canario and Torres sent off (89)

Goals: Pujol (3, 86, 120), Marcelino (24, 87), Zaballa (70)

Goalscorers Fairs Cup 1965/66

7 goals: Karl-Heinz Thielen (FC Köln), Friedhelm Konietzka (München 1860), José Antonio ZALDÚA Urdanavia (CF Barcelona)

6 goals: Johannes Löhr (FC Köln), MARCELINO Martínez Cao (Real Zaragoza)

5 goals: João de Matos Moura Lourenço (Sporting Lisboa), Hans Rebele (München 1860), Robert Paton (Dunfermline), Juan MUÑOZ Cerdá, WALDO Machado da Silva (Valencia CF)

4 goals: Erich Hof (Wiener SK), Hans Siemensmeyer (Hannover 96), Rudolf Brunnenmeier (München 1860), Luis PUJOL Codina, Joaquín RIFÉ Climent, José María FUSTÉ Blanch (CF Barcelona), Eleuterio Santos (Real Zaragoza), Alexander Ferguson (Dunfermline), José María Sánchez RODILLA (Español), Joaquim António Oliveira Duarte, Ernesto Figueiredo (Sporting Lisboa)

3 goals: Mladen Vaha (NK Zagreb), Wolfgang Gayer (Wiener SK), Kurt Hamrin (Fiorentina), Donald Kerrigan, William Wallace (Hearts), Béla Kuharszki, Ferenc Bene (Újpesti Dózsa), Peter Grosser, Alfred Heiss (München 1860), William Bremner, Peter Lorimer (Leeds United), Darcy Canario, Carlos Lapetra, Juan Manuel VILLA Gutiérrez (Zaragoza), Amas (Español), George Graham, Peter Osgood, Terence Venables (Chelsea), Pedro ZABALLA Barquín Marín (CF Barcelona)

2 goals: Thompson (Glentoran), Harris (Everton), Backman (AIK Solna), Peres (Sporting Lisboa), Manuel Antonio (FC Porto), Ertan (Göztepe), Bertini (Fiorentina), Anderson (Hearts), Goran, Ivăncescu (Steagul Roşu), Hradský, Lichtnégl (Spartak Brno), Krauthausen, Overath, Neumann, Sturm (FC Köln), Bandura, Nix (Hannover 96), Daina, Georgy (Servette),

Fortunato, Angelillo, Sormani (Milan), A. Dunai II, Solymosi (Újpesti Dózsa), Fleming (Dunfermline), Van de Velde, Segers (Antwerp), José María, Miralles (Español), J. Charlton (Leeds United), Tambling (Chelsea), Guillot (Valencia CF)

1 goal: Demarteau (FC Liège), Filippou, Konstantinidis (Aris Thessaloniki), Scott, McNamee (Hibernian), Milosević (Crvena Zvezda), Koudas, Mouratidis (PAOK), Van der Linden (DOS Utrecht), Abossolo (Bordeaux), Hauss, Farias, Szczepaniak (Strasbourg), Randoux (Daring Club Brussel), Hamilton (Glentoran), Kanchev (Lokomotiv Plovdiv), Greif (FC Nürnberg), Orlando (Torino), P. Knudsen (Vålerengen), Gabriel (Everton), P. Petersen, C. Andersen (B 1903), Ohlsson, Eriksson, Carlsson, Nilden (AIK Solna), Ferreira Pinto (Sporting Lisboa), Pinto (FC Porto), Cengiz (Göztepe), Tuohy, Fullam (Shamrock Rovers Dublin), Azinovic (NK Zagreb), Rafreider (Wiener SK), Frenzel (SC Leipzig), De Sisti, Nuti, Pirovano, Brugnera (Fiorentina), Hauser, Benthaus (FC Basel), Fernando, Abalroado (CUF Barreiro), Traynor (Hearts), Zaharia, Pescaru, Năftănăilă, Haşoti (Steagul Roşu), Chaloupka, Vojta (Spartak Brno), Müller, Weber (FC Köln), Rodekamp (Hannover 96), Urtiaga, Sánchez Lage (Valencia CF), Makay, Nemeth, Schindelholz (Servette), Amarildo, Rivera, Lodetti, Benigni (Milan), Fazekas, Göröcs (Újpesti Dózsa), Kohlars, Radenkovic (TSV 1860 München), Robertson, T. Callaghan, Edwards (Dunfermline Athletic), Re, Eulogio Martínez (Español), Van Moer, Van der Wee (Antwerp), Johanneson, Cooper, Bell, Storrie, O'Grady, Peacock (Leeds United), Endériz, Reija (Zaragoza), Bridges, Murray (Chelsea), Barison (Roma), Vidal, Benítez, Vergés, Pereda (CF Barcelona)

Own Goals: Noskó (Újpesti Dózsa) for Everton, Torres & Reina (Barcelona) for Chelsea London

FAIRS CUP 1966-67

FIRST ROUND

DJURGARDEN IF STOCKHOLM
v 1.FC LOKOMOTIVE LEIPZIG 1-3 (0-1)

Klocktornet, Stockholm   24.08.66

Referee: Hans Grandlund (Nor)   Attendance: 4,200

DJURGARDEN: Ronney Pettersson; Mats Karlsson, Claes Cronqvist, Jan Erik Sjøberg, Willy Gummesson, Gösta Sandberg, Jan Ohman, Peder Persson, Kay Wiestähl, Sven Lindman, Conny Granqvist. Sub: Inge Karlsson, Jan Svensson. Trainer: Torsten Lindberg

1.FC LOKOMOTIVE: Horst Weigang; Michael Faber, Peter Giessner, Manfred Geisler; Arno Zerbe, Karl Drössler; Dieter Engelhardt, Wolfram Löwe, Henning Frenzel, Jürgen Naumann, Jörg Berger.   Trainer: Hans Studener

Goals: Frenzel (45), Löwe (53), Persson (60), Berger (63)

1.FC LOKOMOTIVE LEIPZIG
v DJURGARDEN IF STOCKHOLM 2-1 (1-0)

Zentralstadion, Leipzig   27.09.66

Referee: Jef F. Dorpmans (Hol)   Attendance: 4,200

1.FC LOKOMOTIVE: Horst Weigang; Michael Faber, Peter Giessner, Manfred Geisler; Arno Zerbe, Karl Drössler; Dieter Engelhardt, Rainer Trölitzsch, Henning Frenzel, Jürgen Naumann, Werner Gase.   Trainer: Hans Studener

DJURGARDEN: Ronney Pettersson; Rolf Fransson, Mats Karlsson, Jan Erik Sjøberg, Willy Gummesson, Claes Cronqvist, Roland Magnusson, Kay Wiestähl, Conny Granqvist, Sven Lindman, Jan Ohman.

Goals: Trölitzsch (24), Karlsson (68 og), Wiestähl (69)

FRIGG FK OSLO
v DUNFERMLINE ATHLETIC 1-3 (1-1)

Bislett, Oslo   24.08.66

Referee: Arnth Jensen (Dan)   Attendance: 6,300

FRIGG: Ebbe Gysler; Anders Svela, Åge Solvang, Jan Birch-Aune, Tore Borrehaug, Tore Fjellstad, Erik Hagen, Arne Bergersen, Eivind Ballangrund, Per Pettersen, Tor Kåre Frafjord.

DUNFERMLINE: Eric Martin; William Callaghan, Alex Totten, James Thomson, Patrick Delaney, Thomas Callaghan, Alexander Edwards, Robert Paton, James Fleming, Alexander Ferguson, Hugh Robertson.

Goals: P. Pettersen (1), T. Callaghan (36), Fleming (46, 50)

DUNFERMLINE ATHLETIC
v FRIGG OSLO 3-1 (3-1)

East End Park, Dunfermline   28.09.66

Referee: James Finney (Eng)   Attendance: 6,300

DUNFERMLINE: Eric Martin; William Callaghan, John Lunn, Roy Barry, James McLean, James Thomson, Alexander Edwards, Robert Paton, Patrick Delaney, Thomas Callaghan, Hugh Robertson.

FRIGG: Ebbe Gysler; Anders Svela, Åge Solvang, Jan Birch-Aune, Tore Borrehaug, Erik Hagen, Tore Fjellstad, Arne Bergersen, Eivind Ballangrund, Per Pettersen, Tor Kåre Frafjord.

Goals: Ballgrund (1), Delaney (10, 40), T. Callaghan (28)

WIENER SK v NAPOLI 1-2 (1-1)

Prater, Wien   1.09.66

Referee: Anton Bucheli (Swi)   Attendance: 4,000

WIENER SK: Zdravko Brkljacic; Anton Linhart, Norbert Hof; Adolf Knoll, Markovic, Helmut Weiss; Friedrich Rafreider, Erich Hof, Kurt Leitner, Peter Schmidt, Johann Hörmayer.

NAPOLI: Claudio Bandoni; Stelio Nardin, Romano Micelli, Amedeo Stenti, Dino Panzanato, Ottavio Bianchi, Jarbas Faustinho Cané, Antonio Juliano, José Altafini, Omar Enrique Sívori, Alberto Orlando.   Trainer: Bruno Pesaola

Goals: Cané (27), Knoll (42), Orlando (73)

NAPOLI v WIENER SK 3-1 (3-1)

San Paolo, Napoli   21.09.66

Referee: Marcel Deckx (Bel)   Attendance: 21,000

NAPOLI: Pacifico Cuman; Stelio Nardin, Antonio Girardo, Amedeo Stenti, Dino Panzanato, Ottavio Bianchi, Jarbas Faustinho Cané, Antonio Juliano, Gastone Bean, Omar Enrique Sívori, Paolo Braca.   Trainer: Bruno Pesaola

WIENER SK: Zdravko Brkljacic; Anton Linhart, Norbert Hof; Adolf Knoll, Markovic, Wilhelm Kainrath; Friedrich Rafreider, Erich Hof, Kurt Leitner, Peter Schmidt, Johann Hörmayer.

Goals: Cané (10), Sívori (25), Bianchi (26), Schmidt (44)

ARIS THESSALONIKI
v JUVENTUS TORINO 0-2 (0-1)

Harilaou, Thessaloniki   11.09.66

Referee: Edgar Deuschel (WG)   Attendance: 27,300

ARIS: Nikos Hristidis; Hristos Kambourlazos, Hristos Nalmpantis, Dimitris Grimbelakos, Sofoklis Semertzis, Vasilis Psifidis, Giorgos Konstantinidis, Manolis Keramidas, Stefanos Demiris, Alekos Alexiadis, Vaggelis Siropoulos.

JUVENTUS: Roberto Anzolin; Adolfo Gori, Gianfranco Leoncini, Giancarlo Bercellino, Ernesto Castano, Sandro Salvadore, Erminio Favalli, Luis Cascajares DEL SOL, Virginio De Paoli, CINESINHO Cunha Coloña, Giampaolo Menichelli.   Trainer: Heriberto Herrera

Goals: Del Sol (30), Menichelli (52)

JUVENTUS TORINO
v ARIS THESSALONIKI 5-0 (2-0)

Stadio Comunale, Torino   21.09.66

Referee: John Wright Paterson (Sco)   Attendance: 9,800

JUVENTUS: Roberto Anzolin; Adolfo Gori, Gianfranco Leoncini, Giancarlo Bercellino, Ernesto Castano, Sandro Salvadore, Erminio Favalli, Luis Cascajares DEL SOL, Virginio De Paoli, CINESINHO Cunha Coloña, Giampaolo Menichelli. Trainer: Heriberto Herrera

ARIS: Nikos Hristidis; Hristos Nalbantis, Theofanis Athanasiadis, Vasilis Psifidis, Dimitris Grimbelakos, Alekos Alexiadis, Giorgos Konstantinidis, Manolis Keramidas, Vaggelis Tsitoumis, Theodoros Spanopoulos, Vaggelis Siropoulos.

Goals: Menichelli (32), Favalli (36, 87), De Paoli (65), A. Gori (81)

DOS UTRECHT v FC BASEL 2-1 (1-1)

Galgenwaard Stadion, Utrecht   13.09.66

Referee: William J. Mullan (Sco)   Attendance: 4,100

DOS: Theo Hoogeveen; Hans De Weerd, Wietse Veenstra, Johan Plageman, Eddy Achterberg, Bennie Aarts, Joop van de Bogert, Leo De Vroet, Arie De Kuyper, Tonny Van der Linden, Henk Wery.   Trainer: Louis van der Bogert

FC BASEL: Marcel Kunz; Josef Kiefer, Bruno Michaud, Hanspeter Stocker, Markus Pfirter, Karl Odermatt, Helmut Benthaus, Anton Schnyder, Helmut Hauser, Roberto Frigerio, Aldo Moscatelli.

Goals: Odermatt (15), Stocker (18 og), Wery (65)

GÖZTEPE IZMIR v AC BOLOGNA 1-2 (0-1)

Alsançak, Izmir   11.09.66

Referee: Luben Spasov (Bul)   Attendance: 23,000

GÖZTEPE: Ali Artuner; Mehmet Aydin, Çaglayan Derebaşi, Mehmet II, Hüseyin Yazici, Nevzat Güzelirmak, Ceyhan Yazar, Ertan Öznur, Fevzi Zemzem, Gürsel Aksel, Halil Kiraz.

BOLOGNA: Rino Rado; Carlo Furlanis, Mario Ardizzon, Manlio Muccini, Francesco Janich, Romano Fogli, Marino Perani, Giacomo Bulgarelli, Harald Nielsen, Helmut Haller, Giovanni Vastola.   Trainer: Luis Antonio Carniglia

Goals: Vastola (17), Nielsen (60), Ceyhan (69)

FC BASEL v DOS UTRECHT 2-2 (0-0)

St.Jakob Stadion, Basel   21.09.66

Referee: Rudolf Kreitlein (WG)   Attendance: 6,300

FC BASEL: Marcel Kunz; Josef Kiefer, Bruno Michaud, Hanspeter Stocker, Markus Pfirter, Karl Odermatt, Helmut Benthaus, Anton Schnyder, Helmut Hauser, Roberto Frigerio, Aldo Moscatelli.

DOS: Theo Hoogeveen; Hans De Weerd, Wietse Veenstra, Johan Plageman, Eddy Achterberg, Bennie Aarts, Joop van de Bogert, Leo De Vroet, Arie De Kuyper, Tonny Van der Linden, Henk Wery.   Trainer: Louis van der Bogert

Goals: Frigerio (59, 62), Wery (69), Van der Linden (78)

AC BOLOGNA v GÖZTEPE IZMIR 3-1 (2-0)

Stadio Comunale, Bologna   28.09.66

Referee: Mathias Frisch (Lux)   Attendance: 10,100

BOLOGNA: Rino Rado; Tazio Roversi, Mario Ardizzon, Francesco Battisodo, Francesco Janich, Romano Fogli, Marino Perani, Giacomo Bulgarelli, Bruno Pace, Helmut Haller, Ezio Pascutti.   Trainer: Luis Antonio Carniglia

GÖZTEPE: Ali Artuner; Mehmet Aydin, Çaglayan Derebaşi, Mehmet II, Huseyin, Nevzat Güzelirmak, Nihat Yayöz, Ertan Öznur, Fevzi Zemzem, Gürsel Aksel, Halil Kiraz.

Goals: Pace (32, 59), Haller (36 pen), Halil (64)

OLIMPIJA LJUBLJANA
v FERENCVÁROS BUDAPEST 3-3 (1-1)

Bezigrad, Ljubljana   14.09.66

Referee: Eduard Babauczek (Aus)   Attendance: 6,900

OLIMPIJA: Anton Zabjek; Atanas Djorlev, Dragan Racić, Rasim Kokot, Miloš Šoškić, Anton Čeh, Josip Franceskin, Milovan Nikolić, Joze Zagorc, Zijad Arslanagić, Rudolf Corn.

FERENCVÁROS: István Géczi; Dezső Novák, Sándor Mátrai, Miklós Páncsics; László Horváth, Lajos Szűcs; János Karába, Gyula Rákosi, Flórián Albert, Lajos Németh, Máté Fenyvesi. Trainer: Sándor Tatrai

Goals: Albert (23, 68), Franceskin (35), Rákosi (66), Kokot (80), Arslanagić (88)

FERENCVÁROS BUDAPEST
v OLIMPIJA LJUBLJANA 3-0 (2-0)

Népstadion, Budapest 5.10.66

Referee: Pavel Spotak (Cze)   Attendance: 68,000

FERENCVÁROS: István Géczi; Dezső Novák, Sándor Mátrai, Miklós Páncsics; István Juhász; Lajos Szűcs; István Szőke, Zoltán Varga, Flórián Albert, László Rátkai, Gyula Rákosi. Trainer: Sándor Tatrai

OLIMPIJA: Borut Škulj; Atanas Djorlev, Rasim Kokot, Čedomir Jovičević; Anton Čeh, Dimitrije Srbu; Josip Franceskin, Milovan Nikolić, Joze Zagorc, Zijad Arslanagić, Rudolf Corn.

Goals: Albert (9), Rákosi (10), Varga (75)

OGC NICE v ÖRGRYTE GÖTEBORG 2-2 (0-1)

Stade du Ray, Nice 21.09.66

Referee: Fabio Monti (Ita)   Attendance: 5,566

OGC NICE: Marcel Aubour; Guy Cauvin, Gérard Segarra, Maurice Serrus, Francis Isnard, Yvon Giner, René Fioroni, Horacio Barrionuevo, Rafaël Santos, André Cristol, Charly Loubet.   Trainer: César Gonzalès

ÖRGRYTE: Åke Bergling; Helge Börjesson, Bo Åkervall, Bert Wåhlin, Vilgot Schwartz, Lars-Göran Johansson, Rolf Hansson, Anders Svensson, Agne Simonsson, Rolf Wetterlind, Claes-Olof Arvidsson.

Goals: Simonsson (42, 55), Santos (66), Loubet (80)

VfB STUTTGART v BURNLEY FC 1-1 (0-1)

Neckarstadion, Stuttgart 20.09.66

Referee: Gilbert Droz (Swi)   Attendance: 10,000

VfB: Günter Sawitzki; Siegfried Böhringer, Günter Seibold, Hartmut Weiss, Theo Hoffmann, Rudi Entenmann, Helmut Huttary, Horst Köppel, Gilbert Gress, Bo Larsson, Manfred Reiner.   Trainer: Rudi Gutendorf

BURNLEY FC: Adam Blacklaw; John Angus, Alexander Elder, Brian O'Neil, Brian Miller, Arthur Bellamy, William Morgan, Andrew Lochhead, William Irvine, Gordon Harris, Ralph Coates. O'Neil sent off (85).   Manager: Harry Potts

Goals: Irvine (17), Weiss (50 pen)

ÖRGRYTE GÖTEBORG v OGC NICE 2-1 (0-0)

Ullevi, Göteborg 27.09.66

Referee: Johannes Malka (WG)   Attendance: 3,000

ÖRGRYTE: Åke Bergling; Helge Börjesson, Bo Åkervall, Bert Wåhlin, Vilgot Schwartz, Lars-Göran Johansson, Jen Söderberg, Anders Svensson, Agne Simonsson, Rolf Wetterlind, Rolf Hansson.

OGC NICE: Marcel Aubour; Guy Cauvin, Bruno Rodzik, Maurice Serrus, Francis Isnard, Gérard Segarra, Jean-Pierre Serra, Horacio Barrionuevo, Yvon Giner, André Cristol, Charly Loubet.   Trainer: César Gonzalès

Goals: Simonsson (52), Hansson (57), Barrionuevo (83)

BURNLEY FC v VfB STUTTGART 2-0 (0-0)

Turf Moor, Burnley 27.09.66

Referee: Einar Boström (Swe)   Attendance: 23,716

BURNLEY FC: Adam Blacklaw; John Angus, John Talbot, Arthur Bellamy, Brian Miller, Samuel Todd, William Morgan, Andrew Lochhead, William Irvine, Gordon Harris, Ralph Coates.   Manager: Harry Potts

VfB: Werner Pfeiffer; Siegfried Böhringer, Theo Hoffmann, Eberhard Pfisterer, Günter Seibold, Hartmut Weiss, Gilbert Gress, Willi Entenmann, Bo Larsson, Helmut Huttary, Manfred Reiner.   Trainer: Rudi Gutendorf

Goals: Coates (57), Lochead (78)

UNION SPORTIVE LUXEMBOURG
v ANTWERP FC 0-1 (0-1)

Stade Municipal, Luxembourg 21.09.66

Referee: Pierre Schwinte (Fra)   Attendance: 1,300

US: Roland Pletschette; Gruneisen, Fernand Remakel, Jean Hardt, Ady Colas, Kohl, René Schneider, Jean-Pierre Hemmerling, Johny Leonard, Jean-Pierre Mertl, Marco Funck.

ANTWERP FC: Willy Coremans; Maurice Renier, Jozef Rens, Florent Bohez, Robert Geens, Raymond Goris, Wilfried Van Moer, Marcel Janssen, Karel Beyers, Ivan Fränkel, Theofiel van de Velde.

Goal: Van Moer (24)

ANTWERP FC
v UNION SPORTIVE LUXEMBOURG 1-0 (1-0)

Bosuil, Antwerp   28.09.66

Referee: Kurt Handwerker (WG)   Attendance: 4,000

ANTWERP FC: Willy Coremans; Maurice Renier, Florent Bohez, Robert Geens, Jozef Rens, Raymond Goris, Karel Beyers, Wilfried Van Moer, Marcel Janssen, Urbain Segers, Theofiel van de Velde.

US: Roland Pletschette, Gruneisen, Ady Colas, Kohl, Jean Hardt, René Piron, Jean-Pierre Hemmerling, René Schneider, Johny Leonard, Jean-Pierre Mertl, Marco Funck.

Goal: Janssen (29)

CRVENA ZVEZDA BEOGRAD
v ATHLETIC BILBAO 5-0 (2-0)

Crvena Zvezda Beograd   21.09.66

Referee: Gusztáv Bircsak (Hun)   Attendance: 35,000

CRVENA ZVEZDA: Dragan Racić; Aleksandar Stojanović, Živorad Jevtić, Vojislav Melić, Aleksandar Marković, Dejan Bekić, Branko Klenkovski, Stevan Ostojić, Jovan Aćimović, Trifun Mihajlović, Dragan Džajić.   Trainer: Miljan Miljanić

ATHLETIC: José Ángel IRÍBAR Cortajarena; José María ORUE Aranguren, Jesús ARANGUREN Merino, Luis María ECHEBERRÍA Igartua, Juan María ZORRIQUETA Azpiazu, José Ramón Martínez LARRAURI, Ignacio ARROYO, Luis María AGUIRRE Vidaurrazaga, Ignacio ARIETA Araunabeña Piedra, José María ARGOITIA Acha, Nicolás ESTÉFANO Montalbán.   Trainer: Agustin Gainza

Goals: Mihajlović (30), Džajić (40, 58 pen), Ostojić (76), Melić (87)

ATHLETIC BILBAO
v CRVENA ZVEZDA BEOGRAD 2-0 (0-0)

Estadio San Mamés, Bilbao   28.09.66

Referee: Roger Barde (Fra)   Attendance: 21,500

ATHLETIC: José Ángel IRÍBAR Cortajarena; José María CENITAGOYA Urien, Jesús ARANGUREN Merino, José Ramón Martínez LARRAURI, Luis María ECHEBERRÍA Igartua, Urra, Ignacio ARROYO, Luis María AGUIRRE Vidaurrazaga, Ignacio ARIETA Araunabeña Piedra, Nicolás ESTÉFANO Montalbán, Pedro LAVÍN Arcocha.   Trainer: Agustin Gainza

CRVENA ZVEZDA: Ratomir Dujković; Aleksandar Stojanović, Živorad Jevtić, Vojislav Melić, Aleksandar Marković, Dejan Bekić, Branko Klenkovski, Stevan Ostojić, Jovan Aćimović, Trifun Mihajlović, Dragan Džajić.   Trainer: Miljan Miljanić

Goals: Estéfano (54, 88)

FC PORTO v GIRONDINS de BORDEAUX 2-1 (0-0)

Estádio das Antas, Porto   21.09.66

Referee: Manuel Gomez Arribas (Spa)   Attendance: 16,700

FC PORTO: RUI Fernando Sousa Teixeira; CARLOS MANUEL Gomes Dias, João Luís Pinto ALMEIDA, José ROLANDO Andrade Gonçalves, David Sucena; Fernando Neves Pavão, Carlos Baptista; JAIME Ferreira Silva, Djalma Freitas, João CUSTÓDIO PINTO, Francisco Lage Pereira da NOBREGA.   Trainer: José Maria Pedroto

GIRONDINS: Christian Montes; Gilbert Moevi, André Chorda, Bernard Baudet, Claude Rey, Guy Calleja, Yves Texier, Mohamed Abdelkader Tayeb, Didier Couécou, Gabriel Abossolo, Laurent Robuschi.   Trainer: Salvador Artigas

Goals: Pinto (58 pen), Pavão (70), Robuschi (82)

GIRONDINS de BORDEAUX v FC PORTO 2-1 (1-1)

Stade Municipal, Bordeaux   5.10.66

Referee: Alessandro d'Agostini (Ita)   Attendance: 10,320

GIRONDINS: Christian Montes; Gilbert Moevi, André Chorda, Robert Peri, Bernard Baudet, Claude Rey, Guy Calleja, Yves Texier, Didier Couécou, Gabriel Abossolo, Laurent Robuschi.   Trainer: Salvador Artigas

FC PORTO: RUI Fernando Sousa Teixeira; João Eleutério Luis ATRACA, João Luís Pinto ALMEIDA, Valdemar Pacheco, David Sucena; José ROLANDO Andrade Gonçalves, Fernando Neves Pavão; MANUEL ANTÓNIO Leitão da Silva, Djalma Freitas, João CUSTÓDIO PINTO, ERNESTO Fernando Pereira.   Trainer: José Maria Pedroto

Goals: Djalma (35), Texier (40), Couécou (78)

Girondins de Bordeaux won on the toss of a coin

FC NÜRNBERG v CF VALENCIA 1-2 (1-2)

Städtisches Stadion, Nürnberg   21.09.66

Referee: Paul Schiller (Aus)   Attendance: 9,000

FC NÜRNBERG: Roland Wabra; Helmut Hilpert, Fritz Popp, Horst Leupold, Ludwig Müller, Karl-Heinz Ferschl, Manfred Greif, Franz Brungs, Heinz Strehl, Jovan Miladinovic, Georg Volkert.   Trainer: Jenő Csaknady

CF VALENCIA: José PESUDO Soler; José Antonio García Conesa "TATONO", Valentín García Pascual "TOTÓ", Francisco García Gómez "PAQUITO", Manuel MESTRE Torres, ROBERTO Gil Esteve, José CLARAMUNT Torres, WALDO Machado da Silva, Fernando ANSOLA Sanmartín, Juan Cruz SOL Oria, Manuel Polinario Muñoz "POLI".   Trainer: Edmundo Suárez Taranco "MUNDO"

Goals: Strehl (17), Claramunt (24), Waldo (41)

CF VALENCIA v FC NÜRNBERG 2-0 (2-0)

Campo de Mestalla, Valencia 5.10.66

Ref: Norman C.H. Burtenshaw (Eng)   Attendance: 50,000

CF VALENCIA: José PESUDO Soler; José Antonio García Conesa "TATONO", Alberto ARNAL Andrés, Francisco García Gómez "PAQUITO", Manuel MESTRE Torres, ROBERTO Gil Esteve, Vicente GUILLOT Fabian, WALDO Machado da Silva, Fernando ANSOLA Sanmartín, Manuel Polinario Muñoz "POLI", José CLARAMUNT Torres.
Trainer: Edmundo Suárez Taranco "MUNDO"

FC NÜRNBERG: Roland Wabra; Ferdinand Wenauer, Helmut Hilpert, Ludwig Müller, Karl-Heinz Ferschl, Fritz Popp, Heinz Müller, Tasso Wild, Manfred Greif, Franz Brungs, Georg Volkert.   Trainer: Jenő Csaknady

Goals: Ansola (3), Waldo (14 pen)

SPARTAK BRNO v DINAMO ZAGREB 2-0 (1-0)

Spartak Brno 28.09.66

Referee: Vasile Dumitrescu (Rom)   Attendance: 2,000

SPARTAK: Padúch, Bohumil Pišek, Karel Kohlík, Karel Komárek, Josef Bouška, Farmačka, Jiří Sýkora, Vlastimil Bubník, Karel Lichtnégl, Šefčík, Jaroslav Vojta.
Trainer: Karel Kolský

DINAMO: Zlatko Škorić; Rudolf Cvek, Petar Lončarić, Filip Blašković, Hrvoje Jukic, Zlatko Mesic, Andjelko Pavic, Ivica Kiš, Slaven Zambata, Stjepan Lamza, Krasnodar Rora.
Trainer: Branko Zebec

Goals: Mesić (10 og), Bubník (79)

DRUMCONDRA DUBLIN v EINTRACHT FRANKFURT 0-2 (0-2)

Dalymount Park, Dublin 21.09.66

Referee: William John Gow (Wal)   Attendance: 8,600

DRUMCONDRA: Michael Eamonn Darcy, Brian Kenny, John Bray, Gordon Atherton, Patrick McGrath, James Morrissey, Con Flanagan, Mike Jackson, J. McGrath, David Brooks, Seamus Doyle.

EINTRACHT: Egon Loy; Karl-Heinz Wirth, Dieter Lindner, Peter Blusch, Lothar Schämer, Jürgen Friedrich, Wilhelm Huberts, Helmut Kraus, Siegfried Bronnert, Jürgen Grabowski, Oskar Lotz.   Trainer: Elek Schwartz

Goals: Lotz (25, 30)

DINAMO ZAGREB v SPARTAK BRNO 2-0 (1-0, 2-0)

Maksimir, Zagreb 5.10.66

Referee: Günter Männig (DDR)   Attendance: 10,800

DINAMO: Zlatko Škorić; Rudolf Cvek, Mirko Braun, Filip Blašković, Marijan Brnčić, Zlatko Mesic, Andjelko Pavic, Hrvoje Jukic, Ivica Kiš, Slaven Zambata, Stjepan Lamza.
Trainer: Branko Zebec

SPARTAK: Padúch, Miroslav Vítů, Lehning, Karel Komárek, Josef Bouška, Farmačka, Jiří Sýkora, Vlastimil Bubník, Píšek, Karel Lichtnégl, Šefčík.   Trainer: Karel Kolský

Goals: Zambata (4), Jukić (73)

Dinamo Zagreb won on the toss of a coin

EINTRACHT FRANKFURT v DRUMCONDRA DUBLIN 6-1 (3-1)

Waldstadion, Frankfurt 5.10.66

Referee: Hubert Burguet (Bel)   Attendance: 4,500

EINTRACHT: Siegbert Feghelm; Karl-Heinz Wirth, Dieter Lindner, Peter Blusch, Lothar Schämer, Fahrudin Jusufi, Jürgen Friedrich, Helmut Kraus, Wilhelm Huberts, Wolfgang Solz, Oskar Lotz.   Trainer: Elek Schwartz

DRUMCONDRA: Michael Eamonn Darcy, Brian Kenny, John Bray, Gordon Atherton, Patrick McGrath, James Morrissey, Joe McGrath, Eddie O'Connell, Eddie Tyrell, John Whelan, Seamus Doyle.

Goals: Kraus (5, 56), Lotz (14), Whelan (20), Kenny (45 og), Huberts (60), Solz (72)

DINAMO PITEŞTI v FC SEVILL 2-0 (2-0)

1 Mai, Piteşti 28.09.66

Referee: Ratko Çanak (Jug)   Attendance: 6,900

DINAMO: Narcis Coman; Ioachim Popescu, Ion Barbu, Ilie Stelian, Constantin Olteanu; Nicolae Dobrin, Ion Ţircovnicu; Constantin Radu, Haralambie Eftimie, Nicolae Nagy, Mihai Ţurcan.   Trainer: Ştefan Vasile

FC SEVILLA: Salvador MUT; ELOY Fernández López, Manuel COSTA Sanromán, Ignacio ACHÚCARRO Ayala, Alfredo REBELLÓN Sáinz; Rafael Bautista Hernández "FELO", Pedro Antonio CABRAL Filartiga; Ángel OLIVEROS Jiménez, Alberto "PIPI" SUÁREZ Suárez, LIZARRALDE, José Carlos DIEGUEZ Bravo.   Trainer: Sabino Barinaga

Goals: Radu (2), Nagy (10)

FC SEVILLA v DINAMO PITEŞTI 2-2 (1-0)

Ramón Sánchez Pizjuan, Sevilla 5.10.66

Referee: Aníbal da Silva Oliveira (Por), Mariano Medina Iglesias, Quinta (Spa) Attendance: 36,000

FC SEVILLA: Salvador MUT; Antonio Rincón López "Toni", Manuel COSTA Sanromán, Alfredo REBELLÓN Sáinz; ELOY Fernández López, Ignacio ACHÚCARRO Ayala; Ángel OLIVEROS Jiménez, LIZARRALDE, Pedro Antonio CABRAL Filartiga, Alberto "PIPI" SUÁREZ Suárez, José Carlos DIÉGUEZ. Trainer: Sabino Barinaga

DINAMO: Narcis Coman; Ioachim Popescu, Ion Barbu, Ilie Stelian, Constantin Badea; Nicolae Dobrin, Ion Ţircovnicu; Constantin Radu, Nicolae Nagy, Mihai Ţurcan, Ion Prepurgel. Trainer: Ştefan Vasile

Goals: Dieguez (14), Prepurgel (65), Nagy (69), Cabral (77)

DWS AMSTERDAM v LEEDS UNITED 1-3 (0-2)

Olympisch, Amsterdam 18.10.66

Referee: Anton Bucheli (Swi) Attendance: 7,000

DWS: Jan Jongbloed; Jan Van der Zande, Tonny Adam, Theo Cornwall, André Pijlman, Jos Vonhof, Piet Boogaard, Pim Waaijenberg, Piet Kruiver, Frans Geurtsen, Rob Rensenbrink. Trainer: László Zalai

UNITED: Gary Sprake; Paul Reaney, Jack Charlton, William Bell, Norman Hunter, William Bremner, Michael O'Grady, James Greenhoff, Paul Madeley, John Giles, Albert Johanneson. Manager: Don Revie

Goals: Bremner (11), Johanneson (27), Greenhoff (46), Boogaard (90)

SECOND ROUND

1.FC LOKOMOTIVE LEIPZIG v RFC LIÈGE 0-0

Zentralstadion, Leipzig 12.10.66

Referee: Josef Tittl (Aus) Attendance: 6,700

1.FC LOKOMOTIVE: Horst Weigang; Michael Faber, Peter Giessner, Manfred Geisler; Karl Drössler, Arno Zerbe; Dieter Engelhardt, Rainer Trölitzsch, Henning Frenzel, Jürgen Naumann, Wolfram Löwe. Trainer: Hans Studener

RFC LIÈGE: Guy Delhasse; Yves Baré, Albert Sulon, Emile Lejeune, Auguste Goessens, Gérard Sulon, Henri Depireux, Günther Genschick, Jacky Stockman, Georget Bertoncello, René Andries.

LEEDS UNITED v DWS AMSTERDAM 5-1 (3-0)

Elland Road, Leeds 26.10.66

Referee: Kurt Handwerker (WG) Attendance: 27,096

UNITED: Gary Sprake; Paul Reaney, William Bell, William Bremner, Jack Charlton, Norman Hunter, James Storrie, Paul Madeley, James Greenhoff, John Giles, Albert Johanneson. Manager: Don Revie

DWS: Piet Schrijvers; Jan Van der Zande, Theo Cornwall, Jan Van de Weijer, André Pijlman, Jos Vonhof, Gérard Hoogenbirk, Frans Geurtsen, Pim Waaijenberg, Piet Kruiver, Rob Rensenbrink. Trainer: László Zalai

Goals: Johanneson (20, 33, 75), Giles (42 pen), Geurtsen (55), Madeley (65)

RFC LIÈGE v 1.FC LOKOMOTIVE LEIPZIG 1-2 (0-1)

Stade Rocourt, Liège 1.11.66

Referee: George McCabe (Eng) Attendance: 13,700

RFC LIÈGE: Guy Delhasse; Yves Baré, Albert Sulon, Emile Lejeune, Auguste Goessens, Gérard Sulon, Denis Houf, Günther Genschick, Jacky Stockman, Horatio Schéna, Henri Depireux.

1.FC LOKOMOTIVE: Horst Weigang; Christoph Franke, Peter Giessner, Manfred Geisler; Michael Faber, Karl Drössler; Dieter Engelhardt, Arno Zerbe, Henning Frenzel, Jürgen Naumann, Wolfram Löwe. Trainer: Hans Studener

Goals: Löwe (31, 66), Genschick (65)

ARA LA GANTOISE v GIRONDINS de BORDEAUX 1-0 (0-0)

Jules Otten stadion, Gand 19.10.66

Referee: Adrianus Aalbrecht (Hol) Attendance: 3,600

ARA LA GANTOISE: Dzenko Vukasovic; Antoine Devreese, Roger Debaets, Lucien Ghellynck, Richard Denaeyer, Roger Tavernier, Norbert Deviaene, Rudi Lippens, Piet Van der Lippe, André De Vos, Eric Lambert.

GIRONDINS: Christian Montes; Robert Peri, Bernard Baudet, Guy Calleja, Claude Rey, Jean-Louis Leonetti, Hector De Bourgoing, Jean-François Villa, Henri Duhayot, Roland Guillas, Jean-Louis Masse. Trainer: Salvador Artigas

Goal: Lippens (80)

GIRONDINS de BORDEAUX v ARA LA GANTOISE 0-0

Stade Municipal, Bordeaux   25.10.66

Referee: Gilbert Droz (Swi)   Attendance: 4,600

GIRONDINS: Christian Montes; Gilbert Moevi, André Chorda, Robert Peri, Bernard Baudet, Guy Calleja, Hervé Othily, Jean-Louis Leonetti, Didier Couécou, Roland Guillas, Laurent Robuschi.   Trainer: Salvador Artigas

ARA LA GANTOISE: Dzenko Vukasovic; Lucien Ghellynck, Roger Debaets, Herman Vermeulen, Richard Denaeyer, Roger Tavernier, Norbert Deviaene, Rudi Lippens, Piet Van der Lippe, André De Vos, Eric Lambert.

LAUSANNE SPORTS v BURNLEY FC 1-3 (1-2)

Stade Olympique de la Pontaise, Lausanne   19.10.66

Referee: Gerhard Kunze (DDR)   Attendance: 4,000

LAUSANNE SPORTS: René Schneider; André Grobéty, Kurt Hunziker, Anton Weibel, Ely Tacchella, Richard Dürr, Pierre-Albert Chapuisat, Pierre Kerkhoffs, Robert Hosp, Kurt Armbruster, Jacques Fragniere.   Trainer: Karl Rappan

BURNLEY FC: Adam Blacklaw; John Angus, Alexander Elder, Brian O'Neil, John Talbut, Brian Miller, William Morgan, Andrew Lochhead, Arthur Bellamy, Gordon Harris, Ralph Coates.   Manager: Harry Potts

Goals: Armbruster (17), Coates (29), Harris (44), Lochead (87)

BURNLEY FC v LAUSANNE SPORTS 5-0 (2-0)

Turf Moor, Burnley   25.10.66

Referee: William J. Gow (Wal)   Attendance: 18,573

BURNLEY FC: Adam Blacklaw; John Angus, Alexander Elder, Brian O'Neil, John Talbut, Brian Miller, William Morgan, Andrew Lochhead, Arthur Bellamy, Gordon Harris, William Irvine.   Manager: Harry Potts

LAUSANNE SPORTS: René Künzi; André Grobety, Anton Weibel, Richard Dürr, Bruno Lüthi, Kurt Hunziker, Albert Bonny, Pierre-Albert Chapuisat, Pierre Kerkhoffs, Kurt Armbruster, Gilbert Fuchs.   Trainer: Karl Rappan

Goals: Lochead (26, 32, 74), O'Neil (55), Irvine (59)

FC TOULOUSE v DINAMO PITEŞTI 3-0 (3-0)

Municipal, Toulouse   19.10.1966

Referee: João Pinto Ferreira (Por)   Attendance: 5,000

FC TOULOUSE: André Giussepin; Hervé Cros, Jean-Antoine Redin, Carlos Monnin, Michel Turraud; Régis Bruneton, Max Richard; Philippe Le Donche, Abderrhaman Soukhane, Jacques Bernard, Pierre Dorsini.   Trainer: Kader Firoud

DINAMO: Narcis Coman; Ioachim Popescu, Ion Barbu, Ilie Stelian, Constantin Badea; Nicolae Dobrin, Ion Ţircovnicu; Constantin Radu, Nicolae Nagy, Mihai Ţurcan, Ion Prepurgel.   Trainer: Ştefan Vasile

Goals: Soukhane (32), Dorsini (42, 44)

DINAMO PITEŞTI v FC TOULOUSE 5-1 (1-1)

1 Mai, Piteşti   26.10.66

Referee: Fabio Monti; Antonio Varengo, Alberto Picasso (Ita)   Attendance: 15,000

DINAMO: Narcis Coman; Ioachim Popescu, Ion Barbu, Ilie Stelian, Constantin David; Nicolae Dobrin, Ion Prepurgel, Constantin Ionescu, Haralambie Eftimie, Mihai Ţurcan, Constantin Radu.   Trainer: Ştefan Vasile

FC TOULOUSE: André Giussepin; Hervé Cros, Jean-Antoine Redin, Carlos Monnin, Michel Turraud; Régis Bruneton, Max Richard; Edouard Wojciak, Abderrhaman Soukhane, Jacques Bernard, Pierre Dorsini.   Trainer: Kader Firoud

Sent off: I. Popescu (11), Dorsini (11)

Goals: David (19), Wojciak (42), Dobrin (50), Radu (55, 59), Ţurcan (90)

ÖRGRYTE GÖTEBORG v FERENCVÁROS BUDAPEST 0-0

Ullevi, Göteborg   19.10.66

Referee: Rolf Hansen (Nor)   Attendance: 5,000

ÖRGRYTE: Åke Bergling; Rolf Wetterlind, Helge Börjesson, Vilgot Schwartz; Bert Wåhlin, Lars-Göran Johansson; Rune Börjesson, Anders Svensson, Agne Simonsson, Rolf Hansson, Claes-Olof Arvidsson.

FERENCVÁROS: István Géczi; Dezső Novák, Sándor Mátrai, Miklós Páncsics; István Juhász, Lajos Szűcs; János Karába, Zoltán Varga, Flórián Albert, László Rátkai, Gyula Rákosi.   Trainer: Sándor Tatrai

FERENCVÁROS BUDAPEST v ÖRGRYTE GÖTEBORG 7-1 (3-0)

Népstadion, Budapest   2.11.66

Referee: Sterev (Bul)   Attendance: 15,000

FERENCVÁROS: István Géczi; Dezső Novák, Miklós Páncsics, László Horváth; István Juhász, Lajos Szűcs; János Karába, Lajos Németh, Flórián Albert, Gyula Rákosi, István Szőke.   Trainer: Sándor Tatrai

ÖRGRYTE: Lars-Olof Gunsskog; Helge Börjesson, Kent Bäck, Vilgot Schwartz; Bert Wåhlin, Lars-Göran Johansson; Carry Magnusson, Rolf Hansson, Rolf Wetterlind, Rune Börjesson, Lindberg.

Goals: Németh (2, 54), Albert (10, 26, 49, 80), Szőke (70), Magnusson (60)

ANTWERP FC v FC KILMARNOCK 0-1 (0-1)

Bosuil, Antwerp   25.10.66

Referee: Gunnar Michaelsen (Dan)   Attendance: 8,800

ANTWERP FC: Willy Coremans; Maurice Renier, Florent Bohez, Robert Geens, Jozef Rens, Raymond Goris, Wilfried Van Moer, Karel Beyers, Theofiel van de Velde, Ivan Fränkel, Urbain Segers.

FC KILMARNOCK: Robert Ferguson, Andrew King, James McFadzean, Pat O'Connor, John McGrory, Frank Beattie, Thomas McLean, John McInally, Carl Bertelsen, Gerald Queen, Craig Watson.   Manager: Malcolm MacDonald

Goal: McInally (15)

FC KILMARNOCK v ANTWERP FC 7-2 (3-0)

Rugby Park, Kilmarnock   2.11.66

Referee: Roger Machin (Fra)   Attendance: 14,000

FC KILMARNOCK: Robert Ferguson, Andrew King, James McFadzean, Pat O'Connor, John McGrory, Frank Beattie, Thomas McLean, John McInally, Carl Bertelsen, Gerald Queen, Craig Watson.   Manager: Malcolm MacDonald

ANTWERP FC: Willy Coremans; Maurice Renier, Florent Bohez, Robert Geens, Jozef Rens, Raymond Goris, Wilfried Van Moer, Karel Beyers, Theofiel van de Velde, Ivan Fränkel, Urbain Segers.

Goals: McInally (6, 49), Queen (17 pen, 51), T. McLean (33 pen, 48), Watson (69), Beyers (73), Van de Velde (79)

B 1909 ODENSE v NAPOLI 1-4 (0-2)

Odense Stadium   25.10.66

Referee: John Adair (NIr)   Attendance: 3,700

B 1909: Erik Bertelsen; Mogens Engstrøm, Jørgen Rask, Arno Hansen, E.Hansen, Poul Eriksen, Per Jacobsen, Mogens Håstrup, Jørgen, Jørgen Thura Hansen, Torben Hansen.

NAPOLI: Pacifico Cuman; Pietro Adorni, Romano Micelli, Flavio Emoli, Dino Panzanato, Amedeo Stenti, Jarbas Faustinho Cané, Antonio Juliano, José Altafini, Omar Enrique Sívori, Alberto Orlando.   Trainer: Bruno Pesaola

Goals: Sívori (9, 20), Haastrup (48), Altafini (49), Cané (52)

NAPOLI v B 1909 ODENSE 2-1 (0-1)

San Paolo, Napoli   2.11.66

Referee: Kurt Tschenscher (WG)   Attendance: 25,000

NAPOLI: Pacifico Cuman (46 Claudio Bandoni); Pietro Adorni, Romano Micelli, Pierluigi Ronzon, Dino Panzanato, Flavio Emoli, Alberto Orlando, Francesco Volpato, José Altafini, Omar Enrique Sívori, Paolo Braca.   Trainer: Bruno Pesaola

B 1909: Erik Bertelsen (46 Svend Aage Rask); Mogens Engström, Jørgen Rask, Erling Linde Larsen, Leif Frandsen, Mogens Håstrup, Arno Hansen, Jørgen Thura Hansen, Palle Kähler, Per Jacobsen, Poul Eriksen.

Goals: Haastrup (8), Braca (84), Altafini (85)

CF BARCELONA v DUNDEE UNITED 1-2 (0-1)

Camp Nou, Barcelona   25.10.66

Referee: Josip Dragomir Horvath (Jug)   Attendance: 16,800

CF BARCELONA: Salvador SADURNÍ Urpi; Julio César BENÍTEZ Amoedo, Francisco Fernández Rodríguez "GALLEGO", ELADIO Silvestre Graells, José María FUSTÉ Blanch, Antonio TORRES García, Jesús María PEREDA Ruiz de Temiño, Lucien MULLER Schmidt, José Antonio ZALDÚA Urdanavia, Narciso MARTÍ FILOSÍA, Joaquín RIFÉ Climent.   Trainer: Roque Olsen

DUNDEE: Sandy Davie; Thomas Millar, James Briggs, Thomas Neilson, Douglas Smith, Lennart Wing, Finn Seeman, William Hainey, Ian Mitchell, Dennis Gillespie, Orjan Persson.   Manager: Jerry Kerr

Goals: Hainey (13), Seeman (58 pen), Fusté (82)

DUNDEE UNITED v CF BARCELONA 2-0 (1-0)

Tannadice Park, Dundee 16.11.66

Referee: Robert Schaut (Bel)   Attendance: 28,000

DUNDEE: Sandy Davie; Thomas Millar, James Briggs, Thomas Neilson, Lennart Wing, Douglas Smith, Finn Seeman, William Hainey, Ian Mitchell, Dennis Gillespie, Orjan Persson. Manager: Jerry Kerr

CF BARCELONA: Salvador SADURNÍ Urpi; Julio César BENÍTEZ Amoedo, Alfonso María Rodríguez Salas "FONCHO", Ramón MONTESINOS Calaf, Francisco Fernández Rodríguez "GALLEGO", Antonio TORRES García, Joaquín RIFÉ Climent, Lucien MULLER Schmidt, Luis VIDAL Planella, José María FUSTÉ Blanch, Pedro María ZABALLA Barquín.   Trainer: Roque Olsen

Goals: Mitchell (17), Hainey (48)

DUNFERMLINE ATHLETIC
v DINAMO ZAGREB 4-2 (1-1)

East End Park, Dunfermline 26.10.66

Referee: Patrick J. Graham (Eire)   Attendance: 8,900

DUNFERMLINE: Eric Martin, William Callaghan, John Lunn, Roy Barry, James McLean, Thomas Callaghan, Alexander Edwards, James Fleming, Patrick Delaney, Alexander Ferguson, Hugh Robertson.

DINAMO: Zlatko Škorić; Rudolf Cvek, Mirko Braun, Branko Gračanin, Marijan Brnčić, Marijan Novak, Hrvoje Jukic, Slaven Zambata, Josip Gucmirtl, Krasnodar Rora, Filip Blašković. Trainer: Branko Zebec

Goals: Delaney (7), Gucmirtl (11), Zambata (55), Edwards (59 pen), Ferguson (75, 83)

DINAMO ZAGREB
v DUNFERMLINE ATHLETIC 2-0 (1-0)

Maksimir, Zagreb 2.11.66

Referee: Tibor Wotava (Hun)   Attendance: 7,000

DINAMO: Zlatko Škorić; Rudolf Cvek, Zlatko Mesic, Branko Gračanin, Marijan Brnčić, Filip Blašković, Marijan Novak, Hrvoje Jukic, Slaven Zambata, Josip Gucmirtl, Krasnodar Rora.   Trainer: Branko Zebec

DUNFERMLINE: Eric Martin, William Callaghan, John Lunn, Roy Barry, James McLean, Thomas Callaghan, Alexander Edwards, James Fleming, Patrick Delaney, Alexander Ferguson, Hugh Robertson.

Goals: Zambata (32, 77)

CF VALENCIA
v CRVENA ZVEZDA BEOGRAD 1-0 (0-0)

Campo de Mestalla, Valencia 25.10.66

Referee: Bruno de Marchi (Ita)   Attendance: 33,300

CF VALENCIA: José PESUDO Soler; Juan Cruz SOL Oria, Francisco VIDAGAÑY Hernández, Francisco García Gómez «PAQUITO», Manuel MESTRE Torres, ROBERTO Gil Esteve, José CLARAMUNT Torres, WALDO Machado da Silva, Fernando ANSOLA Sanmartín, Manuel Polinario Muñoz «POLI», Juan MUÑOZ Cerdá.
Trainer: Edmundo Suárez Taranco "MUNDO"

CRVENA ZVEZDA: Dragan Racić; Milan Čop, Živorad Jevtić, Vojislav Melić, Aleksandar Marković, Dejan Bekić, Branko Klenkovski, Jovan Aćimović, Vojin Lazarević, Trifun Mihajlović, Dragan Džajić.

Goal: Ansola (69)

CRVENA ZVEZDA BEOGRAD
v CF VALENCIA 1-2 (0-2)

Crvena Zvezda Beograd 3.11.66

Referee: Sándor Káposi (Hun)   Attendance: 65,000

CRVENA ZVEZDA: Dragan Racić; Milan Čop, Živorad Jevtić, Vojislav Melić, Aleksandar Marković, Dejan Bekić, Branko Klenkovski, Stevan Ostojić, Vojin Lazarević, Trifun Mihajlović, Dragan Džajić.

CF VALENCIA: José PESUDO Soler; Juan Cruz SOL Oria, Francisco VIDAGAÑY Hernández; Francisco García Gómez "PAQUITO", Manuel MESTRE Torres, ROBERTO Gil Esteve; José CLARAMUNT Torres, WALDO Machado da Silva, Fernando ANSOLA Sanmartín, Manuel Polinario Muñoz "POLI", Vicente GUILLOT Fabian.
Trainer: Edmundo Suárez Taranco "MUNDO"

Goals: Waldo (40, 44), Ostojic (59)

SPARTAK PLOVDIV v BENFICA LISBOA 1-1 (1-1)

9 Septemvri, Plovdiv 26.10.66

Referee: Alois Obtulovič (Cze)   Attendance: 30,000

SPARTAK: Iordan Stankov; Ivan Ivanov, Tobia Momin, Stoian Maznev, Dimov; Georgi Valkov, Georgi Benchev, Dimitar Genov, Hristo Dishkov, Atanas Atanasov, Petar Kolev.

BENFICA: Alfredo NASCIMENTO; Domiciano Barrocal Gomes CAVÉM (Cap), RAÚL Martins Machado, JACINTO José Martins Godinho Santos, Fernando da Conceição CRUZ; JAIME da Silva GRAÇA, JORGE de Oliveira CALADO; JOSÉ AUGUSTO Pinto de Almeida, José Augusto da Costa Senica TORRES, EUSÉBIO Ferreira da Silva, António Fernandes "YAÚCA".   Trainer: Fernando Riera

Goals: Eusébio (4), Dishkov (30)

BENFICA LISBOA v SPARTAK PLOVDIV 3-0 (0-0)

Estádio da Luz, Lisboa 21.11.66

Referee: John Wright Paterson (Sco)   Attendance: 14,200

BENFICA: Alfredo NASCIMENTO; Domiciano Barrocal Gomes CAVÉM (Cap), RAÚL Martins Machado, JACINTO José Martins Godinho Santos, AUGUSTO Lamela da SILVA, JAIME da Silva GRAÇA, JORGE de Oliveira CALADO, JOSÉ AUGUSTO Pinto de Almeida, José Augusto da Costa Senica TORRES, EUSÉBIO Ferreira da Silva, António José SIMÕES da Costa.   Trainer: Fernando Riera

SPARTAK: Iordan Stankov; Ivan Ivanov, Tobia Momin, Dimitar Dimov, Stoian Maznev, Georgi Valkov, Georgi Benchev, Dimitar Genov, Hristo Dishkov, Atanas Atanasov, Georgiev.

Goals: Eusébio (53), Torres (55), Dimov (76 og)

SPARTA PRAHA v AC BOLOGNA 2-2 (1-1)

Stadión na Letnej, Praha 26.10.66

Referee: Gösta Lindberg (Swe)   Attendance: 12,300

SPARTA: Antonín Kramerius; Josef Vojta, Jiří Tichý, Hudcovský, Václav Migas, Laciga, Tomás Pospíchal, Josef Jurkanin, Andrej Kvašnák, Václav Mašek, Pavel Dyba. Trainer: Václav Ježek

BOLOGNA: Giuseppe Spalazzi; Carlo Furlanis, Mario Ardizzon, Manlio Muccini, Francesco Janich, Romano Fogli, Faustino Turra, Giacomo Bulgarelli, Harald Nielsen, Helmut Haller, Ezio Pascutti.   Trainer: Luis Antonio Carniglia

Goals: Turra (3), Mašek (10), Haller (70 pen), Pospichal (81)

AC BOLOGNA v SPARTA PRAHA 2-1 (1-1)

Stadio Comunale, Bologna 27.11.66

Referee: Erich Linemayr (Aus)   Attendance: 12,400

BOLOGNA: Giuseppe Vavassori; Carlo Furlanis, Mario Ardizzon, Faustino Turra, Francesco Janich, Romano Fogli, Giovanni Vastola, Giacomo Bulgarelli, Bruno Pace, Helmut Haller, Ezio Pascutti.   Trainer: Luis Antonio Carniglia

SPARTA: Pavel Kouba (46 Antonín Kramerius); Josef Vojta, Jiří Tichý, Laciga, Pavel Dyba, Václav Migas, Tomás Pospíchal, Josef Jurkanin, Andrej Kvašnák, Václav Mašek, Václav Vrána. Trainer: Václav Ježek

Goals: Haller (9, 46), Jurkanin (21)

DOS UTRECHT v WEST BROMWICH ALBION 1-1 (0-1)

Galgenwaard, Utrecht 2.11.66

Referee: Antoine Queudeville (Lux)   Attendance: 5,500

DOS: Theo Hoogeveen; Hans De Weerd, Eddy Achterberg, Bennie Aarts, Wietse Veenstra, Johan Plageman, Joop van de Bogert, Dick Weyman, Tonny Van der Linden, Arie De Kuyper, Henk Wery.   Trainer: Louis van der Bogert

WEST BROMWICH ALBION: Raymond Potter; Campbell Crawford, Ian Collard, Graham Lovett, Stanley Jones, Douglas Fraser, Graham Williams, Jeffrey Astle, John Kaye, Robert Hope, Clive Clark.   Manager: James Hagan

Goals: Hope (22), Van der Linden (85)

WEST BROMWICH ALBION v DOS UTRECHT 5-2 (1-0)

The Hawthorns, West Bromwich 9.11.66

Referee: Adolfo Bueno Perales (Spa)   Attendance: 19,692

WEST BROMWICH ALBION: Raymond Potter; Campbell Crawford, Ian Collard, Douglas Fraser, Stanley Jones, Graham Williams, Jeffrey Astle, Anthony Brown, John Kaye, Robert Hope, Clive Clark.   Manager: James Hagan

DOS: Theo Hoogeveen; Hans De Weerd, Eddy Achterberg, Bennie Aarts, Johan Plageman, Leo De Vroet, Wietse Veenstra, Rini Block, Joop van de Bogert, Arie De Kuyper, Henk Wery. Trainer: Louis van der Bogert

Goals: Brown (12 pen, 68, 88), Clark (51), De Vroet (58), Kaye (74), De Kuyper (77)

EINTRACHT FRANKFURT v HVIDOVRE KØBENHAVN 5-1 (1-1)

Waldstadion, Frankfurt 9.11.66

Referee: William Syme (Sco)   Attendance: 3,000

EINTRACHT: Siegbert Feghelm; Fahrudin Jusufi, Dieter Lindner, Jürgen Friedrich, Lothar Schämer, Wilhelm Huberts, Dieter Krafcyzk, Oskar Lotz, Siegfried Bronnert, Walter Bechtold, Wolfgang Solz.   Trainer: Elek Schwartz

HVIDOVRE: Jørgen Henriksen; Villy Bang Nielsen, Jørgen Jespersen, John Petersen, John Worbye, Lars Bo Henriksen, John Steen Olsen, Frits Hansen, Leif Sørensen, Allan Hebo Larsen, Knud Andersen.

Goals: Hansen (8), Lotz (18), Huberts (65), Schämer (73), Solz (81), Bronnert (86)

HVIDOVRE KØBENHAVN
v EINTRACHT FRANKFURT 2-2 (2-1)

Hvidovre, København   16.11.66

Referee: Vaclav Davidek (Cze)   Attendance: 3,800

HVIDOVRE: Jørgen Henriksen; Villy Bang Nielsen, Jørgen Jespersen, John Petersen, John Worbye, Lars Bo Henriksen, John Steen Olsen, Frits Hansen, Leif Sørensen, Allan Hebo Larsen, Knud Andersen.

EINTRACHT: Peter Kunter; Karl-Heinz Wirth, Dieter Lindner, Jürgen Friedrich, Lothar Schämer, István Sztani, Dieter Krafczyk, Oskar Lotz, Siegfried Bronnert, Wilhelm Huberts, Wolfgang Solz.   Trainer: Elek Schwartz

Goals: Bronnert (12), Larsen (18), Olsen (33), Schämer (50)

JUVENTUS TORINO v VITÓRIA SETÚBAL 3-1 (0-1)

Stadio Comunale, Torino   9.11.66

Referee: Robert Hélies (Fra)   Attendance: 3,000

JUVENTUS: Roberto Anzolin; Benito Sarti, Gianfranco Leoncini, Giancarlo Bercellino, Ernesto Castano, Sandro Salvadore, Erminio Favalli, Luis Cascajares DEL SOL, Gianfranco Zigoni, CINESINHO Cunha Coloña, Giampaolo Menichelli.   Trainer: Heriberto Herrera

VITÓRIA: Dinis Martins VITAL, Joaquim Adriao José da CONCEIÇÃO, Carlos Alberto Lourenço CARDOSO, Fernando Massano TOMÉ, Carlos TORPES Junior, Manuel Jesus Pereira Leiria, Félix Marques Guerreiro, JOSÉ MARIA Júnior, CARLOS MANUEL Ferreira Cordeiro, Augusto Martins, Pedras. Trainer: Fernando Vaz

Goals: Carlos Manuel (10), Castano (72), Favalli (75), Del Sol (88)

VITÓRIA SETÚBAL v JUVENTUS TORINO 0-2 (0-1)

Estadio do Bonfim, Setúbal   30.11.66

Referee: Ken Dagnall (Eng)   Attendance: 1,600

VITÓRIA: Dinis Martins VITAL, Joaquim Adriao José da CONCEIÇÃO, Carlos Alberto Lourenço CARDOSO, Manuel Jesus Pereira Leiria, Fernando Massano TOMÉ, Carlos TORPES Junior, HERCULANO do Carmo Oliveira, JOSÉ MARIA Júnior, Augusto Martins, Pedras, Jacinto João. Trainer: Fernando Vaz

JUVENTUS: Roberto Anzolin; Benito Sarti, Ernesto Castano, Gianfranco Leoncini, Giancarlo Bercellino, Sandro Salvadore, Erminio Favalli, Luis Cascajares DEL SOL, Gianfranco Zigoni, CINESINHO Cunha Coloña, Giampaolo Menichelli. Trainer: Heriberto Herrera

Goals: Gori (10), De Paoli (51)

THIRD ROUND

KILMARNOCK FC v ARA LA GANTOISE 1-0 (1-0)

Rugby Park, Kilmarnock   14.12.66

Referee: Bertil Lööw (Swe)   Attendance: 10,000

FC KILMARNOCK: Robert Ferguson; Andrew King, James McFadzean, Pat O' Connor, John McGrory, Frank Beattie, Thomas McLean, Gerald Queen, Eric Murray, Craig Watson, Brian McIlroy.   Manager: Malcolm MacDonald

ARA LA GANTOISE: Dzenko Vukasovic; Lucien Ghellinck, Nasret Cerkic, Herman Vermeulen, Richard Denaeyer, Roger Tavernier, Norbert Deviaene, Rudi Lippens, Piet Van der Lippe, André De Vos, Eric Lambert.

Goal: Murray (38)

ARA LA GANTOISE
v KILMARNOCK FC 1-2 (0-0, 1-0) a.e.t.

Jules Ottenstadion, Gent   21.12.66

Referee: Bruno de Marchi (Ita)   Attendance: 9,100

ARA LA GANTOISE: Dzenko Vukasovic; Antoine Devreese, Lucien Ghellinck, Herman Vermeulen, Richard Denaeyer, Roger Tavernier, Norbert Deviaene, Rudi Lippens, Piet Van der Lippe, André De Vos, Eric Lambert.

FC KILMARNOCK: Robert Ferguson; Andrew King, James McFadzean, Pat O' Connor, John McGrory, Frank Beattie, Thomas McLean, Gerald Queen, John McInally, Carl Bertelsen, Brian McIlroy.   Manager: Malcolm MacDonald

Goals: Ghellynck (78), McInally (112), T. McLean (114)

1.FC LOKOMOTIVE LEIPZIG
v BENFICA LISBOA 3-1 (1-1)

Zentralstadion, Leipzig   21.12.66

Referee: Kevin Howley (Eng)   Attendance: 68,000

1.FC LOKOMOTIVE: Horst Weigang; Christoph Franke, Peter Giessner, Manfred Geisler; Michael Faber, Karl Drössler; Dieter Engelhardt, Arno Zerbe, Henning Frenzel, Jürgen Naumann, Wolfram Löwe.   Trainer: Hans Studener

BENFICA: Alfredo NASCIMENTO; Domiciano Barrocal Gomes CAVÉM, RAÚL Martins Machado, JACINTO José Martins Godinho Santos, AUGUSTO Lamela da SILVA; JAIME da Silva GRAÇA, Mário Esteves COLUNA; NÉLSON Fernandes, JOSÉ AUGUSTO Pinto de Almeida, EUSÉBIO Ferreira da Silva, DIAMANTINO José Vieira COSTA. Trainer: Fernando Riera

Goals: Jacinto (25 og), J. Augusto (40), Frenzel (47, 51)

BENFICA LISBOA
v 1.FC LOKOMOTIVE LEIPZIG 2-1 (0-0)

Estádio da Luz, Lisboa   7.03.67

Referee: William Syme (Sco)   Attendance: 50,000

BENFICA: Alberto da COSTA PEREIRA; Domiciano Barrocal Gomes CAVÉM, RAÚL Martins Machado, JACINTO José Martins Godinho Santos, Fernando da Conceição CRUZ; JOSÉ AUGUSTO Pinto de Almeida, Mário Esteves COLUNA (Cap); António Fernandes "YAÚCA", NÉLSON Fernandes, EUSÉBIO Ferreira da Silva, António José SIMÕES da Costa. Trainer: Fernando Riera

1.FC LOKOMOTIVE: Horst Weigang; Christoph Franke, Manfred Geisler, Claus Pfeuffer; Michael Faber, Karl Drössler; Dieter Engelhardt, Arno Zerbe, Henning Frenzel, Jürgen Naumann, Wolfram Löwe.   Trainer: Hans Studener

Goals: Eusébio (65 pen, 88), Frenzel (81)

LEEDS UNITED v CF VALENCIA 1-1 (1-1)

Elland Road, Leeds   18.01.67

Referee: Hans-Joachim Weyland (WG)   Attendance: 40,644

UNITED: Gary Sprake; Paul Reaney, Paul Madeley, William Bremner, Jack Charlton, Norman Hunter, John Giles, Edward Gray, James Greenhoff, Robert Collins, Terence Cooper. Manager: Don Revie

CF VALENCIA: José PESUDO Soler (43 Ángel ABELARDO González); Juan Cruz SOL Oria, Francisco VIDAGAÑY Hernández, ROBERTO Gil Esteve, Manuel MESTRE Torres, Francisco García Gómez "PAQUITO", José CLARAMUNT Torres, WALDO Machado da Silva, Fernando ANSOLA Sanmartín, Manuel Polinario Muñoz "POLI", Vicente GUILLOT Fabian. Trainer: Edmundo Suárez Taranco "MUNDO"

Goals: Greenhoff (11), Claramunt (37)

CF VALENCIA v LEEDS UNITED 0-2 (0-1)

Campo de Mestalla, Valencia   8.02.67

Referee: Robert Hélies (Fra)   Attendance: 45,000

CF VALENCIA: José PESUDO Soler; José Antonio García Conesa «TATONO», Valentín García Pascual «TOTÓ», Francisco García Gómez «PAQUITO», Manuel MESTRE Torres, ROBERTO Gil Esteve, José CLARAMUNT Torres, WALDO Machado da Silva, Fernando ANSOLA Sanmartín, Manuel Polinario Muñoz «POLI», Vicente GUILLOT Fabian. Trainer: Edmundo Suárez Taranco «MUNDO»

UNITED: Gary Sprake; Paul Madeley, William Bell, William Bremner, Jack Charlton, Norman Hunter, John Giles, Peter Lorimer, Rodney Belfitt, Edward Gray, Terence Hibbitt. Manager: Don Revie

Goals: Giles (6), Lorimer (87)

BURNLEY FC v SSC NAPOLI 3-0 (2-0)

Turf Moor, Burnley   18.01.67

Referee: Juan Gardeazabal Garay (Spa)   Attendance: 24,519

BURNLEY FC: Harold Thomson; Frederick Smith, John Angus, Brian O'Neil, Brian Miller, Samuel Todd, William Morgan, Andrew Lochhead, Ralph Coates, Gordon Harris, Leslie Latcham.   Manager: Harry Potts

NAPOLI: Pacifico Cuman; Stelio Nardin, Romano Micelli, Amedeo Stenti, Dino Panzanato, Flavio Emoli, Jarbas Faustinho Cané, Vincenzo Montefusco, Alberto Orlando, José Altafini, Gastone Bean. Panzanato sent off (34). Trainer: Bruno Pesaola

Goals: Coates (2), Latcham (22), Lochead (51)

SSC NAPOLI v BURNLEY FC 0-0

San Paolo, Napoli   8.02.67

Referee: Gyula Emsberger (Hun)   Attendance: 40,000

NAPOLI: Claudio Bandoni; Stelio Nardin, Romano Micelli, Pierluigi Ronzon, Antonio Girardo, Ottavio Bianchi, Alberto Orlando, Antonio Juliano, José Altafini, Omar Enrique Sívori, Paolo Braca.   Trainer: Bruno Pesaola

BURNLEY FC: Harold Thomson; Frederick Smith, Samuel Todd, Brian O'Neil, Brian Miller, David Merrington, William Morgan, Andrew Lochhead, Ralph Coates, Gordon Harris, Leslie Latcham.   Manager: Harry Potts

AC BOLOGNA
WEST BROMWICH ALBION 3-0 (2-0)

Stadio Comunale, Bologna   1.02.67

Ref: Salvador HELIODORO Garcia (Por)   Attendance: 9,500

BOLOGNA: Giuseppe Vavassori; Tazio Roversi, Mario Ardizzon, Carlo Furlanis, Francesco Janich, Faustino Turra, Marino Perani, Giacomo Bulgarelli, Harald Nielsen, Helmut Haller, Ezio Pascutti.   Trainer: Luis Antonio Carniglia

WEST BROMWICH ALBION: John Osborne; Robert Cram, Graham Williams, Ian Collard, John Talbut, Douglas Fraser, Anthony Brown, Jeffrey Astle, John Kaye, Robert Hope, Clive Clark.   Manager: James Hagan

Goals: Turra (37), Nielsen (39), Haller (78)

WEST BROMWICH ALBION
v AC BOLOGNA 1-3 (0-2)

The Hawthorns, West Bromwich   8.03.67

Referee: Vital Loraux (Bel)   Attendance: 27,527

WEST BROMWICH ALBION: John Osborne; Dennis Clarke, Raymond Fairfax, Ian Collard, Edward Colquhoun, Douglas Fraser, Anthony Brown, Jeffrey Astle, John Kaye, Robert Hope, Clive Clark.   Manager: James Hagan

BOLOGNA: Giuseppe Vavassori; Tazio Roversi, Mario Ardizzon, Carlo Furlanis, Francesco Janich, Romano Fogli, Marino Perani, Giacomo Bulgarelli, Harald Nielsen, Helmut Haller, Faustino Turra.   Trainer: Luis Antonio Carniglia

Goals: Nielsen (37, 64), Bulgarelli (43), Fairfax (54)

JUVENTUS TORINO v DUNDEE UNITED 3-0 (1-0)

Stadio Comunale, Torino   8.02.67

Referee: Karl Keller (Swi)   Attendance: 6,800

JUVENTUS: Roberto Anzolin; Adolfo Gori, Gianfranco Leoncini, Benito Sarti, Ernesto Castano, Sandro Salvadore, Gianfranco Zigoni, Luis Cascajares DEL SOL, Virginio De Paoli, CINESINHO Cunha Coloña, Giampaolo Menichelli. Trainer: Heriberto Herrera

DUNDEE UNITED: Sandy Davie; Thomas Millar, James Briggs, Thomas Neilson, Douglas Smith, Lennart Wing, Finn Seeman, William Hainey, Ian Mitchell, Dennis Gillespie, Orjan Persson. Manager: Jerry Kerr

Goals: Cinesinho (27, 67), Menichelli (66)

DUNDEE UNITED v JUVENTUS TORINO 1-0 (0-0)

Tannadice Park, Dundee   8.03.67

Referee: Pieter Paulus Roomer (Hol)   Attendance: 20,500

DUNDEE UNITED: Sandy Davie; Thomas Millar, James Briggs, Thomas Neilson, Douglas Smith, Lennart Wing, William Hainey, Dennis Gillespie, Finn Dossing, Orjan Persson, Finn Seemann.   Manager: Jerry Kerr

JUVENTUS: Roberto Anzolin; Adolfo Gori, Gianfranco Leoncini, Giancarlo Bercellino, Ernesto Castano, Sandro Salvadore, Elio Rinero, Giovanni Sacco, Virginio De Paoli, CINESINHO Cunha Coloña, Giampaolo Menichelli. Trainer: Heriberto Herrera

Goal: Dossing (80)

DINAMO PITEȘTI v DINAMO ZAGREB 0-1 (0-1)

1 Mai, Pitești   19.02.67

Referee: Franz Mayer; Schlachta, Bauer (Aus)   Att: 18,000

DINAMO PITEȘTI: Narcis Coman; Constantin Badea, Ion Barbu, Ilie Stelian, Dumitru Ivan; Ion Prepurgel, Nicolae Dobrin; Constantin Radu, Mihai Țurcan, Nicolae Nagy, Ion Pop.   Trainer: Ștefan Vasile

DINAMO ZAGREB: Zlatko Škorić, Filip Blašković, Mirko Braun, Hrvoje Jukic; Marijan Brnčić, Mladen Ramljak; Stjepan Lamza, Zlatko Mesic, Slaven Zambata, Josip Gucmirtl, Krasnodar Rora.   Trainer: Branko Zebec

Goal: Zambata (17)

DINAMO ZAGREB v DINAMO PITEȘTI 0-0

Maksimir, Zagreb   1.03.67

Referee: Bruno de Marchi; Rino Possogno, Paolo Toselli (Ita) Attendance: 8,200

DINAMO ZAGREB: Zlatko Škorić; Rudolf Cvek, Mirko Braun; Hrvoje Jukic, Marijan Brnčić, Mladen Ramljak; Zlatko Mesic, Marijan Novak, Josip Gucmirtl, Ivica Kiš, Krasnodar Rora.   Trainer: Branko Zebec

DINAMO PITEȘTI: Narcis Coman; Ioachim Popescu, Nicolae Vulpeanu, Ilie Stelian, Dumitru Ivan; Nicolae Dobrin, Ion Prepurgel; Constantin Radu, Mihai Țurcan, Nicolae Nagy, Ion Pop.   Trainer: Ștefan Vasile

EINTRACHT FRANKFURT
v FERENCVÁROS BUDAPEST 4-1 (2-1)

Waldstadion, Frankfurt   21.02.67

Referee: Dragomir Josip Horvath (Jug)   Attendance: 10,000

EINTRACHT: Peter Kunter; Karl-Heinz Wirth, Dieter Lindner, Peter Blusch, Lothar Schämer; Jürgen Friedrich, Wilhelm Huberts; Jürgen Grabowski, Walter Bechtold, Ernst Abbé, Oskar Lotz.   Trainer: Elek Schwartz

FERENCVÁROS: Béla Takács; Dezső Novák, Sándor Mátrai, Miklós Páncsics, Sándor Havasi; Lajos Szűcs, János Karába; Zoltán Varga, Flórián Albert, Gyula Rákosi, Sándor Katona. Trainer: Sándor Tatrai

Goals: Lotz (4), Abbé (9, 68), Albert (45), Huberts (86)

FERENCVÁROS BUDAPEST
v EINTRACHT FRANKFURT 2-1 (1-1)

Népstadion, Budapest   28.02.67

Referee: Ken Dagnall (Eng)   Attendance: 30,000

FERENCVÁROS: István Géczi; Dezső Novák, Sándor Mátrai, Miklós Páncsics; István Juhász, Lajos Szűcs; István Szőke, Zoltán Varga, Flórián Albert, Gyula Rákosi, Máté Fenyvesi. Trainer: Sándor Tatrai

EINTRACHT: Peter Kunter; Karl-Heinz Wirth, Dieter Lindner, Jürgen Friedrich, Peter Blusch; Wilhelm Huberts, Walter Bechtold; Jürgen Grabowski, Ernst Abbé, Wolfgang Solz, Oskar Lotz.   Trainer: Elek Schwartz

Goals: Rákosi (5), Huberts (10), Novák (61 pen)

JUVENTUS TORINO v DINAMO ZAGREB 2-2 (1-1)

Stadio Comunale, Torino   29.03.67

Referee: Joseph Heymann (Swi)   Attendance: 6,000

JUVENTUS: Roberto Anzolin; Adolfo Gori, Gianfranco Leoncini, Elio Rinero, Ernesto Castano, Giovanni Sacco, Gino Stacchini, Luis Cascajares DEL SOL, Gianfranco Zigoni, CINESINHO Cunha Coloňa, Giampaolo Menichelli. Trainer: Heriberto Herrera

DINAMO: Zlatko Škorić; Rudolf Cvek, Marijan Brnčić, Zlatko Mesic, Rudolf Belin, Mladen Ramljak, Marijan Novak, Hrvoje Jukic, Josip Gucmirtl, Stjepan Lamza, Krasnodar Rora. Trainer: Branko Zebec

Goals: Zigoni (4), Jukic (13, 69), Stacchini (77)

QUARTER-FINALS

AC BOLOGNA v LEEDS UNITED 1-0 (0-0)

Stadio Comunale, Bologna   22.03.67

Referee: Gerhard Schulenburg (WG)   Attendance: 20,000

BOLOGNA: Giuseppe Vavassori; Tazio Roversi, Mario Ardizzon, Paride Tumburus, Francesco Janich, Romano Fogli, Faustino Turra, Giacomo Bulgarelli, Harald Nielsen, Helmut Haller, Ezio Pascutti.   Trainer: Luis Antonio Carniglia

UNITED: Gary Sprake; Paul Reaney, William Bell, William Bremner, Jack Charlton, Norman Hunter, Peter Lorimer, Rodney Belfitt, Paul Madeley, John Giles, Terence Cooper. Manager: Don Revie

Goal: Nielsen (64)

DINAMO ZAGREB v JUVENTUS TORINO 3-0 (1-0)

Maksimir, Zagreb   19.04.67

Referee: Paul Schiller (Aus)   Attendance: 27,900

DINAMO: Zlatko Škorić; Rudolf Cvek, Marijan Brnčić, Zlatko Mesic, Rudolf Belin, Mladen Ramljak, Marijan Novak, Hrvoje Jukic, Josip Gucmirtl, Stjepan Lamza, Krasnodar Rora. Trainer: Branko Zebec

JUVENTUS: Roberto Anzolin; Adolfo Gori, Gianfranco Leoncini, Giancarlo Bercellino, Ernesto Castano, Benito Sarti, Gino Stacchini, Luis Cascajares DEL SOL, Gianfranco Zigoni, CINESINHO Cunha Coloňa, Giampaolo Menichelli. Trainer: Heriberto Herrera

Goals: Novak (4), Mesic (67), Belin (73)

LEEDS UNITED v AC BOLOGNA 1-0 (1-0)

Elland Road, Leeds   19.04.67

Referee: Erwin Vetter (DDR)   Attendance: 42,126

UNITED: Gary Sprake; Paul Reaney, Paul Madeley, William Bell, William Bremner, Norman Hunter, John Giles, Rodney Belfitt, James Greenhoff, Edward Gray, Terence Cooper. Manager: Don Revie

BOLOGNA: Giuseppe Vavassori; Tazio Roversi, Mario Ardizzon, Carlo Furlanis, Francesco Janich, Paride Tumburus, Marino Perani, Giacomo Bulgarelli, Helmut Haller, Romano Fogli, Faustino Turra.   Trainer: Luis Antonio Carniglia

Goal: Giles (9 pen)

Leeds United won on the toss of a coin

EINTRACHT FRANKFURT
v BURNLEY FC 1-1 (1-0)

Waldstadion, Frankfurt   4.04.67

Referee: János Biroczki (Hun)   Attendance: 21,000

EINTRACHT: Peter Kunter; Fahrudin Jusufi, Dieter Lindner, Peter Blusch, Lothar Schämer, Jürgen Friedrich, Wilhelm Huberts, Jürgen Grabowski, Walter Bechtold, Wolfgang Solz, Oskar Lotz.   Trainer: Elek Schwartz

BURNLEY FC: Harold Thomson; Frederick Smith, David Merrington, Brian O'Neil, Brian Miller, Leslie Latcham, William Morgan, John Angus, Arthur Bellamy, Gordon Harris, Ralph Coates.   Manager: Harry Potts

Goals: Friedrich (35), Miller (60)

BURNLEY FC
v EINTRACHT FRANKFURT 1-2 (0-1)

Turf Moor, Burnley   18.04.67

Referee: Einar Boström (Swe)   Attendance: 25,161

BURNLEY FC: Harold Thomson; Frederick Smith, Brian Miller, David Merrington, Alexander Elder, Brian O'Neil, Arthur Bellamy, Gordon Harris, William Morgan, Leslie Latcham, Ralph Coates.   Manager: Harry Potts

EINTRACHT: Peter Kunter; Fahrudin Jusufi, Dieter Lindner, Peter Blusch, Lothar Schämer, Wilhelm Huberts, Jürgen Friedrich, Jürgen Grabowski, Ernst Abbé, Walter Bechtold, Oskar Lotz.   Trainer: Elek Schwartz

Goals: Lotz (32), Huberts (72), Miller (86)

1.FC LOKOMOTIVE LEIPZIG
v KILMARNOCK FC 1-0 (1-0)

Zentralstadion, Leipzig   19.04.67

Referee: Adrianus Aalbrecht (Hol)   Attendance: 21,000

1.FC LOKOMOTIVE: Horst Weigang; Michael Faber, Manfred Geisler, Claus Pfeuffer; Arno Zerbe, Roland Krauss; Dieter Engelhardt, Wolfram Löwe, Henning Frenzel, Jürgen Naumann, Jörg Berger.   Trainer: Hans Studener

KILMARNOCK FC: Robert Ferguson, Matthew Watson, William Dickson, Eric Murray, John McGrory, Frank Beattie, Thomas McLean, John McInally, Carl Bertelsen, Gerald Queen, Brian McIlroy.   Manager: Malcolm MacDonald

Goal: Berger (3)

KILMARNOCK FC
v 1.FC LOKOMOTIVE LEIPZIG 2-0 (1-0)

Rugby Park, Kilmarnock   26.04.67

Referee: Joseph Hannet (Bel)   Attendance: 20,000

KILMARNOCK FC: Robert Ferguson; Andrew King, James McFadzean, Eric Murray, John McGrory, Frank Beattie, Thomas McLean, John McInally, Carl Bertelsen, Craig Watson, Brian McIlroy.   Manager: Malcolm MacDonald

1.FC LOKOMOTIVE: Horst Weigang; Michael Faber, Manfred Geisler, Claus Pfeuffer; Arno Zerbe, Karl Drössler; Dieter Engelhardt, Wolfram Löwe, Henning Frenzel, Jürgen Naumann, Jörg Berger.   Trainer: Hans Studener

Goals: Murray (9) McIlroy (64)

SEMI-FINALS

LEEDS UNITED v KILMARNOCK FC 4-2 (4-2)

Elland Road, Leeds   19.05.67

Referee: Jef Dorpmans (Hol)   Attendance: 43,189

UNITED: Gary Sprake; Paul Reaney, William Bell, William Bremner, Paul Madeley, Norman Hunter, Michael O'Grady, Peter Lorimer, Rodney Belfitt, John Giles, Edward Gray.   Manager: Don Revie

KILMARNOCK FC: Robert Ferguson; Andrew King, James McFadzean, Eric Murray, John McGrory, Frank Beattie, Craig Watson, Pat O'Connor, Carl Bertelsen, Gerald Queen, Brian McIlroy.   Manager: Malcolm MacDonald

Goals: Belfitt (1, 4, 31), Giles (38 pen), McIlroy (21, 35)

KILMARNOCK FC v LEEDS UNITED 0-0

Rugby Park, Kilmarnock   24.05.67

Referee: Vital Loraux (Bel)   Attendance: 28,000

KILMARNOCK FC: Robert Ferguson; Andrew King, James McFadzean, Eric Murray, John McGrory, Frank Beattie, Thomas McLean, John McInally, Carl Bertelsen, Gerald Queen, Brian McIlroy.   Manager: Malcolm MacDonald

UNITED: Gary Sprake; Paul Reaney, William Bell, William Bremner, Paul Madeley, Norman Hunter, Peter Lorimer, Edward Gray, Rodney Belfitt, John Giles, Terence Cooper.   Manager: Don Revie

EINTRACHT FRANKFURT
v DINAMO ZAGREB 3-0 (2-0)

Waldstadion, Frankfurt   7.06.67

Referee: Michel Kitabdjian (Fra)   Attendance: 10,000

EINTRACHT: Peter Kunter; Fahrudin Jusufi, Dieter Lindner, Lothar Schämer, Jürgen Friedrich, Wilhelm Huberts, Jürgen Grabowski, Walter Bechtold, Wolfgang Solz, Oskar Lotz, Karl-Heinz Wirth.   Trainer: Elek Schwartz

DINAMO: Zlatko Škorić; Rudolf Cvek, Marijan Brnčić, Zlatko Mesic, Rudolf Belin, Mladen Ramljak, Marijan Novak, Branko Gračanin, Slaven Zambata, Stjepan Lamza, Krasnodar Rora.   Trainer: Branko Zebec

Goals: Grabowski (11 pen), Bechtold (14), Solz (67)

DINAMO ZAGREB
v EINTRACHT FRANKFURT 4-0 (2-0, 3-0)

Maksimir, Zagreb   14.06.67

Referee: Gyula Gere (Hun)   Attendance: 35,000

DINAMO: Zlatko Škorić; Filip Blašković, Marijan Brnčić, Zlatko Mesić, Rudolf Belin, Mladen Ramljak, Marijan Novak, Josip Gucmirtl, Slaven Zambata, Stjepan Lamza, Krasnodar Rora.   Trainer: Branko Zebec

EINTRACHT: Peter Kunter; Fahrudin Jusufi, Dieter Lindner, Lothar Schämer, Jürgen Friedrich, István Sztani, Wilhelm Huberts, Jürgen Grabowski, Walter Bechtold, Wolfgang Solz, Oskar Lotz.   Trainer: Elek Schwartz

Goals: Zambata (14), Novak (15), Gucmirtl (87), Belin (102 pen)

FINAL

NK DINAMO ZAGREB
v LEEDS UNITED AFC 2-0 (1-0)

Maksimir, Zagreb   30.08.67

Referee: Adolfo Bueno Perales (Spa)   Attendance: 31,800

DINAMO: Zlatko Škorić; Branko Gračanin, Marijan Brnčić, Rudolf Belin, Mladen Ramljak; Filip Blašković, Marijan Čerček; Denijal Pirić, Slaven Zambata (Cap), Josip Gucmirtl, Krasnodar Rora.   Trainer: Branko Zebec

UNITED: Gary Sprake; Paul Reaney, Terence Cooper, William Bremner (Cap), Jack Charlton; Norman Hunter, Michael Bates; Peter Lorimer, Rodney Belfitt, Edward Gray, Michael O'Grady.   Manager: Don Revie

Goals: Cercek (39), Rora (59)

LEEDS UNITED AFC v NK DINAMO ZAGREB 0-0

Elland Road, Leeds   6.09.67

Referee: Antonio Sbardella (Ita)   Attendance: 35,604

UNITED: Gary Sprake; William Bell, Terence Cooper, William Bremner (Cap), Jack Charlton; Norman Hunter, Paul Reaney; Rodney Belfitt, James Greenhoff, John Giles, Michael O'Grady.   Manager: Don Revie

DINAMO: Zlatko Škorić; Branko Gračanin, Marijan Brnčić, Rudolf Belin, Mladen Ramljak; Filip Blašković, Marijan Čerček; Denijal Pirić, Slaven Zambata (Cap), Josip Gucmirtl, Krasnodar Rora.   Trainer: Branko Zebec

Goalscorers Fairs Cup 1966/67

8 goals: Florián Albert (Ferencváros)

6 goals: Andrew Lochhead (Burnley), Oskar Lotz (Eintracht), Slaven Zambata (Dinamo Zagreb)

5 goals: Helmut Haller, Harald Nielsen (Bologna), Wilhelm Huberts (Eintracht)

4 goals: Eusébio Ferreira da Silva (Benfica), Waldo Machado da Silva (CF Valencia), Henning Frenzel (1.FC Lokomotive Leipzig), John McInally (FC Kilmarnock), Albert Johanneson, John Giles (Leeds United)

3 goals: Agne Simonsson (Örgryte Göteborg), Patrick Delaney (Dunfermline Athletic), Cané, Sívori (Napoli), Brown (West Bromwich Albion), Constantin Radu (Dinamo Piteşti), Rákosi (Ferencváros), Favalli, Menichelli (Juventus), Coates (Burnley), Löwe (1.FC Lokomotive Leipzig), McIlroy, Thomas McLean (FC Kilmarnock), Jukic (Dinamo Zagreb), Solz (Eintracht), Belfitt (Leeds United)

2 goals: Frigerio (FC Basel), Dorsini (Toulouse), Haastrup (B 1909 Odense), T. Callaghan, Ferguson, Fleming (Dunfermline), Dzajic, Ostojic (Crvena Zvezda Beograd), Wery, Van der Linden (DOS Utrecht), Claramunt, Ansola (CF Valencia), Altafini (Napoli), Hainey (Dundee United), Nagy (Dinamo Piteşti), Németh (Ferencváros), Pace, Turra (Bologna), Cinesinho, Del Sol, De Paoli, Gori (Juventus), Irvine, Miller (Burnley), Berger (1.FC Lokomotive Leipzig), Queen (FC Kilmarnock), Abbé, Bronnert, Schämer, Kraus (Eintracht), Greenhoff (Leeds United), Novak, Gucmirtl, Belin (Dinamo Zagreb), Estéfano (Athletic Bilbao)

1 goal: Persson, Wieståhl (Djurgardens), P.Pettersen, Ballgrund (Frigg Oslo), Knoll, Schmidt (Wiener SK), Ceyhan, Halil (Göztepe Izmir), Odermatt (FC Basel), Franceskin, Kokot, Arslanagic (Olimpija Ljubljana), Weiss (VfB Stuttgart), Santos, Loubet, Barrionuevo (Nice), Pinto, Pavão, Djalma (FC Porto), Strehl (FC Nürnberg), Whelan (Drumcondra), Bubník (Spartak Brno), Dieguez, Cabral (FC Sevilla), Genschick (FC Liège), Boogaard, Geurtsen (DWS Amsterdam), Robuschi, Texier, Couécou (Bordeaux), Armbruster (Lausanne), Wojciak, Soukhane (Toulouse), Magnusson, Hansson (Örgryte), Beyers, Van de Velde, Van Moer, Janssen (Antwerp), Fusté (CF Barcelona), Edwards (Dunfermline Athletic), Mihajlovic, Melic (Crvena Zvezda), Dishkov (Spartak Plovdiv), Mašek, Pospichal, Jurkanin (Sparta Praha), De Vroet, De Kuyper (DOS Utrecht), Hansen, Larsen, Olsen (Hvidovre), Carlos Manuel (Vitória Setúbal), Ghellynck, Lippens (ARA La Gantoise), J.Augusto, Torres (Benfica), Orlando, Bianchi, Braca (Napoli), Fairfax, Hope, Clark, Kaye (West Bromwich Albion), Dossing, Seeman, Mitchell (Dundee United), David, Dobrin, Ţurcan, Prepurgel (Dinamo Piteşti), Novák, Szőke, Varga (Ferencváros), Bulgarelli, Vastola (Bologna), Zigoni, Stacchini, Castano (Juventus), Latcham, Harris, O'Neil (Burnley), Trölitzsch (1.FC Lokomotive Leipzig), McFadzean, Murray, Watson (FC Kilmarnock), Grabowski, Bechtold, Friedrich (Eintracht), Lorimer, Bremner, Madeley (Leeds United), Čerček, Rora, Mesic (Dinamo Zagreb)

Own Goals: I. Karlsson (Djurgardens) for 1.FC Lokomotive Leipzig, Stocker (FC Basel) for DOS Utrecht, Kenny (Drumcondra) for Eintracht, Mesić (Dinamo Zagreb) for Spartak Brno, Dimov (Spartak Plovdiv) for Benfica, Jacinto (Benfica) for 1.FC Lokomotive Leipzig

FAIRS CUP 1967-68

FIRST ROUND

FREM KØBENHAVN
v ATHLETIC BILBAO 0-1 (0-1)

Idraetspark, København   13.09.67

Referee: Antoine Queudeville (Lux)   Attendance: 6,000

FREM: Leif Nielsen; Finn Hansen, Birger Larsen, Knudsen; Sørensen, Kaj Hansen; Jørn Jeppesen (72 Stegler), Ole Mørch, Leif Nielsen, D. Nielsen, Leif Printzlau.   Trainer: Ivan Jeffen

ATHLETIC: José Ángel IRÍBAR Cortajarena; José Ignacio SÁEZ Ruiz, Luis María ECHEBERRÍA Igartua, Jesús ARANGUREN Merino, Juan María ZORRIQUETA Azpiazu, José Ramón Martínez LARRAURI, Ignacio ARROYO (54 Nicolás ESTÉFANO Montalbán), José María ARGOITIA Acha, Antonio María ARIETA Araunabeña Piedra, Fidel URIARTE Macho, José Francisco ROJO I Arroita.
Trainer: Agustin Gainza

Goal: Arroyo (14)

ATHLETIC BILBAO
v FREM KØBENHAVN 3-2 (1-0)

Estadio San Mamés, Bilbao   20.09.67

Referee: Eric Jennings (Eng)   Attendance: 30,000

ATHLETIC: José Ángel IRÍBAR Cortajarena; José Ignacio SÁEZ Ruiz, Luis María ECHEBERRÍA Igartua, Jesús ARANGUREN Merino, Juan María ZORRIQUETA Azpiazu, José Ramón Martínez LARRAURI (53 Luis María ZUGAZAGA Martínez), Enrique Arráiz (75 Pedro LAVÍN Arcocha), José María ARGOITIA Acha, Antonio María ARIETA Araunabeña Piedra, Fidel URIARTE Macho, José Francisco ROJO I Arroita.   Trainer: Agustin Gainza

FREM: Leif Nielsen; Finn Hansen, Sørensen, Birger Larsen, Knudsen, Kaj Hansen, Flemming Mortensen (46 F. Hansen), Ole Mørch, Leif Nielsen, D. Nielsen, Leif Printzlau.
Trainer: Ivan Jeffen

Goals: Arráiz (17), L. Nielsen (20), Uriarte (50), Printzlau (56), Arieta (78)

PAOK THESSALONIKI v RFC LIÈGE 0-2 (0-2)

Toumpas, Thessaloniki   13.09.67

Referee: Fabio Monti (Ita)   Attendance: 27,000

PAOK: Apostolos Savvoulidis; Aristarhos Foudoukidis, Apostolos Vasileiadis, Efstratios Mouratidis, Giannis Giakoumis, Leandros Symeonidis, Emilios Theofanidis, Anastasios Afentoulidis, Giorgos Makris, Onufrios Haralampidis, Stavros Sarafis.

RFC LIÈGE: André Radar; Yves Baré, Albert Sulon, Claude Thompkins, Auguste Goessens, Gérard Sulon, Guido Mallants, Sreten Banovic, Philippe Mardaga, Henri Depireux, René Andries.

Goals: Mardaga (5), Banovic (9)

RFC LIÈGE v PAOK THESSALONIKI 3-2 (2-1)

Stade de Rocourt, Liège   20.09.67

Referee: Kaj Rasmussen (Dan)   Attendance: 3,900

RFC LIÈGE: André Radar; Yves Baré, Albert Sulon, Claude Thompkins, Auguste Goessens, Gérard Sulon, Guido Mallants, Sreten Banovic, Philippe Mardaga, Henri Depireux, René Andries.

PAOK: Gianis Karantaglidis; Aristarhos Foudoukidis, Apostolos Vasileiadis (46 Giorgos Makris), Efstratios Mouratidis, Giannis Giakoumis, Giannis Nikolaidis, Emilios Theofanidis, Anastasios Afentoulidis, Giorgos Tatsis, Lelos, Stavros Sarafis.

Goals: Andries (13, 32), Afendoulidis (27), Mardaga (67), Makris (79)

CLUB BRUGGE v SPORTING LISBOA 0-0

Olympisch, Brugge   13.09.67

Referee: Roger Machin (Fra)   Attendance: 15800

CLUB BRUGGE: Fernand Boone; Brian Hill, André Vanderlinden, Kurt Axelsson, Walter Loske, Erwin Vandendaele, Johnny Thio (46 Alfons Bastijns), Freddy Hinderijckx, Pierre Carteus, Raoul Lambert, Gilbert Bailliu.

SPORTING: Joaquim da Silva CARVALHO; Manuel Pedro Gomes, ARMANDO António Manhiça, JOSÉ CARLOS da Silva José, HILÁRIO Rosário da Conceição, JOSÉ MORAIS, Vítor GONÇALVES, Lourenço Salvador Sitoe, José Rodrigues LEITÃO, Mário da Silva Mateus "MARINHO", Fernando PERES.   Trainer: Fernando Cabrita

SPORTING LISBOA v CLUB BRUGGE 2-1 (1-1)

Estadio José Alvalade, Lisboa   27.09.67

Referee: Mariano Medina Iglesias (Spa)   Attendance: 8,451

SPORTING: Joaquim da Silva CARVALHO; Manuel Pedro Gomes, ARMANDO António Manhiça, JOSÉ CARLOS da Silva José, HILÁRIO Rosário da Conceição, JOSÉ MORAIS, Vítor GONÇALVES, João de Matos Moura LOURENÇO, José Rodrigues LEITÃO, Mário da Silva Mateus "MARINHO", Fernando PERES.   Trainer: Fernando Cabrita

CLUB BRUGGE: Fernand Boone; Brian Hill, André Vanderlinden, Kurt Axelsson, Gabriel Savat, Erwin Vandendaele, Johnny Thio, Freddy Hinderijckx, Pierre Carteus, Raoul Lambert, Gilbert Bailliu.

Goals: Lourenço (34, 68), Lambert (36)

ST. PATRICK's ATHLETIC DUBLIN
v GIRONDINS de BORDEAUX 1-3 (0-2)

Dalymount Park, Dublin   13.09.67

Referee: R.D. Henderson (Sco)   Attendance: 4,800

ST. PATRICK'S: Dinny Lowry, Paddy Dowling, William Roche, David Parkes (46 Dessie Keating), John Campbell, Jack Hennessey, Gerry Monaghan, Edward Ryan, Noel Dunne, Noel Campbell, Eamonn Carroll.

GIRONDINS: Christian Montes; Christian-Jacques Castellan, Robert Péri, André Chorda, Bernard Baudet, Guy Calleja, Jean-Louis Massé (.. Henri Duhayot), Hector De Bourgoing, RUITER Pontes de Oliveira, Didier Couécou, Edouard Wojciak.   Trainer: Jean-Pierre Bakrim

Goals: Chorda (5 pen), Massé (35), Hennessey (71), Couécou (88)

GIRONDINS de BORDEAUX
ST. PATRICK's ATHLETIC DUBLIN 6-3 (3-2)

Stade Municipal, Bordeaux   11.10.67

Referee: Joseph Heymann (Swi)   Attendance: 5,000

GIRONDINS: Christian Montes; Christian-Jacques Castellan (46 Hector de Bourgoing), Didier Desremeaux, André Chorda, Bernard Baudet, Guy Calleja (46 Robert Péri), Didier Couécou, Gabriel Abossolo, RUITER Pontes de Oliveira, Henri Duhayot, Edouard Wojciak.   Trainer: Jean-Pierre Bakrim

ST. PATRICK'S: Dinny Lowry, Paddy Dowling, William Roche, David Parkes (30 Douglas Boucher), Dessie Keating, Jack Hennessey, John Campbell, Noel Bates, Edward Ryan, Noel Campbell, Eamonn Carroll.

Goals: Calleja (13), Ruiter (21), N. Campbell (23, 25), Duhayot (43, 53), Ryan (61), Wojciak (65, 88)

WIENER SK ATLÉTICO MADRID 2-5 (0-2)

Prater, Wien   13.09.67

Referee: Mario Clematide (Swi)   Attendance: 15,000

WIENER SK: Wilhelm Kaipel (55 Zaczek); Wilhelm Kainrath, Webora, Anton Linhart; Peter Schmidt, Norbert Hof; Matousek, Johann Buzek, Erich Hof, Johann Hörmayer, Kurt Leitner.   Trainer: Karl Decker

ATLÉTICO: Roberto Rodríguez García "RODRI"; Julio Santaella Benítez "COLO", Julio IGLESIAS Santamaría, Isacio CALLEJA García; Manuel RUIZ-SOSA, Jesús MARTÍNEZ JAYO; Luis Armando UFARTE Ventosa; LUIS Aragonés Suárez, José Eulogio GÁRATE Ormaechea, José Enrique CARDONA Gutiérrez, Enrique COLLAR Monterrubio (29 José Antonio URTIAGA Albizu).   Trainer: Otto Gloria

Goals: Luis (24), Gárate (42, 70, 78, 89), Calleja (58 og), Leitner (68)

ATLÉTICO MADRID v WIENER SK 2-1 (2-0)

Estadio del Manzanares, Madrid   25.10.67

Referee: George McCabe (Eng) Attendance: 14000

ATLÉTICO: Roberto Rodríguez García "RODRI"; Feliciano RIVILLA Muńoz, Julio IGLESIAS Santamaría, Jesús MARTÍNEZ JAYO (46 Julio Santaella Benítez «COLO»); Isacio CALLEJA García, LUIS Aragonés Suárez (46 Manuel RUIZ-SOSA); Jesús GLARÍA Roldán, José Enrique CARDONA Gutiérrez, José Antonio URTIAGA Albizu, Javier IRURETAgoyena Amiano, Enrique COLLAR Monterrubio.   Trainer: Otto Gloria

WIENER SK: Wilhelm Kaipel; Wilhelm Kainrath (46 Alfred Hala), Webora, Anton Linhart; Helmut Wallner, Norbert Hof; Peter Schmidt, Erich Hof, Kurt Leitner, Johann Hörmayer, Matousek (46 Herbert Onger).   Trainer: Galli

Goals: Cardona (5, 23), Schmidt (65)

DOS UTRECHT v REAL ZARAGOZA 3-2 (2-1)

Galgenwaard, Utrecht   14.09.67

Referee: Einar Boström (Swe)   Attendance: 9,000

DOS: Nico Verrips; Bennie Aarts, Hans de Weerd, Eddie Van Stijn, Bas Peters (46 Johnny van Renswouw), Johan Plageman, Piet Van Oudenallen, Leo van Veen, Abbes van Vliet, Arie de Kuyper, Henk Wery.   Trainer: Van der Laan

REAL ZARAGOZA: Rafael Álvarez ALARCIA; Alfonso María Rodríguez Salas "FONCHO", Severino REIJA Vázquez, José Luis VIOLETA Lajusticia, José DÍAZ Fernández, José Manuel "MANOLO" GONZÁLEZ López, Darcy Silveira dos Santos "CANARIO", Eleuterio SANTOS Brito, MARCELINO Martínez Cao, Juan Manuel VILLA Gutiérrez, José Antonio TEJEDOR Sanz.   Trainer: Roque Olsen

Goals: Van Veen (28), Wery (34), Canario (43), Villa (79), Van Vliet (64)

REAL ZARAGOZA v DOS UTRECHT 3-1 (2-1)

Estadio La Romareda, Zaragoza   *12.10.67*

Referee: Karl Keller (Swi)   Attendance: 35,000

REAL ZARAGOZA: Rafael Álvarez ALARCIA; Alfonso María Rodríguez Salas «FONCHO», Severino REIJA Vázquez, José Luis VIOLETA Lajusticia, José Manuel «MANOLO» GONZÁLEZ López, Antonio PAÍS Castroagudin, Darcy Silveira dos Santos "CANARIO", Eleuterio SANTOS Brito, MARCELINO Martínez Cao, Miguel Ángel BUSTILLO Lafoz, Francisco MOYA Gómez.   Trainer: Roque Olsen

DOS: Nico Verrips (46 Theo Hoogeveen); Bennie Aarts, Hans de Weerd, Arie de Kuyper, Eddie Van Stijn, Piet van Oudenallen, Johnny van Renswouw, Bas Peters (46 Abbes van Vliet), Matthias Maiwald, Leo van Veen, Henk Wery.   Trainer: Van der Laan

Goals: Bustillo (19, 51), Maiwald (30), Moya (36)

MALMÖ FF v LIVERPOOL FC 0-2 (0-1)

Malmö stadion   *19.09.67*

Referee: William Schalks (Hol)   Attendance: 14,314

MALMÖ FF: Nils Hult; Jörgen Ohlin (80 Ulf Kleander), Krister Kristensson, Bertil Elmstedt, Rolf Björklund, Anders Ljungberg, Lars Granström, Anders Svensson, Harry Jönsson, Dag Szepanski, Ingvar Svahn.   Trainer: Antonio Duran

LIVERPOOL: Thomas Lawrence; Christopher Lawler, Gerald Byrne, Thomas Smith, Ronald Yeats, Emlyn Hughes, Ian Callaghan, Roger Hunt, Anthony Hateley, Ian St.John, Peter Thompson.   Manager: Bill Shankly

Goals: Hateley (9, 80)

LIVERPOOL FC v MALMÖ FF 2-1 (2-0)

Anfield Road, Liverpool   *4.10.67*

Referee: Alfred Delcourt (Bel)   Attendance: 39,795

LIVERPOOL: Thomas Lawrence; Christopher Lawler, Gerald Byrne, Thomas Smith, Ronald Yeats, Emlyn Hughes, Ian Callaghan, Roger Hunt, Anthony Hateley, William Stevenson, Peter Thompson.   Manager: Bill Shankly

MALMÖ FF: Nils Hult; Ulf Kleander, Krister Kristensson, Bertil Elmstedt, Rolf Björklund, Anders Ljungberg, Staffan Tapper, Anders Svensson, Björn Friberg, Dag Szepanski, Ingvar Svahn.   Trainer: Antonio Duran

Goals: Yeats (28), Hunt (36), Szepanski (82)

AC BOLOGNA v LYN OSLO 2-0 (1-0)

Stadio Comunale. Bologna   *19.09.67*

Referee: Gottfried Dienst (Swi)   Attendance: 17,200

BOLOGNA: Giuseppe Vavassori; Carlo Furlanis, Mario Ardizzon, Aristide Guarneri, Francesco Janich, Faustino Turra (46 Bruno Pace), Marino Perani, Romano Fogli, Sergio Clerici, Helmut Haller, Ezio Pascutti.   Trainer: Luis Antonio Carniglia

LYN: Svein Bjørn Olsen; Jan Rodvang, Kjell Saga (46 Knut Berg), Sveinung Aarnseth, Knut Kolle, Svein Bredo Östlien, Karl Johan Johannessen, Andreas Morisbak, Jan Berg, Harald Berg, Ola Dybwad Olsen.

Goals: Clerici (42), Pace (53)

LYN OSLO v AC BOLOGNA 0-0

Ulleval, Oslo   *4.10.67*

Referee: Sven Jonsson (Swe)   Attendance: 8,000

LYN: Svein Bjørn Olsen; Jan Rodvang, Kjell Saga, Sveinung Aarnseth (46 Helge Østvold), Knut Kolle, Svein Bredo Östlien, Karl Johan Johannessen, Andreas Morisbak, Jan Berg, Harald Berg, Ola Dybwad Olsen.

BOLOGNA: Giuseppe Vavassori; Tazio Roversi, Mario Ardizzon, Aristide Guarneri, Francesco Janich, Paride Tumburus, Bruno Pace (46 Italo Carminati), Romano Fogli (46 Faustino Turra), Sergio Clerici, Helmut Haller, Ezio Pascutti.   Trainer: Luis Antonio Carniglia

SSC NAPOLI v HANNOVER 96 4-0 (3-0)

San Paolo, Napoli   *19.09.67*

Referee: Dittmar Huber (Swi)   Attendance: 15,500

NAPOLI: Dino Zoff; Stelio Nardin, Luigi Pogliana, Amedeo Stenti, Dino Panzanato, Antonio Girardo, Alberto Bigon, Antonio Juliano, José Altafini, Vincenzo Montefusco, Girardi.   Trainer: Bruno Pesaola

HANNOVER 96: Horst Podlasly; Hans-Josef Hellingrath, Otto Laszig, Peter Anders, Rainer Stiller (46 Jürgen Bandura), Werner Gräber, Hermann Straschitz, Kaj Poulsen, Josef Heynckes, Hans Siemensmeyer, Walter Rodekamp.   Trainer: Horst Buhtz

Goals: Girardo (14), Laszig (17 og), Altafini (37, 73)

HANNOVER 96 v SSC NAPOLI 1-1 (0-1)

Niedersachsenstadion, Hannover   18.10.67

Referee: Adrianus Aalbrecht (Hol)   Attendance: 8,600

HANNOVER 96: Horst Podlasly; Hans-Josef Hellingrath, Peter Anders, Rainer Stiller, Christian Breuer, Hans Siemensmeyer (46 Werner Gräber), Kaj Poulsen, Hermann Straschitz, Wilfried Ahnefeld, Walter Rodekamp, Jürgen Bandura.   Trainer: Horst Buhtz

NAPOLI: Dino Zoff; Stelio Nardin, Luigi Pogliana, Amedeo Stenti, Dino Panzanato, Antonio Girardo, Ivano Bosdaves (46 José Altafini), Antonio Juliano, Alberto Orlando, Vincenzo Montefusco, Paolo Barison.   Trainer: Bruno Pesaola

Goals: Barison (40), Straschitz (65)

DINAMO ZAGREB v PETROLUL PLOIEŞTI 5-0 (0-0)

Maksimir, Zagreb   20.09.67

Referee: Gerhard Kunze (DDR)   Attendance: 20,000

DINAMO: Zlatko Škorić; Branko Graçanin, Marijan Brnčić, Zlatko Mesic, Mladen Ramljak; Denijal Pirić, Marijan Čerček; Ivica Kiš, Slaven Zambata, Hrvoje Jukic, Krasnodar Rora. Trainer: Branko Zebec

PETROLUL: Mihai Ionescu; Gheorghe Pahonţu, Nicolae Ionescu, Gheorghe Florea, Mihai Mocanu; Gheorghe Grozea, Petre Dragomir; Camil Oprişan, Octavian Dincuţă, Alexandru Badea, Ştefan Roman.   Trainer: Ilie Oană

Goals: Jukić (51, 65), Kiss (57, 59), Zambata (77)

PETROLUL PLOIEŞTI v DINAMO ZAGREB 2-0 (1-0)

Petrolul, Ploieşti   27.09.67

Referee: Orhan Gonül (Tur)   Attendance: 10,000

PETROLUL: Mihai Ionescu; Gheorghe Pahonţu, Nicolae Ionescu, Gheorghe Florea, Mihai Mocanu; Eduard Juhasz (46 Gheorghe Grozea), Petre Dragomir; Camil Oprişan (46 Constantin Moldoveanu), Mircea Dridea, Alexandru Badea, Ştefan Roman. Trainer: Ilie Oană

DINAMO: Zlatko Škorić; Branko Graçanin, Mirko Braun; Zlatko Mesic, Mladen Ramljak, Filip Blašković; Marijan Čerček, Rudolf Belin (46 Marijan Novak), Slaven Zambata, Hrvoje Jukic, Krasnodar Rora.   Trainer: Branko Zebec

Goals: M. Dridea (15), Grozea (70)

1.FC LOKOMOTIVE LEIPZIG v LINFIELD BELFAST 5-1 (3-0)

Zentralstadion, Leipzig   20.09.67

Referee: Zdenek Vales (Cze)   Attendance: 8,400

1.FC LOKOMOTIVE: Ulrich Schulze; Christoph Franke, Peter Giessner, Manfred Geisler; Michael Faber, Karl Drössler; Werner Gase, Arno Zerbe, Henning Frenzel, Jürgen Naumann, Wolfram Löwe.   Trainer: Hans Studener

LINFIELD: Robert McGonigal; Ken Gilliland, Thomas Leishman, Isaac Andrews, Samuel Hatton, Stan Gregg, Bryan Hamilton, Philip Scott, Samuel Pavis, Ronald Wood, Thomas Shields (46 Des Cathcart).

Goals: Löwe (1, 84), Zerbe (13, 87), Faber (37), Pavis (53)

LINFIELD BELFAST v 1.FC LOKOMOTIVE LEIPZIG 1-0 (1-0)

Windsor Park, Belfast   4.10.67

Referee: William J. Mullan (Sco)   Attendance: 9,400

LINFIELD: Robert McGonigal; Ken Gilliland, John Patterson, Thomas Leishman, Isaac Andrews, Samuel Hatton, William Ferguson, Bryan Hamilton, Samuel Pavis, Philip Scott, Des Cathcart.

1.FC LOKOMOTIVE: Peter Nauert; Christoph Franke, Peter Giessner, Manfred Geisler; Michael Faber, Karl Drössler; Werner Gase, Arno Zerbe, Henning Frenzel (46 Jörg Berger), Jürgen Naumann, Wolfram Löwe.   Trainer: Hans Studener

Goal: Hamilton (11)

HIBERNIAN EDINBURGH v FC PORTO 3-0 (2-0)

Easter Road Park, Edinburgh   20.09.67

Referee: John Adair (NIr)   Attendance: 14,200

HIBERNIAN: Thomson Allan; Robert Duncan, Joseph Davis, Patrick Stanton, John Madsen, Alan McGraw, Alexander Scott (58 Colin Grant), Patrick Quinn, Colin Stein, Peter Cormack, Eric William Stevenson.   Manager: Bob Shankly

FC PORTO: AMÉRICO Lopes; Valdemar Pacheco, João Luís Pinto ALMEIDA, José ROLANDO Andrade Gonçalves, João Eleutério Luis ATRACA; Mario, João CUSTÓDIO PINTO, Francisco Lage Pereira da NÓBREGA; Fernando Neves Pavão, Djalma Freitas, Serafim Mesquita Pedro "MALAGUETA" (46 MANUEL ANTÓNIO Leitão da Silva). Trainer: José Maria Pedroto

Goals: Cormack (26, 37), Stevenson (46)

FC PORTO v HIBERNIAN EDINBURGH 3-1 (0-1)

Estádio das Antas, Porto   4.10.67

Referee: Antonio Rigo Sureda (Spa)   Attendance: 40,000

FC PORTO: AMÉRICO Lopes; Alberto Festa (46 João Maria RICARDO), João Luís Pinto ALMEIDA, José ROLANDO Andrade Gonçalves, João Eleutério Luis ATRACA; Fernando Neves Pavão, João CUSTÓDIO PINTO (81 Mário); JAIME Ferreira Silva, Djalma Freitas, VALDIR Araújo Sousa, Francisco Lage Pereira da NÓBREGA.
Trainer: José Maria Pedroto

HIBERNIAN: Thomson Allan; Robert Duncan, Joseph Davis, Patrick Stanton, John Madsen, Alan McGraw, Alexander Scott, Patrick Quinn, Colin Stein, Peter Cormack, Eric Stevenson.
Manager: Bob Shankly

Goals: Davis (2 pen), Pinto (54), Valdir (55, 69)

DYNAMO DRESDEN v GLASGOW RANGERS 1-1 (0-0)

Rudolf-Harbig-Stadion, Dresden   20.09.67

Referee: Ratko Çanak (Jug)   Attendance: 40,000

DYNAMO: Manfred Kallenbach; Wolfgang Haustein, Klaus Sammer, Roland May, Siegmar Wätzlich, Meinhard Hemp, Bernd Hofmann, Dieter Riedel, Uwe Ziegler, Hans-Jürgen Kreische, Siegfried Gumz.

RANGERS: Erik Sorensen; Kai Johansen, John Greig, William Jardine, Ronald McKinnon, David Smith, William Henderson, Andrew Penman, Alex Ferguson, Örjan Persson, William Johnston.   Manager: David White

Goals: Ferguson (49), Riedel (66)

GLASGOW RANGERS v DYNAMO DRESDEN 2-1 (1-0)

Ibrox Stadium, Glasgow   4.10.67

Referee: Salvador Garcia Campos (Por)   Attendance: 59,000

RANGERS: Erik Sorensen; Kai Johansen, William Mathieson, John Greig, Ronald McKinnon, David Smith, William Henderson, Andrew Penman, Alex Ferguson, Örjan Persson, William Johnston.   Manager: David White

DYNAMO: Manfred Kallenbach; Wolfgang Haustein, Klaus Sammer, Wolfgang Pfeifer, Siegmar Wätzlich, Meinhard Hemp, Bernd Hofmann, Horst Walter (73 Klaus Engels), Uwe Ziegler, Hans-Jürgen Kreische, Siegfried Gumz.

Goals: Penman (15), Kreische (88), Greig (90)

FC ZÜRICH v CF BARCELONA 3-1 (1-1)

Letzigrund, Zürich   20.09.67

Referee: Roger Barde (Fra)   Attendance: 8,000

FC ZÜRICH: Othmar Iten (46 Karl Grob); Werner Leimgruber, Hubert Münch, Konrad Kyburz, Marcel Tanner, Ettore Trivellin, Pirmin Stierli, Jakob Kuhn, Christian Winiger, Fritz Künzli, Ernst Meyer.   Trainer: Lav Mantula

CF BARCELONA: Miguel REINA Santos; Joaquín BORRÁS Canut, Fernando OLIVELLA Pons, Juan TORRENT Solé, Antonio TORRES García, Francisco Fernández Rodríguez "GALLEGO", Eduardo ENDÉRIZ Cortajarena, Jesús María PEREDA Ruiz de Temiño, Joaquín RIFÉ Climent, José Antonio ZALDÚA Urdanavia, JIMÉNEZ.   Trainer: Salvador Artigas

Goals: Zaldúa (30), Winiger (43, 65), Kuhn (87)

CF BARCELONA v FC ZÜRICH 1-0 (0-0)

Camp Nou, Barcelona   4.10.67

Referee: Anibal Da Silva Oliveira (Por)   Attendance: 34,300

CF BARCELONA: Salvador SADURNÍ Urpi; Julio César BENÍTEZ Amoedo, Ángel OLIVEROS Jiménez, ELADIO Silvestre Graells, Lucien MULLER Schmidt, Antonio TORRES García, Francisco Fernández Rodríguez "GALLEGO", Carlos PELLICER Vázquez (56 Jesús María PEREDA Ruiz de Temiño), José Antonio ZALDÚA Urdanavia, José María FUSTÉ Blanch, Carlos REXACH Cerdá (68 Joaquín RIFÉ Climent).   Trainer: Salvador Artigas

FC ZÜRICH: Karl Grob; Hubert Münch, Jürgen Neumann, Werner Leimgruber, Konrad Kyburz; Jakob Kuhn, Rosario Martinelli, Christian Winiger, Ettore Trivellin (72 Marcel Tanner), Fritz Künzli, Ernst Meyer.   Trainer: Lav Mantula

Goal: Zaldúa (62)

FC ARGEŞ PITEŞTI v FERENCVÁROS BUDAPEST 3-1 (1-1)

1 Mai, Piteşti   20.09.67

Referee: Božidar Botić (Jug)   Attendance: 22,000

FC ARGEŞ: Narcis Coman; Ioachim Popescu, Ion Barbu (Cap), Ilie Stelian, Nicolae Vulpeanu; Ion Prepurgel, Constantin Olteanu; Viorel Kraus, Mihai Ţurcan, Nicolae Dobrin, Radu Jercan.   Trainer: Ion Bălănescu

FTC: István Géczi; László Horváth, Sándor Mátrai, Miklós Páncsics, István Juhász, Lajos Szűcs; István Szőke, Zoltán Varga, Flórián Albert, Gyula Rakosi, Sándor Katona.
Trainer: Károly Lakat. Sent off: Szőke (44).

Goals: Jercan (2), Albert (22), Dobrin (48), Kraus (54)

FERENCVÁROS BUDAPEST
v FC ARGEŞ PITEŞTI 4-0 (1-0)

Népstadion, Budapest 11.10.67

Referee: Vaclav Davidek (Cze) Attendance: 80,000

FERENCVÁROS: Béla Takács; Dezső Novák, Sándor Mátrai, Miklós Páncsics; István Juhász, Lajos Szűcs; János Karába, Zóltán Varga, Flórián Albert, Gyula Rákosi, Máté Fenyvesi (60 Sándor Katona). Trainer: Károly Lakat

FC ARGEŞ: Narcis Coman; Ioachim Popescu, Ion Barbu (Cap), Ilie Stelian, Nicolae Vulpeanu; Ion Prepurgel, Constantin Olteanu; Viorel Kraus, Mihai Ţurcan (54 Constantin Radu), Nicolae Dobrin, Radu Jercan. Trainer: Ion Bălănescu

Goals: Albert (37, 65), Novak (50 pen), Varga (79)

EINTRACHT FRANKFURT/MAIN
v NOTTINGHAM FOREST 0-1 (0-1)

Waldstadion, Frankfurt/Main 20.09.67

Referee: Daniel María Zariquiegui (Spa) Attendance: 4,500

EINTRACHT: Hans Tilkowski; Fahrudin Jusufi, Peter Blusch, Lothar Schämer, Karl-Heinz Wirth, István Sztani, Jürgen Friedrich, Oskar Lotz, Ernst Abbé, Wilhelm Huberts, Helmut Kraus. Trainer: Elek Schwartz

FOREST: Peter Grummitt; Peter Hindley, John Winfield, Terence Hennessey, Robert McKinlay, Robert Chapman, Barry Lyons, Ian Storey-Moore, Joseph Baker, Frank Wignall, Alan Hinton. Wignall sent off (66). Manager: John Carey

Goal: Baker (9)

OGC NICE v AC FIORENTINA FIRENZE 0-1 (0-0)

Stade du Ray, Nice 20.09.67

Referee: Rudolf Kreitlein (WG) Attendance: 16,000

OGC NICE: Marcel Aubour; Guy Cauvin, Bruno Rodzik, Maurice Serrus, Francis Isnard, Régis Bruneton, Jean-Pierre Serra, Gérard Segarra, Jean-Rémy Issembe, Albert Robin, Charles Loubet. Trainer: César Gonzalés

FIORENTINA: Enrico Albertosi; Giovan Battista Pirovano, Bernardo Rogora, Mario Bertini, Ugo Ferrante, Giuseppe Brizi, Mario Maraschi, Claudio Merlo (46 Marzio Magli), Mario Brugnera, AMARILDO Tavares de Silveire, Giancarlo De Sisti. Trainer: Giuseppe Chiapella

Goal: Maraschi (78)

NOTTINGHAM FOREST
v EINTRACHT FRANKFURT/MAIN 4-0 (2-0)

City Ground, Nottingham 17.10.67

Referee: Henry Öberg (Nor) Attendance: 27,090

FOREST: Peter Grummitt; Peter Hindley, John Winfield, Terence Hennessey, Robert McKinlay, Henry Newton, Barry Lyons, John Barnwell (80 William Taylor), Joseph Baker, Robert Chapman, Ian Storey-Moore. Manager: John Carey

EINTRACHT: Hans Tilkowski; Fahrudin Jusufi, Dieter Lindner, Peter Blusch, Helmut Kraus, Günter Keifler, Hermann-Dieter Belutt, Jürgen Grabowski (46 Oskar Lotz), Siegfried Bronnert, Jürgen Friedrich, Heiko Racky. Trainer: Elek Schwartz

Goals: Baker (13, 35), Chapman (47), Lyons (72)

AC FIORENTINA FIRENZE v OGC NICE 4-0 (1-0)

Stadio Comunale, Firenze 11.10.67

Referee: Paul Schiller (Aus) Attendance: 10,000

FIORENTINA: Enrico Albertosi; Marcello Diomedi, Eraldo Mancini, Mario Bertini, Giovan Battista Pirovano, Giuseppe Brizi, Luciano Chiarugi, Claudio Merlo (46 Marzio Magli), Mario Brugnera, Giancarlo De Sisti, Salvatore Esposito. Trainer: Giuseppe Chiapella

OGC NICE: Marcel Aubour; Guy Cauvin, Bruno Rodzik (30 Sylvain Leandri), Maurice Serrus, Francis Isnard, Régis Bruneton, René Fioroni, Albert Robin, Jean-Rémy Issembe, Rafaël Santos, Charles Loubet. Trainer: César Gonzalés

Goals: De Sisti (9), Brugnera (53, 68), Bertini (63)

SERVETTE GENÈVE
v TSV MÜNCHEN 1860 2-2 (2-1)

Stade des Charmilles, Genève 26.09.67

Referee: Alessandro d'Agostini (Ita) Attendance: 5,500

SERVETTE: Enzo Scalena; Georges Martignano, Roger Piguet, Péter Pázmándy, Bernard Mocellin, Didier Makay, Jürgen Sundermann, Valér Németh, Pierre-Maurice Georgy, Philippe Pottier (37 Walter Heuri), Jean-Claude Schindelholz.

TSV MÜNCHEN 1860: Petar Radenković; Manfred Wagner, Rudolf Zeiser, Hans Reich, Rudolf Steiner, Hans Küppers, Željko Perušić (57 Horst Schmidt), Ludwig Bründl, Wolfgang Lex, Peter Grosser, Hans Rebele (33 Wilfried Kohlars). Trainer: Albert Sing

Goals: Georgy (17), Küppers (26 pen), Heuri (44), Grosser (87)

TSV MÜNCHEN 1860
v SERVETTE GENÈVE 4-0 (1-0)

Grünwalderstadion, München   3.10.67

Referee: John Wright Paterson (Sco)   Attendance: 12,000

TSV MÜNCHEN 1860: Petar Radenković; Wilfried Kohlars, Gottfried Peter, Horst Schmidt, Manfred Wagner, Željko Perušić, Hans Küppers, Ludwig Bründl, Wolfgang Lex (46 Max Reichenberger), Peter Grosser (71 Hans-Günther Kroth), Alfred Heiss.   Trainer: Albert Sing

SERVETTE: Jacques Barlie; Georges Martignano, Roger Piguet, Péter Pázmándy, Bernard Mocellin, Jürgen Sundermann, Didier Makay, Valér Németh, Michel Desbiolles, Walter Heuri, Jean-Claude Schindelholz.

Goals: Küppers (33), Grosser (51 pen), Bründl (64), Peter (76)

ROYAL ANTWERP FC v GÖZTEPE IZMIR 1-2 (1-0)

Bosuil, Antwerp   26.09.67

Referee: Adrianus Boogaerts (Hol)   Attendance: 4,500

ROYAL ANTWERP FC: Willy Coremans; Maurice Tillotson, Florent Bohez, Jozef Rens, Robert Geens, Raymond Goris, Karel Beyers, Paul Marter (64 Jozef Van Gorp), Ronny Tielemans, Willy Vander Wee, Ivan Fränkel.

GÖZTEPE: Ali Artuner; Mehmet Aydin, Çaglayan Derebaşi; Hüseyin Yazici (52 Halil Kiraz), Mehmet Tuncer Ergon, Muzar, Ertan Öznur, Gürsel Aksel, Fevzi Zemzem, Ali Ihsan Okçuoglu, Nihat Ertan.   Trainer: Adnan Sovari

Goals: Fränkel (12), Fevzi (51, 80)

GÖZTEPE IZMIR v ROYAL ANTWERP FC 0-0

Alsançak, Izmir   18.10.67

Referee: Vasile Dumitrescu (Rom)   Attendance: 18,000

GÖZTEPE: Ali Artuner; Mehmet Aydin, Çaglayan Derebaşi, Hüseyin Yazici, Mehmet Tuncer Ergon; Muzar, Ertan Öznur, Gürsel Aksel, Fevzi Zemzem, Ali Ihsan Okçuoglu, Nihat Ertan.   Trainer: Adnan Sovari

ROYAL ANTWERP FC: Eddy Braem; Maurice Tillotson, Florent Bohez, Robert Geens, Jozef Rens, Raymond Goris (46 Jozef Van Gool), Wilfried Van Moer, Willy Vander Wee, Karel Beyers, Ronny Tielemans, Paul Marter.

DWS AMSTERDAM v DUNDEE FC 2-1 (2-1)

Olimpisch, Amsterdam   27.09.67

Referee: Franz Geluck (Bel)   Attendance: 6,500

DWS: Piet Schrijvers; Martin Kamminga, Joop Burgers, Jos Dijkstra, André Pijlman, Jos Vonhof, Theo Cornwall, Piet Kruiver, Piet Van den Berg (46 Josip Simokovic), Frans Geurtsen, Rob Rensenbrink.   Trainer: Lesley Talbot

DUNDEE FC: John Arrol; Robert Wilson, Robert Cox, Stephen Murray, George Stewart, Alexander Stuart, William Campbell (46 John Scott), Samuel Wilson, George McLean, James McLean, Alexander Bryce.   Manager: Robert Ancell

Goals: Rensenbrink (2), Van den Berg (17), G. McLean (25)

DUNDEE FC v DWS AMSTERDAM 3-0 (2-0)

Dens Park, Dundee   4.10.67

Referee: John Adair (NIr)   Attendance: 16,000

DUNDEE FC: Alistair Donaldson; George Stewart, Robert Wilson, Alexander Stuart, Stephen Murray, William Campbell, Ron Selway (.. Alex Kinninmonth), Samuel Wilson, George McLean, James McLean, Alexander Bryce.   Manager: Robert Ancell

DWS: Piet Schrijvers; Frits Flinkevleugel, André Pijlman, Jos Dijkstra, Theo Cornwall, Jos Vonhof, Joop Burgers, Piet Kruiver, Piet Van den Berg, Frans Geurtsen, Rob Rensenbrink.   Trainer: Lesley Talbot

Goals: S. Wilson (4), G. McLean (14, 61 pen)

VOJVODINA NOVI SAD
v CUF BARREIRO 1-0 (1-0)

Gradski, Novi Sad   27.09.67

Referee: Dimitar Rumenchev (Bul)   Attendance: 3,600

VOJVODINA: Ilija Pantelić; Rajko Aleksić, Josip Zemko, Stevan Nešticki, Ivan Brzić, Zoran Dakić, Milan Stanić (46 Marinković), Dobrivoje Trivić, Petar Nikezić, Radivoj Radosav, Dimitrije Radović.

CUF: VÍTOR CABRAL Martins; António BAMBO Cassama, António Esteves DURAND, Francisco Abalroado, MÁRIO JOÃO Sousa Alves, António José Santos MEDEIROS, António VIEIRA DIAS, José Monteiro, Fernando Oliveira, Alfredo Agostinho ESPÍRITO SANTO (75 PEDRO Manuel Tavares), Carlos Santos SÉRIO.   Trainer: Anselmo Fernández (Spa)

Goal: Dakic (33 pen)

CUF BARREIRO
v VOJVODINA NOVI SAD 1-3 (1-0)

Estadio Alfredo de Liloa, Barreiro   8.10.67

Referee: Gaspar Pintado Viu (Spa)   Attendance: 4,230

CUF: VÍTOR CABRAL Martins; António BAMBO Cassama, António Esteves DURAND, Francisco Abalroado, António José Santos MEDEIROS, MÁRIO JOÃO Sousa Alves, António VIEIRA DIAS, Carlos Santos SÉRIO, José Monteiro, Fernando Oliveira, Manuel Francisco Cambado CAPITÃO-MOR. Trainer: Anselmo Fernández

VOJVODINA: Ilija Pantelić, Rajko Aleksić, Stevensk, Ivan Brzić, Dorvić, Josip Zemko, Dobrivoje Trivić, Milan Stanić, Radivoj Radosav, Petar Nikezić, Dimitrije Radović.

Goals: Fernando (14), Trivic (72, 73), Zemko (86)

PARTIZAN BEOGRAD
v LOKOMOTIV PLOVDIV 5-1 (1-0)

JNA, Beograd   27.09.67

Referee: Alfred Ott (WG)   Attendance: 5,200

PARTIZAN: Ivan Čurković; Miloš Radaković, Milan Damjanović, Blagoje Paunović (46 Milan Vukelić), Branko Rašović, Ljubomir Mihajlović, Mane Bajić, Vladimir Kovačević, Mustafa Hasanagić, Borcević, Milan Petrović (46 Ljuan Prekazi).   Trainer: Stjepan Bobek

LOKOMOTIV: Trifon Brambarov; Ilia Bekiarov, Vasil Muratov, Gancho Peev, Vasil Ankov, Todor Paunov, Georgi Vasilev, Ivan Boiadjiev, Kanchev, Spas Iliev, Ivan Enchev (73 Tsonio Stoinov).

Goals: Hasanagić (44, 57, 88), Kovačević (46), Iliev (53), Rašović (70)

LOKOMOTIV PLOVDIV
v PARTIZAN BEOGRAD 1-1 (0-1)

9 Septemvri, Plovdiv   25.10.67

Referee: Alfred Ott (WG)   Attendance: 4,000

LOKOMOTIV: Ivan Videnov; Ilia Bekiarov, Georgi Valkov, Gancho Peev; Vasil Ankov, Todor Paunov; Georgi Vasilev, Ivan Boiadjiev (77 Vasil Angelov), Ivan Kanchev, Georgi Mizin, Spas Iliev.

PARTIZAN: Ivan Čurković (53 Marković); Miloš Radaković, Milan Damjanović, Borivoje Djordjević, Blagoje Paunović, Ljubomir Mihajlović; Mane Bajić, Ljuan Prekazi, Milan Petrović, Milan Vukelić (38 Vidović), Josip Pirmajer.   Trainer: Stjepan Bobek

Goals: Petrović (31), Vasilev (57)

FC KÖLN v SLAVIA PRAHA 2-0 (1-0)

Müngersdorfenstadion, Köln   30.09.67

Referee: Erich Linemayer (Aus)   Attendance: 12,000

FC KÖLN: Milutin Soskic; Wolfgang Rausch, Heinz Simmet, Fritz Pott, Wolfgang Weber, Matthias Hemmersbach, Heinz Flohe, Wolfgang Overath, Karl-Heinz Rühl, Karl-Heinz Thielen, Johannes Löhr.   Trainer: Willy Multhaup

SLAVIA: Jiří Vošta; Jan Lála, Bohumil Smolík, Bedrich Tesař, Hildebrand, Emil Hamár, Josef Linhart, Vaclav Novak, Karel Nepomucký, František Veselý, Miroslav Ziegler.   Trainer: F. Hravanek

Goals: Rühl (40), Löhr (49)

SLAVIA PRAHA v FC KÖLN 2-2 (2-0)

Dr. Vacka, Praha   11.10.67

Referee: Gusztáv Bircsak (Hun)   Attendance: 5,200

SLAVIA: Jiří Vošta; Jaroslav Šimek, Hildebrand, Bedrich Tesař, Bohumil Smolík, Jan Lála, Karel Nepomucký, František Veselý, Emil Hamár, Vaclav Novak, Miroslav Ziegler.   Trainer: F. Hravanek

FC KÖLN: Milutin Soskic; Wolfgang Rausch, Wolfgang Weber, Reinhard Roder (46 Jürgen Rumor), Matthias Hemmersbach, Heinz Simmet, Johannes Löhr, Wolfgang Overath, Karl-Heinz Rühl, Heinz Flohe, Heinz Hornig.   Trainer: Willy Multhaup

Goals: Tesař (3), Lála (38), Löhr (50), Rühl (60)

SPORA LUXEMBOURG v LEEDS UNITED 0-9 (0-4)

Stade Municipal, Luxembourg   3.10.67

Referee: Helmut Fritz (WG)   Attendance: 2,500

SPORA: Friedhelm Jesse; Arthur Schmitz, René Schmitt, Mathias Ewen, Pierrot Hut, Jean Kremer (46 Gaston Bauer), Emile Meyer, Carlo Devillet (46 Harald Werwie), Peter Scholtes, Joseph Krier, François Hostert.   Trainer: János Gerdov

LEEDS UNITED: David Harvey; Paul Reaney, Paul Madeley, William Bremner, Jack Charlton, Norman Hunter, James Greenhoff, Peter Lorimer, Michael Jones, Edward Gray, Terence Cooper.   Manager: Don Revie

Goals: Lorimer (14, 24 pen, 29, 54), Bremner (45), Greenhoff (70, 77), Madeley (80), Jones (81)

LEEDS UNITED v SPORA LUXEMBOURG 7-0 (2-0)

Elland Road, Leeds   17.10.67

Referee: Peter Coates (Irl)   Attendance: 15,196

LEEDS UNITED: Gary Sprake; Paul Reaney, Terence Cooper, Paul Madeley (46 Michael Bates), Jack Charlton, Norman Hunter, James Greenhoff, Peter Lorimer, Rodney Belfitt, Terence Hibbitt, Albert Johanneson.   Manager: Don Revie

SPORA: Friedhelm Jesse; Arthur Schmitz, Pierrot Hut, René Schmitt, Mathias Ewen, Dominique Da Fonseca (12 John Hilbert), Carlo Devillet, Peter Scholtes, Joseph Krier, Emile Meyer, François Hostert (46 Jean Kremer).
Trainer: János Gerdov

Goals: Johanneson (10, 35, 80), Greenhoff (51, 70), Cooper (60), Lorimer (68)

NOTTINGHAM FOREST v FC ZÜRICH 2-1 (0-0)

City Ground, Nottingham   31.10.67

Referee: Robert Lacoste (Fra)   Attendance: 32,896

FOREST: Peter Grummitt; Peter Hindley, John Winfield, Terence Hennessey, Robert McKinlay, Henry Newton, Barry Lyons, John Barnwell, Joseph Baker, Frank Wignall, Ian Storey-Moore.   Manager: John Carey

FC ZÜRICH: Karl Grob; Hubert Münch, Konrad Kyburz, Werner Leimgruber, Jürgen Neumann, Ettore Trivellin, Christian Winiger, Rosario Martinelli, Fritz Künzli, Jakob Kuhn, Ernst Meyer.   Trainer: Lav Mantula

Goals: Newton (49), Künzli (59), Storey-Moore (72 pen)

SECOND ROUND

GIRONDINS de BORDEAUX
v ATHLETIC BILBAO 1-3 (0-1)

Stade Municipal, Bordeaux   25.10.67

Referee: Jacques Colling (Lux)   Attendance: 8000

GIRONDINS: Christian Montes; Christian-Jacques Castellan, Bernard Baudet, Robert Peri, Didier Desremeaux (60 Yves Texier), Guy Calleja, Jean-Louis Massé, Hector de Bourgoing, Henri Duhayot, Gabriel Abossolo, Edouard Wojciak.
Trainer: Jean-Pierre Bakrim

ATHLETIC: José Ángel IRÍBAR Cortajarena, José Ignacio SÁEZ Ruiz, Jesús ARANGUREN Merino, Juan María ZORRIQUETA Azpiazu, Luis María ECHEBERRÍA Igartua, José Ramón Martínez LARRAURI, Luis María AGUIRRE Vidaurrazaga, José María ARGOITIA Acha, Antonio María ARIETA Araunabeña Piedra, Fidel URIARTE Macho, José Francisco ROJO I Arroita.   Trainer: Agustin Gainza

Goals: Rojo (18), Arieta (55), Abossolo (74), Uriarte (76)

ATHLETIC BILBAO
v GIRONDINS de BORDEAUX 1-0 (0-0)

Estadio San Mamés, Bilbao   8.11.67

Referee: Hubert Burguet (Bel)   Attendance: 15,000

ATHLETIC: José Ángel IRÍBAR Cortajarena, José Ignacio SÁEZ Ruiz, Luis María ECHEBERRÍA Igartua, Jesús ARANGUREN Merino, José Ramón BETZUÉN Urquiaza, José Ramón Martínez LARRAURI, Antonio María ARIETA Araunabeña Piedra, Nicolás ESTÉFANO Montalbán, José María ARGOITIA Acha, Fidel URIARTE Macho, José Francisco ROJO I Arroita.   Trainer: Agustin Gainza

GIRONDINS: Christian Montes; Christian-Jacques Castellan, Didier Desremeaux, André Chorda, Bernard Baudet, Guy Calleja, Jean-Louis Massé, Hector De Bourgoing (46 Yves Texier), Didier Couécou, Gabriel Abossolo (46 Henri Duhayot), Edouard Wojciak.   Trainer: Jean-Pierre Bakrim

Goal: Estéfano (68)

FC ZÜRICH v NOTTINGHAM FOREST 1-0 (0-0)

Letzigrund, Zürich   14.11.67

Referee: Franz Geluck (Bel)   Attendance: 12,000

FC ZÜRICH: Karl Grob; Hubert Münch, Konrad Kyburz, Werner Leimgruber, Jürgen Neumann, Ettore Trivellin, Christian Winiger, Rosario Martinelli (76 Pirmin Stierli), Fritz Künzli, Jakob Kuhn, Ernst Meyer.   Trainer: Lav Mantula

FOREST: Peter Grummitt; Peter Hindley, John Winfield, Terence Hennessey, Robert McKinlay, Henry Newton, Billy Taylor, John Barnwell, Joseph Baker, Frank Wignall, Robert Chapman.   Manager: John Carey

Goal: Winiger (70)

DUNDEE FC v RFC LIÈGE 3-1 (1-1)

Dens Park, Dundee   1.11.67

Referee: Gösta Lindberg (Swe)   Attendance: 12,000

DUNDEE FC: John Arrol; Robert Wilson, Robert Cox, Stephen Murray, George Stewart, Alexander Stuart, William Campbell, James McLean, Samuel Wilson, Douglas Houston, George McLean.   Manager: Robert Ancell

RFC LIÈGE: Jovan Curcic; Yves Baré, Albert Sulon, Emile Lejeune, Auguste Goessens, Claude Thompkins, Roger De Condé, Alexandre Kozlina, Horatio Schéna, Gérard Sulon, René Andries.

Goals: G. Sulon (7), Stuart (18, 55), S. Wilson (59)

RFC LIÉGE v DUNDEE FC 1-4 (0-2)

Stade Rocourt, Liège   14.11.67

Referee: Rudolf Kreitlein (WG)   Attendance: 12,000

RFC LIÈGE: André Radar; Yves Baré, Albert Sulon, Emile Lejeune, Claude Thompkins, Gérard Sulon, Raymond Corbaye, Horatio Schéna, Philippe Mardaga, Sreten Banovic, René Andries.

DUNDEE FC: John Arrol; Robert Wilson, Robert Cox, Stephen Murray, James Easton, Alexander Stuart, William Campbell, James McLean, Samuel Wilson, George McLean, Douglas Houston.   Manager: Robert Ancell

Goals: G. McLean (13, 41, 58, 80), Lejeune (52)

**REAL ZARAGOZA
v FERENCVÁROS BUDAPEST 2-1** (2-1)

Estadio La Romareda, Zaragoza   1.11.67

Referee: Décio Bentes de Freitas (Por)   Attendance: 30,000

REAL ZARAGOZA: Rafael Álvarez ALARCIA; José Ramón IRUSQUIETA García; José Manuel «MANOLO» GONZÁLEZ López, Severino REIJA Vázquez; Antonio PAÍS Castroagudin, José Luis VIOLETA Lajusticia; MARCELINO Martínez Cao, Eleuterio SANTOS Brito, Miguel Ángel BUSTILLO Lafoz, Juan Manuel VILLA Gutiérrez (55 Antonio HIDALGO de Carlos), Darcy Silveira dos Santos "CANARIO". Trainer: Roque Olsen

FERENCVÁROS: Béla Takács; Dezső Novák, Sándor Mátrai, Miklós Páncsics; Sándor Havasi, Lajos Szűcs, István Szőke, Zoltán Varga, Flórián Albert, Gyula Rákosi, Sándor Katona. Trainer: Károly Lakat

Goals: Marcelino (12, 30), Szőke (32)

**FERENCVÁROS BUDAPEST
v REAL ZARAGOZA 0-0**

Népstadion, Budapest   15.11.67

Referee: Franz Wöhrer (Aus)   Attendance: 30,000

The game was stopped in the 29th minute due to fog

FERENCVÁROS: Béla Takács; Dezső Novák, Sándor Mátrai, Miklós Páncsics; Sándor Havasi, Lajos Szűcs, István Szőke, Zoltán Varga, Flórián Albert, Gyula Rákosi, Sándor Katona. Trainer: Károly Lakat

REAL ZARAGOZA: Andrés Rodríguez «RODRI»; José Ramón IRUSQUIETA García, Francisco SANTAMARÍA Briones, Alfonso María Rodríguez Salas «FONCHO»; José Luis VIOLETA Lajusticia, José Manuel «MANOLO» GONZÁLEZ López; Darcy Silveira dos Santos «CANARIO», Eleuterio SANTOS Brito, MARCELINO Martínez Cao, Antonio PAÍS Castroagudin, Miguel Ángel BUSTILLO Lafoz. Trainer: Roque Olsen

**FERENCVÁROS BUDAPEST
v REAL ZARAGOZA 3-0** (0-0)

Népstadion, Budapest   16.11.67

Referee: Franz Wöhrer (Aus)   Attendance: 50,000

FERENCVÁROS: Béla Takács; Dezső Novák, Sándor Mátrai, Miklós Páncsics; Sándor Havasi, Lajos Szűcs, István Szőke, Zoltán Varga, Flórián Albert, Gyula Rákosi, Sándor Katona. Trainer: Károly Lakat

REAL ZARAGOZA: Andrés Rodríguez «RODRI»; José Ramón IRUSQUIETA García, Francisco SANTAMARÍA Briones, Alfonso María Rodríguez Salas «FONCHO»; José Luis VIOLETA Lajusticia, José Manuel «MANOLO» GONZÁLEZ López; Darcy Silveira dos Santos «CANARIO», Eleuterio SANTOS Brito, MARCELINO Martínez Cao, Antonio PAÍS Castroagudin (46 Manuel FONTENLA Barreiros), Miguel Ángel BUSTILLO Lafoz.   Trainer: Roque Olsen

Sent off: Foncho (74).

Goals: Katona (50 pen), Varga (52), Novák (62)

**VOJVODINA NOVI SAD
v 1.FC LOKOMOTIVE LEIPZIG 0-0**

Gradski, Novi Sad   1.11.67

Referee: Sándor Kaposi (Hun)   Attendance: 5,000

VOJVODINA: Ilija Pantelić (20 Canyi); Rajko Aleksić, Josip Zemko, Stevan Nešticki, Ivan Brzić, Zoran Dakić, Milan Stanić, Radivoj Radosav, Djordjević, Vladimir Savić, Marinković.

1.FC LOKOMOTIVE: Peter Nauert (25 Ulrich Schulze); Christoph Franke, Peter Giessner, Claus Pfeuffer; Michael Faber, Karl Drössler; Werner Gase (70 Jörg Berger), Arno Zerbe, Henning Frenzel, Jürgen Naumann, Wolfram Löwe. Trainer: Hans Studener

**1.FC LOKOMOTIVE LEIPZIG
v VOJVODINA NOVI SAD 0-2** (0-1)

Zentralstadion, Leipzig   22.11.67

Referee: Jef Dorpmans (Hol)   Attendance: 10,000

1.FC LOKOMOTIVE: Ulrich Schulze; Christoph Franke, Peter Giessner, Claus Pfeuffer; Michael Faber, Karl Drössler; Dieter Buckewiz (61 Roland Krauss), Arno Zerbe, Henning Frenzel (76 Jerzy Czieschowitz), Jürgen Naumann, Wolfram Löwe.   Trainer: Hans Studener

VOJVODINA: Ilija Pantelić; Rajko Aleksić, Josip Zemko, Stevan Nešticki, Ivan Brzić, Mladen Vucinić, Radivoj Radosav, Vladimir Savić, Milan Stanić, Dobrivoje Trivić, Zoran Dakić (33 Svemir Djordjić).

Goals: Savić (12), Djordjić (54)

LIVERPOOL FC v TSV MÜNCHEN 1860 8-0 (3-0)

Anfield Road, Liverpool   7.11.67

Referee: Antonio Sbardella (Ita)   Attendance: 44,812

LIVERPOOL: Thomas Lawrence; Christopher Lawler, Gerald Byrne, Thomas Smith, Ronald Yeats, Emlyn Hughes, Ian Callaghan, Roger Hunt, Anthony Hateley, Ian St. John, Peter Thompson.   Manager: Bill Shankly

TSV MÜNCHEN 1860: Petar Radenković; Manfred Wagner (55 Gottfried Peter), Bernd Patzke, Rudolf Steiner, Hans Reich, Željko Perušić, Alfred Heiss (70 Ludwig Bründl), Hans Küppers, Wilfried Kohlars, Rudolf Zeiser, Hans Rebele. Trainer: Albert Sing

Goals: St. John (7), Hateley (9), Smith (43 pen), Hunt (52, 55), Thompson (54), Callaghan (59, 69)

TSV MÜNCHEN 1860 v LIVERPOOL FC 2-1 (1-1)

Grünwalderstadion, München   14.11.67

Referee: Zdenek Vales (Cze)   Attendance: 10,000

TSV MÜNCHEN 1860: Petar Radenković; Manfred Wagner (46 Hans-Günther Kroth), Rudolf Steiner, Rudolf Zeiser, Hans Reich, Bernd Patzke, Alfred Heiss, Horst Schmidt (50 Ludwig Bründl), Wilfried Kohlars, Rudolf Brunnenmeier, Hans Rebele. Trainer: Albert Sing

LIVERPOOL: Thomas Lawrence; Christopher Lawler, Gerald Byrne, Thomas Smith, Ronald Yeats, Emlyn Hughes, Ian Callaghan, Roger Hunt, Anthony Hateley (46 William Stevenson), Ian St.John, Peter Thompson. Manager: Bill Shankly

Goals: Callaghan (5), Kohlars (33, 88)

ATLÉTICO MADRID v GÖZTEPE IZMIR 2-0 (1-0)

Estadio del Manzanares, Madrid   8.11.67

Referee: Robert Hélies (Fra)   Attendance: 20,000

ATLÉTICO: Roberto Rodríguez García "RODRI"; Feliciano RIVILLA Muñoz, Julio IGLESIAS Santamaría, Isacio CALLEJA García; Jesús GLARÍA Roldán, Jesús MARTÍNEZ JAYO; Luis Armando UFARTE Ventosa, LUIS Aragonés Suárez, José Eulogio GÁRATE Ormaechea, ADELARDO Rodríguez Sánchez (75 José Enrique CARDONA Gutiérrez), Enrique COLLAR Monterrubio.   Trainer: Otto Gloria

GÖZTEPE: Ali Artuner; Mehmet Aydin, Çağlayan Derebaşi; Hüseyin Yazici, Mehmet Tuncer Ergon, Nevzat Güzelırmak; Nihat Yayöz, Ertan Öznur, Fevzi Zemzem, Gürsel Aksel, Halil Kiraz.   Trainer: Adnan Sovari

Goals: Gárate (24), Cardona (88)

GÖZTEPE IZMIR v ATLÉTICO MADRID 3-0 (2-0)

Alsançak Stadyumu, Izmir   22.11.67

Referee: Josip Strmečki (Jug)   Attendance: 15,600

GÖZTEPE: Ali Artuner; Halil Kiraz, Çağlayan Derebaşi; Hüseyin Yazici, Mehmet Tuncer Ergon, Nevzat Güzelirmak; Ertan Öznur, Ali Ihsan Okçuoglu, Fevzi Zemzem, Gürsel Aksel, Ceyhan Yazar.   Trainer: Adnan Sovari

ATLÉTICO: Miguel SAN ROMÁN Núñez; Feliciano RIVILLA Muñoz, Julio IGLESIAS Santamaría, Isacio CALLEJA García; Jesús GLARÍA Roldán, Jesús MARTÍNEZ JAYO; Luis Armando UFARTE Ventosa, LUIS Aragonés Suárez, José Eulogio GÁRATE Ormaechea (59 José Antonio URTIAGA Albizu), ADELARDO Rodríguez Sánchez, Enrique COLLAR Monterrubio.   Trainer: Otto Gloria

Collar, Ufarte (66) sent off (14)

Goals: Halil (15 pen, 90), Gürsel (27)

GLASGOW RANGERS v FC KÖLN 3-0 (0-0)

Ibrox Stadium, Glasgow   8.11.67

Referee: Aranth Jensen (Dan)   Attendance: 55,000

RANGERS: Erik Sorensen; Kai Johansen, William Mathieson, John Greig (.. Alex Smith), Ronald McKinnon, David Smith, William Henderson, Andrew Penman, Alex Ferguson, William Johnston, Örjan Persson.   Manager: David White

FC KÖLN: Toni Schumacher; Wolfgang Rausch, Anton Regh, Heinz Simmet, Matthias Hemmersbach, Fritz Pott, Karl-Heinz Rühl, Heinz Flohe, Johannes Löhr, Wolfgang Overath, Heinz Hornig.   Trainer: Willy Multhaup

Goals: Ferguson (51, 72), Henderson (63)

FC KÖLN
v GLASGOW RANGERS 3-1 (1-0, 3-0) a.e.t.

Müngersdorfenstadion, Köln   28.11.67

Referee: Concetto Lo Bello (Ita)   Attendance: 12,000

FC KÖLN: Toni Schumacher; Wolfgang Rausch, Karl-Heinz Thielen, Wolfgang Weber, Heinz Simmet, Matthias Hemmersbach, Fritz Pott, Karl-Heinz Ruhl, Johannes Löhr (72 Heinz Flohe), Wolfgang Overath, Heinz Hornig. Trainer: Willy Multhaup

RANGERS: Erik Sorensen; Kai Johansen, William Mathieson, John Greig, Ronald McKinnon, David Smith, William Henderson, Andrew Penman, Alex Ferguson (.. Robert Watson), William Johnston, Örjan Persson. Manager: David White

Goals: Overath (1), Weber (75), Rühl (79), Henderson (118 pen)

AC BOLOGNA v DINAMO ZAGREB 0-0

Stadio Comunale, Bologna   *15.11.67*

Referee: Norman Burtenshaw (Eng)   Attendance: 28,500

BOLOGNA: Giuseppe Vavassori; Carlo Furlanis, Mario Ardizzon, Aristide Guarneri, Tazio Roversi, Faustino Turra, Marino Perani, Giacomo Bulgarelli (46 Bruno Pace), Sergio Clerici, Helmut Haller, Ezio Pascutti.
Trainer: Luis Antonio Carniglia

DINAMO: Fahrija Dautbegović; Rudolf Cvek, Branko Graçanin, Rudolf Belin, Mladen Ramljak, Filip Blašković, Marijan Čerček, Denijal Pirić, Marijan Novak, Josip Gucmirtl, Krasnodar Rora.   Trainer: Branko Zebec

DINAMO ZAGREB v AC BOLOGNA 1-2 (0-1)

Maksimir, Zagreb   *22.11.67*

Referee: William Syme (Sco)   Attendance: 28,500

DINAMO: Fahrija Dautbegović; Rudolf Cvek, Branko Graçanin, Rudolf Belin, Mladen Ramljak, Filip Blašković (46 Zlatko Mesić), Marijan Čerček, Denijal Pirić, Marijan Novak (46 Ivica Kiš), Josip Gucmirtl, Krasnodar Rora.
Trainer: Branko Zebec

BOLOGNA: Giuseppe Vavassori; Carlo Furlanis, Mario Ardizzon, Aristide Guarneri, Tazio Roversi, Romano Fogli, Marino Perani, Giacomo Bulgarelli (46 Faustino Turra), Bruno Pace, Sergio Clerici (46 Ezio Pascutti), Helmut Haller.
Trainer: Luis Antonio Carniglia

Goals: Haller (45), Belin (68), Pace (88)

NAPOLI v HIBERNIAN EDINBURGH 4-1 (1-0)

Stadio San Paolo, Napoli   *22.11.67*

Referee: Rudolf Scheurer (Swi)   Attendance: 30,000

NAPOLI: Dino Zoff; Stelio Nardin, Luigi Pogliana, Amedeo Stenti, Dino Panzanato, Ottavio Bianchi, Jarbas Faustinho Cané, Antonio Juliano, José Altafini, Vincenzo Montefusco (46 Alberto Orlando), Paolo Barison.   Trainer: Bruno Pesaola

HIBERNIAN: Thomson Allan; Robert Duncan, Joseph Davis, Patrick Stanton, John Madsen, Alan McGraw, Alexander Scott, Patrick Quinn, Colin Stein, Colin Grant, James O'Rourke.
Manager: Bob Shankly

Goals: Cané (20, 50, 85), Altafini (68), Stein (80)

HIBERNIAN EDINBURGH v NAPOLI 5-0 (2-0)

Easter Road, Edinburgh   *29.11.67*

Referee: Antonio Rigo Sureda (Spa)   Attendance: 21,000

HIBERNIAN: William Wilson; Robert Duncan, Joseph Davis, Patrick Stanton, John Madsen, Alan McGraw, Alexander Scott, Patrick Quinn, Colin Stein, Peter Cormack, Eric Stevenson.
Manager: Bob Shankly

NAPOLI: Dino Zoff; Stelio Nardin, Luigi Pogliana, Mario Zurlini, Dino Panzanato, Ottavio Bianchi, Jarbas Faustinho Cané, Antonio Juliano, Alberto Orlando, Vincenzo Montefusco (46 Antonio Girardo), Paolo Barison.   Trainer: Bruno Pesaola

Goals: Duncan (5), Quinn (44), Cormack (66), Stanton (67), Stein (77)

PARTIZAN BEOGRAD v LEEDS UNITED 1-2 (0-1)

JNA, Beograd   *29.11.67*

Referee: Dogan Babacan (Tur)   Attendance: 8,000

PARTIZAN: Ivan Curković; Miloš Radaković, Milan Damjanović, Borivoje Djordjević (27 Milan Vukelić), Blagoje Paunović, Ljubomir Mihajlović, Mane Bajić, Ljuan Prekazi, Mustafa Hasanagić, Idriz Hosić, Josip Pirmajer.
Trainer: Stjepan Bobek

LEEDS UNITED: David Harvey; Paul Reaney, Terence Cooper, William Bremner, Jack Charlton, Norman Hunter, James Greenhoff, Peter Lorimer, Paul Madeley, Rodney Belfitt, Edward Gray (46 Michael Bates). Bates sent off (79).
Manager: Don Revie

Goals: Lorimer (24), Belfitt (53), Paunović (87)

LEEDS UNITED v PARTIZAN BEOGRAD 1-1 (1-0)

Elland Road, Leeds   *6.12.67*

Referee: Dittmar Huber (Swi)   Attendance: 34,258

LEEDS UNITED: Gary Sprake, Paul Reaney, Terence Cooper, William Bremner, Jack Charlton, Norman Hunter, James Greenhoff, Peter Lorimer, Paul Madeley, Terence Hibbitt (46 Albert Johanneson), Edward Gray.   Manager: Don Revie

PARTIZAN: Ivan Curković; Miloš Radaković, Milan Damjanović, Milan Vukelić, Blagoje Paunović, Ljubomir Mihajlović, Mane Bajić, Ljuan Prekazi, Milan Petrović, Idriz Hosić, Josip Pirmajer (46 Ivica Pogarić).
Trainer: Stjepan Bobek

Goals: Lorimer (29), Petrović (60)

SPORTING LISBOA
v AC FIORENTINA FIRENZE 2-1 (1-0)

Estadio José Alvalade, Lisboa   6.12.67

Referee: Kurt Handwerker (WG)   Attendance: 16,735

SPORTING: Joaquim da Silva CARVALHO; João Pedro
BARNABÉ, HILÁRIO Rosário da Conceição, ARMANDO
António Manhiça, JOSÉ CARLOS da Silva José; Carlos
BARÃO, Vítor Gonçalves; Ernesto Figueiredo, João de Matos
Moura Lourenço, Mário da Silva Mateus "MARINHO" (82 José
Rodrigues LEITÃO), Fernando PERES.
Trainer: Fernando Cabrita

FIORENTINA: Enrico Albertosi; Giovan Battista Pirovano,
Eraldo Mancini, Mario Bertini, Ugo Ferrante, Giuseppe Brizi,
Mario Maraschi, Claudio Merlo (82 Pierluigi Cencetti), Mario
Brugnera, Giancarlo De Sisti, Luciano Chiarugi (46 Marzio
Magli).   Trainer: Giuseppe Chiapella

Goals: Lourenço (4), Magli (62), Peres (74 pen)

AC FIORENTINA FIRENZE
v SPORTING LISBOA 1-1 (1-0)

Stadio Comunale, Firenze   13.12.67

Referee: Tibor Wotava (Hun)   Attendance: 8,200

FIORENTINA: Enrico Albertosi; Giovan Battista Pirovano,
Eraldo Mancini, Mario Bertini (52 Cortesi), Ugo Ferrante,
Pierluigi Cencetti, Mario Maraschi (61 Luciano Chiarugi),
Claudio Merlo, Mario Brugnera, Giancarlo De Sisti,
AMARILDO Tavares de Silveire.   Trainer: Giuseppe Chiapella

SPORTING: Joaquim da Silva CARVALHO; João Pedro
BARNABÉ, HILÁRIO Rosário da Conceição, ARMANDO
António Manhiça, JOSÉ CARLOS da Silva José; Carlos BARÃO,
Vítor Gonçalves; Carlos Adriano Santos "CARLITOS" (67 José
ALEXANDRE da Silva BAPTISTA), Armenio Alberto "ADÉ",
João de Matos Moura Lourenço, Fernando PERES.
Trainer: Fernando Cabrita

Goals: Maraschi (20), Peres (57)

THIRD ROUND

FERENCVÁROS BUDAPEST
v LIVERPOOL FC 1-0 (1-0)

Népstadion, Budapest   28.11.67

Referee: Alessandro d'Agostini (Ita)   Attendance: 30,000

FERENCVÁROS: Béla Takács; Dezső Novák, Miklós Páncsics,
Sándor Havasi; István Juhász, Lajos Szűcs; István Szőke, Zoltán
Varga, László Branikovits, Gyula Rákosi, Sándor Katona.
Trainer: Károly Lakat

LIVERPOOL: Thomas Lawrence; Christopher Lawler, Gerald
Byrne, Thomas Smith; Ronald Yeats, Emlyn Hughes; Ian
Callaghan, Roger Hunt, Anthony Hateley, William Stevenson,
Peter Thompson.   Manager: Bill Shankly

Goal: Katona (44)

LIVERPOOL FC
v FERENCVÁROS BUDAPEST 0-1 (0-1)

Anfield Road, Liverpool   9.01.68

Referee: Gerhard Schulenburg (WG)   Attendance: 46,892

LIVERPOOL: Thomas Lawrence; Christopher Lawler, Gerald
Byrne, Thomas Smith; Ronald Yeats, Emlyn Hughes; Ian
Callaghan, Roger Hunt, Geoffrey Strong, Ian St.John, Peter
Thompson.   Manager: Bill Shankly

FERENCVÁROS: Béla Takács; Dezső Novák, Miklós Páncsics,
Sándor Havasi; István Juhász, Lajos Szűcs; István Szőke, Zoltán
Varga, László Branikovits, Gyula Rákosi, Sándor Katona.
Trainer: Károly Lakat

Goal: Branikovits (19)

LEEDS UNITED
v HIBERNIAN EDINBURGH 1-0 (1-0)

Elland Road, Leeds   20.12.67

Referee: John Russell (NIr)   Attendance: 31,522

LEEDS UNITED: Gary Sprake; Paul Reaney (46 Paul
Madeley), Terence Cooper, William Bremner, Jack Charlton,
James Greenhoff, Norman Hunter, Peter Lorimer, Michael
Jones, John Giles, Edward Gray.   Manager: Don Revie

HIBERNIAN: William Wilson; Robert Duncan, Joseph Davis,
Patrick Stanton, John Madsen, Alan McGraw, Alexander
Scott, Patrick Quinn, Colin Stein (30 James O'Rourke), Peter
Cormack, Eric Stevenson.   Manager: Bob Shankly

Goal: E. Gray (4)

HIBERNIAN EDINBURGH
v LEEDS UNITED 1-1 (1-0)

Easter Road, Edinburgh   10.01.68

Referee: Clive Thomas (Wal)   Attendance: 30,000

HIBERNIAN: William Wilson; Robert Duncan, Joseph Davis,
Patrick Stanton, John Madsen, Alan McGraw, Alexander Scott,
Patrick Quinn, Colin Stein, Peter Cormack, Eric Stevenson.
Manager: Bob Shankly

LEEDS UNITED: Gary Sprake, Paul Reaney, Terence Cooper,
William Bremner, Jack Charlton, James Greenhoff, Norman
Hunter, Peter Lorimer, Michael Jones, John Giles, Edward
Gray.   Manager: Don Revie

Goals: Stein (4), Charlton (87)

VOJVODINA NOVI SAD
v GÖZTEPE IZMIR 1-0 (0-0)

Gradski, Novi Sad   21.02.68

Referee: Aurelio Angonese (Ita)   Attendance: 2,500

VOJVODINA: Ilija Pantelic; Tomce Stamenski, Mladen
Vucinic, Josip Zemko, Ivan Brzic, Stevan Nešticki, Milan
Stanic, Radivoj Radosav, Dobrivoje Trivic, Vladimir Savic, Vasa
Pušibrk (46 Svemir Djordjic).

GÖZTEPE: Ali Artuner; Mehmet Aydin, Çaglayan Derebaşi;
Hüseyin Yazici, Halil Kiraz, Nevzat Güzelirmak; Ertan Öznur,
Ali Ihsan Okçuoglu, Fevzi Zemzem, Gürsel Aksel, Nihat Yayöz.
Trainer: Adnan Sovari

Goal: Savić (47)

GÖZTEPE IZMIR
v VOJVODINA NOVI SAD 0-1 (0-0)

Alsançak, Izmir   28.02.68

Referee: Franz Wöhrer (Aus)   Attendance: 21,400

GÖZTEPE: Ali Artuner; Mehmet Aydin, Çaglayan Derebaşi;
Hüseyin Yazici, Halil Kiraz, Nevzat Güzelirmak; Ertan Öznur,
Ali Ihsan Okçuoglu, Fevzi Zemzem, Gürsel Aksel, Nihat Yayöz.
Trainer: Adnan Sovari

VOJVODINA: Ilija Pantelic, Tomce Stamenski, Mladen
Vucinic, Josip Zemko, Ivan Brzic, Stevan Nešticki, Milan
Stanic, Radivoj Radosav, Dobrivoje Trivic, Vladimir Savic,
Svemir Djordjic.

Goal: Trivić (71)

FC ZÜRICH v SPORTING LISBOA 3-0 (2-0)

Letzigrund, Zürich   28.02.68

Referee: Wolfgang Riedel (DDR)   Attendance: 11,300

FC ZÜRICH: Karl Grob; Jürgen Neumann, Hubert Münch,
Pirmin Stierli, Werner Leimgruber, Xavier Stierli, Rosario
Martinelli, Jakob Kuhn, Christian Winiger, Fritz Künzli, Ernst
Meyer.   Trainer: Lav Mantula

SPORTING: Joaquim da Silva CARVALHO; Manuel Pedro
Gomes, HILÁRIO Rosário da Conceição, ARMANDO António
Manhiça, JOSÉ CARLOS da Silva José; Daniel Afonso da
Silva DANI, Vítor Gonçalves (73 Francisco Caló); Ernesto
Figueiredo (62 João Carlos), João de Matos Moura Lourenço,
Mário da Silva Mateus "MARINHO", Manuel Duarte.
Trainer: Fernando Cabrita

Goals: Winiger (6), Meyer (42), Neumann (89)

SPORTING LISBOA v FC ZÜRICH 1-0 (1-0)

Estadio José Alvalade, Lisboa   13.03.68

Referee: Alfred Ott (WG)   Attendance: 19,426

SPORTING: Joaquim da Silva CARVALHO; Manuel Pedro
Gomes, HILÁRIO Rosário da Conceição, ARMANDO António
Manhiça, JOSÉ CARLOS da Silva José; Daniel Afonso da Silva
DANI, Vítor Gonçalves; Mário da Silva Mateus "MARINHO",
Ernesto Figueiredo, João de Matos Moura Lourenço, Carlos
Adriano Santos "CARLITOS" (55 JOSÉ MORAIS).
Trainer: Fernando Cabrita

FC ZÜRICH: Karl Grob; Hubert Münch, Jürgen Neumann,
Werner Leimgruber, Xavier Stierli, Pirmin Stierli, Jakob Kuhn,
Christian Winiger, Rosario Martinelli, Fritz Künzli, Ernst
Meyer.   Trainer: Lav Mantula

Goal: Carlitos (22)

QUARTER-FINALS

FERENCVÁROS BUDAPEST
v ATHLETIC BILBAO 2-1 (2-0)

Népstadion, Budapest   13.03.68

Referee: Vital Loraux (Bel)   Attendance: 30,000

FERENCVÁROS: Béla Takács; Sándor Havasi, László Bálint,
László Horváth; Dezső Novák, Lajos Szűcs; János Karába,
Zoltán Varga, Flórián Albert, Gyula Rákosi, Máté Fenyvesi.
Trainer: Károly Lakat

ATHLETIC: José Ángel IRÍBAR Cortajarena; José Ignacio
SÁEZ Ruiz, Luis María ECHEBERRÍA Igartua, Jesús
ARANGUREN Merino, José Ramón Martínez LARRAURI;
Luis María AGUIRRE Vidaurrazaga, Luis María ZUGAZAGA
Martínez; Antonio María ARIETA Araunabeña Piedra, José
María ARGOITIA Acha, Fidel URIARTE Macho (13 José
Ramón BETZUÉN Urquiaza), José Francisco ROJO I Arroita.
Trainer: Agustin Gainza

Goals: Albert (14), Novák (30 pen), Aranguren (59)

ATHLETIC BILBAO
v FERENCVÁROS BUDAPEST 1-2 (0-0)

Estadio San Mamés, Bilbao   27.03.68

Referee: John Taylor (Eng)   Attendance: 40,000

ATHLETIC: José Ángel IRÍBAR Cortajarena; José Ignacio SÁEZ Ruiz, Luis María ECHEBERRÍA Igartua, Jesús ARANGUREN Merino; José Ramón Martínez LARRAURI, Luis María AGUIRRE Vidaurrazaga (46 José Ramón BETZUÉN Urquiaza), Luis María ZUGAZAGA Martínez; Antonio María ARIETA Araunabeña Piedra, José María ARGOITIA Acha, Nicolás ESTÉFANO Montalbán, José Francisco ROJO I Arroita (79 Francisco Javier Ormaza Garay). Trainer: Agustin Gainza

FERENCVÁROS: Béla Takács; Dezső Novák, László Bálint, Sándor Havasi; László Horváth, Lajos Szűcs; János Karába, László Branikovits, Flórián Albert, Gyula Rákosi, Máté Fenyvesi.   Trainer: Károly Lakat

Goals: Betzuén (68), Branikovits (69), dr. Fenyvesi (86)

GLASGOW RANGERS v LEEDS UNITED 0-0

Ibrox Stadium, Glasgow   26.03.68

Referee: Gottfried Dienst (Swi)   Attendance: 60,000

RANGERS: Erik Sørensen; Kai Johansen, William Mathieson, John Greig, Ronald McKinnon, David Smith, Alex Ferguson, Alexander Smith, William Henderson, William Johnston, Örjan Persson.   Manager: David White

LEEDS UNITED: Gary Sprake; Paul Reaney, Terence Cooper, William Bremner, Jack Charlton, Norman Hunter, James Greenhoff (3 Rodney Belfitt), Peter Lorimer, Michael Jones, John Giles, Paul Madeley.   Manager: Don Revie

LEEDS UNITED v GLASGOW RANGERS 2-0 (2-0)

Elland Road, Leeds   9.04.68

Referee: Kurt Tschenscher (WG)   Attendance: 50,498

LEEDS UNITED: David Harvey; Paul Reaney, Terence Cooper, William Bremner, Jack Charlton, Norman Hunter, James Greenhoff, Paul Madeley, Michael Jones, John Giles, Peter Lorimer.   Manager: Don Revie

RANGERS: Erik Sørensen; Kai Johansen, William Mathieson, John Greig, Ronald McKinnon, David Smith, Alex Ferguson, Alexander Willoughby (68 Andrew Penman), William Henderson, William Johnston, Örjan Persson. Manager: David White

Goals: Giles (25 pen), Lorimer (31)

DUNDEE FC v FC ZÜRICH 1-0 (0-0)

Dens Park, Dundee   27.03.68

Referee: Jef F. Dorpmans (Hol)   Attendance: 18,000

DUNDEE FC: Alistair Donaldson; Robert Wilson, George Stewart, Douglas Houston, James Easton, Stephen Murray, James McLean, William Campbell, Samuel Wilson (46 Roddy Georgeson), George McLean, John Scott.
Manager: Robert Ancell

FC ZÜRICH: Karl Grob; Jürgen Neumann, Hubert Münch, Pirmin Stierli, Werner Leimgruber, Xavier Stierli, Rosario Martinelli, Jakob Kuhn, Christian Winiger, Fritz Künzli, Ernst Meyer.   Trainer: Lav Mantula

Goal: Easton (80)

FC ZÜRICH v DUNDEE FC 0-1 (0-1)

Letzigrund, Zürich   3.04.68

Referee: Raymond Poncin (Fra)   Attendance: 24,000

FC ZÜRICH: Karl Grob; Hubert Münch, Jürgen Neumann, Werner Leimgruber, Pirmin Stierli, Xavier Stierli, Jakob Kuhn, Christian Winiger, Rosario Martinelli, Fritz Künzli, Ernst Meyer.   Trainer: Lav Mantula

DUNDEE FC: Alistair Donaldson; Robert Wilson, Douglas Houston, Stephen Murray, James Easton, George Stewart, William Campbell, James McLean, Samuel Wilson, George McLean, John Scott.   Manager: Robert Ancell

Goal: S. Wilson (37)

AC BOLOGNA v VOJVODINA NOVI SAD 0-0

Stadio Comunale, Bologna   27.03.68

Referee: Anibal Da Silva Oliveira (Por)   Attendance: 15,000

BOLOGNA: Giuseppe Vavassori; Carlo Furlanis (46 Faustino Turra), Mario Ardizzon, Aristide Guarneri, Francesco Janich, Romano Fogli, Marino Perani (46 Marcello Tentorio), Giacomo Bulgarelli, Sergio Clerici, Helmut Haller, Bruno Pace. Trainer: Luis Antonio Carniglia

VOJVODINA: Ilija Pantelić; Tomce Stamenski, Mladen Vucinić, Josip Zemko, Ivan Brzić, Stevan Nešticki, Vladimir Savić (46 Dimitrije Radović), Radivoj Radosav, Racić (46 Petar Nikezić), Dobrivoje Trivić, Svemir Djordjić.

119

VOJVODINA NOVI SAD v AC BOLOGNA 0-2 (0-0)

Gradski, Novi Sad   9.04.68

Referee: Ferdinand Marschall (Aus)   Attendance: 20,000

VOJVODINA: Ilija Pantelić; Tomce Stamenski, Mladen Vucinić (46 Dimitrije Radović), Josip Zemko, Ivan Brzić, Stevan Nešticki, Vladimir Savić, Radivoj Radosav, Petar Nikezić, Dobrivoje Trivić, Svemir Djordjić.

BOLOGNA: Giuseppe Vavassori; Carlo Furlanis, Mario Ardizzon, Aristide Guarneri, Francesco Janich, Romano Fogli, Faustino Turra, Giacomo Bulgarelli, Sergio Clerici, Helmut Haller, Bruno Pace (46 Augusto Scala).
Trainer: Luis Antonio Carniglia

Goals: Pace (49), Clerici (87)

SEMI-FINALS

DUNDEE FC v LEEDS UNITED 1-1 (1-1)

Dens Park, Dundee   1.05.68

Referee: Gerhard Schulenburg (WG)   Attendance: 30,000

DUNDEE FC: Alistair Donaldson; Robert Wilson, Dave Swan, Stephen Murray, James Easton, George Stewart, William Campbell, James McLean, Samuel Wilson, George McLean, Alexander Kinninmonth.   Manager: Robert Ancell

LEEDS UNITED: David Harvey; Paul Reaney, Terence Cooper, Jack Charlton, William Bremner, Paul Madeley, Norman Hunter, James Greenhoff, Peter Lorimer, John Giles, Edward Gray.   Manager: Don Revie

Goals: Madeley (26), R. Wilson (36)

LEEDS UNITED v DUNDEE FC 1-0 (0-0)

Elland Road, Leeds   15.05.68

Referee: Willem Schalks (Hol)   Attendance: 23,830

LEEDS UNITED: Gary Sprake; Paul Reaney, Terence Cooper, William Bremner, Paul Madeley, Norman Hunter, James Greenhoff, Peter Lorimer, Michael Jones, John Giles, Edward Gray.   Manager: Don Revie

DUNDEE FC: Alistair Donaldson; Ron Selway, Douglas Houston, Stephen Murray, James Easton, George Stewart, William Campbell, James McLean, Samuel Wilson, George McLean, John Scott (84 Alexander Stuart).
Manager: Robert Ancell

Goal: E. Gray (81)

**FERENCVÁROS BUDAPEST
v AC BOLOGNA 3-2** (1-2)

Népstadion, Budapest   22.05.68

Referee: Anton Bucheli (Swi)   Attendance: 20,000

FERENCVÁROS: István Géczi; Dezső Novák, László Bálint, Sándor Havasi; István Juhász (.. János Karába), Miklós Páncsics; István Szőke, Zoltán Varga, Lajos Szűcs, László Branikovits, Sándor Katona.   Trainer: Károly Lakat

BOLOGNA: Giuseppe Vavassori; Carlo Furlanis, Mario Ardizzon, Aristide Guarneri; Francesco Janich, Faustino Turra (.. Romano Fogli), Marino Perani; Giacomo Bulgarelli, Sergio Clerici, Helmut Haller, Bruno Pace.
Trainer: Luis Antonio Carniglia

Goals: Clerici (1), Perani (34), Branikovits (37, 56), Varga (80)

**AC BOLOGNA
v FERENCVÁROS BUDAPEST 2-2** (1-1)

Stadio Comunale, Bologna   27.05.68

Referee: Kurt Tschenscher (WG)   Attendance: 30,000

BOLOGNA: Giuseppe Vavassori; Carlo Furlanis, Mario Ardizzon, Aristide Guarneri; Francesco Janich, Marcello Tentorio, Marino Perani; Giacomo Bulgarelli (.. Romano Fogli, .. Paolo Ferrario), Sergio Clerici, Helmut Haller, Bruno Pace.
Trainer: Luis Antonio Carniglia

FERENCVÁROS: István Géczi; Dezső Novák, Miklós Páncsics, László Horváth; Sándor Havasi, Lajos Szűcs; János Karába (.. Sándor Katona), Zoltán Varga, Flórián Albert, László Branikovits, István Szőke.   Trainer: Károly Lakat

Goals: Varga (24), Perani (43), Tentorio (59), Havasi (69)

FINAL

**LEEDS UNITED
v FERENCVÁROS BUDAPEST 1-0** (1-0)

Elland Road, Leeds   7.08.68

Referee: Rudolf Scheurer (Swi)   Attendance: 25,268

LEEDS UNITED: Gary Sprake; Paul Reaney, John "Jack" Charlton, Norman Hunter; Terence Cooper, William Bremner (Cap); Peter Lorimer, Paul Madeley, Michael Jones (46 Rodney Belfitt), John Giles (46 James Greenhoff), Edward Gray.
Manager: Don Revie

FERENCVÁROS: István Géczi; Dezső Novák (Cap), Miklós Páncsics, Sándor Havasi; István Juhász, Lajos Szűcs; István Szőke, Zoltán Varga, Flórián Albert, Gyula Rákosi, Máté Fenyvesi (65 László Branikovits).   Trainer: Károly Lakat

Goal: Jones (41)

FERENCVÁROS BUDAPEST v LEEDS UNITED 0-0

Népstadion, Budapest 11.09.68

Referee: Gerhard Schulenburg (WG)   Attendance: 76,000

FERENCVÁROS: István Géczi; Dezső Novák (Cap), Miklós Páncsics, Sándor Havasi; István Juhász, Lajos Szűcs; István Szőke (60 János Karába), Zoltán Varga, Flórián Albert, Gyula Rákosi, Sándor Katona.   Trainer: Károly Lakat

LEEDS UNITED: Gary Sprake; Paul Reaney, John "Jack" Charlton, Norman Hunter, Terence Cooper, William Bremner (Cap), Michael O'Grady, Peter Lorimer, Michael Jones, Paul Madeley, Terence Hibbitt (62 Michael Bates).
Manager: Don Revie

Goalscorers Fairs Cup 1967/68

8 goals: Peter Lorimer (Leeds United)

5 goals: José Gárate (Atlético Madrid), George McLean (Dundee FC)

4 goals: Christian Winiger (FC Zürich), Flórián Albert, László Branikovits, Zoltán Varga (Ferencváros), James Greenhoff (Leeds United)

3 goals: Joseph Baker (Nottingham Forest), Karl-Heinz Rühl (FC Köln), José Altafini, Jarbas Faustinho Cané (Napoli), Mustafa Hasanagić (Partizan Beograd), Peter Cormack, Colin Stein (Hibernian), Ian Callaghan, Anthony Hateley, Roger Hunt (Liverpool), Alex Ferguson (Glasgow Rangers), Dobrivoje Trivic (Vojvodina), Samuel Wilson (Dundee FC), Sergio Clerici, Bruno Pace (Bologna), Dezső Novák (Ferencváros), Albert Johanneson (Leeds United), Cardona (Atlético Madrid), João de Matos Moura Lourenço (Sporting Lisboa)

2 goals: N. Campbell (St.Patrick's), Valdir (FC Porto), Zaldúa (CF Barcelona), Duhayot, Wojciak (Bordeaux), Andries, Mardaga (FC Liège), Marcelino, Bustillo (Real Zaragoza), Kohlars, Küppers, Grosser (München 1860), Löhr (FC Köln), Jukic, Kiss (Dinamo Zagreb), Petrović (Partizan Beograd), Löwe, Zerbe (1.FC Lokomotive Leipzig), Maraschi, Brugnera (Fiorentina), Stanton (Hibernian), Halil, Fevzi (Göztepe Izmir), Peres (Sporting Lisboa), Arieta, Uriarte (Athletic Bilbao), Henderson (Glasgow Rangers), Savic (Vojvodina), J.McLean, Stuart (Dundee FC), Perani (Bologna), Katona (Ferencváros), Jones, Madeley, E.Gray (Leeds United)

1 goal: L. Nielsen, Printzlau (Frem København), Afendoulidis, Makris (PAOK), Lambert (Club Brugge), Hennessey, Ryan (St.Patrick's), Leitner, Schmidt (Wiener SK), Maiwald, Van Veen, Wery, Van Vliet (DOS Utrecht), Szepanski (Malmö FF), Straschitz (Hannover 96), M.Dridea, Grozea (Petrolul Ploieşti), Pavis, Hamilton (Linfield Belfast), Pinto (FC Porto), Kreische, Riedel (Dynamo Dresden), Jercan, Dobrin, Kraus (FC Argeş Piteşti), Georgy, Heuri (Servette Genève), Fränkel (Antwerp), Rensenbrink, Van den Berg (DWS Amsterdam), Fernando (CUF Barreiro), Iliev, Vasilev (Lokomotiv Plovdiv), Tesař, Lála (Slavia Praha), Newton, Storey-Moore, Chapman, Lyons (Nottingham Forest), Abossolo, Chorda, Masse,

Couécou, Calleja, Ruiter (Bordeaux), G. Sulon, Lejeune, Banovic (FC Liège), Canario, Moya, Villa (Real Zaragoza), Bründl, Peter (München 1860), Luis (Atlético Madrid), Overath, Weber (FC Köln), Belin, Zambata (Dinamo Zagreb), Barison, Girardo (Napoli), Paunović, Kovacević, Rasović (Partizan Beograd), Faber (1.FC Lokomotive Leipzig), Magli, De Sisti, Bertini (Fiorentina), Duncan, Quinn, Stevenson (Hibernian Edinburgh), Gürsel (Göztepe Izmir), Carlitos (Sporting Lisboa), St.John, Smith, Thompson, Yeats (Liverpool), Aranguren, Betzuén, Rojo, Estéfano, Arráiz, Arroyo (Athletic Bilbao), Penman, Greig (Glasgow Rangers), Meyer, Neumann, Künzli, Kuhn (FC Zürich), Djordjic, Dakic, Zemko (Vojvodina), Easton, R.Wilson (Dundee FC), Tentorio, Haller (Bologna), Havasi, Fenyvesi, Szőke (Ferencváros), Giles, Charlton, Belfitt, Bremner, Cooper (Leeds United)

Own Goals: Calleja (Atlético Madrid) for Wiener SK, Laszig (Hannover 96) for Napoli

FAIRS CUP 1968-69

FIRST ROUND

WACKER INNSBRUCK v EINTRACHT FRANKFURT am MAIN 2-2 (1-1)

Tivoli, Innsbruck 10.09.68

Referee: Alfred Delcourt (Bel)   Attendance: 5,000

WACKER: Herbert Rettensteiner (66 Leo Tschenett); Anton Urban, Roland Eschlmüller, Heinz Binder, Karl Prowaznik (.. Dieter Lederer); Josef Obert, Helmut Senekowitsch; Johannes Ettmayer, Michael Vogel, Franz Wolny, Peter Aust. Trainer: Branko Elsner

EINTRACHT: Peter Kunter; Karl-Heinz Wirth, Hermann-Dieter Bellut, Dieter Lindner, Lothar Schämer, Jürgen Kalb, Helmut Kraus (.. Günter Keifler), Jürgen Grabowski, Ernst Abbé, Bernd Nickel (60 Oskar Lotz), Heiko Racky.
Trainer: Erich Ribbeck

Goals: Aust (20), Abbé (26), Grabowski (65 pen), Lotz (81 og)

EINTRACHT FRANKFURT am MAIN v WACKER INNSBRUCK 3-0 (1-0)

Wald-Stadion, Frankfurt am Main 1.10.68

Referee: James Finney (Eng)   Attendance: 900

EINTRACHT: Hans Tilkowski; Karl-Heinz Wirth, Dieter Lindner, Friedel Lutz, Lothar Schämer, Hermann-Dieter Bellut, Jürgen Kalb, Oskar Lotz, Bernd Nickel, Wilhelm Huberts, Heiko Racky.   Trainer: Erich Ribbeck

WACKER: Herbert Rettensteiner; Karl Prowaznik, Heinz Binder, Roland Eschlmüller, Werner Kriess; Helmut Senekowitsch (.. Iwanusch), Dieter Lederer, Josef Obert; Michael Vogel, Peter Aust, Johannes Ettmayer.
Trainer: Branko Elsner

Goals: Kalb (8), Nickel (47, 85)

NEWCASTLE UNITED
v FEYENOORD ROTTERDAM 4-0 (3-0)

St. James' Park, Newcastle   11.09.68

Referee: Hans Carlsson (Swe)   Attendance: 46,300

UNITED: William McFaul, David Craig, John McNamee, Alwyn Burton, Frank Clark, Thomas Gibb, James Scott, Bryan Robson, Wyn Davies, David Elliott, Geoffrey Allen. Manager: Joseph Harvey

FEYENOORD: Eddy Pieters Graafland; Frans Van der Heide, Rinus Israël, Theo Laseroms, Cor Veldhoen, Jan Boskamp, Wim Jansen, Wim Van Hanegem (67 Ruud Geels), Henk Wery, Ove Kindvall, Coen Moulijn.   Trainer: Benjamin Peeters

Goals: Scott (6), Robson (34), Gibb (42), Davies (72)

FEYENOORD ROTTERDAM
v NEWCASTLE UNITED 2-0 (1-0)

Feyenoord, Rotterdam   17.09.68

Referee: Helmut Fritz (WG)   Attendance: 48,000

FEYENOORD: Eddy Pieters Graafland; Piet Romeijn, Rinus Israël, Theo Laseroms (23 Frans Van der Heide), Cor Veldhoen, Jan Boskamp, Wim Jansen, Wim Van Hanegem, Henk Wery, Ove Kindvall, Coen Moulijn.   Trainer: Benjamin Peeters

UNITED: William McFaul; David Craig, John McNamee, Alwyn Burton, Frank Clark (85 James Iley), Thomas Gibb, James Scott, Bryan Robson, Wyn Davies, David Elliott, Geoffrey Allen.   Manager: Joseph Harvey

Goals: Kindvall (28), Van der Heide (54)

RAPID BUCUREŞTI v O.F.K. BEOGRAD 3-1 (1-1)

Republicii, Bucureşti   11.09.68

Referee: Nejat Sener (Tur)   Attendance: 15,000

RAPID: Adrian Rămureanu; Vasile Ştefan, Nicolae Lupescu, Dan Coe, Ilie Greavu; Iordan Angelescu, Ion Dumitru; Constantin Năsturescu, Marian Popescu (79 Ion Pop), Alexandru Neagu, Teofil Codreanu. Trainer: Valentin Stănescu

OFK: Hodzic; Stojan Vukašinović, Zdravko Jokic; Slobodan Mesanovic, Blagomir Krivokuća, Dragoslav Stepanovic; Bogdan Turudija, Dušan Maravic, Slobodan Santrac, Ilija Mitic, Ilija Petkovic.   Trainer: Mihajlovic & Sava Antic

Goals: Stepanovic (13), Neagu (28, 90), Năsturescu (85)

O.F.K. BEOGRAD
v RAPID BUCUREŞTI 6-1 (3-1, 3-1) a.e.t.

Omladinski, Beograd   18.09.68

Referees: Konstantin Zecević; Ratko Çanak, Aleksander Škorić (Jug)   Attendance: 2,000

OFK: Hodzic; Stojan Vukašinović, Zdravko Jokic; Slobodan Mesanovic, Blagomir Krivokuća, Dragoslav Stepanovic; Bogdan Turudija, Milutinovic, Slobodan Santrac, Dragoslav Šekularac, Ilija Petkovic.   Trainer: Mihajlovic

RAPID: Răducanu Necula; Vasile Ştefan, Nicolae Lupescu, Dan Coe (108 Ion Motroc), Ilie Greavu; Iordan Angelescu, Ion Dumitru; Ion Pop; Constantin Năsturescu, Alexandru Neagu, Teofil Codreanu (107 Marian Popescu). Trainer: Valentin Stănescu

Goals: Santrac (4, 13, 104, 107), Turudija (11, 100), Codreanu (29)

ARIS THESSALONIKI
v HIBERNIANS PAOLA 1-0 (1-0)

Thessaloniki   11.09.68

Referee: Josip Strmecki (Jug)   Attendance: 18,000

ARIS: Giorgos Gandinas; Aggelos Spiridon, Anastasios Aslanidis, Dimitris Raptopoulos, Hristos Nalbantis, Petros Grosis, Vaggelis Siropoulos, Manolis Keramidas, Alekos Alexiadis, Kostas Papaioannou, Klimis Gounaris.

HIBERNIANS: Freddie Debono; John Privitera, Alfred Mallia; Edgar Azzopardi, Edgar Caruana, Charles Gatt; Lawrence Young, Edward Aquilina, Salvu Bonello, Edward Theobald, Victor Cassar.

Goal: Alexiadis (22)

HIBERNIANS PAOLA
v ARIS THESSALONIKI 0-6 (0-2)

The Stadium, Gzira   22.09.68

Referee: George McCabe (Eng)   Attendance: 30,000

HIBERNIANS: Freddie Debono (.. A.Borg); John Privitera, Alfred Mallia; Edward Theobald, Edgar Caruana, Charles Gatt; Lawrence Young, Norman Buckle (..Alfred Delia), Francis Mifsud, Edward Aquilina, Victor Cassar.

ARIS: Giorgos Gandinas; Aggelos Spiridon, Klimis Gounaris, Dimitris Grimbelakos, Manolis Keramidas, Hristos Nalbantis, Anastasios Aslanidis, Petros Grosis, Kostas Papaioannou, Alekos Alexiadis, Vaggelis Siropoulos.

Goals: Grimbelakos (4), Papaioannou (30, 80, 89), Siropoulos (51), Alexiadis (84)

BEERSCHOT ANTWERPEN
v DWS AMSTERDAM 1-1 (1-0)

Stedelijk Olympisch, Antwerp   11.09.68

Referee: Leo Callaghan (Wal)   Attendance: 5,000

BEERSCHOT: Jozef Smolders; Yvan Deferm, Guillaume Raskin, Wilfried Willems, Julien Van Opdorp, Jan Verheyen, Marcel Hermans, Kaj Poulsen, Léon Ritzen (80 René Desaeyere), Herman Houben, Ivan Pintaric (80 Rosidar Ranogajec).

DWS: Jan Jongbloed; Frits Flinkevleugel, Rob Bianchi, André Pijlman, Jos Dijkstra, Hans Deen, Frits Soetekouw, Kick Van der Vall, Frans Geurtsen, Finn Seemann, Rob Rensenbrink. Trainer: Lesley Talbot

Goals: Houben (34), Van der Vall (56 pen)

DWS AMSTERDAM
v BEERSCHOT ANTWERP 2-1 (1-1)

Olympisch, Amsterdam   25.09.68

Referee: John Adair (NIr)   Attendance: 3,500

DWS: Jan Jongbloed; Frits Flinkevleugel, Jos Dijkstra, Niels Overweg, André Pijlman, Rob Bianchi, Frits Soetekouw, Kick Van der Vall, Frans Geurtsen, Finn Seemannn, Rob Rensenbrink.   Trainer: Lesley Talbot

BEERSCHOT: Willy Mortier; Yvan Deferm, Wilfried Willems, Guillaume Raskin, Julien Van Opdorp, Jan Verheyen, René Desaeyere, Kaj Poulsen, Léon Ritzen, Herman Houben, Robert Weyn.

Goals: Pijlman (23), Houben (27), Rensenbrink (80)

DOS UTRECHT v FC DUNDALK 1-1 (1-0)

Galgenwaard, Utrecht   11.09.68

Referee: Joseph Minnoy (Bel)   Attendance: 4,000

DOS: Branislav Veljković; Hans De Weerd, Jan Gerritse, Johan Plageman, Piet Van Oudenallen, Arie De Kuyper, Eddie Van Stijn, Tonny Nieuwenhuys, Nico Hardeman (.. Arie Lagendijk), Leo Van Veen, Djordje Milic. Trainer: Friedrich Donenfeld (Aus)

DUNDALK: Pat Lawless; Des O'Reilly, Kevin Murray, Francis Brennan, Patrick McKeown (.. Brendan Hannigan), Michael Millington, James Morrissey, Larry Gilmore, Turlough O'Connor, Derek Stokes, Frank Campbell.

Goals: Van Veen (27), Stokes (74)

FC DUNDALK
v DOS UTRECHT 2-1 (1-1, 1-1) a.e.t.

Oriel Park, Dundalk   1.10.68

Referee: Thomas Wharton (Sco)   Attendance: 12,000

DUNDALK: Pat Lawless (.. Kevin Blount); John Murphy, James Morrissey, Kevin Murray, Francis Brennan, Michael Millington, Laurence Gilmore (.. Patrick Turner), Turlough O'Connor, Derek Stokes, Anthony O'Connell, Brendan Hannigan.

DOS: Nico Verrips; Rini Block, Hans De Weerd, Johan Plageman, Arie Witzand, Arie De Kuyper, Eddie Van Stijn, Tonny Nieuwenhuys, George In't Veld, Leo Van Veen (.. Arie Lagendijk), Matthias Maiwald. Trainer: Friedrich Donenfeld

Goals: Stokes (8), Nieuwenhuys (20), Morrissey (109)

SSC NAPOLI v GRASSHOPPER ZÜRICH 3-1 (3-0)

San Paolo, Napoli   11.09.68

Referee: Arthur Lentini (Mal)   Attendance: 20,000

NAPOLI: Dino Zoff; Stelio Nardin, Florio, Mario Zurlini, Aristide Guarneri, Ottavio Bianchi, Egidio Salvi, Vincenzo Montefusco, Harald Nielsen, José Altafini, Claudio Sala. Trainer: Giuseppe Chiapella

GRASSHOPPER: René Deck; Heinz Ingold, Hansruedi Fuhrer, Roland Citherlet, Marc Berset, Kurt Rüegg, Herbert Hunger, Rudolf Schneeberger (46 Kurt Soom), Hansruedi Staudenmann, Ove Grahn, René Thurnherr.

Goals: Altafini (6), Salvi (12, 33), Rüegg (78)

GRASSHOPPER ZÜRICH v SSC NAPOLI 1-0 (0-0)

Hardturm, Zürich   23.10.68

Referee: Robert Lacoste (Fra)   Attendance: 10,000

GRASSHOPPER: Enrico Borrini; Heinz Ingold, Roland Citherlet, Peter Scheibel, Kurt Aerni, Arild Gulden (46 Hansruedi Staudenmann), Isidor Cina, Hansruedi Fuhrer, Ove Grahn, Rolf Blättler, Rudolf Schneeberger (80 Kurt Soom).

NAPOLI: Pacifico Cuman; Stelio Nardin (46 Florio), Mario Zurlini, Amedeo Stenti, Dino Panzanato, Ottavio Bianchi, Egidio Salvi, Vincenzo Montefusco, Harald Nielsen (60 Claudio Sala), José Altafini, Jarbas Faustinho CANÉ. Trainer: Giuseppe Chiapella

Goal: Grahn (58)

GÖZTEPE IZMIR
v OLYMPIQUE MARSEILLE 2-0 (1-0)

Alsançak, Izmir   11.09.68

Referees: Konstantin Zecević, Tatipnić, Medić (Jug)
Attendance: 20,000

GÖZTEPE: Ali Artuner; Mehmet Kiraz, Caglayan Derebaşi; Hüseyin Yazici, B.Mehmet, Ali Ihsan Okçuoglu; Ertan Öznur, Nihat Yayöz, Fevzi Zemzem, Gürsel Aksel, Halil Kiraz. Trainer: Adnan Süvari

OLYMPIQUE: Jean-Paul Escale; André Tassonne, Jacky Novi, Jules Zvunka, Jean Djorkaeff, Jean-Pierre Lopez, Jean-Pierre Destrumelle, Roger Magnusson, Yegba Maya «Joseph», Christian Donnat, Hubert Guéniche (85 Franck Fiawoo). Trainer: Robert Domergue

Goals: Halil (20, 46)

OLYMPIQUE MARSEILLE
v GÖZTEPE IZMIR 2-0 (0-0, 2-0) a.e.t.

Stade Vélodrome, Marseille   2.10.68

Referee: Concetto Lo Bello (Ita)   Attendance: 7,411

OLYMPIQUE: Jean-Paul Escale; André Tassone, Jean Djorkaeff, Jacky Novi; Jules Zvunka, Jean-Pierre Destrumelle (108 Christian Donnat), Ange Di Caro, Joseph Bonnel, Yegba Maya «Joseph», Hubert Guéniche, Franck Fiawoo. Trainer: Robert Domergue

GÖZTEPE: Ali Artuner; Mehmet Kiraz, Caglayan Derebaşi; Hüseyin Yazici, Mehmet B, Ali Ihsan Okçuoglu; Ertan Öznur, Nihat Yayöz, Fevzi Zemzem, Gürsel Aksel, Halil Kiraz. Trainer: Adnan Süvari

Goals: Joseph (75), Guéniche (83)

Göztepe qualified on the toss of a coin

SLAVIA SOFIA v ABERDEEN FC 0-0

Sofia   17.09.68

Referee: Sándor Petri (Hun)   Attendance: 18,000

SLAVIA: Simeon Simeonov; Stoian Aleksiev, Petar Petrov, Viktor Ionov; Ivan Davidov, Georgi Haralampiev; Iancho Dimitrov, Liuben Tasev, Bozhidar Grigorov, Nikola Krastev (46 Iordan Lechev), Stoian Kotzev.

ABERDEEN: Robert Clark; James Hermiston, Alistair Shewan, Jens Petersen, Thomas McMillan, Thomas Craig, Thomas Rae, David Robb, James Forrest, James Smith, Martin Buchan.   Manager: Edward Turnbull

ABERDEEN FC v SLAVIA SOFIA 2-0 (2-0)

Pittodrie, Aberdeen   2.10.68

Referee: Curt Liedberg (Swe)   Attendance: 29.000

ABERDEEN: Robert Clark; James Hermiston, Alistair Shewan, Jens Petersen, Thomas McMillan, Thomas Craig (.. Martin Buchan), Thomas Rae, David Robb, James Forrest, James Smith, Ian Taylor.   Manager: Edward Turnbull

SLAVIA: Simeon Simeonov; Ilia Chalev, Petar Petrov, Viktor Ionov; Ivan Davidov, Petar Hristov, Georgi Haralampiev (.. Manchov), Aleksandar Vasilev, Bozhidar Grigorov, Liuben Tasev (.. Stanov), Iordan Lechev.

Goals: Robb (7), Taylor (39)

SKEID OSLO v AIK SOLNA 1-1 (1-1)

Oslo   18.09.68

Referee: Aranth Jensen (Dan)   Attendance: 10,000

SKEID: Kjell Kaspersen (80 Tom Holter); Ragnar Naess, Frank Olafsen, Kjell Wangen, Finn Haglund, Terje Gulbrandsen, Erik Johansen, Jörn Stople, Jan Mathisen, Kai Sjöberg, Terje Kristoffersen.

AIK: Leif Hult; Curt Edenvik, Ove Ohlsson, Olavus Olsson, Roland Grip, Kurt Andersson, Jim Nildén, Tord Grip, Kent Persson (46 Björn Carlsson), Roland Lundblad, Lennart Backman.

Goals: K. Andersson (22), J. Mathisen (36)

AIK SOLNA v SKEID OSLO 2-1 (0-1)

Nya Råsunda, Solna   26.09.68

Referee: Erik Beijar (Fin)   Attendance: 812

AIK: Leif Hult, Curt Edenvik, Ove Ohlsson, Olavus Olsson, Roland Grip, Jim Nildén, Kurt Andersson, Jan Nilsson, Sven Billman (.. Tord Grip), Roland Lundblad, Kent Persson.

SKEID: Kjell Kaspersen (56 Tom Holter); Ragnar Naess, Frank Olafsen, Kjell Wangen, Finn Haglund, Terje Gulbrandsen, Erik Mejlo, Erik Johansen, Jörn Stople, Kai Sjöberg, Jan Mathisen.

Goals: Sjøberg (30), Lundblad (55), O. Ohlsson (70)

CHELSEA LONDON
v GREENOCK MORTON 5-0 (2-0)

Stamford Bridge, London   18.09.68

Referee: Kurt Tschenscher (WG)   Attendance: 28,736

CHELSEA: Peter Bonetti; Ronald Harris, Edward McCreadie, John Hollins, David Webb, John Boyle, Thomas Baldwin, Charles Cooke, Peter Osgood, Alan Birchenall, Robert Tambling.   Manager: Dave Sexton

MORTON: Robert Russell; Borge Thorup, John Loughlan, Preben Arentoft, Hugh Strachan, Billy Gray, Joseph Harper (69 Bjarne Jensen), Gerald Sweeney, Joseph Mason (69 William Allan), Morris Stevenson, Anthony Taylor.
Manager: Haldane Stewart

Goals: Osgood (44), Birchenall (45), Cooke (50), Boyle (67), Hollins (84)

GREENOCK MORTON
v CHELSEA LONDON 3-4 (3-3)

Cappielow Park, Greenock   30.09.68

Referee: Willem Schalks (Hol)   Attendance: 8,000

MORTON: Andy Crawford (46 Robert Russell); Borge Thorup, Gerald Sweeney, Preben Arentoft, Billy Gray, Hugh Strachan, Joseph Harper, Stan Rankin, Joseph Mason, William Allan, Anthony Taylor.   Manager: Haldane Stewart

CHELSEA: Peter Bonetti; Marvin Hinton, Edward McCreadie, John Hollins, David Webb, Ronald Harris, Thomas Baldwin, Robert Tambling, Peter Osgood, Alan Birchenall, Peter Houseman.   Manager: Dave Sexton

Goals: Baldwin (3), Thorup (6), Mason (9), Taylor (26), Birchenall (34), Houseman (42), Tambling (84)

FC METZ v HAMBURGER SV 1-4 (1-1)

Stade Municipal, Metz   18.09.68

Referee: Franz Geluck (Bel)   Attendance: 15,645

METZ: Jean-Marie Lawniczak; Georges Zvunka, Jacques Lemée, Gilbert Le Chenadec, Fernand Jeitz, André Bailet (40 Jacques Pauvert), Gérard Hitz, Richard Krawczyk (87 Michel Heinrich), Johnny Leonard, Robert Szczepaniak, Gérard Hausser.   Trainer: Pierre Flamion

HAMBURGER SV: Özcan Arkoc; Holger Dieckmann, Egon Horst, Willi Schulz, Jürgen Kurbjuhn, Hans Schulz, Klaus Fock (57 Helmut Sandmann), Werner Krämer, Franz-Josef Hönig, Uwe Seeler, Gert Dörfel.   Trainer: Georg Knöpfle

Goals: Hausser (20), Dörfel (21), Seeler (Zvunka og) (56), Krämer (63), Hönig (82)

HAMBURGER SV v FC METZ 3-2 (2-1)

Volksparkstadion, Hamburg   1.10.68

Referee: Henry Öberg (Nor)   Attendance: 10,000

HAMBURGER SV: Özcan Arkoc; Helmut Sandmann, Egon Horst, Willi Schulz, Jürgen Kurbjuhn, Hans Schulz, Jürgen Dringelstein, Werner Krämer, Franz-Josef Hönig, Uwe Seeler, Gert Dörfel.   Trainer: Georg Knöpfle

METZ: Jean-Marie Lawniczak; Georges Zvunka, Michel Heinrich, Gilbert Le Chenadec (52 Jacques Lemée), Fernand Jeitz, Jacques Pauvert, Gérard Hitz, Roger Niesser, Johnny Leonard, Robert Szczepaniak, Sadek Boukhalfa.
Trainer: Pierre Flamion

Goals: Hönig (7), Krämer (18), Hitz (40), Niesser (85), Seeler (88)

ATHLETIC BILBAO v LIVERPOOL FC 2-1 (2-0)

Estadio San Mamés, Bilbao   18.09.68

Referee: Eugen Boller (Swi)   Attendance: 28,004

ATHLETIC: José Ángel IRÍBAR Cortajarena; José Ignacio SÁEZ Ruiz, Jesús ARANGUREN Merino, Luis María AGUIRRE Vidaurrazaga (52 Luis María ZUGAZAGA Martínez), Luis María ECHEBERRÍA Igartua, José Ramón Martínez LARRAURI, Pedro LAVÍN Arcocha, Nicolás ESTÉFANO Montalbán, Javier ORMAZA Garay, José María ARGOITIA Acha, José Francisco ROJO I Arroitia (46 Javier CLEMENTE Lázaro).   Trainer: Agustín GAINZA Vicandi

LIVERPOOL: Thomas Lawrence; Christopher Lawler, Peter Wall, Thomas Smith, Ronald Yeats, Emlyn Hughes, Ian Callaghan, Roger Hunt, Robert Graham (48 Geoffrey Strong), Ian St. John (80 Ian Ross), Peter Thompson.
Manager: Bill Shankly

Goals: Estéfano (15), Ormaza (39), Hunt (66)

LIVERPOOL FC v ATHLETIC BILBAO 2-1 (0-1)

Anfield Road, Liverpool   2.10.68

Referee: Kurt Tschenscher (WG)   Attendance: 49,567

LIVERPOOL: Thomas Lawrence; Christopher Lawler, Peter Wall, Thomas Smith, Ronald Yeats, Emlyn Hughes, Ian Callaghan, Roger Hunt, Alun Evans, Ian St. John, Peter Thompson.   Manager: Bill Shankly

ATHLETIC: José Ángel IRÍBAR Cortajarena; José Ignacio SÁEZ Ruiz, Jesús ARANGUREN Merino, Luis María AGUIRRE Vidaurrazaga, Luis María ECHEBERRÍA Igartua (65 Luis María ZUGAZAGA Martínez), José Ramón Martínez LARRAURI, Juan María ZORRIQUETA Azpiazu, José María ARGOITIA Acha, Antonio María ARIETA II Araunabeña Piedra (52 José Ramón BETZUÉN Urquiaza), Fidel URIARTE Macho, José Francisco ROJO I Arroitia.
Trainer: Agustín GAINZA Vicandi

Goals: Argoitia (32), Lawler (78), Hughes (87)

Athletic Bilbao won on the toss of a coin

DINAMO ZAGREB
v AC FIORENTINA FIRENZE 1-1 (1-0)

Maksimir, Zagreb 18.09.68

Referee: Erich Linemayr (Aus)   Attendance: 20,000

DINAMO: Fahrija Dautbegovic; Rudolf Cvek, Branko Gračanin, Denijal Pirić, Rudolf Belin, Filip Blašković, Marijan Čerček, Josip Gucmirtl, Slaven Zambata, Ivica Kiš, Krasnodar Rora.

FIORENTINA: Francesco Superchi; Bernardo Rogora, Eraldo Mancini, Giovan Battista Pirovano, Ugo Ferrante, Giuseppe Brizi, Giorgio Mariani (46 Salvatore Esposito), Francesco Rizzo, Mario Maraschi, Giancarlo De Sisti, Luciano Chiarugi.   Trainer: Bruno Pesaola

Goals: Zambata (18), Pirovano (83)

AC FIORENTINA FIRENZE
v DINAMO ZAGREB 2-1 (2-0)

Stadio Communale, Firenze 2.10.68

Referee: Robert Schaut (Bel)   Attendance: 20,000

FIORENTINA: Francesco Superchi; Bernardo Rogora, Eraldo Mancini, Giovan Battista Pirovano, Ugo Ferrante, Giuseppe Brizi, Francesco Rizzo (46 Lucio Bertogna), Claudio Merlo, Mario Maraschi, Giancarlo De Sisti, AMARILDO Tavares de Silveire (79 Salvatore Esposito).   Trainer: Bruno Pesaola

DINAMO: Fahrija Dautbegović; Rudolf Cvek, Branko Gračanin, Rudolf Belin (55 Damir Valec), Mladen Ramljak, Filip Blašković, Marijan Čerček, Denijal Pirić, Slaven Zambata, Ivica Kiš (56 Marijan Novak), Krasnodar Rora.

Goals: Amarildo (1), Maraschi (37), Novak (64)

SPORTING LISBOA v CF VALENCIA 4-0 (1-0)

Estádio José Alvalade, Lisboa 18.09.68

Referee: Robert Lacoste (Fra)   Attendance: 27,500

SPORTING: Vítor Manuel Afonso DAMAS de Oliveira; Manuel PEDRO GOMES, ARMANDO António Manhiça, JOSÉ CARLOS da Silva José, HILÁRIO Rosário da Conceição; JOSÉ MORAIS, José Maria de Freitas Pereira "PEDRAS"; Francisco Delfim Dias Faria CHICO, ERNESTO Francisco de Sousa, João de Matos Moura LOURENÇO, Vítor Manuel de Almeida GONÇALVES (46 Mário da Silva Mateus "MARINHO").   Trainer: Fernando CAIADO

VALENCIA: José PESUDO Soler; José Antonio García Conesa "TATONO", Jesús MARTÍNEZ Rivadeneyra, Emilio González Morán "PANCHULO"; Juan Cruz SOL Oria, ANÍBAL Pérez Miers, José CLARAMUNT Torres, Fernando ANSOLA Sanmartín, WALDO Machado da Silva, Francisco García Gómez "PAQUITO", Ángel Iglesias Domínguez "MACHICHA".   Trainer: Edmundo Suarez Trabanco "MUNDO"

Goals: Lourenço (26, 73), Gonçalves (56), Ernesto (81)

CF VALENCIA
v SPORTING LISBOA 4-1 (2-0, 4-0) a.e.t.

Campo de Mestalla, Valencia 2.10.68

Referee: Aurelio Angonese (Ita)   Attendance: 30,000

CF VALENCIA: José PESUDO Soler; Juan Cruz SOL Oria, Luis VILAR Botet, José Antonio García Conesa «TATONO» (31 Francisco VIDAGAÑY Hernández); Jesús MARTÍNEZ Rivadeneyra, Francisco García Gómez «PAQUITO»; Vicente GUILLOT Fabián (31 Manuel Polinario Muñoz «POLI»), José CLARAMUNT Torres, Fernando ANSOLA Sanmartín, WALDO Machado da Silva, Francisco Ramón Delhom BLAYET.   Trainer: Edmundo Suarez Trabanco "MUNDO"

SPORTING: Vítor Manuel Afonso DAMAS de Oliveira; Manuel PEDRO GOMES, ARMANDO António Manhiça, JOSÉ CARLOS da Silva José; HILÁRIO Rosário da Conceição, JOSÉ MORAIS; Vítor Manuel de Almeida GONÇALVES (.. JOÃO CARLOS Conceição), José Maria de Freitas Pereira "PEDRAS", Francisco Delfim Dias Faria CHICO, Mário da Silva Mateus "MARINHO" (..José ALEXANDRE da Silva BAPTISTA), João de Matos Moura LOURENÇO.   Trainer: Fernando CAIADO

Goals: Claramunt (19), Blayet (31, 71), Sol (87), Chico Faria (112)

AC BOLOGNA v FC BASEL 4-1 (1-0)

Stadio Communale, Bologna 18.09.68

Referee: Décio de Freitas (Por)   Attendance: 8,349

BOLOGNA: Giuseppe Vavassori; Tazio Roversi, Mario Ardizzon, Francesco Cresci, Francesco Janich, Ivan Gregori, Marino Perani (50 Bruno Pace), Giacomo Bulgarelli, Giuseppe Savoldi, Faustino Turra, Ezio Pascutti.   Trainer: Cervellati

FC BASEL: Jean-Paul Laufenberger; Josef Kiefer, Bruno Michaud, Walter Mundschin, Peter Ramseier, Karl Odermatt, Helmut Benthaus, Jürgen Sundermann, Otto Demarmels (72 Paul Fischli), Janos Konrad, Peter Wenger.

Goals: Turra (12), Konrad (48), Cresci (50), Pace (53), Savoldi (83)

FC BASEL v AC BOLOGNA 1-2 (1-0)

St. Jakob, Basel 2.10.68

Referee: Roger Barde (Fra)   Attendance: 10,000

FC BASEL: Jean-Paul Laufenberger; Josef Kiefer, Bruno Michaud, Peter Ramseier, Roland Paolucci, Helmut Benthaus, Helmut Hauser, Jürgen Sundermann, Dieter Rüefli (46 Peter Wenger), Paul Fischli, Janos Konrad.

BOLOGNA: Giuseppe Vavassori; Tazio Roversi, Mario Ardizzon, Francesco Cresci, Francesco Janich, Ivan Gregori, Bruno Pace, Giacomo Bulgarelli (43 Francesco Battisodo), Lucio Mujesan, Faustino Turra, Roberto Quadalti (46 Giuseppe Savoldi).   Trainer: Cervellati

Goals: Hauser (42), Pace (46), Savoldi (63)

TRAKIA PLOVDIV v REAL ZARAGOZA 3-1 (1-0)

9 Septemvri, Plovdiv   18.09.68

Referee: Doğan Babacan (Tur)   Attendance: 25,000

TRAKIA: Mihail Karushkov; Neno Georgiev, Raiko Stoinov, Vangel Delev; Gluhchev, Ivan Zaduma; Georgi Popov, Dinko Dermendjiev, Dobrin Nenov, Dimitar Kostadinov, Petar Radkov.   Trainer: Georgi Chakarov

REAL ZARAGOZA: Enrique YARZA Soraluce; José Luis VIOLETA Lajusticia, Francisco SANTAMARÍA Briones (80 José DÍAZ Fernández), José Luis RICO Ibáñez; Antonio PAÍS Castroagudin, José Manuel GONZÁLEZ López; Juan Manuel VILLA Gutiérrez, Manuel FONTENLA Barreiros, Miguel Ángel BUSTILLO Lafoz, Carlos LAPETRA Coarasa, José Antonio TEJEDOR Sanz.   Trainer: Roque OLSEN Fontana

Goals: Gluhchev (32), Dermendjiev (65), Popov (78), Tejedor (88)

OGC NICE v HANSA ROSTOCK 2-1 (0-0)

Stade Municipal du Ray, Nice   2.10.68

Referee: Eugen Boller (Swi)   Attendance: 6,855

OGC NICE: Charly Marchetti; Guy Cauvin, Maurice Serrus, Francis Isnard, Régis Bruneton, Gérard Segarra, Patrick Barthélemy, René Fioroni, Fernand Goeyvaerts, Jean-Rémy Issembe (46 Albert Robin), Roger Jouve.
Trainer: César Gonzales

HANSA: Manfred Schröbler; Gerd Sackritz, Klaus-Dieter Seehaus, Helmut Hergesell, Dieter Wruck, Gerhard Brümmer, Herbert Pankau (.. Dieter Schneider), Kurt Habermann, Wolfgang Barthels, Jürgen Decker (70 Gerd Kostmann), Werner Drews.   Trainer: Gerhard Gläser

Goals: Goeyvaerts (47 pen), Robin (65), Drews (80)

REAL ZARAGOZA v TRAKIA PLOVDIV 2-0 (1-0)

Estadio La Romareda, Zaragoza   2.10.68

Referee: Gilbert Droz (Swi)   Attendance: 20,000

REAL ZARAGOZA: Rafael Álvarez ALARCIA; José Ramón IRUSQUIETA García, José DÍAZ Fernández (67 José Luis VIOLETA Lajusticia), Severino REIJA Vázquez; Manuel FONTENLA Barreiros, José Manuel GONZÁLEZ López; José Antonio TEJEDOR Sanz, Eleuterio SANTOS Brito, Miguel Ángel BUSTILLO Lafoz, MARCELINO Martínez Cao, Carlos LAPETRA Coarasa.   Trainer: Roque OLSEN Fontana

TRAKIA: Mihail Karushkov (88 Dragan Radenkov); Neno Georgiev, Gluhchev, Raiko Stoinov; Vangel Delev, Ivan Zaduma; Georgi Popov, Dinko Dermendjiev, Dobrin Nenov, Viden Apostolov (79 Dimitar Kostadinov), Petar Radkov.   Trainer: Georgi Chakarov

Goals: Bustillo (24, 76)

OLIMPIJA LJUBLJANA v HIBERNIAN EDINBURGH 0-3 (0-2)

Bezigrad, Ljubljana   18.09.68

Referee: Franz Wöhrer (Aus)   Attendance: 3,000

OLIMPIJA: Borut Škulj (55 Anton Zabjek); Gyor, Velimir Sombolac, Rasim Kokot, Miloš Šoškić, Milovan Nikolić, Danilo Popivoda, Milorad Lazović, Viliam Amersek, Branko Oblak, Živorad Spasojević.

HIBERNIAN: Wilson; Christopher Shevlane, Joseph Davis, John Henderson Blackley, Alan Cousin, Patrick Stanton, Peter Marinello, Patrick Quinn, Colin Stein, Peter Cormack, Eric William Stevenson.

Goals: Stevenson (32), Stein (36), Marinello (71)

HANSA ROSTOCK v OGC NICE 3-0 (1-0)

Ostseestadion, Rostock   18.09.68

Referee: Arie Van Gemert (Hol)   Attendance: 12,000

HANSA: Manfred Schröbler; Gerhard Brümmer, Dieter Wruck, Klaus-Dieter Seehaus, Helmut Hergesell, Herbert Pankau, Wolfgang Barthels, Gerd Kostmann, Jürgen Decker, Kurt Habermann, Werner Drews.   Trainer: Gerhard Gläser

OGC NICE: Marcel Aubour; Guy Cauvin, Richard Moussu, Maurice Serrus, Francis Isnard, Régis Bruneton, Charles Loubet, Gérard Segarra, Fernand Goeyvaerts, Sylvain Leandri, Jean-Rémy Issembe.   Trainer: César Gonzales

Goals: Drews (23), Decker (52, 90)

HIBERNIAN EDINBURGH v OLIMPIJA LJUBLJANA 2-1 (0-1)

Easter Road Park, Edinburgh   2.10.68

Referee: Jack Russell (NIr)   Attendance: 10,445

HIBERNIAN: Wilson; Christopher Shevlane, Joseph Davis, John Henderson Blackley, Alan Cousin, Patrick Stanton, Peter Marinello, Patrick Quinn, Colin Stein, Peter Cormack, Eric William Stevenson.

OLIMPIJA: Anton Zabjek; Rasim Kokot, Atanas Djorlev, Dragan Rogić, Branislav Jovanović, Mahmut Kapidžić, Danilo Popivoda, Milovan Nikolić, Milorad Lazović, Branko Oblak, Viliam Amersek.

Goals: Popivoda (4), Davis (61 pen, 68 pen)

WIENER SK v SLAVIA PRAHA 1-0 (1-0)

Sportclub-Platz, Wien   18.09.68

Referee: János Biroczki (Hun)   Attendance: 4,000

WIENER SK: Wilhelm Kaipel; Anton Linhart, Horst Blankenburg, Haider; Johann Schmidradner, Norbert Hof; Finn Laudrup, Anton Herzog (46 Herbert Onger), Erich Hof, Johann Buzek, Johann Hörmayer.

SLAVIA: Jiří Vošta; Jan Lála, Karel Knesl, Bedrich Tesař, Bohumil Smolík; Karel Nepomucký, Zdenek Konečný; František Veselý, Emil Hamár, Ivan Kopecký, Miroslav Ziegler.   Trainer: F. Havránek

Goal: Buzek (15)

SLAVIA PRAHA v WIENER SK 5-0 (2-0)

Stadion Dr. Vacka, Praha   2.10.68

Referee: Joseph Heymann (Swi)   Attendance: 4,000

SLAVIA: Jiří Vošta; Jan Lála (46 Ivan Kopecký), Hildebrandt, Karel Knesl, Bohumil Smolík; Karel Nepomucký, Bedrich Tesař; František Veselý, Jaroslav Šimek, Zdenek Konečný, Miroslav Ziegler.   Trainer: F. Havránek

WIENER SK: Wilhelm Kaipel; Anton Linhart, Horst Blankenburg, Haider; Johann Schmidradner, Norbert Hof; Alfred Hala, Helmut Wallner, Finn Laudrup, Anton Herzog, Johann Hörmayer.

Goals: Nepomucký (29,76), Tesař (44), Ziegler (65), Kopecký (86)

GLASGOW RANGERS
v VOJVODINA NOVI SAD 2-0 (1-0)

Ibrox Stadium, Glasgow   18.09.68

Referee: Raymond Poncin (Fra)   Attendance: 60,000

RANGERS: Norman Martin; Colin Jackson, William Mathieson, John Greig, Ronald McKinnon, Roger Hynd, William Henderson, Andrew Penman, William Jardine, William Johnston, Örjan Persson.   Manager: David White

VOJVODINA: Ilija Pantelić; Rajko Aleksić, Tomce Stamenski, Josip Zemko, Ivan Brzić, Nikolić, Vladimir Rakić (.. Zoran Dakić), Dobrivoje Trivić, Radivoj Radosav, Josip Pirmajer, Vladimir Savić.

Goals: Greig (28 pen), Jardine (84)

VOJVODINA NOVI SAD
v GLASGOW RANGERS 1-0 (0-0)

Gradski, Novi Sad   2.10.68

Referee: Aurel Bentu (Rom)   Attendance: 7,000

VOJVODINA: Ilija Pantelić; Rajko Aleksić, Tomce Stamenski, Vladimir Savić, Ivan Brzić, Zoran Dakić, Zvonko Ivezić (.. Petar Nikezić), Radivoj Radosav, Dobrivoje Trivić, Josip Pirmajer, Vasa Pušibrk.

RANGERS: Norman Martin; Colin Jackson, William Mathieson, John Greig, Ronald McKinnon, Roger Hynd, William Henderson, Andrew Penman (.. David Smith), William Jardine, William Johnston, Örjan Persson. Trainer: David White

Goal: Nikezic (66)

LAUSANNE SPORTS
v JUVENTUS TORINO 0-2 (0-1)

Stade Olympique de la Pontaise, Lausanne   18.09.68

Referee: René Vigliani (Fra)   Attendance: 8,000

LAUSANNE SPORTS: René Schneider; Christian Delay, Charles Hertig, Anton Weibel, Ely Tacchella, Richard Dürr, Pierre-Albert Chapuisat, Robert Hosp, Georges Vuilleumier, André Bosson, Pierre Kerkhoffs.

JUVENTUS: Roberto Anzolin; Luigi Pasetti, Sandro Salvadore, Giancarlo Bercellino, Gianluigi Roveta, Gianfranco Leoncini, Erminio Favalli, Luis Cascajares Del Sol, Pietro Anastasi, Romeo Benetti, Gianfranco Zigoni. Trainer: Heriberto Herrera

Goals: Zigoni (17), Leoncini (63)

JUVENTUS TORINO
v LAUSANNE SPORTS 2-0 (1-0)

Stadio Comunale, Torino   9.10.68

Referee: Božidar Botić (Jug)   Attendance: 10,000

JUVENTUS: Roberto Anzolin; Luigi Pasetti, Sandro Salvadore, Gianluigi Roveta, Ernesto Castano, Gianfranco Leoncini, Erminio Favalli, Luis Cascajares Del Sol, Pietro Anastasi, Romeo Benetti (61 Giovanni Sacco), Gianfranco Zigoni.   Trainer: Heriberto Herrera

LAUSANNE SPORTS: René Schneider; Christian Delay, Charles Hertig (46 François Kaeser), Anton Weibel, Vinko Cuzzi, Gilbert Fuchs, Pierre-Albert Chapuisat, Robert Hosp, Pierre Kerkhoffs, André Bosson, Pierre-André Zappella.

Goals: Benetti (43), Del Sol (74)

VITÓRIA SETÚBAL v LINFIELD BELFAST 3-0 (1-0)

Estadio do Bonfim, Setúbal 18.09.68

Referee: Manuel Gomez Arribas (Spa)   Attendance: 8,000

VITÓRIA: Dinis Martins VITAL; Joaquim Adriao José da CONCEIÇÃO, Manuel Luís dos Santos "CARRIÇO", VAGNER Canotilho (51 VITOR Manuel Ferreira BAPTISTA), Carlos Alberto Lourenço CARDOSO, HERCULANO do Carmo Oliveira, Fernando Massano TOMÉ, JOSÉ MARIA Júnior, Ernesto FIGUEIREDO, António Ilídio de Sousa "PETITA", JACINTO JOÃO.   Trainer: Fernando VAZ

LINFIELD: Robert McGonigal; Ken Gilliland, John Patterson, Isaac Andrews, Samuel Hatton, Eric Bowyer, William Millen, Bryan Hamilton (75 Ken Coulter), Samuel Pavis, Philip Scott, Des Cathcart.

Goals: Tomé (18), Figueiredo (63), Carriço (81)

LINFIELD BELFAST v VITÓRIA SETÚBAL 1-3 (1-3)

Windsor Park, Belfast 9.10.68

Referee: Norman Burtenshaw (Eng)   Attendance: 20,000

LINFIELD: Robert McGonigal; Ken Gilliland, John Patterson, Isaac Andrews, Samuel Hatton, Eric Bowyer, Ken Coulter (.. William Ferguson), Bryan Hamilton, Samuel Pavis, Philip Scott, Des Cathcart.

VITÓRIA: Dinis Martins VITAL; Joaquim Adriao José da CONCEIÇÃO, Manuel Luís dos Santos "CARRIÇO", VAGNER Canotilho (60 Fernando Massano TOMÉ), Carlos Alberto Lourenço CARDOSO, HERCULANO do Carmo Oliveira, JOSÉ MARIA Júnior, VITOR Manuel Ferreira BAPTISTA, Ernesto FIGUEIREDO, Joaquim Leonardo Quinta ARCANJO, JACINTO JOÃO.   Trainer: Fernando VAZ

Goals: Figueiredo (2), Vitor Baptista (24), Scott (26), Arcanjo (29)

STANDARD LIÉGE v LEEDS UNITED 0-0

Stade Maurice Dufrasne Sclessin, Liège 18.09.68

Referee: Gerhard Kunze (DDR)   Attendance: 35,000

STANDARD: Jean Nicolay; Jacques Beurlet, Nicolas Dewalque, Léon Jeck, Jean Thissen, Wilfried Van Moer, Henri Depireux, Louis Pilot; Léon Semmeling, Erwin Kostedde, Antal Nagy.   Trainer: René Hauss

UNITED: Gary Sprake; Paul Reaney, Jack Charlton, Terence Cooper, William Bremner, Norman Hunter; Michael O'Grady, Peter Lorimer, Michael Jones, Paul Madeley, Terence Hibbitt.
Manager: Don Revie

LEEDS UNITED v STANDARD LIÉGE 3-2 (0-1)

Elland Road, Leeds 23.10.68

Referee: Gunnar Michaelsen (Dan)   Attendance: 24,178

UNITED: Gary Sprake; Paul Reaney, Jack Charlton, Terence Cooper (46 Michael Bates), William Bremner, Norman Hunter; Michael O'Grady, Peter Lorimer, Michael Jones, Paul Madeley, Terence Hibbitt (64 Edward Gray).
Manager: Don Revie

STANDARD: Jean Nicolay; Danny Blaise, Nicolas Dewalque, Léon Jeck, Jean Thissen, Wilfried Van Moer, Henri Depireux, Louis Pilot; Léon Semmeling, Erwin Kostedde, Milan Galic.
Trainer: René Hauss

Goals: Kostedde (44), Galic (50), Charlton (52), Lorimer (75), Bremner (88)

LEIXÕES PORTO v FC ARGEŞ PITEŞTI 1-1 (1-0)

Estádio das Antas, Porto 19.09.68

Referees: Medina Iglesias, M. Banegas, L. Camacho (Spa)
Attendance: 5,000

LEIXÕES: João Francisco FONSECA dos Santos; GERALDO Melo Medeiros, ADRIANO Fernandes Tato, NICOLAU Barbosa Lopes Vaqueiro, RAÚL Martins MACHADO, GENTIL Carreiro, Benedito Lacerda Ribeiro "BENE" (82 Fernando José Carmo MONTOIA), António Monteiro Teixeira de BARROS (70 ALBERTINO Eduardo Pereira), HORÁCIO Delfim Dias Faria, Ricardo, Manuel Gonçalves Gomes "NECA".
Trainer: José Águas

FC ARGEŞ: Spiridon Niculescu; Ion Ioniţă, Ion Barbu, Remus Vlad, Dumitru Ivan, Ion Prepurgel, Petre Nuţu, Constantin Radu, Viorel Kraus, Nicolae Dobrin, Radu Jercan.
Trainer: Ion Bălănescu

Goals: Horácio (18), Nuţu (73)

FC ARGEŞ PITEŞTI v LEIXÕES PORTO 0-0

1 Mai, Piteşti 2.10.68

Referees: Paul Schiller; Josef Tittl, Bauer (Aus)
Attendance: 15,000

FC ARGEŞ: Spiridon Niculescu; Ion Păciulete, Ion Barbu, Remus Vlad, Dumitru Ivan; Ion Ioniţă, Constantin Olteanu; Constantin Radu (76 Mihai Ţurcan), Viorel Kraus, Nicolae Dobrin, Radu Jercan.   Trainer: Ion Bălănescu

LEIXÕES: João Francisco FONSECA dos Santos; António Monteiro Teixeira de BARROS, ADRIANO Fernandes Tato, RAÚL Martins MACHADO, NICOLAU Barbosa Lopes Vaqueiro (76 LAZARO Branco Neves); MANUEL Fernando Martins MOREIRA, JORGE de Oliveira CALADO; Benedito Lacerda Ribeiro "BENE", ALBERTINO Eduardo Pereira (65 Manuel Gonçalves Gomes "NECA"), HORÁCIO Delfim Dias Faria, João Maia RICARDO.   Trainer: José Aguas

ATLÉTICO MADRID v SV WAREGEM 2-1 (1-1)

Estadio del Manzanares, Madrid 25.09.68

Referee: Antonio Sbardella (Ita)   Attendance: 15,000

ATLÉTICO: Jesús María ZUBIARRAIN Arguiñano; Julio Santaella Benítez «COLO», Jorge Bernardo GRIFFA Monferoni, Isacio CALLEJA García, Javier IRURETAgoyena Amiano, Julio IGLESIAS Santamaría, José Enrique CARDONA Gutiérrez (46 Fernando BARRIOCANAL Sanmartín), LUIS Aragonés Suárez, José Eulogio GÁRATE Ormaechea (82 Jesús MARTÍNEZ JAYO), ADELARDO Rodríguez Sánchez, Enrique COLLAR Monterrubio.   Trainer: MIGUEL González Pérez

WAREGEM: Georges De Meyer; Eric Ghyselinck, André Van Maldeghem, Christiaan Strobbe, Rafael Hostijn, Prudent Bettens, Christian De Smet, Guy Lammens, Eric Lambert, Jacky Stockman, Lucas Van Moerkerke.
Trainer: Freddy Chaves de Aguilar

Goals: Luis (21 pen), Bettens (42), Barriocanal (49)

SV WAREGEM v ATLÉTICO MADRID 1-0 (0-0)

Regenboogstadion, Waregem 2.10.68

Referee: William O'Neill (Irl)   Attendance: 20,000

WAREGEM: Georges De Meyer; Eric Ghyselinck, André Van Maldeghem, Christiaan Strobbe, Rafael Hostijn, Prudent Bettens, Christian De Smet, Guy Lammens, Eric Lambert, Jacky Stockman, Lucas Van Moerkerke.
Trainer: Freddy Chaves de Aguilar

ATLÉTICO: Jesús María ZUBIARRAIN Arguiñano; Francisco Faleato Ochoantesana "PAQUITO", Isacio CALLEJA García, Javier IRURETAgoyena Amiano, Jorge Bernardo GRIFFA Monferoni, Julio IGLESIAS Santamaría, José Armando UFARTE Ventoso, LUIS Aragonés Suárez, José Eulogio GÁRATE Ormaechea, ADELARDO Rodríguez Sánchez, Enrique COLLAR Monterrubio.
Trainer: MIGUEL González Pérez

Goal: Bettens (53)

DARING CLUB BRUSSEL v PANATHINAIKOS ATHINA 2-1 (1-0)

Oscar Bossaert, Brussel 25.09.68

Referee: Robert Holley Davidson (Sco)   Attendance: 5,000

DARING CLUB: François Cuypers; Roland Coclet, Julien Wauters, Donald De Vlegelaere, Jean Van Capellen, Etienne Coppens, Roland Beelen, Armand Randoux, Roger Foulon (82 Alex Lafont), Brian Etheridge, Ingvar Svahn.

PANATHINAIKOS: Takis Oikonomopoulos; Victoras Mitropoulos, Dimitris Dimitriou (32 Giorgos Rokidis), Panagiotis Filakouris, Aristeidis Kamaras, Fragkiskos Sourpis, Giorgos Gonios, Kostas Eleutherakis, Giannis Frantzis (46 Giannis Kalaitzidis), Mimis Domazos, Harilaos Grammos.
Trainer: Vasilis Petropoulos

Goals: Randoux (6), Gonios (64), Coppens (67)

PANATHINAIKOS ATHINA v DARING CLUB BRUSSEL 2-0 (0-0)

Stadio Apostolos Nikolaidis, Athina 9.10.68

Referee: Alessandro d'Agostini (Ita)   Attendance: 15,000

PANATHINAIKOS: Takis Oikonomopoulos; Victoras Mitropoulos, Kostas Athanasopoulos, Panagiotis Filakouris, Aristeidis Kamaras, Zaharias Pitihoutis, Giorgos Gonios (68 Giannis Frantzis), Fragkiskos Sourpis, Giorgos Rokidis, Mimis Domazos, Harilaos Grammos, Antonis Antoniadis.
Trainer: Vasilis Petropoulos

DARING CLUB: Ghislain Verhulst; Roland Coclet, Julien Wauters, Donald De Vlegelaere, Jean Van Capellen, Etienne Coppens (53 Ludo De Schutter), Roland Beelen, Roger Foulon, Alex Lafont, Brian Etheridge, Ingvar Svahn.

Goals: Rokidis (83), Frantzis (87)

HANNOVER 96 v B 1909 ODENSE 3-2 (3-0)

Niedersachsenstadion Hannover 1.10.68

Referee: Bo Nilsson (Swe)   Attendance: 5,000

HANNOVER 96: Horst Podlasly; Hans-Josef Hellingrath, Klaus Bohnsack, Peter Anders, Christian Breuer, Rainer Stiller, Hans Siemensmeyer, Rainer Zobel (.. Klaus Plitschke), Josef Heynckes, Josip Skoblar, Jürgen Bandura.
Trainer: Zlatko Cajkovski

B 1909: Svend Aage Rask; Jørgen Larsen, Petersen, Arno Hansen, H.Lindholm, Flemming Johansen, Torben Hansen, Walther Richter, Mogens Haastrup, Bent Outzen, Dyrholm.

Goals: Siemensmeyer (15), Heynckes (25), Skoblar (30), Richter (46), Torben Hansen (53)

B 1909 ODENSE v HANNOVER 96 0-1 (0-0)

Odense Stadion 9.10.68

Referee: Jef F. Dorpmans (Hol)   Attendance: 5,500

B 1909: Svend Aage Rask; Jørgen Larsen, Petersen, Arno Hansen, H. Lindholm, Flemming Johansen, Torben Hansen, Walther Richter, Mogens Haastrup, Bent Outzen, Dyrholm.

HANNOVER 96: Horst Podlasly; Hans-Josef Hellingrath, Rainer Stiller, Peter Anders, Christian Breuer, Peter Loof, Rainer Zobel, Josef Heynckes, Hans Siemensmeyer, Josip Skoblar, Jürgen Bandura.   Trainer: Zlatko Cajkovski

Goal: Siemensmeyer (80)

LEGIA WARSZAWA
v TSV 1860 MÜNCHEN 6-0 (3-0)

Wojska Polskiego, Warszawa   2.10.68

Referee: Gyula Emsberger (Hun)   Attendance: 8,000

LEGIA: Wladyslaw Grotynski, Wladyslaw Stachurski, Andrzej Zygmunt, Feliks Niedziólka, Antoni Trzaskowski, Kazimierz Deyna, Bernard Blaut, Janusz Zmijewski, Lucjan Brychczy, Jan Pieszko, Robert Gadocha.

TSV 1860: Petar Radenković; Manfred Wagner, Hans Reich, Bernd Patzke, Rudolf Steiner, Jürgen Schütz, Željko Perušić, Hans-Günther Kroth, Helmut Roth (63 Rudolf Zeiser), Hans Linsenmayer (22 Klaus Fischer), Alfred Heiss.
Trainer: Albert Sing

Goals: Pieszko (1, 41), Blaut (21), Deyna (46), Zmijewski (52), Gadocha (57)

TSV 1860 MÜNCHEN
v LEGIA WARSZAWA 2-3 (2-1)

Grünwalderstadion, München   9.10.68

Referee: Rudolf Scheurer (Swi)   Attendance: 6,000

TSV 1860: Herbert Schweers; Helmut Roth, Hans Reich, Bernd Patzke, Rudolf Zeiser, Max Reichenberger, Jürgen Schütz, Peter Kittel (42 Bernd Gerstner), Wilfried Kohlars, Peter Grosser (43 Klaus Fischer), Alfred Heiss.
Trainer: Albert Sing

LEGIA: Wladyslaw Grotynski, Wladyslaw Stachurski, Andrzej Zygmunt, Feliks Niedziólka, Antoni Trzaskowski, Kazimierz Deyna, Bernard Blaut, Janusz Zmijewski (.. Henryk Apostel), Jan Pieszko, Lucjan Brychczy, Robert Gadocha.

Goals: B. Blaut (8), Patzke (30 pen), Schutz (40), Pieszko (57), Brychczy (89)

OLYMPIQUE LYON
v ACADÉMICA COIMBRA 1-0 (0-0)

Stade Municipal de Gerland, Lyon   2.10.68

Referee: Joseph Moscado (Lux)   Attendance: 10,000

OLYMPIQUE: Yves Chauveau; Lucien Degeorges, Robert Nouzaret, Yves Flohic, Jacques Glyczinski, André Perrin, Mohamed Lekkak, Hector Maison (61 Bernard L'homme), André Guy, François Felix, Angel Rambert.
Trainer: Aimé Mignot

ACADÉMICA: Armelim Ferreira VIEGAS; António José CURADO, RUI Gouveia Pinto RODRIGUES, António Pereira MARQUES, Vasco Manuel Vieira Pereira GERVÁSIO, António Francisco VIEIRA NUNES, MÁRIO Alberto Domingos CAMPOS, MANUEL ANTÓNIO Leitão da Silva (.. José António Pinto BELO), ARTUR JORGE Braga Melo Teixeira, VÍTOR José Domingos CAMPOS, Fernando PERES.
Trainer: Mario Wilson

Goal: Guy (85)

ACADÉMICA COIMBRA
v OLYMPIQUE LYON 1-0 (0-0, 1-0) a.e.t.

Estadio Municipal Calhabe, Coimbra   9.10.68

Referee: Adolfo Bueno Perales (Spa)   Attendance: 6,500

ACADÉMICA: Armelim Ferreira VIEGAS; José António Pinto BELO, António José CURADO, Vasco Manuel Vieira Pereira GERVÁSIO, RUI Gouveia Pinto RODRIGUES; António Francisco VIEIRA NUNES, MANUEL ANTÓNIO Leitão da Silva, Joaquim José Ventura da Silva "QUIM"; Augusto Francisco ROCHA, ARTUR JORGE Braga Melo Teixeira, VÍTOR José Domingos CAMPOS.   Trainer: Mario Wilson

OLYMPIQUE: Yves Chauveau; Lucien Degeorges, Robert Nouzaret, Yves Flohic, Jacques Glyczinski, André Perrin, Mohamed Lekkak, Hector Maison, André Guy, François Felix, Angel Rambert.   Trainer: Aimé Mignot

Goal: Manuel António (75)

Olympique Lyon won on the toss of a coin

SECOND ROUND

ABERDEEN FC v REAL ZARAGOZA 2-1 (1-0)

Pittodrie, Aberdeen   23.10.68

Referee: Robert Schaut (Bel)   Attendance: 25,000

ABERDEEN: Robert Clark; James Hermiston, Alistair Shewan, Jens Petersen, Thomas McMillan, Thomas Craig, David Johnston, James Smith, James Forrest, Martin Buchan, Ian Taylor.   Manager: Edward Turnbull

REAL ZARAGOZA: José Manuel Fernández NIEVES; José Luis RICO Ibáñez, Severino REIJA Vázquez, José Luis VIOLETA Lajusticia, José Manuel GONZÁLEZ López, Joaquín BORRÁS Canut, Ángel OLIVEROS Jiménez, Antonio PAÍS Castroagudin (70 Francisco Javier PLANAS Abad), MARCELINO Martínez Cao, José Antonio TEJEDOR Sanz, Carlos LAPETRA Coarasa.   Trainer: Roque OLSEN Fontana

Goals: Forrest (32), Smith (64), Tejedor (72)

REAL ZARAGOZA v ABERDEEN FC 3-0 (2-0)

Estadio La Romareda, Zaragoza   30.10.68

Referee: Lousada Rodrigues (Por)   Attendance: 25,000

REAL ZARAGOZA: José Manuel Fernández NIEVES, José Luis RICO Ibáñez (52 Miguel Ángel BUSTILLO Lafoz), Severino REIJA Vázquez (46 Francisco Javier PLANAS Abad), José Luis VIOLETA Lajusticia, José Manuel GONZÁLEZ López, Joaquín BORRÁS Canut, José Antonio TEJEDOR Sanz, Eleuterio SANTOS Brito, MARCELINO Martínez Cao, Juan Manuel VILLA Gutiérrez, Carlos LAPETRA Coarasa.
Trainer: Roque OLSEN Fontana

ABERDEEN: Robert Clark; James Hermiston, Alistair Shewan, Jens Petersen, Thomas McMillan, Thomas Craig, David Robb, James Smith, James Forrest, Martin Buchan, Ian Taylor.   Manager: Edward Turnbull

Goals: Marcelino (35), Tejedor (43), Villa (78)

CHELSEA LONDON v DWS AMSTERDAM 0-0

Stamford Bridge, London   23.10.68

Referee: Ejnar Espersen (Dan)   Attendance: 28,428

CHELSEA: Peter Bonetti; John Boyle, Edward McCreadie, John Hollins, David Webb, Ronald Harris, Charles Cooke, Robert Tambling (59 Peter Osgood), Thomas Baldwin, Alan Birchenall, Peter Houseman.   Manager: Dave Sexton

DWS: Jan Jongbloed; Theo Cornwall, Jos Dijkstra, Niels Overweg, André Pijlman, Rob Bianchi, Martin Kamminga, Joop Burgers, Finn Seemannn, Piet Van den Berg, Frans Geurtsen.   Trainer: Lesley Talbot

DWS AMSTERDAM v CHELSEA LONDON 0-0 a.e.t.

Olympisch, Amsterdam   30.10.68

Referee: Gusztáv Bircsak (Hun)   Attendance: 8,000

DWS: Jan Jongbloed; Theo Cornwall, André Pijlman, Niels Overweg, Rob Bianchi, Martin Kamminga (.. Frits Flinkevleugel), Joop Burgers, Jos Dijkstra, Finn Seemann, Frans Geurtsen, Rob Rensenbrink (.. Piet Van den Berg).   Trainer: Lesley Talbot

CHELSEA: Peter Bonetti; Marvin Hinton, Ronald Harris, Edward McCreadie, John Boyle, Robert Tambling, Alan Birchenall, Charles Cooke, Thomas Baldwin, Peter Osgood, David Webb.   Manager: Dave Sexton

DWS won on the toss of a coin

GÖZTEPE IZMIR v FC ARGEŞ PITEŞTI 3-0 (3-0)

Alsançak, Izmir   30.10.68

Referee: Bohumil Smejkal; Slama, Mitrik (Cze)   Att: 13,000

GÖZTEPE: Ali Artuner; Mehmet Kiraz, Caglayan Derebaşi; Hüseyin Yazici, B.Mehmet I, Ali Ihsan Okçuoglu (51 Ceyhan Yazar); Nihat Yayöz, Ertan Öznur, Fevzi Zemzem, Gürsel Aksel (77 Sabahattin Kuruoglu), Halil Kiraz.   Trainer: Adnan Süvari

FC ARGEŞ: Spiridon Niculescu; Dumitru Ciolan, Ion Barbu, Remus Vlad, Dumitru Ivan; Ion Ioniţă, Petre Nuţu, Viorel Kraus, Cornel Pavlovici (61 Mihai Ţurcan), Nicolae Dobrin, Radu Jercan (80 Ion Păciulete).   Trainer: Ion Bălănescu

Goals: Ertan (3), Gürsel (10,35)

FC ARGEŞ PITEŞTI v GÖZTEPE IZMIR 3-2 (0-1)

1 Mai, Piteşti   13.11.68

Referee: Leonidas Vamvakopoulos (Gre)   Attendance: 8,000

FC ARGEŞ: Spiridon Niculescu; Ion Păciulete, Ion Barbu, Remus Vlad, Dumitru Ivan; Ion Prepurgel, Constantin Olteanu, Petre Nuţu, Viorel Kraus (46 Radu Jercan), Nicolae Dobrin, Constantin Radu.   Trainer: Ion Bălănescu

GÖZTEPE: Ali Artuner; Mehmet Kiraz, Caglayan Derebaşi; Hüseyin Yazici, B.Mehmet I (5 Sabahattin Kuruoglu), Ali Ihsan Okçuoglu; Nihat Yayöz, Ertan Öznur, Fevzi Zemzem, Gürsel Aksel, Halil Kiraz.   Trainer: Adnan Süvari

Goals: Ertan (9), Prepurgel (56 pen), Caglayan (58 og), Jercan (65), Fevzi (77)

GLASGOW RANGERS v DUNDALK FC 6-1 (2-1)

Ibrox Stadium, Glasgow   30.10.68

Referee: Kurt Nystrand (Swe)   Attendance: 30,000

RANGERS: Norman Martin; Kai Johansen, William Mathieson, John Greig, Ronald McKinnon, David Smith, William Henderson, Andrew Penman, Alex Ferguson, William Johnston, Örjan Persson.   Manager: David White

DUNDALK: Pat Lawless; John Murphy, Morrissey, Kevin Murray, Francis Brennan, Michael Millington, Patrick Turner, Turlough O'Connor, Derek Stokes, Brendan Hannigan, Anthony O'Connell.

Goals: Henderson (13, 26), Murray (43), Greig (50), Ferguson (55, 90), Brennan (88 og)

DUNDALK FC v GLASGOW RANGERS 0-3 (0-1)

Oriel Park, Dundalk   13.11.68

Referee: Kåre Sirevaag (Nor)   Attendance: 8,000

DUNDALK: Pat Lawless; Des O'Reilly, Francis Brennan (.. John Murphy), Kevin Murray, Andy Keogh, Michael Millington, Patrick Turner, Turlough O'Connor, Derek Stokes, James Morrissey, Laurence Gilmore.

RANGERS: Norman Martin; Kai Johansen, William Mathieson, Roger Hynd, Colin Jackson, David Smith, William Henderson, Alex Ferguson (.. Alfred Conn), Colin Stein, William Johnston, Örjan Persson.   Trainer: David White

Goals: Mathieson (45), Stein (64, 81)

VITÓRIA SETÚBAL v OLYMPIQUE LYON 5-0 (2-0)

Estadio do Bonfim, Setúbal   30.10.68

Referee: Alfred Delcourt (Bel)   Attendance: 10,000

VITÓRIA: Dinis Martins VITAL; Joaquim Adriao José da CONCEIÇÃO, ALFREDO Teixeira Moreira, Manuel Luís dos Santos "CARRIÇO", Fernando Massano TOMÉ, Carlos Alberto Lourenço CARDOSO, VAGNER Canotilho, JOSÉ MARIA Júnior, Ernesto FIGUEIREDO (.. Félix Marques Guerreiro), Joaquim Leonardo Quinta ARCANJO (.. António Ilídio de Sousa "PETITA"), JACINTO JOÃO.   Trainer: Fernando VAZ

OLYMPIQUE: Yves Chauveau; Lucien Degeorges, Yves Flohic, Jacques Glyczinski, Bernard Lhomme, Hector Maison, Robert Nouzaret, Mohamed Lekkak, André Guy, André Perrin, Angel Rambert.   Trainer: Aimé Mignot

Goals: Carriço (30), Tomé (32, 57, 70), Petita (81 pen)

OLYMPIQUE LYON v VITÓRIA SETÚBAL 1-2 (1-1)

Stade Municipal de Gerland, Lyon   13.11.68

Referee: Daniel Zariquiegui (Spa)   Attendance: 5,000

OLYMPIQUE: Yves Chauveau; Erwin Kuffer, Yves Flohic (66 Jacques Glyczinski), Marcel Le Borgne, Bernard Lhomme, Hector Maison, Robert Nouzaret, Mohamed Lekkak, André Guy, François Felix, Angel Rambert.   Trainer: Aimé Mignot

VITÓRIA: Dinis Martins VITAL; Joaquim Adriao José da CONCEIÇÃO, ALFREDO Teixeira Moreira, Manuel Luís dos Santos «CARRIÇO», Fernando Massano TOMÉ, Carlos Alberto Lourenço CARDOSO, VAGNER Canotilho (69 VITOR Manuel Ferreira BAPTISTA), JOSÉ MARIA Júnior, Ernesto FIGUEIREDO, Joaquim Leonardo Quinta ARCANJO, JACINTO JOÃO.   Trainer: Fernando VAZ

Goals: Figueiredo (11), Felix (29), Arcanjo (59 pen)

SPORTING LISBOA v NEWCASTLE UNITED 1-1 (0-1)

Estádio de José Alvalade, Lisboa   30.10.68

Referee: Erwin Vetter (DDR)   Attendance: 9,000

SPORTING: Vítor Manuel Afonso DAMAS de Oliveira; CELESTINO da Silva Martins Bárbara, HILÁRIO Rosário da Conceição, Vítor Manuel de Almeida GONÇALVES (46 Mário da Silva Mateus «MARINHO»), ARMANDO António Manhiça, JOSÉ CARLOS da Silva José, Francisco Delfim Dias Faria CHICO, ERNESTO Francisco de Sousa, João de Matos Moura LOURENÇO, JOSÉ MORAIS, José Maria de Freitas Pereira "PEDRAS".   Trainer: Fernando CAIADO

UNITED: William McFaul; David Craig, Frank Clark, Thomas Gibb, Graham Winstanley, Robert Moncur, James Scott, Bryan Robson, Wyn Davies, Alwyn Burton, Alan Foggon (73 Keith Dyson).   Manager: Joseph Harvey

Goals: Scott (31), João Morais (89)

NEWCASTLE UNITED v SPORTING LISBOA 1-0 (1-0)

St. James' Park, Newcastle   20.11.68

Referee: Gerhard Schulenburg (WG)   Attendance: 53,650

UNITED: William McFaul; David Craig, Frank Clark, Thomas Gibb, Alwyn Burton, Robert Moncur, James Scott, Bryan Robson, Wyn Davies, David Elliott, Keith Dyson (75 Albert Bennett).   Manager: Joseph Harvey

SPORTING: Vítor Manuel Afonso DAMAS de Oliveira; CELESTINO da Silva Martins Bárbara, ARMANDO António Manhiça, JOSÉ CARLOS da Silva José, HILÁRIO Rosário da Conceição, JOSÉ MORAIS, José Maria de Freitas Pereira "PEDRAS", Francisco Delfim Dias Faria CHICO, João de Matos Moura LOURENÇO (60 Lourenço Salvador SITOE), Mário da Silva Mateus "MARINHO", JOÃO CARLOS Conceição.   Trainer: Fernando CAIADO

Goal: Robson (10)

KSV WAREGEM v LEGIA WARSZAWA 1-0 (1-0)

Regenboogstadion, Waregem   6.11.68

Referee: Mario Clematide (Swi)   Attendance: 20,000

WAREGEM: Georges De Meyer; Eric Ghyselinck, André Van Maldeghem, Christiaan Strobbe, Christian De Smet, Prudent Bettens, Marc Millecamps (75 Lucas Van Moerkerke), Guy Lammens, Eric Lambert, Jacky Stockman, Pierre van de Velde.   Trainer: Freddy Chaves de Aguilar

LEGIA: Wladyslaw Grotynski; Wladyslaw Stachurski (.. Antoni Mahseli), Feliks Niedziólka, Antoni Trzaskowski, Andrzej Zygmunt, Bernard Blaut, Janusz Zmijewski, Kazimierz Deyna, Lucjan Brychczy, Jan Pieszko, Robert Gadocha.

Goal: Lambert (38 pen)

LEGIA WARSZAWA v KSV WAREGEM 2-0 (0-0)

Wojska Polskiego, Warszawa   12.11.68

Referee: Gheorghe Popovici (Rom)   Attendance: 10,000

LEGIA: Wladyslaw Grotynski; Wladyslaw Stachurski, Feliks Niedziólka, Antoni Trzaskowski, Andrzej Zygmunt, Bernard Blaut, Janusz Zmijewski, Kazimierz Deyna, Lucjan Brychczy (80 Henryk Apostel), Jan Pieszko, Robert Gadocha.

WAREGEM: Georges De Meyer; Eric Ghyselinck, André Van Maldeghem, Christian De Smet, André Van Horenbeke, Prudent Bettens, Guy Lammens, Pierre van de Velde (88 Marc Millecamps), Eric Lambert, Jacky Stockman, Lucas Van Moerkerke.   Trainer: Freddy Chaves de Aguilar

Goals: Deyna (68), Gadocha (89)

ARIS THESSALONIKI
v ÚJPESTI DÓZSA BUDAPEST 1-2 (0-1)

Harilaou, Thessaloniki   6.11.68

Referee: Alessandro d'Agostini (Ita)   Attendance: 15,000

ARIS: Nikos Hristidis; Theodoros Pallas, Aggelos Spiridon, Hristos Nalbantis, Dimitris Raptopoulos; Merkurios Giantzis, Giorgos Konstantinidis; Manolis Keramidas, Alekos Alexiadis, Klimis Gounaris (.. Dimitris Grimbelakos), Kostas Papaioannou.

ÚJPESTI DÓZSA: Antal Szentmihályi; Benő Káposzta, Ernő Solymosi, István Bánkuti, Ede Dunai III, Ernő Noskó; László Fazekas, János Göröcs, Ferenc Bene, Antal Dunai II, Sándor Zámbó.   Trainer: Lajos Baróti

Goals: Bene (7), Konstantinidis (57), Dunai II (80)

ÚJPESTI DÓZSA BUDAPEST
v ARIS THESSALONIKI 9-1 (4-1)

Megyeri út, Budapest   20.11.68

Referee: Ertugrul Dilek (Tur)   Attendance: 10,000

ÚJPESTI DÓZSA: Antal Szentmihályi; Benő Káposzta, Ernő Solymosi, István Bánkuti; Ede Dunai III (.. László Nagy), Ernő Noskó; Péter Juhász, János Göröcs (.. Béla Kuharszki), Ferenc Bene, Antal Dunai II, Sándor Zámbó.   Trainer: Lajos Baróti

ARIS: Nikos Hristidis; Theodoros Pallas, Aggelos Spiridon, Theofilos Kourtidis, Dimitris Raptopoulos, Merkurios Giantzis (30 Klimis Gounaris), Giorgos Konstantinidis, Manolis Keramidas, Alekos Alexiadis, Vaggelis Siropoulos, Stefanos Demiris (46 Kostas Papaioannou).

Goals: Dunai II (1, 16, 46, 70), Dunai III (9), Bene (25), Siropoulos (40), Kuharszki (48), Solymosi (55 pen), L. Nagy (76)

OFK BEOGRAD v AC BOLOGNA 1-0 (1-0)

Omladinski, Beograd   6.11.68

Referee: Milivoje Gugulović (Jug)   Attendance: 10,000

OFK: Bratislav Djordjević, Stojan Vukašinović, Zdravko Jokić, Sredojević, Slobodan Mesanović, Dragoslav Stepanović, Bogdan Turudija, Dragan Stojanović, Slobodan Santrac, Dragoslav Šekularac, Matković (46 Dušan Maravić).

BOLOGNA: Giuseppe Vavassori; Tazio Roversi, Mario Ardizzon, Francesco Cresci, Francesco Janich, Ivan Gregori, Bruno Pace, Giacomo Bulgarelli, Lucio Mujesan, Faustino Turra, Giuseppe Savoldi.   Trainer: Cervellati

Goal: Santrac (32)

AC BOLOGNA v OFK BEOGRAD 1-1 (1-0)

Stadio Communale, Bologna   20.11.68

Referee: Jacques Colling (Lux)   Attendance: 6,893

BOLOGNA: Giuseppe Vavassori; Tazio Roversi, Mario Ardizzon, Francesco Cresci, Francesco Janich, Ivan Gregori, Bruno Pace, Giacomo Bulgarelli, Lucio Mujesan, Faustino Turra, Ezio Pascutti (52 Francesco Battisodo). Trainer: Cervellati

OFK: Bratislav Djordjević, Stojan Vukašinović, Zdravko Jokić, Sredojević (81 Dušan Maravić), Slobodan Mesanović, Dragoslav Stepanović, Bogdan Turudija, Dragan Stojanović, Slobodan Santrac, Dragoslav Šekularac, Matković.

Goals: Mujesan (40), Santrac (80)

JUVENTUS TORINO
v EINTRACHT FRANKFURT am MAIN 0-0

Stadio Comunale, Torino   6.11.68

Referee: Juan Gardeazabal (Spa)   Attendance: 25,000

JUVENTUS: Roberto Anzolin; Sandro Salvadore, Gianfranco Leoncini, Gianluigi Roveta, Ernesto Castano, Luis Cascajares Del Sol, Erminio Favalli, Romeo Benetti (46 Luigi Pasetti), Pietro Anastasi, Helmut Haller, Gianfranco Zigoni. Trainer: Heriberto Herrera

EINTRACHT: Hans Tilkowski; Karl-Heinz Wirth, Hermann-Dieter Bellut, Friedel Lutz, Lothar Schämer, Jürgen Kalb, Helmut Kraus (46 Wilhelm Huberts), Oskar Lotz, Ernst Abbé (70 Heiko Racky), Bernd Nickel, Bernd Hölzenbein. Trainer: Erich Ribbeck

EINTRACHT FRANKFURT am MAIN
v JUVENTUS TORINO 1-0 (0-0)

Wald-Stadion, Frankfurt   21.11.68

Referee: Lado Jakse (Jug)   Attendance: 18,000

EINTRACHT: Hans Tilkowski; Karl-Heinz Wirth, Friedel Lutz, Dieter Lindner, Lothar Schämer, Hermann-Dieter Bellut (75 Ernst Abbé), Bernd Hölzenbein, Jürgen Grabowski, Walter Bechtold, Bernd Nickel, Wilhelm Huberts. Trainer: Erich Ribbeck

JUVENTUS: Roberto Anzolin; Sandro Salvadore, Gianluigi Roveta, Giancarlo Bercellino (91 Luigi Pasetti), Ernesto Castano, Gianfranco Leoncini, Gianfranco Zigoni, Romeo Benetti, Pietro Anastasi, Helmut Haller, Giampaolo Menichelli. Trainer: Heriberto Herrera

Goal: Bechtold (120)

AIK SOLNA v HANNOVER 96 4-2 (0-0)

Nya Råsunda, Solna   12.11.68

Referee: William Mullan (Sco)   Attendance: 514

AIK: Leif Hult; Curt Edenvik, Jim Nildén, Olavus Olsson, Roland Grip, Bo Holmberg, Ove Ohlsson, Kurt Andersson, Tord Grip, Roland Lundblad, Kent Persson (.. Jan Nilsson).

HANNOVER 96: Horst Podlasly, Peter Anders, Hans-Josef Hellingrath, Klaus Bohnsack, Christian Breuer, Rainer Stiller, Rainer Zobel, Josef Heynckes, Hans Siemensmeyer, Josip Skoblar, Jürgen Bandura.   Trainer: Zlatko Cajkovski

Goals: Anders (48), Ohlsson (54, 65, 85), T. Grip (57), Siemensmeyer (77)

HANNOVER 96 v AIK SOLNA 5-2 (2-1)

Niedersachsenstadion, Hannover   19.11.68

Referee: Robert Schaut (Bel)   Attendance: 5,000

HANNOVER 96: Bernd Helmschrot (26 Horst Podlasly); Peter Anders, Christian Breuer, Rainer Stiller, Klaus Bohnsack (61 Peter Loof), Jürgen Bandura, Hans-Josef Hellingrath, Rainer Zobel, Josef Heynckes, Josip Skoblar, Hans Siemensmeyer. Trainer: Zlatko Cajkovski

AIK: Leif Hult; Göran Åberg, Jim Nildén, Olavus Olsson, Roland Grip, Kurt Andersson, Jan Nilsson (52 Tord Grip), Bo Holmberg, Kent Persson, Roland Lundblad, Owe Ohlsson.

Goals: Nilsson (12), Skoblar (16, 17), Heynckes (49, 51, 77), Lundblad (70)

HIBERNIAN EDINBURGH v 1.FC LOKOMOTIVE LEIPZIG 3-1 (3-0)

Easter Road, Edinburgh   13.11.68

Referee: Joseph Heymann (Swi)   Attendance: 11,000

HIBERNIAN: Wilson; Christopher Shevlane, Joseph Davis, Alan Cousin, Patrick Stanton, James O'Rourke, Patrick Quinn, Alexander Scott, Joseph McBride, Colin Grant, Eric William Stevenson.

1.FC LOKOMOTIVE: Peter Nauert; Christoph Franke, Michael Faber, Peter Giessner, Eberhard Harms; Dieter Buckewiz (46 Jürgen Fritsch), Jürgen Naumann, Werner Gase; Heinz Stamer, Henning Frenzel, Wolfram Löwe. Trainer: Hans Studener

Goals: McBride (3, 7, 44), Fritsch (65)

1.FC LOKOMOTIVE LEIPZIG v HIBERNIAN EDINBURGH 0-1 (0-1)

Zentralstadion, Leipzig   20.11.68

Referee: Arie Van Gemert (Hol)   Attendance: 10,000

1.FC LOKOMOTIVE: Werner Friese; Christoph Franke, Peter Giessner, Jerzy Czieschowitz, Michael Faber; Werner Gase (59 Dieter Buckewiz), Arno Zerbe, Jürgen Naumann (75 Eberhard Harms); Heinz Stamer, Henning Frenzel, Jürgen Fritsch. Trainer: Hans Studener

HIBERNIAN: Wilson; Christopher Shevlane, Joseph Davis, Alan Cousin, Patrick Stanton, James O'Rourke, Patrick Quinn, Peter Cormack, Joseph McBride, Colin Grant, Eric William Stevenson.

Goal: Grant (3)

LEEDS UNITED v SSC NAPOLI 2-0 (2-0)

Elland Road, Leeds   13.11.68

Referee: Paul Schiller (Aus)   Attendance: 26,967

UNITED: Gary Sprake; Paul Reaney, Paul Madeley, William Bremner, Jack Charlton, Norman Hunter, Michael O'Grady, Michael Jones, Rodney Belfitt, John Giles, Peter Lorimer. Manager: Don Revie

NAPOLI: Dino Zoff; Stelio Nardin, Dino Panzanato, Amedeo Stenti, Aristide Guarneri, Mario Zurlini, José Altafini, Antonio Juliano, Harald Nielsen (76 Claudio Sala), Enrique Omar Sívori, Paolo Barison.   Trainer: Giuseppe Chiapella

Goals: Charlton (23, 25)

SSC NAPOLI v LEEDS UNITED 2-0 (1-0, 2-0) a.e.t.

San Paolo, Napoli   27.11.68

Referee: Rudolf Glöckner (DDR)   Attendance: 15,000

NAPOLI: Dino Zoff; Stelio Nardin, Luigi Pogliana (91 Romano Micelli), Mario Zurlini, Dino Panzanato, Ottavio Bianchi, Egidio Salvi, Antonio Juliano, Claudio Sala, Enrique Omar Sívori (46 Vincenzo Montefusco), Paolo Barison. Trainer: Giuseppe Chiapella

UNITED: Gary Sprake (82 David Harvey); Paul Reaney, Terence Cooper, William Bremner, Jack Charlton, Norman Hunter, Michael O'Grady, Paul Madeley (61 Rodney Belfitt), Michael Jones, John Giles, Edward Gray. Manager: Don Revie

Goals: Sala (14), Juliano (83 pen)

Leeds won on the toss of a coin

HANSA ROSTOCK
v AC FIORENTINA FIRENZE 3-2 (0-0)

Ostseestadion, Rostock   13.11.68

Referee: Laurens van Ravens (Hol)   Attendance: 15,000

HANSA: Dieter Schneider; Gerd Sackritz (51 Jürgen Decker), Manfred Rump, Helmut Hergesell, Klaus-Dieter Seehaus, Herbert Pankau, Wolfgang Barthels, Gerhard Brümmer, Gerd Kostmann, Kurt Habermann, Werner Drews.
Trainer: Gerhard Gläser

FIORENTINA: Francesco Superchi; Giovan Battista Pirovano, Paolo Stanzial, Salvatore Esposito, Ugo Ferrante, Bernardo Rogora, Francesco Rizzo, Claudio Merlo, Mario Maraschi, Giancarlo De Sisti, Luciano Chiarugi.
Trainer: Bruno Pesaola

Goals: Kostmann (69), Maraschi (70), Barthels (80), Rizzo (84), Hergesell (90)

AC FIORENTINA FIRENZE
v HANSA ROSTOCK 2-1 (1-1)

Stadio Communale, Firenze   27.11.68

Referee: Robert Lacoste (Fra)   Attendance: 12,000

FIORENTINA: Claudio Bandoni; Bernardo Rogora, Paolo Stanzial, Claudio Merlo, Ugo Ferrante, Giuseppe Brizi, Giancarlo Danova, Francesco Rizzo, Mario Maraschi, Giancarlo De Sisti, AMARILDO Tavares de Silveire.
Trainer: Bruno Pesaola

HANSA: Dieter Schneider; Gerhard Brümmer, Manfred Rump, Gerd Sackritz, Klaus-Dieter Seehaus, Helmut Hergesell, Wolfgang Barthels (51 Jürgen Decker), Herbert Pankau, Gerd Kostmann, Kurt Habermann, Werner Drews.
Trainer: Gerhard Gläser

Goals: Kostmann (26), Rizzo (36), Merlo (68)

HAMBURGER SV v SLAVIA PRAHA 4-1 (3-1)

Volksparkstadion, Hamburg   20.11.68

Referee: David Smith (Eng)   Attendance: 8,000

HAMBURGER SV: Özcan Arkoc (46 Gert Girschkowski); Helmut Sandmann, Holger Dieckmann, Egon Horst, Jürgen Kurbjuhn, Werner Krämer, Hans Schulz, Jürgen Dringelstein, Klaus Fock, Franz-Josef Hönig, Gert Dörfel.
Trainer: Georg Knöpfle

SLAVIA: Jiří Vošta; Milos Tolar, Bohumil Smolík, Karel Knesl, Hildebrand, Jaroslav Šimek, Bedrich Tesař, František Veselý, Karel Nepomucký, Josef Linhart, Zigler (68 Ivan Kopecký).
Trainer: F. Havránek

Goals: Schulz (17), Fock (29), Krämer (34, 80 pen), Tesař (40)

SLAVIA PRAHA v HAMBURGER SV 3-1 (2-1)

Stadion dr. Vacka, Praha   27.11.68

Referee: Erich Linemayr (Aus)   Attendance: 7,500

SLAVIA: Jiří Vošta; Milos Tolar, Hildebrand, Bedrich Tesař, Bohumil Smolík, Josef Linhart, Karel Nepomucký, František Veselý, Jaroslav Šimek, Zdenek Konečný, Ivan Kopecký (46 Stefan Lukáč).   Trainer: F. Havránek

HAMBURGER SV: Özcan Arkoc (46 Gert Girschkowski); Helmut Sandmann, Holger Dieckmann, Egon Horst, Jürgen Kurbjuhn, Werner Krämer, Hans Schulz, Jürgen Dringelstein, Robert Pötzschke, Franz-Josef Hönig, Gert Dörfel.
Trainer: Georg Knöpfle

Goals: Kopecký (13), Veselý (19), Hönig (34), Lukáč (80)

PANATHINAIKOS ATHINA
v ATHLETIC BILBAO 0-0

Stadio Apostolos Nikolaidis, Athina   20.11.68

Referee: Ratko Çanak (Jug)   Attendance: 25,000

PANATHINAIKOS: Takis Oikonomopoulos; Victoras Mitropoulos, Aristeidis Kamaras, Dimitris Dimitriou, Kostas Athanasopoulos; Giorgos Rokidis (74 Kostas Eleutherakis), Zaharias Pitihoutis, Mimis Domazos; Giorgos Gonios, Giannis Frantzis (70 Panagiotis Papadimitriou), Harilaos Grammos.
Trainer: Vasilis Petropoulos

ATHLETIC: Juan Antonio DEUSTO Olagorta; José Ignacio SÁEZ Ruiz, Luis María ECHEBERRÍA Igartua, Jesús ARANGUREN Merino; Luis María ZUGAZAGA Martínez, José Ramón Martínez LARRAURI (46 Juan María ZORRIQUETA Azpiazu); Antonio María ARIETA Araunabeña Piedra, José María ARGOITIA Acha, Javier ORMAZA Garay, Fidel URIARTE Macho, José Francisco ROJO I Arroitia.
Trainer: Rafael IRIONDO

ATHLETIC BILBAO
v PANATHINAIKOS ATHINA 1-0 (1-0)

Estadio San Mamés, Bilbao   27.11.68

Referee: Michel Kitabdjian (Fra)   Attendance: 25,551

ATHLETIC: Juan Antonio DEUSTO Olagorta; Juan María ZORRIQUETA Azpiazu (.. Pedro LAVÍN Arcocha), Luis María ECHEBERRÍA Igartua, Jesús ARANGUREN Merino; Luis María ZUGAZAGA Martínez, José Ramón BETZUÉN Urquiaza; Antonio María ARIETA Araunabeña Piedra, José María ARGOITIA Acha, Javier ORMAZA Garay, Fidel URIARTE Macho (.. José María IGARTUA Mendizábal), José Francisco ROJO I Arroitia.   Trainer: Rafael IRIONDO

PANATHINAIKOS: Takis Oikonomopoulos; Victoras Mitropoulos, Aristeidis Kamaras, Dimitris Dimitriou, Kostas Athanasopoulos; Fragkiskos Sourpis, Harilaos Grammos (70 Giorgos Gonios); Zaharias Pitihoutis, Panagiotis Filakouris (75 Giorgos Rokidis), Mimis Domazos, Giannis Frantzis.
Trainer: Vasilis Petropoulos

Sent off: Rojo (87)

Goal: Rojo (43)

THIRD ROUND

HAMBURGER SV
v HIBERNIAN EDINBURGH 1-0 (1-0)

Volksparkstadion, Hamburg 18.12.68

Referee: Joseph Hannet (Bel)   Attendance: 7,000

HAMBURGER SV: Gert Girschkowski; Helmut Sandmann, Holger Dieckmann, Egon Horst, Jürgen Kurbjuhn, Hans Schulz, Werner Krämer, Jürgen Dringelstein, Uwe Seeler, Franz-Josef Hönig, Gert Dörfel.   Trainer: Georg Knöpfle

HIBERNIAN: Thomson Allan; Christopher Shevlane, Patrick Stanton, John Madsen, Joseph Davis, Alan Cousin, Patrick Quinn, James O'Rourke, Joseph McBride, Peter Cormack, Eric William Stevenson.

Goal: Hönig (6)

HIBERNIAN EDINBURGH
v HAMBURGER SV 2-1 (0-0)

Easter Road, Edinburgh 15.01.69

Referee: Sven Jonsson (Swe)   Attendance: 27,399

HIBERNIAN: Thomson Allan; Robert Duncan, Patrick Stanton, John Madsen, Joseph Davis, Alan Cousin, Patrick Quinn, Alexander Scott, Joseph McBride, Peter Cormack, Eric William Stevenson.

HAMBURGER SV: Özcan Arkoc; Helmut Sandmann, Willi Schulz (46 Jürgen Dringelstein), Egon Horst, Jürgen Kurbjuhn, Hans Schulz, Werner Krämer, Franz-Josef Hönig, Hubert Schöll, Uwe Seeler, Gert Dörfel.   Trainer: Georg Knöpfle

Goals: McBride (67, 87), Seeler (79)

VITÓRIA SETÚBAL
v AC FIORENTINA FIRENZE 3-0 (2-0)

Estadio do Bonfim, Setúbal 18.12.68

Referee: Thomas Wharton (Sco)   Attendance: 10,000

VITÓRIA: Dinis Martins VITAL; HERCULANO do Carmo Oliveira, Manuel Luís dos Santos "CARRIÇO", VAGNER Canotilho, Carlos Alberto Lourenço CARDOSO, ALFREDO Teixeira Moreira, Félix Marques Guerreiro, JOSÉ MARIA Júnior, Ernesto FIGUEIREDO (65 António Ilídio de Sousa "PETITA"), Joaquim Leonardo Quinta ARCANJO, JACINTO JOÃO.   Trainer: Fernando VAZ

FIORENTINA: Francesco Superchi; Paolo Stanzial, Eraldo Mancini, Claudio Merlo, Ugo Ferrante, Bernardo Rogora, Salvatore Esposito, Francesco Rizzo, Mario Maraschi, Giancarlo De Sisti, AMARILDO Tavares de Silveire.   Trainer: Bruno Pesaola

Goals: José Maria (13, 52), Arcanjo (36)

AC FIORENTINA FIRENZE
v VITÓRIA SETÚBAL 2-1 (2-0)

Stadio Communale, Firenze 22.01.69

Referee: Mario Clematide (Swi)   Attendance: 7,000

FIORENTINA: Francesco Superchi; Bernardo Rogora, Eraldo Mancini, Salvatore Esposito, Ugo Ferrante, Giuseppe Brizi, Luciano Chiarugi (68 Giancarlo Danova), Francesco Rizzo, Mario Maraschi, Giancarlo De Sisti, AMARILDO Tavares de Silveire.   Trainer: Bruno Pesaola

VITÓRIA: Dinis Martins VITAL; Joaquim Adriao José da CONCEIÇÃO, Manuel Luís dos Santos "CARRIÇO", HERCULANO do Carmo Oliveira (46 Fernando Massano TOMÉ), Carlos Alberto Lourenço CARDOSO, ALFREDO Teixeira Moreira, Félix Marques Guerreiro, JOSÉ MARIA Júnior, Ernesto FIGUEIREDO (75 VITOR Manuel Ferreira BAPTISTA), VAGNER Canotilho, JACINTO JOÃO.   Trainer: Fernando VAZ

Goals: Amarildo (12), Rogora (36), Mancini (90 og)

LEEDS UNITED v HANNOVER 96 5-1 (2-0)

Elland Road, Leeds 18.12.68

Referee: Adolfo Bueno Perales (Spa)   Attendance: 25,162

UNITED: Gary Sprake; Paul Reaney, Paul Madeley, William Bremner, Norman Hunter, Jack Charlton, Michael O'Grady (64 Terence Hibbitt), Peter Lorimer, Michael Jones, John Giles, Edward Gray.   Manager: Don Revie

HANNOVER 96: Horst Podlasly; Hans-Josef Hellingrath, Peter Anders, Christian Breuer, Klaus Bohnsack, Rainer Stiller, Jürgen Bandura, Rainer Zobel, Josef Heynckes, Josip Skoblar, Hans Siemensmeyer (46 Peter Loof).
Trainer: Zlatko Cajkovski

Goals: O'Grady (4), Hunter (35), Lorimer (52, 64), Charlton (62), Hellingrath (86)

HANNOVER 96 v LEEDS UNITED 1-2 (0-2)

Niedersachsenstadion, Hannover 4.02.69

Referee: Jef F. Dorpmans (Hol)   Attendance: 15,000

HANNOVER: Bernd Helmschrot; Hans-Josef Hellingrath, Peter Anders, Christian Breuer, Peter Loof, Rainer Stiller, Jürgen Bandura, Rainer Zobel (60 Winfried Wottka), Josef Heynckes, Claus Brune, Bernd Kettler (23 Kurt Ritter).   Trainer: Zlatko Cajkovski

UNITED: Gary Sprake; Paul Reaney, Terence Cooper, William Bremner, Jack Charlton, Norman Hunter, Michael O'Grady, Peter Lorimer, Michael Jones, Rodney Belfitt, Edward Gray. Cooper sent off (74).   Manager: Don Revie

Goals: Belfitt (5), Jones (16), Heynckes (87)

REAL ZARAGOZA
v NEWCASTLE UNITED 3-2 (2-2)

Estadio La Romareda, Zaragoza   1.01.69

Referee: Alfred Ott (WG)   Attendance: 15,000

REAL ZARAGOZA: José Manuel Fernández NIEVES;
Joaquín BORRÁS Canut, José Ramón IRUSQUIETA García,
Francisco Javier PLANAS Abad, Armando MARTÍN Suárez,
Francisco SANTAMARÍA Briones, Eleuterio SANTOS Brito
(51 José Luis VIOLETA Lajusticia), Francisco MOYA Gómez
(74 Miguel PLANAS Abad), José Manuel GONZÁLEZ López,
Miguel Ángel BUSTILLO Lafoz, MARCELINO Martínez Cao.
Trainer: CESAR Rodríguez

UNITED: William McFaul; David Craig, Frank Clark, Thomas
Gibb, Alwyn Burton, Robert Moncur, Keith Dyson, Bryan
Robson, Wyn Davies, James Scott, Alan Foggon.
Manager: Joseph Harvey

Goals: Santos (5), Robson (6), Bustillo (15), Davies (32),
F. Planas (57)

NEWCASTLE UNITED
v REAL ZARAGOZA 2-1 (2-1)

St. James Park, Newcastle   15.01.69

Referee: Roger Barde (Fra)   Attendance: 56,200

UNITED: William McFaul; David Craig (46 Ronald Guthrie),
Frank Clark, Thomas Gibb, Alwyn Burton, Robert Moncur,
Keith Dyson, Bryan Robson, Wyn Davies, James Scott, Alan
Foggon.   Manager: Joseph Harvey

REAL ZARAGOZA: José Manuel Fernández NIEVES (29
Rafael Álvarez ALARCIA); José Luis RICO Ibáñez, José Ramón
IRUSQUIETA García, Joaquín BORRÁS Canut, Francisco
SANTAMARÍA Briones, José Manuel GONZÁLEZ López,
Armando MARTÍN Suárez, José Luis VIOLETA Lajusticia,
Miguel Ángel BUSTILLO Lafoz, Eleuterio SANTOS Brito,
Manuel FONTENLA Barreiros (71 José Antonio TEJEDOR
Sanz).   Trainer: CESAR Rodríguez

Goals: Robson (2), Gibb (28), Martin (42)

OFK BEOGRAD v GÖZTEPE IZMIR 3-1 (1-0)

Omladinski, Beograd   2.01.69

Referee: Wolfgang Riedel (DDR)   Attendance: 10,000

OFK: Bratislav Djordjević, Stojan Vukašinović, Zdravko
Jokić; Sredojević, Slobodan Mesanović, Dragoslav Stepanović;
Bogdan Turudija, Milutinović, Slobodan Santrac, Dragan
Stojanović, Matković.

GÖZTEPE: Ali Artuner; Mehmet Kiraz, Caglayan Derebaşi;
Hüseyin Yazici, Mehmet B, Ali Ihsan Okçuoglu; Ertan Öznur,
Cenap Oztezel, Fevzi Zemzem, Gürsel Alsel, Halil Kiraz.
Trainer: Adnan Süvari

Goals: Santrac (21, 60, 76), Fevzi (87)

GÖZTEPE IZMIR v OFK BEOGRAD 2-0 (2-0)

Alsançak, Izmir   29.01.69

Referees: Todor Betchkirov; Petar Nikolov, Gocho Rusev (Bul)
Attendance: 9,500

GÖZTEPE: Ali Artuner; Mehmet Kiraz, Caglayan Derebaşi;
Hüseyin Yazici, B.Mehmet, Ali Ihsan Okçuoglu; Ertan Öznur,
Nihat Yayöz, Fevzi Zemzem, Gürsel Aksel, Halil Kiraz.
Trainer: Adnan Süvari

OFK: Djordjecar, Stojan Vukašinović, Zdravko Jokić;
Sredojević, Slobodan Mesanović, Dragoslav Stepanović;
Bogdan Turudija, Dušan Maravic, Slobodan Santrac, Dragan
Stojanović, Matković.

Goals: Fevzi (5), Ertan (14)

ATHLETIC BILBAO
v EINTRACHT FRANKFURT am MAIN 1-0 (1-0)

Estadio San Mamés, Bilbao   8.01.69

Referee: Alessandro d'Agostini (Ita)   Attendance: 33,111

ATHLETIC: José Ángel IRÍBAR Cortajarena; José Ignacio
SÁEZ Ruiz, Luis María ECHEBERRÍA Igartua, Jesús
ARANGUREN Merino, José María IGARTUA Mendizábal,
Luis María ZUGAZAGA Martínez, Nicolás ESTÉFANO
Montalbán, José María ARGOITIA Acha, Antonio María
ARIETA Araunabeña Piedra, Javier CLEMENTE Lázaro, Fidel
URIARTE Macho.   Trainer: Rafael IRIONDO

EINTRACHT: Hans Tilkowski; Karl-Heinz Wirth, Dieter
Lindner, Wilhelm Huberts, Günter Keifler, Friedel Lutz, Jürgen
Kalb, Jürgen Grabowski, Walter Bechtold, Bernd Nickel,
Helmut Kraus.   Trainer: Erich Ribbeck

Goal: Uriarte (27)

EINTRACHT FRANKFURT am MAIN
v ATHLETIC BILBAO 1-1 (1-1)

Waldstadion, Frankfurt   29.01.69

Referee: Joseph Heymann (Swi)   Attendance: 10,000

EINTRACHT: Peter Kunter; Karl-Heinz Wirth, Friedel Lutz
(63 Bernd Hölzenbein), Wilhelm Huberts, Lothar Schämer,
Jürgen Kalb, Hermann-Dieter Bellut, Jürgen Grabowski, Ernst
Abbé, Bernd Nickel, Oskar Lotz.   Trainer: Erich Ribbeck

ATHLETIC: José Ángel IRÍBAR Cortajarena; Luis María
ZUGAZAGA Martínez, Luis María ECHEBERRÍA Igartua,
Jesús ARANGUREN Merino, José María IGARTUA
Mendizábal, Juan María ZORRIQUETA Azpiazu, José María
ARGOITIA Acha, Fidel URIARTE Macho, Antonio María
ARIETA Araunabeña Piedra, Javier CLEMENTE Lázaro, José
Francisco ROJO I Arroitia.   Trainer: Rafael IRIONDO

Goals: Lotz (4), Igartua (5)

DWS AMSTERDAM
v GLASGOW RANGERS 0-2 (0-1)

Olympisch, Amsterdam   15.01.69

Referee: Vital Loraux (Bel)   Attendance: 20,000

DWS: Jan Jongbloed; Niels Overweg, Frits Soetekouw, Martin Kamminga, André Pijlman, Theo Cornwall, Kick Van der Vall, Jos Dijkstra, Finn Seemannn, Frans Geurtsen, Rob Rensenbrink.
Trainer: Lesley Talbot

RANGERS: Norman Martin; Kai Johansen, William Mathieson, John Greig, Ronald McKinnon, Robert Watson, William Henderson, William Johnston, Andrew Penman, Colin Stein, Örjan Persson (.. David Smith).
Manager: David White

Goals: Johnston (38), Henderson (53)

GLASGOW RANGERS
v DWS AMSTERDAM 2-1 (2-1)

Ibrox Stadium, Glasgow   22.01.69

Referee: Hans-Joachim Weyland (WG)   Attendance: 63,443

RANGERS: Norman Martin; Kai Johansen, John Greig, Robert Watson, Ronald McKinnon, David Smith (.. William Jardine), William Henderson, Andrew Penman, Colin Stein, William Johnston, Alex MacDonald.   Manager: David White

DWS: Jan Jongbloed; Frits Flinkevleugel, Frits Soetekouw, Niels Overweg, André Pijlman, Theo Cornwall, Jos Dijkstra, Kick Van der Vall, Frans Geurtsen, Finn Seemann, Rob Rensenbrink.   Trainer: Lesley Talbot

Goals: Smith (8), Geurtsen (12), Stein (21)

LEGIA WARSZAWA
v ÚJPESTI DÓZSA BUDAPEST 0-1 (0-0)

Wojska Polskiego, Warszawa   23.02.69

Referee: Bohumil Smejkal (Cze)   Attendance: 7,000

LEGIA: Wladyslaw Grotynski; Wladyslaw Stachurski, Andrzej Zygmunt, Feliks Niedziólka, Antoni Trzaskowski; Kazimierz Deyna, Bernard Blaut; Janusz Zmijewski, Lucjan Brychczy, Jan Pieszko, Robert Gadocha (7 Zygfryd Blaut).

ÚJPESTI DÓZSA: Antal Szentmihályi; Benő Káposzta, Ernő Solymosi, István Bánkuti, Ede Dunai III, Ernő Noskó, László Fazekas, Ferenc Bene, Antal Dunai II, Sándor Zámbó, János Göröcs.   Trainer: Lajos Baróti

Goal: A. Dunai II (85)

ÚJPESTI DÓZSA BUDAPEST
v LEGIA WARSZAWA 2-2 (0-2)

Megyeri út, Budapest   26.02.69

Referee: Erich Linemayr (Aus)   Attendance: 12,000

ÚJPESTI DÓZSA: Antal Szentmihályi; Benő Káposzta, Ernő Solymosi, István Bánkuti; Ede Dunai III, János Göröcs, Ernő Noskó; László Fazekas, Ferenc Bene, Antal Dunai II, Sándor Zámbó.   Trainer: Lajos Baróti

LEGIA: Wladyslaw Grotynski; Wladyslaw Stachurski, Feliks Niedziólka, Andrzej Zygmunt, Antoni Trzaskowski; Robert Gadocha, Kazimierz Deyna; Bernard Blaut, Janusz Zmijewski, Lucjan Brychczy, Jan Pieszko.

Goals: Stachurski (40), Zmijewski (42), A. Dunai II (66), Solymosi (75 pen)

QUARTER-FINALS

LEEDS UNITED
v ÚJPESTI DÓZSA BUDAPEST 0-1 (0-0)

Elland Road, Leeds   5.03.69

Referee: Robert Hélies (Fra)   Attendance: 30,906

UNITED: Gary Sprake; Paul Reaney, Paul Madeley, William Bremner, Jack Charlton, Norman Hunter, Michael O'Grady (60 Peter Lorimer), Rodney Belfitt, Michael Jones, John Giles, Edward Gray.   Manager: Don Revie

ÚJPESTI DÓZSA: Antal Szentmihályi; Benő Káposzta, Ernő Solymosi, István Bánkuti, Ede Dunai, Ernő Noskó; László Fazekas, János Göröcs, Ferenc Bene, Antal Dunai, Sándor Zámbó.   Trainer: Lajos Baróti

Goal: A. Dunai (71)

ÚJPESTI DÓZSA BUDAPEST
v LEEDS UNITED 2-0 (0-0)

Megyeri út, Budapest   19.03.69

Referee: Heinz Siebert (WG)   Attendance: 30,000

ÚJPESTI DÓZSA: Antal Szentmihályi; Benő Káposzta, Ernő Solymosi, István Bánkuti, Ede Dunai, Ernő Noskó, László Fazekas, János Göröcs, Ferenc Bene, Antal Dunai, Sándor Zámbó.   Trainer: Lajos Baróti

UNITED: Gary Sprake; William Bremner, Paul Madeley, Norman Hunter, Terence Cooper; John Giles, Michael Bates, Edward Gray; Peter Lorimer (70 Terence Yorath), Rodney Belfitt, Michael Jones (85 Terence Hibbitt).   Manager: Don Revie

Goals: Solymosi (63 pen), Bene (75)

NEWCASTLE UNITED
VITÓRIA SETÚBAL 5-1 (2-0)

St. James Park, Newcastle   12.03.69

Referee: Curt Liedberg (Swe)   Attendance: 57,633

UNITED: William McFaul; John Craggs, Frank Clark, Thomas Gibb, Alwyn Burton, Robert Moncur, Bryan Robson, Arthur Horsfield (68 John Sinclair), Wyn Davies, James Scott, Alan Foggon.   Manager: Joseph Harvey

VITÓRIA: Dinis Martins VITAL; HERCULANO do Carmo Oliveira, Manuel Luís dos Santos "CARRIÇO", VAGNER Canotilho, Carlos Alberto Lourenço CARDOSO, ALFREDO Teixeira Moreira, VITOR Manuel Ferreira BAPTISTA, JOSÉ MARIA Júnior, Ernesto FIGUEIREDO, Joaquim Leonardo Quinta ARCANJO (56 António Ilídio de Sousa "PETITA"), JACINTO JOÃO (63 Fernando Massano TOMÉ).
Trainer: Fernando VAZ

Goals: Foggon (23), Robson (36, 75), Davies (60), José Maria (84), Gibb (89)

GLASGOW RANGERS
v ATHLETIC BILBAO 4-1 (2-1)

Ibrox Stadium, Glasgow   19.03.69

Referee: Bruno de Marchi (Ita)   Attendance: 60,000

RANGERS: Norman Martin; Kai Johansen, William Mathieson, John Greig, Ronald McKinnon, David Smith, William Henderson, Andrew Penman, Colin Stein, Alex Ferguson (73 Örjan Persson), William Johnston.
Manager: David White

ATHLETIC: José Ángel IRÍBAR Cortajarena; Luis María ZUGAZAGA Martínez, José Ignacio SÁEZ Ruiz, José María IGARTUA Mendizábal, Luis María ECHEBERRÍA Igartua, José Ramón Martínez LARRAURI, José María ARGOITIA Acha (46 José Ramón BETZUÉN Urquiaza), Fidel URIARTE Macho, Antonio María ARIETA Araunabeña Piedra, Javier CLEMENTE Lázaro, José Francisco ROJO I Arroitia.
Trainer: Rafael IRIONDO

Goals: Ferguson (7), Penman (27), Clemente (29), Persson (86), Stein (87)

VITÓRIA SETÚBAL
v NEWCASTLE UNITED 3-1 (1-1)

Estádio de José Alvalade, Lisboa   26.03.69

Referee: Dittmar Huber (Swi)   Attendance: 35,000

VITÓRIA: Dinis Martins VITAL; Joaquim Adriao José da CONCEIÇÃO, Carlos Alberto Lourenço CARDOSO (47 António Ilídio de Sousa «PETITA»), ALFREDO Teixeira Moreira, Manuel Luís dos Santos «CARRIÇO», VITOR Manuel Ferreira BAPTISTA, VAGNER Canotilho (.. Fernando Massano TOMÉ), JOSÉ MARIA Júnior, Ernesto FIGUEIREDO, Joaquim Leonardo Quinta ARCANJO, JACINTO JOÃO.
Trainer: Fernando VAZ

UNITED: William McFaul; John Craggs, Frank Clark, Thomas Gibb, Alwyn Burton (.. John McNamee), Robert Moncur, John Sinclair, Bryan Robson, Wyn Davies, James Scott, Alan Foggon. Manager: Joseph Harvey

Goals: Arcanjo (27), Davies (40), Petita (60), Figueiredo (66)

ATHLETIC BILBAO
v GLASGOW RANGERS 2-0 (1-0)

Estadio San Mamés, Bilbao   2.04.69

Referee: Willem Schalks (Hol)   Attendance: 25,578

ATHLETIC: José Ángel IRÍBAR Cortajarena; José Ramón BETZUÉN Urquiaza, José Ignacio SÁEZ Ruiz, José María IGARTUA Mendizábal, Luis María ECHEBERRÍA Igartua, José Ramón Martínez LARRAURI, Nicolás ESTÉFANO Montalbán, Ricardo IBÁÑEZ Conde, Antonio María ARIETA Araunabeña Piedra, Fidel URIARTE Macho, José Francisco ROJO I Arroitia.
Trainer: Rafael IRIONDO

RANGERS: Norman Martin; Kai Johansen, William Mathieson, Colin Jackson, Ronald McKinnon, John Greig, William Henderson, Andy Penman, Colin Stein, David Smith, William Johnston.   Manager: David White

Sent off: Betzuén and Johnston (80)

Goals: Estéfano (10), Ibáñez (54)

SEMI-FINALS

GÖZTEPE IZMIR
v ÚJPESTI DÓZSA BUDAPEST 1-4 (1-2)

Alsançak, Izmir 23.04.69

Referee: Francesco Francescon (Ita)   Attendance: 25,000

GÖZTEPE: Ali Artuner; Mehmet Aydin, Caglayan Derebaşi, Ali Ihsan Okçuoglu; B. Mehmet, Nevzat Güzelirmak; Cenap Oztezel, Ertan Öznur, Fevzi Zemzem, Gürsel Aksel, Halil Kiraz. Trainer: Adnan Süvari

ÚJPESTI DÓZSA: Antal Szentmihályi; Benő Káposzta, Ernő Solymosi, Ernő Noskó; Ede Dunai III, Sándor Zámbó; László Fazekas, János Göröcs, Ferenc Bene, Antal Dunai II, László Nagy. Trainer: Lajos Baróti

Goals: Bene (12, 32), Caglayan (15 pen), Dunai II (63, 81)

ÚJPESTI DÓZSA BUDAPEST
v GÖZTEPE IZMIR 4-0 (1-0)

Megyeri út, Budapest 30.04.69

Referee: Kurt Tschenscher (WG)   Attendance: 20,000

ÚJPESTI DÓZSA: László Borbély; Benő Káposzta, József Horváth, Ernő Noskó; Ede Dunai III (.. István Nyiró), Sándor Zámbó, Péter Juhász, János Göröcs (.. László Fazekas), Ferenc Bene, Antal Dunai II, László Nagy. Trainer: Lajos Baróti

GÖZTEPE: Güngör Celikciler; Mehmet Kiraz, Caglayan Derebaşi (.. Sabahattin Kuruoglu), Hüseyin Yazici; Mehmet B, Ali Ihsan Okçuoglu; Cenap Oztezel, Ertan Öznur, Fevzi Zemzem (.. Nevzat Güzelirmak), Gürsel Aksel, Halil Kiraz. Trainer: Adnan Süvari

Goals: Bene (24, 55, 78), L. Nagy (56)

GLASGOW RANGERS v NEWCASTLE UNITED 0-0

Ibrox Stadium, Glasgow 14.05.69

Referee: John Adair (NIr)   Attendance: 76,083

RANGERS: Gerhardt Neef; Kai Johansen, David Provan, John Greig, Colin Jackson, David Smith, William Henderson, Andrew Penman, Colin Stein, William Jardine, Örjan Persson. Manager: David White

UNITED: William McFaul; John Craggs, Frank Clark, Thomas Gibb, John McNamee, Robert Moncur, James Scott (75 John Sinclair), Bryan Robson, Wyn Davies, Preben Arentoft, Alan Foggon. Manager: Joseph Harvey

NEWCASTLE UNITED
v GLASGOW RANGERS 2-0 (0-0)

St.James'Park, Newcastle 21.05.69

Referee: William John Gow (Wal)   Attendance: 60,000

UNITED: William McFaul; David Craig, Frank Clark, Thomas Gibb, Alwyn Burton, Robert Moncur, James Scott, Bryan Robson, Wyn Davies, Preben Arentoft, John Sinclair. Manager: Joseph Harvey

RANGERS: Gerhardt Neef; Kai Johansen, William Mathieson, John Greig, Ronald McKinnon (65 David Provan), David Smith, William Henderson, Andrew Penman, Colin Stein, William Johnston, Örjan Persson.   Manager: David White

Goals: Scott (52), Sinclair (77)

FINAL

NEWCASTLE UNITED
v ÚJPESTI DÓZSA BUDAPEST 3-0 (0-0)

St. James Park, Newcastle 29.05.69

Referee: Joseph Hannet (Bel)   Attendance: 59,500

UNITED: William McFaul; David Craig, Frank Clark, Thomas Gibb, Alwyn Burton; Robert Moncur (Cap), Preben Arentoft; James Scott, Bryan Robson, Wyn Davies, John Sinclair (70 Alan Foggon). Manager: Joseph Harvey

ÚJPESTI DÓZSA: Antal Szentmihályi; Benő Káposzta, Ernő Solymosi, István Bánkuti, Ernő Noskó; Ede Dunai, János Göröcs, László Fazekas, Ferenc Bene, Antal Dunai, Sándor Zámbó. Trainer: Lajos Baróti

Goals: Moncur (63, 72), Scott (83)

ÚJPESTI DÓZSA BUDAPEST
v NEWCASTLE UNITED 2-3 (2-0)

Megyeri út, Budapest 11.06.69

Referee: Joseph Heymann (Swi)   Attendance: 37,000

ÚJPESTI DÓZSA: Antal Szentmihályi; Benő Káposzta, Ernő Solymosi, István Bánkuti, Ernő Noskó; Ede Dunai, János Göröcs, László Fazekas, Ferenc Bene, Antal Dunai, Sándor Zámbó. Trainer: Lajos Baróti

UNITED: William McFaul; David Craig, Alwyn Burton, Robert Moncur (Cap), Frank Clark; Thomas Gibb, Preben Arentoft; James Scott (69 Alan Foggon), Bryan Robson, Wyn Davies, John Sinclair. Manager: Joseph Harvey

Goals: Bene (29), Göröcs (44), Moncur (46), Arentoft (52), Foggon (70)

Goalscorers Fairs Cup 1968/69

10 goals: Antal Dunai (Újpesti Dózsa Budapest)

9 goals: Slobodan Santrac (OFK Beograd), Ferenc Bene (Újpesti Dózsa Budapest)

6 goals: Bryan Robson (Newcastle United)

5 goals: Joseph McBride (Hibernian Edinburgh), Josef Heynckes (Hannover 96)

4 goals: Owe Ohlsson (AIK Solna), Colin Stein (Glasgow Rangers), Franz-Josef Hönig, Werner Krämer (Hamburger SV), Joaquim Leonardo Quinta ARCANJO, Fernando Massano TOMÉ, Ernesto FIGUEIREDO (Vitória Setúbal), Jack Charlton (Leeds), Wyn Davies, James Scott (Newcastle)

3 goals: Hans Siemensmeyer, Josip Skoblar (Hannover 96), Miguel Ángel BUSTILLO Lafoz, José Antonio TEJEDOR Sanz (Real Zaragoza), Fevzi Zemzem, Ertan Öznur, Gürsel Aksel (Göztepe), Alex Ferguson, William Henderson (Rangers), Uwe Seeler (Hamburger SV), JOSÉ MARIA Júnior (Vitória Setúbal), Peter Lorimer (Leeds), Jan Pieszko (Legia), Ernő Solymosi (Újpesti Dózsa), Thomas Gibb, Robert Moncur (Newcastle), Kostas Papaioannou (Aris Thessaloniki)

2 goals: Neagu (Rapid Bucureşti), Houben (Beerschot), Blayet (Valencia CF), Stokes (FC Dundalk), Lourenço (Sporting Lisboa), Bettens (Waregem), Siropoulos, Alexiadis (Aris Thessaloniki), Pace, Savoldi (Bologna), Lundblad (AIK Solna), Salvi (Napoli), Kostmann, Drews, Decker (Hansa Rostock), Tesař, Kopecký, Nepomucký (Slavia Praha), Davis (Hibernian), Amarildo, Rizzo, Maraschi (Fiorentina), Nickel (Eintracht), Estéfano (Athletic Bilbao), Greig (Rangers), Turudija (OFK Beograd), Birchenall (Chelsea), Carriço, Petita (Vitória Setúbal), Zmijewski, Deyna, Gadocha, B. Blaut (Legia), L. Nagy (Újpesti Dózsa), Foggon (Newcastle)

1 goal: Aust (Wacker Innsbruck), Kindvall, Van der Heide (Feyenoord), Grahn, Rüegg (Grasshopper) Năsturescu, Codreanu (Rapid Bucureşti), Nieuwenhuys, Van Veen (DOS Utrecht), Joseph, Guéniche (Marseille), K. Sjöberg, J. Mathisen (Skeid Oslo), Thorup, Taylor, Mason (Morton), Hitz, Niesser, Hausser (Metz), Lawler, Hughes, Hunt (Liverpool), Zambata, Novak (Dinamo Zagreb), Claramunt, Sol (Valencia CF), Konrad, Hauser (FC Basel), Dermendjiev, Gluhchev, Popov (Trakia Plovdiv), Goyvaerts, Robin (OGC Nice), Popivoda (Olimpija Ljubljana), Buzek (Wiener SK), Nikezic (Vojvodina), Scott (Linfield), Kostedde, Galic (Standard Liège), Horacio (Leixões Porto), Luis, Barriocanal (Atletico Madrid), Randoux, Coppens (Daring Brussel), Gonios, Rokidis, Frantzis (Panathinaikos), Patzke, Schutz (München 1860), Manuel António (Academica Coimbra), Richter, Torben Hansen (BK Odense), Forrest, Smith, Robb, Taylor (Aberdeen), Prepurgel, Jercan, Nuţu (FC Argeş), Murray, Morrissey (FC Dundalk), Felix, Guy (Lyon), José Morais, Chico Faria, Gonçalves, Ernesto (Sporting Lisboa), Lambert (Waregem), Konstantinidis, Grimbelakos (Aris Thessaloniki), Benetti, Del Sol, Zigoni, Leoncini (Juventus), Mujesan, Turra, Cresci (Bologna), Grip, Nilsson, K.Andersson (AIK Solna), Fritsch (Lokomotiv Leipzig), Sala, Juliano, Altafini (Napoli), Barthels, Helmut Hergesell (Hansa Rostock), Veselý, Lukáč, Ziegler

(Slavia Praha), Grant, Stevenson, Stein, Marinello (Hibernian), Rogora, Merlo, Pirovano (Fiorentina), Hellingrath, Anders (Hannover 96), Martin, Santos, Planas, Marcelino, Villa (Real Zaragoza), Lotz, Bechtold, Kalb, Abbé, Grabowski (Eintracht), Geurtsen, Pijlman, Rensenbrink, Van der Vall (DWS Amsterdam), Halil, Caglayan (Göztepe), Stepanovic (OFK Beograd), Igartua, Uriarte, Rojo, Argoitia, Ormaza, Clemente, Ibáñez (Athletic Bilbao), Penman, Persson, Smith, Johnston, Mathieson, Jardine (Rangers), Osgood, Cooke, Boyle, Hollins, Baldwin, Houseman, Tambling (Chelsea), Schulz, Fock, G.Dörfel (Hamburger SV), Vitor Baptista (Vitória Setúbal), O'Grady, Hunter, Belfitt, Jones, Bremner (Leeds), Stachurski, Brychczy (Legia), Dunai III, Kuharszki, Göröcs (Újpesti Dózsa), Arentoft, Sinclair (Newcastle)

Own Goals: Lotz (Eintracht) for Wacker Innsbruck, Caglayan (Göztepe) for FC Argeş, Brennan (Dundalk) for Rangers, Mancini (Fiorentina) for Vitória Setúbal

FAIRS CUP 1969-70

FIRST ROUND

TSV MÜNCHEN 1860 v SKEID OSLO 2-2 (1-0)

Grünwalderstadion, München   3.09.69

Referee: Rudolf Scheurer (SWI)   Attendance: 3,000

TSV 1860: Petar Radenkovic; Hans-Günther Kroth, Max Reichenberger, Rudolf Zeiser, Wolfgang Lex, Franz Hiller, Bernd Gerstner (.. Horst Schmidt), Ferdinand Keller, Klaus Fischer, Dieter Schumacher, Helmut Roth.
Trainer: Fritz Langner

SKEID: Kjell Kaspersen; Leif Syversen, Tor Albiniusen (60 Stig Mathisen), Frank Olafsen, Kjell Wangen, Trygve Bornø, Terje Gulbrandsen, Terje Kristoffersen, Kai Sjøberg, Pål Saetrang, Erik Johansen.

Goals: K. Fischer (40, 79), E. Johansen (78), Sjøberg (82)

SKEID OSLO v TSV MÜNCHEN 1860   2-1 (1-1)

Ullevål, Oslo   16.09.69

Referee: Preben Christophersen (DAN)   Attendance: 13,000

SKEID: Bjørn Kristiansen; Ragnar Naess, Leif Syversen, Frank Olafsen, Kjell Wangen, Trygve Bornø, Terje Gulbrandsen, Torgeir Naess, Kai Sjøberg, Erik Johansen, Pål Saetrang.

TSV 1860: Franz-Josef Pauly; Hans-Günther Kroth, Rudolf Zeiser, Max Reichenberger, Horst Blankenburg, Željko Perušić, Dieter Schumacher, Horst Berg, Ferdinand Keller, Klaus Fischer, Horst Schmidt.   Trainer: Fritz Langner

Goals: Keller (39), Sjøberg (32), Reichenberger (77 og)

RSC CHARLEROI v NK ZAGREB 2-1 (2-1)

Stade du Mambourg, Charleroi   3.09.69

Referee: Antoine Queudeville (LUX)   Attendance: 20,000

RSC CHARLEROI: Antonio Tosini; Jean-Marie Termolle, Lucien Spronck, Claude Collard, René Hutmacher; André Colasse, Guy Verbist (66 Tony Van Schoonbeek), Marcel Vandenbossch, Jean Boulet (79 Ivan Pintaric), Claude Bissot, Georget Bertoncello.

NK ZAGREB: Nježić; Suša, Kovac (46 Mestrović), Ivić, Milanović; Zdravko Smajlović, Mijo Markulin; Stanković, Stanislav Bubanj, Mladen Vaha, Zutelija.

Goals: Bissot (6), Boulet (39), Bubanj (42)

NK ZAGREB v RSC CHARLEROI 1-3 (0-1)

Zagreb   24.09.69

Referee: Ferdinand Marschall (AUS)   Attendance: 2,000

NK ZAGREB: Nježić; Vastenić, Saja, Ivić (35 Mijo Markulin); Suša, Kicić (65 Karan), Milanović; Stanković, Stanislav Bubanj, Mladen Vaha, Zutelija.

RSC CHARLEROI: André Sumera; Jean-Marie Termolle, Lucien Spronck, Claude Collard, René Hutmacher; Henri Majchrowski, André Colasse; Ivan Pintaric (73 Guy Verbist), Jean Boulet, Claude Bissot, Georget Bertoncello (73 Claude Surin).

Goals: Bertoncello (29), Bissot (49, 73), Huttmacher (67 og)

VOJVODINA NOVI SAD
v GWARDIA WARSZAWA 1-1 (0-1)

Gradski, Novi Sad   4.09.69

Referee: Giorgos Katsoras (GRE)   Attendance: 1,000

VOJVODINA: Nikolovski (.. Krivokapić); Rajko Aleksić, Josip Zemko, Zoran Dakić, Jovicević, Karamahmedović, Pal Laszlo, Vladimir Savić (.. Stevan Kurcinac), Radivoj Radosav, Dobrivoje Trivić, Zvonko Ivezić.

GWARDIA: Zbigniew Pocialik; Jan Sroka, Roman Jurczak, Ryszard Kielak, Adam Lipinski (.. Zbigniew Hertel), Bogdan Wisniewski, Jerzy Krasucki, Edward Lipinski (.. Krzysztof Marczak), Bogdan Masztaler, Ryszard Szymczak, Edward Biernacki.

Goals: Wisniewski (18), Dakic (49 pen)

GWARDIA WARSZAWA
v VOJVODINA NOVI SAD 1-0 (1-0)

Gwardia, Warszawa   17.09.69

Referee: Nicolae Rainea (ROM)

GWARDIA: Leszek Nowicki; Jan Sroka, Roman Jurczak (.. Krystian Michalik), Adam Lipinski, Ryszard Kielak, Edward Lipinski, Stanislaw Dawidczynski, Bogdan Masztaler, Ryszard Szymczak, Edward Biernacki, Wyszomirski.

VOJVODINA: Krivokapić; Rajko Aleksić, Jovicević, Vladimir Savić (.. Radivoj Radosav), Josip Zemko, Karamahmedović, Zvonko Ivezić, Dobrivoje Trivić, Petar Nikezić, Josip Pirmajer, Zoran Dakić (.. Birovier).

Goal: E. Lipinski (16)

ARSENAL FC LONDON
v GLENTORAN FC BELFAST 3-0 (3-0)

Highbury, London   9.09.69

Referee: Clive Thomas (WAL)   Attendance: 24,292

ARSENAL: Robert Wilson; Peter Storey, Robert McNab (68 Samuel Nelson), Frank McLintock, Peter Simpson, George Graham, James Robertson, David Court (16 Edward Kelly), Robert Gould, Jonathan Sammels, George Armstrong.
Manager: Bertie Mee

GLENTORAN: Albert Finlay; Roy Coyle, Billy McKeag, Roy Stewart, William McCullough, Anthony Macken, James Weatherup, Walter Bruce, Ian Henderson (46 Syd Patterson), Thomas Morrow, John Hill.   Manager: Peter McParland

Goals: Graham (15, 25), Gould (42)

GLENTORAN FC BELFAST
v ARSENAL FC LONDON 1-0 (1-0)

The Oval, Belfast   29.09.69

Referee: Robert Holley Davidson (SCO)   Attendance: 13,000

GLENTORAN: Albert Finlay; John Hill, Billy McKeag, Roy Coyle, William McCullough, Anthony Macken, James Weatherup, Roy Stewart (80 James Lemon), Walter Bruce, Ian Henderson (64 Syd Patterson), Thomas Morrow.
Manager: Peter McParland

ARSENAL: Malcolm Webster; Patrick Rice, Robert McNab, David Court, Terence Neill, Peter Simpson, James Robertson, Jonathan Sammels, John Radford (61 Raymond Kennedy), Robert Gould, Charles George.   Manager: Bertie Mee

Goal: Henderson (2 pen)

FC ROUEN v FC TWENTE ENSCHEDE 2-0 (1-0)

Stade Robert Diochon, Rouen   9.09.69

Referee: Alfred Delcourt (BEL)   Attendance: 5,625

FC ROUEN: Pierre Rigoni; Jacques Largouet, Patrice Rio, Michel Sénéchal, André Mérelle; Arnaud Dos Santos (26 Charles Gosselin), Daniel Druda; Dominique Rustichelli, Jean-François Douis, Jean-François Villa (30 François Bruant), Tomás Pospíchal.   Trainer: André Gérard

TWENTE: Piet Schrijvers; Kees Van Ierssel, Epi Drost, Willem De Vries, Izzy Ten Donkelaar, Eddy Achterberg, Kick Van der Vall (46 Ferry Pirard), René Notten (60 Jan Streuer), Uwe Blotenberg, Jan Jeuring, Antal Nagy.   Trainer: Kees Rijvers

Goals: Pospíchal (27 pen), Rustichelli (57)

FC TWENTE ENSCHEDE v FC ROUEN 1-0 (1-0)

Diekman Stadion, Enschede   30.09.69

Referee: Alfred Ott (WG)   Attendance: 12,000

TWENTE: Piet Schrijvers; Kees Van Ierssel, Epi Drost, Willem De Vries, Jan Streurer, Eddy Achterberg, Kick Van der Vall, René Notten, Uwe Blotenberg, Jan Jeuring, Antal Nagy (46 Theo Pahlplatz).   Trainer: Kees Rijvers

FC ROUEN: Pierre Rigoni; Jacques Largouet, Patrice Rio, Michel Sénéchal, André Mérelle, Tomás Pospíchal, Arnaud Dos Santos, Daniel Druda, Jean-François Douis (53 Robert Pintenat), Joseph Szczyrba, Jean-François Villa. Trainer: André Gérard

Goal: Drost (43)

RSC ANDERLECHT BRUSSEL
v VALUR REYKJAVÍK 6-0 (4-0)

Parc Astrid, Brussel   10.09.69

Referee: Willem J.M. Schalks (HOL)   Attendance: 5,300

ANDERLECHT: Hugo Vandenbossche (46 Christian Rigaut); George Heylens, Raymond Wilms, Johnny Velkeneers, Jean Cornelis; Julien Kialunda, Maurice Martens; Gerard Bergholtz, Thomas Nordahl, Paul Van Himst, Wilfried Puis. Trainer: Pierre Sinibaldi

VALUR: Sigurdur Dagsson; Sigurdur Olafsson, Torsteinn Fridtjófsson, Samúel Örn Erlingsson, Páll Ragnarsson; Miksson, Ingvar Elísson; Sigurdur Jónsson, Bergsveinn Alfonsson, Alexander Johannesson, Bjarsson.

Goals: Nordahl (5, 30), Van Himst (15, 22, 28, 50)

VALUR REYKJAVÍK
v RSC ANDERLECHT BRUSSEL 0-2 (0-1)

Jules Ottenstadion, Gent   19.09.69

Referee: Ferdinand Biwersi (WG)   Attendance: 2,600

VALUR: Sigurdur Dagsson; Sigurdur Olafsson, Torsteinn Fridtjófsson, Samúel Örn Erlingsson, Páll Ragnarsson; Miksson, Ingvar Elísson; Sigurdur Jónsson, Bergsveinn Alfonsson, Alexander Johannesson, Bjarsson.

ANDERLECHT: Hugo Vandenbossche, George Heylens, Johnny Velkeneers, Pierre Hanon, Jean Cornelis; Thomas Nordahl, Raymond Wilms; Gerard Bergholtz, Jan Mulder, Paul Van Himst, Wilfried Puis (46 Maurice Martens). Trainer: Pierre Sinibaldi

Goals: Nordahl (7), Mulder (78)

VITÓRIA GUIMARÃES
v BANÍK OSTRAVA 1-0 (1-0)

Estádio Municipal, Guimarães   10.09.69

Referee: Adolfo Bueno Perales (SPA)   Attendance: 10,000

VITÓRIA: Mario ROLDÃO Carvalho Pinto; José Fernando Silva « COSTEADO », Manuel Campos PINTO, JOAQUIM António JORGE, Manuel Joaquim Pereira da SILVA; ARTUR da Rocha, António Francisco Jesus Moreira "PERES"; José Marques Silva « ZEZINHO », MANUEL Martins de Sousa (84 António Silva MENDES), AUGUSTO Martins, CARLOS MANUEL Teixeira.   Trainer: Gilberto Carvalho « GIBA »

BANÍK: František Schmucker; Jiří Večerek, Bohumil Pišek, Jan Kniezek (60 Rostislav Sionko), K. Weiss; Karel Herot, Jünger, Josef Kolečko (80 Milan Poštulka); Ladislav Michalík, Valerian Bartalský, Mazanik.   Trainer: J. Rubáš

Goal: Carlos Manuel (10)

BANÍK OSTRAVA
v VITÓRIA GUIMARÃES 1-1 (0-0)

Stadión na Bazaloch, Ostrava   2.10.69

Referee: Constantin Bărbulescu (ROM)   Attendance: 9,000

BANÍK: František Schmucker; Jiří Večerek, Karel Herot, Jan Kniezek, Weiss; Jünger, Petr Křižák; Rudolf Guzik, Josef Kolečko, Valerian Bartalský, Ladislav Michalík (70 Milan Poštulka).   Trainer: J. Rubáš

VITÓRIA: Mario ROLDÃO Carvalho Pinto; José Fernando Silva « COSTEADO », Manuel Campos PINTO, JOAQUIM António JORGE, Manuel Joaquim Pereira da SILVA; ARTUR da Rocha, António Francisco Jesus Moreira "PERES", Francisco José BILREIRO da Silva; MANUEL Martins de Sousa, António Silva MENDES, CARLOS MANUEL Teixeira. Trainer: Fernando CAIADO

Goals: Guzik (73), Artur (80)

DUNDEE UNITED v NEWCASTLE UNITED 1-2 (0-0)

Tannadice Park, Dundee 15.09.69

Referee: Peter Coates (IRL) Attendance: 21,000

DUNDEE: Donald Mackay (72 Jed Reilly); Andy Rolland, Jim Cameron, Dennis Gillespie, Douglas Smith, Stuart Markland (63 James Briggs), David Wilson, Alexander Reid, Kenneth Cameron, Ian Scott, Ian Mitchell. Manager: Jerry Kerr

NEWCASTLE: William McFaul; John Craggs, Frank Clark, Thomas Gibb, Alwyn Burton, Robert Moncur, Bryan Robson, Keith Dyson, Wyn Davies, Preben Arentoft, James Smith. Manager: Joe Harvey

Goals: Davies (56, 62), Scott (76)

NEWCASTLE UNITED v DUNDEE UNITED 1-0 (0-0)

St. James' Park, Newcastle 1.10.69

Referee: Leo Callaghan (WAL) Attendance: 37,470

NEWCASTLE: William McFaul; David Craig, Frank Clark, Thomas Gibb, John McNamee, Robert Moncur, Bryan Robson, Keith Dyson, Wyn Davies, James Smith, Alan Foggon (64 Preben Arentoft). Manager: Joe Harvey

DUNDEE: Donald Mackay; Andy Rolland, Jim Cameron, Dennis Gillespie, Douglas Smith, Stuart Markland, David Hogg, Alexander Reid, Alan Gordon, Ian Scott, Ian Mitchell. Manager: Jerry Kerr

Goal: Dyson (90)

WIENER SK v RUCH CHORZÓW 4-2 (3-1)

Sportclub-Platz, Wien 16.09.69

Referee: Dittmar Huber (SWI) Attendance: 3,000

WIENER SK: Wilhelm Kaipel; Helmut Wallner, Johann Schmidradner, Kovacic, Haider; Herbert Onger, Anton Herzog; Josef Pribil, Finn Laudrup, Günther Kaltenbrunner, Johann Hörmayer.

RUCH: Henryk Pietrek; Antoni Piechniczek (.. Józef Janduda), Bernard Bem, Antoni Nieroba, Jerzy Wyrobek (.. Piotr Drzewiecki), Józef Bon, Bronislaw Bula, Józef Gomoluch, Edward Herman, Joachim Marx, Eugeniusz Faber. Trainer: Jerzy Nikiel

Goals: Pribil (12), Marx (30), Onger (35), Laudrup (40), Gomoluch (64), Hörmayer (80)

RUCH CHORZÓW v WIENER SK 4-1 (2-0)

Slaski, Chorzów 30.09.69

Referee: Todor Gerov (BUL) Attendance: 30,000

RUCH: Henryk Pietrek; Antoni Piechniczek, Jerzy Wyrobek, Antoni Nieroba, Bernard Bem, Józef Gomoluch, Bronislaw Bula, Józef Bon, Joachim Marx, Edward Herman, Eugeniusz Faber. Trainer: Jerzy Nikiel

WIENER SK: Wilhelm Kaipel; Helmut Wallner, Johann Schmidradner, Haider, Peter Clement (60 Reitbauer); Herbert Onger, Josef Pribil, Anton Herzog, Finn Laudrup, Alfred Hala, Johann Hörmayer.

Goals: Piechniczek (5), E. Faber (16), Marx (51), Herman (55), Laudrup (72)

LIVERPOOL FC v DUNDALK FC 10-0 (5-0)

Anfield Road, Liverpool 16.09.69

Referee: John G.D. Lewis (WAL) Attendance: 32,656

LIVERPOOL: Raymond Clemence; Christopher Lawler, Geoffrey Strong, Thomas Smith, Ronald Yeats, Emlyn Hughes, Ian Callaghan, Robert Graham, Alec Lindsay, Alun Evans, Peter Thompson. Manager: William Shankly

DUNDALK: Maurice Swan; Francis Brennan, Des O'Reilly, Kevin Murray, Thomas McConville, Charles Hendricks, Laurence Gilmore (46 Derek Stokes), Patrick Turner, Turlough O'Connor, Anthony Bartley, Eamonn Carroll. Manager: Liam Tuohy

Goals: Evans (1, 38), Lawler (10), Smith (24, 67), Graham (36, 82), Lindsay (56), Thompson (69), Callaghan (76)

DUNDALK FC v LIVERPOOL FC 0-4 (0-2)

Oriel Park, Dundalk 30.09.69

Referee: Thomas Wharton (SCO) Attendance: 6,000

DUNDALK: Maurice Swan; Francis Brennan, Des O'Reilly, Kevin Murray, Thomas McConville, Michael Millington, Thomas Kinsella (66 Laurence Gilmore), Patrick Turner, Turlough O'Connor, Anthony Bartley, Eamonn Carroll (66 Derek Stokes). Manager: Liam Tuohy

LIVERPOOL: Raymond Clemence; Christopher Lawler, Geoffrey Strong, Thomas Smith, Larry Lloyd, Emlyn Hughes, Peter Thompson (46 Ian Callaghan), Robert Graham (58 Roger Hunt), Ian St. John, Alun Evans, Philip Boersma. Manager: William Shankly

Goals: Thompson (13, 31), Graham (48), Callaghan (81)

**DUNFERMLINE ATHLETIC
v GIRONDINS de BORDEAUX 4-0** (1-0)

East End Park, Dunfermline   16.09.69

Referee: Kenneth Howard Burns (ENG)   Attendance: 11,363

ATHLETIC: William Duff; William Callaghan, John McGarty, Douglas Baillie, John Lunn, Robert Paton, Alexander Edwards, William Renton, Barrie Mitchell, Patrick Gardner, George McLean.   Manager: George Farm

GIRONDINS: Christian Montes; Didier Desremeaux, Gérard Papin (.. Yves Texier), Claude Andrien, Georges Grabowski, Félix Burdino, Jacques Simon, André Betta, Claude Petyt, Carlos Ruiter, Réginald Dortomb.
Trainer: Jean-Pierre Bakrim

Goals: Paton (26, 74), Mitchell (67), Gardner (84)

**GIRONDINS de BORDEAUX
v DUNFERMLINE ATHLETIC 2-0** (1-0)

Stade Municipal, Bordeaux   1.10.69

Referee: Francis Rion (BEL)   Attendance: 13,592

GIRONDINS: Christian Montes; Didier Desremeaux, Gérard Papin, Yves Texier, Georges Grabowski, Jacques Simon, André Betta, Hervé Othily, Carlos Ruiter, Réginald Dortomb, Edouard Wojciak.   Trainer: Jean-Pierre Bakrim

ATHLETIC: William Duff; William Callaghan, John McGarty, Douglas Baillie, John Lunn, Robert Paton, Alexander Edwards, William Renton, Barrie Mitchell, Patrick Gardner, George McLean.   Manager: George Farm

Goals: Otchily (19), Wojciak (88)

FC ZÜRICH v KILMARNOCK FC 3-2 (2-2)

Letzigrund, Zürich   16.09.69

Referee: Wolfgang Riedel (DDR)   Attendance: 13,500

FC ZÜRICH: Karl Grob; René Hasler, Rosario Martinelli, Michele Rebozzi, Jakob Kuhn, Konrad Kyburz, Christian Winiger, Kurt Grünig, Fritz Künzli, René-Pierre Quentin, Georg Volkert.

KILMARNOCK: Alex McLaughlan; Andrew King, William Dickson, Hugh Strachan, John McGrory, Frank Beattie, Thomas McLean, John Gilmour, Edward Morrison, James McLean, Ross Mathie.

Goals: J. McLean (1), Mathie (14), Volkert (26 pen), Künzli (30), Grünig (47)

KILMARNOCK FC v FC ZÜRICH 3-1 (1-0)

Rugby Park, Kilmarnock   30.09.69

Referee: Rolf Hennum Andersen (NOR)   Attendance: 13,000

KILMARNOCK: Alex McLaughlan; Andrew King, William Dickson, John Gilmour, Hugh Strachan, John McGrory, Thomas McLean, Edward Morrison, James McLean (.. Frank Beattie), Ross Mathie, James Cook.

FC ZÜRICH: Karl Grob; Hubert Münch, René Hasler, Michele Rebozzi, Jakob Kuhn, Konrad Kyburz, Christian Winiger, Kurt Grünig, Fritz Künzli, René-Pierre Quentin, Georg Volkert.

Goals: McGrory (42), Morrison (46), Grünig (63), T. McLean (74)

**FC CARL ZEISS JENA
v ALTAY GENÇLIK IZMIR 1-0** (1-0)

Ernst-Abbe-Sportfeld, Jena   16.09.69

Referee: Willem J.M. Schalks (HOL)   Attendance: 8,000

FC CARL ZEISS: Wolfgang Blochwitz; Helmut Stein, Werner Krauss, Peter Rock, Udo Preusse, Michael Strempel, Rainer Schlutter, Harald Irmscher, Peter Ducke, Dieter Scheitler, Roland Ducke (78 Bernd Krauss).   Trainer: Georg Buschner

ALTAY: Tanzer Sencer; Oguz Böke, Oktay Akgün, Zinnur Sari, Necdet Tunca, Ali Riza Şenol, Ayfer Elmastaşoglu, Aytekin Erhanoglu (76 Mustafa Kalpakaslan), K. Cihat, D. Mustafa, Behzat Çinar.

Goal: Stein (42)

**ALTAY GENÇLIK IZMIR
v FC CARL ZEISS JENA 0-0**

Alsançak, Izmir   1.10.69

Referee: Paul Bonett (MAL)   Attendance: 20,000

ALTAY: Tanzer Sencer, Oktay Akgün, Necdet Tunca, Ali Riza Şenol, Zinnur Sari, Ayfer Elmastaşoglu, Mithat Mihçi, Aytekin Erhanoglu (78 Yilmaz Canlisoy), Mustafa Kalpakaslan, D. Mustafa, Behzat Çinar.

FC CARL ZEISS: Wolfgang Blochwitz; Udo Preusse, Werner Krauss, Michael Strempel, Jürgen Werner, Harald Irmscher, Peter Rock, Gerd Brunner, Roland Ducke, Helmut Stein, Dieter Scheitler.   Trainer: Georg Buschner

HANNOVER 96 v AJAX AMSTERDAM 2-1 (2-1)

Niedersachsenstadion, Hannover   17.09.69

Referee: Vital Loraux (BEL)   Attendance: 26,000

HANNOVER 96: Horst Podlasly; Peter Loof, Rainer Stiller, Hans-Josef Hellingrath, Hans Siemensmeyer, Jürgen Bandura, Zvezdan Cebinac, Rainer Zobel, Josef Heynckes, Josip Skoblar, Claus Brune (60 Kurt Ritter).   Trainer: Zlatko Cajkovski

AJAX: Gerrit Bals; Wim Suurbier, Velibor Vasovic, Ruud Krol, Nico Rijnders, Ben Muller, Gerrie Mühren, Sjaak Swart, Tom Søndergaard, Dick Van Dijk, Ruud Suurendonk (46 Ton Pronk).   Trainer: Marinus Michels

Goals: Heynckes (20), Swart (32), Skoblar (41)

FLORIANA FC v DINAMO BACĂU 0-1 (0-0)

Valletta   28.09.69

Referee: Fabio Monti (ITA)   Attendance: 8,000

FLORIANA: George Borg; Charles Galea, Charles Farrugia, Anton Camilleri, Alfred Debono; Frankie Micallef, Saviour Borg; William Vassallo, Louis Arpa, Raymond Xuereb, Hughie Caruana.

DINAMO: Aristide Ghiţă; Madocsa Kiss, Mircea Nedelcu, Laurenţiu Velicu, Constantin David; Constantin Duţan, Nicolae Vătafu; Alexandru Comănescu (82 Vasile Panait), Daniel Ene, Emerich Dembrovschi, Petre Băluţă (68 Francisc Neumayer).   Trainer: Valeriu Neagu

Goal: D. Ene (32)

AJAX AMSTERDAM v HANNOVER 96 3-0 (1-0)

Olympisch, Amsterdam   24.09.69

Referee: John Keith Taylor (ENG)   Attendance: 19,923

AJAX: Gerrit Bals; Wim Suurbier, Velibor Vasovic, Barry Hulshoff, Ruud Krol, Nico Rijnders, Gerrie Mühren, Sjaak Swart, Johan Cruijff, Dick Van Dijk, Piet Keizer (80 Ben Muller).   Trainer: Marinus Michels

HANNOVER 96: Horst Podlasly; Peter Loof, Klaus Bohnsack, Rainer Stiller, Hans-Josef Hellingrath, Hans Siemensmeyer, Jürgen Bandura, Zvezdan Cebinac (46 Rainer Zobel), Josef Heynckes, Josip Skoblar (67 Kurt Ritter), Claus Brune.   Trainer: Zlatko Cajkovski

Goals: Cruijff (22), Swart (47), G.Mühren (69)

HANSA ROSTOCK v PANIONIOS ATHINA 3-0 (1-0)

Ostseestadion, Rostock   17.09.69

Referee: Bo Nilsson (SWE)   Attendance: 8,000

HANSA: Peter Below, Gerhard Brümmer, Dieter Wruck, Klaus-Dieter Seehaus, Helmut Hergesell, Hernert Pankau, Werner Drews, Wolfgang Barthels (72 Klaus-Peter Stein), Joachim Streich, Helmut Kleiminger, Lothar Hahn.   Trainer: Horst Sass

PANIONIOS: Dimitris Maniakis; Giorgos Skrekis, Haralampos Intzoglou, Kostas Negris, Dimitris Dounias, Panagiotis Karagiannopoulos, Stathis Haitas, Stavros Tripkovits (68 Giorgos Dedes), Giorgos Spiropoulos, Thanasis Intzoglou, Roulis.

Goals: Drews (20,75), Pankau (85 pen)

DINAMO BACĂU v FLORIANA FC 6-0 (3-0)

23 August, Bacău   17.09.69

Referee: Kostas Xanthos (GRE)   Attendance: 8,000

DINAMO: Aristide Ghiţă; Madocsa Kiss, Mircea Nedelcu, Laurenţiu Velicu, Constantin David; Nicolae Vătafu, Constantin Duţan; Petre Băluţă, Emerich Dembrovschi, Daniel Ene, Alexandru Comănescu (46 Francisc Neumayer).   Trainer: Valeriu Neagu

FLORIANA: Charles Zerafa; Charles Galea, Joe Grima, Anton Camilleri, Alfred Debono; Charles Farrugia, Nazzareno Alamango (46 Raymond Xuereb); William Vassallo, Louis Arpa, Frankie Micallef, Hughie Caruana.

Goals: Grima (1 og), Dembrovschi (11, 73 pen, 86), Băluţă (24), D. Ene (87)

PANIONIOS ATHINA v HANSA ROSTOCK 2-0 (0-0)

Nea Smirni, Athina   30.09.69

Referee: Alessandro d'Agostini (ITA)   Attendance: 6,200

PANIONIOS: Dimitris Maniakis; Giorgos Skrekis, Haralampos Intzoglou, Kostas Negris, Giorgos Spiropoulos, Stathis Haitas, Thanasis Intzoglou, Stavros Tripkovits (46 Ahileas Athanasiadis), Panagiotis Karagiannopoulos, Giorgos Dedes, Roulis.

HANSA: Dieter Schneider; Gerd Sackritz, Dieter Wruck, Klaus-Dieter Seehaus, Helmut Hergesell, Herbert Pankau, Axel Bergmann, Jürgen Decker, Wolfgang Barthels, Klaus-Peter Stein, Lothar Hahn (64 Joachim Streich).   Trainer: Horst Sass

Goals: Spiropoulos (50), Dedes (60)

VfB STUTTGART v MALMÖ FF 3-0 (1-0)

Neckarstadion, Stuttgart   17.09.69

Referee: Robert Franciel (FRA)   Attendance: 5,000

VfB: Dieter Feller; Reinhold Zech, Hans Arnold, Herbert Höbusch, Theo Hoffmann, Jan Olsson, Manfred Weidmann, Gilbert Gress, Willi Entenmann, Horst Haug, Roland Weidle.
Trainer: Franz Seybold

MALMÖ FF: Nils Hult; Roland Andersson, Krister Kristensson, Bertil Elmstedt, Ulf Kleander, Roy Andersson, Staffan Tapper, Rolf Björklund, Curt Olsberg, Kent Andersson (.. Roland Rasmusson), Harry Jönsson.

Goals: Björklund (36 og), J. Olsson (50), Haug (87)

MALMÖ FF v VfB STUTTGART 1-1 (0-1)

Malmo stadion   1.10.69

Referee: Tage Sørensen (Dan)   Attendance: 2,800

MALMÖ FF: Nils Hult; Bertil Elmstedt, Krister Kristensson, Ulf Kleander, Rolf Björklund, Lars Granström, Roy Andersson, Harry Jönsson (.. Kent Andersson), Staffan Tapper, Bo Larsson, Tommy Larsson.

VfB: Gerhard Heinze; Hans Eisele, Hans Mayer, Roland Weidle, Reinhold Zech, Jan Olsson, Manfred Weidmann, Gilbert Gress, Willi Entenmann, Hans Arnold, Horst Haug.
Trainer: Franz Seybold

Goals: Weidemann (15), Bo Larsson (65)

CF BARCELONA v B 1913 ODENSE 4-0 (3-0)

Camp Nou, Barcelona   17.09.69

Referee: José Alexandre (POR)   Attendance: 45,000

CF BARCELONA: Miguel REINA Santos; José FRANCH Xargay, Ramón Díaz Cruz «RAMONÍ», Francisco Fernández Rodríguez «GALLEGO», ELADIO Silvestre Graells (89 Francisco ROMEA Hernando); MARCIAL Pina Morales, Santiago CASTRO Anido; Carlos PELLICER Vázquez, José Antonio ZALDÚA Urdanavia (46 Carlos REXACH Cerdá), Narciso MARTÍ FILOSÍA, Luis PUJOL Codina.
Trainer: Salvador ARTIGAS Sahagún

B 1913: Knud Engedahl; Christiansen, Nielsen, Finn Helweg, John Ejlertsen, Kent Hansen, Jack Hansen; Erik Dyrholm, Nøttrup, Bent Jensen, Sørensen (59 Jørgen Rasmussen).
Trainer: Willy Schone

Goals: Ejlersen (12 og), Zaldúa (18), Martí Filosía (30, 73)

B 1913 ODENSE v CF BARCELONA 0-2 (0-0)

Odense stadium   1.10.69

Referee: Theo Boosten (HOL)   Attendance: 5,000

BK 1913: Knud Engedahl; Christiansen, Nielsen, Finn Helweg, John Ejlertsen; Nottrup, Jack Hansen; Jørgen Rasmussen, Bent Jensen, Ole Steffensen, Erik Dyrholm.
Trainer: Willy Schone

CF BARCELONA: Salvador SADURNÍ Urpi; José FRANCH Xargay, Ramón Díaz Cruz "RAMONÍ", Francisco Fernández Rodríguez "GALLEGO", Antonio TORRES García (65 SANJUÁN); JUAN CARLOS Pérez López, Pedro María ZABALZA Inda (46 Pablo GARCÍA CASTANY); Carlos PELLICER Vázquez, José María FUSTÉ Blanch, Narciso MARTÍ FILOSÍA, Carlos REXACH Cerdá.
Trainer: Salvador ARTIGAS Sahagún

Goals: Pellicer (54), Rexach (89)

JEUNESSE d'ESCH v COLERAINE FC 3-2 (0-1)

Luxembourg   18.09.69

Referee: Joseph Minnoy (BEL)   Attendance: 1,400

JEUNESSE: René Hoffmann; Robert Da Grava, Henri Kosmala, Johny Hoffmann, Mario Morocutti, Feyder, Daniel Drouet, Guy Allamano, Dominique Di Genova, Pierre Langer, Bartolatti.

COLERAINE: Victor Hunter; John McCurdy, Alan Campbell, Tony O'Doherty, David Jackson, Ivan Murray, Sean Dunlop, Anthony Curley, Samuel Wilson, Des Dickson, Brian Jennings (.. Derek McQuillan).

Goals: Curley (16), Allamann (48, 53, 89), Murray (60)

COLERAINE FC v JEUNESSE d'ESCH 4-0 (1-0)

The Showgrounds, Coleraine   1.10.69

Referee: William A. O'Neill (IRL)   Attendance: 6,000

COLERAINE: Victor Hunter; John McCurdy (.. David Gordon), Alan Campbell, Tony O'Doherty, David Jackson, Ivan Murray, Sean Dunlop, Anthony Curley, Samuel Wilson, Des Dickson, Brian Jennings.

JEUNESSE: René Hoffmann; Robert Da Grava (.. Jeannot Schaul), Henri Kosmala, Johny Hoffmann, Mario Morocutti, Daniel Drouet, Feyder, Guy Allamano, Dominique di Genova, Pierre Langer, Bartolatti.

Goals: S. Wilson (11), Dickson (73, 85), Jennings (87)

ROSENBORG TRONDHEIM BK v SOUTHAMPTON FC 1-0 (1-0)

Lerkendal, Trondheim   17.09.69

Referee: Sven Jonsson (SWE)   Attendance: 20,338

ROSENBORG: Tor Røste Fossen; Kåre Rønnes, Bjørn Rime, Nils Arne Eggen, Kjell Hvidsand, Jan Christiansen, Erling Naess, Tore Pedersen, Odd Iversen, Harald Sunde (85 Svein Haagenrud), Per Loraas (63 Kjell Øyasaether).
Trainer: George Curtis

SOUTHAMPTON: Eric Martin; Kenneth Jones, Joseph Kirkup, Hugh Fisher, James Gabriel, David Walker, Terence Paine, Michael Channon, Ronald Davies (46 Frank Saul), Robert Stokes, Anthony Byrne.   Manager: Ted Bates

Goal: Sunde (36)

SOUTHAMPTON FC v ROSENBORG BK TRONDHEIM 2-0 (1-0)

The Dell, Southampton   1.10.69

Referee: Robert Héliès (FRA)   Attendance: 22,329

SOUTHAMPTON: Eric Martin; Joseph Kirkup, Dennis Hollywood, Frederick Kemp, John McGrath, James Gabriel, Terence Paine, Robert Stokes, Ronald Davies (85 Hugh Fisher), Anthony Byrne, John Sydenham.   Manager: Ted Bates

ROSENBORG: Tor Røste Fossen; Kåre Rønnes, Bjørn Rime, Nils Arne Eggen, Kjell Hvidsand, Jan Christiansen, Erling Naess, Tore Pedersen, Odd Iversen, Harald Sunde, Kjell Øyasaether (86 Frode Sjøvold).   Trainer: George Curtis

Goals: R. Davies (34), Paine (60)

C.D. SABADELL v CLUB BRUGGE 2-0 (1-0)

Estadio Nova Creu Alta, Sabadell   17.09.69

Referee: Francesco Francescon (ITA)   Attendance: 12,000

SABADELL: Ismael COMAS Solanot; ISIDRO Sánchez García Figueras, Ramón MONTESINOS Calaf, Mario Rolando PINI Stagi, Alberto ARNAL Andrés; Luis MUÑOZ Grau, Jesús María PEREDA Ruiz de Temiño; Pedro ZABALLA Barquín, José PALAU Busquet, José Luis GARZÓN Fito, José CRISTO Vázquez.   Trainer: Bernardino Pérez Elizarán "PASIEGUITO"

CLUB BRUGGE: Fernand Boone; Alfons Bastijns, Gilbert Marmenout, Kurt Axelsson, John Moulaert; Henk Houwaart, Erwin Vandendaele; Johnny Thio, Pierre Carteus, Raoul Lambert, Rob Rensenbrink.   Trainer: De Munk

Goals: Zaballa (38), José Cristo (88)

CLUB BRUGGE v C.D. SABADELL 5-1 (3-0)

Albert Dyserynck, Brugge   1.10.69

Referee: Alistair McKenzie (SCO)   Attendance: 18,000

CLUB BRUGGE: Fernand Boone; Alfons Bastijns (65 Freddy Hinderijckx), Kurt Axelsson, Erwin Vandendaele, John Moulaert; Henk Houwaart, Pierre Carteus; Walter Loske (75 Johnny Thio), Tom Turesson, Raoul Lambert, Rob Rensenbrink.   Trainer: De Munk

SABADELL: Ismael COMAS Solanot; ISIDRO Sánchez García Figueras, Alberto ARNAL Andrés, Ramón de Pablo MARAÑÓN, Mario Rolando PINI Stagi, Luis MUÑOZ Grau (46 José Luis ROMERO Robledo), Ramón MONTESINOS Calaf, Fernando ORTUÑO Blasco, José PALAU Busquet, José Luis GARZÓN Fito, Pedro ZABALLA Barquín.
Trainer: Bernardino Pérez Elizarán "PASIEGUITO"

Goals: Carteus (12), Lambert (24 pen, 41), Turesson (48, 64), Palau (55)

SLAVIA SOFIA v VALENCIA CF 2-0 (1-0)

Slavia, Sofia   17.09.69

Referee: Tibor Wotava (HUN)   Attendance: 5,000

SLAVIA: Simeon Simeonov; Aleksandar Shalamanov, Georgi Hristakiev, Atanas Gerov; Ivan Davidov, Todor Kolev; Emil Lukach (66 Georgi Manolov), I. Georgiev, Bozhidar Grigorov, Atanas Mikhailov (51 Nikola Krastev), Stoian Kotzev.
Trainer: Mirko Tashkov

VALENCIA CF: José PESUDO Soler; José Antonio García Conesa "TATONO" (67 Luis VILAR Botet), Fernando BARRACHINA Plo, Francisco VIDAGAÑY Hernández; Juan Cruz SOL Oria, Antonio Martínez Morales "ANTÓN"; Manuel POLInario Muñoz, José CLARAMUNT Torres, Fernando ANSOLA Sanmartín (65 José NEBOT Navarro), Francisco García Gómez "PAQUITO", Enrique COLLAR Monterrubio.
Trainer: JOSEÍTO

Goals: Grigorov (42), Kolev (68 pen)

VALENCIA CF v SLAVIA SOFIA 1-1 (0-1)

Campo de Mestalla, Valencia   1.10.69

Referee: Roger Mouton (FRA)   Attendance: 40,000

VALENCIA CF: José PESUDO Soler; Juan Cruz SOL Oria, Fernando BARRACHINA Plo, Francisco VIDAGAÑY Hernández, ROBERTO Gil Esteve (46 Francisco García Gómez «PAQUITO»), Antonio Martínez Morales "ANTÓN"; José CLARAMUNT Torres, Manuel POLInario Muñoz (71 Vicente GUILLOT Fabián), Fernando ANSOLA Sanmartín, WALDO Machado da Silva, Enrique COLLAR Monterrubio.
Trainer: JOSEÍTO

SLAVIA: Simeon Simeonov; Aleksandar Shalamanov, Georgi Hristakiev, Atanas Gerov, Ivan Davidov, Nikola Krastev; Iancho Dimitrov, Todor Kolev, Bozhidar Grigorov, Iv. Georgiev, Stoian Kotzev (73 Petar Tsolov).   Trainer: Mirko Tashkov

Simeonov sent off (73)

Goals: Grigorov (33), Ansola (75)

ARIS THESSALONIKI v CAGLIARI 1-1 (1-0)

Thessaloniki 17.09.69

Referee: Ratko Çanak (JUG)   Attendance: 10,000

ARIS: Nikos Hristidis; Theodoros Pallas, Hristos Nalbantis, Aggelos Spiridon, Dimitris Raptopoulos, Vasilis Psifidis, Giorgos Konstantinidis (65 Sokratis Petkakis), Manolis Keramidas, Alekos Alexiadis, Efstratios Sakellaridis, Kostas Papaioannou.

CAGLIARI: Enrico Albertosi; Mario Martiradonna, Giulio Zignoli, Pierluigi Cera, Comunardo Niccolai, Giuseppe Tomasini, Angelo Domenghini, Mario Brugnera, Sergio Gori, Ricciotti Greatti, Luigi Riva.   Trainer: Manlio Scopigno

Goals: Spiridon (12), Martiradonna (82)

CAGLIARI v ARIS THESSALONIKI 3-0 (2-0)

Stadio Sant Elia, Cagliari   1.10.69

Referee: Marcel Despland (SWI)   Attendance: 15,000

CAGLIARI: Enrico Albertosi; Mario Martiradonna, Giulio Zignoli, Pierluigi Cera (72 Cesare Poli), Comunardo Niccolai, Giuseppe Tomasini, Angelo Domenghini, Mario Brugnera, Sergio Gori, Ricciotti Greatti, Luigi Riva (27 Corrado Nastasio).   Trainer: Manlio Scopigno

ARIS: Nikos Hristidis; Theodoros Pallas, Vasilis Psifidis (64 Klimis Gounaris), Aggelos Spiridon, Dimitris Raptopoulos, Manolis Keramidas (11 Kostas Papaioannou), Giorgos Kostandinidis, Efstratios Sakellaridis, Alekos Alexiadis, Vaggelis Siropoulos, Sokratis Petkakis.

Goals: Domenghini (10), Riva (13), Gori (76p)

* The match was abandoned after 76 minutes due to irregularities.

INTERNAZIONALE MILANO
v SPARTA PRAHA 3-0 (0-0)

San Siro, Milano   17.09.69

Referee: János Biroczki (HUN)   Attendance: 20,000

INTERNAZIONALE: Lido Vieri; Tarciso Burgnich, Giacinto Facchetti, Gianfranco Bedin, Mauro Bellugi, Spartaco Landini, Giovanni Vastola (46 Alberto Reif), Alessandro Mazzola, Roberto Boninsegna, Mario Bertini, Mario Corso (46 Luis SUÁREZ Miramontes).   Trainer: Heriberto Herrera

SPARTA: Antonín Kramerius; Ján Tenner, Václav Migas, Vladimír Táborský (18 Josef Bouška), František Chovanec, Eduard Kessel, Bohumil Veselý (70 Pavel Dyba), Josef Jurkanin, František Gögh, Svatopluk Bouška, Josef Jarabinský.   Trainer: M. Navara

Goals: Boninsegna (68, 79), Reif (84)

SPARTA PRAHA
v INTERNAZIONALE MILANO 0-1 (0-1)

Stadion na Letnej, Praha   1.10.69

Referee: Eugen Boller (SWI)   Attendance: 25,000

SPARTA: Antonín Kramerius; Tibor Semendák, Václav Migas, Hudcovský, František Chovanec, Svatopluk Bouška, Bohumil Veselý, Josef Jurkanin, Pavel Dyba (78 Josef Bouška), František Gögh, Ivan Voborník.   Trainer: M. Navara

INTERNAZIONALE: Lido Vieri; Tarciso Burgnich, Giacinto Facchetti, Gianfranco Bedin (78 Mauro Bellugi), Spartaco Landini, Luis SUÁREZ Miramontes, Alessandro Vanello, Alessandro Mazzola, Roberto Boninsegna, Mario Bertini, Mario Corso.   Trainer: Heriberto Herrera

Goal: Boninsegna (6)

FC METZ v NAPOLI 1-1 (0-1)

Saint-Symphorien, Metz   17.09.69

Referee: Heinz Siebert (WG)   Attendance: 12,000

FC METZ: Albert Duchêne; Georges Zvunka, Denis Bauda, Jacques Pauvert, Fernand Jeitz, Robert Péri, Henning Jensen, Patrice Vicq (68 Jacques Lemée), Guy Lassalette, Robert Szczepaniak, Gérard Hausser.   Trainer: Pierre Flamion

NAPOLI: Dino Zoff; Luciano Monticolo, Luigi Pogliana, Mario Zurlini, Stelio Nardin, Ottavio Bianchi, Ivano Bosdaves, Antonio Juliano, José Altafini (20 Paolo Barison, 68 Pierpaolo Manservisi), Vincenzo Montefusco, Virginio Canzi.   Trainer: Giuseppe Chiapella

Goals: Bosdaves (8), Szczepaniak (67)

NAPOLI v FC METZ 2-1 (1-0)

Stadio San Paolo, Napoli 1.10.69

Referee: Fernando Santos Nunes Leite (POR)   Att: 20,000

NAPOLI: Dino Zoff, Luciano Monticolo, Luigi Pogliana, Mario Zurlini, Giacomo Vianello (56 Stelio Nardin), Ottavio Bianchi, Pierpaolo Manservisi (46 Ivano Bosdaves), Antonio Juliano, Paolo Barison, Giovanni Improta, Virginio Canzi.   Trainer: Giuseppe Chiapella

FC METZ: Albert Duchêne; Georges Zvunka, Denis Bauda, Jacques Pauvert, Fernand Jeitz, Marcel Jurczak (67 Robert Szczepaniak), Henning Jensen (66 Mario Confente), Robert Péri, Jacques Lemée, Patrice Vicq, Gérard Hausser.   Trainer: Pierre Flamion

Goals: Bianchi (41), Improta (60 pen), Hausser (70)

JUVENTUS TORINO
v LOKOMOTIV PLOVDIV 3-1 (2-1)

Stadio Comunale, Torino   17.09.69

Referee: Josip Strmecki (JUG)   Attendance: 15,000

JUVENTUS: Roberto Tancredi; Sandro Salvadore, Gianfranco Leoncini, Francesco Morini (46 Elio Rinero), Ernesto Castano, Giuseppe Furino, Erminio Favalli, Helmut Haller, Pietro Anastasi (46 Gianfranco Zigoni), Roberto Vieri, Lamberto Leonardi.   Trainer: Luis Antonio Carniglia

LOKOMOTIV: Panitsa Hadzhilski (46 Stancho Bonchev); Ilia Bekiarov, Nedialko Stamboliev, Gancho Peev, Georgi Valkov, Todor Paunov, Georgi Vasilev, Hristo Bonev, Vasil Ankov, Spas Iliev, Lukanov (76 Vasil Valentinov).

Goals: Vasilev (3), Vieri (27 pen) Leonardi (31), Castano (71)

LOKOMOTIV PLOVDIV
v JUVENTUS TORINO 1-2 (0-1)

Plovdiv   1.10.69

Referee: Franz Wöhrer (AUS)   Attendance: 10,000

LOKOMOTIV: Stancho Bonchev; Georgi Valkov (79 Ilia Bekiarov), Ivan Boiadjiev, Gancho Peev, Nedialko Stamboliev, Todor Paunov, Georgi Vasilev, Hristo Bonev, Vasil Ankov, Spas Iliev, Lukanov (78 Peiko Manov).

JUVENTUS: Roberto Tancredi (63 Roberto Anzolin); Sandro Salvadore, Gianfranco Leoncini, Francesco Morini, Ernesto Castano, Elio Rinero, Erminio Favalli, Giuseppe Furino, Pietro Anastasi, Roberto Vieri, Lamberto Leonardi (46 Gianfranco Zigoni).   Trainer: Luis Antonio Carniglia

Goals: Leonardi (21), Vasilev (62), Anastasi (75)

UD LAS PALMAS v HERTHA BERLIN SC 0-0

Estadio Insular, Las Palmas   17.09.69

Referee: José Rosa Dias Nunes (POR)   Attendance: 20,000

UD LAS PALMAS: Ignacio OREGUI Urriastegui; MARTÍN II Marrero de la Cruz, Antonio Alfonso Moreno «TONONO», Guillermo HERNÁNDEZ Robayna; Francisco CASTELLANO Rodríguez, Juan GUEDES Rodríguez; José María LEÓN Talavera, JUSTO GILBERTO González, Felipe Ojeda del Rosario «TRONA», GERMÁN Dévora Ceballos, GILBERTO Rodríguez Pérez.   Trainer: Luís MOLOWNY Arbelo

HERTHA: Gernot Fraydl; Lothar Groβ, Bernd Patzke, Peter Enders, Uwe Witt; Karl-Heinz Ferschl, Hans-Joachim Altendorff (46 Jürgen Weber); Werner Ipta, Lorenz Horr, Wolfgang Gayer, Arno Steffenhagen.   Trainer: Helmut Kronsbein

Guedes sent off (65)

HERTHA BERLIN SC v UD LAS PALMAS 1-0 (0-0)

Olympiastadion, Berlin   1.10.69

Referee: Zdeněk Valeš (CZE)   Attendance: 20,000

HERTHA: Volkmar Groβ; Bernd Patzke, Uwe Witt, Tasso Wild (23 Hermann Bredenfeld), Lothar Gross, Hans-Joachim Altendorff (65 Jürgen Weber), Wolfgang Gayer, Peter Enders, Werner Ipta, Franz Brungs, Arno Steffenhagen.   Trainer: Helmut Kronsbein

UD LAS PALMAS: Ignacio OREGUI Urriastegui; Guillermo HERNÁNDEZ Robayna, Francisco CASTELLANO Rodríguez, Antonio Alfonso Moreno "TONONO", JOSE LUIS Hernández Ortega, JUSTO GILBERTO González, Dionisio Nuez Robayna "NIZ", GERMÁN Dévora Ceballos, José María LEÓN Talavera, Felipe Ojeda del Rosario "TRONA" (54 JOSÉ JUAN Gutiérrez Deniz), GILBERTO Rodríguez Pérez.   Trainer: Luís MOLOWNY Arbelo

Goal: Patzke (70 pen)

LAUSANNE SPORTS v RÁBA ETO GYÖR 1-2 (1-2)

Stade Olympique de la Pontaise, Lausanne   17.09.69

Referee: Georges Uhlen (FRA)   Attendance: 8,000

LAUSANNE SPORTS: Georges Favre; Anton Weibel, Ely Tacchella, Jan Lala, Charles Hertig; Richard Dürr, Pierre-Albert Chapuisat, François Kaeser; Pierre-André Zappella (.. Eric Polencent), Georges Vuilleumier, Pierre Kerkhoffs (.. Jean-Pierre Claude).

RÁBA ETO: Lajos Tóth; László Keglovich, Arpád Orbán, Béla Horváth, László Izsáki; József Somogyi, Zoltán Kiss, János Máté; Gyula Nagy (.. Róbert Glázer), László Györffi, István Korsós.   Trainer: József Mészáros

Goals: Györffi (1, 30), Chapuisat (16)

RÁBA ETO GYÖR v LAUSANNE SPORTS 2-1 (0-0)

Györ Stadion   1.10.69

Referee: Alois Kessler (AUS)   Attendance: 12,000

RÁBA ETO: Lajos Tóth; László Keglovich, Arpád Orbán, Béla Horváth, László Izsáki; József Somogyi, Zoltán Kiss; Tibor Varsányi, László Györffi, István Korsós (.. Gyula Nagy), Lajos Magyar.   Trainer: József Mészáros

LAUSANNE SPORTS: Daniel Gautschi; Charles Hertig, Pierre-Albert Chapuisat, Anton Weibel, Jean-Paul Loichat; Richard Dürr, Eric Polencent, Robert Hosp; Pierre-André Zappella, Georges Vuilleumier (.. François Kaeser), Jean-Pierre Claude.

Goals: Korsós (55), Somogyi (60), Dürr (64)

151

PARTIZAN BEOGRAD
v ÚJPESTI DÓZSA BUDAPEST 2-1 (0-0)

JNA, Beograd   18.09.69

Referee: Erich Linemayr (AUS)   Attendance: 25,000

PARTIZAN: Ivan Curković; Mane Bajić, Blagoje Paunović, Milan Damjanović; Borivoje Djordjević, Ljubomir Mihajlović; Ilija Katić, Vladimir Kovacević, Momčilo Vukotić, Nenad Bjeković (.. Miloš Radakovic), Milan Petrović.

ÚJPESTI DÓZSA: Antal Szentmihályi; Benő Káposzta, Ernő Solymosi, Sándor Zámbó, Ernő Noskó; Ede Dunai III, János Göröcs; László Fazekas, Ferenc Bene, Antal Dunai II, László Nagy.   Trainer: Lajos Baróti

Goals: Djordjević (.., ..), Dunai III (80)

ÚJPESTI DÓZSA BUDAPEST
v PARTIZAN BEOGRAD 2-0 (0-0)

Megyeri út, Budapest   1.10.69

Referee: Jan Lazowski (POL)   Attendance: 25,000

ÚJPESTI DÓZSA: László Borbély; Benő Káposzta, Ernő Solymosi, Sándor Zámbó, Ernő Noskó; Ede Dunai III, János Göröcs; László Fazekas, Ferenc Bene, Antal Dunai II, László Nagy.   Trainer: Lajos Baróti

PARTIZAN: Ivan Curković; Ljubomir Mihajlović, Mane Bajić (.. Djordjić), Blagoje Paunović, Miloš Radaković, Milan Damjanović (.. Djuro Marić); Ilija Katić, Borivoje Djordjević, Vladimir Kovacević; Momčilo Vukotić, Nenad Bjeković.

Goals: Bene (61), Dunai III (66)

VITÓRIA de SETÚBAL
v RAPID BUCUREŞTI 3-1 (1-0)

Estádio José Alvalade, Lisboa   18.09.69

Referees: Daniel M. Zariquiegui; Martin Álvarez, David Aguado (Spa)   Attendance: 10,000

VITÓRIA: Dinis Martins VITAL; Joaquim Adriao José da CONCEIÇÃO, Carlos Alberto Lourenço CARDOSO (65 HERCULANO do Carmo Oliveira), ALFREDO Teixeira Moreira, Manuel Luís dos Santos "CARRIÇO"; Fernando Massano TOMÉ, JOSÉ MARIA Júnior, VAGNER Canotilho; Félix Marques GUERREIRO, Joaquim Leonardo Quinta ARCANJO (65 Ernesto FIGUEIREDO), JACINTO JOÃO.   Trainer: Jose-Maria Pedroto

RAPID: Răducanu Necula; Ion Pop, Nicolae Lupescu, Dan Coe, Ilie Greavu; Iordan Angelescu, Ion Dumitru, Iosif Ştraţ (66 Teofil Codreanu); Constantin Năsturescu, Alexandru Neagu, Marian Petreanu.   Trainer: Marin Bărbulescu

Goals: José Maria (41, 87), Guereiro (64), Neagu (71)

RAPID BUCUREŞTI
v VITÓRIA de SETÚBAL 1-4 (0-2)

23 August, Bucureşti   1.10.69

Referees: Muzafer Sarvan; Turan Kundakci, Sani Gullu (TUR)   Attendance: 70,000

RAPID: Răducanu Necula; Ilie Greavu, Nicolae Lupescu, Dan Coe (71 Ion Pop), Constantin Muşat; Marin Stelian, Ion Dumitru; Marian Petreanu, Iosif Ştraţ (46 Constantin Năsturescu), Alexandru Neagu, Teofil Codreanu.   Trainer: Marin Bărbulescu

VITÓRIA: Dinis Martins VITAL; Joaquim Adriao José da CONCEIÇÃO, Carlos Carlos Alberto Lourenço CARDOSO, HERCULANO do Carmo Oliveira, Manuel Luís dos Santos "CARRIÇO"; Fernando Massano TOMÉ, JOSÉ MARIA Júnior, VAGNER Canotilho (64 VITOR Manuel Ferreira BAPTISTA); Félix Marques GUERREIRO, Ernesto FIGUEIREDO (76 Joaquim Leonardo Quinta ARCANJO), JACINTO JOÃO.   Trainer: Jose-Maria Pedroto

Goals: Vagner (23 pen, 61 pen), José Maria (34), Lupescu (64 og), Marin Stelian (78)

HVIDOVRE BK KØBENHAVN
v FC PORTO 1-2 (1-0)

København   24.09.69

Referee: Curt Nystrand (SWE)   Attendance: 2,000

HVIDOVRE: Heinz Hildebrandt; Claus Larsen, Bjarne Jensen, Claus Petersen, Kaj Pedersen, Esben Pedersen, Kent Olsen, Leif Sørensen, Steen Petersen, Birger Pedersen, Jørgen Petersen (.. Kaj Svendsen).

FC PORTO: ANÍBAL Martins; Manuel GUALTER Martins da Costa, VALDEMAR de Barros Pacheco, António Francisco VIEIRA NUNES, David Figueiredo Guerra SUCENA; Fernando Pascoal Neves "PAVÃO", HÉLDER José Costa ERNESTO; LISBOA Alberto Dias, RONALDO Brito (61 Arsenio Rodrigues Jardim "SENINHO"), João CUSTÓDIO PINTO, Francisco Lage Pereira da NÓBREGA.   Trainer: Elek Schwartz

Goals: Leif Sørensen (29 pen), Hélder Ernesto (62, 70)

FC PORTO
v HVIDOVRE BK KØBENHAVN 2-0 (1-0)

Estádio das Antas, Porto   1.10.69

Referee: Mariano Medina Iglesias (SPA)   Att: 30,000

FC PORTO: ANÍBAL Martins; Manuel GUALTER Martins da Costa, VALDEMAR de Barros Pacheco, António Francisco VIEIRA NUNES, David Figueiredo Guerra SUCENA; Fernando Pascoal Neves "PAVÃO", José ROLANDO Andrade Gonçalves; HÉLDER José Costa ERNESTO, Rubens dos Santos "SALIM", João CUSTÓDIO PINTO, Francisco Lage Pereira da NÓBREGA.   Trainer: Elek Schwartz

HVIDOVRE: Heinz Hildebrandt; Claus Larsen, Bjarne Jensen, Claus Petersen, Kaj Pedersen, Esben Pedersen, Leif Sørensen, Steen Petersen, Birger Pedersen, Jørgen Petersen, Kaj Svendsen.

Goals: Salim (24), Rolando (74)

SPORTING LISBOA v LINZER ASK 4-0 (1-0)

Estádio José de Alvalade, Lisboa   24.09.69

Referee: David W. Smith (ENG)   Attendance: 30,000

SPORTING: Vitor Manuel Afonso DAMAS de Oliveira; Manuel PEDRO GOMES, José Fernandes CALÓ, HILÁRIO Rosário da Conceição, Vitor Manuel de Almeida GONÇALVES (79 CELESTINO da Silva Martins), José ALEXANDRE da Silva BAPTISTA, Fernando PERES da Silva, JOSÉ MORAIS (83 João de Matos Moura LOURENÇO), José Maria de Freitas Pereira PEDRAS, NÉLSON Fernandes, Mário da Silva Mateus "MARINHO".   Trainer: Fernando VAZ

LASK: Wilhelm Harreither; Karl Kiesenebner, Gerhard Sturmberger, Manfred Pichler, Franz Viehböck; Titus Bubernik, Wieger, M.Leitner (86 Carlos Chico Lima); Alfred Wurdinger (46 Bauer), Kurt Leitner, Medvid.

Goals: Pedras (8), Gonçalves (60), Peres (72 pen), Lourenço (75)

LINZER ASK v SPORTING LISBOA 2-2 (1-1)

Linzer Stadion   1.10.69

Referee: Helmut Bader (DDR)   Attendance: 10,000

LASK: Wilhelm Harreither; Karl Kiesenebner, Gerhard Sturmberger, Manfred Pichler (38 Schmidt), Franz Viehböck; Carlos Chico Lima, Titus Bubernik (62 M.Leitner); Alfred Wurdinger, Wieger, Kurt Leitner, Medvid.

SPORTING: Vitor Manuel Afonso DAMAS de Oliveira; Manuel PEDRO GOMES, José Fernandes CALÓ, HILÁRIO Rosário da Conceição, Vitor Manuel de Almeida GONÇALVES, José ALEXANDRE da Silva BAPTISTA, Fernando PERES da Silva (68 CELESTINO da Silva Martins), JOSÉ MORAIS, NÉLSON Fernandes, José Maria de Freitas Pereira PEDRAS, Mário da Silva Mateus "MARINHO" (62 João de Matos Moura LOURENÇO).   Trainer: Fernando VAZ

Goals: Gonçalves (39), Wurdinger (44), Lourenço (77), K. Leitner (82)

SECOND ROUND

RÁBA ETO GYÖR v CF BARCELONA 2-3 (1-2)

Györ Stadion   21.10.69

Referee: Alessandro d'Agostini (ITA)   Attendance: 20,000

RÁBA ETO: Lajos Tóth; László Keglovich, Arpád Orbán, Béla Horváth, László Izsáki; József Somogyi, Zoltán Kiss; Tibor Varsányi, István Korsós (71 László Györffi), Gyula Nagy, Lajos Magyar.   Trainer: József Mészáros

CF BARCELONA: Miguel REINA Santos; Antonio TORRES García, José FRANCH Xargay, Francisco Fernández Rodríguez «GALLEGO», Pedro María ZABALZA Inda, ELADIO Silvestre Graells, Carlos REXACH Cerdá, Carlos PELLICER Vázquez (70 Pablo GARCÍA CASTANY), JUAN CARLOS Pérez López (25 Ramón Díaz Cruz «RAMONÍ»); José Antonio ZALDÚA Urdanavia, Santiago CASTRO Anido.   Trainer: José SEGUER Sanz

Goals: Varsányi (5), Pellicer (12), Zaldúa (31, 71), Orbán (82)

CF BARCELONA v RÁBA ETO GYÖR 2-0 (1-0)

Camp Nou, Barcelona   26.11.69

Referee: Christos Mihas (GRE)   Attendance: 15,000

CF BARCELONA: Miguel REINA Santos; Antonio TORRES García, Francisco Fernández Rodríguez "GALLEGO", Ramón Díaz Cruz "RAMONÍ"; ELADIO Silvestre Graells, MARCIAL Pina Morales (70 Santiago CASTRO Anido), Pedro María ZABALZA Inda; Ramón ALFONSEDA Pous, José Antonio ZALDÚA Urdanavia, Pablo GARCÍA CASTANY (46 José María FUSTÉ Blanch), Luis PUJOL Codina.   Trainer: José SEGUER Sanz

RÁBA ETO: Lajos Tóth; László Keglovich, Arpád Orbán, Béla Horváth, László Izsáki; József Somogyi, Zoltán Kiss; János Stolcz, Gyula Nagy, László Györffi (.. Zoltán Varga), István Korsós.   Trainer: József Mészáros

Goals: Orbán (43 og), Zaldúa (62)

SKEID OSLO v DINAMO BACĂU 0-0

Ullevål, Oslo   22.10.69

Referee: Einar Espersen (Dan)   Attendance: 7,250

SKEID: Bjørn Kristiansen; Leif Syversen, Stig Mathisen, Frank Olafsen, Kjell Wangen; Trygve Bornø, Terje Gulbrandsen; Naess, Kai Sjøberg, Erik Johansen, Setrang.

DINAMO: Aristide Ghiţă; Alexandru Comănescu, Mircea Nedelcu, Laurenţiu Velicu, Constantin David; Nicolae Vătafu, Emerich Dembrovschi; Daniel Ene, Mihai Rugiubei, Constantin Duţan, Petre Băluţă.   Trainer: Valeriu Neagu

DINAMO BACĂU v SKEID OSLO 2-0 (0-0)

23 August, Bacău   *29.10.69*

Referee: János Almasi (HUN)   Attendance: 12,000

DINAMO: Aristide Ghiță; Alexandru Comănescu, Mircea Nedelcu, Laurențiu Velicu, Constantin David; Nicolae Vătafu (75 Francisc Neumayer), Constantin Duțan; Daniel Ene, Emerich Dembrovschi, Mihai Rugiubei, Petre Băluță. Trainer: Valeriu Neagu

SKEID: Bjørn Kristiansen; Leif Syversen, Stig Mathisen, Frank Olafsen, Kjell Wangen (85 Erik Mejlo); Trygve Bornø, Terje Gulbrandsen; Naess, Kai Sjøberg, Erik Johansen, Setrang (73 Tor Albiniusen).

Goals: Dembrovschi (47 pen, 68)

RSC CHARLEROI v FC ROUEN 3-1 (3-1)

Stade du Mambourg, Charleroi   *29.10.69*

Referee: Thomas Wharton (SCO)   Attendance: 15,000

RSC CHARLEROI: Antonio Tosini; Jean-Marie Termolle, Lucien Spronck, Claude Collard, Guy Verbist, André Colasse, Jean-Paul Spaute, Marcel Vandenbossche, Jean Boulet, Claude Bissot, Georget Bertoncello.

FC ROUEN: Pierre Rigoni; Jacques Largouet, André Mérélle, Patrice Rio, Michel Sénéchal, Daniel Druda, Arnaud Dos Santos, Dominique Rustichelli, Jean-François Douis, Jean-François Villa, Robert Pintenat.   Trainer: André Gérard

Goals: Bissot (23, 31), Spaute (27), Villa (40)

FC ROUEN v RSC CHARLEROI 2-0 (1-0)

Stade Robert Diochon, Rouen   *19.11.69*

Referee: Jacques Colling (LUX)   Attendance: 5,940

FC ROUEN: Pierre Rigoni; Jacques Largouet, Patrice Rio, Michel Sénéchal, Jean-Claude Dubouil, Arnaud Dos Santos, Daniel Druda, Dominique Rustichelli (.. Jean-François Douis), Jean-François Villa, Tomás Pospíchal, Robert Pintenat. Trainer: André Gérard

RSC CHARLEROI: Antonio Tosini; Jean-Marie Termolle, Claude Collard, Lucien Spronck (40 Claude Bissot), Guy Verbist, Jean-Paul Spaute, René Hutmacher, Tony Van Schoonbeek, Ivan Pintaric (14 Marcel Vandenbossche), Jean Boulet, Georget Bertoncello.

Goals: Rustichelli (10), Villa (54)

SPORTING LISBOA v ARSENAL FC LONDON 0-0

Estádio de José Alavalde, Lisboa   *29.10.69*

Referee: Dittmar Huber (SWI)   Attendance: 32,000

SPORTING: Vitor Manuel Afonso DAMAS de Oliveira; Manuel PEDRO GOMES, José Fernandes CALÓ, JOSÉ CARLOS da Silva José, HILÁRIO Rosário da Conceição, Vitor Manuel de Almeida GONÇALVES, Fernando PERES da Silva, JOSÉ MORAIS (46 CELESTINO da Silva Martins), NÉLSON Fernandes, João de Matos Moura LOURENÇO (67 Daniel Afonso da Silva "DANI"), Mário da Silva Mateus "MARINHO". Trainer: Fernando VAZ

ARSENAL: Geoffrey Barnett; Peter Storey, Robert McNab, David Court, Terence Neill, Peter Simpson, James Robertson, Jonathan Sammels, John Radford, George Graham, George Armstrong.   Manager: Bertie Mee

ARSENAL FC v SPORTING LISBOA   3-0 (2-0)

Highbury, London   *26.11.69*

Referee: Heinz Siebert (WG)   Attendance: 35,253

ARSENAL: Geoffrey Barnett; Peter Storey, Robert McNab, David Court, Terence Neill, Peter Simpson, James Robertson, Jonathan Sammels, John Radford, George Graham, George Armstrong.   Manager: Bertie Mee

SPORTING: Vitor Manuel Afonso DAMAS de Oliveira; Manuel PEDRO GOMES, CELESTINO da Silva Martins, Vitor Manuel de Almeida GONÇALVES, José ALEXANDRE da Silva BAPTISTA, José Fernandes CALÓ, JOSÉ MORAIS (46 Carlos Alberto MANACA Dias), NÉLSON Fernandes (68 João de Matos Moura LOURENÇO), Mário da Silva Mateus "MARINHO", Fernando PERES da Silva, Joaquim António DINIS.   Trainer: Fernando VAZ

Goals: Radford (20), Graham (43, 53)

CLUB BRUGGE
v ÚJPESTI DÓZSA BUDAPEST 5-2 (2-1)

Albert Dyserynck, Brugge   *29.10.69*

Referee: Peter Coates (IRL)   Attendance: 23,000

CLUB BRUGGE: Fernand Boone; Freddy Hinderijckx, Erwin Vandendaele, Kurt Axelsson, John Moulaert, Stefan Reisch (46 Gilbert Marmenout), Pierre Carteus, Henk Houwaart, Tom Turesson, Raoul Lambert, Rob Rensenbrink. Trainer: De Munk

ÚJPESTI DÓZSA: Antal Szentmihályi; Benő Káposzta, Ernő Solymosi, Ernő Noskó; Ede Dunai III, Sándor Zámbó; Péter Juhász, László Fazekas, Ferenc Bene, László Nagy, András Tóth. Trainer: Lajos Baróti

Goals: Rensenbrink (4, 36, 87), Juhász (33), Turesson (48, 73), Fazekas (90)

ÚJPESTI DÓZSA BUDAPEST
v CLUB BRUGGE KV 3-0 (1-0)

Megyeri út, Budapest 26.11.69

Referee: Kurt Tschenscher (WG)   Attendance: 30,000

ÚJPESTI DÓZSA: Antal Szentmihályi; Benő Káposzta, Ernő Solymosi, István Bánkuti; Ede Dunai III; Ernő Noskó; László Fazekas, János Göröcs, Ferenc Bene, Antal Dunai II (.. László Nagy), Sándor Zámbó.   Trainer: Lajos Baróti

CLUB BRUGGE: Luc Sanders; Freddy Hinderijckx, Kurt Axelsson, Erwin Vandendaele, John Moulaert, Henk Houwaart, Gilbert Marmenout (80 Alfons Bastijns), Johnny Thio (75 Gilbert Bailliu), Pierre Carteus, Tom Turesson, Rob Rensenbrink.   Trainer: De Munk

Sent off: Turesson (45)

Goals: Fazekas (47, 64), Bene (57)

VITÓRIA GUIMARÃES
v SOUTHAMPTON FC 3-3 (1-1)

Estádio Municipal, Guimarães 4.11.69

Referee: Pius Kamber (SWI)   Attendance: 10,000

VITÓRIA: Francisco Diamantino RODRIGUES; BERNARDO Oliveira DA VELHA, Manuel Campos PINTO, JOAQUIM António JORGE, José Fernando Silva "COSTEADO", ARTUR da Rocha, Francisco José BILREIRO da Silva, MANUEL Martins de Sousa, António Silva MENDES, António Francisco Jesús Moreira "PERES", CARLOS MANUEL Teixeira (46 ADEMIR Melo Silva).   Trainer: Fernando CAIADO

SOUTHAMPTON: Eric Martin; Joseph Kirkup, Anthony Byrne, Hugh Fisher (76 Denis Hollywood), John McGrath, James Gabriel, Terence Paine, Michael Channon (86 Frank Saul), Ronald Davies, David Walker, John Sydenham. Manager: Ted Bates

Goals: Mendes (12, 58), Channon (13), Davies (63), Paine (82), Pinto (88 pen)

SOUTHAMPTON FC
v VITÓRIA GUIMARÃES 5-1 (1-0)

The Dell, Southampton 12.11.69

Referee: Robert Franciel (FRA)   Attendance: 21,414

SOUTHAMPTON: Eric Martin; Joseph Kirkup, Anthony Byrne, Hugh Fisher, John McGrath, James Gabriel, Terence Paine, Michael Channon, Ronald Davies, David Walker, John Sydenham.   Manager: Ted Bates

VITÓRIA: Francisco Diamantino RODRIGUES; BERNARDO Oliveira DA VELHA, Manuel Campos PINTO, JOAQUIM António JORGE, José Fernando Silva "COSTEADO", ADEMIR Melo Silva, ARTUR da Rocha, Francisco José BILREIRO da Silva, MANUEL Martins de Sousa, António Silva MENDES, António Francisco Jesús Moreira "PERES" (70 AUGUSTO Martins).   Trainer: Fernando CAIADO

Goals: Costeado (13 og), Davies (54 pen, 87), Gabriel (55), Ademir (68), Channon (85)

DUNFERMLINE ATHLETIC
v GWARDIA WARSZAWA 2-1 (1-0)

East End Park, Dunfermline 5.11.69

Referee: Joseph Minnoy (BEL)   Attendance: 11,137

DUNFERMLINE: Bent Martin; William Callaghan, John McGarty, Douglas Baillie, John Lunn, William Renton, George McKimmie (.. Hugh Robertson), Barrie Mitchell, Alexander Edwards, Patrick Gardner, George McLean. Manager: George Farm

GWARDIA: Zbigniew Pocialik; Jan Sroka, Roman Jurczak, Ryszard Kielak, Krystian Michalik, Bogdan Wisniewski, Ryszard Szymczak, Stanislaw Dawidczynski, Krzysztof Marczak, Bogdan Masztaler, Edward Biernacki (.. Krystian Hanke).

Goals: G. McLean (8), Marczak (62), Gardner (73)

GWARDIA WARSZAWA
v DUNFERMLINE ATHLETIC 0-1(0-1)

Gwardia Warszawa 18.11.69

Referee: György Müncz (HUN)   Attendance: 8,000

GWARDIA: Zbigniew Pocialik; Jan Sroka, Roman Jurczak, Ryszard Kielak, Krystian Michalik, Edward Lipinski (.. Edward Biernacki), Bogdan Wisniewski, Stanislaw Dawidczynski, Bogdan Masztaler (.. Marian Szarama), Ryszard Szymczak, Krzysztof Marczak.

DUNFERMLINE: Bent Martin; William Callaghan, John McGarty, Douglas Baillie, John Lunn, William Renton, Robert Paton, Barrie Mitchell, Alexander Edwards, Patrick Gardner, George McLean.   Manager: George Farm

Goal: Renton (5)

ANDERLECHT BRUSSEL
v COLERAINE FC 6-1 (3-1)

Parc Astrid, Brussel 11.11.69

Referee: Theo Boosten (HOL)   Attendance: 10,000

ANDERLECHT: Hugo Vandenbossche; George Heylens, Johnny Velkeneers, Jacques Van Welle, Jean Cornelis; Pierre Hanon, Pirmin Stierli; Gilbert Van Binst, Jan Mulder, Paul Van Himst, Maurice Martens (75 Johan Devrindt). Trainer: Pierre Sinibaldi

COLERAINE: Victor Hunter; John McCurdy, Tony O'Doherty, David Jackson, Alan Campbell; Ivan Murray, Samuel Wilson (80 David Irwin); Sean Dunlop, Des Dickson, Anthony Curley, Brian Jennings.

Goals: Van Himst (5, 47), Mulder (23, 41), Murray (26), Hanon (70), Devrindt (82)

COLERAINE FC
v RSC ANDERLECHT BRUSSEL 3-7 (0-6)

The Showgrounds, Coleraine   20.11.69

Referee: Clive Thomas (WAL)   Attendance: 3,500

COLERAINE: Victor Hunter; John McCurdy, David Gordon, David Jackson, Alan Campbell; Ivan Murray, David Irwin; Sean Dunlop, Des Dickson, Anthony Curley, Brian Jennings.

ANDERLECHT: Hugo Vandenbossche (46 Gerard Maïr), George Heylens, Johnny Velkeneers, Julien Kialunda, Pirmin Stierli; Pierre Hanon, Thomas Nordahl; Johan Devrindt, Jan Mulder, Paul Van Himst, Wilfried Puis.
Trainer: Pierre Sinibaldi

Goals: Van Himst (1, 4, 23), Puis (15, 27, 52), Devrindt (16), Dickson (46, 71), Irwin (2-7)

FC CARL ZEISS JENA v CAGLIARI 2-0 (0-0)

Ernst-Abbe-Sportfeld, Jena   12.11.69

Referee: Paul Schiller (AUS)   Attendance: 18,000

FC CARL ZEISS: Wolfgang Blochwitz; Jürgen Werner, Peter Rock, Helmut Stein, Werner Krauss, Michael Strempel, Rainer Schlutter, Harald Irmscher, Peter Ducke, Dieter Scheitler, Roland Ducke.   Trainer: Georg Buschner

CAGLIARI: Enrico Albertosi; Mario Martiradonna, Eraldo Mancini, Pierluigi Cera, Comunardo Niccolai, Giuseppe Tomasini, Angelo Domenghini, Cláudio Olinto de Carvalho NENÉ, Sergio Gori, Ricciotti Greatti, Mario Brugnera.
Trainer: Manlio Scopigno

Goals: Rock (63), Irmscher (73 pen)

HANSA ROSTOCK
v INTERNAZIONALE MILANO 2-1 (0-1)

Ostseestadion, Rostock   12.11.69

Referee: Arie van Gemert (HOL)   Attendance: 30,000

HANSA: Jürgen Heinsch; Gerd Sackritz, Manfred Rump, Gerhard Brümmer, Helmut Hergesell, Herbert Pankau, Klaus-Dieter Seehaus, Joachim Streich, Klaus-Peter Stein, Helmut Schühler, Lothar Hahn.   Trainer: Horst Sass

INTERNAZIONALE: Lido Vieri; Tarciso Burgnich, Giacinto Facchetti, Gianfranco Bedin, Spartaco Landini, Giancarlo Cella, Luis SUÁREZ Miramontes, Alessandro Mazzola, Roberto Boninsegna, Mario Bertini, Alberto Reif.
Trainer: Heriberto Herrera

Goals: Boninsegna (1), Hergesell (63), Sackritz (89)

CAGLIARI v FC CARL ZEISS JENA 0-1 (0-1)

Stadio Sant'Elia, Cagliari   26.11.69

Referee: Daniel M. Zariquiegui (SPA)   Attendance: 5,900

CAGLIARI: Enrico Albertosi; Mario Martiradonna, Giulio Zignoli, Cláudio Olinto de Carvalho NENÉ, Comunardo Niccolai, Giuseppe Tomasini, Angelo Domenghini, Mario Brugnera, Sergio Gori (46 Cesare Poli), Ricciotti Greatti (82 Eraldo Mancini), Corrado Nastasio. Trainer: Manlio Scopigno

FC CARL ZEISS: Wolfgang Blochwitz; Jürgen Werner, Peter Rock, Helmut Stein, Werner Krauss, Michael Strempel, Rainer Schlutter, Harald Irmscher, Peter Ducke, Dieter Scheitler, Roland Ducke.   Trainer: Georg Buschner

Goal: Stein (8)

INTERNAZIONALE MILANO
v HANSA ROSTOCK 3-0 (3-0)

San Siro, Milano   26.11.69

Referee: Norman C.H. Burtenshaw (ENG)   Att: 48,000

INTERNAZIONALE: Lido Vieri; Tarciso Burgnich, Giacinto Facchetti, Gianfranco Bedin, Spartaco Landini, Luis SUÁREZ Miramontes, JAIR da Costa, Alessandro Mazzola (73 Alessandro Vanello), Roberto Boninsegna, Mario Bertini, Mario Corso.   Trainer: Heriberto Herrera

HANSA: Jürgen Heinsch; Gerd Sackritz, Manfred Rump, Gerhard Brümmer, Helmut Hergesell, Herbert Pankau, Klaus-Dieter Seehaus, Joachim Streich, Klaus-Peter Stein (67 Werner Drews), Helmut Schühler, Lothar Hahn.   Trainer: Horst Sass

Goals: Jair (5), Suárez (23), Mazzola (32)

VfB STUTTGART v NAPOLI 0-0

Neckarstadion, Stuttgart   12.11.69

Referee: Michel Kitabdjian (FRA)   Attendance: 25,000

VfB: Dieter Feller; Hans Eisele, Hans Mayer, Reinhold Zech, Theo Hoffmann, Willi Entenmann, Manfred Weidmann, Gilbert Gress, Jan Olsson, Hans Arnold, Horst Haug.
Trainer: Franz Seybold

NAPOLI: Dino Zoff; Luigi Pogliana, Salvatore Albano, Mario Zurlini, Dino Panzanato, Ottavio Bianchi, Pierpaolo Manservisi (44 Giovanni Improta), Antonio Juliano, José Altafini, Vincenzo Montefusco, Paolo Barison.
Trainer: Giuseppe Chiapella

NAPOLI v VfB STUTTGART 1-0 (0-0)

San Paolo, Napoli   26.11.69

Referee: José Rosa Dias Nunes (POR)   Attendance: 10,000

NAPOLI: Dino Zoff; Luciano Monticolo, Luigi Pogliana, Mario Zurlini, Dino Panzanato, Ottavio Bianchi, Ivano Bosdaves (78 Pierpaolo Manservisi), Antonio Juliano, Paolo Barison, Vincenzo Montefusco, Virginio Canzi (78 Giovanni Improta).   Trainer: Giuseppe Chiapella

VfB: Dieter Feller; Hans Eisele, Hans Mayer, Reinhold Zech, Willi Entenmann, Hans-Jürgen Wittfort, Manfred Weidmann, Gilbert Gress, Jan Olsson, Hans Arnold (79 Herbert Höbusch), Horst Haug.   Trainer: Franz Seybold

Goal: Canzi (75)

VITÓRIA SETÚBAL v LIVERPOOL FC 1-0 (1-0)

Estádio do Bonfim, Setúbal   12.11.69

Referee: Antonio Sbardella (ITA)   Attendance: 16,000

VITÓRIA: Dinis Martins VITAL; Joaquim Adriao José da CONCEIÇÃO, Carlos Alberto Lourenço CARDOSO, ALFREDO Teixeira MOREIRA (46 Joaquim Leonardo Quinta ARCANJO), Manuel Luís dos Santos "CARRIÇO", Fernando Massano TOMÉ, VAGNER Canotilho, JOSÉ MARIA Júnior, Félix Marques GUERREIRO, Ernesto FIGUEIREDO, JACINTO JOÃO.   Trainer: José Maria Pedroto

LIVERPOOL: Thomas Lawrence; Christopher Lawler, Peter Wall, Thomas Smith, Ronald Yeats, Emlyn Hughes, Ian Callaghan, Ian Ross, Robert Graham (61 Ian St. John), Geoffrey Strong, Peter Thompson.   Manager: William Shankly

Goal: Tomé (40)

HERTHA BERLIN SC
v JUVENTUS TORINO 3-1 (2-1)

Olympiastadion, Berlin   12.11.69

Referee: Kenneth Howard Burns (ENG)   Attendance: 30,000

HERTHA: Gernot Fraydl; Bernd Patzke (46 Lothar Gross), Karl-Heinz Ferschl, Peter Enders, Uwe Witt, Tasso Wild, Arno Steffenhagen, Hans-Joachim Altendorff, Franz Brungs, Wolfgang Gayer, Jürgen Weber.   Trainer: Helmut Kronsbein

JUVENTUS: Roberto Anzolin; Antonello Cuccureddu, Gianfranco Leoncini (3 Erminio Favalli), Giampietro Marchetti, Francesco Morini, Gianluigi Roveta, Lamberto Leonardi, Roberto Vieri, Pietro Anastasi (24 Paolo Vigano), Luis Cascajares DEL SOL, Helmut Haller. Trainer: Luis Antonio Carniglia

Goals: Anastasi (13), Gayer (17), Wild (31), Steffenhagen (79)

LIVERPOOL FC v VITÓRIA SETÚBAL 3-2 (0-1)

Anfield Road, Liverpool   26.11.69

Referee: Alfred Delcourt (BEL)   Attendance: 41,633

LIVERPOOL: Thomas Lawrence; Christopher Lawler, Geoffrey Strong, Thomas Smith, Ronald Yeats, Emlyn Hughes, Ian Callaghan, Stephen Peplow (46 Roger Hunt), Robert Graham (46 Alun Evans), Ian St. John, Peter Thompson. Manager: William Shankly

VITÓRIA: Dinis Martins VITAL; Francisco Silva REBELO, Carlos Alberto Lourenço CARDOSO, ALFREDO Teixeira MOREIRA, Manuel Luís dos Santos "CARRIÇO", Fernando Massano TOMÉ, VAGNER Canotilho, JOSÉ MARIA Júnior, Félix Marques GUERREIRO (77 Carlos Alberto CORREIA), Joaquim Leonardo Quinta ARCANJO (66 Ernesto FIGUEIREDO), JACINTO JOÃO.   Trainer: José Maria Pedroto

Goals: Vagner (23 pen), Strong (56 og), Smith (60 pen), Evans (88), Hunt (90)

JUVENTUS TORINO v HERTHA BERLIN SC 0-0

Stadio Comunale, Torino   26.11.69

Referee: Milivoje Gugulović (JUG)   Attendance: 20,000

JUVENTUS: Roberto Tancredi; Sandro Salvadore, Giuseppe Furino, Ernesto Castano, Francesco Morini, Giampietro Marchetti, Lamberto Leonardi, Luis Cascajares DEL SOL, Gianfranco Zigoni, Helmut Haller, Antonello Cuccureddu. Trainer: Luis Antonio Carniglia

HERTHA: Volkmar Gross; Bernd Patzke, Karl-Heinz Ferschl, Peter Enders, Uwe Witt, Tasso Wild, Hans-Joachim Altendorff (65 Hermann Bredenfeld), Arno Steffenhagen, Franz Brungs (78 Bernd Laube), Wolfgang Gayer, Jürgen Weber. Trainer: Helmut Kronsbein

AJAX AMSTERDAM v RUCH CHORZÓW 7-0 (2-0)

Olympisch, Amsterdam   19.11.69

Referee: Henry Øberg (NOR)   Attendance: 14,836

AJAX: Gerrit Bals; Wim Suurbier, Barry Hulshoff, Velibor Vasovic, Ruud Krol, Sjaak Swart, Nico Rijnders, Gerrie Mühren, Johan Cruijff, Dick Van Dijk, Piet Keizer. Trainer: Marinus Michels

RUCH: Henryk Pietrek; Antoni Piechniczek, Antoni Nieroba, Jerzy Wyrobek, Bernard Bem, Józef Gomoluch, Zygmunt Maszczyk, Bronislaw Bula, Joachim Marx, Edward Herman, Eugeniusz Faber.   Trainer: Jerzy Nikiel

Goals: Vasovic (43,76 pen), Swart (44), Cruijff (56, 70), Van Dijk (63, 80)

RUCH CHORZÓW v AJAX AMSTERDAM 1-2 (1-1)

Ruch, Chorzów   26.11.69

Referee: Stoian Chomakov (BUL)   Attendance: 9,400

RUCH: Henryk Pietrek (31 Jerzy Sokolik); Antoni Piechniczek, Antoni Nieroba, Jerzy Wyrobek (64 Józef Janduda), Bernard Bem, Józef Gomoluch, Zygmunt Maszczyk, Bronislaw Bula, Joachim Marx, Edward Herman, Eugeniusz Faber.   Trainer: Jerzy Nikiel

AJAX: Gerrit Bals; Ton Pronk, Wim Suurbier, Barry Hulshoff, Ruud Krol, Sjaak Swart, Nico Rijnders, Gerrie Mühren, Johan Cruijff, Dick Van Dijk, Piet Keizer.   Trainer: Marinus Michels

Goals: G. Mühren (15), Piechniczek (43), Van Dijk (89)

FC PORTO v NEWCASTLE UNITED 0-0

Estádio das Antas, Porto   19.11.69

Referee: Roland Marendaz (SWI)   Attendance: 25,000

FC PORTO: RUI Fernando Sousa Teixeira; Manuel GUALTER Martins da Costa, VALDEMAR de Barros Pacheco, António Francisco VIEIRA NUNES, David Figueiredo Guerra SUCENA; José ROLANDO Andrade Gonçalves, Rubens dos Santos "SALIM"; Fernando Pascoal Neves "PAVÃO", Arsenio Rodrigues Jardim "SENINHO", João CUSTÓDIO PINTO, Francisco Lage Pereira da NÓBREGA. Trainer: Elek Schwartz

NEWCASTLE: William McFaul; David Craig, Frank Clark, Thomas Gibb, Alwyn Burton, Robert Moncur, Bryan Robson, Keith Dyson, Wyn Davies, Ronald Guthrie (71 James Scott), Preben Arentoft.   Manager: Joe Harvey

NEWCASTLE UNITED v FC PORTO 1-0 (1-0)

St. James' Park, Newcastle   26.11.69

Referee: Wolfgang Riedel (DDR)   Attendance: 44,800

NEWCASTLE: William McFaul; David Craig, Frank Clark, Thomas Gibb, Alwyn Burton, Robert Moncur, James Scott, Bryan Robson, Wyn Davies, Preben Arentoft, Alan Foggon. Manager: Joe Harvey

FC PORTO: RUI Fernando Sousa Teixeira; Manuel GUALTER Martins da Costa, VALDEMAR de Barros Pacheco, António Francisco VIEIRA NUNES, David Figueiredo Guerra SUCENA; José ROLANDO Andrade Gonçalves (80 JOÃO Tavares Domingues), Rubens dos Santos "SALIM"; Fernando Pascoal Neves "PAVÃO", ALBANO da Silva Soares (50 ACÁCIO António Duarte Carniero), João CUSTÓDIO PINTO, Francisco Lage Pereira da NÓBREGA.   Trainer: Elek Schwartz

Goal: Scott (22)

KILMARNOCK FC v SLAVIA SOFIA 4-1 (2-0)

Rugby Park, Kilmarnock   19.11.69

Referee: Curt Nystrand (SWE)   Attendance: 12,500

KILMARNOCK: Alex McLaughlan; Andrew King, William Dickson, John Gilmour, John McGrory, Frank Beattie, Thomas McLean, Edward Morrison, Ross Mathie, James McLean (.. William Waddell), James Cook.

SLAVIA: Petar Tsolov; Aleksandar Shalamanov, Georgi Hristakiev, Stoian Aleksiev, Petar Petrov, Ivan Davidov, Iancho Dimitrov, Iv. Georgiev, Atanas Mikhailov, Todor Kolev, Stoian Kotzev.   Trainer: Mirko Tashkov

Goals: Mathie (6, 75), Cook (11), Gilmour (76), Shalamanov (88)

SLAVIA SOFIA v KILMARNOCK FC 2-0 (2-0)

Sofia   26.11.69

Referee: Bohumil Smejkal (CZE)   Attendance: 10,000

SLAVIA: Petar Tsolov; Atanas Gerov, Petar Petrov, Stoian Aleksiev, Ivan Davidov, Todor Kolev, Iancho Dimitrov (80 Georgi Manolov), Iv. Georgiev, Atanas Mikhailov, Bozhidar Grigorov, Stoian Kotzev.   Trainer: Mirko Tashkov

KILMARNOCK: Alex McLaughlan; Andrew King, William Dickson, John Gilmour, John McGrory, Frank Beattie, Thomas McLean, Edward Morrison, Ross Mathie, Hugh Strachan, James Cook.

Goals: Mikhailov (1), Kotzev (24)

THIRD ROUND

NAPOLI v AJAX AMSTERDAM 1-0 (1-0)

San Paolo, Napoli   10.12.69

Referee: Anton Bucheli (SWI)   Attendance: 15,400

NAPOLI: Dino Zoff; Luciano Monticolo, Luigi Pogliana, Mario Zurlini, Dino Panzanato, Ottavio Bianchi, Kurt Hamrin (77 Ivano Bosdaves), Antonio Juliano, Pierpaolo Manservisi, José Altafini, Vincenzo Montefusco. Trainer: Giuseppe Chiapella

AJAX: Gerrit Bals; Velibor Vasovic, Wim Suurbier, Barry Hulshoff, Ruud Krol, Nico Rijnders, Gerrie Mühren, Sjaak Swart, Tom Søndergaard, Dick Van Dijk, Ben Muller. Trainer: Marinus Michels

Goal: Manservisi (37)

AJAX AMSTERDAM v NAPOLI 4-0 (1-0, 1-0) a.e.t.

Olympisch, Amsterdam 21.01.70

Referee: Rudolf Glöckner (DDR) Attendance: 40,132

AJAX: Gerrit Bals; Velibor Vasovic, Wim Suurbier, Barry Hulshoff, Ruud Krol, Nico Rijnders, Gerrie Mühren, Sjaak Swart, Johan Cruijff, Dick Van Dijk (91 Ruud Suurendonk), Piet Keizer (110 Ben Muller). Trainer: Marinus Michels

NAPOLI: Dino Zoff; Stelio Nardin, Luigi Pogliana, Giacomo Vianello (46 Giovanni Improta), Dino Panzanato, Luciano Monticolo, Ivano Bosdaves (46 Virginio Canzi), Antonio Juliano, Pierpaolo Manservisi, Ottavio Bianchi, Paolo Barison. Trainer: Giuseppe Chiapella

Goals: Swart (35), Suurendonk (109, 113, 116)

FC ROUEN v ARSENAL FC LONDON 0-0

Stade Robert Diochon, Rouen 17.12.69

Referee: Franz Geluck (BEL) Attendance: 12,093

FC ROUEN: Pierre Rigoni; Jacques Largouet, Patrice Rio, Michel Sénéchal, André Mérelle, Arnaud Dos Santos, Tomás Pospíchal, Dominique Rustichelli, Jean-François Villa, Claude Le Roy, François Bruant. Trainer: André Gérard

ARSENAL: Robert Wilson; Peter Storey, Robert McNab, David Court, Terence Neill, Peter Simpson, James Robertson, Jonathan Sammels, John Radford, George Graham (46 Edward Kelly), George Armstrong. Manager: Bertie Mee

KILMARNOCK FC v DINAMO BACĂU 1-1 (0-0)

Rugby Park, Kilmarnock 17.12.1969

Referee: Francis Rion (BEL) Attendance: 25,000

KILMARNOCK: Alex McLaughlan; John McGrory, Andrew King, William Dickson, Gilmore, Frank Beattie, James Cook, Ross Mathie, William Waddell, Edward Morrison, Thomas McLean.

DINAMO: Aristide Ghiță; Alexandru Comănescu, Mircea Nedelcu, Laurențiu Velicu, Madocsa Kiss (81 Constantin David); Nicolae Vătafu, Constantin Duțan; Mircea Pană, Emerich Dembrovschi, Daniel Ene, Petre Băluță. Trainer: Valeriu Neagu

Goals: Mathie (50), Băluță (73)

ARSENAL FC LONDON v FC ROUEN 1-0 (0-0)

Highbury, London 13.01.70

Referee: Adrianus Boogaerts (HOL) Attendance: 38,018

ARSENAL: Robert Wilson; Peter Storey, Samuel Nelson, David Court (22 George Graham), Terence Neill, Peter Simpson, Peter Marinello, Jonathan Sammels, John Radford, Charles George, George Armstrong. Manager: Bertie Mee

FC ROUEN: Pierre Rigoni; Jacques Largouet, Patrice Rio, Michel Sénéchal, André Mérelle, Arnaud Dos Santos, Daniel Druda, Dominique Rustichelli, Jean-François Villa, Tomás Pospíchal, François Bruant (60 Jean-François Douis). Trainer: André Gérard

Goal: Sammels (89)

DINAMO BACĂU v KILMARNOCK FC 2-0 (1-0)

23 August, Bacău 13.01.70

Referees: István Zsolt; Tibor Wotawa, P. Sandor (HUN) Attendance: 7,000

DINAMO: Aristide Ghiță; Alexandru Comănescu, Mircea Nedelcu, Laurențiu Velicu, Madocsa Kiss; Nicolae Vătafu, Constantin Duțan; Mircea Pană, Emerich Dembrovschi, Daniel Ene, Petre Băluță (79 Francisc Neumayer). Trainer: Valeriu Neagu

KILMARNOCK: Alex McLaughlan; John McGrory, Andrew King, Hugh Strachan, William Dickson; Gilmore (55 George Maxwell), James McLean; Thomas McLean, Ross Mathie, Edward Morrison, Ronald Sheed.

Goals: D. Ene (27, 79)

NEWCASTLE UNITED v SOUTHAMPTON FC 0-0

St. James' Park, Newcastle 17.12.69

Referee: Robert Holley Davidson (SCO) Attendance: 37,580

NEWCASTLE: William McFaul; David Craig, Frank Clark, Thomas Gibb, Alwyn Burton, Robert Moncur, Bryan Robson, Keith Dyson, Wyn Davies, Preben Arentoft, James Scott (55 Alan Foggon). Manager: Joe Harvey

SOUTHAMPTON: Eric Martin; Joseph Kirkup, Anthony Byrne, Hugh Fisher, John McGrath (23 Robert Stokes), James Gabriel, Terence Paine, Michael Channon, Ronald Davies, David Walker, Thomas Jenkins. Manager: Ted Bates

SOUTHAMPTON FC
v NEWCASTLE UNITED 1-1 (1-0)

The Dell, Southampton   13.01.70

Referee: William John Gow (WAL)   Attendance: 25,182

SOUTHAMPTON: Eric Martin; Joseph Kirkup, Anthony Byrne, Hugh Fisher, James Gabriel, David Walker, Thomas Jenkins, Michael Channon, Ronald Davies, Terence Paine, John Sydenham (83 Robert Stokes).   Manager: Ted Bates

NEWCASTLE: William McFaul; David Craig, Frank Clark, Thomas Gibb, Robert Moncur, John McNamee, Bryan Robson, James Smith, Wyn Davies, David Young (81 Ronald Guthrie), David Ford.   Manager: Joe Harvey

Goals: Channon (29), Robson (84)

RSC ANDERLECHT BRUSSEL
v DUNFERMLINE ATHLETIC 1-0 (1-0)

Parc Astrid, Brussel   17.12.69

Referee: Dittmar Huber (SWI)   Attendance: 11,700

ANDERLECHT: Hugo Vandenbossche; George Heylens, Johnny Velkeneers, Julien Kialunda, Jean Cornelis; Thomas Nordahl, Alfons Peeters; Gerard Bergholtz (46 Pierre Hanon), Jan Mulder, Johan Devrindt, Wilfried Puis.
Trainer: Pierre Sinibaldi

DUNFERMLINE: William Duff; William Callaghan, David McNicoll, Douglas Baillie, John Lunn; George McLean, William McLaren; Alexander Edwards, Patrick Gardner, Barrie Mitchell, Hugh Robertson.   Manager: George Farm

Goal: Devrindt (45)

DUNFERMLINE ATHLETIC
v RSC ANDERLECHT BRUSSEL 3-2 (1-0)

East End Park, Dunfermline   14.01.70

Referee: Mariano Medina Iglesias (SPA)   Attendance: 11,773

DUNFERMLINE: William Duff; William Callaghan, David McNicoll, Douglas Baillie, John Lunn; George McLean, William McLaren; Alexander Edwards, Patrick Gardner, Barrie Mitchell, James Gillespie.   Trainer: George Farm

ANDERLECHT: Jean Trappeniers; George Heylens, Johnny Velkeneers, Julien Kialunda, Jean Cornelis; Werner Deraeve, Thomas Nordahl, Alfons Peeters; Jan Mulder, Paul Van Himst, Wilfried Puis.   Trainer: Pierre Sinibaldi

Goals: McLean (9, 88), Mitchell (46), Van Himst (75), Mulder (85)

VITÓRIA SETÚBAL
v HERTHA BERLIN SC 1-1 (1-1)

Estádio do Bonfim, Setúbal   30.12.69

Referee: Anton Bucheli (SWI)   Attendance: 10,000

VITÓRIA: Dinis Martins VITAL; Joaquim Adriao José da CONCEIÇÃO, Carlos Alberto Lourenço CARDOSO, ALFREDO Teixeira MOREIRA, Manuel Luís dos Santos "CARRIÇO", Fernando Massano TOMÉ, JOSÉ MARIA Júnior, VAGNER Canotilho, Joaquim Leonardo Quinta ARCANJO, Félix Marques GUERREIRO, JACINTO JOÃO.
Trainer: José Maria Pedroto

HERTHA: Volkmar Gross; Bernd Patzke, Tasso Wild, Uwe Witt, Karl-Heinz Ferschl, Peter Enders, Wolfgang Gayer, Arno Steffenhagen, Franz Brungs, Lorenz Horr, Jürgen Weber.
Trainer: Helmut Kronsbein

Goals: Tomé (10), Horr (30)

HERTHA BERLIN SC
v VITÓRIA SETÚBAL 1-0 (0-0)

Olympia stadion, Berlin   7.01.70

Referee: James Finney (ENG)   Attendance: 20,000

HERTHA: Gernot Fraydl; Bernd Patzke, Uwe Witt, Tasso Wild, Karl-Heinz Ferschl, Hans-Joachim Altendorff, Wolfgang Gayer, Ipta (46 Arno Steffenhagen), Franz Brungs, Lorenz Horr, Jürgen Weber.   Trainer: Helmut Kronsbein

VITÓRIA: Dinis Martins VITAL; Joaquim Adriao José da CONCEIÇÃO, Carlos Alberto Lourenço CARDOSO, ALFREDO Teixeira MOREIRA, Manuel Luís dos Santos "CARRIÇO", Fernando Massano TOMÉ (60 VÍTOR Manuel Ferreira BAPTISTA), JOSÉ MARIA Júnior, VAGNER Canotilho, Joaquim Leonardo Quinta ARCANJO, Félix Marques GUERREIRO, JACINTO JOÃO (60 Ernesto FIGUEIREDO).
Trainer: José Maria Pedroto

Goal: Steffenhagen (59)

FC CARL ZEISS JENA
v ÚJPESTI DÓZSA BUDAPEST 1-0 (0-0)

Ernst-Abbe-Sportfeld, Jena   14.01.70

Referee: Theo Boosten (HOL)   Attendance: 16,000

FC CARL ZEISS: Wolfgang Blochwitz; Harald Irmscher, Peter Rock, Michael Strempel, Werner Krauss; Helmut Stein, Jürgen Werner; Roland Ducke, Rainer Schlutter; Peter Ducke, Dieter Scheitler.   Trainer: Georg Buschner

ÚJPESTI DÓZSA: László Borbély; Benő Káposzta, Ernő Solymosi, Sándor Zámbó, Ernő Noskó; Ede Dunai III, János Göröcs; László Fazekas, Ferenc Bene, Antal Dunai II, László Nagy.   Trainer: Lajos Baróti

Goal: W. Kraus (87)

ÚJPESTI DÓZSA BUDAPEST
v FC CARL ZEISS JENA 0-3 (0-2)

Megyeri út, Budapest   21.01.70

Referee: Bruno de Marchi (ITA)   Attendance: 10,000

ÚJPESTI DÓZSA: László Borbély; Benő Káposzta, Ernő Solymosi, Sándor Zámbó, Ernő Noskó; Ede Dunai III, János Göröcs; László Fazekas, Ferenc Bene, Antal Dunai II, László Nagy (46 István Bánkuti).   Trainer: Lajos Baróti

FC CARL ZEISS: Wolfgang Blochwitz; Harald Irmscher, Peter Rock, Michael Strempel, Werner Krauss; Helmut Stein, Jürgen Werner; Roland Ducke, Rainer Schlutter; Peter Ducke, Dieter Scheitler.   Trainer: Georg Buschner

Goals: Scheitler (4), Stein (43), P. Ducke (53)

CF BARCELONA
v INTERNAZIONALE MILANO 1-2 (1-2)

Camp Nou, Barcelona   14.01.70

Referee: John Keith Taylor (ENG)   Attendance: 80,000

CF BARCELONA: Miguel REINA Santos; Joaquín RIFÉ Climent, ELADIO Silvestre Graells, Antonio TORRES García, Francisco Fernández Rodríguez "GALLEGO", JUAN CARLOS Pérez López, Carlos REXACH Cerdá, Santiago CASTRO Anido, Narciso MARTÍ FILOSÍA, José María FUSTÉ Blanch (22 Pablo GARCÍA CASTANY, 57 Francisco ROMEA Hernando), Luis PUJOL Codina.   Trainer: Victor Frederik Buckingham

INTERNAZIONALE: Lido Vieri; Tarciso Burgnich, Giacinto Facchetti, Mauro Bellugi, Spartaco Landini, Giancarlo Cella, Luis SUÁREZ Miramontes, Alessandro Mazzola, Roberto Boninsegna, Mario Bertini, Mario Corso. Trainer: Heriberto Herrera

Goals: Boninsegna (7), Fusté (20), Bertini (32)

INTERNAZIONALE MILANO
v CF BARCELONA 1-0

San Siro, Milano   28.01.70

Referee: Kurt Tschenscher (WG)   Attendance: 10,000

INTERNAZIONALE: Lido Vieri; Tarcisio Burgnich, Giacinto Facchetti, Gianfranco Bedin; Spartaco Landini, Giancarlo Cella; Alberto Reif, Luis Suárez, Roberto Boninsegna, Mario Bertini, Mario Corso.   Trainer: Heriberto Herrera

CF BARCELONA: Miguel REINA Santos; Joaquín RIFÉ Climent, Francisco Fernández Rodríguez "GALLEGO", ELADIO Silvestre Graells; Antonio TORRES García, Pedro María ZABALZA; Carlos REXACH Cerdá, JUAN CARLOS Pérez, Ramón ALFONSEDA Pous, Santiago CASTRO Anido, Luis PUJOL Codina.   Trainer: Victor Frederik Buckingham

Goal: Boninsegna (15)

This match stopped due to fog and was replayed on 4-02-1970

INTERNAZIONALE MILANO
v CF BARCELONA 1-1 (1-1)

San Siro, Milano   4.02.70

Referee: Kurt Tschenscher (WG)   Attendance: 15,000

INTERNAZIONALE: Lido Vieri; Tarciso Burgnich, Giacinto Facchetti, Mauro Bellugi, Spartaco Landini, Giancarlo Cella, JAIR da Costa (42 Alberto Reif), Alessandro Mazzola, Roberto Boninsegna, Mario Bertini, Luis SUÁREZ Miramontes (36 Mario Corso).   Trainer: Heriberto Herrera

CF BARCELONA: Miguel REINA Santos; Joaquín RIFÉ Climent, ELADIO Silvestre Graells, Antonio TORRES García, Francisco Fernández Rodríguez "GALLEGO", José María FUSTÉ Blanch, Carlos REXACH Cerdá, JUAN CARLOS Pérez López, Narciso MARTÍ FILOSÍA, Ramón ALFONSEDA Pous, Luis PUJOL Codina (46 Santiago CASTRO Anido).   Trainer: Victor Frederik Buckingham

Goals: Boninsegna (18), Rexach (29)

QUARTER-FINALS

FC CARL ZEISS JENA
v AJAX AMSTERDAM 3-1 (3-0)

Ernst-Abbe-Sportfeld, Jena   4.03.70

Referee: Francesco Francescon (ITA)   Attendance: 22,000

FC CARL ZEISS: Wolfgang Blochwitz; Michael Strempel, Jürgen Werner, Peter Rock, Helmut Stein, Werner Krauss, Harald Irmscher, Rainer Schlutter, Roland Ducke, Dieter Scheitler, Peter Ducke.   Trainer: Georg Buschner

AJAX: Gerrit Bals; Wim Suurbier (54 Ruud Suurendonk), Velibor Vasovic, Barry Hulshoff, Ruud Krol, Nico Rijnders, Gerrie Mühren, Sjaak Swart, Johan Cruijff, Dick Van Dijk, Piet Keizer.   Trainer: Marinus Michels

Goals: R. Ducke (22), Stein (27), P. Ducke (33), Vasovic (87)

AJAX AMSTERDAM
v FC CARL ZEISS JENA 5-1 (3-1)

Olympisch, Amsterdam   11.03.70

Referee: Norman C.H. Burtenshaw (ENG)   Att: 50,896

AJAX: Gerrit Bals; Wim Suurbier, Velibor Vasovic, Barry Hulshoff, Ruud Krol, Nico Rijnders, Gerrie Mühren, Sjaak Swart, Johan Cruijff, Dick Van Dijk (85 Ruud Suurendonk), Piet Keizer.   Trainer: Marinus Michels

FC CARL ZEISS: Wolfgang Blochwitz; Helmut Stein, Peter Rock, Jürgen Werner, Werner Krauss, Michael Strempel, Rainer Schlutter, Harald Irmscher, Roland Ducke (67 Udo Preusze), Dieter Scheitler, Peter Ducke. Trainer: Georg Buschner

Goals: Scheitler (16), Vasovic (21), Swart (24, 53), Keizer (44), Cruijff (71)

HERTHA BERLIN SC
v INTERNAZIONALE MILANO 1-0 (1-0)

Olympiastadion, Berlin   4.03.70

Referee: Gilbert Droz (SWI)   Attendance: 40,000

HERTHA: Volkmar Gross; Bernd Patzke, Karl-Heinz Ferschl, Uwe Witt, Tasso Wild, Hans-Joachim Altendorff (46 Hermann Bredenfeld), Arno Steffenhagen, Wolfgang Gayer, Franz Brungs, Lorenz Horr, Jürgen Weber.
Trainer: Helmut Kronsbein

INTERNAZIONALE: Sergio Girardi; Spartaco Landini, Enzo Vecchié, Dionisio Collavini (46 Luis SUÁREZ Miramontes), Aristide Guarneri, Giancarlo Cella, JAIR da Costa, Gianfranco Bedin, Roberto Boninsegna, Mario Bertini, Mario Corso.
Trainer: Heriberto Herrera

Goal: Horr (22)

INTERNAZIONALE MILANO
v HERTHA BERLIN SC 2-0 (0-0)

San Siro, Milano   18.03.70

Referee: Georges Uhlen (FRA)   Attendance: 15.000

INTERNAZIONALE: Lido Vieri (32 Sergio Girardi); Mauro Bellugi, Giacinto Facchetti, Mario Bertini, Aristide Guarneri, Spartaco Landini, JAIR da Costa, Alessandro Mazzola, Roberto Boninsegna, Luis SUÁREZ Miramontes, Alessandro Vanello.
Trainer: Heriberto Herrera

HERTHA: Gernot Fraydl; Bernd Patzke, Karl-Heinz Ferschl, Tasso Wild, Uwe Witt, Hans-Joachim Altendorff, Arno Steffenhagen, Wolfgang Gayer, Franz Brungs, Lorenz Horr, Jürgen Weber.   Trainer: Helmut Kronsbein

Goals: Boninsegna (47, 60 pen)

RSC ANDERLECHT BRUSSEL
v NEWCASTLE UNITED 2-0 (1-0)

Parc Astrid, Brussel   11.03.70

Referee: Paul Schiller (AUS)   Attendance: 19,000

ANDERLECHT: Jean Trappeniers; George Heylens, Johnny Velkeneers, Julien Kialunda, Maurice Martens; Thomas Nordahl, Gérard Desanghere; Johan Devrindt, Jan Mulder, Paul Van Himst, Wilfried Puis.   Trainer: Pierre Sinibaldi

NEWCASTLE: William McFaul; John Craggs, John McNamee (77 Alwyn Burton), Robert Moncur, Ronald Guthrie; Thomas Gibb, Alan Foggon; Bryan Robson, James Smith (72 David Elliott), Wyn Davies, Keith Dyson.   Managers: Joe Harvey

Goals: Desanghere (32), Puis (61)

NEWCASTLE UNITED
v RSC ANDERLECHT BRUSSEL 3-1 (2-0)

St. James' Park, Newcastle   18.03.70

Referee: Helmut Fritz (WG)   Attendance: 57, 500

NEWCASTLE: William McFaul; David Craig, Frank Clark (25 David Young), Robert Moncur, Alwyn Burton; Thomas Gibb, Alan Foggon; Bryan Robson, Ronald Guthrie, Wyn Davies, Keith Dyson.   Manager: Joe Harvey

ANDERLECHT: Jean Trappeniers; George Heylens, Johnny Velkeneers, Julien Kialunda, Maurice Martens; Thomas Nordahl, Gérard Desanghere; Johan Devrindt, Jan Mulder, Paul Van Himst, Wilfried Puis.   Trainer: Pierre Sinibaldi

Goals: Robson (4, 20), Dyson (85), Nordahl (87)

DINAMO BACĂU v ARSENAL LONDON 0-2 (0-0)

23 August, Bacău   11.03.70

Refs: Gyula Emsberger, Sándor Kaposi, János Piroczki (HUN)
Attendance: 20,000

DINAMO: Aristide Ghiţă; Alexandru Comănescu, Mircea Nedelcu, Laurenţiu Velicu, Madocsa Kiss; Nicolae Vătafu, Constantin Duţan; Francisc Neumayer, Mircea Pană, Daniel Ene, Constantin David (55 Gheorghe Sinăuceanu).
Trainer: Valeriu Neagu

ARSENAL: Robert Wilson; Peter Storey, Robert McNab, Edward Kelly, Frank McLintock, Peter Simpson, Peter Marinello, Jonathan Sammels, John Radford, Charles George, George Graham.   Manager: Bertie Mee

Goals: Sammels (58), Radford (81)

ARSENAL LONDON v DINAMO BACĂU 7-1 (4-1)

Highbury, London   18.03.70

Referee: Willem J.M. Schalks (HOL)   Attendance: 35,342

ARSENAL: Robert Wilson, Peter Storey, Robert McNab, Edward Kelly, Frank McLintock, Peter Simpson, Peter Marinello, Jonathan Sammels, John Radford, Charles George, George Graham (46 George Armstrong).
Manager: Bertie Mee

DINAMO: Aristide Ghiţă; Alexandru Comănescu, Mircea Nedelcu, Laurenţiu Velicu, Constantin David; Nicolae Vătafu, Constantin Duţan; Mircea Pană, Emerich Dembrovschi, Daniel Ene, Petre Băluţă.   Trainer: Valeriu Neagu

Goals: Radford (7, 77), George (24, 26), Băluţă (33), Graham (45), Sammels (59, 83)

SEMI-FINALS

RSC ANDERLECHT BRUSSEL
v INTERNAZIONALE MILANO 0-1 (0-0)

Parc Astrid, Brussel   1.04.70

Referee: Thomas Wharton (SCO)   Attendance: 31,500

ANDERLECHT: Jean Trappeniers; George Heylens, Johnny Velkeneers, Alfons Peeters, Maurice Martens; Thomas Nordahl, Gerard Desanghere; Gerard Bergholtz, Jan Mulder, Johan Devrindt, Wilfried Puis.   Trainer: Pierre Sinibaldi

INTERNAZIONALE: Lido Vieri; Giancarlo Cella, Tarciso Burgnich, Giacinto Facchetti, Gianfranco Bedin; Spartaco Landini, Mario Bertini; Luis SUÁREZ Miramontes, Alessandro Mazzola, Roberto Boninsegna, Mario Corso. Trainer: Heriberto Herrera

Goal: Boninsegna (48)

INTERNAZIONALE MILANO
v RSC ANDERLECHT BRUSSEL 0-2 (0-2)

San Siro, Milano   15.04.70

Referee: Rudolf Glöckner (DDR)   Attendance: 25,000

INTERNAZIONALE: Lido Vieri; Tarciso Burgnich, Giacinto Facchetti, Gianfranco Bedin, Spartaco Landini, Giancarlo Cella, Luis SUÁREZ Miramontes, Alessandro Mazzola, Roberto Boninsegna, Mario Bertini (55 JAIR da Costa), Mario Corso.   Trainer: Heriberto Herrera

ANDERLECHT: Jean Trappeniers; George Heylens, Maurice Martens, Thomas Nordahl, Johnny Velkeneers, Julien Kialunda, Gerard Desanghere; Gerard Bergholtz, Johan Devrindt, Paul Van Himst, Wilfried Puis. Trainer: Pierre Sinibaldi

Goals: Bergholtz (3, 45)

ARSENAL FC LONDON
v AJAX AMSTERDAM 3-0 (1-0)

Highbury, London   8.04.70

Referee: Kurt Tschenscher (WG)   Attendance: 46,269

ARSENAL: Robert Wilson; Peter Storey, Robert McNab, Edward Kelly, Frank McLintock, Peter Simpson, Peter Marinello (65 George Armstrong), Jonathan Sammels, John Radford, Charles George, George Graham. Manager: Bertie Mee

AJAX: Gerrit Bals; Wim Suurbier, Velibor Vasovic, Barry Hulshoff, Ruud Krol, Nico Rijnders, Gerrie Mühren, Sjaak Swart, Johan Cruijff, Dick Van Dijk, Piet Keizer (46 Ruud Suurendonk).   Trainer: Marinus Michels

Goals: George (16, 84 pen), Sammels (80)

AJAX AMSTERDAM
v ARSENAL FC LONDON 1-0 (1-0)

Olympisch, Amsterdam 15.04.70

Referee: Paul Schiller (AUS)   Attendance: 39,349

AJAX: Gerrit Bals; Wim Suurbier, Velibor Vasovic, Barry Hulshoff, Ruud Krol, Nico Rijnders, Gerrie Mühren, Sjaak Swart, Johan Cruijff, Dick Van Dijk, Piet Keizer. Trainer: Marinus Michels

ARSENAL: Robert Wilson; Peter Storey, Robert McNab, Edward Kelly, Frank McLintock, Peter Simpson, George Armstrong, Jonathan Sammels, John Radford, Charles George, George Graham.   Manager: Bertie Mee

Goal: G. Mühren (17)

FINAL

RSC ANDERLECHT BRUSSEL
v ARSENAL FC LONDON 3-1 (2-0)

Parc Astrid, Brussel   22.04.70

Referee: Rudolf Scheurer (SWI)   Attendance: 27,000

ANDERLECHT: Jean Trappeniers; Georges Heylens, Jean Cornelis (68 Alfons Peeters), Johnny Velkeneers, Julien Kialunda, Gerard Desanghere, Thomas Nordahl; Johan Devrindt, Jan Mulder, Paul Van Himst (Cap), Wilfried Puis. Trainer: Pierre Sinibaldi (Fra)

ARSENAL: Robert Wilson; Peter Storey, Robert McNab, Edward Kelly, Frank McLintock (Cap); Peter Simpson, George Armstrong; Jonathan Sammels, John Radford, Charles George (80 Raymond Kennedy), George Graham. Manager: Bertie Mee

Goals: Devrindt (25), Mulder (30, 77), Kennedy (84)

ARSENAL FC LONDON
v RSC ANDERLECHT 3-0 (1-0)

Highbury, London   28.04.70

Referee: Gerhard Kunze (DDR)   Attendance: 51,612

ARSENAL: Robert Wilson; Peter Storey, Robert McNab, Edward Kelly, Frank McLintock (Cap); Peter Simpson, George Armstrong; Jonathan Sammels, John Radford, Charles George, George Graham.   Manager: Bertie Mee

ANDERLECHT: Jean Trappeniers; Georges Heylens, Maurice Martens, Johnny Velkeneers, Julien Kialunda; Gérard Desanghere, Thomas Nordahl; Johan Devrindt, Jan Mulder, Paul Van Himst (Cap), Wilfried Puis. Trainer: Pierre Sinibaldi

Goals: Kelly (25), Radford (70), Sammels (73)

Goalscorers Fairs Cup 1969/70

10 goals: Paul Van Himst (Anderlecht Brussel)

9 goals: Roberto Boninsegna (Inter Milano)

6 goals: Sjaak Swart (Ajax Amsterdam), Jonathan Sammels (Arsenal London), Jan Mulder (Anderlecht Brussel)

5 goals: Claude Bissot (Charleroi), George Graham, John Radford (Arsenal London), Emeric Dembrovschi (Dinamo Bacău), 4: Tom Turesson (Club Brugge), Ronald Davies (Southampton), José Antonio Zaldúa (FC Barcelona), Helmut Stein (Carl Zeiss), Daniel Ene (Dinamo Bacău), Johan Cruijff, Velibor Vasovic (Ajax Amsterdam), Johan Devrindt, Thomas Nordahl, Wilfried Puis (Anderlecht Brussel), Charles George (Arsenal London)

4 goals: Des Dickson (Coleraine), Ross Mathie (Kilmarnock)

3 goals: Guy Allamann (Jeunesse d'Esch), Rob Rensenbrink (Club Brugge), Michael Channon (Southampton), George McLean (Dunfermline), Vagner, José Maria (Vitória Setúbal), László Fazekas (Újpesti Dózsa), Alun Evans, Robert Graham, Thomas Smith, Peter Thompson (Liverpool), Petre Băluță (Dinamo Bacău), Bryan Robson (Newcastle United), Gerrie Mühren, Ruud Suurendonk, Dick Van Dijk (Ajax Amsterdam)

2 goals: K. Fischer (München 1860), Laudrup (Wiener SK), Grönig (FC Zürich), Vasilev (Lokomotiv Plovdiv), Györffi (Rába ETO Györ), Djordjevic (Partizan Beograd), K. Sjöberg (Skeid Oslo), Lourenço, Nelson (Sporting Lisboa), Lambert (Club Brugge), Mendes (Vitória Guimarães), Murray (Coleraine), Drews (Hansa Rostock), Anastasi, Leonardi (Juventus Torino), Piechniczek, Marx (Ruch Chorzów), Hélder Ernesto (FC Porto), Grigorov (Slavia Sofia), Paine (Southampton), Mitchell, Gardner, Paton (Dunfermline Athletic), Tomé (Vitória Setúbal), Bene, E. Dunai III (Újpesti Dózsa), Pellicer, Martí Filosía, Rexach (FC Barcelona), Rustichelli, Villa (Rouen), Callaghan (Liverpool), P. Ducke, Scheitler (Carl Zeiss), Horr, Steffenhagen (Hertha Berlin), Dyson, Wyn Davies (Newcastle United), Bergholtz (Anderlecht Brussel)

1 goal: Keller (München 1860), Bubanj (NK Zagreb), Dakic (Vojvodina), Henderson (Glentoran), Drost (Twente Enschede), Guzik (Baník Ostrava), Scott (Dundee United), Pribil, Onger, Hörmayer (Wiener SK), Otchily, Wojciak (Bordeaux), Volkert, Künzli (FC Zürich), Heynckes, Skoblar (Hannover 96), Spiropoulos, Dedes (Panionios), Larsson (Malmö FF), Sunde (Rosenborg), Zaballa, José Cristo, Palau (CD Sabadell), Ansola (Valencia CF), Neagu, Marin Stelian (Rapid Bucureşti), Spiridon (Aris Thessaloniki), Szczepaniak, Hausser (Metz), Chapuisat, Dürr (Lausanne), Leif Sørensen (Hvidovre), Wurdinger, K. Leitner (Linzer ASK), Orbán, Varsányi, Korsós, Somogyi (Rába ETO Györ), E.Johansen (Skeid Oslo), Spaute, Boulet, Bertoncello (Charleroi), Gonçalves, Peres (Sporting Lisboa), Carteus (Club Brugge), Pinto, Ademir, Artur, Carlos Manuel (Vitória Guimarães), Marczak, E. Lipinski, Wisniewski (Gwardia), Irwin, Curley, S. Wilson, Jennings (Coleraine), Pankau, Hergesell, Sackritz (Hansa Rostock), Martiradonna, Domenghini, Riva, Gori (Cagliari), Haug, Weidemann, J. Olsson (VfB Stuttgart), Vieri,

Castano (Juventus Torino), Gomoluch, E. Faber, Herman (Ruch Chorzów), Salim, Rolando (FC Porto), Mikhailov, Shalamanov, Kolev (Slavia Sofia), Manservisi, Canzi, Bosdaves, Bianchi, Improta (Napoli), Cook, Gilmour, J. McLean, McGrory, T. McLean, Morrison (Kilmarnock), Gabriel (Southampton), Guereiro (Vitória Setúbal), Renton (Dunfermline), Juhász (Újpesti Dózsa), Fusté (FC Barcelona), Pospíchal (Rouen), Hunt, Lawler, Lindsay (Liverpool), R. Ducke, W. Kraus, Rock, Irmscher (Carl Zeiss), Gayer, Wild, Patzke (Hertha Berlin), Scott (Newcastle United), Bertini, Jair, Suárez, Mazzola, Reif (Inter Milano), Keizer (Ajax Amsterdam), Kennedy, Kelly, Gould (Arsenal), Desanghere, Hanon (Anderlecht)

Own Goals: Reichenberger (München 1860) for Skeid Oslo, Hutmacher (Charleroi) for NK Zagreb, Grima (Floriana) for Dinamo Bacău, Björklund (Malmö FF) for VfB Stuttgart, Ejlersen (B 1913) for Barcelona, Lupescu (Rapid Bucureşti) for Vitória Setúbal, Orbán (Rába ETO) for Barcelona, Strong (Liverpool) for Vitória Setúbal, King (Kilmarnock) for Slavia Sofia, Costeado (Vitória Guimarães) for Southampton

FAIRS CUP 1970-71

FIRST ROUND

AEK ATHINA v FC TWENTE ENSCHEDE 0-1 (0-1)

Karaiskaki, Athina   2.09.70

Referee: Josip Strmecki (Jug)   Attendance: 26,400

AEK: Stelios Konstantinidis, Karapoulitidis, Apostolos Toskas, Triantafillou, Nikos Stathopoulos, Stelios Skevofilax (63 Papaemmanouil), Giorgos Lavaridis, Panagiotis Ventouris, Kostas Nikolaidis, Dimitris Papaioannou, Spiros Pomonis.

TWENTE: Piet Schrijvers; Kees Van Ierssel, Epi Drost, Willem De Vries, Benno Huve, Eddy Achterberg, Kick Van der Vall, Jan Jeuring, Theo Pahlplatz (.. Jan Streuer), Antal Nagy, René van de Kerkhof.   Trainer: Kees Rijvers

Goal: René van de Kerkhof (12)

FC TWENTE ENSCHEDE v AEK ATHINA 3-0 (2-0)

Diekman Stadion, Enschede   8.09.70

Referee: Kenneth Howard Burns (Eng)   Attendance: 16,000

TWENTE: Piet Schrijvers; Kees Van Ierssel, Epi Drost, Willem De Vries, Benno Huve (.. Izzy Ten Donkelaar), Eddy Achterberg, Kick Van der Vall, Antal Nagy, Jan Jeuring, Theo Pahlplatz, René van de Kerkhof (.. Willy van de Kerkhof). Trainer: Kees Rijvers

AEK: Stelios Konstantinidis (31 Stelios Serafeidis), Giorgos Kefalidis, Apostolos Toskas (87 Stefanos Theodoridis), Triantafillou, Nikos Stathopoulos, Stelios Skevofilax, Giorgos Lavaridis, Panagiotis Ventouris, Kostas Nikolaidis, Dimitris Papaioannou, Spiros Pomonis.

Goals: Pahlplatz (37, 50), René van de Kerkhof (43)

ARA LA GANTOISE v HAMBURGER SV 0-1 (0-1)

Jules Ottenstadion, Gent   2.09.70

Referee: Alistair McKenzie (Sco)   Attendance: 10,900

ARA LA GANTOISE: Zdravko Brkljacic; Gilbert De Groote, François Konter, Lucien Ghellynck, Robert Mahieu, Norbert Deviaene, Eric Delmulle, Jef Jurion, Moise Dos Santos, Jean Leonard, Francisco Benedito "Bene" (65 István Sztany).

HAMBURGER SV: Gert Girschkowski; Helmut Sandmann, Jürgen Kurbjuhn, Peter Nogly (46 Gerd Klier), Hans-Werner Kremer, Hans-Jürgen Hellfritz, Franz-Josef Hönig, Klaus Zaczyk, Hans Schulz, Uwe Seeler, Gert Dörfel. Trainer: Klaus-Dieter Ochs

Goal: Nogly (25)

HAMBURGER SV v ARA LA GANTOISE 7-1 (3-0)

Volksparkstadion, Hamburg   15.09.70

Referee: Stefan Eksztajn (Pol)   Attendance: 5,000

HAMBURGER SV: Özcan Arkoc; Helmut Sandmann, Hans-Werner Kremer, Hans-Jürgen Ripp, Heinz Bonn (28 Wolfgang Kampf); Hans Schulz, Klaus Zaczyk, Franz-Josef Hönig (67 Georg Volkert), Gerd Klier, Robert Pötzschke, Gert Dörfel. Trainer: Klaus-Dieter Ochs

ARA LA GANTOISE: Zdravko Brkljacic; Roger Tavernier, François Konter, Lucien Ghellynck, Robert Mahieu, István Sztany, Norbert Deviaene, Jef Jurion, Moise Dos Santos (14 Francisco Benedito "Bene"), Jean Leonard (46 Josef Vacenovski), Eric Delmulle.

Goals: Dörfel (3, 22, 59, 61), Hönig (26), Zaczyk (56 pen), Volkert (83), Bene (89)

ZELJEZNICAR SARAJEVO v RSC ANDERLECHT BRUSSEL 3-4 (1-1)

Kosevo, Sarajevo   2.09.70

Referee: Günter Männig (DDR)   Attendance: 4,600

ZELJEZNICAR: Vasilije Radović; Kadrić, Velija Bećirspahić, Blagoje Bratić, Josip Katalinski; Horvat, Fikret Mujkić, Ivan Osim; Josip Bukal, Edin Sprečo, Bajić (46 Božidar Jankovic).

ANDERLECHT: Jean Trappeniers; George Heylens, Alfons Peeters, Gerard Desanghere, Maurice Martens; André Colasse, Thomas Nordahl; Inge Ejderstedt (46 Gilbert Van Binst), Jan Mulder, Paul Van Himst, Wilfried Puis. Trainer: Pierre Sinibaldi

Goals: Osim (4), Puis (34, 82), Spreco (58), Mujkić (59), Mulder (60), Van Binst (89)

RSC ANDERLECHT BRUSSEL v ZELJEZNICAR SARAJEVO 5-4 (2-3)

Parc Astrid, Brussel   16.09.70

Referee: Thomas Wharton (Sco)   Attendance: 17,000

ANDERLECHT: Jean Trappeniers; Alfons Peeters, Johnny Velkeneers, Gerard Desanghere, Maurice Martens; André Colasse, Thomas Nordahl; Inge Ejderstedt, Jan Mulder, Paul Van Himst, Wilfried Puis.   Trainer: Pierre Sinibaldi

ZELJEZNICAR: Vasilije Radović; Kadrić, Velija Bećirspahić (55 Horvat), Blagoje Bratić, Josip Katalinski; Enver Hadžiabdić, Avdija Deraković; Božidar Janković, Josip Bukal, Edin Sprečo, Fikret Mujkić.

Goals: Ejderstedt (11, 61, 75), Bukal (20, 25), Van Himst (23), Spreco (36, 60), Puis (55)

SEVILLA FC v ESKIŞEHIRSPOR 1-0 (0-0)

Ramón Sánchez Pizjuán, Sevilla   5.09.70

Referee: Jacques Colling (Lux)   Attendance: 20,600

SEVILLA: José Rodríguez Domínguez «RODRI»; AnTONIo Rincón Gómez, Manuel COSTA Sanromán, Juan López HITA; ELOY Matute Urbano, SANTOS Bedoya López; Enrique LORA Millán, Manuel Muñoz Blanco «BLANQUITO», Bernardo ACOSTA Miranda, Juan LEBRÓN Lainez (76 ANTONIO López Martínez), Pedro BERRUEZO Martín. Trainer: Max Merkel

ESKIŞEHIRSPOR: Mümin Özkasap; Abdurrahman Temel, Ismail Arca, Faik Sentasler; Kamuran Yavuz, Süreyya; Dogan Senoglu, Burhan Ipek (76 Mustafa), Fethi Heper, Vahap Özbayar, Ender Konca.   Trainer: Abdulah Gegić (Jug)

Goal: Eloy (61)

ESKIŞEHIRSPOR v SEVILLA FC 3-1 (0-0)

Atatürk, Eskişehir   16.09.70

Referee: Gerhard Kunze (DDR)   Attendance: 10,700

ESKIŞEHIRSPOR: Mümin Özkasap; Ilhan Çolak, Abdurrahman Temel, Kamuran Yavuz, Ismail Arca, Süreyya, Dogan Senoglu, Burhan Ipek, Fethi Heper, Vahap Özbayar, Ender Konca.   Trainer: Abdulah Gegić

SEVILLA: José Rodríguez Domínguez; AnTONIo Rincón Gómez (.. AZUAGA), Juan López HITA, Manuel COSTA Sanromán, Hermínio Rafael TOÑANEZ; SANTOS Bedoya López; Enrique LORA Millán, Manuel Muñoz Blanco «BLANQUITO» (46 ANTONIO López Martínez), Bernardo ACOSTA Miranda, ELOY Matute Urbano, Pedro BERRUEZO Martín.   Trainer: Max Merkel

Goals: Acosta (79), Fethi (80, 82, 92)

COLERAINE FC v KILMARNOCK FC 1-1 (0-0)

The Showgrounds, Coleraine   15.09.70

Referee: Kevin Howley (Eng)   Attendance: 7,000

COLERAINE: Edward Crossan; John McCurdy, David Gordon, Alan Campbell, David Jackson, Ivan Murray, Tony O'Doherty, Sean Dunlop, Samuel Wilson, Des Dickson, Brendan Mullan.

KILMARNOCK: Alistair Hunter; Robin Arthur, William Dickson, John Gilmour, John McGrory, Brian Rodman, Thomas McLean, Edawrd Morrison, Ross Mathie, George Maxwell, James Cook.

Goals: Mathie (56), Mullan (60)

KILMARNOCK FC v COLERAINE FC 2-3 (2-0)

Rugby Park, Kilmarnock   29.09.70

Referee: Thomas H.C. Reynolds (Wal)   Attendance: 5,500

KILMARNOCK: Alistair Hunter; Robin Arthur, William Dickson, John Gilmour (.. Dave Swan), John McGrory, Alan MacDonald, Thomas McLean, George Maxwell, Edward Morrison, James McSherry, Ross Mathie (.. James Cook).

COLERAINE: Edward Crossan; John McCurdy, David Gordon, Anthony Curley, David Jackson, Ivan Murray, Tony O'Doherty, Sean Dunlop, Des Dickson, Brendan Mullan, Brian Jennings (.. Kenny McCandless).

Goals: McLean (16), Morrison (22), Dickson (48, 52, 60)

1.FC KÖLN v CS SEDAN ARDENNES 5-1 (2-0)

Müngersdorferstadion, Köln   15.09.70

Referee: Leonardus W. van der Kroft (Hol)   Att: 10,400

FC KÖLN: Milutin Soskic; Karl-Heinz Thielen, Werner Biskup, Wolfgang Weber, Matthias Hemmersbach; Hans-Josef Kapellmann, Heinz Flohe, Heinz Simmet; Bernd Rupp, Thomas Parits, Johannes Löhr (74 Hans-Jürgen Lex). Trainer: Ernst Ocwirk

RACING: Pierre Tordo; Gerald Zamojski, Maryan, Mohamed Salem, Marc Rastoll; Michel Cardoni, Jacky Le Bihan, Maurice Hardouin; Jean Luc Fugaldi (57 Claude Pierron), Roger Wicke, Serge Dellamore. Tr: Louis Duguauguez

Goals: Parits (26), Thielen (35), Rupp (47, 70), Lex (82), Pierron (69)

CS SEDAN ARDENNES v 1.FC KÖLN 1-0 (0-0)

Stade Émile-Albeau, Sedan   29.09.70

Referee: Karl Göppel (Swi)   Attendance: 5,715

RACING: Pierre Tordo; Jean Luc Fugaldi, Maryan Synakowski, Mohamed Salem, Gérald Zamojski; Michel Cardoni, Jacky Le Bihan; Claude Pierron (85 Marc Rastoll), Roger Wicke (46 Pierre Barre), Maurice Hardouin, Serge Dellamore.   Trainer: Louis Duguauguez

FC KÖLN: Manfred Manglitz; Karl-Heinz Thielen, Werner Biskup, Wolfgang Weber, Heinz Flohe, Manfred Classen, Heinz Simmet; Bernd Rupp, Thomas Parits (46 Wolfgang John), Jürgen Lex, Hans-Josef Kapellmann.   Trainer: Ernst Ocwirk

Goal: Dellamore (87 pen)

SARPSBORG FK v LEEDS UNITED 0-1 (0-0)

Sarpsborg Stadion   15.09.70

Referee: Preben Christophersen (Dan)   Attendance: 8,769

SARPSBORG: Kolbjørn Nilsen; Ingar Løken, Bjørn Woodruff, Sigmund Johansen, Per Anker Holth, Åge Gjerlaugsen, Dag Navestad, Terje Andresen (70 Åge Johansen), Egil Roger Olsen, Knut Spydevold, Kai Kjønnigsen. Trainer: Bjørn Spydevold

UNITED: Gary Sprake; Paul Madeley, Terence Cooper, William Bremner, David Kennedy, Edward Gray, Peter Lorimer, Rodney Belfitt, Michael Jones, Michael Bates, Terence Hibbitt.   Manager: Don Revie

Goal: Lorimer (76)

LEEDS UNITED v SARPSBORG FK 5-0 (1-0)

Elland Road, Leeds   29.09.70

Referee: Mario Gomes Alves (Por)   Attendance: 19,283

UNITED: Gary Sprake; Paul Madeley, Terence Cooper (46 Paul Reaney), William Bremner, Jack Charlton, Norman Hunter, Peter Lorimer, Allan Clarke, Rodney Belfitt, Michael Bates, Edward Gray.   Manager: Don Revie

SARPSBORG: Kolbjørn Nilsen; Ingar Løken, Finn Johansen (.. Per Anker Holth), Bjørn Woodruff, Åge Gjerlaugsen, Sigmund Johansen, Kai Kjønnigsen (.. Arne Melby), Terje Andresen, Egil Roger Olsen, Knut Spydevold, Dag Navestad. Trainer: Bjørn Spydevold

Goals: Charlton (22, 61), Bremner (71, 88), Lorimer (90)

SPARTAK TRNAVA
v OLYMPIQUE MARSEILLE 2-0 (1-0)

Spartak Trnava 15.09.70

Referee: Aurel Bentu (Rom) Attendance: 7,000

SPARTAK: Jozef Púchly; Karol Dobias, Kamil Majerník, Stanislav Jarábek; Vladimír Hagara, Anton Hrusecky; Vojtech Varadín (38 Valentovic), Stanislav Martinkovic, Jaroslav Masrna, Alojz Fandel, Dušan Kabát. Trainer: Valerián Švec

OLYMPIQUE: Jean-Paul Escale; Jean-Pierre Lopez, Jean-Louis Hodoul, Jules Zvunka, Edouard Kula; Jacky Novi, Joseph Bonnel; Roger Magnusson, Didier Couécou, Josip Skoblar, Charly Loubet. Trainer: Mario Zatelli

Goals: Dobias (31 pen), Masrna (48)

OLYMPIQUE MARSEILLE
v SPARTAK TRNAVA 2-0 (1-0) 3-4 on penalties

Vélodrome, Marseille 29.09.70

Referee: H. Marques da Silva (Por) Attendance: 35,367

OLYMPIQUE: Jean-Paul Escale; Jean-Pierre Lopez, Jean-Louis Hodoul, Jules Zvunka, Edouard Kula; Jacky Novi, Joseph Bonnel; Roger Magnusson, Josip Skoblar, Didier Couécou, Charly Loubet. Trainer: Mario Zatelli

SPARTAK: Josef Geryk; Karol Dobias, Kamil Majerník, Stanislav Jarábek (78 Vlastimil Božik), Vladimír Hagara; Ladislav Kuna, Anton Hrusecky; Stanislav Martinkovic, Alojz Fandel, Jaroslav Masrna, Dušan Kabát. Trainer: Valerián Švec

Couécou (97) sent off

Goals: Couécou (13), Skoblar (73)

Penalties: 1-0 Magnusson, 1-1 Kuna, 2-1 Kula, 2-2 Dobiaš, Skoblar, 2-3 Hrušeký, Novi, Fandel, 3-3 Hodoul, 3-4 Kabát

LIVERPOOL FC
v FERENCVÁROS TC BUDAPEST 1-0 (1-0)

Anfield Road, Liverpool 15.09.70

Referee: Roland Marendaz (Swi) Attendance: 37,531

LIVERPOOL: Raymond Clemence; Christopher Lawler, Alec Lindsay, Thomas Smith, Larry Lloyd, Emlyn Hughes, Ian Callaghan, Alun Evans, Robert Graham, John McLaughlin, Peter Thompson. Manager: Bill Shankly

FERENCVÁROS: István Géczi; László Bálint, Miklós Páncsics, Arpád Horváth, István Megyesi; István Juhász, Gyula Rákosi; János Füsi, László Branikovits, Flórián Albert (73 Lajos Kü), József Mucha. Trainer: Jenő Dálnoki

Goal: Graham (17)

FERENCVÁROS TC BUDAPEST
v LIVERPOOL FC 1-1 (0-0)

Népstadion, Budapest 29.09.70

Referee: Walter Horstmann (WG) Attendance: 25,000

FERENCVÁROS: István Géczi; László Bálint, Miklós Páncsics, István Megyesi; István Juhász (88 Tamás Selenka), Arpád Horváth (29 Deszö Novak), István Szőke, Gyula Rákosi; Flórián Albert, József Mucha, Sándor Katona. Trainer: Ferenc Csanádi

LIVERPOOL: Raymond Clemence; Christopher Lawler, Thomas Smith, Larry Lloyd, Alec Lindsay; Brian Hall, John McLaughlin (55 Douglas Livermore), Emlyn Hughes; Alun Evans, Robert Graham, Peter Thompson. Manager: Bill Shankly

Goals: Mucha (47), Hughes (65)

LAUSANNE SPORTS
v VITÓRIA SETÚBAL 0-2 (0-0)

Stade Olympique de la Pontaise, Lausanne 15.09.70

Referee: Robert Wurtz (Fra) Attendance: 4,600

SPORTS: Erich Burgener; Jacky Ducret, Pierre-Albert Chapuisat, Pierre Richard, Jan Lala; Daniel Dufour, Richard Dürr, Anton Weibel, Raffaële Nembrini, Georges Vuilleumier (76 Pierre-André Zappella), Pierre Kerkhoffs.

VITÓRIA: JOAQUIM Manuel Conceição TORRES; Francisco Silva REBELO, Carlos Alberto Lourenço CARDOSO, José Jesus MENDES, Manuel Luis dos Santos "CARRIÇO"; Pedro (68 Carlos BARÃO), JOSÉ MARIA Júnior, VAGNER Canotilho; Felix Marques GUERREIRO, VITOR Manuel Ferreira BAPTISTA (76 Joaquim Leonardo Quinta ARCANJO), JACINTO JOÃO. Trainer: José Maria PEDROTO

Goals: Vitor Baptista (61), João Jacinto (63)

VITÓRIA SETÚBAL
v LAUSANNE SPORTS 2-1 (2-1)

Estádio do Bonfim, Setúbal 30.09.70

Referee: Antonio Sánchez Rios (Spa) Attendance: 8,300

VITÓRIA: JOAQUIM Manuel Conceição TORRES; Francisco Silva REBELO, Carlos Alberto Lourenço CARDOSO, José Jesus MENDES, Manuel Luis dos Santos "CARRIÇO", Pedro, JOSÉ MARIA Júnior, VAGNER Canotilho, Felix Marques GUERREIRO, Joaquim Leonardo Quinta ARCANJO, JACINTO JOÃO. Trainer: José Maria PEDROTO

SPORTS: Erich Burgener; Jacky Ducret, Pierre Richard, Pierre-Albert Chapuisat, Jan Lala, Anton Weibel (46 Yvan Cuenoud), Daniel Dufour, Richard Dürr, Raffaële Nembrini, Georges Vuilleumier (47 Franco Cucinotta), Pierre Kerkhoffs.

Goals: José Maria (21), Dufour (40), V. Baptista (45)

DUNDEE UNITED
v GRASSHOPPER-CLUB ZÜRICH 3-2 (0-1)

Tannadice Park, Dundee   15.09.70

Referee: Curt Nystrand (Swe)   Attendance: 8,400

UNITED: Donald Mackay; Andy Rolland, Jim Cameron, Stuart Markland, Douglas Smith, James Henry, Thomas Traynor, Alexander Reid, Ian Reid, Alan Gordon (.. Dennis Gillespie), David Wilson.

GRASSHOPPER: René Deck; Hansruedi Staudenmann, Bernard Mocellin, Roland Citherlet, Kurt Rüegg, Fredy Gröbli, Peter Meier, André Meyer, Rainer Ohlhauser, Ove Grahn, Rudolf Schneeberger.

Goals: Grahn (35), Meier (50), I. Reid (65), Markland (81), A. Reid (90)

GRASSHOPPER-CLUB ZÜRICH
v DUNDEE UNITED 0-0

Hardturm, Zürich   30.09.70

Referee: Franz Geluck (Bel)   Attendance: 4,500

GRASSHOPPER: René Deck; Hansruedi Staudenmann, Bernard Mocellin, Roland Citherlet, Kurt Rüegg, Fredy Gröbli (63 Adolf Noventa), Peter Meier, André Meyer, Rainer Ohlhauser, Ove Grahn, Rudolf Schneeberger.

UNITED: Donald Mackay; Andy Rolland, Jim Cameron, Stuart Markland, Douglas Smith, James Henry, David Wilson, Alexander Reid, Alan Gordon, Morris Stevenson, Thomas Traynor.

LAZIO ROMA v ARSENAL LONDON 2-2 (0-0)

Stadio Olimpico, Roma   16.09.70

Referee: Gerhard Schulenburg (WG)   Attendance: 31,000

LAZIO: Michelangelo Sulfaro; Franco Nanni, Mario Facco, Nello Governato (77 Giuliano Fortunato), Giuseppe Papadopulo, Giuseppe Wilson, Pierpaolo Manservisi (54 Giancarlo Morrone), Ferruccio Mazzola, Giorgio Chinaglia, Giuseppe Massa, Arrigo Dolso.   Trainer: Juan Carlos Lorenzo

ARSENAL: Bob Wilson; Patrick Rice, Robert McNab, Edward Kelly, Frank McLintock, John Roberts, George Armstrong, Peter Storey, John Radford, Raymond Kennedy, George Graham.   Manager: Bertie Mee

Goals: Radford (52, 56), Chinaglia (85, 89 pen)

ARSENAL LONDON v LAZIO ROMA 2-0 (1-0)

Highbury, London   23.09.70

Referee: Rudolf Glöckner (DDR)   Attendance: 53,013

ARSENAL: Bob Wilson; Patrick Rice, Robert McNab, Edward Kelly, Frank McLintock, John Roberts, George Armstrong, Peter Storey, John Radford, Raymond Kennedy, George Graham (84 Samuel Nelson).   Manager: Bertie Mee

LAZIO: Michelangelo Sulfaro; Giuseppe Wilson, Mario Facco, Nello Governato, Luigi Polentes, Franco Nanni (31 Gaetano Legnaro), Giuseppe Massa, Ferruccio Mazzola, Giorgio Chinaglia, Pierpaolo Manservisi, Giuliano Fortunato (46 Giancarlo Morrone).   Trainer: Juan Carlos Lorenzo

Goals: Radford (11), Armstrong (73)

GKS KATOWICE v CF BARCELONA 0-1 (0-0)

Stadion Śląski, Chrozów   16.09.70

Referee: Karl Riegg (WG)   Attendance: 85,000

GKS: Franciszek Sput; Eryk Anczok, Stanisław Zuzok, Jerzy Geszlecht, Alojzy Lysko, Wiesław Migdal (.. Norbert Wowra), Jacek Góralczyk, Jan Glük (.. Andrzej Strzelczyk), Lechosław Olsza, Eugeniusz Pluta, Gerard Rother.   Trainer: Marcel Strezykalski

CF BARCELONA: Salvador SADURNÍ Urpi; Joaquín RIFÉ Climent, Francisco Fernández Rodríguez "GALLEGO", ELADIO Silvestre Graells, Antonio TORRES García, Pedro María ZABALZA Inda, Carlos REXACH Cerdá, JUAN CARLOS Pérez López, Narciso MARTÍ FILOSÍA, José María FUSTÉ Blanch, Luis PUJOL Codina.   Trainer: Victor Frederik Bucingham

Goal: Rexach (82)

CF BARCELONA v GKS KATOWICE 3-2 (0-2)

Camp Nou, Barcelona   23.09.70

Referee: René Vigliani (Fra)   Attendance: 70,000

CF BARCELONA: Salvador SADURNÍ Urpi; Joaquín RIFÉ Climent, Francisco Fernández Rodríguez «GALLEGO», ELADIO Silvestre Graells, Antonio TORRES García, Pedro María ZABALZA Inda, Carlos REXACH Cerdá, JUAN CARLOS Pérez López, Narciso MARTÍ FILOSÍA, José María FUSTÉ Blanch (46 MARCIAL Pina Morales), Luis PUJOL Codina.   Trainer: Victor Frederik Bucingham

GKS: Franciszek Sput; Lechosław Olsza, Stanisław Zuzok, Jerzy Geszlecht (63 Eryk Anczok), Alojzy Lysko (72 Wiesław Migdal), Jerzy Nowok, Jan Glük, Andrzej Strzelczyk, Jacek Góralczyk, Eugeniusz Pluta, Gerard Rother.   Trainer: Marcel Strezykalski

Goals: Rother (8), Nowok (41 pen), Pujol (51), M. Filosia (60), Rexach (84)

CORK HIBERNIANS v VALENCIA CF 0-3 (0-2)

Flower Lodge, Cork   16.09.70

Referee: Alfred Delcourt (Bel)   Attendance: 10,500

HIBERNIANS: Joe O'Grady; David Bacuzzi, Noel O'Mahony, Frank Connolly, John Herrick, John Lawson, Sonny Sweeney (46 Matthew Donovan), Jeremiah Dennehy, David Wigginton, Brendan Draper, Gus Eadie (46 Terry Young).
Trainer: David Bacuzzi (Eng)

VALENCIA: Ángel ABELARDO González; Juan Cruz SOL Oria, ANÍBAL Pérez Miers, Antonio Martínez Morales "ANTÓN" (77 Francisco VIDAGAŇY Hernández), Jesús MARTÍNEZ Rivadeneyra, Francisco García Gómez "PAQUITO", José CLARAMUNT I Torres, Manuel POLInario Muñoz, Fernando ANSOLA Sanmartín (66 Fernando BARRACHINA Plo), Carlos PELLICER Vázquez, SERGIO Manzanera Lloret.   Trainer: Alfredo DI STÉFANO Lahule

Goals: Claramunt I (13, 22), Barrachina (75)

VALENCIA CF v CORK HIBERNIANS 3-1 (2-1)

Campo de Mestalla, Valencia   29.09.70

Referee: David W. Smith (Eng)   Attendance: 12,000

VALENCIA: José PESUDO Soler; Juan Cruz SOL Oria, Francisco VIDAGAŇY, Fernando BARRACHINA Plo (46 José Antonio García Conesa "TATONO"), ANÍBAL Pérez Miers, Francisco García Gómez "PAQUITO", José CLARAMUNT I Torres, Manuel POLInario Muñoz (46 Fernando ANSOLA Sanmartín), José Vicente FORMENT Fáez, Vicente Anastasio JARA Segovia, SERGIO Manzanera Lloret.
Trainer: Alfredo DI STÉFANO Lahule

HIBERNIANS: Joe O'Grady; David Bacuzzi, Noel O'Mahony, Frank Connolly, John Herrick, John Lawson, Matthew Donovan (61 Sonny Sweeney), Jeremiah Dennehy (70 Gus Eadie), David Wigginton, Carl Davenport, John Lambie.
Trainer: David Bacuzzi (Eng)

Goals: Jara (12), Sergio (19, 46), Wigginton (40)

AKADEMISK KØBENHAVN v SLIEMA WANDERERS 7-0 (2-0)

København   16.09.70

Referee: Sven Jonsson (Swe)   Attendance: 1,960

AB: Poul Werner Henriksen; Jan Larsen, Søren Jessen, Niels Yde, Erik Sandvad; Flemming Hansen, K.Knudsen; Ove Carlsen, A.Hansen, Henrik Bernburg, Benny Nielsen, Andersen (.. Johnny Petersen).

SLIEMA: Michael Sultana, Charles Spiteri, Joseph Aquilina, Lawrence Borg, Emanuel Micallef (.. Joe Serge), Edward Darmanin, Ronald Cocks, Carmel Camenzuli (.. Peter Langridge), John Bonnett, Jimmy Briffa, Franz Falzon.

Goals: F. Hansen (..,..), Carlsen (..,..), Nielsen (..), Petersen (..), Joseph Sultana (.. og)

SLIEMA WANDERERS v AKADEMISK KØBENHAVN 2-3 (1-2)

Valletta   29.09.70

Referee: Fulvio Pieroni (Ita)   Attendance: 5,000

SLIEMA: Alfred Vella (.. Albert Pearson), Charles Spiteri, Emanuel Micallef, Edward Darmanin, Joseph Aquilina, Lawrence Borg, Peter Langridge, Ronald Cocks, Joseph Cini, John Bonnett, Carmel Camenzuli.

AB: Poul Werner Henriksen; Jan Larsen, Søren Jessen, Flemming Hansen, Niels Yde, Erik Sandvad, Johnny Petersen, Ove Carlsen, Benny Nielsen, Aage Hansen, Andersen.

Goals: B. Nielsen (.., ..), A. Hansen (..), Joseph Cini (..), Jessen (.. og)

PARTIZAN BEOGRAD v DYNAMO DRESDEN 0-0

JNA, Beograd   16.09.70

Referee: Franz Wöhrer (Aus)   Attendance: 9,600

PARTIZAN: Ivan Curković; Miloš Radaković, Milan Damjanović (46 Milan Petrović), Nadoveza, Blagoje Paunović, Nikola Budisić, Miodrag Živaljević (60 Ilija Katić), Borivoje Djordjević, Momčilo Vukotić, Djordjić, Nenad Bjeković.

DYNAMO: Manfred Kallenbach; Frank Ganzera, Joachim Kern, Klaus Sammer, Wolfgang Haustein, Meinhard Hemp, Uwe Ziegler, Hans-Jürgen Kreische, Gerd Heidler, Frank Richter (78 Eduard Geyer), Rainer Sachse (60 Dieter Riedel).   Trainer: Walter Fritzsch

DYNAMO DRESDEN v PARTIZAN BEOGRAD 6-0 (4-0)

Rudolf Harbig Stadion, Dresden   30.09.70

Referee: Robert Holley Davidson (Sco)   Attendance: 30,500

DYNAMO: Manfred Kallenbach; Frank Ganzera, Joachim Kern, Klaus Sammer, Wolfgang Haustein, Uwe Ziegler, Meinhard Hemp, Hans-Jürgen Kreische, Gerd Heidler (62 Dieter Riedel), Frank Richter (25 Eduard Geyer), Rainer Sachse.   Trainer: Walter Fritzsch

PARTIZAN: Ivan Curković; Miloš Radaković, Vladimir Pejović, Nadoveza, Blagoje Paunović, Nikola Budisić, Milan Petrović (46 Djuro Marić), Djordjić, Ilija Katić, Momčilo Vukotić, Nenad Bjeković (46 Miodrag Živaljević).

Goals: Kreische (16, 37 pen, 43 pen, 71 pen), K. Sammer (25), Sachse (85)

BAYERN MÜNCHEN
v GLASGOW RANGERS 1-0 (1-0)

Grünwalderstadion, München   16.09.70

Referee: Arie van Gemert (Hol)   Attendance: 23,000

BAYERN: Josef Maier; Herward Koppenhöfer, Peter Pumm, Johnny Hansen, Franz Beckenbauer; Paul Breitner (65 Uli Hoeness), Franz Roth, Rainer Zobel; Gerd Müller, Karl-Heinz Mrosko, Dieter Brenninger.   Trainer: Udo Lattek

RANGERS: Peter McCloy; William Jardine, Alex Miller, John Greig, Ronald McKinnon; Colin Jackson, Graham Fyfe, Alfred Conn; Colin Stein (55 William Henderson), Alex MacDonald, William Johnston.

Goal: Beckenbauer (21)

GLASGOW RANGERS
v BAYERN MÜNCHEN 1-1 (0-0)

Ibrox, Glasgow   30.09.70

Referee: Pius Kamber (Swi)   Attendance: 70,000

RANGERS: Peter McCloy; William Jardine, Alex Miller, John Greig, Ronald McKinnon, Colin Jackson (60 Derek Johnstone); Graham Fyfe (46 William Henderson), Alfred Conn, Colin Stein, Alex MacDonald, William Johnston.

BAYERN: Josef Maier; Johnny Hansen, Peter Pumm (76 Peter Kupferschmidt), Georg Schwarzenbeck, Franz Beckenbauer, Rainer Zobel, Herward Koppenhöfer, Franz Roth (30 Paul Breitner), Gerd Müller, Karl-Heinz Mrosko, Dieter Brenninger.   Trainer: Udo Lattek

Goals: Müller (80), Stein (81)

SPARTA PRAHA v ATHLETIC BILBAO 2-0 (1-0)

Stadión na Letnej, Praha   16.09.70

Referee: Giorgos Gianopoulos (Gre)   Attendance: 16,400

SPARTA: Antonín Kramerius; Pavel Melichar, Václav Migas, Oldřich Urban; Tibor Semendák, František Chovanec; Bohumil Veselý, Petr Uličný, František Gögh, Josef Jurkanin, Václav Vrána.   Trainer: Karel Kolsky

ATHLETIC: José Ángel IRÍBAR Cortajarena; José Ignacio SÁEZ Ruiz, Luis María ECHEBERRÍA Igartua, Jesús ARANGUREN Merino, José María IGARTUA Mendizábal, José Ramón Martínez LARRAURI, Félix ZUBIAGA Acha, Fidel URIARTE Macho, Antonio María ARIETA Araunabeña Piedra (75 CARLOS Ruiz Herrero), José Ramón BETZUÉN Urquiaza, José Francisco ROJO Arroitia.   Trainer: Ronnie Allen

Goals: Migas (19 pen), Gögh (61)

ATHLETIC BILBAO v SPARTA PRAHA 1-1 (0-0)

Estadio San Mamés, Bilbao   30.09.70

Referee: Clive Thomas (Wal)   Attendance: 29,300

ATHLETIC: José Ángel IRÍBAR Cortajarena; José Ignacio SÁEZ Ruiz, Jesús ARANGUREN Merino, José María IGARTUA Mendizábal, Luis María ECHEBERRÍA Igartua (73 José Ramón BETZUÉN Urquiaza, José Ramón Martínez LARRAURI, Antonio María ARIETA Araunabeña Piedra, Félix ZUBIAGA Acha (58 José María ARGOITIA Acha), CARLOS Ruiz Herrero, Fidel URIARTE Macho, José Francisco ROJO Arroitia.   Trainer: Ronnie Allen

SPARTA: Antonín Kramerius; Pavel Melichar, Václav Migas, Oldřich Urban, Václav Vrána; František Chovanec, Josef Jurkanin, Václav Mašek; Bohumil Veselý, Petr Uličný, Jaroslav Barton.   Trainer: Karel Kolsky

Goals: Chovanec (53), Uriarte (65 pen)

WIENER SK v SK BEVEREN-WAAS 0-2 (0-0)

Sportclub-Platz, Wien   16.09.70

Referee: Gusztáv Bircsak (Hun)   Attendance: 1,200

WIENER SK: Wilhelm Kaipel; Peter Clement, Johann Schmidradner, Kovacic, Haider; Herbert Onger, Anton Herzog, Norbert Hof (46 Helmut Wallner); Bauer, Alfred Hala (46 Hafner), Johann Hörmayer.

BEVEREN: Luksa Poplekovic; Maurice Renier, Freddy Buyl, Paul Van Genechten, André Vanderlinden, Jaak Roelandt, Raymond Goossens, Robert Vande Sompel, Robert Rogiers, Hugo De Raeymaecker, Jean Janssens.
Trainer: Edward Volckaert

Goals: Rogiers (58), Janssens (74)

SK BEVEREN-WAAS v WIENER SK 3-0 (1-0)

Stade de Klapperstraat, Beveren   30.09.70

Referee: Norbert Rolles (Lux)   Attendance: 5,300

BEVEREN: Luksa Poplekovic, Maurice Renier, Freddy Buyl (75 William Verdonck), Paul Van Genechten, André Vanderlinden, Robert Vande Sompel, Richard Verelst, Raymond Goossens, Robert Rogiers, Hugo De Raeymaecker, Jean Janssens (72 Freddy Van Gremberghe).
Trainer: Edward Volckaert

WIENER SK: Wilhelm Kaipel; Peter Clement, Johann Schmidradner, Kovacic, Haider; Herbert Onger (.. Hafner), Anton Herzog, Norbert Hof; Alfred Hala, Helmut Wallner (.. Karl Bauer), Eric Barber.

Goals: Rogiers (41 pen), Van der Linden (54), Janssens (70)

FC ILVES TAMPERE v SK STURM GRAZ 4-2 (2-1)

Ratina, Tampere   16.09.70

Referee: Marian Kuston (Pol)   Attendance: 300

ILVES: Harri Holli; Jussi Ristimäki, Aarno Rinne, Matti Laine, Simo Lehtonen; Jan-Erik Lundberg, Markku Wacklin, Veikko Hovivuori, Matti Mäkelä, Kalevi Nupponen, Semi Nuoranen.

STURM: Fritz Benko; Franz Reiter, Heinz Schilcher, Walter Fuchs, Heinz Russ; Helmut Wagner, Loske; Dietrich Albrecht, Alfred Murlasits, Robert Kaiser, Heinz Zamut (.. Erwin Solleder).   Trainer: János Szep

Goals: Rinne (2 og), Lundberg (3), Nuoranen (40, 47), Nupponen (53), Kaiser (54)

SK STURM GRAZ v FC ILVES TAMPERE 3-0 (2-0)

Bundesstadion Liebenau, Graz   30.09.70

Referee: Gocho Rusev (Bul)   Attendance: 5,600

STURM: Fritz Benko; Erwin Solleder, Heinz Schilcher, Walter Fuchs, Heinz Russ; Helmut Wagner, Helmut Huberts; Dietrich Albrecht, Alfred Murlasits, Robert Kaiser, Heinz Zamut. Trainer: János Szep

ILVES: Harri Holli; Jussi Ristimäki, Matti Laine, Kari Korpelainen, Simo Lehtonen, Jan-Erik Lundberg, Markku Wacklin, Veikko Hovivuori, Matti Mäkelä, Kalevi Nupponen, Semi Nuoranen.

Goals: Murlasits (13), Albrecht (32), Kaiser (49)

BARREIRENSE v DINAMO ZAGREB 2-0 (1-0)

Barreiro   16.09.70

Referee: Georges Uhlen (Fra)   Attendance: 4,700

BARREIRENSE: Manuel Galrinho BENTO, Francisco CANDEIAS Cardoso (80 Luis Manuel MIRA), João Luís Pinto ALMEIDA, Antonio Alfredo Costa BANDEIRA, Antonio Tavares SERRA Santos, JOÃO CARLOS Conceição, VALTER Manuel Pereira Costa (57 Joaquim Manuel Rodrigues Silva Marques NELINHO), JOSE JOÃO Fernandes, JOSÉ CARLOS Gonçalves Silva, Henrique Raul CÂMPORA Carmu, Manuel SERAFIM Monteiro Pereira.   Trainer: Edsel Fernandes (Bra)

DINAMO: Fahrija Dautbegović; Zlatko Mesić, Mladen Ramljak, Filip Blašković, Branko Gračanin, Denijal Pirić, Drago Vabec, Josip Lalić (46 Terecrić), Rozić (63 Ivica Miljković), Josip Gucmirtl, Krasnodar Rora.

Goals: Serafim (30), Câmpora (89)

DINAMO ZAGREB v BARREIRENSE 6-1 (0-1)

Maksimir, Zagreb   30.09.70

Referee: Helmut Bader (DDR)   Attendance: 9,300

DINAMO: Fahrija Dautbegović; Zlatko Mesić, Mladen Ramljak, Filip Blašković, Branko Gračanin; Josip Lalić, Denijal Pirić; Drago Vabec, Josip Gucmirtl, Marijan Novak, Krasnodar Rora.

BARREIRENSE: Manuel Galrinho BENTO; Antonio Tavares SERRA Santos, João Luís Pinto ALMEIDA, Antonio Alfredo Costa BANDEIRA, José Manuel Copas MURRAÇAS; JOÃO CARLOS Conceição, Joaquim Manuel Rodrigues Silva Marques NÉLINHO; JOSÉ CARLOS Gonçalves Silva, JOSÉ JOÃO Fernandes (75 ROGÉRIO Gonçalves Delgadinho), Manuel SERAFIM Monteiro Pereira (72 VALTER Manuel Pereira Costa), Henrique Raul CÂMPORA Carmu. Trainer: Edsel Fernandes

Goals: Câmpora (38), Novak (50, 55, 70, 84), Lalić (72, 75)

B 1901 NYKÖBING
v HERTHA BSC BERLIN 2-4 (1-2)

Nyköbing   16.09.70

Referee: Kjell Wahlen (Nor)   Attendance: 8,000

B 1901: Henriksen; K.Larsen, Jørn Nielsen, Erik Nielsen, Henryk Andersen; Niels Boesen, Morten Olsen; Niels Erik Rasmussen (46 Frimann), Gotfred Fredriksen, Hans Eward Hansen, John Rasmussen (46 Paul Hansen).

HERTHA: Volkmar Gross (75 Michael Kellner); Bernd Patzke, Uwe Witt, Jürgen Rumor, Karl-Heinz Ferschl; László Gergely, Jürgen Weber; Hans-Jürgen Sperlich, Franz Brungs, Lorenz Horr (46 Wolfgang Gayer), Arno Steffenhagen. Trainer: Helmut Kronsbein

Goals: Brungs (19, 28), Olsen (25), Gayer (68), Steffenhagen (70), Hans E. Hansen (78)

HERTHA BSC BERLIN
v B 1901 NYKÖBING 4-1 (1-1)

Olympiastadion, Berlin   30.09.70

Referee: Georg Krutelev (Fin)   Attendance: 2,135

HERTHA: Michael Kellner; Jürgen Rumor, Uwe Witt, Tasso Wild, Karl-Heinz Ferschl; László Gergely, Wolfgang Gayer, Arno Steffenhagen, Lorenz Horr (46 Franz Brungs), Jürgen Weber, Norbert Janzon.   Trainer: Helmut Kronsbein

B 1901: Henriksen; K.Larsen, Erik Nielsen, Henryk Andersen, Jørn Nielsen, Niels Erik Rasmussen, Niels Boesen, Madsen (60 John Rasmussen), Gotfred Fredriksen, Hans Eward Hansen, Frimann (74 Torben Rasmussen).

Goals: Horr (9), N. Rasmussen (31), Brungs (55, 82), Gergely (87)

HIBERNIAN EDINBURGH v MALMÖ FF 6-0 (2-0)

Easter Road, Edinburgh   16.09.70

Referee: Pablo Augusto Sánchez Ibáñez (Spa)   Att: 11,165

HIBERNIAN: Gordon Marshall; Christopher Shevlane, Eric Schaedler, Patrick Stanton, Jim Black, John Hamilton, Arthur Duncan, Jim Blair, Joseph McBride, William McEwan, Alexander Cropley.   Manager: Dave Ewing

MALMÖ FF: Nils Hult; Roland Andersson, Christer Jakobsson, Staffan Tapper, Krister Kristensson, Roy Andersson, Björn Friberg, Curt Olsberg, Tommy Andersson, Bo Larsson, Ingvar Svahn.

Goals: Blair (31), McBride (33, 57, 59), A. Duncan (62, 75)

MALMÖ FF v HIBERNIAN EDINBURGH 2-3 (0-1)

Malmö stadion   30.09.70

Referee: Koen Brouwer (Hol)   Attendance: 1,900

MALMÖ FF: Nils Hult; Christer Jakobsson, Staffan Tapper, Ulf Kleander, Gert Sigfridsson, Roland Rasmussen, Lars Granström, Curt Olsberg, Tommy Andersson, Bo Larsson, Harry Jönsson.

HIBERNIAN: Gordon Marshall; Robert Duncan, Eric Schaedler, John Brownlie, Patrick Stanton, William McEwan, Kenny Davidson, Mervyn Jones, Joseph McBride (.. John Graham), Jim Blair (.. John Hamilton), Arthur Duncan. Manager: Dave Ewing

Goals: Larsson (23), B. Duncan (46), McEwan (77), Jönsson (79), Stanton (85)

VITÓRIA GUIMARÃES v AS ANGOULÊME 3-0 (0-0)

Estádio Municipal, Guimarães   16.09.70

Referee: Ettore Carminati (Ita)   Attendance: 5,500

VITÓRIA: João Ferreira GOMES; ARTUR da Rocha, José Fernando Silva "COSTEADO", JOAQUIM António JORGE, Manuel Joaquim Pereira da SILVA, BERNARDO Oliveira DA VELHA, António Francisco Jesús Moreira "PERES", Firminio Sardinha "OSVALDINHO" (72 AUGUSTO Martins), José Marques Silva "ZEZINHO", ADEMIR Melo Silva, António Silva MENDES.   Trainer: Jorge Vieira (Bra)

AS ANGOULÊME: Pavel Kouba; Henri Ansaldo, Daniel Solas, Robert Peri, Jean-Marie Gester, Gilbert Le Chenadec, Jean-Louis Leonetti, Jean Gallice, Jean Deloffre, Gérard Grizzetti, Frantz Edom.   Trainer: Claude Hugues

Goals: Bernardo da Velha (46, 82), Peres (55)

AS ANGOULÊME v VITÓRIA GUIMARÃES 3-1 (2-0)

Stade Camille Lebon, Angoulême   30.09.70

Referee: John Carpenter (Irl)   Attendance: 6,300

AS ANGOULÊME: Pavel Kouba; Henri Ansaldo, Jacques Glycinski, Robert Peri, Jean-Marie Gester; Jean-Louis Leonetti, Daniel Solas; Chriastian Castellan, Gérard Grizzetti, Jean Gallice, Frantz Edom.   Trainer: Claude Hugues

VITÓRIA: João Ferreira GOMES; ARTUR da Rocha, José Fernando Silva "COSTEADO", JOAQUIM António JORGE, Manuel Joaquim Pereira da SILVA; BERNARDO Oliveira DA VELHA, António Francisco Jesús Moreira "PERES"; José Marques Silva "ZEZINHO", ADEMIR Melo Silva (61 AUGUSTO Martins), António Silva MENDES, Firminio Sardinha "OSVALDINHO".   Trainer: Jorge Vieira (Bra)

Artur Rocha sent off (61)

Goals: Castellan (25, 39), Ademir (51), Gallice (67)

RUCH CHORZOW v FIORENTINA FIRENZE 1-1 (0-0)

Slaski, Chorzow   16.09.70

Referee: Josef Bucek (Aus)   Attendance: 85,000

RUCH: Piotr Czaja; Jan Rudnow, Antoni Nieroba, Bernard Bem, Jerzy Wyrobek, Zygmunt Maszczyk, Józef Gomoluch, Joachim Marx, Bronislaw Bula, Edward Herman, Eugeniusz Faber.

FIORENTINA: Francesco Superchi; Paolo Stanzial, Mario Bozzi, Salvatore Esposito, Ugo Ferrante, Giuseppe Brizi, Giorgio Mariani, Claudio Merlo, Giampietro Vitali, Giancarlo De Sisti, Luciano Chiarugi.   Trainer: Bruno Pesaola

Goals: Faber (46), Vitali (53)

FIORENTINA FIRENZE v RUCH CHORZOW 2-0 (1-0)

Stadio Comunale, Firenze   30.09.70

Referee: Petar Kostovski (Jug)   Attendance: 25,000

FIORENTINA: Francesco Superchi; Paolo Stanzial, Mario Bozzi, Salvatore Esposito, Ugo Ferrante, Giuseppe Brizi, Giorgio Mariani, Claudio Merlo, Giampietro Vitali, Giancarlo De Sisti, Luciano Chiarugi.   Trainer: Bruno Pesaola

RUCH: Piotr Czaja; Antoni Piechniczek, Antoni Nieroba, Bernard Bem (80 Eugeniusz Nagiel), Jerzy Wyrobek, Zygmunt Maszczyk, Józef Gomoluch, Joachim Marx, Bronislaw Bula, Edward Herman, Eugeniusz Faber.

Goals: Chiarugi (42), Mariani (47)

JUVENTUS TORINO
v UNION SPORTIVE RÜMELANGE 7-0 (5-0)

Stadio Comunale, Torino   16.09.70

Referee: Karl Göppel (Swi)   Attendance: 10,700

JUVENTUS: Massimo Piloni; Luciano Spinosi, Sandro Salvadore (46 Gianluigi Roveta), Giuseppe Furino, Francesco Morini (70 Franco Causio), Giuseppe Zaniboni, Helmut Haller, Antonello Cuccureddu, Pietro Anastasi, Gianluigi Savoldi, Roberto Bettega.   Trainer: Armando Picchi

US RÜMELANGE: Nico Halsdorf, Kieffer, Eisenbarth, Rongoni, Marius Pawlowski, Marcel Bertoldo, René Cardoni, Minelli (50 Kerschen), Norbert Leszczynski, Furio Cardoni, Gérard Mordenti.

Goals: Pablowsky (9 og), Bettega (15,74), Anastasi (19, 27, 43, 70)

UNION SPORTIVE RÜMELANGE
v JUVENTUS TORINO 0-4 (0-3)

Stade Municipal, Rümelange   30.09.70

Referee: Robert Wurtz (Fra)   Attendance: 2,000

US RÜMELANGE: Nico Halsdorf, Eisenbarth, Kieffer, Jean Schlutter (46 Rongoni), Marius Pawlowski, Marcel Bertoldo, René Cardoni (65 Roger Philippi), Kerschen, Norbert Leszczynski, Furio Cardoni, Jankovic.

JUVENTUS: Roberto Tancredi; Luciano Spinosi, Giampietro Marchetti, Antonello Cuccureddu (46 Gianluigi Savoldi), Gianluigi Roveta, Giuseppe Zaniboni, Adriano Novellini, Franco Causio, Fausto Landini, Fabio Capello, Roberto Bettega (46 Roberto Montorsi).   Trainer: Armando Picchi

Goals: Novellini (30, 44, 87), Landini (37)

TRAKIA PLOVDIV v COVENTRY CITY 1-4 (0-2)

9 Septemvri, Plovdiv   16.09.70

Referee: Joseph M. Cassar Naudi (Mal)   Attendance: 10,400

TRAKIA: Mihail Karushkov (46 Dragan Radenkov); Vangel Delev, Ivan Gluhchev, Viden Apostolov, Ivan Zaduma, Christofor Marinov, Georgi Popov, Dinko Dermendjiev, Georgi Ubinov, Bogomir Stanoev, Petar Radkov.
Trainer: Vasil Spasov

COVENTRY: William Glazier; Mick Coop, Wilfred Smith, Ernest Machin, Jeffrey Blockley, Geoffrey Strong, Roger Hunt, William Carr, Neil Martin, John O'Rourke, David Clements.
Manager: Noel Cantwell

Goals: O'Rourke (39, 67, 89), Martin (43), Radkov (75)

COVENTRY CITY v TRAKIA PLOVDIV 2-0 (2-0)

Highfield Road, Coventry   30.09.70

Referee: Francis Rion (Bel)   Attendance: 20,771

COVENTRY: William Glazier; Mick Coop, Dietmar Bruck, David Clements, Jeffrey Blockley, Geoffrey Strong, Roger Hunt, William Carr, Brian Joicey (53 Bill Rafferty), John O'Rourke, Brian Alderson.   Manager: Noel Cantwell

TRAKIA: Dragan Radenkov (23 Mihail Karushkov); Vangel Delev, Ivan Gluhchev, Viden Apostolov, Christofor Marinov, Ivan Zaduma, Georgi Popov, Dinko Dermendjiev, Dobrin Nenov, Bogomir Stanoev, Georgi Ubinov.

Goals: Joicey (30), Blockley (35)

UNIVERSITATEA CRAIOVA
v PÉCSI DÓZSA 2-1 (0-0)

Central, Craiova   16.09.70

Referees: Efstathios Papavasiliou, E. Pagurtzis, Emmanouil Platopoulos (Gre)   Attendance: 15,000

UNIVERSITATEA: Teodor Pilcă; Victor Niculescu, Petre Deselnicu, Constantin Mincă, Ion Velea; Lucian Strîmbeanu, Nicolae Ivan; Ion Niţă (46 Florea Martinovici), Decebal Neagu, Ion Oblemenco, Teodor Ţarălungă.   Trainer: Ştefan Coidum

PÉCSI DÓZSA: István Kollár; Ferenc Hernádi, László Maurer, János Konrád, Viktor Kincses; István Kocsis, József Tóth (66 István Rónai); Ferenc Bérczesi, László Daka, János Máté, Lajos Rádi.   Trainer: Mihály Czibulka

Goals: Máté (67), Ţarălungă (68), Strîmbeanu (80)

PÉCSI DÓZSA
v UNIVERSITATEA CRAIOVA 3-0 (3-0)

PVSK, Pécs   30.09.70

Referees: Walter Fercher; Georg Höck, Johan Artner (Aus)   Attendance: 18,000

PÉCSI DÓZSA: Imre Rapp; Ferenc Hernádi, László Maurer, János Konrád, Viktor Kincses; István Kocsis, József Tóth, Ferenc Bérczesi, Csaba Tüske, János Máté, János Dunai.   Trainer: Mihály Czibulka

UNIVERSITATEA: Teodor Pilcă; Victor Niculescu, Petre Deselnicu, Constantin Mincă, Constantin Bîtlan; Lucian Strîmbeanu, Nicolae Ivan; Florea Martinovici, Iulian Bălan, Ion Oblemenco (70 Ion Niţă), Teodor Ţarălungă.

Goals: Kocsis (16, 25), Máté (22)

DINAMO BUCUREŞTI v P.A.O.K. THESSALONIKI 5-0 (1-0)

Dinamo Bucureşti   16.09.70

Referees: Sándor Petri; József Katona, Zoltán Scaban (Hun)   Attendance: 20,000

DINAMO: Mircea Constantinescu; Florin Cheran, Mircea Stoenescu, Cornel Dinu, Augustin Pax Deleanu; Viorel Sălceanu (73 Alexandru Moldovan), Radu Nunweiller; Petre Nuţu (46 Doru Popescu); Gavril Both, Florea Dumitrache, Mircea Lucescu.   Trainer: Dumitru Nicolae Nicuşor

PAOK: Hristodoulou; Giannis Gounaris, Aristarhos Foudoukidis, Papahristoudis, P. Papadopoulos; Bellis, Dramalis; Stavros Sarafis, Giorgos Koudas, Giannis Mantzourakis, Dimitris Paridis.   Sent off: Bellis.   Trainer: Horvath

Goals: Dumitrache (8, 49, 73), D. Popescu (64, 83)

P.A.O.K. THESSALONIKI v DINAMO BUCUREŞTI 1-0 (0-0)

Toumpas, Thessaloniki   30.09.70

Referees: Sergio Gonella, Trono Antonio, Vacato Salvadore (Ita)   Attendance: 12,400

PAOK: Hristodoulou (46 Pirtsos); Giannis Gounaris, Kontogiorgos, P. Papadopoulos, Dramalis; Vergos, Ahilleas Aslanidis; Stavros Sarafis, Giorgos Koudas, Gianis Mantzourakis, Dimitris Paridis.   Trainer: Horvath

DINAMO: Mircea Constantinescu; Florin Cheran, Mircea Stoenescu, Cornel Dinu, Augustin Pax Deleanu; Radu Nunweiller (82 Petre Nuţu), Alexandru Mustăţea; Viorel Sălceanu (70 Mircea Lucescu), Gavril Both, Florea Dumitrache, Ioan Haidu.   Trainer: Dumitru Nicolae Nicuşor

Goal: Koudas (80)

HAJDUK SPLIT v JSK SLAVIA SOFIA 3-0 (2-0)

Hajduk Split   16.09.70

Referee: László Vizhanyo (Hun)   Attendance: 6,600

HAJDUK: Radomir Vukčević; Vilson Dzoni, Marino Lemešic; Ivica Hlevnjak, Dragan Holcer, Luka Peruzović; Miroslav Vardić, Jure Jerković, Petar Nadoveza, Micun Jovanić, Ivan Pavlica.

SLAVIA: Petar Tsolov; Aleksandar Shalamanov, Petar Petrov, Stoian Aleksiev; Ivan Davidov, Nikola Krastev; Iancho Dimitrov, Todor Kolev, Bozhidar Grigorov, Liuben Tasev (.. Atanas Gerov), Stoian Kotsev.

Goals: Jerković (22), Pavlica (39), Jovanić (89)

JSK SLAVIA SOFIA v HAJDUK SPLIT 1-0 (1-0)

Sofia   30.09.70

Referee: Muzafer Sarvan (Tur)   Attendance: 10,000

SLAVIA: Petar Tsolov; Aleksandar Shalamanov (46 Atanas Gerov), Petar Petrov, Stoian Aleksiev; Ivan Davidov, Georgi Georgiev; Iancho Dimitrov, Liuben Tasev (46 Nikola Krastev), Bozhidar Grigorov, Atanas Mikhailov, Stoian Kotsev.

HAJDUK: Radomir Vukčević; Vilson Dzoni, Marino Lemešic; Ivica Hlevnjak, Dragan Holcer, Luka Peruzović; Miroslav Vardić, Jure Jerković, Petar Nadoveza, Micun Jovanić, Ivan Pavlica.

Goal: Davidov (18)

SPARTA ROTTERDAM v IA AKRANES 6-0 (3-0)

Feyenoord, Rotterdam   23.09.70

Referee: David W. Smith (Eng)   Attendance: 8,000

SPARTA: Pim Doesburg; Hans Venneker, Hans Eijkenbroek, Gerrie Ter Horst, Dries Visser, Stef Walbeek, Jan Van der Veen, Nol Heijerman, Aad Koudijzer (.. Henny Wijs), Janusz Kowalik, Jørgen Kristensen.   Trainer: Georg Kessler

IA AKRANES: Einar Gudleifsson; Benedikt Valtysson, Jón Gunnlaugsson, Thröstur Stefánsson, Jón Alfredsson, Hjalmarsson, Haraldur Sturlaugsson, Eyleifur Hafsteinsson, Matthias Hallgrimsson, Teitur Thordarsson, Gudjón Gudmundsson.

Goals: Venneker (2), Kowalik (11), Koudijzer (44), Heijerman (48, 57 pen), Walbeek (87)

IA AKRANES v SPARTA ROTTERDAM 0-9 (0-5)

Zuiderpark, Den Haag   29.09.70

Referee: Keith E. Walker (Eng)   Attendance: 1,800

IA AKRANES: Einar Gudleifsson; Benedikt Valtysson, Jón Gunnlaugsson, Thröstur Stefánsson, Jón Alfredsson, Hjalmarsson, Haraldur Sturlaugsson, Eyleifur Hafsteinsson, Matthias Hallgrimsson, Teitur Thordarsson, Gudjón Gudmundsson.

SPARTA: Pim Doesburg; Hans Venneker, Hans Eijkenbroek, Gerrie Ter Horst (.. Peter Drijver), Dries Visser, Stef Walbeek, Jan Van der Veen, Nol Heijerman (.. Arie Van Staveren), Jan Klijnjan, Janusz Kowalik, Jørgen Kristensen.   Trainer: Georg Kessler

Goals: Klijnjan (24, 31, 74), Kristensen (29), Kowalik (32, 61, 65), Van der Veen (34), Venneker (82)

INTERNAZIONALE MILANO
v NEWCASTLE UNITED 1-1 (0-1)

Stadio San Siro, Milano   23.09.70

Referee: Heinz Siebert (WG)   Attendance: 14,460

INTER: Lido Vieri; Tarcisio Burgnich, Giacinto Facchetti, Bernardino Fabbian, Mario Giubertoni, Giancarlo Cella, Sergio Pellizzaro, Sandro Mazzola, Marco Achilli, Mario Frustalupi, Mario Corso (66 JAIR da Costa). Trainer: Giovanni Invernizzi

UNITED: William McFaul; David Craig, Frank Clark, Thomas Gibb, Alwyn Burton, Robert Moncur, Bryan Robson, Keith Dyson, Wyn Davies, Preben Arentoft, David Young. Manager: Joe Harvey

Goals: W. Davies (44), Cella (84)

NEWCASTLE UNITED
v INTERNAZIONALE MILANO 2-0 (1-0)

St. James' Park, Newcastle   30.09.70

Referee: Joseph Minnoy (Bel)   Attendance: 56,800

UNITED: William McFaul; David Craig, Frank Clark, Thomas Gibb, Alwyn Burton, Robert Moncur, Bryan Robson, Keith Dyson, Wyn Davies, Preben Arentoft, David Young. Manager: Joe Harvey

INTER: Lido Vieri; Oscar Righetti, Giacinto Facchetti, Mauro Bellugi, Mario Giubertoni, Giancarlo Cella, JAIR da Costa, Bernardino Fabbian, Roberto Boninsegna, Marco Achilli (32 Ivano Bordon), Mario Corso. Vieri sent off (32).   Trainer: Giovanni Invernizzi

Goals: Moncur (29), Davies (70)

SECOND ROUND

HIBERNIAN EDINBURGH
v VITÓRIA GUIMARÃES 2-0 (1-0)

Easter Road, Edinburgh   14.10.70

Referee: Theo Boosten (Hol)   Attendance: 11,400

HIBERNIAN: Roy Baines; Christopher Shevlane, Eric Schaedler, John Brownlie, Jim Black, Patrick Stanton, Kenny Davidson (.. Alex Cropley), John Blackley (.. William McEwan), Joseph McBride, Johnny Graham, Arthur Duncan. Manager: Dave Ewing

VITÓRIA: Francisco Diamantino RODRIGUES; BERNARDO Oliveira DA VELHA, Manuel Joaquim Pereira da SILVA, António Francisco Jesús Moreira "PERES", José Fernando Silva "COSTEADO", JOAQUIM António JORGE, José Marques Silva "ZEZINHO", AUGUSTO Martins, ADEMIR Melo Silva, JORGE GONÇALVES, Firminio Sardinha "OSVALDINHO". Trainer: Jorge Vieira (Bra)

Goals: A. Duncan (45), Stanton (90)

VITÓRIA GUIMARÃES
v HIBERNIAN EDINBURGH 2-1 (2-0)

Estádio Municipal, Guimarães   28.10.70

Referee: Sergio Gonella (Ita)   Attendance: 5,700

VITÓRIA: Francisco Diamantino RODRIGUES; BERNARDO Oliveira DA VELHA, Manuel Joaquim Pereira da SILVA, António Francisco Jesús Moreira "PERES", José Fernando Silva "COSTEADO", JOAQUIM António JORGE, Firminio Sardinha "OSVALDINHO", José Marques Silva "ZEZINHO", ADEMIR Melo Silva, JORGE GONÇALVES, ARTUR da Rocha. Trainer: Jorge Vieira (Bra)

HIBERNIAN: Roy Baines; Christopher Shevlane, Eric Schaedler, John Blackley, Jim Black, Patrick Stanton, John Hamilton (.. Kenny Davidson), Joseph McBride (.. Jim Blair), Johnny Graham, William Hunter, Arthur Duncan. Manager: Dave Ewing

Goals: Gonçalves (20), Ademir (43), Graham (75)

BAYERN MÜNCHEN v COVENTRY CITY 6-1 (4-1)

Grünwalderstadion, München   20.10.70

Referee: Francesco Francescon (Ita)   Attendance: 12,000

BAYERN: Josef Maier; Johnny Hansen, Georg Schwarzenbeck, Franz Beckenbauer, Herward Koppenhöfer, Franz Roth, Rainer Zobel, Karl-Heinz Mrosko, Edgar Schneider, Gerd Müller, Dieter Brenninger. Trainer: Udo Lattek

COVENTRY: Eric McManus; Mick Coop, Chris Cattlin, Ernest Machin, Jeffrey Blockley, Geoffrey Strong, Roger Hunt, William Carr, Neil Martin, John O'Rourke, David Clements. Trainer: Noel Cantwell

Goals: Schneider (3, 12), Hunt (9), Schwarzenbeck (15), Müller (19, 89), Roth (75)

COVENTRY CITY v BAYERN MÜNCHEN 2-1 (1-0)

Highfield Road, Coventry   3.11.70

Referee: Antonio Sánchez Ríos (Spa)   Attendance: 26,033

COVENTRY: William Glazier; Mick Coop, Wilfred Smith, Dennis Mortimer, Jeffrey Blockley, Brian Hill, Roger Hunt (61 Brian Joicey), William Carr, Neil Martin, John O'Rourke, David Clements.   Trainer: Noel Cantwell

BAYERN: Josef Maier; Johnny Hansen, Georg Schwarzenbeck, Franz Beckenbauer, Herward Koppenhöfer, Uli Hoeness, Rainer Zobel, Peter Pumm, Karl-Heinz Mrosko, Gerd Müller, Dieter Brenninger.   Trainer: Udo Lattek

Goals: Martin (35), Hoeness (47), O'Rourke (85)

FIORENTINA FIRENZE v 1.FC KÖLN 1-2 (1-1)

Stadio Comunale, Firenze   20.10.70

Referee: Anton Bucheli (Swi)   Attendance: 9,600

FIORENTINA: Francesco Superchi; Paolo Stanzial, Giuseppe Longoni, Ennio Pellegrini, Ugo Ferrante, Giuseppe Brizi, Giorgio Mariani, Claudio Merlo, Giampietro Vitali, Giancarlo De Sisti, Luciano Chiarugi.   Trainer: Pugliese

FC KÖLN: Manfred Manglitz; Heinz Simmet, Matthias Hemmersbach, Bernd Cullmann, Werner Biskup, Wolfgang Weber, Hans-Josef Kapellmann, Heinz Flohe, Thomas Parits, Wolfgang Overath, Bernd Rupp.   Trainer: Ernst Ocwirk

Goals: Mariani (20), Flohe (25, 46)

1.FC KÖLN v FIORENTINA FIRENZE 1-0 (1-0)

Müngersdorferstadion, Köln   3.11.70

Referee: Franz Geluck (Bel)   Attendance: 11,800

FC KÖLN: Manfred Manglitz; Karl-Heinz Thielen (52 Bernd Cullmann), Matthias Hemmersbach (46 Kurt Kowalski), Heinz Simmet, Werner Biskup, Wolfgang Weber, Hans-Josef Kapellmann, Heinz Flohe, Thomas Parits, Wolfgang Overath, Bernd Rupp.   Trainer: Ernst Ocwirk

FIORENTINA: Francesco Superchi; Francesco Carpenetti, Giuseppe Longoni, Salvatore Esposito, Ugo Ferrante, Giuseppe Brizi, Giorgio Mariani, Claudio Merlo (11 Fabrizio Berni), Giampietro Vitali, Giancarlo De Sisti, Giorgio Gennari.   Trainer: Pugliese

Goal: Biskup (33 pen)

CF BARCELONA v JUVENTUS TORINO 1-2 (0-1)

Camp Nou, Barcelona   20.10.70

Referee: John K. Taylor (Eng)   Attendance: 36,000

CF BARCELONA: Salvador SADURNÍ Urpi; Joaquín RIFÉ Climent, José Luis ROMERO Robledo, Antonio TORRES García, Francisco Fernández Rodríguez "GALLEGO", Pedro María ZABALZA Inda, Carlos REXACH Cerdá, JUAN CARLOS Pérez López, Narciso MARTÍ FILOSÍA, MARCIAL Pina Morales, Luis PUJOL Codina.   Trainer: Victor Frederik Bucingham

JUVENTUS: Roberto Tancredi; Luciano Spinosi, Giuseppe Furino, Antonello Cuccureddu, Francesco Morini, Sandro Salvadore, Roberto Bettega, Giampietro Marchetti (82 Franco Causio), Pietro Anastasi (74 Adriano Novellini), Fabio Capello, Helmut Haller.   Trainer: Armando Picchi

Goals: Haller (12), Bettega (55), Marcial (76)

JUVENTUS TORINO v CF BARCELONA 2-1 (2-0)

Stadio Comunale, Torino   4.11.70

Referee: Günter Männig (DDR)   Attendance: 25,800

JUVENTUS: Roberto Tancredi; Luciano Spinosi, Giuseppe Furino, Antonello Cuccureddu (74 Franco Causio), Gianluigi Roveta, Sandro Salvadore, Roberto Bettega, Giampietro Marchetti, Adriano Novellini (46 Fausto Landini), Fabio Capello, Helmut Haller.   Trainer: Armando Picchi

CF BARCELONA: Salvador SADURNÍ Urpi; Joaquín RIFÉ Climent, José Luis ROMERO Robledo, Antonio TORRES García, Francisco Fernández Rodríguez "GALLEGO", Pedro María ZABALZA Inda, Carlos REXACH Cerdá, JUAN CARLOS Pérez López (76 Pablo GARCÍA-CASTANY), Ramón ALFONSEDA Pous, MARCIAL Pina Morales (46 Narciso MARTÍ FILOSÍA), Luis PUJOL Codina.   Trainer: Victor Frederik Bucingham

Goals: Bettega (3), Capello (23), Pujol (83)

SPARTA ROTTERDAM v COLERAINE 2-0 (2-0)

Feyenoord, Rotterdam   20.10.70

Referee: Antoine Queudeville (Lux)   Attendance: 7,000

SPARTA: Pim Doesburg; Hans Venneker, Hans Eijkenbroek, Gerrie Ter Horst, Dries Visser, Stef Walbeek, Jan Van der Veen, Nol Heijerman, Janusz Kowalik, Jan Klijnjan, Jørgen Kristensen.   Trainer: Georg Kessler

COLERAINE: Edward Crossan; John McCurdy, David Jackson, David Gordon, Tony O'Doherty, Ivan Murray, Sean Dunlop, Brendan Mullan (.. Anthony Curley), Samuel Wilson, Des Dickson, Brian Jennings.

Goals: Klijnjan (19, 44)

COLERAINE v SPARTA ROTTERDAM 1-2 (1-2)

The Showgrounds, Coleraine   4.11.70

Referee: Kurt Sørensen (Dan)   Attendance: 5,000

COLERAINE: Edward Crossan; John McCurdy, David Jackson, David Gordon, Tony O'Doherty, Ivan Murray, Sean Dunlop, Brendan Mullan, Samuel Wilson, Des Dickson, Brian Jennings (.. Anthony Curley).

SPARTA: Pim Doesburg; Hans Venneker, Hans Eijkenbroek (.. Peter Drijver), Gerrie Ter Horst, Dries Visser, Jan Van der Veen, Stef Walbeek, Nol Heijerman, Aad Koudijzer, Jan Klijnjan, Jørgen Kristensen.   Trainer: Georg Kessler

Goals: Koudijzer (15), Kristensen (26), Jennings (28)

HERTHA BSC BERLIN
v SPARTAK TRNAVA 1-0 (0-0)

Olympiastadion, Berlin   21.10.70

Referee: Constantin Petrea (Rom)   Attendance: 15,129

HERTHA: Volkmar Gross; Bernd Patzke, Uwe Witt, Jürgen Rumor, Karl-Heinz Ferschl; Hans-Joachim Altendorff (55 Jürgen Weber), Wolfgang Gayer; Hans-Jürgen Sperlich, Lorenz Horr, Zoltán Varga, Arno Steffenhagen (56 Franz Brungs).   Trainer: Helmut Kronsbein

SPARTAK: Josef Geryk; Karol Dobias, Vlastimil Bozík, Stanislav Jarábek, Vladimír Hagara (74 Valentovic); Anton Hrusecky, Ladislav Kuna, Alojz Fandel; Stanislav Martinkovic, Vojtech Varadín, Dušan Kabát.   Trainer: Valerián Švec

Goal: L. Horr (85)

SPARTAK TRNAVA
v HERTHA BSC BERLIN 3-1 (2-0)

Spartak Trnava   28.10.70

Referee: Karl Göppel (Swi)   Attendance: 10,700

SPARTAK: Jozef Púchly; Karol Dobias, Kamil Majerník, Vlastimil Bozík, Vladimír Hagara; Anton Hrusecky, Ladislav Kuna, Alojz Fandel; Stanislav Martinkovic, Vojtech Varadín, Dušan Kabát.   Trainer: Valerián Švec

HERTHA: Volkmar Gross; Bernd Patzke, Uwe Witt, Jürgen Rumor, Tasso Wild; Peter Enders, Lorenz Horr, Franz Brungs (46 Hans-Jürgen Sperlich); Wolfgang Gayer, Arno Steffenhagen, Jürgen Weber (64 Hans-Joachim Altendorff). Trainer: Helmut Kronsbein

Goals: Kuna (7), Martinkovic (36), Bozik (76), Gayer (71)

SK STURM GRAZ v ARSENAL LONDON 1-0 (0-0)

Bundesstadion Liebenau, Graz   21.10.70

Referee: Bohumil Smejkal (Cze)   Attendance: 18,000

STURM: Fritz Benko; Erwin Solleder, Franz Reiter, Heinz Schilcher, Heinz Russ; Helmut Wagner, Walter Fuchs; Dietrich Albrecht, Robert Kaiser, Alfred Murlasits, Heinz Zamut. Trainer: János Szep

ARSENAL: Bob Wilson; Patrick Rice, Robert McNab, Edward Kelly, Frank McLintock, John Roberts, George Armstrong, Peter Storey, John Radford, Raymond Kennedy, George Graham.   Manager: Bertie Mee

Goal: Zamut (48)

ARSENAL LONDON v SK STURM GRAZ 2-0 (1-0)

Highbury, London   4.11.70

Referee: Theo Boosten (Hol)   Attendance: 37,677

ARSENAL: Bob Wilson; Patrick Rice, Robert McNab, Edward Kelly, Frank McLintock, John Roberts, George Armstrong, Peter Storey, John Radford, Raymond Kennedy, George Graham.   Manager: Bertie Mee

STURM: Damir Grloci (40 Fritz Benko); Erwin Solleder, Heinz Schilcher, Franz Reiter, Heinz Russ; Walter Fuchs, Alfred Murlasits, Helmut Wagner (74 Helmut Huberts); Dietrich Albrecht, Robert Kaiser, Heinz Zamut.   Trainer: János Szep

Goals: Kennedy (9), Storey (90 pen)

LEEDS UNITED v DYNAMO DRESDEN 1-0 (0-0)

Elland Road, Leeds   21.10.70

Referee: Alfred Delcourt (Bel)   Attendance: 21,292

UNITED: David Harvey; Nigel Davey, Terence Cooper, William Bremner, Jack Charlton, Norman Hunter, Peter Lorimer, Allan Clarke, Michael Jones, Rodney Belfitt (75 Christopher Galvin), Paul Madeley.   Manager: Don Revie

DYNAMO: Manfred Kallenbach; Hans-Jürgen Dörner, Frank Ganzera, Klaus Sammer, Joachim Kern, Wolfgang Haustein, Uwe Ziegler, Hans-Jürgen Kreische, Meinhard Hemp, Gerd Heidler, Frank Richter.   Trainer: Walter Fritzsch

Goal: Lorimer (57 pen)

DYNAMO DRESDEN v LEEDS UNITED 2-1 (1-1)

Rudolf Harbig Stadion, Dresden   4.11.70

Referee: Ferdinand Marschall (Aus)   Attendance: 32,800

DYNAMO: Manfred Kallenbach; Hans-Jürgen Dörner, Frank Ganzera, Klaus Sammer, Wolfgang Haustein, Uwe Ziegler, Hans-Jürgen Kreische, Meinhard Hemp, Dieter Riedel (77 Eduard Geyer), Frank Richter, Rainer Sachse (46 Gerd Heidler).   Trainer: Walter Fritzsch

UNITED: Gary Sprake; Nigel Davey, Paul Madeley, William Bremner, Jack Charlton, Norman Hunter, Peter Lorimer, Allan Clarke, Michael Jones, John Giles, Michael Bates. Manager: Don Revie

Bates & Geyer sent off (83)

Goals: Hemp (15), Jones (31), Kreische (64)

SPARTA PRAHA v DUNDEE UNITED 3-1 (1-1)

Stadión na Letnej, Praha   21.10.70

Referee: Dogan Babacan (Tur)   Attendance: 17,600

SPARTA: Antonín Kramerius; Pavel Melichar, Oldřich Urban, Tibor Semendák, Václav Migas, František Chovanec, Bohumil Veselý, Jaroslav Barton, Václav Mašek (.. Petr Uličný), Josef Jurkanin, Václav Vrána.   Trainer: Karel Kolsky

UNITED: Donald Mackay (.. Hamish McAlpine); Andy Rolland, Jim Cameron, Stuart Markland, Douglas Smith, James Henry, David Wilson, Alexander Reid, Alan Gordon (.. Ian Scott), Morris Stevenson, Thomas Traynor.

Goals: Vrana (19), Traynor (25), Jurkanin (71, 89)

DUNDEE UNITED v SPARTA PRAHA 1-0 (1-0)

Tannadice Park, Dundee   4.11.70

Referee: Kjell Wahlen (Nor)   Attendance: 9,000

UNITED: Hamish McAlpine; Stuart Markland, Jim Cameron, Dennis Gillespie, Douglas Smith, James Henry, David Wilson, Alexander Reid, Alan Gordon, Morris Stevenson, Thomas Traynor.

SPARTA: Antonín Kramerius; Pavel Melichar, Oldřich Urban, Eduard Kessel, Václav Migas, František Chovanec, Bohumil Veselý, Jaroslav Barton, Václav Vrána, Josef Jurkanin, Petr Uličný.   Trainer: Karel Kolsky

Goal: Gordon (31)

NEWCASTLE UNITED v PÉCSI DÓZSA 2-0 (1-0)

St. James' Park, Newcastle   21.10.70

Referee: Hans-Joachim Weyland (WG)   Attendance: 50,550

UNITED: William McFaul; David Craig, Frank Clark, Thomas Gibb, David Young, Robert Moncur, Bryan Robson, Keith Dyson, Wyn Davies, James Smith, David Ford.   Manager: Joe Harvey

DÓZSA: Imre Rapp; László Maurer, Ferenc Hernádi, István Kocsis, János Konrád, Viktor Kincses; László Daka, József Tóth; Ferenc Bérczesi, János Máté, István Rónai (79 Csaba Tüske).   Trainer: Mihály Czibulka

Goals: Davies (44, 58)

PÉCS DÓZSA
v NEWCASTLE UNITED 2-0 (1-0, 2-0) 5-2 penalties

PVSK, Pécs   4.11.70

Referee: Roland Marendaz (Swi)   Attendance: 20,000

DÓZSA: Imre Rapp; Ferenc Hernádi, László Maurer, János Konrád, Viktor Kincses; István Kocsis, László Daka, József Tóth; Ferenc Bérczei (118 János Dunai), János Máté, István Rónai (91 Csaba Tüske).   Trainer: Mihály Czibulka

UNITED: William McFaul; David Craig, Frank Clark, Thomas Gibb, John McNamee, Robert Moncur, Bryan Robson, Keith Dyson (85 Gordon Hindson), Wyn Davies, David Young, David Ford (106 Ian Mitchell).   Manager: Joe Harvey

Goals: Máté (18, 82)

Penalties: 1-0 Konrád, Robson, 2-0 Daka, Mitchell, 3-0 Tüske, Gibb, 4-0 Dunai, 4-1 Clark, 5-1 Tóth, 5-2 McFaul

LIVERPOOL FC v DINAMO BUCUREŞTI 3-0 (0-0)

Anfield Road, Liverpool   21.10.70

Referee: Roger Machin (Fra)   Attendance: 36,525

LIVERPOOL: Raymond Clemence; Christopher Lawler, Ronald Yeats, Thomas Smith (Cap); Larry Lloyd, Emlyn Hughes; Brian Hall, Alec Lindsay, Steve Heighway (79 Ian St.John), John McLaughlin, Peter Thompson.   Manager: Bill Shankly

DINAMO: Mircea Constantinescu; Florin Cheran, Mircea Stoenescu, Cornel Dinu, Augustin Pax Deleanu; Viorel Sălceanu, Alexandru Mustăţea, Radu Nunweiller; Mircea Lucescu (67 Doru Popescu), Florea Dumitrache, Ioan Haidu.   Trainer: Dumitru Nicolae Nicuşor

Goals: Lindsay (60), Lawler (76), Hughes (83)

DINAMO BUCUREŞTI v LIVERPOOL FC 1-1 (1-0)

23 August, Bucureşti   4.11.70

Referees: Erich Linemayr, Ench Höltein, Stefan Koler (Aus)   Attendance: 50,000

DINAMO: Mircea Constantinescu; Florin Cheran, Ion Nunweiller, Mircea Stoenescu, Augustin Pax Deleanu; Cornel Dinu, Radu Nunweiller; Viorel Sălceanu, Doru Popescu (30 Alexandru Mustăţea), Florea Dumitrache, Ioan Haidu.   Trainer: Dumitru Nicolae Nicuşor

LIVERPOOL: Raymond Clemence; Christopher Lawler, Thomas Smith (Cap), Larry Lloyd, Alec Lindsay; Emlyn Hughes, John McLaughlin; Brian Hall, Alun Evans (13 Philip Boersma), Steve Heighway, Peter Thompson.   Manager: Bill Shankly

Goals: Sălceanu (34), Boersma (48)

DINAMO ZAGREB v HAMBURGER SV 4-0 (2-0)

Maksimir, Zagreb   21.10.70

Referee: Dimitris Protonotarios (Gre)   Attendance: 13,500

DINAMO: Fahrija Dautbegović, Mladen Ramljak, Branko Gračanin, Denijal Pirić, Josip Gucmirtl (21 Ivica Miljković), Filip Blašković, Marijan Čerček, Josip Lalić (.. Barsić), Marijan Novak, Drago Vabec, Krasnodar Rora.

HAMBURGER SV: Özcan Arkoc; Hans-Jürgen Hellfritz, Helmut Sandmann (76 Heinz Bonn), Jürgen Kurbjuhn, Hans-Jürgen Ripp, Klaus Zaczyk, Peter Nogly, Franz-Josef Hönig, Robert Potzschke, Uwe Seeler (46 Hans Schulz), Gert Dörfel.   Trainer: Klaus-Dieter Ochs

Goals: Lalić (2, 24), Čerček (73), Schulz (83 og)

HAMBURGER SV v DINAMO ZAGREB 1-0 (1-0)

Volksparkstadion, Hamburg   4.11.70

Referee: José Augusto Ismael Baltasar (Por)   Att: 11,000

HAMBURGER SV: Özcan Arkoc; Helmut Sandmann, Jürgen Kurbjuhn, Peter Nogly, Heinz Bonn (15 Hans-Werner Kremer), Hans-Jürgen Ripp, Hans Schulz, Klaus Zaczyk, Gerd Klier, Franz-Josef Hönig (70 Robert Pötzschke), Gert Dörfel. Trainer: Klaus-Dieter Ochs

DINAMO: Fahrija Dautbegović; Ivica Miljković, Branko Gračanin, Denijal Pirić, Mladen Ramljak, Filip Blašković, Drago Vabec, Josip Lalić (46 Bradvić), Marijan Novak (67 Barcić), Josip Gucmirtl, Krasnodar Rora.

Goal: Hönig (35)

AKADEMISK BOLDCLUB KØBENHAVN v RSC ANDERLECHT BRUSSEL 1-3 (1-3)

Idraetsparken, København   21.10.70

Referee: David W. Smith (Eng)   Attendance: 5,500

AB: Poul Werner Henriksen; Jørgen Collaitz, Niels Yde, K. Knudsen, Erik Sandvad; Flemming Hansen, Ove Carlsen; H. Hansen, Henrik Bernburg, Benny Nielsen, Andersen (46 Johnny Petersen).

ANDERLECHT: Leen Barth; Gerard Desanghere, Jean Plaskie, Johnny Velkeneers, Jean Cornelis; André Colasse (46 Julien Kialunda), Thomas Nordahl; Inge Ejderstedt, Jan Mulder, Paul Van Himst, Wilfried Puis. Trainer: Pierre Sinibaldi

Goals: Mulder (30), Nielsen (33), Ejderstedt (35), Yde (38 og)

RSC ANDERLECHT BRUSSEL v AKADEMISK BOLDCLUB KØBENHAVN 4-0 (2-0)

Parc Astrid, Brussel   4.11.70

Referee: William Anderson (Sco)   Attendance: 9,000

ANDERLECHT: Leen Barth, Gerard Desanghere, Jean Plaskie, Johnny Velkeneers, Maurice Martens; André Colasse, Thomas Nordahl; Gilbert Van Binst (46 Antonio Elizeu), Jan Mulder, Paul Van Himst (63 Inge Ejderstedt), Wilfried Puis. Trainer: Pierre Sinibaldi

AB: Poul Werner Henriksen; Jørgen Collaitz, Niels Yde, Søren Jessen, Erik Sandvad; Flemming Hansen, Johnny Petersen; Ove Carlsen, H.Hansen, Benny Nielsen, Andersen.

Goals: Van Himst (12), Nordahl (33,55), Elizeu (82)

VITÓRIA SETÚBAL v HAJDUK SPLIT 2-0 (0-0)

Estádio do Bonfim, Setúbal   21.10.70

Referee: Alfred Ott (WG)   Attendance: 6,900

VITÓRIA: JOAQUIM Manuel Conceição TORRES, Francisco Silva REBELO, Carlos Alberto Lourenço CARDOSO, José Jesus MENDES, Manuel Luis dos Santos "CARRIÇO", Pedro (23 Joaquim Leonardo Quinta ARCANJO), JOSÉ MARIA Júnior, VAGNER Canotilho, VITOR Manuel Ferreira BAPTISTA, Felix Marques GUERREIRO (74 OCTÁVIO Joaquim Coelho Machado), JACINTO JOÃO.   Trainer: José Maria PEDROTO

HAJDUK: Radomir Vukčević; Vilson Dzoni (40 Mario Boljat), Marino Lemešic, Buljan, Dragan Holcer, Luka Peruzović, Muzinić, Ivica Hlevnjak, Petar Nadoveza (74 Mladen Matijanić), Jure Jerković, Ivan Pavlica.

Goals: José Maria (59), Boljat (82 og)

HAJDUK SPLIT v VITÓRIA SETÚBAL 2-1 (0-1)

Plinada, Split   4.11.70

Referee: Jan Lazowski (Pol)   Attendance: 11,800

HAJDUK: Radomir Vukčević; Miroslav Bošković, Dragan Holcer, Ivica Hlevnjak, Marino Lemešic, Luka Peruzović (59 Buljan), Micun Jovanić, Jure Jerković, Miroslav Vardić, Petar Nadoveza, Ivan Pavlica.

VITÓRIA: JOAQUIM Manuel Conceição TORRES, Francisco Silva REBELO, Carlos Alberto Lourenço CARDOSO, José Jesus MENDES, Manuel Luis dos Santos "CARRIÇO", OCTÁVIO Joaquim Coelho Machado (74 Carlos Alberto CORREIA), JOSÉ MARIA Júnior, VAGNER Canotilho, Felix Marques GUERREIRO, VITOR Manuel Ferreira BAPTISTA (74 Joaquim Leonardo Quinta ARCANJO), JACINTO JOÃO. Trainer: José Maria PEDROTO

Goals: José Maria (23), Nadoveza (63), Buljan (72)

VALENCIA CF v BEVEREN-WAAS 0-1 (0-0)

Campo de Mestalla, Valencia   *22.10.70*

Referee: Robert Wurtz (Fra)   Attendance: 45,000

VALENCIA: Ángel ABELARDO González; Francisco VIDAGAÑY Hernández, Juan Cruz SOL Oria, Antonio Martínez Morales "ANTÓN"; ANÍBAL Pérez Miers, José CLARAMUNT Torres I, SERGIO Manzanera Lloret, Manuel POLInario Muñoz (46 Fernando ANSOLA Sanmartín), Enrique CLARAMUNT II Torres (75 Vicente Anastasio JARA Segovia), Carlos PELLICER Vázquez, Óscar Rubén VALDEZ Ferrero.   Trainer: Alfredo DI STÉFANO Lahule

BEVEREN: Luksa Poplekovic, Maurice Renier (57 William Verdonck), Freddy Buyl, Paul van Genechten, André Vanderlinden, Jaak Roelandt, Robert vande Sompel, Raymond Goossens, Robert Rogiers, Hugo de Raeymaecker, Jean Janssens. Trainer: Edward Volckaert

Goal: De Raeymaecker (76)

BEVEREN-WAAS v VALENCIA CF 1-1 (0-0)

Stedelijk Olympisch, Antwerp   *4.11.70*

Referee: Curt Nystrand (Swe)   Attendance: 15,000

BEVEREN: Luksa Poplekovic; Maurice Renier, Freddy Buyl, Paul van Genechten, André Vanderlinden, Jaak Roelandt, Robert vande Sompel, Raymond Goossens, Robert Rogiers, Hugo de Raeymaecker, Jean Janssens. Trainer: Edward Volckaert

VALENCIA: Ángel ABELARDO González; José Antonio García Conesa "TATONO", Juan Cruz SOL Oria, Antonio Martínez Morales "ANTÓN"; ANÍBAL Pérez Miers, Enrique CLARAMUNT II Torres, SERGIO Manzanera Lloret (46 José CLARAMUNT Torres I), Francisco García Gómez "PAQUITO", José Vicente FORMENT Fáez, Carlos PELLICER Vázquez (62 José NEBOT Navarro), Óscar Rubén VALDEZ Ferrero. Trainer: Alfredo DI STÉFANO Lahule

Goals: De Raeymaecker (59), Forment (82)

ESKİŞEHIRSPOR v TWENTE ENSCHEDE 3-2 (2-0)

Atatürk, Eskişehir   *28.10.70*

Referee: Marijan Raus (Jug)   Attendance: 25,000

ESKİŞEHIRSPOR: Taskin Yilmaz; Abdurrahman Temel, Faik Sentasler, Kamuran Yavuz, Ismail Arca, Nuri Toygun, Ender Konca, Nihat Atacan (.. Burhan Ipek), Fethi Heper, Vahap Özbayar, Halil Gundögan.   Trainer: Abdulah Gegić

TWENTE: Piet Schrijvers; Kees Van Ierssel, Epi Drost, Willem De Vries, Benno Huve (.. Izzy Ten Donkelaar), Willy van de Kerkhof, Lloyd Rooks, Kick Van der Vall, Theo Pahlplatz, Jan Jeuring, René van de Kerkhof (.. Jan Streuer). Trainer: Kees Rijvers

Goals: Halil (42), Fethi (44, 89), Pahlplatz (72), René van de Kerkhof (87)

TWENTE ENSCHEDE v ESKİŞEHIRSPOR 6-1 (3-1)

Diekman Stadion, Enschede   *4.11.70*

Referee: Rudolf Glöckner (DDR)   Attendance: 24,500

TWENTE: Piet Schrijvers; Kees Van Ierssel, Epi Drost, Willem De Vries, Benno Huve, René Notten, Kick Van der Vall, Willy van de Kerkhof, Jan Jeuring (.. Antal Nagy), Theo Pahlplatz, René van de Kerkhof (.. Jan Streuer).   Trainer: Kees Rijvers

ESKİŞEHIRSPOR: Taskin Yilmaz; Ilhan Çolak, Faik Sentasler, Abdurrahman Temel, Ismail Arca, Mustafa, Kamuran Yavuz, Vahap Özbayar, Ender Konca (.. Nihat Atacan), Fethi Heper, Halil Gundögan. Trainer: Abdulah Gegić

Goals: Jeuring (1, 12, 60), Fethi (26), René van de Kerkhof (44), Streuer (85), Nagy (88)

THIRD ROUND

SPARTAK TRNAVA v 1.FC KÖLN 0-1 (0-1)

Spartak Trnava   *25.11.70*

Referee: Nikola Mladenović (Jug)   Attendance: 13,000

SPARTAK: Jozef Púchly; Karol Dobias, Vlastimil Bozík, Stanislav Jarábek, Vladimír Hagara; Anton Hrusecky, Alojz Fandel, Ladislav Kuna; Stanislav Martinkovic, Jaroslav Masrna (70 Valentovic), Dušan Kabát.   Trainer: Valerián Švec

FC KÖLN: Manfred Manglitz; Karl-Heinz Thielen, Werner Biskup, Wolfgang Weber, Matthias Hemmersbach; Heinz Simmet, Heinz Flohe, Bernd Cullmann; Thomas Parits, Bernd Rupp, Kurt Kowalski.   Trainer: Ernst Ocwirk

Goal: Dobias (8 og)

1.FC KÖLN v SPARTAK TRNAVA 3-0 (1-0)

Müngersdorferstadion, Köln   *9.12.70*

Referee: Joseph Minnoy (Bel)   Attendance: 8,000

FC KÖLN: Manfred Manglitz; Kurt Kowalski (57 Hans-Jürgen Lex), Matthias Hemmersbach, Werner Biskup, Heinz Simmet; Wolfgang Weber, Bernd Rupp, Thomas Parits, Bernd Cullmann (25 Manfred Classen), Wolfgang Overath, Johannes Löhr.   Trainer: Ernst Ocwirk

SPARTAK: Jozef Púchly; Karol Dobias, Stanislav Jarábek, Kamil Majerník, Vladimír Hagara; Alojz Fandel, Ladislav Kuna; Stanislav Martinkovic, Vojtech Varadín, Anton Hrusecky (77 Valentovic), Dušan Kabát.   Trainer: Valerián Švec

Goals: Biskup (33 pen), Hemmersbach (59), Rupp (72)

BAYERN MÜNCHEN
v SPARTA ROTTERDAM 2-1 (0-1)

Grünwalderstadion, München   25.11.70

Referee: José Rosa Dias Nunez (Por)   Attendance: 10,300

BAYERN: Josef Maier; Johnny Hansen, Georg
Schwarzenbeck, Franz Beckenbauer, Peter Pumm, Franz
Roth, Uli Hoeness (55 Peter Kupferschmidt), Rainer Zobel,
Karl-Heinz Mrosko (46 Edgar Schneider), Gerd Müller, Dieter
Brenninger.   Trainer: Udo Lattek

SPARTA: Pim Doesburg; Hans Venneker, Hans Eijkenbroek,
Gerrie Ter Horst, Dries Visser, Jan Van der Veen, Stef Walbeek,
Nol Heijerman, Janusz Kowalik (65 Peter De Quant), Jan
Klijnjan, Jørgen Kristensen.   Trainer: Georg Kessler

Goals: Heijerman (16), Schneider (56), Müller (88)

SPARTA PRAHA v LEEDS UNITED 2-3 (0-2)

Stadión na Letnej, Praha   9.12.70

Referee: Aurelio Angonese (Ita)   Attendance: 25,000

SPARTA: Vladimír Brabec; Pavel Melichar, Oldřich Urban,
Eduard Kessel, Václav Migas, František Chovanec, Bohumil
Veselý, Jaroslav Barton, Václav Mašek, Josef Jurkanin, Václav
Vrána.   Trainer: Karel Kolsky

UNITED: Gary Sprake (46 David Harvey); Paul Reaney,
Terence Cooper, William Bremner, Paul Madeley, Norman
Hunter (46 Terence Yorath), Peter Lorimer, Allan Clarke,
Rodney Belfitt, Michael Bates, Edward Gray.
Manager: Don Revie

Goals: E. Gray (12), Clarke (32), Belfitt (35), Barton (65),
Urban (85)

SPARTA ROTTERDAM
v BAYERN MÜNCHEN 1-3(1-2)

Feyenoord, Rotterdam   9.12.70

Referee: Antonio Camacho Jiménez (Spa)   Att: 45,000

SPARTA: Pim Doesburg; Hans Venneker (75 Peter Drijver),
Gerrie Ter Horst, Hans Eijkenbroek, Dries Visser, Jan Van der
Veen, Stef Walbeek, Jan Klijnjan, Nol Heijerman (59 Arie Van
Staveren), Janusz Kowalik, Jørgen Kristensen.
Trainer: Georg Kessler

BAYERN: Josef Maier; Johnny Hansen, Georg
Schwarzenbeck, Franz Beckenbauer, Herward Koppenhöfer,
Rainer Zobel, Franz Roth (46 Dieter Brenninger), Uli
Hoeness, Karl-Heinz Mrosko, Gerd Müller, Edgar Schneider.
Trainer: Udo Lattek

Goals: Müller (23, 40, 66), Kristensen (32)

ARSENAL LONDON v BEVEREN-WAAS 4-0 (2-0)

Highbury, London   2.12.70

Referee: Pius Kamber (Swi)   Attendance: 33,444

ARSENAL: Bob Wilson; Patrick Rice, Robert McNab,
Jonathan Sammels, Frank McLintock, Peter Simpson, George
Armstrong, Peter Storey, John Radford, Raymond Kennedy,
George Graham.   Manager: Bertie Mee

BEVEREN: Luksa Poplekovic; William Verdonck, Freddy
Buyl, Paul Van Genechten, André Vanderlinden, Jaak Roelandt,
Robert Vande Sompel, William Maes, Robert Rogiers, Cyriel
Braem (46 Roland Debadts), Jean Janssens.
Trainer: Edward Volckaert

Goals: Graham (10), Kennedy (29, 77), Sammels (54)

LEEDS UNITED v SPARTA PRAHA 6-0 (5-0)

Elland Road, Leeds   2.12.70

Referee: Koen Brouwer (Hol)   Attendance: 25,500

UNITED: Gary Sprake; Paul Madeley, Terence Cooper,
William Bremner, Jack Charlton, Norman Hunter, Peter
Lorimer, Allan Clarke, Rodney Belfitt (21 Paul Reaney), John
Giles, Edward Gray.   Manager: Don Revie

SPARTA: Antonín Kramerius; Pavel Melichar, Václav Migas,
Eduard Kessel, Oldřich Urban, František Chovanec, Bohumil
Veselý (72 Tibor Semendák), František Gögh, Václav Mašek
(46 Petr Uličný), Josef Jurkanin, Václav Vrána.
Trainer: Karel Kolsky

Goals: Clarke (19), Chovanec (24 og), Bremner (26),
E. Gray (28, 36), Charlton (54)

BEVEREN-WAAS v ARSENAL LONDON 0-0

Stedelijk Olympisch, Antwerp   16.12.70

Referee: Gerd Hennig (WG)   Attendance: 9,000

BEVEREN: Luksa Poplekovic; Richard Verelst, Freddy Buyl,
Paul Van Genechten, André Vanderlinden, Jaak Roelandt
(80 Roland Debadts), Raymond Goossens, Robert Vande
Sompel, Robert Rogiers (70 William Maes), Hugo De
Raeymaecker, Jean Janssens.   Trainer: Edward Volckaert

ARSENAL: Bob Wilson; Patrick Rice, Robert McNab,
Jonathan Sammels, John Roberts, Peter Simpson, George
Armstrong (57 Peter Marinello), Peter Storey, John Radford
(46 Charles George), Raymond Kennedy, George Graham.
Manager: Bertie Mee

PÉCS DÓZSA v JUVENTUS TORINO 0-1 (0-1)

PVSK, Pécs 3.12.70

Referee: Ferdinand Biwersi (WG)   Attendance: 22,000

DÓZSA: Imre Rapp; Ferenc Hernádi, Viktor Kincses, István Kocsis, János Konrád, László Maurer, Ferenc Bérczesi, József Tóth, László Daka (77 János Dunai), János Máté, István Rónai (46 Csaba Tüske).   Trainer: Mihály Czibulka

JUVENTUS: Roberto Tancredi; Luciano Spinosi, Giuseppe Furino, Antonello Cuccureddu, Francesco Morini, Sandro Salvadore, Franco Causio, Giampietro Marchetti, Pietro Anastasi, Fabio Capello, Fausto Landini (46 Adriano Novellini, 78 Gianluigi Savoldi).   Trainer: Armando Picchi

Goal: Causio (31)

JUVENTUS TORINO v PÉCS DÓZSA 2-0 (0-0)

Stadio Comunale, Torino 16.12.70

Referee: Kenneth Howard Burns (Eng)   Attendance: 15,000

JUVENTUS: Roberto Tancredi; Luciano Spinosi, Giuseppe Furino, Antonello Cuccureddu (35 Giampietro Marchetti), Francesco Morini, Sandro Salvadore, Helmut Haller; Franco Causio, Pietro Anastasi, Fabio Capello, Roberto Bettega. Trainer: Armando Picchi

DÓZSA: Imre Rapp; Ferenc Hernádi, Viktor Kincses II, István Kocsis, János Konrád, László Maurer, Ferenc Bérczesi, János Máté, László Köves, Csaba Tüske, József Tóth. Trainer: Mihály Czibulka

Goals: Anastasi (85, 87)

DINAMO ZAGREB v TWENTE ENSCHEDE 2-2 (2-1)

Maksimir, Zagreb 9.12.70

Referee: Josef Bucek (Aus)   Attendance: 17,000

DINAMO: Fahrija Dautbegović; Ivica Miljković, Branko Gračanin, Denijal Pirić, Mladen Ramljak, Filip Blašković, Marijan Čerček, Josip Lalić, Krasnodar Rora, Josip Gucmirtl, Drago Vabec.

TWENTE: Piet Schrijvers; Kees Van Ierssel, Epi Drost, Willem De Vries, Benno Huve, René Notten (.. Lloyd Rooks), Kick Van der Vall, Theo Pahlplatz, René van de Kerkhof, Jan Jeuring, Antal Nagy (.. Willy van de Kerkhof).   Trainer: Kees Rijvers

Goals: Gucmirtl (17, 37), Pahlplatz (41), R. van de Kerkhof (88)

TWENTE ENSCHEDE v DINAMO ZAGREB 1-0 (1-0)

Diekman Stadion, Enschede 16.12.70

Referee: Daniel J. Lyden (Eng)   Attendance: 12,500

TWENTE: Piet Schrijvers; Kees Van Ierssel, Epi Drost, Willem De Vries (.. René Notten), Kalle Oranen, Benno Huve, Kick Van der Vall, Theo Pahlplatz, Willy van de Kerkhof, Jan Jeuring, René van de Kerkhof (.. Lloyd Rooks).   Trainer: Kees Rijvers

DINAMO: Fahrija Dautbegović; Ivica Miljković, Branko Gračanin, Denijal Pirić (.. Petar Bručić), Mladen Ramljak, Filip Blašković (.. Damir Valec), Marijan Čerček, Josip Lalić, Krasnodar Rora, Josip Gucmirtl, Drago Vabec.

Goal: Jeuring (21)

HIBERNIAN EDINBURGH v LIVERPOOL FC 0-1 (0-0)

Easter Road, Edinburgh 9.12.70

Referee: Rudolf Glöckner (DDR)   Attendance: 30,296

HIBERNIAN: Roy Baines; John Brownlie, Eric Schaedler, John Blackley, Jim Black, Patrick Stanton, Kenny Davidson (.. Joseph McBride), William McEwan, Eric Stevenson (.. John Hamilton), Jim Blair, Arthur Duncan.   Manager: Dave Ewing

LIVERPOOL: Raymond Clemence; Christopher Lawler, Alec Lindsay (80 Ian Ross), Thomas Smith, Larry Lloyd, Emlyn Hughes, Brian Hall, John McLaughlin, Steve Heighway, John Toshack, Peter Thompson.   Manager: Bill Shankly

Goal: Toshack (75)

LIVERPOOL FC v HIBERNIAN EDINBURGH 2-0 (1-0)

Anfield Road, Liverpool 22.12.70

Referee: István Zsolt (Hun)   Attendance: 37,815

LIVERPOOL: Raymond Clemence; Christopher Lawler, Roy Evans, Thomas Smith, Larry Lloyd, Emlyn Hughes, Brian Hall, John McLaughlin, Steve Heighway, Philip Boersma, Ian Callaghan.   Manager: Bill Shankly

HIBERNIAN: Roy Baines; John Brownlie, Mervyn Jones, John Blackley, Jim Black, Patrick Stanton, Arthur Duncan, William McEwan, Joseph McBride, Jim Blair (61 Johnny Graham), Eric Stevenson (73 John Hamilton). Manager: Dave Ewing

Goals: Heighway (23), Boersma (50)

ANDERLECHT BRUSSEL
v VITÓRIA SETÚBAL 2-1 (1-1)

Parc Astrid, Brussel 9.12.70

Referee: John Wright Paterson (Sco)   Attendance: 16,200

ANDERLECHT: Leen Barth; George Heylens, Jean Plaskie, Johnny Velkeneers, Maurice Martens; André Colasse, Thomas Nordahl; Inge Ejderstedt, Jan Mulder, Paul Van Himst, Wilfried Puis.   Trainer: Pierre Sinibaldi

VITÓRIA: JOAQUIM Manuel Conceição TORRES; Francisco Silva REBELO, Carlos Alberto Lourenço CARDOSO, José Jesus MENDES, Manuel Luis dos Santos "CARRIÇO"; OCTÁVIO Joaquim Coelho Machado, JOSÉ MARIA Júnior; VAGNER Canotilho, VITOR Manuel Ferreira BAPTISTA, Felix Marques GUERREIRO, JACINTO JOÃO.
Trainer: José Maria PEDROTO

Goals: Ejderstedt (9), Vagner (32), Mulder (66)

VITÓRIA SETÚBAL
v ANDERLECHT BRUSSEL 3-1 (1-0, 2-1) a.e.t

Estádio do Bonfim, Setúbal 23.12.70

Referee: Robert Franciel (Fra)   Attendance: 14,300

VITÓRIA: JOAQUIM Manuel Conceição TORRES; Francisco Silva REBELO, Carlos Alberto Lourenço CARDOSO, José Jesus MENDES, Manuel Luis dos Santos "CARRIÇO"; OCTÁVIO Joaquim Coelho Machado (65 Pedro), JOSÉ MARIA Júnior; VAGNER Canotilho (65 Arnaldo), VITOR Manuel Ferreira BAPTISTA, Felix Marques GUERREIRO, JACINTO JOÃO.
Trainer: José Maria PEDROTO

ANDERLECHT: Leen Barth; Jean Plaskie, George Heylens, Johnny Velkeneers (72 André Colasse), Julien Kialunda; Maurice Martens, Gerard Desanghere; Thomas Nordahl, Wilfried Puis, Jan Mulder, Paul Van Himst.
Trainer: Pierre Sinibaldi

Goals: Guerreiro (24, 120), Desanghere (52), Baptista (70)

TWENTE ENSCHEDE
v JUVENTUS TORINO 2-2 (1-0, 2-0)

Diekman stadion, Enschede 17.02.71

Referee: Erich Linemayr (Aus)   Attendance: 22,800

TWENTE: Piet Schrijvers; Kees Van Ierssel (85 Izzy Ten Donkelaar), Epi Drost, Willem De Vries, Kalle Oranen, Kick Van der Vall, Benno Huve (93 René Notten), Theo Pahlplatz, Willy van de Kerkhof, Jan Jeuring, René van de Kerkhof.   Trainer: Kees Rijvers

JUVENTUS: Roberto Tancredi; Luciano Spinosi, Sandro Salvadore, Giuseppe Furino, Francesco Morini, Gianluigi Roveta, Franco Causio, Giampietro Marchetti, Pietro Anastasi (106 Adriano Novellini), Fabio Capello (106 Antonello Cuccureddu), Roberto Bettega.   Trainer: Armando Picchi

Goals: Pahlplatz (11), Drost (49), Anastasi (96, 98)

ARSENAL LONDON v 1.FC KÖLN 2-1 (1-1)

Highbury, London 9.03.71

Referee: István Zsolt (Hun)   Attendance: 40,007

ARSENAL: Bob Wilson; Patrick Rice, Frank McLintock, Peter Simpson, Robert McNab, Peter Storey, Jonathan Sammels (46 George Graham), Charles George, George Armstrong, John Radford, Raymond Kennedy.   Manager: Bertie Mee

FC KÖLN: Manfred Manglitz; Karl-Heinz Thielen (76 Kurt Kowalski), Bernd Cullmann, Werner Biskup, Matthias Hemmersbach, Heinz Simmet, Heinz Flohe, Wolfgang Overath, Thomas Parits (44 Hans-Josef Kapellmann), Bernd Rupp, Johannes Löhr.   Trainer: Ernst Ocwirk

Goals: McLintock (24), Thielen (44), Storey (69)

QUARTER-FINALS

JUVENTUS TORINO
v TWENTE ENSCHEDE 2-0 (1-0)

Stadio Comunale, Torino 27.01.71

Referee: José Maria Ortiz de Mendebil (Spa)   Att: 14,200

JUVENTUS: Roberto Tancredi; Luciano Spinosi, Giuseppe Furino, Antonello Cuccureddu, Francesco Morini, Sandro Salvadore, Helmut Haller, Franco Causio, Pietro Anastasi (59 Adriano Novellini), Fabio Capello, Roberto Bettega (80 Roberto Montorsi).   Trainer: Armando Picchi

TWENTE: Piet Schrijvers; Kees Van Ierssel, Epi Drost, Willem De Vries, Kalle Oranen, Kick Van der Vall, Benno Huve, Theo Pahlplatz, Willy van de Kerkhof (73 Jan Streuer), Jan Jeuring, René van de Kerkhof (86 René Notten).
Trainer: Kees Rijvers

Goals: Haller (8), Novellini (80)

1.FC KÖLN v ARSENAL LONDON 1-0 (1-0)

Müngersdorferstadion, Köln 23.03.71

Referee: Constantin Petrea (Rom)   Attendance: 46,200

FC KÖLN: Manfred Manglitz; Karl-Heinz Thielen, Werner Biskup, Wolfgang Weber, Matthias Hemmersbach (67 Kurt Kowalski), Heinz Simmet, Heinz Flohe, Wolfgang Overath, Hans-Josef Kapellmann, Bernd Rupp, Johannes Löhr.
Trainer: Ernst Ocwirk

ARSENAL: Bob Wilson; Patrick Rice, Frank McLintock, Peter Simpson, Robert McNab, Peter Storey, George Graham, Charles George, George Armstrong, John Radford, Raymond Kennedy.   Manager: Bertie Mee

Goal: Biskup (4 pen)

LIVERPOOL FC v BAYERN MÜNCHEN 3-0 (1-0)

Anfield Road, Liverpool   10.03.71

Referee: Franz Geluck (Bel)   Attendance: 45,616

LIVERPOOL: Raymond Clemence; Christopher Lawler, Alec Lindsay, Thomas Smith, Larry Lloyd, Emlyn Hughes, Philip Boersma, Alun Evans, Steve Heighway, John Toshack (66 Robert Graham), Brian Hall.   Manager: Bill Shankly

BAYERN: Josef Maier; Johnny Hansen, Herward Koppenhöfer, Georg Schwarzenbeck, Franz Roth, Franz Beckenbauer, Paul Breitner (46 Karl-Heinz Mrosko), Rainer Zobel, Gerd Müller, Uli Hoeness (65 Edgar Schneider), Dieter Brenninger.   Trainer: Udo Lattek

Goals: A. Evans (30, 50, 73)

BAYERN MÜNCHEN v LIVERPOOL FC 1-1 (0-0)

Grünwalderstadion, München   24.03.71

Referee: Robert Wurtz (Fra)   Attendance: 22,000

BAYERN: Josef Maier; Paul Breitner, Georg Schwarzenbeck, Franz Beckenbauer, Herward Koppenhöfer, Franz Roth (86 Peter Kupferschmidt), Rainer Zobel, Uli Hoeness (65 Jürgen Ey), Edgar Schneider, Gerd Müller, Dieter Brenninger.   Trainer: Udo Lattek

LIVERPOOL: Raymond Clemence; Christopher Lawler, Thomas Smith, Larry Lloyd, Alec Lindsay, Emlyn Hughes, Ian Callaghan, John McLaughlin, Alun Evans, Ian Ross, John Toshack (78 Peter Thompson).   Manager: Bill Shankly

Goals: Ross (74), Schneider (77)

LEEDS UNITED v VITÓRIA SETÚBAL 2-1 (1-1)

Elland Road, Leeds   10.03.71

Referee: Günter Männig (DDR)   Attendance: 27,143

UNITED: David Harvey; Paul Reaney, Nigel Davey (79 Terence Yorath), Michael Bates, Jack Charlton, Norman Hunter, Peter Lorimer, Rodney Belfitt, Michael Jones (69 Joseph Jordan), John Giles, Paul Madeley. Manager: Don Revie

VITÓRIA: JOAQUIM Manuel Conceição TORRES; Francisco Silva REBELO, Carlos Alberto Lourenço CARDOSO, José Jesus MENDES, Manuel Luis dos Santos "CARRIÇO", OCTÁVIO Joaquim Coelho Machado, JOSÉ MARIA Júnior, VAGNER Canotilho, VITOR Manuel Ferreira BAPTISTA, Felix Marques GUERREIRO, JACINTO JOÃO (74 Carlos Alberto CORREIA).   Trainer: José Maria PEDROTO

Goals: Baptista (2), Lorimer (19), Giles (75 pen)

VITÓRIA SETÚBAL v LEEDS UNITED 1-1 (0-1)

Estádio do Bonfim, Setúbal   24.03.71

Referee: Roland Marendaz (Swi)   Attendance: 30,000

VITÓRIA: JOAQUIM Manuel Conceição TORRES; Joaquim Adriao José da CONCEIÇÃO (26 Joaquim Leonardo Quinta ARCANJO), Carlos Alberto Lourenço CARDOSO, Francisco Silva REBELO, José Jesus MENDES, OCTÁVIO Joaquim Coelho Machado (70 Mateus), VAGNER Canotilho, JOSÉ MARIA Júnior, VITOR Manuel Ferreira BAPTISTA, Felix Marques GUERREIRO, JACINTO JOÃO.   Trainer: José Maria PEDROTO

UNITED: David Harvey (82 Gary Sprake); Paul Reaney, Jack Charlton, Norman Hunter, Terence Cooper, Michael Bates, John Giles, Peter Lorimer, Allan Clarke, Michael Jones, Paul Madeley.   Manager: Don Revie

Goals: Lorimer (17), Baptista (84)

SEMI-FINALS

LIVERPOOL FC v LEEDS UNITED 0-1 (0-0)

Anfield Road, Liverpool   14.04.71

Referee: Jef F. Dorpmans (Hol)   Attendance: 52,577

LIVERPOOL: Raymond Clemence; Christopher Lawler, Alec Lindsay, Thomas Smith, Larry Lloyd, Emlyn Hughes, Ian Callaghan (68 Robert Graham), Alun Evans (69 Peter Thompson), Steve Heighway, John Toshack, Brian Hall.   Manager: Bill Shankly

UNITED: Gary Sprake; Paul Reaney (83 Nigel Davey), Terence Cooper, William Bremner, Jack Charlton, Norman Hunter, Michael Bates, Allan Clarke, Michael Jones, John Giles, Paul Madeley.   Manager: Don Revie

Goal: Bremner (67)

LEEDS UNITED v LIVERPOOL FC 0-0

Elland Road, Leeds   28.04.71

Referee: Thomas Wharton (Sco)   Attendance: 40,462

UNITED: Gary Sprake; Paul Madeley, Terence Cooper, William Bremner, Jack Charlton, Norman Hunter, Michael Bates, Allan Clarke (46 Paul Reaney), Michael Jones (53 Joseph Jordan), John Giles, Edward Gray.   Manager: Don Revie

LIVERPOOL: Raymond Clemence; Christopher Lawler, Ronald Yeats, Thomas Smith, Larry Lloyd, Emlyn Hughes, Peter Thompson, Brian Hall, Steve Heighway, Ian Callaghan, John Toshack.   Manager: Bill Shankly

1.FC KÖLN v JUVENTUS TORINO 1-1 (0-1)

Müngersdorferstadion, Köln   14.04.71

Referee: Anton Bucheli (Swi)   Attendance: 50,500

FC KÖLN: Manfred Manglitz; Karl-Heinz Thielen, Werner Biskup, Wolfgang Weber, Matthias Hemmersbach, Wolfgang Overath (30 Bernd Cullmann), Heinz Simmet, Heinz Flohe, Hans-Josef Kapellmann, Bernd Rupp, Johannes Löhr. Trainer: Ernst Ocwirk

JUVENTUS: Massimo Piloni; Luciano Spinosi, Sandro Salvadore, Francesco Morini, Giampietro Marchetti, Franco Causio, Fabio Capello, Giuseppe Furino, Helmut Haller, Adriano Novellini (77 Fausto Landini), Roberto Bettega. Trainer: Cestimir Vycpalek

Goals: Bettega (37), Thielen (87)

JUVENTUS TORINO v 1.FC KÖLN 2-0 (1-0)

Stadio Comunale, Torino   28.04.71

Referee: Roger Machin (Fra)   Attendance: 64,738

JUVENTUS: Massimo Piloni; Luciano Spinosi, Francesco Morini, Sandro Salvadore, Giampietro Marchetti, Franco Causio, Giuseppe Furino, Fabio Capello, Helmut Haller (86 Adriano Novellini), Roberto Bettega, Pietro Anastasi. Trainer: Cestimir Vycpalek

FC KÖLN: Manfred Manglitz; Karl-Heinz Thielen, Wolfgang Weber, Werner Biskup, Matthias Hemmersbach, Heinz Simmet, Heinz Flohe, Bernd Cullmann, Hans-Josef Kapellmann, Bernd Rupp, Johannes Löhr (41 Thomas Parits). Trainer: Ernst Ocwirk

Goals: Capello (2), Anastasi (84)

FINAL

JUVENTUS TORINO v LEEDS UNITED 0-0

Stadio Comunale, Torino   26.05.71

Referee: Laurens van Ravens (Hol)   Attendance: 46,342

JUVENTUS: Massimo Piloni; Luciano Spinosi, Giampietro Marchetti, Giuseppe Furino, Francesco Morini; Sandro Salvadore (Cap), Helmut Haller, Franco Causio; Pietro Anastasi, Fabio Capello, Roberto Bettega. Trainer: Cestimir Vycpalek

LEEDS UNITED: Gary Sprake; Paul Reaney, Paul Madeley, Terence Cooper, William Bremner (Cap), John "Jack" Charlton, Norman Hunter, Peter Lorimer, Allan Clarke, Michael Jones, John Giles, Edward Gray (21 Terence Yorath). Manager: Don Revie

Match abandoned after 51 minutes due to a waterlogged pitch

JUVENTUS TORINO v LEEDS UNITED 2-2 (1-0)

Stadio Comunale, Torino   28.05.71

Referee: Laurens van Ravens (Hol)   Attendance: 58,553

JUVENTUS: Massimo Piloni; Sandro Salvadore (Cap), Luciano Spinosi, Francesco Morini, Giampietro Marchetti, Giuseppe Furino, Helmut Haller, Franco Causio, Pietro Anastasi (72 Adriano Novellini), Fabio Capello, Roberto Bettega. Trainer: Cestimir Vycpalek

LEEDS UNITED: Gary Sprake; Paul Reaney, John "Jack" Charlton, Norman Hunter, Terence Cooper; William Bremner (Cap), John Giles; Paul Madeley, Peter Lorimer, Allan Clarke, Michael Jones (72 Michael Bates). Manager: Don Revie

Goals: Bettega (27), Madeley (48), Capello (55), Bates (76)

LEEDS UNITED v JUVENTUS TORINO 1-1 (1-1)

Elland Road, Leeds   3.06.71

Referee: Rudolf Glöckner (DDR)   Attendance: 42,483

LEEDS UNITED: Gary Sprake; Paul Reaney, John "Jack" Charlton, Norman Hunter, Terence Cooper; William Bremner (Cap), John Giles; Paul Madeley (56 Michael Bates), Peter Lorimer, Allan Clarke, Michael Jones. Manager: Don Revie

JUVENTUS: Roberto Tancredi; Sandro Salvadore (Cap), Luciano Spinosi, Francesco Morini, Giampietro Marchetti, Giuseppe Furino, Helmut Haller, Franco Causio; Pietro Anastasi, Fabio Capello, Roberto Bettega. Trainer: Cestimir Vycpalek

Goals: Clarke (13), Anastasi (19)

Goalscorers Fairs Cup 1970/71

10 goals: Pietro Anastasi (Juventus Torino)

7 goals: Gerd Müller (Bayern München)

6 goals: Fethi Heper (Eskişehirspor), Roberto Bettega (Juventus Torino)

5 goals: Hans-Jürgen Kreische (Dynamo Dresden), Jan Klijnjan (Sparta Rotterdam), Inge Ejderstedt (Anderlecht), Theo Pahlplatz, René van de Kerkhof (Twente Enschede), Vitor Baptista (Vitória Setúbal), Peter Lorimer (Leeds United)

4 goals: John O'Rourke (Coventry City), Franz Brungs (Hertha Berlin), Wyn Davies (Newcastle), Gert Dörfel (Hamburger SV), Benny Nielsen (AB København), Janusz Kowalik (Sparta Rotterdam), János Máté (Pécsi Dózsa), Lalić, Marijan Novak (Dinamo Zagreb), Arthur Duncan (Hibernian), Jan Jeuring (Twente Enschede), Edgar Schneider (Bayern München), José Claramunt (Valencia CF), William Bremner (Leeds United), Adriano Novellini (Juventus Torino)

3 goals: Spreco (Zeljeznicar Sarajevo), Des Dickson (Coleraine), Florea Dumitrache (Dinamo Bucureşti), Nol Heijerman, Jørgen Kristensen (Sparta Rotterdam), Joseph McBride (Hibernian), Jan Mulderm, Wilfried Puis (Anderlecht), Raymond Kennedy, John Radford (Arsenal London), José Maria (Vitória Setúbal), Alun Evans (Liverpool), Werner Biskup, Bernd Rupp, Karl-Heinz Thielen (FC Köln), Edward Gray, Allan Clarke, Jack Charlton (Leeds United), Fabio Capello (Juventus Torino)

2 goals: Bukal (Zeljeznicar Sarajevo), Chinaglia (Lazio Roma), Nuoranen (Ilves Tampere), Câmpora (Barreirense), Castellan (Angoulême), Ademir (Vitória Guimarães), Martin (Coventry City), Mariani (Fiorentina), Pujol, Rexach (FC Barcelona), Gayer, Horr (Hertha Berlin), Kaiser (Sturm Graz), D.Popescu (Dinamo Bucureşti), B. Hönig (Hamburger SV), F.Hansen, Carlsen (AB København), Koudijzer, Venneker (Sparta Rotterdam), Jurkanin (Sparta Praha), Rogiers, De Raeymaecker, Janssens (Beveren), Kocsis (Pécsi Dózsa), Gucmirtl (Dinamo Zagreb), Stanton (Hibernian), Nordahl, Van Himst (Anderlecht), Storey (Arsenal London), Guerreiro (Vitória Setúbal), Barrachina (Valencia CF), Boersma, Hughes (Liverpool), Flohe (FC Köln), Haller (Juventus Torino)

1 goal: Bene (ARA La Gantoise), Osim, Mujkic (Zeljeznicar), Eloy, Acosta (FC Sevilla), Mathie, T. McLean, Morrison (Kilmarnock), Dellamore, Pierron (RC Paris-Sedan), Couécou, Skoblar (Olympique Marseille), Mucha (Ferencváros), Dufour (Lausanne), Grahn, Meier (Grasshopper), Rother, Nowok (GKS Katowice), Wigginton (Cork Hibernians), J. Cini (Sliema), Stein (Glasgow Rangers), Uriarte (Athletic Bilbao), Lundberg, Nupponen (Ilves Tampere), Serafim (Barreirense), Olsen, Hans E. Hansen, N. Rasmussen (B 1901 Nyköbing), Larsson, Jönsson (Malmö FF), Gallice (Angoulême), Faber (Ruch Chorzow), Radkov (Trakia Plovdiv), Davidov (Slavia Sofia), Ţarălungă, Strîmbeanu (Universitatea Craiova), Koudas (PAOK Thessaloniki), Cella (Inter Milano), Gonçalves, Bernardo da Velha, Peres (Vitória Guimarães), Hunt, Joicey, Blockley (Coventry City), Vitali, Chiarugi (Fiorentina), Marcial, M.Filosia (FC Barcelona), Mullan, Jennings (Coleraine), Steffenhagen, Gergely (Hertha Berlin), Zamut, Murlasits, Albrecht (Sturm Graz), Hemp, K.Sammer, Sachse (Dynamo Dresden), Gordon, Traynor, I. Reid, Markland, A. Reid (Dundee United), Moncur (Newcastle United), Sălceanu (Dinamo Bucureşti), Nogly, Zaczyk, Volkert (Hamburger SV), Petersen, A. Hansen (AB København), Nadoveza, Buljan, Jerković, Pavlica, Jovanic (Hajduk Split), Halil (Eskişehirspor), Kuna, Martinkovic, Bozik, Dobias, Masrna (Spartak Trnava), Walbeek, Van der Veen (Sparta Rotterdam), Barton, Urban, Vrana, Migas, Gögh, Chovanec (Sparta Praha), Van der Linden (Beveren), Čerček (Dinamo Zagreb), Graham, Blair, McEwan (Hibernian Edinburgh), Desanghere, Elizeu, Van Binst (Anderlecht), Drost, Streuer, Nagy (Twente Enschede), McLintock, Graham, Sammels, Armstrong (Arsenal London), Hoeness, Schwarzenbeck, Roth, Beckenbauer (Bayern München), Vagner, João Jacinto (Vitória Setúbal), Buyl (Valencia CF), Ross, Toshack, Heighway, Lindsay, Lawler, Graham (Liverpool), Hemmersbach, Parits, Lex (FC Köln), Madeley,

Bates, Giles, Belfitt, Jones (Leeds United), Causio, Landini (Juventus)

Own Goals: Jessen (AB København) for Sliema, Sultana (Sliema) for AB København, Rinne (Ilves) for Sturm Graz, Péri (Angoulême) for Vitória Guimarães, Pablowsky (US Rumelange) for Juventus, Schulz (Hamburger SV) for Dinamo Zagreb, Yde (AB København) for Anderlecht, Boljat (Hajduk Split) for Vitória Setúbal, Dobias (Spartak Trnava) for FC Köln, Chovanec (Sparta Praha) for Leeds United

ALL-TIME FAIRS CUP FINAL

After season 1970-71, the autonomous committee sponsored by FIFA which had organized the Fairs Cup was replaced in this function by UEFA. The European football organism preserved the competition format of this tournament, but renamed it UEFA Cup and created a new trophy for the winner. In order to decide which team would keep the old Fairs Cup trophy permanently, a game was played between the first ever winner of this competition (Barcelona CF, 1958) and the last one (Leeds United AFC, 1971).

CF BARCELONA v LEEDS UNITED 2-1 (0-0)

Camp Nou, Barcelona   22.09.1971

Referees: István Zsolt (Hun); Martín Álvarez (Spa), Ceel (Eng)   Attendance: 35,000

CF BARCELONA: Salvator SADURNÍ Urpi; Joaquín RIFÉ Climent, Francisco Fernández Rodríguez "GALLEGO", Antonio TORRES García, ELADIO Silvestre Graells, Enrique Álvarez COSTAS, JUAN CARLOS Pérez López, Carlos REXACH Cerdá, MARCIAL Pina Morales, Teófilo DUEÑAS Samper, Juan Manuel ASENSI Ripoll (79 José María FUSTÉ Blanch).   Trainer: Marinus Michels

LEEDS UNITED: Gary Sprake; Paul Reaney, John «Jack» Charlton, Norman Hunter, Nigel Davey, William Bremner, John Giles, Peter Lorimer, Joseph Jordan, Rodney Belfitt, Christopher Galvin.   Trainer: Donald George Revie

Goals: Duenas (51, 83), Jordan (53)